o|s Ordnance S

STREET
West
Sussex

Contents

iii *Key to map symbols*
IV-V *Key to map pages*
VI *Administrative and post code boundaries*
1 *Street maps*
207 *Extra-large-scale map of Brighton town centre*
208 *Town maps of Eastbourne and Hastings*
209 *Town maps of Lewes and Royal Tunbridge Wells*
210 *Index of hospitals, railway stations, schools, shopping centres, street names and universities*
246 *Town and village index*

PHILIP'S

First edition published 1994
First colour edition published 1997
Reprinted in 1999, 2000 by

George Philip Ltd, a division of
Octopus Publishing Group Ltd
2-4 Heron Quays, London E14 4JP

ISBN 0-540-07327-X (pocket)

© Crown copyright 1997
© George Philip Ltd 1997

**The mapping between pages 1 and 209 (inclusive) in this
atlas is derived from Ordnance Survey® OSCAR® and
Land-Line® data, and Landranger® mapping.**

Ordnance Survey, OSCAR, Land-line and Landranger are
registered trade marks of Ordnance Survey, the national
mapping agency of Great Britain.

Printed and bound in Spain by Cayfosa

Digital Data

The exceptionally high-quality mapping
found in this book is available as
digital data in TIFF format, which is
easily convertible to other bit-mapped
(raster) image formats.

The index is also available in digital
form as a standard database table.
It contains all the details found in the
printed index together with the
National Grid reference for the map
square in which each entry is named
and feature codes for places of
interest in eight categories such as
education and health.

For further information and to discuss
your requirements, please contact
Philip's on 020 7531 8440 or
george.philip@philips-maps.co.uk

Symbol	Description
(22a)	**Motorway** (with junction number)
	Primary route (dual carriageway and single)
	A road (dual carriageway and single)
	B road (dual carriageway and single)
	Minor road (dual carriageway and single)
	Other minor road
- - -	**Road under construction**
	Railway
	Tramway, miniature railway
	Rural track, private road or narrow road in urban area
—‖—	**Gate or obstruction to traffic** (restrictions may not apply at all times or to all vehicles)
- - -	**Path, bridleway, byway open to all traffic, road used as a public path**
	The representation in this atlas of a road, track or path is no evidence of the existence of a right of way
200 / **156** ▶ / **207** ▼	**Adjoining page indicators**
	The map area within the pink band is shown at a larger scale on the page indicated by the red block and arrow

	British Rail station
⇌	**British Rail station**
(🚂)	**Private railway station**
⬤	**Bus, coach station**
◆	**Ambulance station**
◆	**Coastguard station**
◆	**Fire station**
◆	**Police station**
✚	**Casualty entrance to hospital**
✝	**Church, place of worship**
H	**Hospital**
i	**Information centre**
P	**Parking**
PO	**Post Office**
Chichester High Sch for Girls	**Important buildings, schools, colleges, universities and hospitals**
·—·—·	**County boundaries**
River Arun	**Water name**
	Stream
	River or canal (minor and major)
	Water
	Tidal water
	Woods
	Houses
Arundel Castle	**Non-Roman antiquity**
ROMAN VILLA	**Roman antiquity**

Acad	**Academy**	Mon	**Monument**
Cemy	**Cemetery**	Mus	**Museum**
C Ctr	**Civic Centre**	Obsy	**Observatory**
CH	**Club House**	Pal	**Royal Palace**
Coll	**College**	PH	**Public House**
Ent	**Enterprise**	Rec Gd	**Recreation Ground**
Ex H	**Exhibition Hall**	Resr	**Reservoir**
Ind Est	**Industrial Estate**	Ret Pk	**Retail Park**
Inst	**Institute**	Sch	**School**
Ct	**Law Court**	Sh Ctr	**Shopping Centre**
L Ctr	**Leisure Centre**	Sta	**Station**
LC	**Level Crossing**	TH	**Town Hall/House**
Liby	**Library**	Trad Est	**Trading Estate**
Mkt	**Market**	Univ	**University**
Meml	**Memorial**	YH	**Youth Hostel**

■ The dark grey border on the inside edge of some pages indicates that the mapping does not continue onto the adjacent page

■ The small numbers around the edges of the maps identify the 1 kilometre National Grid lines

The scale of the maps is 3.92 cm to 1 km (2¹/₂ inches to 1 mile)

0	¹/₄	¹/₂	³/₄	1 mile
0	250m 500m 750m	1 kilometre		

The scale of the map on page numbered in red is 7.84 cm to 1 km (5 inches to 1 mile)

0	220 yards	440 yards	660 yards	¹/₂ mile
0	125m 250m	375m	¹/₂ kilometre	

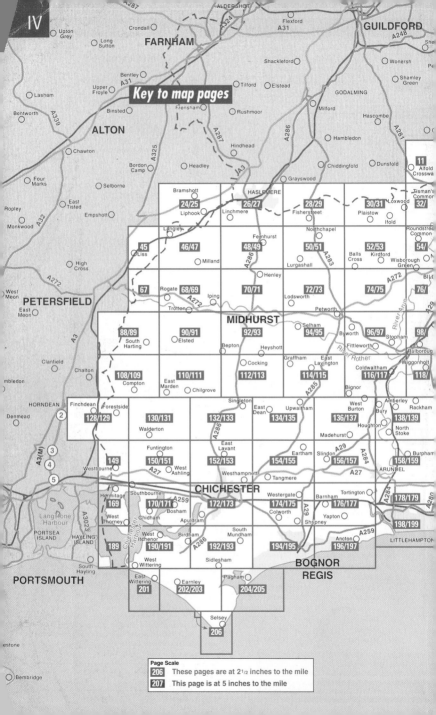

Key to map pages

IV

Page Scale
206 These pages are at 2½ inches to the mile
207 This page is at 5 inches to the mile

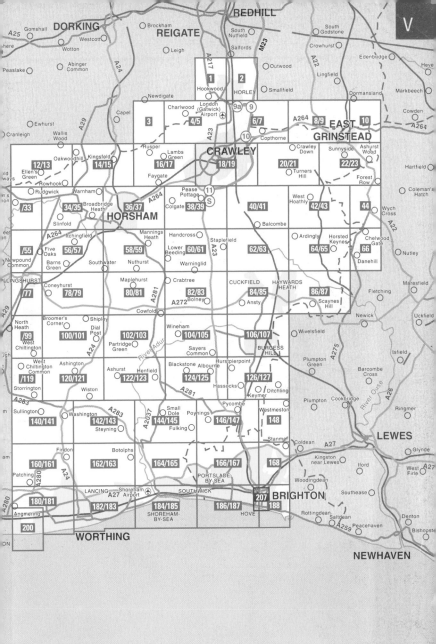

KEY MAP SCALE

| 0 | 1 | 2 | 3 | 4 | 5 | 6 | 7 | 8 | Km |

| 0 | 1 | 2 | 3 | 4 | 5 | Miles |

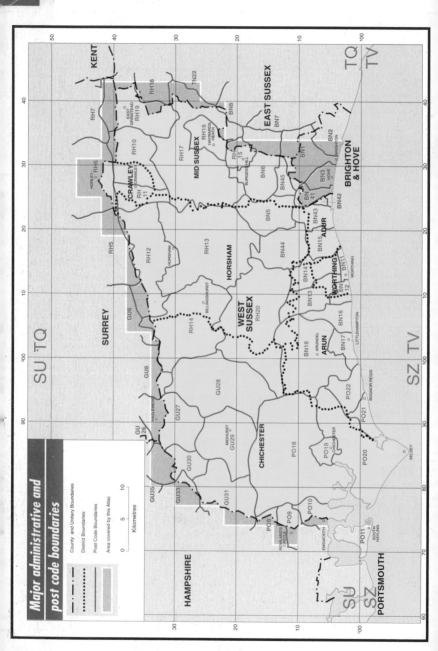

Major administrative and post code boundaries

- ·—·— County and Unitary Boundaries
- District Boundaries
- ·········· Post Code Boundaries
- Area covered by this Atlas

Kilometres

0   5   10

Newdigate

Cudworth Manor

Holly Farm

Hillside Farm

Green Lane Farm

Ash Farm

Cudworth

8

Beam Brook

Cudworth Copse

Green's La

7

Greens Farm

41

Acorn Wood

Cidermill Farm

Ockley Lodge

Tanhurst Farm

The Birches

6

Lodge Farm

Home Cottage

DUKE'S DR

Newdigate Place

Arnewood Farm

Newhouse Farm

5

Boothlands Farm

40

Marelands Farm

HEATH RD

Rose Cottage

Alder Gill

mple ande

CH

Melton Hall Farm

4

TEMPLE LA

Golf Course

Marshlands Cottages

Duke's Copse

Jordan's Wood

East Wood

Chaffolds Copse

The Jordans

Oaklands Park Farm

Ivyhouse Farm

emple Wood

3

Oldhouse Gill

North Barn

Medlands Farm

Orltons

39

Chaffold's farm

Jordans

2

Lyne Farm

Little Copse

ORLTONS LA

yne use

Sussex Border Path

1

Cowix Furzefield

Waffles Corner

Cophatch Corner

Dumbrels Copse

CAPEL RD

Cowix Farm

Nutshell Farm

38

A   B   20   C   D   21   E   F

3

A B C D E F

Gildings Farm
Beggarshouse La
BEGGARSHOUSE LA
STAN HILL
NORMAN HOUSE RD
Charlwood Place
8

Greenings Farm
Greenings
Little Greenings
Barfield Farm
PUDDING LA
Spottles Farm
Charlwood Cty Fst Sch

7

Furzefield Farm
Pagewood
Charlwood
RECTORY LA
PO
PH
THE STREET
ROSEMARY LA
ORCHARD COTTS
SEWILL CL
CHAPEL RD
LOW CHART
HORLEY RD

41

WELLAND GILL
GLOVER'S RD
GLENFIELD COTTS
Gatwick Zoo
DOLBY TERR
CHALMERS CT
Charlwood Place Farm

Glover's Plantation
Glover's Wood
Welling Barn Farm
Betchworth Works
Spicer's Bridge
Tilter's Farm

6

COUNCIL COTTS
Sussex Border Path

RUSS HILL
WEST RD
LOWFIELD HEATH RD

5

Mountnoddy Wood
Russ Hill Farm

CHARLWOOD LA
40
Westlands
Waggoners Farm
Gatwick Wena Hotel
Birchfield

Westlands Farm
4

Upper Prestwood Farm
Great Burlands
Little Park Farm

Prestwood Copse
Burlands
LITTLE PARK ENTERPRISES

Man's Brook
Furze Field
3

Water Hall

Scrag Copse
Burlands Copse
Naldretts Farm
Red Gables

39
PRESTWOOD LA
CHARLWOOD RD
Ifield Wood

Orltons Copse
Lower Prestwood Farm
Oak Tree Farm
Cophall Wood
2

Gotwick Farm
Ifield Court Farm
Ifield Court Hotel

Tilgate
1

THE MOUNT
HILLY BARN RD
Ifieldwood
IFIELD WOOD
The Druids

Langhurst Farm
LANGHURST LA
The Mount Farm
Hilly Barn Farmhouse
Pockney's Farm

38
22 A B 23 C D 24 E F

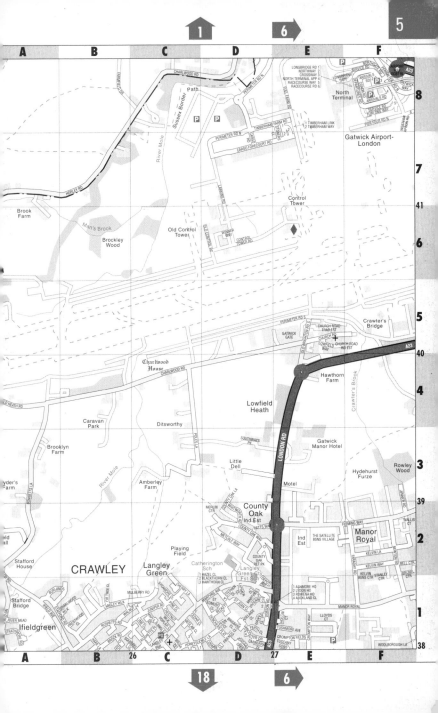

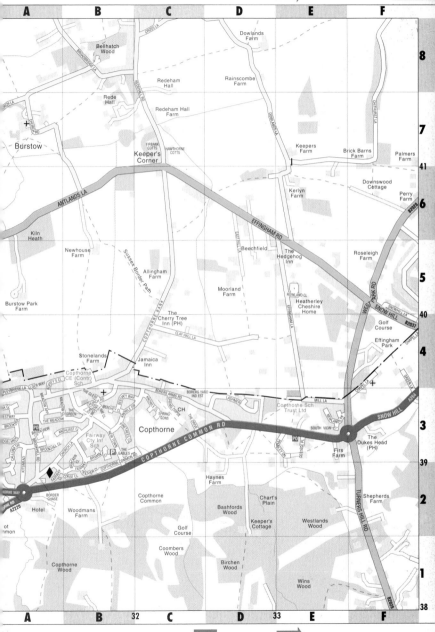

Dowlands Farm

Bellhatch Wood

CROSS LA

BROOKSIDE LA

Redeham Hall

Rainscombe Farm

REDEHAM RD

Rede Hall

DOWNLANDS LA

CHITHURST LA

Redeham Hall Farm

DIXON LA

CHAPEL RD

Burstow

Keeper's Corner

FIRBANK COTTS
HAWTHORNE COTTS

Keepers Farm

Brick Barns Farm

Palmers Farm

Kerlyn Farm

Downswood Cottage

Perry Farm

B2028

ANTLANDS LA

EFFINGHAM RD

Kiln Heath

Sussex Border Path

Newhouse Farm

EAST HILL L

Beechfield

The Hedgehog Inn

Roseleigh Farm

Allingham Farm

Moorland Farm

ROWLAND CL

EFFINGHAM LA

Heatherley Cheshire Home

WEST PARK RD

SNOWHILL LA

Burstow Park Farm

COPTHORNE BANK

The Cherry Tree Inn (PH)

CLAY HALL LA

Snow Hill

Golf Course

B2037

Effingham Park

CHAPEL L

Stonelands Farm

Jamaica Inn

Copthorne CE (Contr.) Sch.

BORERS ARMS RD

BORERS YARD IND EST

LASHMERE

MILL LA

CORNER

BEVELEY RD

PLEYPRIDGE LA

GER WAY

THE GLEBE

BORERS YARD IND EST

CH

Copthorne Sch Trust Ltd

MAPLE RD

HAZEL RD

CATS BANK

ASHURST CL

BROOKSIDE

COPSE RD

WESTWAY

THE MEADOW

ANKHURST CL

SPRING SONS

COPSE CL

CH

SOUTH VIEW

CLAYS

Copthorne

COPTHORNE COMMON RD

SNOW HILL

The Dukes Head (PH)

Fairway Cty Inf Sch

THE GABLES

BROCK RD

BROADWAY

COGEL LANE

CALTHORPE RD

KITE ROAD

BROOKSIDE CL

BROCKENHURST

SHELTER LA

BRINSLE

GORSE LA

PATHER CL

COPTHORNE COMMON RD

FIRS LA

COBBLE PL

GATEHOUSE PL

Firs Farm

TURNERS HILL RD

B2028

THORNE WAY

BORDER CHASE

A2220

Hotel

Woodmans Farm

Copthorne Common

Haynes Farm

Bashfords Wood

Chart's Plain

Keeper's Cottage

Westlands Wood

Shepherds Farm

Copthorne Wood

Golf Course

Coombers Wood

Birchen Wood

Wins Wood

C1
1 THE BROWNINGS
2 BYRON GR
3 CHAUCER AVE
4 TENNYSON RISE
5 THE SAYERS
6 WORDSWORTH RISE

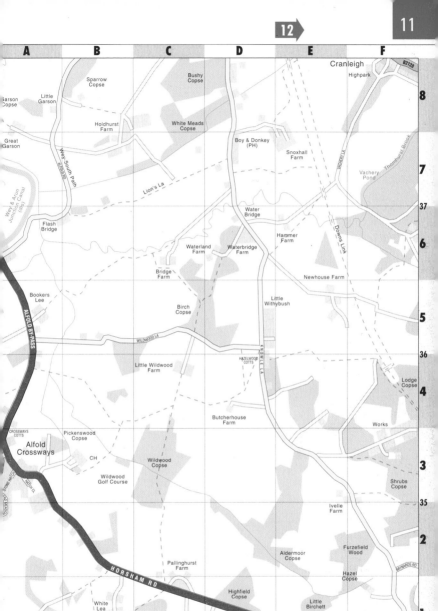

Cranleigh
Highpark
B2128

Sparrow Copse
Little Garson
Garson Copse
Holdhurst Farm
Bushy Copse
White Meads Copse
Great Garson
Boy & Donkey (PH)
Snoxhall Farm

Way South Path
ARUN RD
Lion's La.
Thornhurst Brook
VACHERY LA.
Vachery Pond

Way & Arun Junction Canal (Dis)
Flash Bridge
Water Bridge
Hammer Farm
Downs Link

Waterland Farm
Waterbridge Farm

Bridge Farm
Newhouse Farm

Bookers Lee
Birch Copse
Little Withybush

WILDWOOD LA.
KNOWLE LA.
Lodge Copse

ALFOLD BY-PASS
Little Wildwood Farm
HAZELWOOD COTTS
Works

CROSSWAYS COTTS
Pickenswood Copse
Butcherhouse Farm
Shrubs Copse

Alfold Crossways
CH
Wildwood Copse
Ivelle Farm

PECTOL.
Wildwood Golf Course
Furzefield Wood

Aldermoor Copse
Hazel Copse
REYNARDS RD.

HORSHAM RD
Pallinghurst Farm
Highfield Copse
Little Birchett

Alfold Farm
White Lea
HILLHOUSE LA.
Sussex Border Path
COOK'S HILL

Hook St.
White's Copse
A281
GUILDFORD RD

Males Farm
Lower Hill House

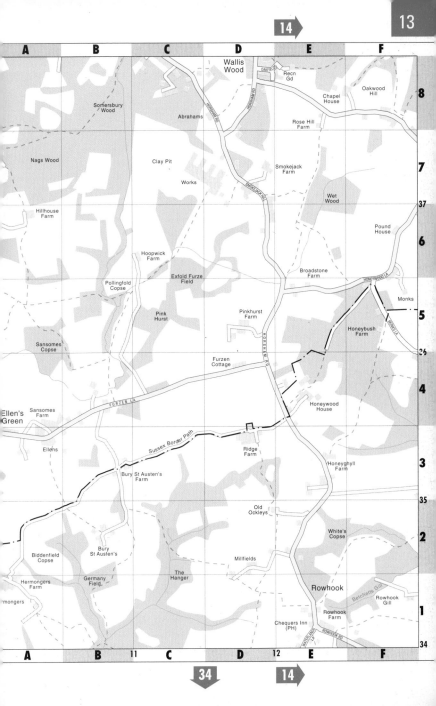

A   B   C   D   E   F

Wallis Wood

Recn Gd

OAKFIELD

Chapel House

Oakwood Hill

8

Somersbury Wood

Abrahams

Rose Hill Farm

HORSHAM RD

Nags Wood

Clay Pit

Works

Smokejack Farm

SMOKEJACK RD

7

Wet Wood

37

Hillhouse Farm

Pound House

6

Hoopwick Farm

Broadstone Farm

HONEYWOOD LA

Monks

Pollingfold Copse

Exfold Furze Field

Pinkhurst Farm

Honeybush Farm

5

Pink Hurst

HORSHAM RD

Sansomes Copse

Furzen Cottage

26

Ellen's Green

Sansomes Farm

FURZEN LA

Honeywood House

4

Ellens

Sussex Border Path

Ridge Farm

Honeyghyll Farm

3

Bury St Austen's Farm

Old Ockleys

35

White's Copse

2

Biddenfield Copse

Bury St Austen's

Millfields

The Hanger

Rowhook

Betchetts Gill

Rowhook Gill

Hermongers Farm

Germany Field

Rowhook Farm

1

mongers

Chequers Inn (PH)

WHITELANDS LA

ROWHOOK RD

34

A   B 11 C   D 12 E   F

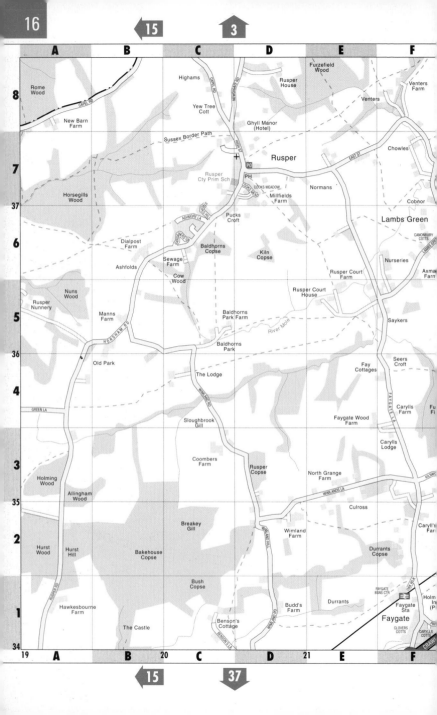

A B C D E F

8 Rome Wood

Highams

Yew Tree Cott

Furzefield Wood

Rusper House

Venters Farm

Venters

New Barn Farm

Ghyll Manor (Hotel)

Chowles

Sussex Border Path

EAST ST

Rusper

7 Horsegills Wood

PO

PH

Rusper Cty Prim Sch

COOKS MEADOW

Millfields Farm

Normans

Cobnor

37

Lambs Green

Pucks Croft

CANONBURY COTTS

6 Dialpost Farm

Baldhorns Copse

Kiln Copse

Nurseries

JAMES GUT

Axma Farm

Sewage Farm

Ashfolds

Cow Wood

Rusper Court Farm

Nuns Wood

Rusper Court House

Saykers

5 Rusper Nunnery

Manns Farm

Baldhorns Park Farm

River Mole

36

Old Park

Baldhorns Park

Fay Cottages

Seers Croft

The Lodge

4 GREEN LA

Sloughbrook Gill

Carylls Farm

Fu Fi

Faygate Wood Farm

Carylls Lodge

3 Holming Wood

Coombers Farm

Rusper Copse

North Grange Farm

Allingham Wood

WIMLANDS LA

35

Culross

Caryll's Far

2 Hurst Wood

Hurst Hill

Breakey Gill

Wimland Farm

Durrants Copse

Bakehouse Copse

1 Bush Copse

Budd's Farm

Durrants

FRYGATE BSNS CTR

Hawkesbourne Farm

Benson's Cottage

Faygate Sta

Holm In (P

The Castle

Faygate

CLOVERS COTTS

CARYLLS COTTS

34

CRAW

19 A 20 B C D 21 E F

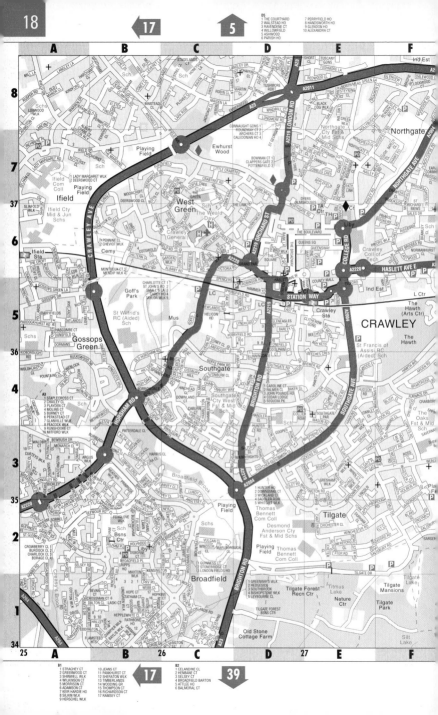

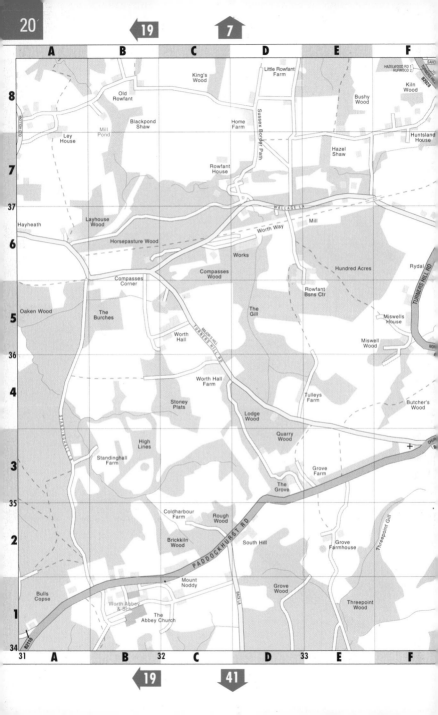

F8
1 MIDDLE ROW
2 FOREST LODGE
3 SACKVILLE CT
4 GREAT HOUSE CT
5 PORTLAND HO
6 CORNWALL GDNS

7 NORMANDY CL
8 WILLOW MEAD
9 KINGS COPSE
10 REGAL DR
11 BECKETT WAY

A   B   C   D   E   F

8 Great Wood

Coles Wood

CHAUDER

SMOLLETTS
CLOSE
THE CLOSE

CHRISTIE

BRICKLEHURST RD

B2110

WEST HILL
WEST HILL
WEST LA

QUEEN'S WK
WEST ST
GARDEN WOOD RD
CAMBRIDGE
DEXTER DR
THE DAKINS
ELMSTEAD
HIGH
Liby

WEST HILL
JUDGE'S
TERR
BELL
HAMMER

VIEW
HERONTYE

7 Hill Place Farm
Brook House
High Grove
Crockshed Wood

Brook House Farm

EAST
GRINSTEAD

Sunnyside

HIGH HICKWOOD LA
HURST FARM RD
HARVEST HILL
SOUTHLANDS
THE MEADS
Cty Prim Sch
MILL-COTTS

ACORN CL

CORONATION RD

37 HAZELDEN CROSS

Coombe Hall Sch

Bulrushes Farm

Dunnings Mill
L Complex

Tobias Sch
of Art

Eurythmy
Sch

MEWS
CT

MORTON RD
STOCKWELL RD
FOREST VIEW RD

6 Hazelden Farm

TURNER'S HILL RD

Coombe Hall
Farm

Coombe Hall
Rd

Imberley

Dunning's Wood

The
Beechcroft
Towse

Boyles
Farm

5 The Plantation
Playing Field
High Wood

Rockwood
Park

Playing Field

Rockingshill
Wood

Rushett's
Shaw

36 B2110
The Rough

SAINT HILL RD

Saint Hill Green

Jenkin's
Wood

Busses
Farm

4 Ridge Hill
Manor

Hen Robin
Wood

Saint Hill
Manor

Saint Hill
Farm

WEST HEATH RD

Standen
Farm

Standen
(National Trust)

Jenhurst
Wood

3 Mary
Wood

Cock Robin
Wood

Busses
Wood

River Medway

35 Mill Place
Farm

Stone Hill
House

ADMIRAL'S BRIDGE LA

Sussex Border Path

Weir Wood Resr

2 Bluebell Rly

Pit
Shaw

Willet's
Bridge

Admiral's Bridge
Wood

1 Birch Farm
Nursery

GRINSTEAD LA

Neylands
Farm

LEDGSHEATH LA

Weir Wood Resr
(Nature Reserve)

Charlwood
Farm

Alder
Moors

34

37 A   B   38 C   39 D   E   F

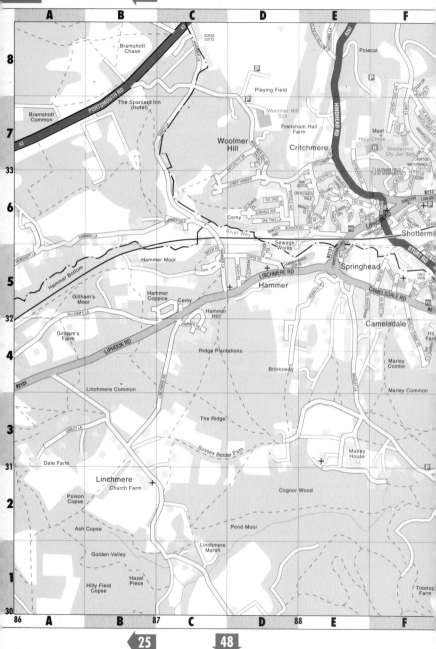

25

A B C D E F

8

7

33

6

32

5

4

3

31

2

1

30

Bramshott Chase

GORSE COTTS

Bramshott Common

PORTSMOUTH RD

The Spaniard Inn (Hotel)

A3

Playing Field

Woolmer Hill Sch

Woolmer Hill

Frensham Hall Farm

Critchmere

Polecat

HINDHEAD RD

A287

Mast

Holy Cross

H

Shottermill City Jun Sch

CROFTON

WEYSPRINGS

B2131

LION GN

JUNCTION

LIPHOOK

Shotterm

LOWER HANGER

OAK COTTS

CRITCHMERE VALE

FIR TREE

SUNVALE AVE

Cemy

OAK TREE LA

BORDER RD

River Wey

Sewage Works

B2131

HAMMER LA

HAMMER VALE

Hammer Moor

MOOR RD

HEATH RD

COPSE RD

LINCHMERE RD

Hammer

Springhead

CAMELSDALE RD

B2131

DALE VIEW

STURT RD

B213

Camelsdale

Marley Combe

HEWSHOTT LA

Hammer Bottom

Gillham's Moor

Hammer Coppice

Cemy

Hammer Hill

GILLHAM'S LA

Gillham's Farm

LIPHOOK RD

B2131

Ridge Plantations

Brinksway

Marley Common

Hil Far

Linchmere Common

LINCHMERE RD

DANLEY LA

The Ridge

Sussex Border Path

Marley House

Dale Farm

Linchmere

Church Farm

Cognor Wood

Poison Copse

Ash Copse

Pond Moor

Golden Valley

Hazel Piece

Linchmere Marsh

Hilly Field Copse

Treetop Farm

86 A B 87 C D 88 E F

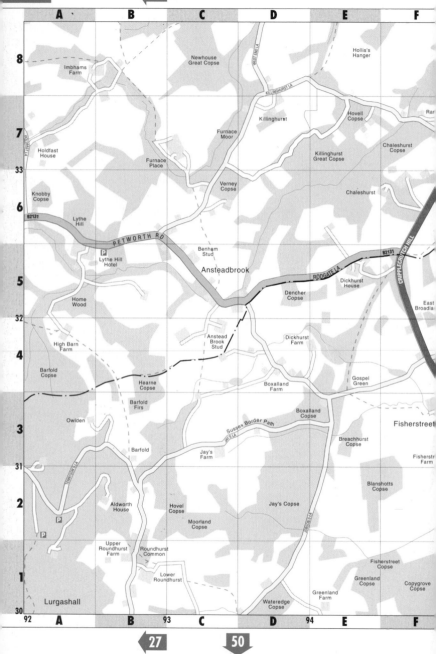

A B C D E F

Windmill Copse

Hungry Corner

Great Copse

Sparkes Copse

Tugley Farm

Fisherlane Hanger

Rovehurst Wood

Griggs Bottom

Gostrode Farm

Fisher Lane Nursery

Surrey Copse

Robins Farm

Little Tugley

Sussex Border Path

GOOSTRODE LA

Ramsnest Common

White's Hill

Works

dlands Farm

Furze Field

Surrey Belt

CH

Surrey Rough

Big Copse

Pollane Farm

Shillinglee Park Golf Course

Downlands

Downlands Wood

Walk Copse

Upper North Pond

Shillinglee Park

Parkgate

Lower North Pond

Shillinglee Home Farm

Manorhill Copse

Stilland Farm

Gaston's Farm

Newhouse Farm

Turnour's Wood

Deer Tower

New Copse

Nine Acre Rew

Beanfield Copse

Little Hayman's Farm

Eastland Farm

Twenty Four Acres

Haymans Farm

China Bridge

The Lake

Mill Copse

Frith Lodge

Park Mill Farm

The Plantation

Frith Wood

Frith Hill

Dale's Farm Hanger

Dale's Farm

A B 96 C D 97 E F

A B C D E F

8

7

33

6

5

32

4

3

31

2

1

30

Old
Lands

Oaken
Wood

Canterbury
Copse

Ireland

Hurlands
Copse

Burntwood
Kennels

Peartree
Hanger

Tugley
Wood

Oak
Wood

The
Hatchetts

Inside
Copse

PLAISTOW RD

Durfold
Hall

Tidy's
Copse

Durfold Hatch
Cottage

Birch
Copse

FISHER LA

Dungate
Farm

Upper Ifold
Wood

Oakhurst
Farm

Sussex Border Path

Weald Barkfold
Copse

Fisherlane
Wood

Durfold
Wood

DURFOLD WOOD

Downlands
Wood

Shortland
Copse

Barkfold
Hanger

DURFOLD RD

East End
Farm

Ashpark
Wood

Weald
Barkfold

Oakhurst

Works

Short's
Farm

Highbridge
House

Lyon's
Farm

COUNCIL
COTTS

Plaistow Cty
Inf Sch

Kingspark
Wood

P

LOXWOOD RD

THE STREET

DURFOLD RD

Plaistow

Beggar
Copse

Ifold
Copse

Birchfold
Copse

RICKMAN'S LA

Sparwood Hanger

Rumbolds
Farm

Rumbold
Wood

Chilsfold
Farm

98 A B 99 C D 00 E F

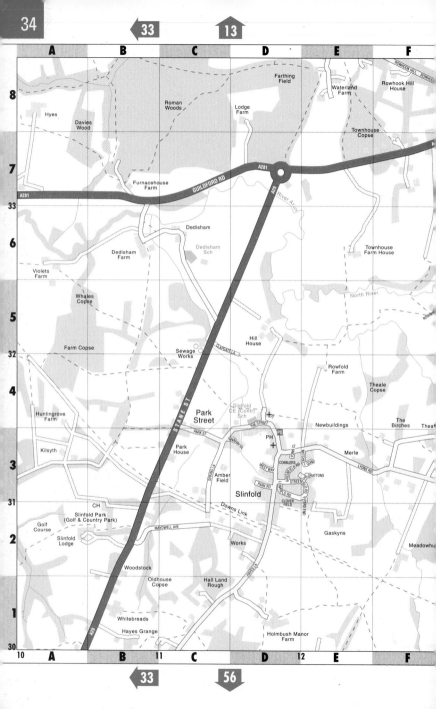

A   B   C   D   E   F

8

Farthing
Field

Hyes

Davies
Wood

Roman
Woods

Lodge
Farm

Waterland
Farm

Rowhook Hill
House

ROWHOOK HILL

7

A281

A281   GUILDFORD RD

Townhouse
Copse

33

Furnacehouse
Farm

River Avon

A29

6

Dedisham

Dedisham
Farm

Dedisham
Sch

Townhouse
Farm House

Violets
Farm

North River

NOWH

Whales
Copse

5

Farm Copse

Sewage
Works

CLARGATE LA

Hill
House

Rowfold
Farm

32

Theale
Copse

4

Huntingrove
Farm

STANE ST

Park
Street

Slinfold
CE (Contr)
Sch

THE STREET

Newbuildings

The
Birches

Theal

Kilsyth

PARK ST

Park
House

TANGLEY CL

PH

COBBLERS

MITCHELL RD

LYONS RD

Merle

3

SPRING LA

Amber
Field

WEST WAY

PARK RD

STREET

GRATTONS

31

CH

Slinfold

CLOVER
FIELD

Slinfold Park
(Golf & Country Park)

Downs Link

Golf
Course

MAYDWELL AVE

2

Slinfold
Lodge

Works

Gaskyns

Meadowhu

Woodstock

Oldhouse
Copse

Hall Land
Rough

1

Whitebreads

A29

Hayes Grange

Holmbush Manor
Farm

30

10   A   B   11   C   D   12   E   F

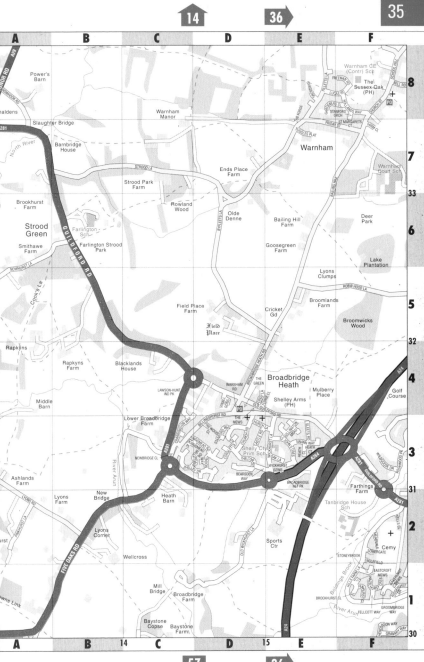

A | B | C | D | E | F

RONNINGTON RD
A29
Power's Barn
haldens
Slaughter Bridge
North River
A281
Barnbridge House
Warnham Manor
Warnham CE (Contr) Sch
The Sussex Oak (PH)
PO
FREEMAN
LUCAS
STANFORD ORCH
ST MARGARETS CT.
FRIDAY ST
Warnham

Brookhurst Farm
STROOD LA
Strood Park Farm
Rowland Wood
Ends Place Farm
Olde Denne
Bailing Hill Farm
Warnham Court Sch

Strood Green
GUILDFORD RD
Farlington Sch
Smithawe Farm
Farlington Strood Park
Goosegreen Farm
Deer Park

NOWHURST LA
Lyons Clumps
Lake Plantation

Rapkyns
Cook's La
Rapkyns Farm
Blacklands House
Field Place Farm
Cricket Gd
Field Place
Broomlands Farm
ROBIN HOOD LA
Broomwicks Wood

Middle Barn
LAWSON-HUNT IND PK
WARNHAM RD
THE GREEN
Broadbridge Heath
Mulberry Place
Golf Course

Lower Broadbridge Farm
PO
Shelley Arms (PH)
THE MEWS
Shelley Cty Prim Sch
SWANN WAY
HEATH
NEWBRIDGE CL
OAK LA
WICKHURST GDNS
Broadbridge Ret Pk
Farthings Farm
GILLMANS RD
A281

Ashlands Farm
River Arun
New Bridge
Heath Barn
BEARSDEN WAY
Tanbridge House Sch
Cemy
GOMERGATE
ENGLEFIELD

Lyons Farm
LYONS RD
FIVE OAKS RD
Lyons Corner
Wellcross
OLD WICKHURST LA
Sports Ctr
STONEYBROOK
EASTCROFT MEWS
GROOMBRIDGE WAY
BROCKHURST CL

Downs Link
Mill Bridge
Broadbridge Farm
Baystone Copse
Baystone Farm
A24
River Arun
FELLCOTT WAY
GRANARY WAY

8
7
33
6
5
32
4
3
31
2
1
30

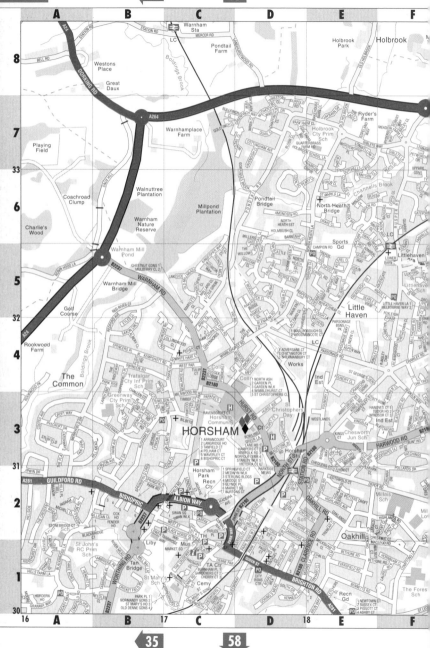

A **B** **C** **D** **E** **F**

8

Square Wood

Old House Farm

Wayside

Duckyls

Bird's Eye Wood

Giffard's Wood

7

Old House

Longwood Slip

The White Hart (PH)

Stonelands

Duckyls Farm

Rocks Wood

SELSFIELD RD

Whitestone Wood

33

Pearcelands

Chiddinglye Farm

Chiddinglye

CHANT RD

THE BROAD

West Hoathly CE (Contr) Sch

West Hoathly

Cat Inn (PH)

Shagswell Wood

6

Sheepwash Wood

Chiddinglye Wood

Lower Barn

Priest Ho (Mus)

GARDEN HEAD

CHURCH RD

THE POST LN

VINOLEI CROSS

HOATHLY HILL

5

Pearcelands Wood

SELSFIELD RD

Philpots Manor Sch

Philpots

Ashurst Wood

32

Boundary Wood

Philpots Farm

Langridge Farm House

Langridge Wood

ASHURST COTTS

4

P

Stonehurst

Coneyburrow Wood

HOOK LA

Courtland Wood

East Wood

Cob Brook

West Wood

South Wood

Barnland Wood

Hook Farm

Grovelands Farm

Newlands Cotts

HAWKENBURY RD

3

Fulling Mill Farm

Ludwell Farm

Whitestone

31

TILLINGHURST LA

Hoathly Shaw

2

Gardeners Arms (PH)

Little London

Scott's Wood

Horncombe

HOOK LA

Whitestone Wood

Furtherhouse Wood

1

COB LA

Pickeridge Farm

Holly Farm

WATNEY COTTS

30

The Showground

Long Shaw

Moorlands Wood

Highbrook

Hudds Wood

34   **A** **B** **35** **C** **D** **36** **E** **F**

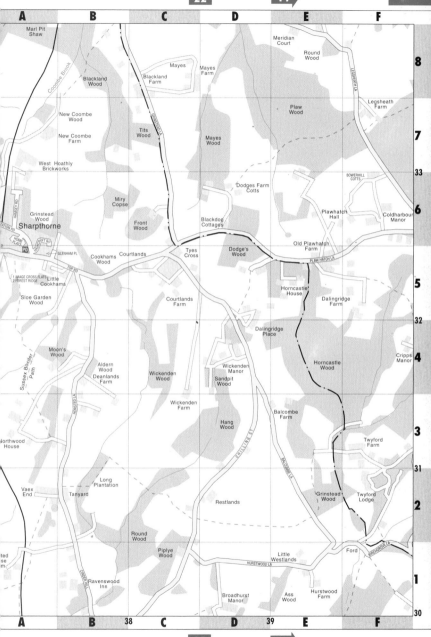

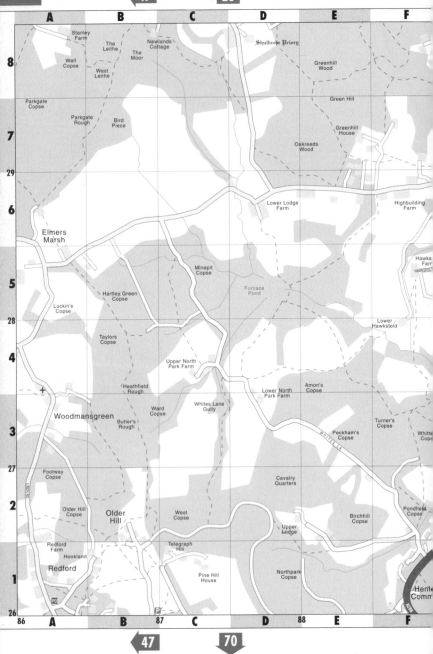

A B C D E F

8
7
29
6
5
28
4
3
27
2
1
26

Stanley
Farm
The
Leithe
Newlands
Cottage
Shulbrede Priory
Well
Copse
The
Moor
Greenhill
Wood
West
Leithe
Green Hill
Parkgate
Copse
Greenhill
House
Parkgate
Rough
Bird
Piece
Oakreeds
Wood
Lower Lodge
Farm
Highbuilding
Farm
Elmers
Marsh
Hawks
Farm
HAWKSFO
Minepit
Copse
Hartley Green
Copse
Furnace
Pond
Luckin's
Copse
Lower
Hawksfold
Taylors
Copse
Upper North
Park Farm
Heathfield
Rough
Lower North
Park Farm
Amon's
Copse
Whites Lane
Gully
Turner's
Copse
Woodmansgreen
Ward
Copse
Butler's
Rough
Peckham's
Copse
WHITES LA
Whitte
Cops
Footway
Copse
Cavalry
Quarters
Older Hill
Copse
Older
Hill
West
Copse
Birchhill
Copse
Pondfield
Copse
Upper
Lodge
Redford
Farm
Hookland
Telegraph
Hill
Redford
Pine Hill
House
Northpark
Copse
Henle
Comm

A B C D E F

Mitchell Park Farm

Hammer Cottages

8

A283

PH

PIPERS LA

Piper's Copse

Northchapel Cy Prim Sch

ST MICHAELS CL

Peacock's Farm

+

7

Northchapel

Hortons Farm

Garlands

SANDROCK COTTS

Beacon

Freehold Copse

29

Little Wood

Kiln Copse

6

Wet Wood

Freehold Farmhouse

Burrell's Wood

Mercers Copse

Goff's Farm

Mercers Furze

Pheasant Court Farm

5

Chafold Copse

Ebernoe House

STREEL'S LA

28

Old School House

Ashfold Copse

+

4

Colhook Farm

Ebernoe

Furnace Pond

School House Farm

Swedes Copse

Willand Wood

3

Kentfield's Lodge

Sibland Farm

Copsegreen

Little London

Ebernoe Common

27

Lodgefield Copse

Blind La

2

Colhook Common

Blackwool Farm

Hook Copse

1

Chillinghurst Plantations

Greyhound Plantation

Birch Copse

A283

COLHOOK IND PK

Palfrey Copse

Chillinghurst

Redhill House

26

A B 96 C D 97 E F

Piper's Cottages

Upper Frithfold Farm

Sparrwood Farm

Red Copse

The Mount

Limekiln Wood

Hardnip Barn

Hard Co

Roundwick Copse

Frithfold Farm

Roundwyck House

Roundwyck Copse

Howick Farm

Thornhouse Farm

Middleground Copse

Ainsworth Copse

Accold's Farm

SCRATCHINGS LA

Scratchings Farm

Benefold Row

Little Slifehurst Wood

Steer's Common

Whitt Planta

Wassell Mill

STREELS LA

Highnoons Farm

Hills Green Farm

Little Slifehurst

The Hoe

PITTLES LA

Hills Green Rough

Slifehurst

Hoe Bridge

Beal House Farm

Butcherland Farm

Kiln Copse Farm

Staples Hill

Parso Far

Hilland Farm

Halfway House

Stapleshill Copse

High Buildings Farm

Allfields Farm

Little Allfields Farm

River Kird

Idolsfold Copse

Rookery Copse

Bittles Field

Isling Bridge

Waytown Cottage

Sladelands

Stag Inn (PH)

Balls Cross

ELKHAM CNR

Elkham Farm

Crawford Farm

River Ki

Langhurst Hill

98   99   00

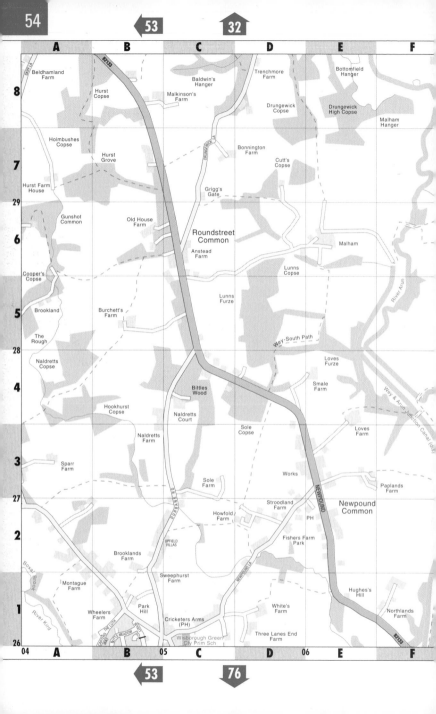

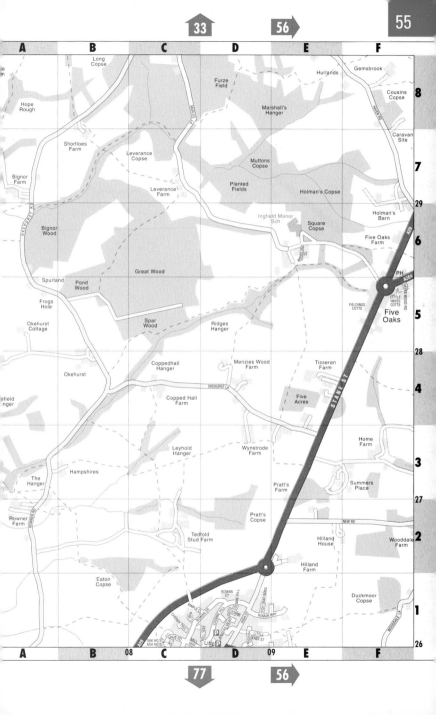

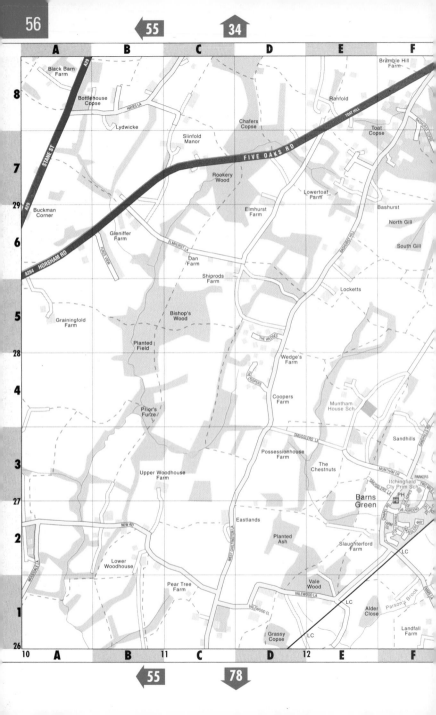

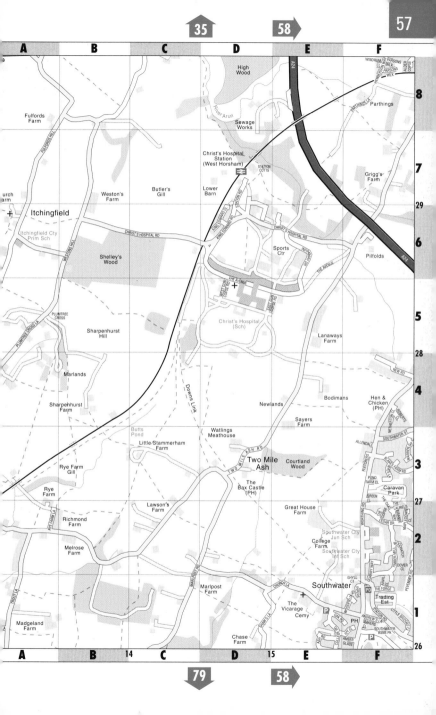

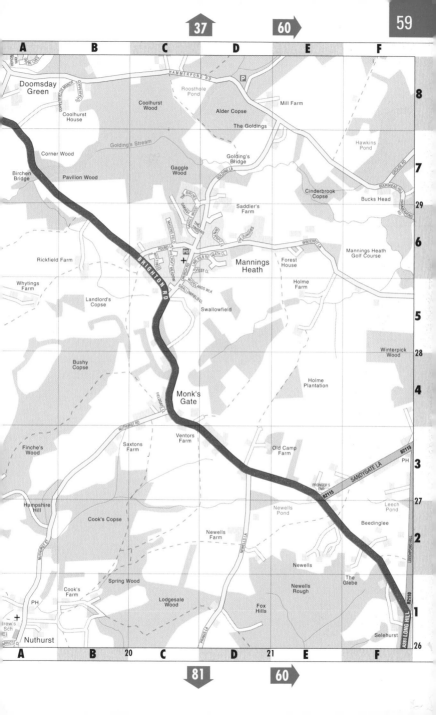

A   B   C   D   E   F

Doomsday
Green

Coolhurst
House

Coolhurst
Wood

HAMMERPOND RD

Roosthole
Pond

Alder Copse

Mill Farm

The Goldings

8

Corner Wood

Golding's Stream

Golding's
Bridge

Hawkins
Pond

7

Birchen
Bridge

Pavilion Wood

Gaggle
Wood

GOLDING LA

Cinderbrook
Copse

Bucks Head

BUCKSHEAD RD

29

Saddler's
Farm

Rickfield Farm

BRIGHTON RD

POUND

WHYTINGS

Mannings
Heath

WINTERPIT LA

Forest
House

Mannings Heath
Golf Course

6

Whytings
Farm

Landlord's
Copse

SWALLOWFIELD CL

Swallowfield

Holme
Farm

30

Bushy
Copse

Holme
Plantation

Winterpick
Wood

28

5

Monk's
Gate

FIELDGATE CL

4

Finche's
Wood

NUTHURST RD

Saxtons
Farm

Ventors
Farm

Old Camp
Farm

SANDYGATE LA

B2115

PH

3

Hampshire
Hill

NUTHURST LA

Cook's Copse

Newells
Pond

PRONGER'S CNR

B2115

Leech
Pond

27

Beedinglee

LEECHPOOL HILL

2

Spring Wood

Cook's
Farm

Lodgesale
Wood

Newells
Farm

NEWELLS LA

FRIDAYS CL

Newells

Newells
Rough

Fox
Hills

The
Glebe

A281 LONG HILL

B2110

Selehurst

1

PH

drew's
Sch
(E)

Nuthurst

RRIOT LA

26

A   B   20   C   D   21   E   F

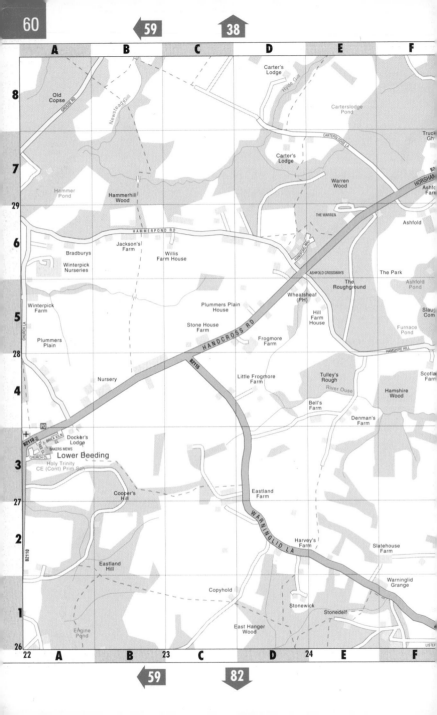

A B C D E F

8

Carter's
Lodge

Hyde Gill

Old
Copse

Carterslodge
Pond

Truck
Gh

BROOSE RD

Newstead Gill

CARTERSLODGE LA

7

HORSHAM RD

Ashfo
Farr

B2

Carter's
Lodge

Warren
Wood

Hammer
Pond

Hammerhill
Wood

29

THE WARREN

Ashfold

HAMMERPOND RD

Jackson's
Farm

Willis
Farm House

CARTERSLODGE

6

ASHFOLD CROSSWAYS

The Park

Ashfold
Pond

Bradburys

Winterpick
Nurseries

The
Roughground

Wheatsheaf
(PH)

Slau
Com

Winterpick
Farm

Plummers Plain
House

Hill
Farm
House

5

Stone House
Farm

Furnace
Pond

HANDCROSS RD

Plummers
Plain

Frogmore
Farm

HAMPSHIRE HILL

CHURCH LA

28

B2115

Little Frogmore
Farm

Tulley's
Rough

Scotla
Farm

River Ouse

4

Nursery

Hamshire
Wood

Bell's
Farm

Denman's
Farm

Docker's
Lodge

B2110

BRICK KILN

BAKERS MEWS

Lower Beeding

CHURCH CL

3

Holy Trinity
CE (Cont) Prim Sch

Eastland
Farm

27

Cooper's
Hill

WARNINGLID LA

B2110

2

Harvey's
Farm

Slatehouse
Farm

Eastland
Hill

Warninglid
Grange

1

Copyhold

Stonewick

Stonedelf

26

Engine
Pond

East Hanger
Wood

LISTEF

22 A B 23 C D 24 E F

	A	B	C	D	E	F

8
Hoadlands Wood
Chodd's Farm
Cow Wood
THE PLATT
OAKLEY COTTS
1 THE FORGE
2 THE PLATT
PH
Handcross

7
HORSHAM RD
HIGHBURY COTTS
WARREN COTTS
BRIGHTON RD
B2110
B2114
NYMANS COTTS
COVERT MEAD
PYLE PARK
Nymans (National Trust)
Dillion's Farm
Oldhouse

29
Farthings
Hill House Farm
Tanyard Wood

6
West Park Farm
Homestead Wood
Slaugham Park
Orange Gill
East Park
East Park Cottages
Tanyard Cottages
Stapleford Court

5
WOOD LA
PARK RD
The Chequers Inn (PH)
Slaugham
Slaugham Common
The Jolly Tanners (PH)
TANYARD MEAD
St Mark's CE (Contr) Prim Sch
PO
BRANTRIDGE LA
Staplefield Place Sch
Staplefield

28
STAPLEFIELD RD
Home Farm
STAPLEFIELD RD
CUCKFIELD RD
B2114

4
Pond Tail Farmhouse
Slaugham Place (remains of)
Slaugham Manor
River Ouse
Little Ashfold

3
Slaughamplace Farm
Old Park Farm
Stanbridge House
STAPLEFIELD RD
North Hall

27
Old Park House
Warninglid Cty Prim Sch
Stanbridge Grange Farm

2
MALLION'S LA
Mallion's Farm

1
Upper Barn
Warninglid
Anne's Wood
Beacon Hall
White House Farm
SLOUGHGREEN LA

26
Hollingbury Court Sch
CUCKFIELD LA
Portways Farm
B2115
A23
B2115
B2115

A B C D E F

8

Brantridge Sch

Bury Wood

Northland Wood

Jarretts Farm

Brook Wood

Kemps Farm

LONDON RD

B2036

Northlands Farm

Norfolk Cottage

Rowhill Wood

WELTER RD

Allen's Farm

Seyron Wood

7

Soles Coppice

Pilstye Wood

29

Washlands Farm

Long Wood

Furze Wood

Brownings

Little Sion Wood

Upper Pilstye Cottages

6

Brightwell Farm

WHITEHOUSE LA

White House

Spicer's Farm

BRANTRIDGE LA

Court Farm

Pilstye Farm

Old Hall

5

CHERRY LA

STONECOURT COTTS

Tyes Place

ROSE COTTAGE LA

28

Upper Staplefield Common

River Ouse

Hillside

Sidnye Cottages

Chiffley Grange

Sidnye Farm

4

The Old Kennels

B2114

Hammerhill Bridge

Barrack Cottages

3

Toll Shaw

HAMMER HILL

Collin's Farm

Bigges Farm

Hammer Hill

Hammerhill Copse

27

CUCKFIELD RD

Holmsted Manor

SPARKS LA

2

Cleaver's Cottages

Mizbrook's Farm

Lower Spark's Farm

BROOK ST

Holmsted Farm

STUBBLE LA

Tanyard Farm

Brook Street

BROOK LANE

1

B2036

Slough Green

Little Mizbrooks

Taylors Barn

HOLMSTED HILL

Slough Place Farm

Slough Place

B2114

26

B2115

28 A B 29 C D 30 E F

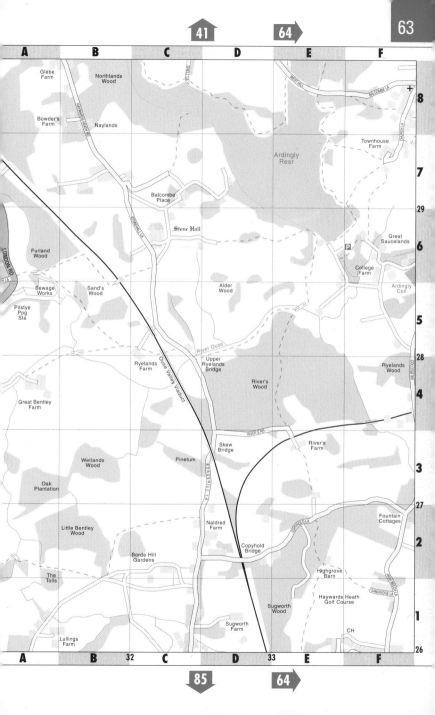

63
42

	A	B	C	D	E	F

8

St Peter's CE (Contr) Prim Sch
Recn Gd
Hapstead Wood
Hapstead House
Withyland
Brookhouse Wood
Hammenden Farm
Lucasland Wood
Brook House Farm

Ardingly
Inn

7

Brook House
Burstow
Upper Sheriff Farm
Orchard Wood

Berry
29
LINDFIELD RD

6

Ardingly Coll
Playing Fields
Great Lywood Farm
Lywood Common
Burstow Hill
Sheriff Farm
High Wood
Cockhaise Brook

Standgrove Wood
Horse Wood
Nobles Farmhouse

5

28
Flat Wood
Goddenwick Farm

4

ROAD LA
Goddard's Farm
Stone Cross
Goddenwick Wood

Bursteye Farm
Hill House Farm
STONE CROSS
STONECROSS LA
REVFORD LA

Avins Farm
Lower Ryelands Bridge
THE COURTYARD
Buxshalls
Den's Barn Farm
WOODSLAND CROSS
Woodsland
Woodsland Farm

3
27

Kenwards Farm
Fullingmill Farm
Bridge Wood
BUXSHALLS HILL
Convent
Court Wood
PARK LA
Quarry Shaw
PLUMMERDEN LA

2

River Ouse
Grange Farm
Paxhill Park

Town Wood
GRAHAM'S COTTS
Lindfield Bridge
Nunnery Wood
Skein Winders
Great Plummerden Farm

1
26
FINCHES GORSE
Mill

34
	A	B	C	D	E	F
35
36

63
86

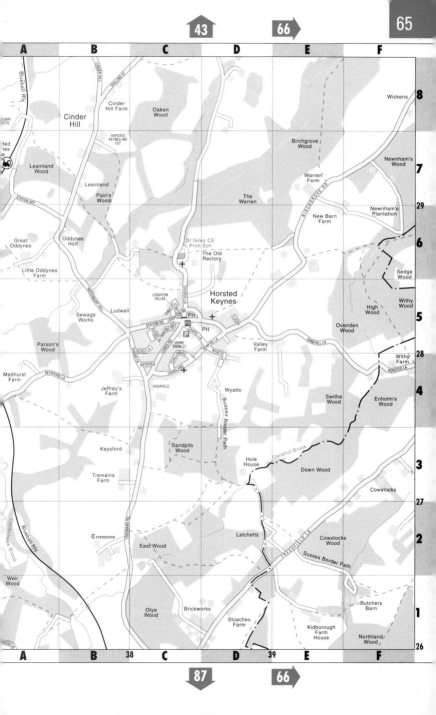

8

Wickens

Cinder Hill Farm

Oaken Wood

Cinder Hill

Birchgrove Wood

HORSTED KEYNES IND EST

Newnham's Wood

7

Leamland Wood

Warren Farm

Leamland

Pain's Wood

The Warren

New Barn Farm

Newnham's Plantation

29

Great Oddynes

Oddynes Holt

St Giles CE Prim Sch

The Old Rectory

6

Little Oddynes Farm

Sedge Wood

Withy Wood

LEIGHTON VILLAS

Horsted Keynes

High Wood

Ludwell

Sewage Works

5

PH

PH

Ovenden Wood

Parson's Wood

P

PO

HOME FARM CT

Valley Farm

Withy Farm

28

Medhurst Farm

HORSTED LA

4

Jeffrey's Farm

HIGHFIELD

Wyatts

Swithe Wood

Enholm's Wood

Sussex Border Path

Keysford

Sandpits Wood

Danehill Brook

3

Hole House

Down Wood

Tremains Farm

Cowstocks

27

Tremains

Latchetts

Cowstocks Wood

2

East Wood

Sussex Border Path

Weir Wood

Bluebell Rly

Cuckfield Brook

Otye Wood

Brickworks

Stoaches Farm

Kidborough Farm House

Butchers Barn

Northland Wood

1

26

A B C D E F

65
44

67
46

A B C D E F

8

Tulliecombe

Wiseland
Hill

Tulliecombe
(Picnic Place)

Trotton
Marsh

7

Fyning
Hill

Cair
Wool

25

Rondle
Wood

Redhill
Copse

BORDEN LA

Fyning
Common

Borden

6

Rogate
Lodge

Halecommon

Home
Farm

TEMPLE RSE

Dangstein

Ship
Copse

Stonehous

5

Terwick
Common

Home
Farm

Cumber's La

FYNING LA

CATTERSS

24

Fyning

Rogate

PH

EAST
LODGE

4

PO

OLD HOUSE CT

Rogate
CE
(Contr)
Prim Sch

HABIN HILL

GARDEN TCE

Mill's Farm House

Terwick
Land

HUGO PLATT

A272

PURCELL HAUS

3

Fyning
Moor

Souter's
Copse

Sewage
Works

23

Haben
Farm

Habin
Bridge

Wakeham
Farm

2

Mizzards

Habin

Fair
Oak

River Rother

Sandhill
Farm

Sandhill
House

1

The
Mount

New
Barn

22

Sandilands
Equestrian Ctr

80 A B 81 C D 82 E F

8
7
25
6
5
24
4
3
23
2
1
22

A B C D E F

PH
Henley
Verdleyhill
Verdley Farm
Poor's Common
Scotland Knob
Whitters Copse
North Heath
Sowters Gate
Kemp's Hill
WICK LA
Budgenor Lodge
CANADA COTTS
Midhurst Intermediate Sch
Easebourne CE (Contr) Prim Sch
Cemy
BIRTHDAY RD
PH
Easebourne
CH
Conifers Sch
1 EVERSLEIGH CT
2 RED OAK CT
3 EGMONT HO
DODSLEY LA
EASEBOURNE LA
KENER RD
Lower Elidge
Overnoons
Gunters Farm
Slong Hanger
Eldridge Farm
Bexleyhill
HIGHSTEAD LA
Knights Copse
Bexleyhill Common
Fenced Common
Ovis Copse
Vining Rough
Grevatts
Hoe Hill
EASEBOURNE ST
Sowter's Hanger
Vining Farm
Lower Vining
Loves Farm
Sowter's Farm
Gosdens Farm
The Race
BLAKERS LA
Cowdray Park
Oaters Wood
Broomhill Plantation
Steward's Pond
Heathend Copse
Lime Bottom
Cowdray Park Golf Course
New Barn
Benbow Pond
High Field Copse
A272

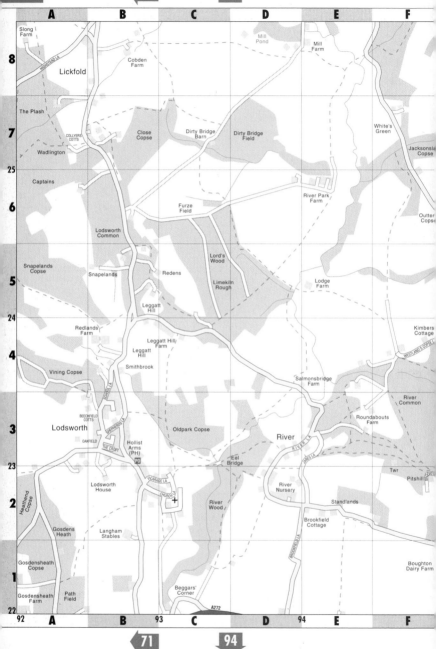

A B C D E F

8

Slong Farm

HIGHSTEAD LA

Lickfold

Cobden Farm

Mill Pond

Mill Farm

7

The Plash

COLLYERS COTTS

Wadlington

Close Copse

Dirty Bridge Barn

Dirty Bridge Field

White's Green

Jacksonsla Copse

25

Captains

6

Lodsworth Common

Furze Field

River Park Farm

Outter Copse

Snapelands Copse

Snapelands

Redens

Lord's Wood

Limekiln Rough

Lodge Farm

5

24

Redlands Farm

Leggatt Hill

Leggatt Hill Farm

Kimbers Cottage

WESTLANDS COPSE LA

4

Vining Copse

Leggatt Hill

Smithbrook

SCHOOL LA

Salmonsbridge Farm

River Common

BEECONFIELD COTTS

Lodsworth

OAKFIELD

HEATHERS LA

THE CROFT

Hollist Arms (PH)

PO

Oldpark Copse

River

RIVER LA

Roundabouts Farm

3

23

Eel Bridge

Twr

Pitshill

Heatherd Copse

Lodsworth House

SCARAGE LA

CHURCH

River Wood

River Nursery

Standlands

PROVIDERS LA

2

Gosdens Heath

Langham Stables

Brookfield Cottage

Gosdensheath Copse

Beggars' Corner

Boughton Dairy Farm

1

Gosdensheath Farm

Path Field

A272

22

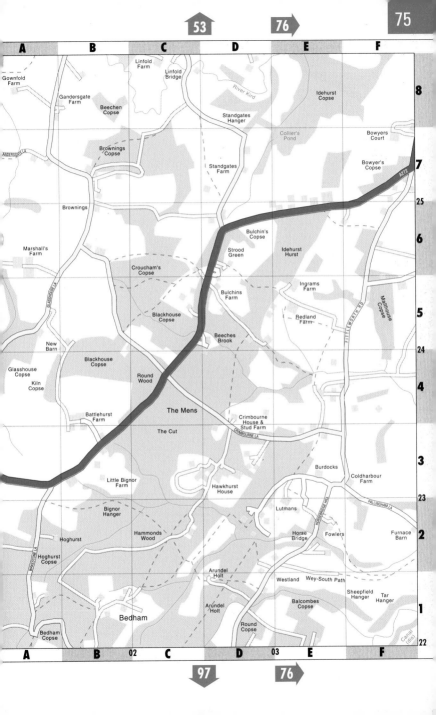

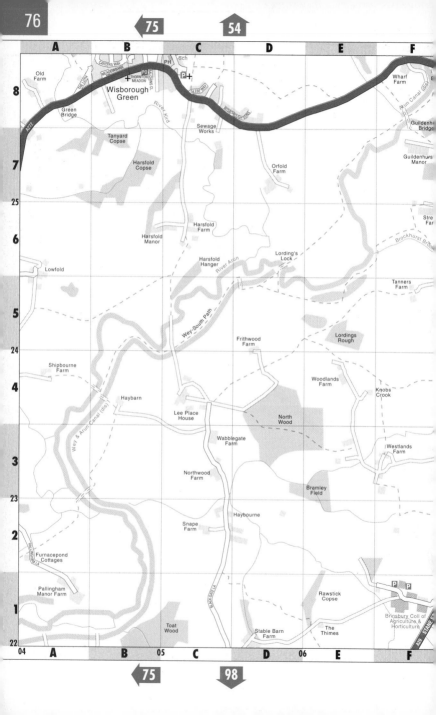

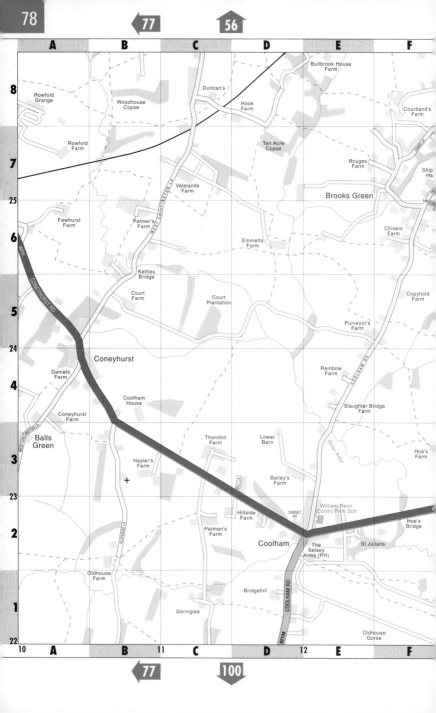

Limekiln
Wood

Alicelands
House

Long
Wood

Cripps
Wood

Nutham
Wood

Fox End
Farm

Furzefield
Wood

Elliotts

Elliotts
Farm

Gaveston
Hall

Goffs
Copse

Copsale
Court

Copsale

The
Bridge House
(PH)

Jamesland
Farm

Pollardshill
Farm

Copsale
Farm

STEEDS
CNR

Maplehurst

HAMP
COT

The
White Horse
(PH)

Great Steed
Farm

Shuckers
Farm

Sheepwash
Farm

ABINGER
COTTS

POLLARD'S HILL

Downs Link

Stead's
Plantation

Blake's
Farm

Maplehurst
Farm

New Brook
Farm

COURTUP HILL

Little
Tuckmans

WORTHING RD

Abinger
Hill

Bar Cover
Furzefield

Tuckmans
Farm

Joles
Farm

The Bar

Haven
Bridge

Upper Soil
Gill

Coate's
Wood

New House
Farm

Smallham
Farm

Buck
Wood

Crawley & Horsham
Kennels

Pondtail
Farm

Freeman's
Wood

A272

MODEL BUILDINGS
COTTS

BUCKBARN
CROSSROADS

BUCK BARN
BGLWS

A272

KIPPENS LA

COWFOLD RD

RAILWAY
COTTS

KENNEL LA

Park Farm
(The Sussex
Stud)

Gatelands

PENNS LA

Hill House
Farm

Park Covert

Furzefield
Wood

8

Lydhurst

Hogstolt
Hill

New
Pond

Riflema
Inn
(PH)

Leonardslee
Gardens

Barland's
Farm

Freechase
Hill

Free
Chase
Farm

Crabtree

Minepits
Wood

The
Lake

7

Free
Chase

Furnace
Pond

The
Crabtree
Inn
(PH)

MILL LA

25

Steep
Wood

Peppersgate
Farm

Drewitts

6

PERRYFIELD LA

Round
Wood

Den
Wood

EWINGS LA

Goodgers

Bushy
Platts

5

Long
House

Denwood
House

CROSS COLWOOD LA

Chatesgro

Graffields

Hookland
Farm

Bull's
Wood

Westle

North
Farm

24

Colwood
Manor
Farm

Chargrove

Barnfield
Wood

PICT'S LA

4

Spronkett's

Pict's
Farm

Aglands

SPRONKETT'S LA

BULL'S LA

Walhurst
Manor

Homefields

SMITH'S
CROSS

3

Kings
Hill

Barnfield
House

Upper
Barn

Cooper's
Farm

23

Six Acre
Shaw

New
Barn

Homewood
House

2

Lyelands

Greenacres
Farm

Oakendene
Manor

Southlands
Farm

A272

Bugshole
Copse

OAKDENE
IND EST

KENT STREET LA

BRINSBURY LA

1

Taintfield
Wood

Nye's
Copse

Red
House

SLOUGHGREEN LA
B2114
B2115
STAPLEFIELD RD
Upper Sparks Farm
Old Deaks Farm
Henmead
Deakes Manor
Old Beech Farm
Mill Hall Oral Sch for the Deaf
BURRELL COTTS 1
RHOULES COTTS 2
IVY COTTS 3
HALLEIGHS 4
HIGHLANDS COTTS 1
FARR CL 2
BURRELL GN 3
STOCKLANDS CL 4
LONGACRE CRES 5
WHITEMANS GN
CROUCHLANDS FARM
CHERRY TREES
TOLLGATE LA
Whitemans Green
Beech Farm
THE KNOWLE
Wyllies Wood
Henmead Wood
The Shanty
New England Wood
POLESTUB LA
ORCHARD COTT 1
GLEBE/TWITTEN 2
YEW TREE CT 3
LONDON RD
B2184
LONDON LA
Holy CE Pri
The Wylies
Walks Wood
Recn Gd
LEDGERS MEADOW
NORTHERN BREACH
MYTTEN CL
Hotel
Liby Mus
PO
PH
BROAD ST
COURTMEAD RD
Cuckfield Park
CUCKFIELD
Cemy
Warden Sch
Cuckfield Park
NEWBURY LA
Newbury Pond
Pondtail
Westup Wood
Oldmill Cottage
B2036
Laines Farm
Court House
Sewage Works
Furze Field
Hoadsherf Farm
High Bridge
Highbridge Mill
Mackrell's
Lodge Farm
COPTHALL LA
Copyhold Farm
Pickwell Shaw
Inholms Wood
PO
The Green Cross (PH)
B2036
GREEN CROSS
ANSTY RD
Ansty
Pickwell Farm
Butler's Wood
Butler's Farm
Heaseland Hanger
A272
Foxashes
Pink's Wood
West Riddens
West Riddens Farm
Upper Ridges
Harvest Hill
Hilders Cottage
Brewhouse Pond
HARVEST HILL
Bishopstone Farm
Legh Manor
Moonhill Place
Moonhill Farm
B2036

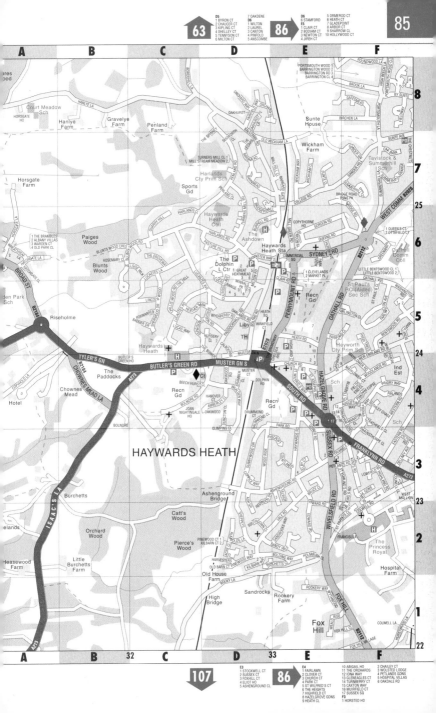

85
64

85

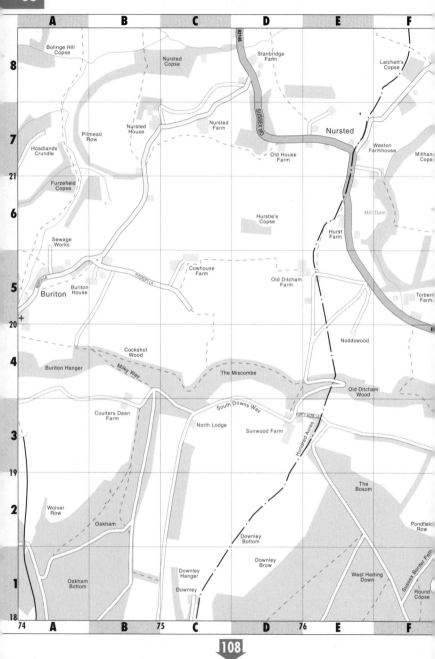

A | **B** | **C** | **D** | **E** | **F**

Bolinge Hill Copse

Nursted Copse

Stanbridge Farm

Latchett's Copse

8

Hoadlands Crundle

Pilmead Row

Nursted House

Nursted Farm

Nursted

Weston Farmhouse

Millham Copse

7

21

Furzefield Copse

Old House Farm

6

Sewage Works

Hurstle's Copse

Hurst Farm

Mill Dam

Buriton

Buriton House

PITCROFT LA

Cowhouse Farm

Old Ditcham Farm

Torberry Farm

5

NORTH LA

Noddswood

20

Cockshot Wood

Buriton Hanger

Milky Way

The Miscombe

Old Ditcham Wood

4

Coulters Dean Farm

North Lodge

South Downs Way

Sunwood Farm

FORTY ACRE LA

3

Hundred Acres

19

The Bosom

Wolver Row

2

Oakham

Downley Bottom

Downley Brow

Pondfield Row

Oakham Bottom

Downley Hanger

Downley

West Harting Down

Sussex Border Path

Round Copse

1

18

74 **A** | **B** 75 **C** | **D** 76 **E** | **F**

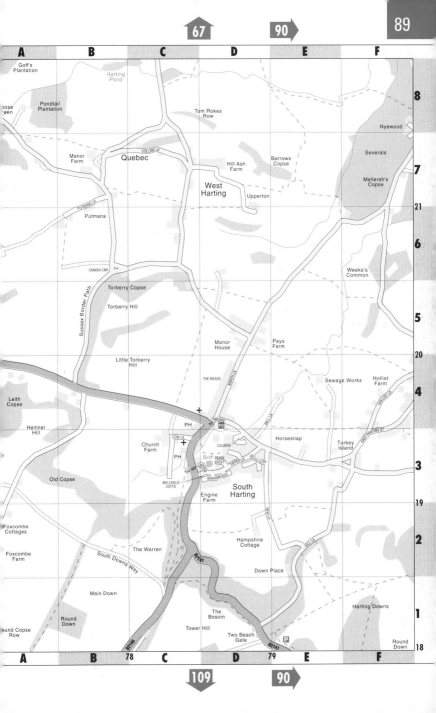

89
68

A B C D E F

8

7

6

5

4

3

2

1

21

20

19

18

Dumpford LA

Southdowns
Hotel

Works

Clarefield
Copse

Little Barn

Dumpford
Farm

Dumpford

Nyewood

Dumpford
Manor
Farm

Champs
Farm

Horne's
Farm

Dumpford Park
Farm

Great
Plantation

Hayters
Plantation

Park
Copse

Woodhouse
Farm

Loaders Copse

The
Hassocks

Elsted
Rough

Tye Oak
Farm

ST
RICHARD'S
COTTR

Elsted Rd

Ti
Inh

Sheepwash
Copse

Manor
Farm

Elsted
Green

Ladymead
Cottage

Oak
Wood

ORCHARD

HILL
VIEW

Three Horse Shoes
(PH)

Elsted

Grevatts

Mill
Barn

Westfield
Hangar

Knightsfield

Cemy

Redlands

Caseys
Copse

Hump Back
Plantation

Manor
Farm

Treyford

Harting
Downs

Bramshott Bottom

South Downs Way

Beacon
Hill

Pen Hill

South Downs Way

Mount
Sinai

Elsted
Hangar

Rook
Clift

80 A 81 B C 82 D E F

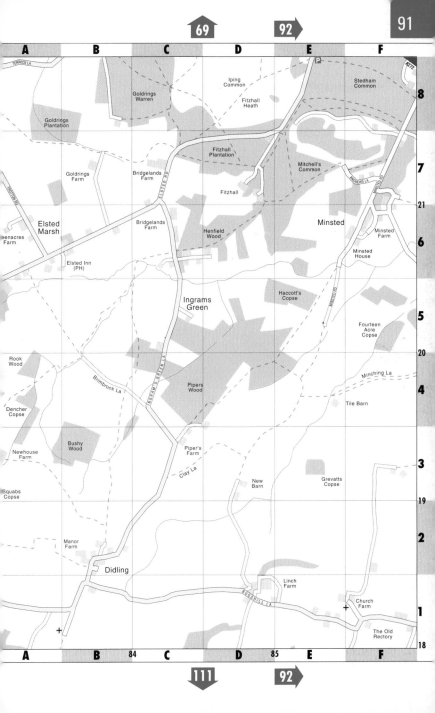

A   B   C   D   E   F

Terwick La

P

Iping
Common

Stedham
Common

A272

8

Goldrings
Warren

Fitzhall
Heath

Goldrings
Plantation

Fitzhall
Plantation

Mitchell's
Common

BEPTON RD

7

Goldrings
Farm

Bridgelands
Farm

ELSTED RD

Fitzhall

Brookwis La

Minsted Rd

21

Elsted
Marsh

Bridgelands
Farm

Henfield
Wood

Minsted

Minsted
Farm

6

Greenacres
Farm

Elsted Inn
(PH)

Minsted
House

Ingrams
Green

Haccott's
Copse

Minsted Rd

5

Rook
Wood

Fourteen
Acre
Copse

20

Brimbrook La

INGRAM SURMILL La

Pipers
Wood

Minching La

4

Dencher
Copse

Tile Barn

Newhouse
Farm

Bushy
Wood

Piper's
Farm

New
Barn

Grevatts
Copse

3

Squabs
Copse

Clay La

19

Manor
Farm

2

Didling

Linch
Farm

Church
Farm

BURGHILL LA

1

+

The Old
Rectory

18

+

A   B   84   C   D   85   E   F

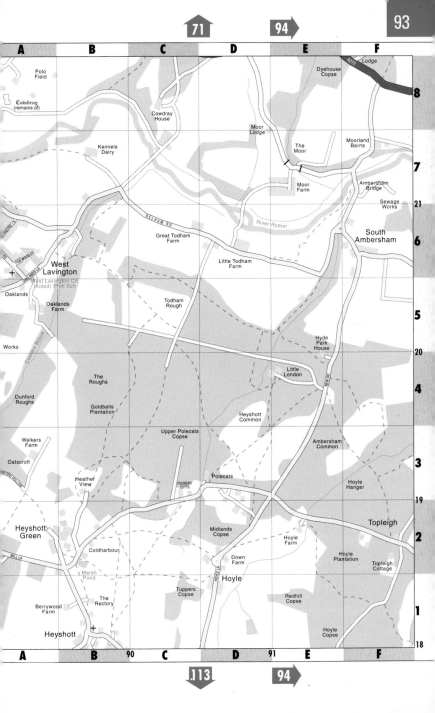

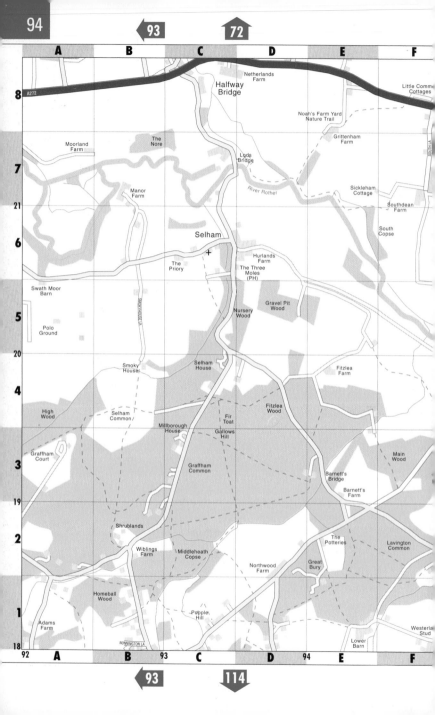

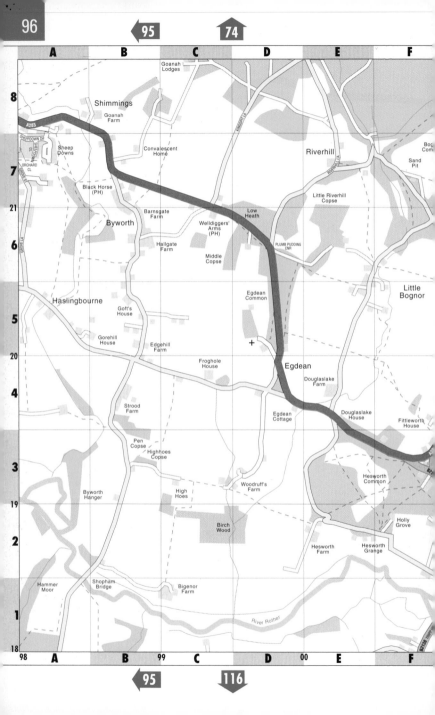

A   **B**   **C**   **D**   **E**   **F**

8

Goanah
Lodges

Shimmings

Goanah
Farm

A283

Sheep
Downs

SHEEPDOWN DR

ORCHARD
CL

Convalescent
Home

Riverhill

Bog
Com

Sand
Pit

7

Black Horse
(PH)

21

Barnsgate
Farm

Byworth

Little Riverhill
Copse

Low
Heath

Welldiggers'
Arms
(PH)

PLUMB PUDDING
CNR

Hallgate
Farm

Middle
Copse

6

Haslingbourne

Goff's
House

Egdean
Common

Little
Bognor

5

Gorehill
House

Edgehill
Farm

20

Froghole
House

Egdean

Douglaslake
Farm

+

4

Strood
Farm

Egdean
Cottage

Douglaslake
House

Fittleworth
House

Pen
Copse

Highhoes
Copse

3

Byworth
Hanger

High
Hoes

Woodruff's
Farm

Hesworth
Common

19

Birch
Wood

Holly
Grove

2

Hesworth
Farm

Hesworth
Grange

Hammer
Moor

Shopham
Bridge

Bigenor
Farm

1

River Rother

18

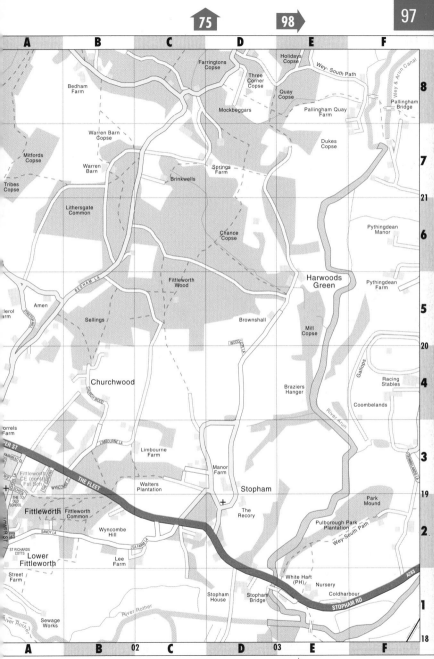

A B C D E F

8

Farringtons Copse
Holidays Copse
Wey- South Path
Bedham Farm
Three Corner Copse
Quay Copse
Pallingham Bridge
Mockbeggars
Pallingham Quay Farm

Warren Barn Copse
Dukes Copse
7

Warren Barn
Springs Farm
21
Brinkwells

Lithersgate Common
Pythingdean Manor
6
Chance Copse

Amen
Fittleworth Wood
Harwoods Green
Pythingdean Farm

lerol arm
Sellings
Brownshall
Mill Copse
5

Churchwood
20
Braziers Hanger
Racing Stables

4
Coombelands

orrels Farm
River Arun
Limbourne La
Limbourne Farm

PER ST
FAIRHEAD CL
Fittleworth CE (cont'd) Fst Sch
THE FLEET
Walters Plantation
Manor Farm
Stopham
Park Mound
3
19

THE OLD SCHOOL
Fittleworth
Fittleworth Common
The Recory
Pulborough Park Plantation
Wey-South Path
2

LOWFR ST
ST RICHARDS COTTS
SANDY LA
Wyncombe Hill
LEA FARM LA
White Hart (PH)
Nursery
Coldharbour
A283

Lower Fittleworth
Lee Farm
Street Farm
Stopham House
Stopham Bridge
STOPHAM RD
1
18

River Roj
Sewage Works
River Rother

A B 02 C D 03 E F

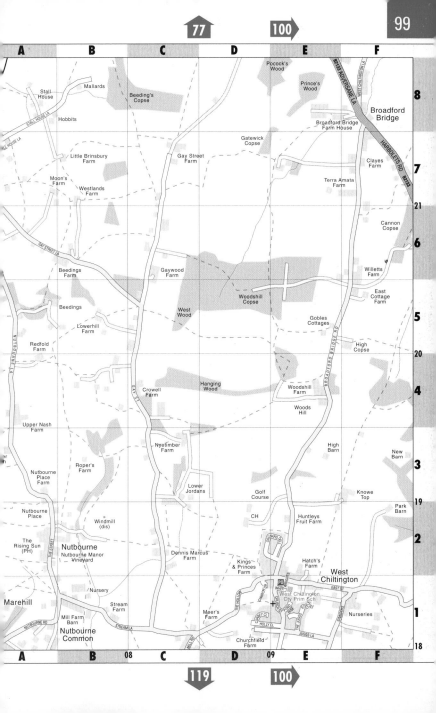

	A	B	C	D	E	F	

8

School La
King's Platt
King's Windmill
Shipley
Capp's Bridge
Church Farm South
Knepp Castle
New Lodge
Kneppmill Pond

Whitehall
Hampshires Farm
COUNTRYMAN LA
POUND CNR.
Pound Farm

7

Smoke House Farm
The Countryman (PH)
SMITHERS HILL LA
Tenchford
Charlwood Barn

21

Hammer Farm
River Adur

6

Pen Bridge
Lower Barn
Hammer Pond
Honeypools Barn

5

Lancing Brook
New Barn Farm
Jackson's Wood
Swallows Farm
WORTHING RD

Brookhouse Farm

20

Bentons Place Farm

4

Tory Copse
Dial Post
Sewage Works
BENTONS LA
Crown Inn (PH)
WORTHING RD

3

HOOKLANDS LA
Blonks Farm
Oakwood Farm Cottages

19

Woodmans Stud
Thistleworth Farm

Oakwood
Percyland Farm

2

Furzefield Wood
Hookland Wood
Honeybridge Poultry Farm
HONEYBRIDGE LA
Grinder's Wood
omhole opse

1

BASING HILL
Wincaves Park Caravan & Camping Site
Round Wood
Oxcopse Barn

18

	A	B	14	C	D	15	E	F	

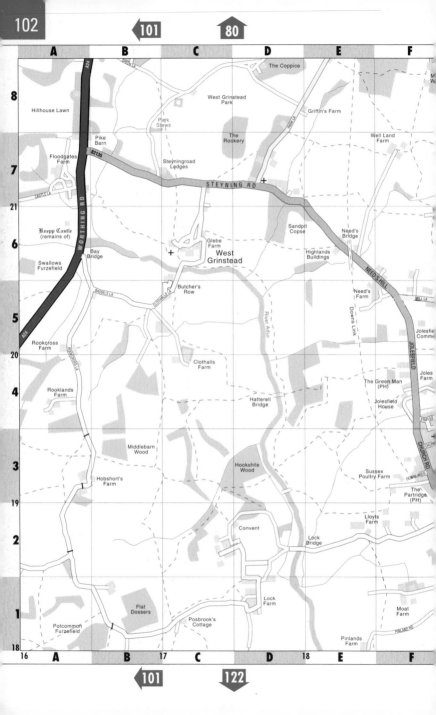

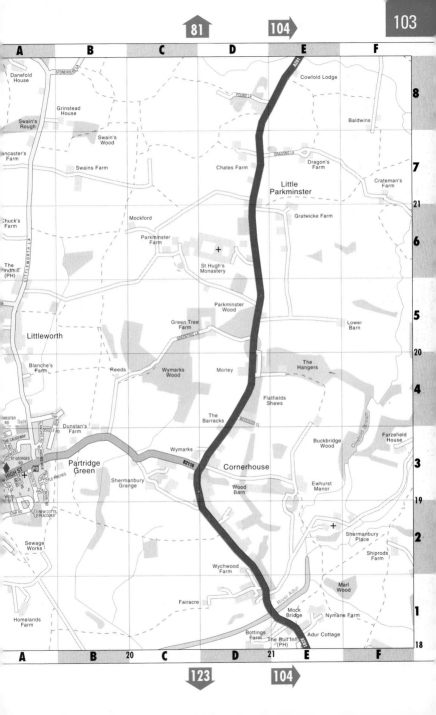

A   B   C   D   E   F

Holmbush
Wood

Brooklands
Farm

Holmbush
Farm

Holmbush
Cottages

ISAAC'S LA

Folly
Farm

Kiln
Wood

FOX HILL
VILLAGE

BRACE HILL
TERR

Fox & Hounds
(PH)

Cleavewaters
Farm

Clearwaters
Farm

Roger's
Farm

8

Vale
Bridge

CLEARWATERS LA

Lunce's
Common

7

Goose
Pit

Tilebarn
Wood

Brook
Lodge

Wivelsfield
Cty Prim Sch

21

Big
Wood

Bedelands Farm
Local Nature
Reserve

Bedelands
Farm

VALEBRIDGE

Antye
Farm

Theobalds

CHURCH LA

Lunces
Hall

6

Lowlands
Farm

Works

CHARLWOOD

HAWTHORN CL

LAUREL

Great Ote
Hall

Works

Great Otehall
Wood

SPRINGFIELDS FARM
IND EST

5

Recn
Gd

Manor Field
Cty Prim Sch

BARKDALE LA

World's
End

Ote Hall
Farm

JANES LA

20

Wivelsfield
Sta

STIRLING

THE CLOSE

Bankside
Farm

The Royal Oak
(PH)

4

WOODLAND DRIVE
WALKWAY

ST ANDREWS RD

St George's
Retreat

3

LCS

Works
Clay
Pit

1 YEW TREE COTTS
2 OAK TREE COTTS
3 WRENTHAM HO

1 HUMPHREY LODGE
2 KELSEY CT
3 WARE CT
4 SCRASE LODGE
5 BENJAMIN LODGE
6 PAYTON HO
7 WATTS LODGE

Hope
Farm

St Mary's
House

19

Liby

Mkt

QUEEN ELIZABETH AVE

MARKET

Burgess
Hill
Sta

WOLSTONBURY 1
WOLSTONBURY WAY 2

WYNNSTAY

Burgess Hill
Sch

Meeds
n Sch

on Meed
Prim Sch

STATION RD

KEYMER RD

Stubs
Copse

Ditchling
Common

BURGESS
HILL

Freckborough
Manor

2

Meoick
House Sch

Pollards
Farm

Ditchling Common
Country Park

Ind Est

1

BEECHWOODS

Folders
Farm

FOLDERS LA

B2113

B2112

18

A   B   32   C   33   D   E   F

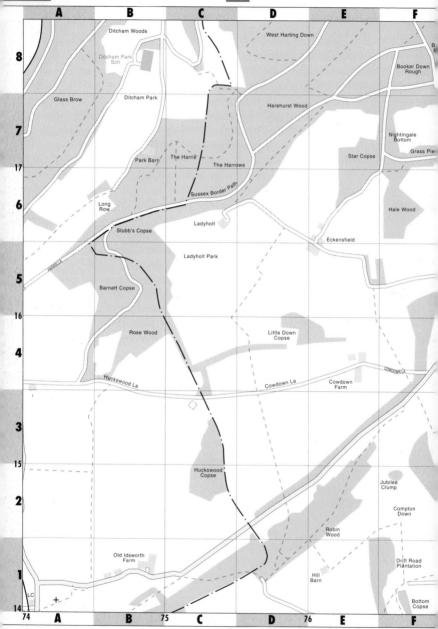

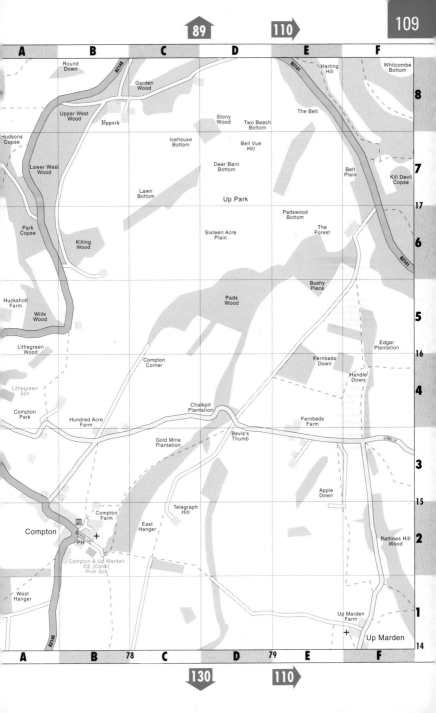

109
90

8

Bramshott Bottom

South Downs Way

Little Round Down

Millpond Bottom

Buriton Farm

Treyford Hill

Telegraph House

7

Buriton Hanger

Devil's Jumps

South Downs Way

Philliswood Down

17

Monk Copi

6

North Marden Down

B2141

Germanleith Copse

Bushy Piece

Philliswood Farm

Monk Far

5

North Marden

Royal Oak (PH)

Gutteridge Row

+

Meredon Farm

Hill Lands Farm

Hooksway

16

Phillis Wood

4

Stubbs Copse

Batten Hanger

3

LONG LA

Long La

Fourways

Newbuildings

15

Upton Farm

Manor Place

2

The Glebe House

East Marden

The White Horse (PH)

+

East Marden Farm

HILLSIDE COTTS

Bow Hill Farm

Chilgrove Hill

Chilgrove

Sm

1

Faraway

East Marden Down

Hill Barn

Whitelands Copse

14

109
131

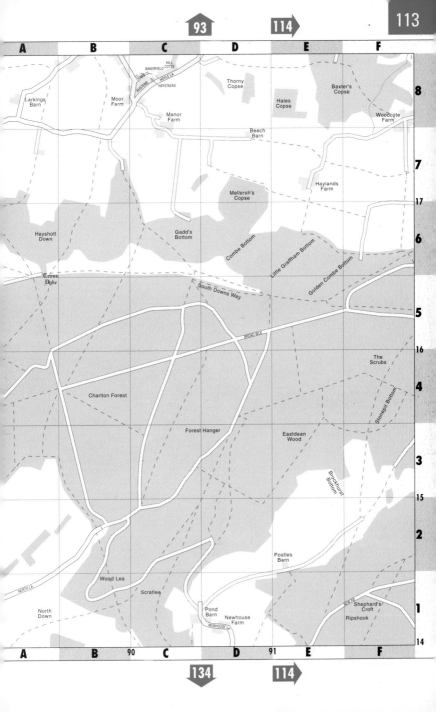

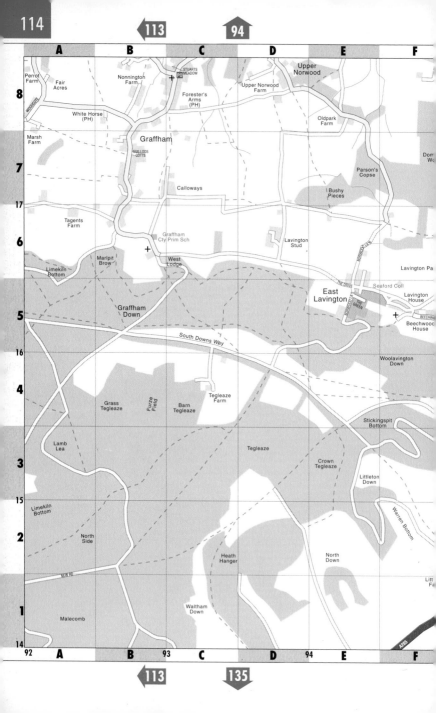

8

Ridlington
Farm

Redlands
Farm

Black
Pond

Newpiece
Moor

Burton Mill
Pond

Duncton

Burton
Park

Chingford
Pond

The
Moor

7

Duncton
CE (Contr)
Prim Sch

Crouch
Farm

Ridlington
Copse

East
Wood

Half Moon
Copse

17

DUNCTON HIGH ST

The Cricketers
(PH)

Lodge
Copse

Brickfield
Copse

6

Playing
Fields

Manor
Farm

Duncton
Mill

Fountain
Copse

BEECHWOOD LA

Pond
Places

Furze
Field

Fryan's
Hanger

P

Duncton
Hanger

Limekiln
Copse

Barlavington

5

Springs

Barlavington
Farm

Jerrymores
Copse

16

Barlavington
Hanger

Chalk
Pit

op's
g

Duncton Down

Haslands
Farm

SCHOOL LA

4

Barlavington Down

Northcomb
Barn

Sutton

Northcomb
Wood

COUNCIL
COTTS

The White Horse
(PH)

3

DOG
KENNELS

Court Farm

GREENFIELD

15

Hazel
Comb

Farm Wood

2

Farm Hill

South Downs Way

New Barn

1

GLATTING LA

Glatting
Farm

14

A   B   C   D   E   F

8

Ravesland
Copse

Coates

Lower
Horncroft

Welchs
Common

Coates
Castle

Tripphill
Farm

7

The
Warren

Broad
Halfpenny

Lord's
Piece

Sutton
Common

Coates
Common

Horncroft
Farm

17

Tooths
Plantation

6

Keyzaston
Farm

Collumn Hill

Bignor Park
Cott

Badland
Wood

Horncroft
Common

Coldwaltham
Wood

Sutton
End

Decoy
Copse

Newoods
Farm

5

Winters
Copse

Bury Gate
House

16

Hospital
Copse

Bowler's Crab
Wood

Ridge
Copse

4

The
Swares

Bignor Park

Bowler's
Copse

Bury Gate
Farm

Dukes
Copse

Downview
Farm

Bignor Park
House

Hammond's
Copse

3

Courthill
Wood

15

Bignor
Mill

Grevatt
Wood

Bury Mill
Farm

2

Bignor

Manor
Farm

ROMAN VILLA
(remains of)

Hadworth
Farm

Hale Hill
Farm

COOTES COTTS

Jay's
Farm

1

Upper
House

14

98   A   B   99   C   D   00   E   F

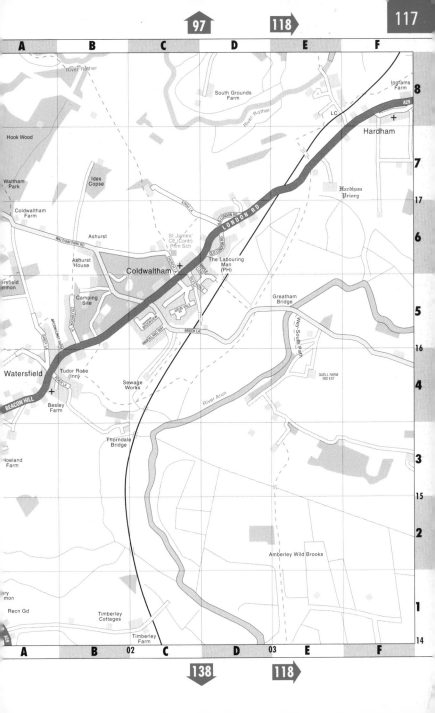

119 100

8

Nursery

Town House
Farm

Cray's
Farm

Bramblefield

Woolvens
Farm

B2133 BILLINGHURST RD

Westlands
Farm

Thakeham
Cty Prim Sch

The Street

7

Chesswood
Nursery

White Lion
Inn
(PH)

Thakeham

Thakeham
Place

Mill
Copse

West Wolves
Farm

WOODLAND
COTTS

17

HAREBARROW
WOODS

HIGH BAR

Manor House
Buildings

Warminghurst Farm

Warminghurst

Oast House
Farm

6

PURSE
COMMON RD

Abingworth

GUYHURST
SPINNEY

Nursery

RECTORY LA

Meiros
Farm

PENN
GONS

Ashingtons
CE (Cont)
Prim Sch

STORRINGTON RD

JACKET'S HILL

Nursery

5

Lancing Brook

STRAWBERRY LA

Guyhurst
Copse

Park Barn

PARK LA

Green Dene
Farm

16

Pelham
House

Little
Thakeham

Church
Farm

4

The
Maples

Newhouse
Farm

Nursery

MERRYWOOD LA

MERRYWOOD HO

Jinkes
Farm

Mitchbourne

3

Orchardway
Farm

WOODLANDS

HENFIELD

MUTTON'S LA

Lower
Barn

Malthouse
Farm

B2139

15

The Rydon
Com Sch

BUNBURY CL

BRACKEN LA

HAZELWOOD CL

OLD BANK CL

ROCK RD

Mutton's
Farm

Nursery

LONDON RD

2

HILLSIDE RD

SANDGATE LA

**Heath
Common**

Longbury
Hill

Nurseries

Nursery

CROSS GORS

1

Sand Pit

THE DELL

BLACK HILL

LANE TURRY LA

Washington
Common

RISA LA

Rock Place
Farm

Rock
Farm

SANDY LA

Sandgate Park

B2133

14

119 141

A   B   C   D   E   F

Wincave Farm

Cow Barn

The Plantation

Windsor Common

Buckells Farm

8

Hooklands Farm

Woodman's Farm

netts arm

Nursery

BASING HILL

Capite Wood

7

stlands Farm

Spear Hill

Calves Croft

Coombewick

Lion's Wood

Daylands Farm

17

Holmbush House

Binser's Barn

6

Martins Farm

Hook Farm

B2133

GREENACRES

East Wolves Farm

Baldwin's Wood

Frenchland Cottage

5

VICTORY LA

America Wood

THE CLOSE

Ashington

Brownhill

Jessops Farm

16

BROADBRIDGE COTTS

Broadbridge Farm

Brownhill Wood

1 BLACKSMITHS CL
2 MORLEYS

4

Sewage Works

Common Copse

KENSETT'S CNR

Nursery

Fairoak Furzefield Wood

Hawking Sopers

3

Trickles Wood

Little Wood

Guesses Farm

15

Birch Copse

HOLE ST

NORTH LA

Hole Street Farm

2

Upper Chancton Farm

Lower Holestreet Barn

Abbott's Farm

Fair Oak Farm

SMITHANDLE LA

Guessgate Farm

stelands arm

STOCKS FIELD

Upper Buncton House

1

WATER LA

Wiston

14

A   B   14   C   D   15   E   F

123
104

| A | B | C | D | E | F |

8

B2116

ALBOURNE RD

B2116

Hollinger

Heatenthorn Farm

Paynesfield

FIRSLAND PARK EST

Morley Farm

Blackstone Gate Wood

B2116

7

Park Farm

Woodhouse Wood

Blackstone Gate Farm

High Cross

17

Woolfly Wood

BLACKSTONE LA

6

Woodhouse

Kingsfold

Furze Field

Woodhouse Farm

Trusler's Hill Farm

5

FURNERS LA

Bylsborough

Blackstone RISE

NORTH VIEW

PO

16

Furners Farm

Bilsborough Barn

Blackstone Grange

BLACKSTONE ST

Blackstone

4

Swains Farm

Bassells

Four Elms

Wick Farm

Henfield Common

A281

BRIGHTON RD

3

Holedean Farm

Hundred Steddle

BLACKSTONE LA

15

Woodmancote Place

West Wood

East Woo

Eastout

Kentons Farmhouse

Woodmancote

2

A2037

The Pools

Hole Farm

TERRY'S CROSS

Nutknowle Farm

1

HENFIELD BSNS PK

Golf Course

BRAMLANDS LA

14

Oreham Common

HORN LA

Bramlands

Holmbush Farm

A2

| 22 | A | B | 23 | C | D | 24 | E | F |

123
145

A B C D E F

8

Ruckford House

Clayton Priory

Hammond's Mill Farm

Hurstpierpoint Coll

Highfields Farm

Mill Nursery

New Close Farm

7

Recn Gd

MILL RACE

New Barn Farm

17

Big Edgerley

St CHRISTOPHER'S RD

Little Park Farm

6

Lawrence CE Sch Liby

Hurst Wickham

Clayton Wickham Farm

Friar's Oak Hotel

Hurstpierpoint

HIGH ST

THE GLEBE
THE TIBBETTS
TIBBETTS HO

Friar's Oak Farm

WILLOW HO 1
GRACE CT 2

THE BRAMBLES
THE CROFT
MEADOWS

5

WEST FURLONG CT

HASSOCKS RD

HIGHFIELD
WICKHAM DR

Hurst Wickham CL
Hurst Wickham Stables

BELMONT LA

Belmont

Hassocks

Parkview
Downsview
HALTON SHAWS

Tott Farm

16

Cemy

WICKHAM HILL

CLYNTON CL

HURST RD

Ham Farm

THE CROSSWAYS

STANFORD CL
STANFORD AVE

THE GENISTOS
THE WILLOWS POINT HO
WOODSLAND RD

CROWN
Hassocks Sch

4

KNABBIDDLES CL

PINE TREES CT

CHALLOW CL
NORTH BANK

KEYMER RD

THE ORCHARD

Bedlam Street

Nursery

STONEPOUND
CROSSROAD

Hassocks Sta

SOUTH BANK

ROUND GATE

ROSE CT 1
CLAYTON PARK 2
STANFORD TERR 3
STATION COTTS 4
DUNCTON RD 5

OCKENDEN WAY

HERON'S EYE 1
SANDBROOK 2
ORION CT 3
FITZJOHN CT 4

3

Danny Lake

LAGWOOD

15

Ockenden's Wood

Butcher's Wood

2

Old Wood

Danny

Furzefield

Lag Wood

Halfway

Little Danny

BRIGHTON RD

Coldharbour Farm

Hautboyes

1

The Jack & Jill (PH)

NEW RD

B2112

A273

14

28 A B 29 C D 30 E F

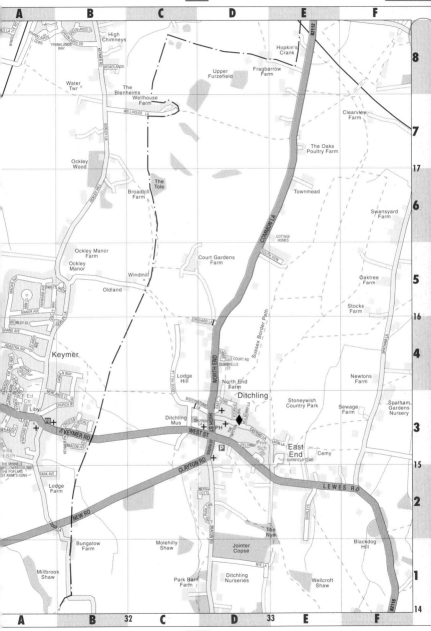

| | A | B | C | D | E | F |

8

7

17

6

5

16

4

3

15

2

1

14

| A | B | C | D | E | F |

A   **B**   **C**   **D**   **E**   **F**

Blendworth House
Blendworth Farm
Wick Farm
Oxleys Copse
Wick Hanger
Rectory
Blendworth CE-Inf Sch
St Giles Farm
Murrants Copse
Blendworth
Cadlington House
Nobles Farm
Idsworth House
Idsworth Park
Finchdean
Finchdean Farm
ROWLANDS CASTLE RD
Eastlands
Woodhouse
Treadwheel Farm
TREADWHEEL RD
Pyle Farm
Motleys Copse
Calf Dell
Cherry Row
The Holt
MAGPIE COTTS
Woodhouse Ashes Farm
Sussex Border Path & Stanton Way
Great Wellsworth
Stein Wood
HOLT GDNS
WELLSWORTH LA
Horsefoot Hill
GREATFIELD WAY
LINKS CL
Recn Gd
Rowlands Castle Sta
The Sling
Havant Thicket
Long Wood
Golf Course
P
THE FAIRWAY
PO
CH
Staunton Country Park
The Forest
Rowland's Castle
Furzy Plain
MANOR LODGE RD
CASTLE RD
Red Hill
LINKS CL
THE DRIFT
BRAMBLING RD 1
NUTHATCH CL 2
P LAND RD
HILL BROW CL
Red Hill Farm
Upper Lake
HAZELDEAN DR
Nightingale Bottom

B2149

71   **A**   **B**   **72**   **C**   **D**   **73**   **E**   **F**

A B C D E F

8

Old Idsworth
Garden

Markwells
Wood

Manor
Copse

Lostlabour
Copse

Horsley
Farm

West Marden
Hall

High
Copse

Grub
Copse

7

13

South Holt
Farm

OLDHOUSE LA

Shortleys
Copse

Adam's
Copse

Northwood
Farm

Lodge
Farm

6

Bottom
Copse

Forestside

Woods
Copse

Forestside
Farm

5

Deanlane
End

Warren
Down

12

Drews
Farm

Firtree
Piece

Batty's
Park

Wythy
Piece

4

Rosamond's
Hill

Stanstead
Forest

Long
Copse

3

Forest
Hanger

Lumley
Seat

11

Hare
Warren

Lumley
Wood

2

North
Coopers
Wood

Stansted
Park

sepasture
Farm

Orange
Grove

The Avenue   Monarch's Way

Sussex Border Path

Lyels
Wood

The
Slip

South
Coopers
Wood

Stansted
House

1

Saw
Mill

10

129
109

B2146

DOWN COTTS

PH

**West
Marden**

Sewage
Works

8

Locksash
Farm

Grevitts
Copse

Hill
Farm

Blinkard
Copse

7

Malthouse
Copse

Dolly's
Hanger

LOCKSASH LA

Lower
Farm

Wheatcroft

13

Nore Down

Lowerfarm
Copse

OLD HOUSE LA

6

Fanny's
Row

Lyecommon

Cabragh
House

Haslett
Copse

Pitlands
Farm

5

Birchin
Copse

Warren
Copse

Busto
Copse

Watergate
Farm

Woodbarn

12

Watergate
Hanger

Holmes
Row

Inholmes
Wood

4

Watergate Park

Piglegged
Row

Broadreed
Farm

Dundarroch

3

Oak
Copse

Mitchamer
Farm

11

MIT
G

WOODLANDS LA

Monarch's Way

Manor
Farm

2

Woodlands
Cottages

Lordington
Copse

COOKS LA

The
BarleyMow
(PH)

BROOKLANDS
COTTS

Walderton

River Ems

Park
Slip

1

B2146

Walderton
Down

Walderton
Hill Plantation

10

129
150

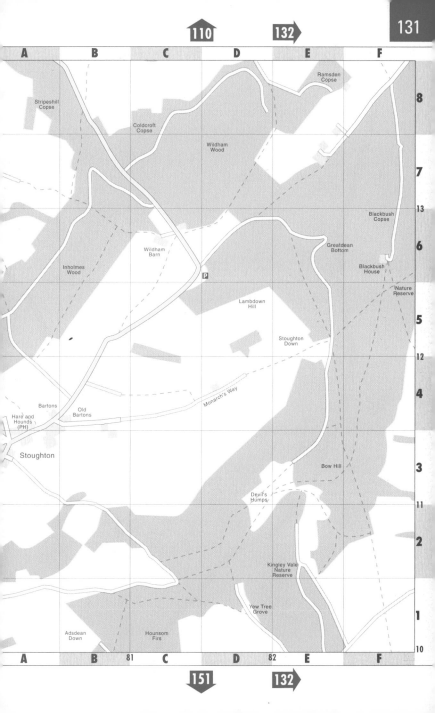

A B C D E F

8

Stripeshill
Copse

Ramsden
Copse

Coldcroft
Copse

Wildham
Wood

7

13

Blackbush
Copse

Wildham
Barn

Inholmes
Wood

P

Greatdean
Bottom

6

Blackbush
House

Nature
Reserve

Lambdown
Hill

5

Stoughton
Down

12

Monarch's Way

4

Bartons

Old
Bartons

Hare and
Hounds
(PH)

Stoughton

Bow Hill

3

11

Devil's
Humps

2

Kingley Vale
Nature
Reserve

Yew Tree
Grove

1

Adsdean
Down

Hounsom
Firs

10

A B 81 C D 82 E F

A   B   C   D   E   F

8

Hylters

Monarch's Way

Lodge Hill Farm

Double Barn

Withy Bed

7

Warren Down

Warren Hanger

Brickkiln Cottages

Warren Barn

13

Whitedown Plantation

Highde Planta

6

Heathbarn Down

Brickkiln Farm

Whiteland Cottages

Whiteland Copse

WARREN COTTS

Little Home Farm

Goosehill Camp

PHEASANT COTTS

West Dean CE (contr) Prim Sch

PH PO

5

Hasler's Steading

HASLER'S LA

Manor Farm

12

Bottom Barn

4

Hensbush Copse

Dean Cottages

River Lavant

Lawrence Copse

Rummages Barn

3

Preston Farm

Binderton Lane

Crows Hall Farm

Crows Hall Copse

11

Welldown Cottages

BINDERTON LA

2

Welldown

Binderton House

Ox Barn

1

Slate Barn

Langford Farm

10

83   A   B   84   C   D   85   E   F

131   152

133

113

A   **B**   **C**   **D**   **E**   **F**

8

Court Hill

Halfmoon
Piece

New Barn

Highdown
Croft   High Down

Green Hill

7

PH

13

CHARLTON RD

DROKE LA

Manor Farm

PO

East Dean

6

Wallerdean
Hill

Bubholts

5

Shotter's Ground

Chiseldown

Potch

12

Charlton
Park

Park
Hill

Monarch's Way

4

Eastdean
Park

Eastdean
Hill

Goodwood
Country Park

SELHURSTPARK RD

Pilleygreen
Lodges

Picnic
Area

3

Open
Winkins

Appletree
Bottom

11

The
Plantation

Red
Copse

2

Molecomb
Peak

Little
Copse

Ladys
Winkins

Halnaker
Park

1

Hat Hill

Denge
Bottom

10

Molecomb

133

154

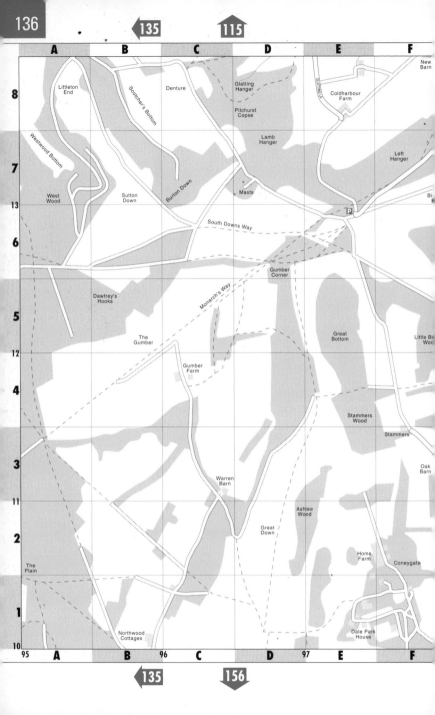

116
138

A B C D E F

West
Burton

Cookes
House

Southview
Farm

8

Hillside
Nursery

Nursery

WEST BURTON RD

WEST BURTON LA

Bignortail
Wood

Bury
CE (Aided)
Prim Sch

A29

Egg Bottom
Coppice

7

The
White Horse
(PH)

13

Westburton
Hill

Bury Manor
Farm

6

BURY HILL

King's
Buildings

Barkhale
Wood

South Downs Way

Bury
Hill

5

Coombe
Wood

12

Langham
Buildings

The Denture

Wapelgate
Corner

4

Houghton
Forest

Langham
Wood

ner's
se

Trot
Row

Monarch's Way

3

P
B2139

11

P

B2139

Parletts
Farm

Picnic
Area

A284

Whiteways
Lodge

2

Madehurst

Lower
Farm

LONDON RD

A29 FAIRMILE BOTTOM

Rewell Hill
Wood

Whiteways
Plantation

A284

1

Newbarn
Farm

Cemy

10

A B 99 C D 00 E F

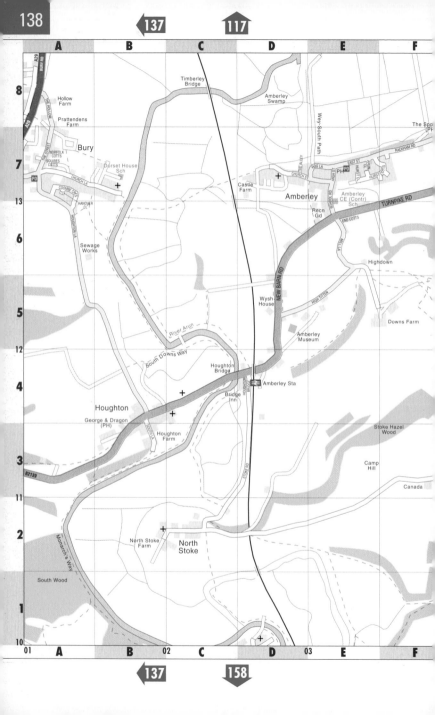

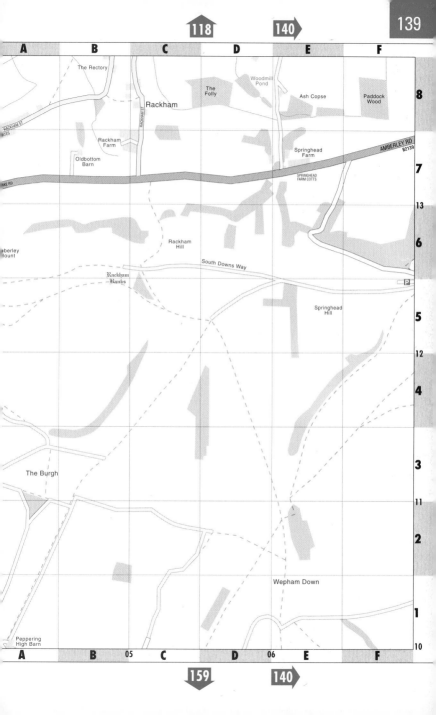

A B C D E F

The Rectory

The Folly

Woodmill
Pond

Ash Copse

Paddock
Wood

8

Rackham

RACKHAM ST

RACKHAM ST

Rackham
Farm

Oldbottom
Barn

AMBERLEY RD
B2139

Springhead
Farm

SPRINGHEAD
FARM COTTS

7

KE RD

13

berley
ount

Rackham
Hill

6

South Downs Way

Rackham
Banks

P

Springhead
Hill

5

12

4

The Burgh

3

11

2

Wepham Down

1

Peppering
High Barn

10

A B 05 C D 06 E F

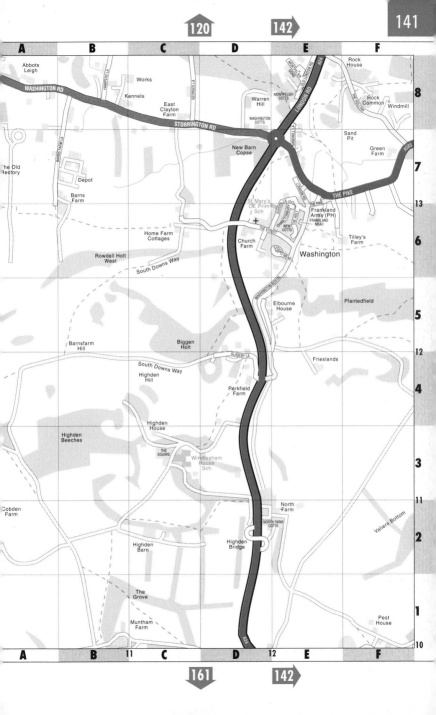

141 121

8

The Rough

Sevier's Barn

+ WATER LA

Buncton

Buncton Manor Farm

Refuse Tip

A283 THE PIKE

WASHINGTON RD

The Falconers

7

Lower Chancton Farm

BUNCTON CROSSWAYS

Model Cottages

Copyhold Wood

13

Newcommon Copse

Bushovel Farm

Rokers

Weppons

CHANCTONBURY RING RD

6

Lock's Farm

Wiston Park

MOUSE LA

Owlscroft Barn

P Picnic Area

Wiston House

Wiston

Combe Holt

Great Barn Farm

+

5

Chanctonbury Ring

Chanctonbury Hill

12

Chalkpit Wood

4

Well Bottom

Lion's Bank

Court Plantation

3

South Downs Way

11

2

Middle Brow

Buddington Bottom

Stump Bottom

Steyning Valley

1

Findon Park House

10

141 162

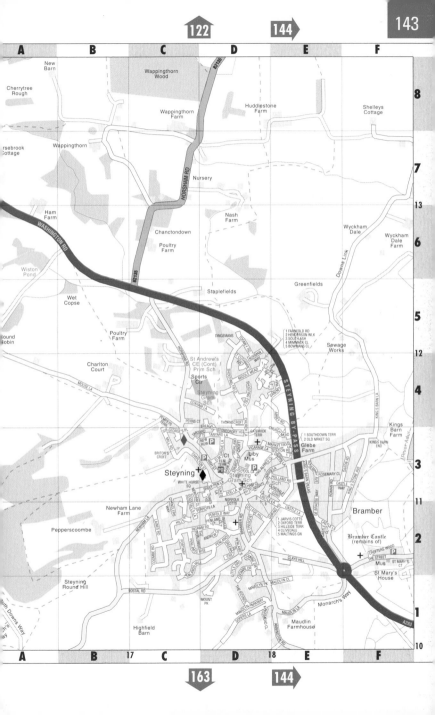

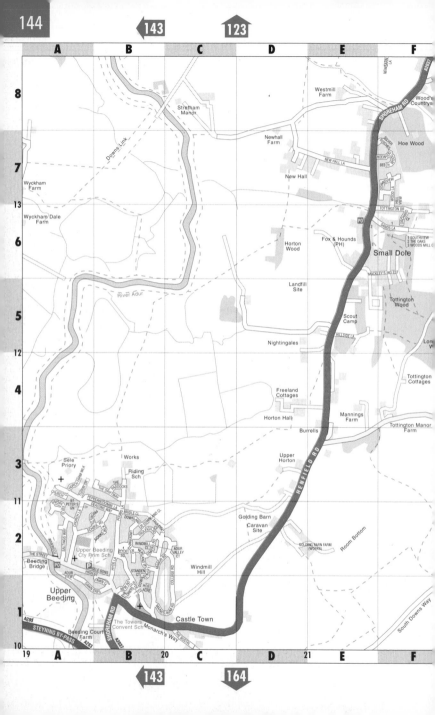

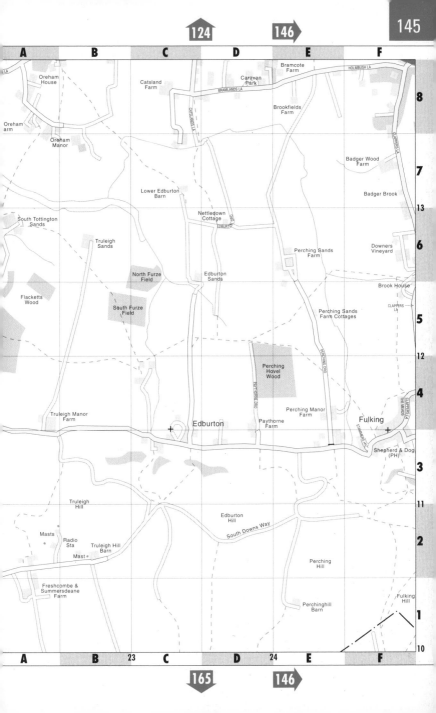

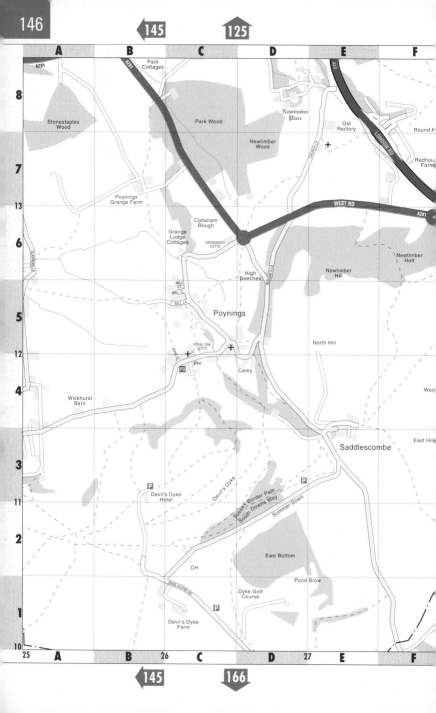

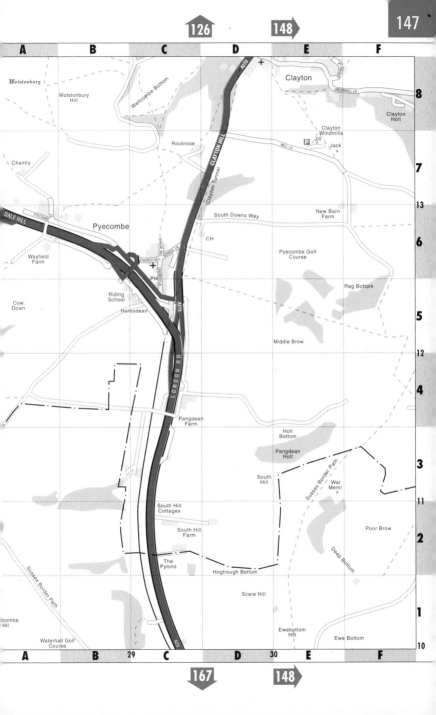

147 127

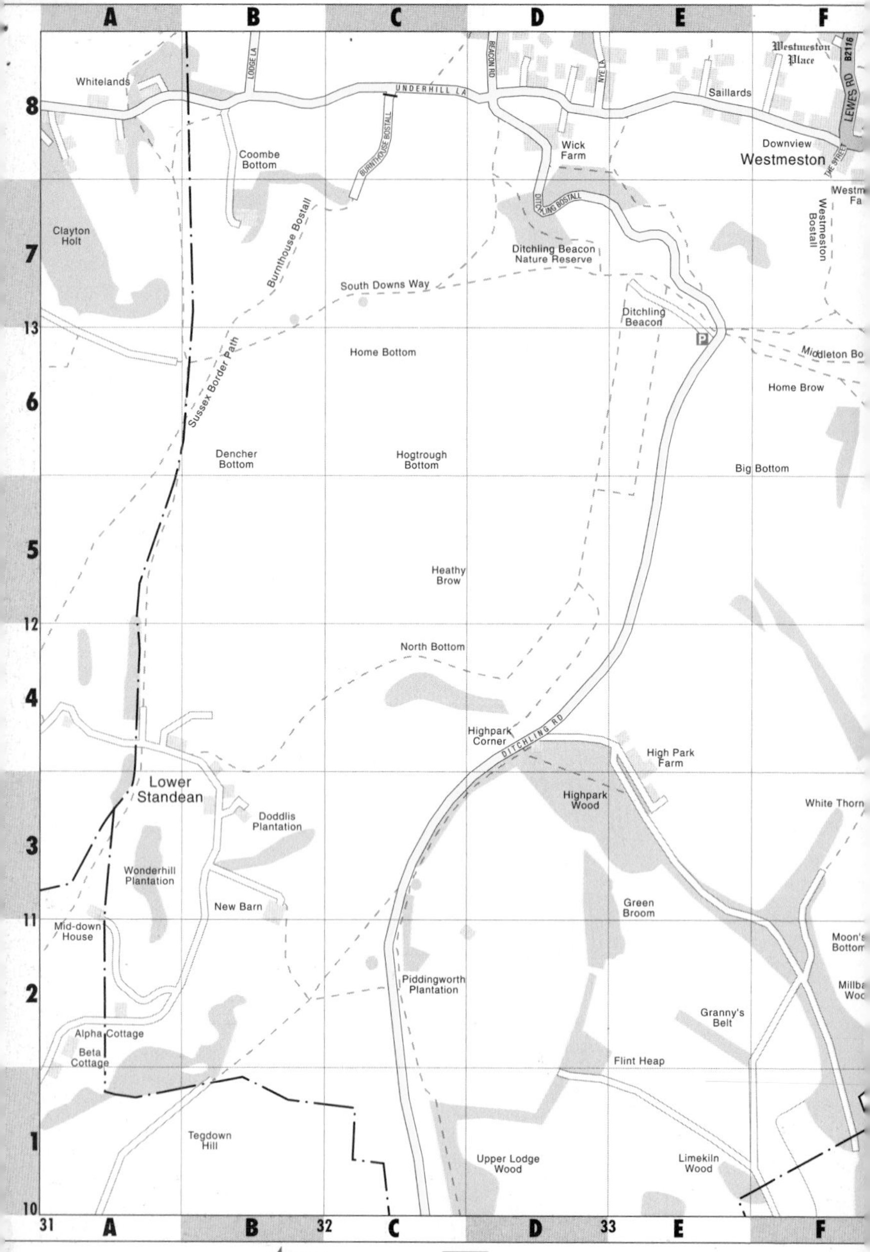

A B C D E F

Westmeston Place

Whitelands

UNDERHILL LA

LEWES RD B2116

Saillards

Coombe Bottom

Downview

Westmeston

BEACON RD

RYE LA

Wick Farm

Westm Fa

Clayton Holt

Westmeston Bostall

Ditchling Beacon Nature Reserve

South Downs Way

BURNTHOUSE BOSTALL

Home Bottom

Ditchling Beacon

Middleton Bo

Home Brow

Dencher Bottom

Hogtrough Bottom

Big Bottom

Sussex Border Path

Heathy Brow

North Bottom

Highpark Corner

DITCHLING RD

High Park Farm

White Thorn

Lower Standean

Highpark Wood

Doddlis Plantation

Wonderhill Plantation

New Barn

Green Broom

Moon's Bottom

Mid-down House

Piddingworth Plantation

Granny's Belt

Millba Wo

Alpha Cottage

Beta Cottage

Flint Heap

Tegdown Hill

Upper Lodge Wood

Limekiln Wood

31 A B 32 C D 33 E F

147 168

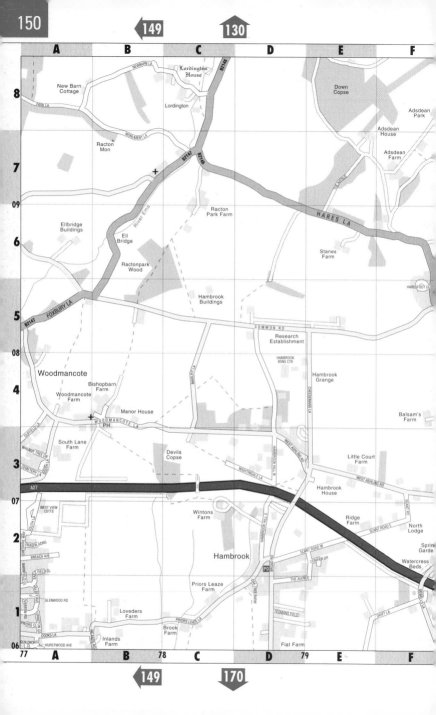

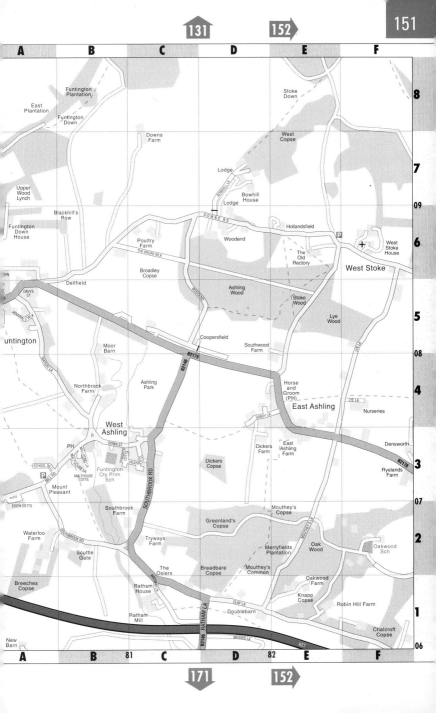

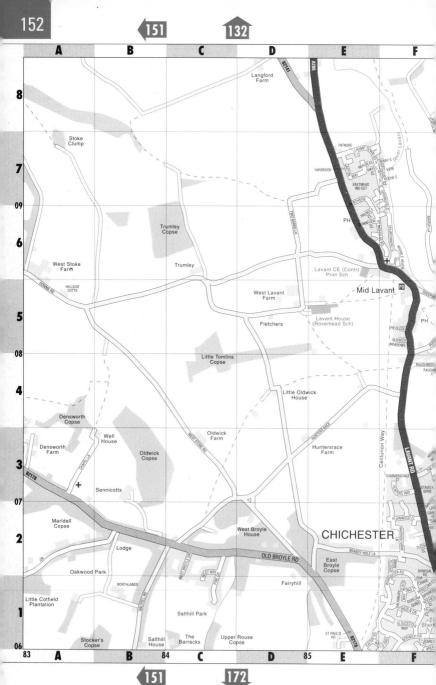

Langford Farm

Stoke Clump

Trumley Copse

West Stoke Farm

HILLSIDE COTTS

DOWNS RD

Trumley

Lavant CE (Contr) Prim Sch

Mid Lavant

PATNORE

LAVANT DOWN

ST MARY'S CL

MEWS CL

MAYES CL

EAST VIEW

ROCHE'S CL

YARBROOK

EASTMEAD IND EST

PORTSIDE

TRINDLES RD

DOWNVIEW CL

CHURCHMEAD CL

PH

River Lavant

MARSH LA

PO

TWO BARNS LA

West Lavant Farm

West Lavant Farm

Fletchers

Lavant House (Rosemead Sch)

THE CLOSE

OLDWICK MEADOWS

PH

SHEEP

RAUGHMERE

RAUGH C

Little Tomlins Copse

Little Oldwick House

Densworth Copse

Well House

Oldwick Farm

HUNTERS RACE

Huntersrace Farm

Centurion Way

LAVANT RD

Densworth Farm

CH LA

Oldwick Copse

WEST STOKE RD

SUMMERSDALE

HUNTERS WAY

STAVELEY GDNS

B2178

Sennicotts

Marldell Copse

Lodge

WEST BROYLE DR

West Broyle House

OLD BROYLE RD

CHICHESTER

BRANDY HOLE LA

East Broyle Copse

PLAINWOOD CL

Oakwood Park

NORTHLANDS

CALDY RD

FIR TREE AVE

ST WAY

Fairhill

TUDOR CL

DONEGAL CL

Little Cotfield Plantation

Salthill Park

The Barracks

Upper Rouse Copse

ST PAUL'S RD

B2178

GLOUCESTER WAY

RESWICK RD

Stocker's Copse

Salthill House

A   B   C   D   E   F

8

Halnaker Park

Bushey
Clump

Hathill Copse
West

Denge
Barn

Denge Bottom

Ha

7

Rook Wood

09

Halnaker
Park

The
Cockpit

Stone
Dell

Home
Farm

Seeley
Copse

Little
Halnaker

Warehead
Farm

Stud
Farm

Halnaker House
(remains of)

Warehead
House

6

Goodwood
Park

Home Farm
Dairy

Ou
B

Sandpit
Copse

The
Folly

Boxgrove Commo

5

Redvins Copse
West

Redvin's
Copse

Hotel

Halnaker

Waterbeach

Inkpen
Furze

Redvin's
Shaw

The
Anglesey Arms
(PH)

PARK LA

HEYDWOOD LA

08

Redvin's
Barn

Keeper's
House

4

The
Old Granary

NEW RD

Boxgrove
CE Prim Sch

THE
ALMSHOUSES

Priory
Farm

STRETTINGTON LA

STANE ST

Strettington

CROUCH CROSS LA

CHURCH LA

Boxgrove

3

Strettington
Farm

Temple
Bar

BARN
ELM

THE STREET

BOXGROVE
HO

07

SARLAND

Pear Tree
Knap

East Hampnett

A285

EDWARDS
AVE

Tangmere
Cty Prim Sch

EAST HAMPNETT LA

2

NETTLETON AVE

CITY
FIELDS

CAMBERRA

Chestnut
Farm

The
Bader Arms
(PH)

MALCOLM RD

SPITFIRE
RD

CHURCHWOOD DR

Sewage
Works

MANNOCK
RD

DERWENT
AVE

CHESTNUT

WOODFIELD

WHITBREAM
WAY

1

A27

BARNCROFT CL
THE GLEBE

Church Farm
House

CHURCH LA

Tangmere

06

SAXON
MEADOW

HARESFIELD TERR
GAMECOCK TERR

Mus

Nursery

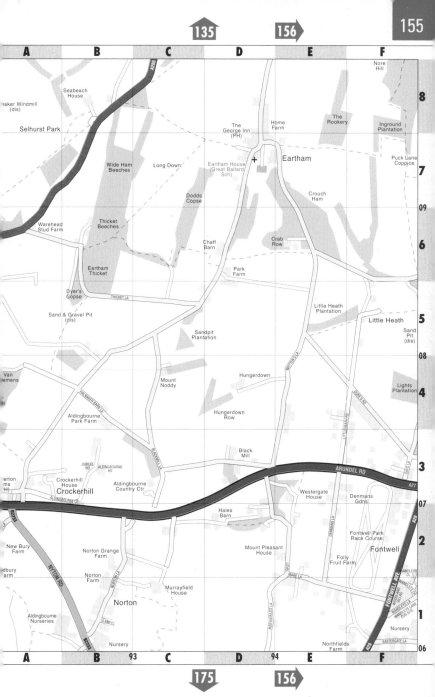

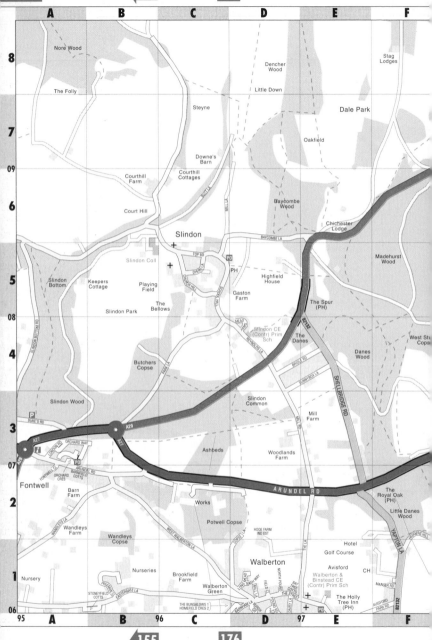

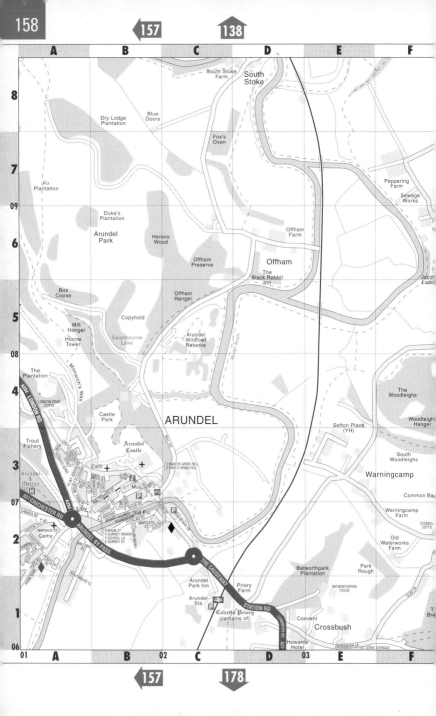

8
7
09
6
5
08
4
3
07
2
1
06

A   B   C   D   E   F

01   02   03

South Stoke
Farm
South
Stoke

Dry Lodge
Plantation
Blue
Doors

Fox's
Oven

Fir
Plantation

Duke's
Plantation

Arundel
Park

Herons
Wood

Offham
Preserve

Offham
Farm

Offham

Peppering
Farm

Sewage
Works

The
Black Rabbit
Inn

Box
Copse

Offham
Hanger

Jaco
Lade

Copyhold

Mill
Hanger

Hiorne
Tower

Swanbourne
Lake

Arundel
Wildfowl
Reserve

River Arun

The
Woodleighs

Woodleigh
Hanger

The
Plantation

London Road
Cotts

A284 LONDON RD

Monarch's Way

Castle
Park

Arundel
Castle

ARUNDEL

Sefton Place
(YH)

South
Woodleighs

Warningcamp

Trout
Fishery

Cath

1 BAKERS ARMS HILL
2 KING'S ARMS HILL

Common Ba

Arundel
& District

H

Mus

Warningcamp
Farm

COUNCIL
COTTS

A27 CHICHESTER RD

Lib

Ind Est

Martlets

ARUNDEL BY-PASS

CANADA RD

Cemy

WARWICK CT

DALTONS
PL

SALTHOUSE CL

3 ARUN ST
4 SURREY WHARF
5 SCHOOL LA
6 SURREY ST

Old
Waterworks
Farm

THE CAUSEWAY

Arundel
Park Inn

Priory
Farm

Batworthpark
Plantation

BATWORTHPARK
HOUSE

Park
Rough

Arundel
Sta

STATION RD

Calcete Priory
(remains of)

Convent

Crossbush

A27

Howards
Hotel

CROSSBUSH LA
THE TERRACE

T
Bre

8

7

09

6

5

08

4

07

3

2

1

06

A   B   C   D   E   F

New Barn

New Buildings

Pigeonhouse Plantation

Worthing Crem

Kempe's Plantation

King's Wood

Broad Wood

North End

NORTH END COTTS

Gallops Farm

Blackpatch Covert

Coventry Plantation

Kingswood

HORSHAM RD
A24

The Downs

Gallops

The Gibbet

Tolmare Farm

The Kennels

A280

OLD COTTS

The Willows

Findon

Convent

LONG FURLONG

North Park Gate

Monarch's Way

North Park

St John Baptist Prim Sch

Cemy

GREYPOINT HO 1
NEPCOTE PAR 2
SHEPHERDS CROFT 3
SOUTHVIEW RD 4

DOWNLAND CL

WESTVIEW TERR

PADDOCK WAY

Nepcote Green

Church Hill

Findon Place

HERMIT TERR

NORTHVIEW TERR

STEEP LA

Nepcote

Cissbury

South Park

STEEP CL

FINDON BY-PASS

NEPFIELD CL

Church Hill Shaw

Findon Nurseries

New Plantation

The Vale

Roger's Farm

Richardson's Wood

The Oaks

Mast West Hill

No Man's Land

STORRINGTON RISE

FINDON RD

Grub Ride

WEST HILL CL

Salvington Hill

The Sanctuary

FURZEHOLME

The Gallops

Vale C'ty Fst & Mid Sch

Clapham Wood

WORTHING

Windmill

DOWNLANDS

Cote Bottom

Bushfield Copse

Munery's Copse

PALMER

SOUTHWOLD

Cote Nurseries

CHERRY WLK

MAPLE CL

High Salvington

WOODLAND AVE

PANKAMS

New
Barn

Church
Wood

Findon Park
Farm

No Man's
Land

Ne
B

8

7

Gallops

Monarch's Way

Park
Brow

09

Lychpole
Bottom

6

P

Canada
Bottom

5

Cissbury
Ring

08

Cissbury
Farm

Hill Barn
Covert

Lychpole
Farm

4

Cissbury
Plantation

Shipdens
Holt

Deep
Bottom

Lychpole
Hill

Vineyard
Hill

3

LONG MEADOW

CENTRAL AVE

CISSBURY GDNS

HOLMBURY GDNS

SHEPHERDS MEAD

Sheepcombe
Hanger

Tenants
Hill

07

CISSBURY
AVE

Mount
Carvey

2

Findon
Valley

COOMBE RISE

P

LIME TREE AVE

Liby

ALDSUICK CRES

ASHFOLD AVE

KESSLE Dr

Worthing
Golf Course

FRANKLANDS
CL

ALLENDALE
AVE

1

GREYSTOKE RD

A 24 FINDON RD

FLORAL DEAN
CL

MAYFIELD CL

Lambleys
Barn

LAMBLEYS LA

06

CH

A B C D E F

8

Upper Maudlyn
Farm

ANNINGTON
COMMERCIAL CTR

Annington
Mere Farm

Botolphs

Steyning
Bowl

P

Monarch's Way   SOPERS LA

Annington
Hill

Annington
Farm

7

South Downs Way

Winding
Bottom

09

Annington Hill
Barn

6

Coombehead
Wood

Coombe
Head

5

08

4

Steep
Down

Valley
Barn

Beggars
Bush

3

TITCH HILL

07

Refuse
Tip

Refuse
Destructor

2

Lancing
Hill

Titch Hill
Farm

Hill Barn
Farm

Lancing
Ring
P

P

1

The
Mountain

THAKEHAM LA

P

HOWARD RD

HEATHER RD
ALANDALE RD
HILLSIDE RD
MOUNTSIDE RD
SUNBURY DR

...VIEW
HILLBARN
AVE

HONEYSUCKLE CL

FIRLE RD

MOUNT WAY

FAIRVIEW RD

SUNNY VALE DR

HOE CT

06

A B C D E F

17 18

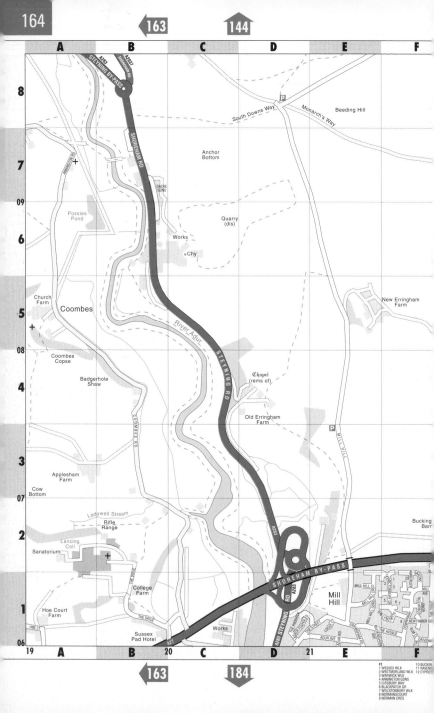

A283 STEYNING BY-PASS

A2037 SHOREHAM RD

SHOREHAM RD

ANNINGTON RD

DACRE GDNS

Possies Pond

Church Farm

Coombes

Coombes Copse

Badgerhole Shaw

COOMBES RD

River Adur

STEYNING RD

South Downs Way

Monarch's Way

Beeding Hill

Anchor Bottom

Quarry (dis)

Works

Chy

New Erringham Farm

Chapel (rems of)

Old Erringham Farm

MILL HILL

Applesham Farm

Cow Bottom

Ladywell Stream

Rifle Range

Lancing Coll

Sanatorium

College Farm

THE DRIVE

Hoe Court Farm

HOE CT

Sussex Pad Hotel

A27

Works

SHOREHAM BY-PASS

A283

A283 STEYNING

Mill Hill

Bucking Barr

MILL HILL CL

HANCTONBURY DR

AMBERLEY

THE AVENUE

NEWTIMBER GD

THE STREET

LOCKET CL

ADUR AVE RD

ERRINGHAM RD

F1
1 WESSEX WLK
2 WESTMORLAND WLK
3 WARWICK WLK
4 ANNINGTON GDNS
5 CISSBURY WAY
6 BLACKPATCH GR
7 WOLSTONBURY WLK
8 NORMANSCOURT
9 NORMAN CRES

10 BUCKIN
11 RAVENS
12 CYPRES

the rren

Bushy Bottom

Summers Deane

Tenant Hill

Hazelhalt Bottom

Cockroast Hill

Thundersbarrow Hill

Sussex Border Path

Mossy Bottom

Whitelot Bottom

Cockroast Bottom

Mileoak Barn

Mile Oak Farm

A27

y Bottom Barn

Monarch's Way

Crooked Moon

Mile Oak

WESTWAY
WESTVIEW CL
OAKDENE RISE
NURSERY CL

GORSE CL
THORNHILL RISE
GRAHAM CL
GRAHAM DR
GRAHAM CRES

OAKDENE
WAY
OAKDENE AVE
OAKDENE MEWS

HEATHFIELD DR
FOXDOWN RD
WARMDENE CL

SEFTON RD

Mile Oak Cty Prim Sch

CHALKY RD

Col

COMPASS CT

Southwick Hill

SHOREHAM BY-PASS

HAZELHOLT 1
PADDOCK CL 2
BEECH CL 3
HILLBANK CL 4

RICKYARD RISE

WARMDENE RD

MAUDLYN PK

Slonk Hill

NEW BARN CL 1
MARJORAM PL 2
FENNEL WLK 2
BERBERIS CT 4

5 JUNIPER WLK
6 SAFFRON CL
7 BERGAMOT CRES
8 THYME CL

1 LOWER DR
2 WINDMILL DR

Superstore

Herons Dale Sch

Holmbush Cty Jun Sch

BRIGHT CL
MILL RISE

NAN
PARADE CL

HILL FARM WAY

DROVE CRT
LODGE CL

Church House CL

Cemy

UPTON AVE

SLONK HILL RD

DOWNSIDE

TRULEIGH WAY
KINGS WAY
MUSTANG

WAYS CRES

ROSEMARY
WAY
CRES

HOLMBUSH WAY

MILLCROFT GDNS

EASTBANK

PARKSIDE

JASMINE WAY

KINGSTON BROADWAY

MILLER
RD
MALIN RD

WHITELOT CL
KINGSTON CL

QUEENS RD

THE WILDY
WILBY AVE

RIDGEWAY

HIGHDOWN

FAIRWAY

kingham Park Recn Gd

A270 UPPER SHOREHAM RD

Royal George Par

Kingston Way

BUCI CRES

FRANKLIN RD

DOWNLAND AVE

OLD SHOREHAM RD A270

SOUTHVIEW RD

ASH CT

Southlands General

UPPER SHOREHAM RD

FAIRFIELD CT

E2
1 ROBINIA LODGE
2 SCEPTRE
3 TIVOLI
4 TOWER HO
5 CLERMONT CT
6 LYNDEN CT
7 STAMFORD LODGE
8 CUMBERLAND LODGE
9 CENTENARY HO

E2
10 SHAWCROSS HO
11 CARLTON HO
12 HARRINGTON MANSIONS
13 HARRINGTON CT
E3
1 THE CEDARS
2 THE APPROACH
3 WITHDEAN HALL
4 LEAHURST CT

5 CHERRYWOOD
6 CEDARWOOD
7 MAPLEWOOD
8 PINEWOOD
9 BEECHWOOD
10 WITHDEAN CT
11 WELLINGTONIA CL

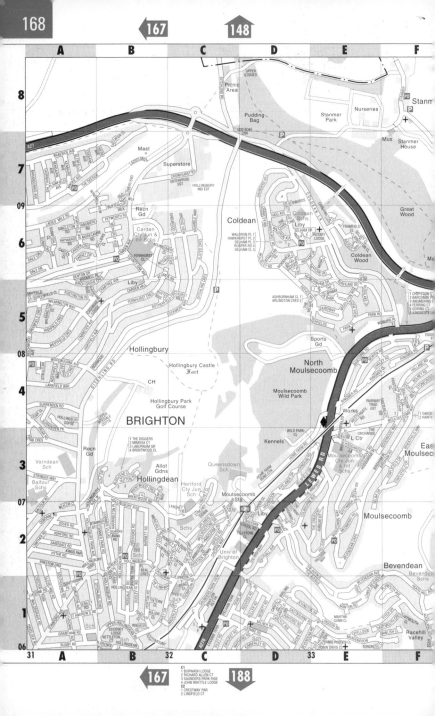

167   188

C1
1 BURWASH LODGE
2 RICHARD ALLEN CT
3 SAUNDERS PARK RISE
4 JOHN WHITTLE LODGE
C2
1 CRESTWAY PAR
2 LINDFIELD CT

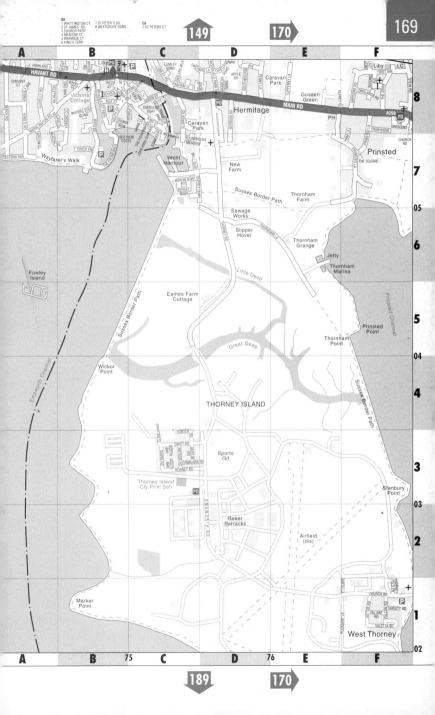

B8
1 WHITTINGTON CT
2 ST JAMES RD
3 CHURCH PATH
4 MEADOW CT
5 WARWICK CT
6 KING'S TERR

7 ST PETER'S SQ
8 WESTGROVE GDNS

C8
1 ST PETERS CT

149
170
189
170

A   B   C   D   E   F

HAVANT RD

Convent
CT

Victoria
Cottage

Western Par

Wayfarer's Walk

CREEK END

SEA VIEW
COTTS

Yacht
Harbour

HERON QUAY

AVOCET
QUAY

Fowley
Island

Sussex Border Path

Emsworth Channel

LUMLEY
GDNS

Caravan
Park

Hermitage

Caravan
Park

ROUNDHOUSE
MEADOW

New
Farm

Sussex Border Path

Sewage
Works

Slipper
Hovel

Little Deep

Eames Farm
Cottage

Great Deep

Wickor
Point

THORNEY ISLAND

HUNTER RD

SWIFT RD

CANBERRA RD

HORNET RD

Thorney Island
Cty Prim Sch

Sports
Gd

Baker
Barracks

Marker
Point

MAIN RD

Gosden
Green

PH

Prinsted

THE SQUARE

Thornham
Farm

Thornham
Grange

Jetty
Thornham
Marina

Prinsted
Point

Thornham
Point

Sussex Border Path

Prinsted Channel

Stanbury
Point

Airfield
(dis)

CHURCH RD

VARSITY RD

VALIANT RD

VALETTA RD

West Thorney

A259

Liby

CHURCH
RD

8

7

05

6

5

04

4

3

03

2

1

02

75   76

Southbourne Halt
LODGEBURY CL
Southbourne Cty Jun & Inf Schs
INLANDS RD
Southbourne
LC
Caravan Site
MOSDELL RD
A259
Ham Brook
Works
Nutbourne Halt
LC
Longacres
NINTT LA
LC
FLAT RD
BROAD RD
Flat Farm
The Bosham Inn
PO
POTTERY LA
BROAD MEADOW
MAIN RD
MANSFIELD COTTS
PH
Nursery
HYGIENE CRES
Nutbourne
MAYBUSH DR
BELL HO
FARM LA

Marsh Farm

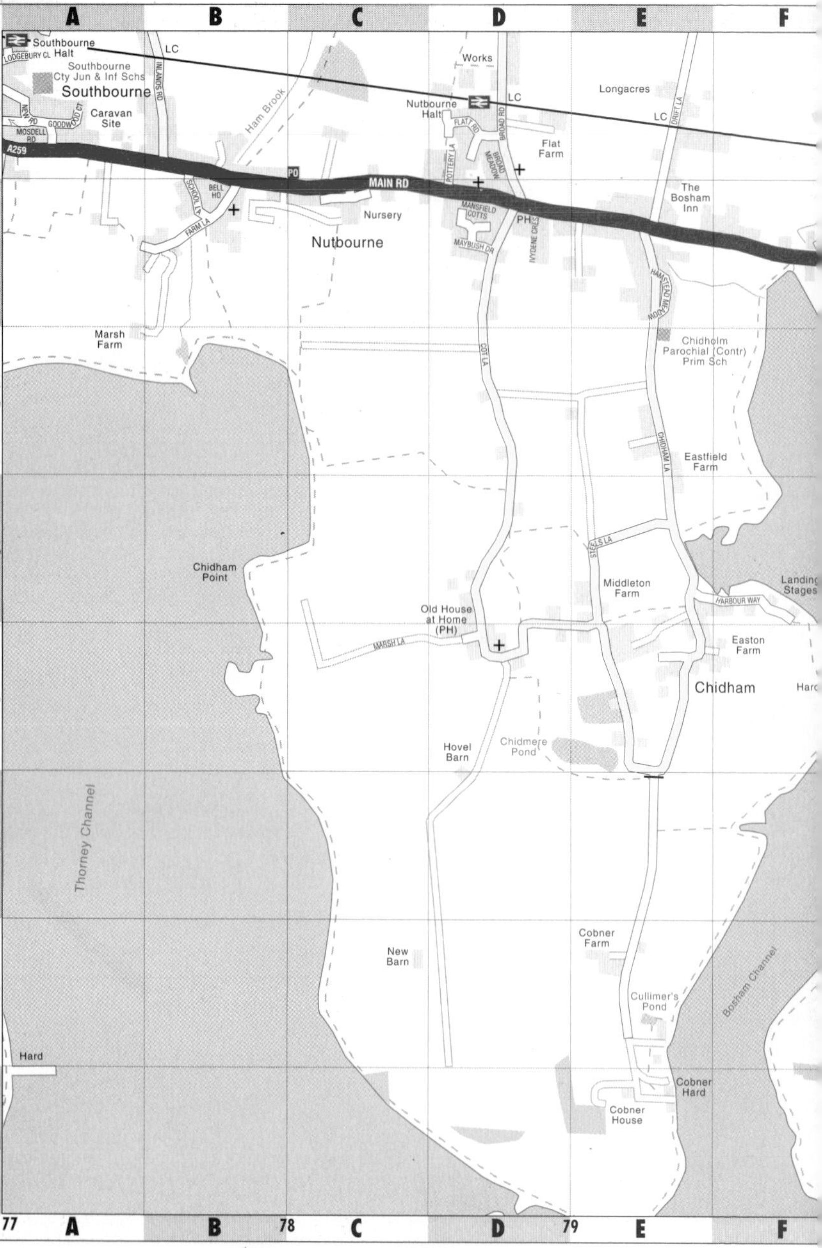

CEL LA
HAM FARM WOODS
Chidholm Parochial (Contr) Prim Sch

CHIDHAM LA
Eastfield Farm

Chidham Point

Thorney Channel

CEL S LA
Middleton Farm
Landing Stages
HARBOUR WAY
Old House at Home (PH)
Easton Farm
Chidham
Hard
MARISH LA

Hovel Barn
Chidmere Pond

New Barn

Cobner Farm

Bosham Channel
Cullimer's Pond

Hard

Cobner Hard
Cobner House

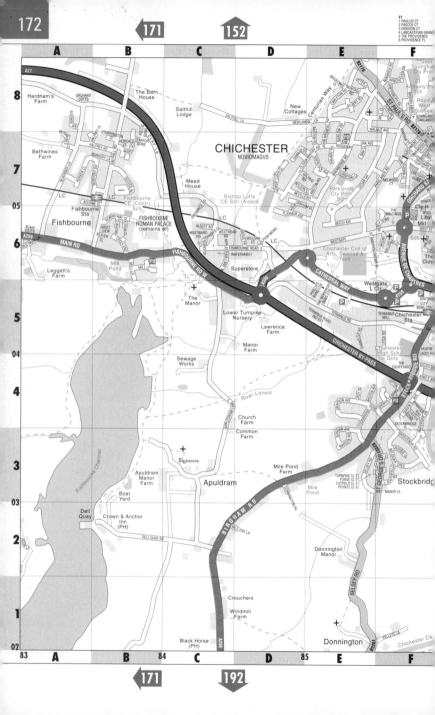

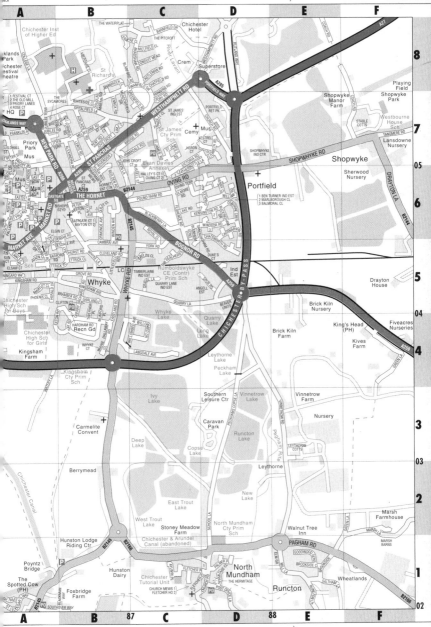

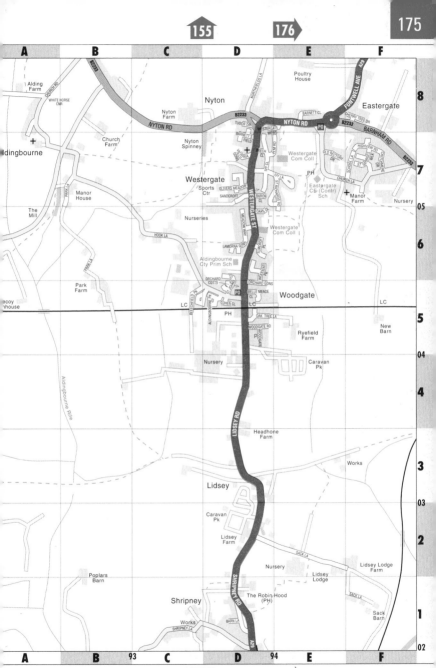

A B C D E F

8
7
05
6
5
04
4
3
03
2
1
02

Aldingbourne

Alding Farm
CHURCH RD
WHITE HORSE CNR
B2233
Church Farm
NYTON RD
Nyton Farm
Nyton
Nyton Spinney

NORTHMEAD LA
Poultry House

FONTWELL AVE
A29
CHERRY TREE DR
Eastergate

BARNETT CL.
NYTON RD
PO
B2233
BARNHAM RD
B2233

HIGHVIEW RD
COLTHORNE
SCHOOL LA
ST

Westergate
Sports Ctr
OLIVERS MEADOW
SANDCROFT

Westergate Com Coll

WESTERGATE ST

IVY LA
ST AUGUSTINE'S RD

OLD RECTORY DR
PH
Eastergate CE (Contr) Sch
CHURCH LA
Manor Farm
Nursery

Manor House
The Mill

TREE LA
FPATH

Park Farm

HOOK LA

Nurseries

MEADOW WAY

LAMORNA GDNS

Westergate Com Coll
OAKS

Aldingbourne Cty Prim Sch

ORCHARD GDNS

Woodgate

LC

ORCHARD COTTS
PO
BELLE MEADE
COHEN CL.
PH
BEECHFIELD
ALDINGBOURNE RD

LC

LC

OAK TREE LA
WOODGATE RD
WOODGATE
Ryefield Farm

New Barn

Nursery
Caravan Pk

acoy
rhouse

Aldingbourne Rife

04

LIDSEY RD

Headbone Farm

Works

Lidsey

03

Caravan Pk

Lidsey Farm

SACK LA

Nursery
Lidsey Lodge
Lidsey Lodge Farm

SACK LA

Sack Barn

Poplars Barn

SHRIPNEY RD

The Robin Hood (PH)

Shripney

Works
SHRIPNEY LA
BARN LA

A29

A B 93 C D 94 E F

175
156

A   B   C   D   E   F

8

Binsted
Park

Lake
Copse

Manor
House

Priory
(remains of)

Meadow
Lodge

New
Barn

Oakley
Cottages

Fairmeads
Farm

Tortington

New England
Coll

7

Slate Barn
Farm

Goose
Green

05

Manor
Farm

Lower
Farm

Marsh
Farm

6

LC

Sunnymead
Farm

GAUGEMASTER WAY   THE WILLOWS

Arundel
Arms
(PH)

5

North End

Wicks
Farm

Ford
Sta

LC

WICKS
COTTS

Wicks
Farm

Trad
Est

Camping
Gd

04

EAST
BANK

FORD LA

Marina

Caravan
Park

River Arun

4

Lower
Farm

Ford

Works

1 THE POPLARS
2 THE LIMES

1 KINGS CL
2 VICTORIA VILLAS
3 HOLKHAM COTTS
4 WAREMERE CT

FORD AIRFIELD IND EST

WILSON CT

3

03

Burndell

BURNDELL RD

HM Prison

HM
Prison

2

Ford Aerodrome
(disused)

RUDFORD
IND EST

Church
Farm

YAPTON RD

Horsemere
Green

HORSEMERE GREEN LA

Nursery

1

B2233

Climping

Northwood
Farm

Hall

02

A   B   99   C   D   00   E   F

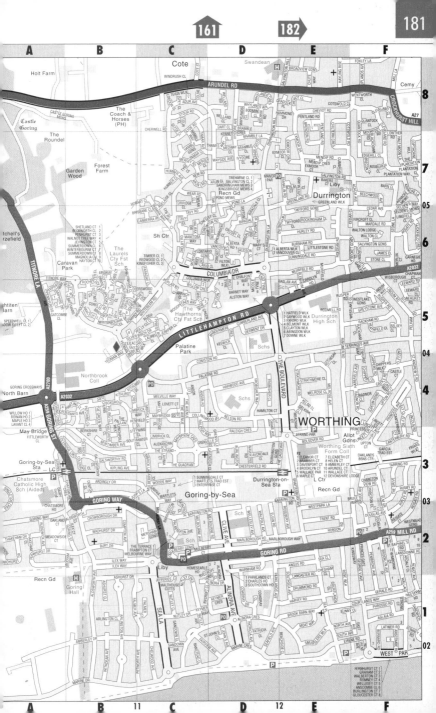

A1
1 CHICHESTER CT
2 EXETER CT
3 LICHFIELD CT
4 CARDINAL CT
5 WINDLESHAM CT
6 BELMER CT

7 DOWNVIEW CT
8 WINCHELSEA CT
9 HASTINGS CT
10 SUN CT
11 DAVIES CT
12 DOLPHIN LODGE
13 MARINE POINT

A2
1 CHESTER LODGE
2 RAGLAN CT
3 PARHAM CT
4 LANGHAM CT
A3
1 STATION PAR

A3
2 WESTDOWN CT
3 RUGBY CT
4 WADHURST CT
5 CAMARGUE CT
6 QUEENSBOROUGH CT

A5
1 ELIZABETH HO
2 PELHAM CT
3 FAIRDAN CT
4 DORSET PL
B1
1 FULMER CT

2 WILLMINGTON CT
3 BEVERLEY CT
4 SEAVIEW CT
5 NORMANDY CT
6 SEABRIGHT
7 BALCOMBE CT

B2
1 REDCOTTS
2 CHAPPELL CROFT
3 THE MANOR
4 WESTBURY CT
5 GREENTREES
6 HARLEY CT

7 HOMEPIER HG
8 AIREDALE CT

B3
1 PILGRIMS CL
2 ST BOTOLPHS CT
C1
1 SANDOWN CT
2 MILTON CT
3 EDINBURGH COTTS
4 BURLEIGH CT

5 BELMAINE CT
6 WYVERN CT
C2
1 WESSEX CT
2 OAKLAND CT
3 AVILA HO
4 CAMBOURNE CT
5 HOPEDENE CT

6 CRANLEIGH CT
7 GREENA
C3
1 NORFOLK CT
2 VICTORIA PARK GDNS
3 VICTORIA CT
4 CLIFTON CT
5 PIGGOTT'S BSNS PK

C3
1 CHARLES CT
C4
1 GAINSBOROUGH LODGE
2 LOXLEY GDNS
3 BEECH GDNS
4 HENTY CL
5 CENTRECOURT CL

D1
1 CALEDONIAN PL
2 NEW ST
3 PROSPECT PL
4 AUGUSTA HO
B2
1 EAST HILL CT
2 STOKE ABBOTT CT

3 GROSVENOR RD
4 HUMPHRYS PL
5 GRAFTON PL
6 FIELD ROW
7 LIVERPOOL BLDGS
8 MONTAGUE CT
9 BANK PASS
10 MARKET ST

11 THE GUILDBOURNE CTR
D4
1 COURIER CT
2 FAIRFIELDS
3 HOMESTEYNE HO
4 CAXTON CT
D5
1 STEYNING HO

2 ALFRISTON HO
3 BURY HO
4 ASHINGTON CT
F2
1 ST GEORGE'S GDNS
2 WESTMINSTER CT
3 CLARENCE CT

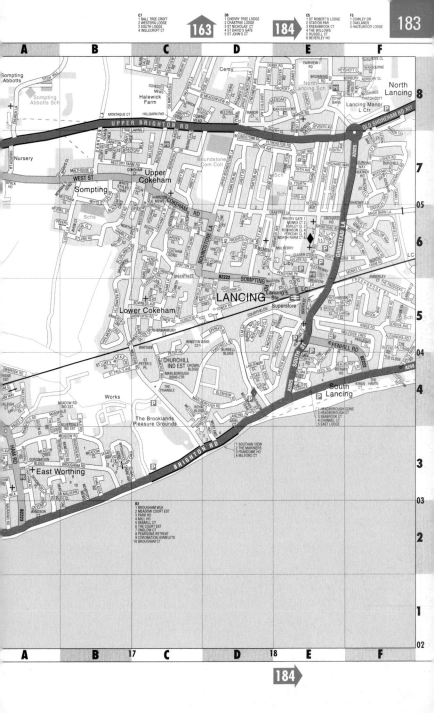

F7
1 CLEMENT'S CT
2 WEPPONS
3 CECIL NORRIS HO
4 NORMANHURST
5 OAKLAND CT
6 TINTAGEL CT

7 SWANBOROUGH CT
8 MANNINGS
9 GLYNDEBOURNE CT
10 PASHLEY CT
11 RIVERSIDE BSNS CTR

8

7

05

6

5

04

4

3

03

2

1

02

19   A   B   20   C   D   21   E   F

OLD SHOREHAM RD

Old Shoreham
Bridge

Withy Patch
Caravan Park

Honeyman's
Hole

Old
Shoreham

Brighton, Hove & Worthing
Municipal Airport

New Monks
Farm

Daniel's
Barn

North Barn
Farm

Old
Salts
Nursery

North Barn
Kennels

Broadway
Park

East
Lancing
Recn Gd

DOWNS CL 1
DRAKES CL 2
TUDOR CL 3

BROOKLANDS 1
OLD FARM CT 2

New Salts
Farm

Mus

Adur
Recn Gd

Norfolk
Bridge

NEW SALTS FARM RD

BRIGHTON RD

WEST BEACH RD

Lancing Beach

Widewater

WILLOWBROOK
PK

Happy Days
Caravan Park

THE
PLOVERS

SOUTH BANK

A259

Caravan
Park

Lakeside

OLD SALTS FARM RD

OLD SALTS FARM RD

C3
1 WIDEWATER CL
2 WILLOW CL
3 SWALLOWS CL
4 WENDELING COTTS
5 ADUR CT
6 ADUR CL
7 WIDEWATER CT

1 MARINE CT
2 FISHERMANS WLK
3 MARINERS CT
4 SEAHAVEN GDNS
5 KINGS CT
6 NELSON CT

SHOREHAM-BY-SI

ST NICOLAS CT 1
TOLLBRIDGE HO 2

ST NICOLAS LA

UPPER SHOREHAM RD

OLD SHOREHAM RD

Cemy

Shoreham
City
Fst Sch

Buckin

1 OXEN CT
2 SEAFIELDS

Shoreham-
by-Sea
Sta

Mus

HIGH ST

BRIGHTON RD

River

Draw-bridge

E7
1 ASTON HO
2 HOMEHAVEN CT
3 VICTORIA CT
4 LONGCROFT
5 WHITE LION CT
6 ST MARY'S TERR
8 ST JOHN'S MEWS COTTS
8 LITTLE HIGH ST

F6
1 ADMIRALS WLK
2 COLLINGWOOD CT
3 PACIFIC CT
4 ATLANTIC CT
5 CHATSWORTH CT
6 SOUTH BEACH

RIVER CL

BEACH RD

BEACH RD

KINGS WLK

A7 (top)
7 STEYNING CT
8 BRAMBER CT
9 EATON CT
10 GRANVILLE CT
11 HADDINGTON ST
12 MALVERN ST
13 MONMOUTH ST

C7
1 DEVONSHIRE CT
2 CORNWALL CT
3 SOMERSET CT
4 JANESTON CT
5 STIRLING CT
6 BRECON CT

7 ELIZABETH CT
8 PHILIP CT
9 BALTIMORE CT
10 DRIVE LODGE
11 EATON MANOR
12 VERIC
13 VALVERDE HO

14 VALENTINE CT
15 HEREFORD CT
16 GAINSBOROUGH HO
17 EATON GATE
18 CHARIS CT
19 EATON HALL
20 EATON GARDENS MANSIONS

C7
21 VANBRUGH CT
D7
1 COWDRAY CT
2 GOODWOOD CT
3 CROMWELL CT
4 WILLOW CT

D7
5 KINSALE CT
6 PALMEIRA HO
7 BELL MEAD
8 AMBER CT
9 CONISTON CT
10 SOMERHILL CT

11 BERESFORD CT
12 ST ANN'S CT

Bottom index

HEIM CT
ROKE CT
OVER GRANGE
IR HO
HIN CT
CES CT
MANOR
AWNS
LOY LODGE

10 BLUEBIRD CT
11 LANCASTER CT
C6
1 MARLBOROUGH CT
2 COPTHORNE CT
3 NORMANDY HO
4 BOWEN CT
5 GROVE CT
6 THE AMBASSADORS
7 WILBURY GRANGE

8 HAREWOOD CT
9 VICTORIA GR
10 WILBURY LODGE
12 ASHDOWN
13 SUSSEX CT
14 THE ATHENAEUM
15 SANDRINGHAM LODGE
16 HATFIELD CT
17 AMBER CT

18 PALMEIRA MANSIONS
19 AVENUE CT
20 PALMEIRA CT
21 VICTORIA CT
22 COOMBE LEA
23 GRAND AVENUE MANSIONS
24 ALBERT MEWS
D6
1 ABERGAVENNY HO
2 ROCHESTER CL

3 ROCHESTER CT
4 GWYDYR MANSIONS
5 KITLEAR CT
6 SOMERHILL LODGE
57 ANNES WELL HO
8 FARM MEWS
9 LANSDOWNE MEWS
E5
1 LITTLE WESTERN ST
2 NORFOLK BLDGS

3 NORFOLK MEWS
4 NORFOLK ST
5 WESTERN TERR
6 SILLWOOD HALL
7 SILLWOOD ST
8 OSPREY HO
9 SILLWOOD PL
10 FRED EMERY CT
11 KINGSLEY CT
12 CAVENDISH HO

13 BEDFORD TOWERS
14 HAMPTON ST
15 MITRE HO
16 REGENCY MEWS

17 RUSSELL MEWS
18 SUSSEX HEIGHTS
19 METROPOLE CT
20 ABBOTS
21 ASTRA HO
E6
1 THE VINERIES
2 WORCESTER CT
3 KENYA CT
4 VERNON CT

5 BRAEMAR HO
6 MONTPELIER PL
7 MONTPELIER LODGE
8 HEATHER CT
9 MONTPELIER TERR
10 VICTORIA PL
E7
1 WESTCOMBE
2 BERKELEY CT
3 DERBY CT

4 WARWICK CT
5 RICHMOND CT
6 MARSTON CT
7 CHESTER CT
8 YORK CT
10 WINDLESHAM CT
11 PAVILION CT
12 WESTMORLAND CT

For full street detail of the highlighted area see page 207.

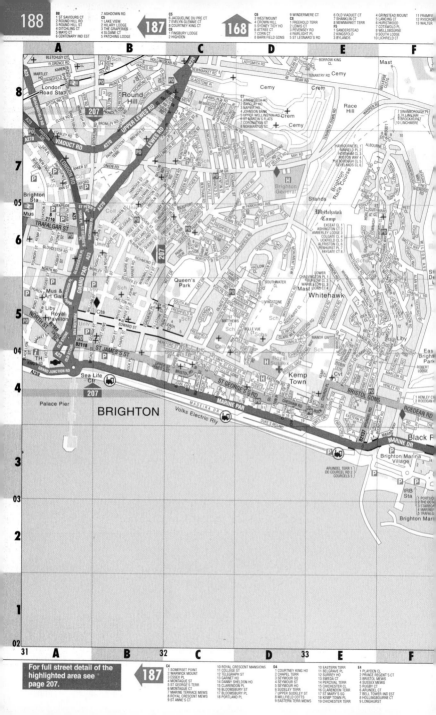

For full street detail of the highlighted area see page 207.

188

187 ▲

168 ▲

B8
1 ST SAVIOURS CT
2 ROUND HILL RD
3 ROUND HILL ST
4 DITCHLING ST
5 MAYO CT
6 CENTENARY IND EST
7 ASHDOWN RD

C5
1 LAKE VIEW
2 HILARY LODGE
3 THE GRAPERIES
4 SLOANE CT
5 PATCHING LODGE
6 JACQUELINE DU PRE CT
7 EVELYN GLENNIE CT
8 COURTNEY KING CT

C6
1 FINSBURY LODGE
2 HIGHDEN
3 WESTMOUNT
4 CROWN HILL
5 SYDNEY TIDY HO
6 ATTREE CT
7 CORN CT
8 BARN FIELD GDNS
9 WINDERMERE CL

C8
1 LAINSWORTH HO
2 BANCA AV HO
3 NAPIER HO
4 JOHNSON BANK
5 UPPER WELLINGTON RD
6 ST MARTIN'S FLATS
7 CORNINGTON ST
8 NORMANTON ST

C8
3 PEVENSEY RD
4 FAIRLIGHT PL
5 ST LEONARD'S RD

D
2 LEWIS CT

E
6 OLD VIADUCT CT
7 SHANKLIN CT
8 NEWMARKET TERR

F5
1 SANDERSTEAD
2 KINGSFOLD
3 BYLANDS

4 GRINSTEAD MOUNT
5 LANCING CT
6 HURSTWOOD
7 COTSWOLD PL
8 WELL SBOURNE
9 SOUTH LODGE
10 LICHFIELD CT

11 FRAMFIE...
12 RYECROE...
13 WALTER

7 SWANBOROUGH...
8 TILLINGTON
9 BROOKHURST
10 LINCHMERE

HAYBOURNE CL 1
TURNFIELD PL 2
HORSHAM CL 3
AYSTON WAY 4
PILEBOROUGH CL 5
SEVELANDS CL 6

EXCEAT CL 1
ASHINGTON CT 2
AMBERLEY COURT 3
COLGATE CL 4
UCKFIELD CL 5
ALFRISTON CL 6
PENHURST PL 7
RAYGATE CT 8

LOWER CHADVINGTON PL 1
HARLOW CL 2
WARB LETON CL 3
JONES CT 4

187 ◀

C4
1 SOMERSET POINT
2 WARWICK MOUNT
3 ESSEX PL
4 MONTAGUE ST
5 ST GEORGE'S TERR
6 MONTAGUE CT
7 MARINE TERRACE MEWS
8 ROYAL CRESCENT MEWS
9 ST ANNE'S CT
10 ROYAL CRESCENT MANSIONS
11 COLLEGE ST
12 TELEGRAPH ST
13 GARNET HO
14 DANNY SHELDON HO
15 CLARENDON PL
16 BLOOMSBURY ST
17 BLOOMSBURY PL
18 PORTLAND PL

D4
1 COURTNEY KING HO
2 CHAPEL TERR
3 SEYMOUR SQ
4 SEYMOUR ST
5 SEYMOUR HO
6 SUDELEY TERR
7 UPPER SUDELEY ST
8 MILLFIELD COTTS
9 EASTERN TERRA MEWS
10 EASTERN TERR
11 BELGRAVE PL
12 SURREY HO
13 SWEDA CT
14 PERCIVAL TERR
15 CHICHESTER CL
16 CLARENDON TERR
17 ST MARY'S SQ
18 KEMP TOWN PL
19 CHICHESTER TERR

E4
1 PLAYDEN CL
2 PRINCE REGENT'S CT
3 BRISTOL MEWS
4 SUSSEX MEWS
5 RUGBY CT
6 ARUNDEL CT
7 BELL TOWER IND EST
8 HOLLINGBOURNE CT
9 LONGHURST

BRIGHTON

189
170

A B C D E F

8

Cobnor
Point

Chichester
Harbour

Chichester Char

Thorney Channel

Chalkdock
Point

Fe

7

Itchenor
Park

West
Itchenor

S
I

01

FARM
COTTS

6

Pilsey
Island

Itchenor
House

5

00

4

Rookwood
House

ROOKW

Rookwood Lane
House

Redlands

Ella
Nore

Wicks Farm
Caravan Park

Tara

Lane End
House

3

Gate
Lodge

Walnut Tree
House

MALTHOUSE
COTTS

99

ELMLEA LA

ROOKWOOD RD

ACRE ST

2

ROMAN LANDING

SUMMERFIELD RD

PO

Nunnington Farm
Caravan Park

Holmes
Farm

West Wittering
Parochial (Contr)
Prim Sch

ELMSTEAD
GDNS

ELMLEA LA

Speedscroft

Snow
Hill

COASTGUARDS
COTTS

COASTGUARD LA

POND RD

PH

Home
Farm

1

West
Wittering

98

P

CAKEHAM RD

SEAWARD DR

WC

77 A B 78 C D 79 E F

189
201

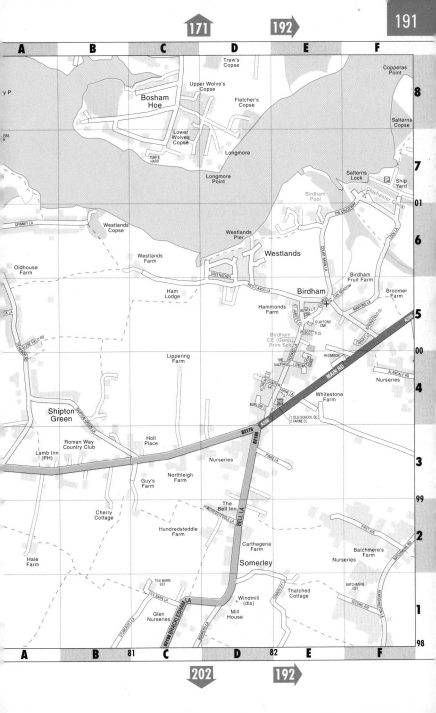

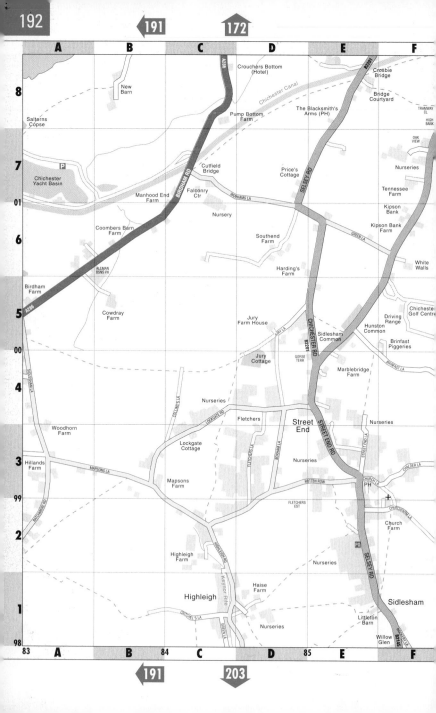

| A | B | C | D | E | F |

Crouchers Bottom
(Hotel)

Chichester Canal

New
Barn

Salterns
Copse

8

Pump Bottom
Farm

The Blacksmith's
Arms (PH)

Crosbie
Bridge

Bridge
Courtyard

TRAMWAY
CL

HIGH
BANK

OAK
VIEW

P

7

Chichester
Yacht Basin

Cutfield
Bridge

Price's
Cottage

Nurseries

01

Manhood End
Farm

BIRDHAM RD

Falconry
Ctr

MORHAMS LA

SELSEY RD

Tennessee
Farm

Kipson
Bank

Nursery

Kipson Bank
Farm

6

Coombers Barn
Farm

GREEN LA

White
Walls

ALLEMAN
BSNS PK

Southend
Farm

Birdham
Farm

A286

Harding's
Farm

Chichester
Golf Centre

5

Cowdray
Farm

Jury
Farm House

Driving
Range

JURY LA

CHICHESTER RD

Sidlesham
Common

Hunston
Common

Brinfast
Piggeries

00

Jury
Cottage

GORSE
TERR

B2201

BRINFAST LA

4

Woodhorn
Farm

COLLINS LA

Nurseries

LOCKGATE RD

Fletchers

FLETCHERS LA

BIRDHAM LA

Street
End

Marblebridge
Farm

STREET END RD

Nurseries

3

Hillands
Farm

BOTCHMBE RD

MAPSONS LA

Lockgate
Cottage

Nurseries

ROTTEN ROW

STREET END RD

PH

CALDER LA

99

Mapsons
Farm

FLETCHERS
EST

CHURCH LA

CHURCHFARM LA

2

Highleigh
Farm

KEYNOR RD

Church
Farm

PO

SELSEY RD

Haise
Farm

Nurseries

1

Highleigh

CRUTCHFIELD S LA

Keynor Rife

GREEN LA

Nurseries

Littleton
Barn

Sidlesham

98

Willow
Glen

B2145

| A | B | 84 | C | D | 85 | E | F |

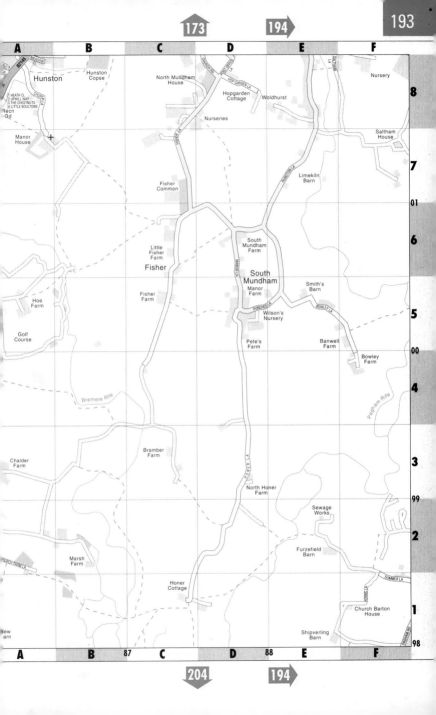

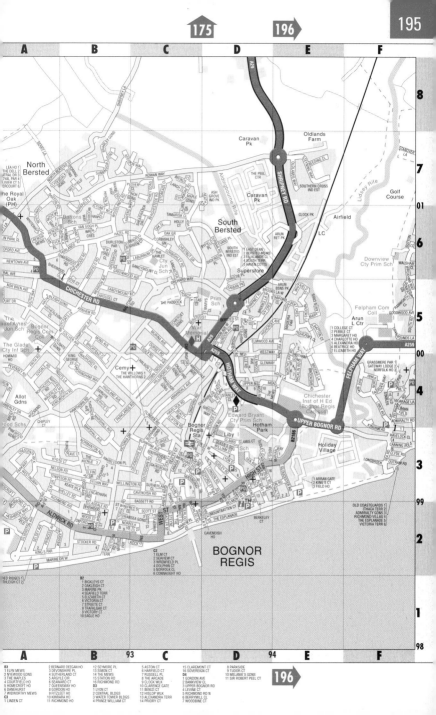

Map Grid Reference Points

North Bersted

The Royal Oak (PH)

Caravan Pk
Oldlands Farm

THE PEEL CTR
SOUTHERN CROSS IND EST

Clock Pk

Airfield

Golf Course

South Bersted

Caravan Pk

Downview Cty Prim Sch

Arun L Ctr

Felpham Com Coll

CHICHESTER RD

The Hamlet Cty Jun Sch

Prim Sch

Superstore

EAST DEAN
BERSTED MEWS
FALKLANDS CL
SOUTH TERR
HAVEN COTES

1 COLLEGE CT
2 PEBBLE CT
3 MARGARET HO
4 CHARLOTTE HO
5 ALEXANDRA HO
6 BEATRICE HO
7 ELIZABETH HO

GRASSMERE PAR 1
GATEWAY LODGE 2
NORFOLK HO 3

Bognor Regis Com Coll

War Memorial

The Glade Cty Inf Sch

Cemy

THE WILLOWS 1
THE HAWTHORNS 2

Allot Gdns

FELPHAM WAY

HOTHAM WAY

Chichester Inst of H Ed (Bognor Regis Campus)

UPPER BOGNOR RD

Edward Bryant Cty Prim Sch

Hotham Park

Holiday Village

Bognor Regis Sta

Liby

1 ARRAN GATE
2 KING'S CT
3 FIELD HO

ALDWICK RD

OLD COASTGUARDS 1
ADMIRALTY GDNS 3
RICHMOND VILLAS 4
THE ESPLANADE 5
VICTORIA TERR 6

WEST ST

THE ESPLANADE

BERKELEY CT

CAVENDISH CL

BOGNOR REGIS

C2
1 ELM CT
2 SEAVEW CT
3 WRENFIELD PL
4 DOLPHIN CT
5 NORFOLK CL
6 CONNAUGHT HO

B2
1 BICKLEYS CT
2 OAKLEIGH CT
3 MARINE PK
4 SEAFIELD TERR
5 ELIZABETH CT
6 VICTORIA CT
7 STREETE CT
8 TRAFALGAR CT
9 VICTORY CT
10 EAGLE HO

RED RIDGES 1
THE LEIGH CT 2

B3
1 ELFN MEWS
2 NYEWOOD GDNS
3 THE MAPLES
4 COURTFIELD HO
5 HOMECROFT HO
6 DANEHURST
7 WIDWORTHY MEWS

C3
1 LINDEN CT

2 BERNARD DEEGAN HO
3 DEVONSHIRE PL
4 SUTHERLAND CT
5 ARGYLE CIR
6 SEAWARD CT
7 QUEENSWAY HO
8 GORDON HO
9 FITZLEET HO
10 KINRARA HO
11 RICHMOND HO

12 SEYMORE PL
13 SIMON CT
14 THE MEWS
15 STATION RD
16 RICHMOND RD

D3
1 LYON CT
2 CENTRAL BLDGS
3 WATER TOWER BLDGS
4 PRINCE WILLIAM CT

5 ASTON CT
6 HARFIELD CT
7 RUSSELL PL
8 THE ARCADE
9 CLOCK WLK
10 CLARENCE GATE
11 BENIZ CT
12 HISLOP WLK
13 ALEXANDRA TERR
14 PRIORY CT

15 CLAREMONT CT
16 SOVEREIGN CT

D4
1 GORDON AVE
2 BANKVIEW CL
3 UPPER BOGNOR RD
4 LEVINE CT
5 RICHMOND RD N
6 BERRYMILL CL
7 WOODBINE CT

8 PARKSIDE
9 TUDOR CT
10 MELANIE'S GDNS
11 SIR ROBERT PEEL CT

Weststone Bridge
Bilsham
Ryebank Rife
B2132
GREVATT'S LA W
BILSHAM LA
BIRNHAM RD
Hoe Barn
BILSHAM CNR
White Rails
Flansham
Poultry Houses
WORMS LA
GREVATT'S LA
STANOVER LA
HOE LA
Sheepwash Barn
YAPTON RD
Guernsey Farm
Golf Course
BOGNOR REGIS
1 ULLSWATER GR
2 DERWENT GR
3 OUTERWYKE GDNS
4 AMBLESIDE CL
FLANSHAM LA
MIDDLETON BSNS PK
ANCTON CL
WALSHAM CL
WHITELANDS
WRIOXHAM WAY
SILVER BIRCH DR
WEST AVE
1 ST NICHOLAS
2 GRANGE CT
FELPHAM WAY
MIDDLETON RD
MERRY END
ILEX WAY
FIRST AVE
ELMER GDNS
KINGFISHER CT
NIGHTINGALE CT
ST NICHOLAS LA
SHAW CL
ROSE AVE
Felpham
Middleton-on-Sea
SEA WAY
Middleton Point
A259
OLD SCHOOL MEWS
MANOR CL
TURRET HO
GROVE
THE MEWS
THE CRESCENT
COPELAND
MINTON RD
FIRST AVE
SECOND AVE
STRAND WAY
SEA DR
NEPTUNE CT
BEREWEEKE RD
CULVER RD
DAVENPORT RD
1 OLD RECTORY FLATS
2 THE OLD RECTORY
3 OAKLAND CT

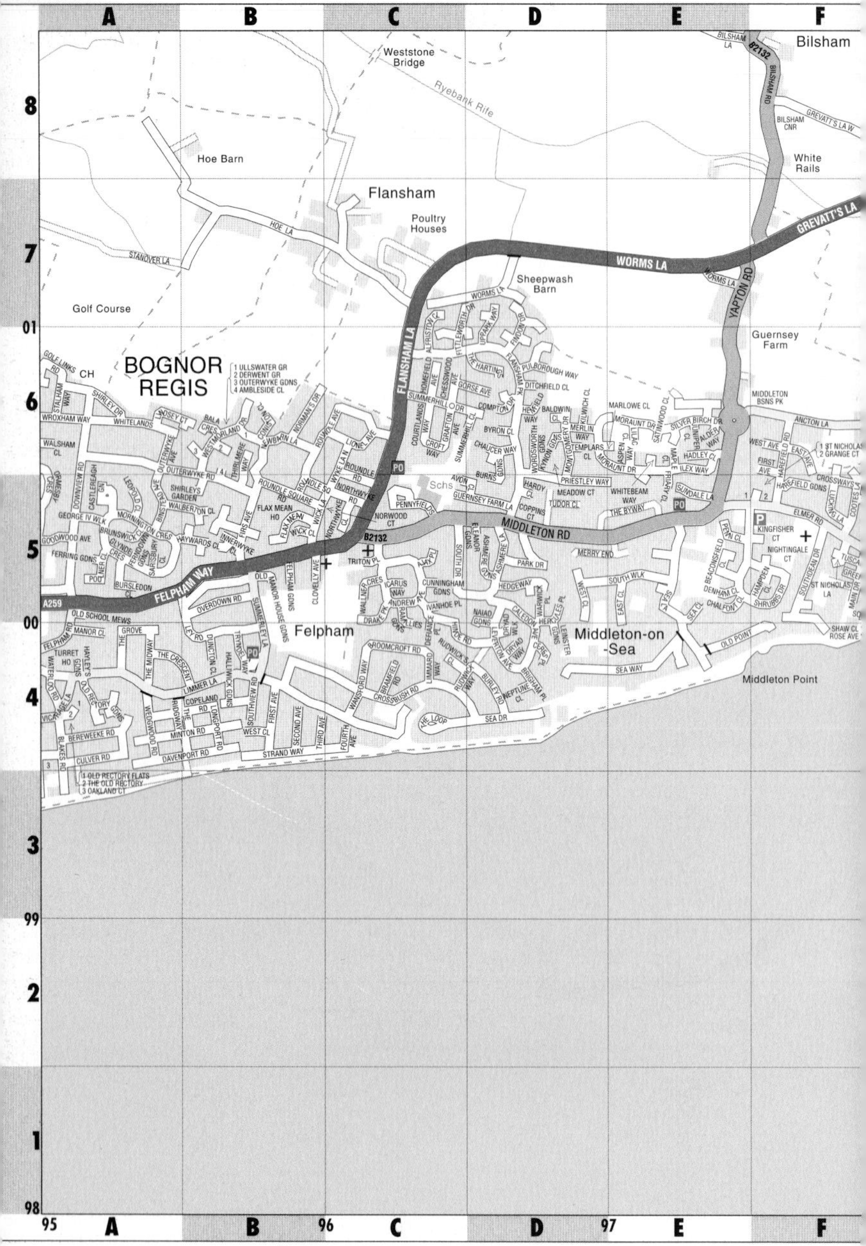

179
200

B3
1 ALDWICK C
2 CLUMPING CT
3 PACKHAM RD
4 FITZALAN CT
5 PETWORTH CT
6 DOWNSIDE CT
7 HOWARDS WAY
B4
1 NORDSETER LODGE
2 MARIGOLDS LODGE
3 KIRDFORD CL

C4
1 KNIGHTSCROFT CL
5 BEACH CT
6 SELSEY CT
7 COPPETS WOOD
8 NORFOLK CT
9 RAWSON CT
B5
1 HIGHFIELD GDNS
2 CLARE LODGE
3 RICHMOND CT

C4
1 ILEX HO
2 FLINT HO
3 MERON'S COURT CL
4 SHAFTESBURY CT
5 SEAVIEW GDNS
6 HAWTHORN CL
7 RAVENS CROFT
C5
1 STERLING PAR
2 BROADMARK PAR
3 CHURCHILL CT

4 BROADMARK HO
9 WHITECROFT
6 EASTERGATE GN
7 FITTLEWORTH GDN
8 CHICHESTER CT
9 ARUNDEL GDN
C6
1 MENDIP CT
2 DONNINGTON CL

D6
1 ST ANTHONY'S WAY
2 SHIRLANDS CT

E6
1 RICHMOND CL
2 THORNTON CT
3 MUNMERE WAY
4 COPPER HALL CL
5 CRUNDENS CNR
6 STATION PAR

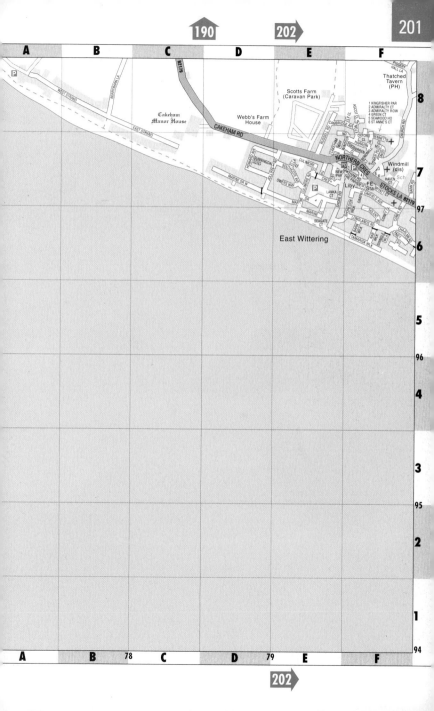

A   B   C   D   E   F

8

PIGGERY
HALL LA
Thatched
Tavern
(PH)

1 KINGFISHER PAR
2 ADMIRALTY CT
3 ADMIRALTY ROW
4 GREEN CT
5 SEAWOOD HO
6 ST ANNE'S CT

Scotts Farm
(Caravan Park)

WEST STRAND

HAWTHORN LA

B2179

Cakeham
Manor House

Webb's Farm
House

CAKEHAM RD

EAST STRAND

ASCOT CL

CAMBRIDGE CL

OXFORD CL

KENNETT'S

NORTHERN CRES

Windmill
(dis)

Haven
Sch

7

MARINE DR W

SUNNINGDALE
ROUND

CULIMORE

SCHOOL
PAR

NEW RD

CAKEHAM
PAR

NEW PARADE

OWERS WAY

CHEYNE

FERRY
Sta

STOCKS LA B2179

97

MARINE DR

LANKA
ST

SHORE RD

OAKFIELD AVE

Liby

LONGLANDS

CHALK LA

SEAGATE

SEA WALK

MARINE

TAMARISK WLK

WEBB

THIMBLE

LONGLANDS RD

CHALK MEAD

6

East Wittering

5

96

4

3

95

2

1

94

A   B   78   C   D   79   E   F

8

Mus
CH FARM LA
CHURCH
FARM
CT
Stubcroft
Farm
HILTON LA
EAST WITTERING
BSNS CTR
Cherry
Tree
Farm
THIRD AVE
Batchmere
Estate
Almoding

Somerley
Farm
EARNLEY RD
MANHOOD
COTTS

7

FIELD
RD
CLAYTON LA
STUBCROFT LA
BRACKLESHAM LA
Holiday
Centre
Earnley
Grange
Grange
Farm
EASTON LA

SOUTHDOWN
EARNLEY MANOR CL
CHURCH
COTTS
Manor
Farm

97
B2179
Camping
Site
BRACKLESHAM
CT
CLAPPERS LA
Earnley
KIMBRIDGE
PK
ON WAY
GRAYSWOOD

6
STOCKS
B2179
PERKLEY CL
B2179
ELM CL
Bracklesham
Grange Rife

WEST BRACKLESHAM DR
B2179
MARSH
LA
Marsh Barn

5
WESTERLEY GDNS
AZARA PK
P
FIRST AVE
FARM RD
WILTON
AVEBURY CL
BRACKLESHAM
Marsh
Farm
Sussex Beach
Holiday Village

96
LEIGH
CT
BYWAVES

4

3
Bracklesham Bay

95

2

1

94
80   **A**   **B**   81   **C**   **D**   82   **E**   **F**

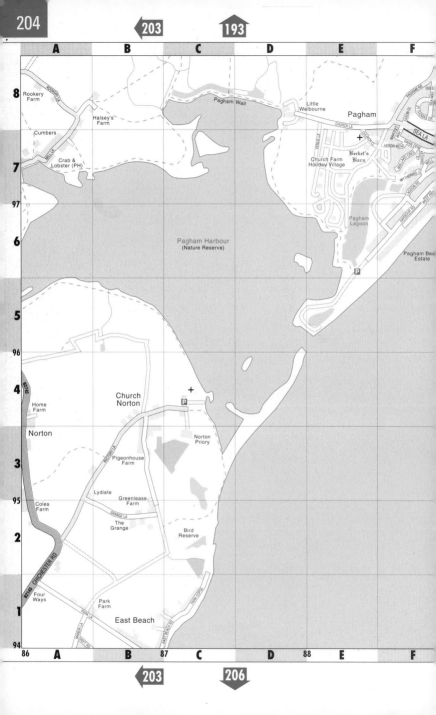

BOGNOR REGIS

Aldwick Bay Estate

1 ST THOMAS CT
2 CHURCHILL WLK
3 MULBERRY CT

203 204

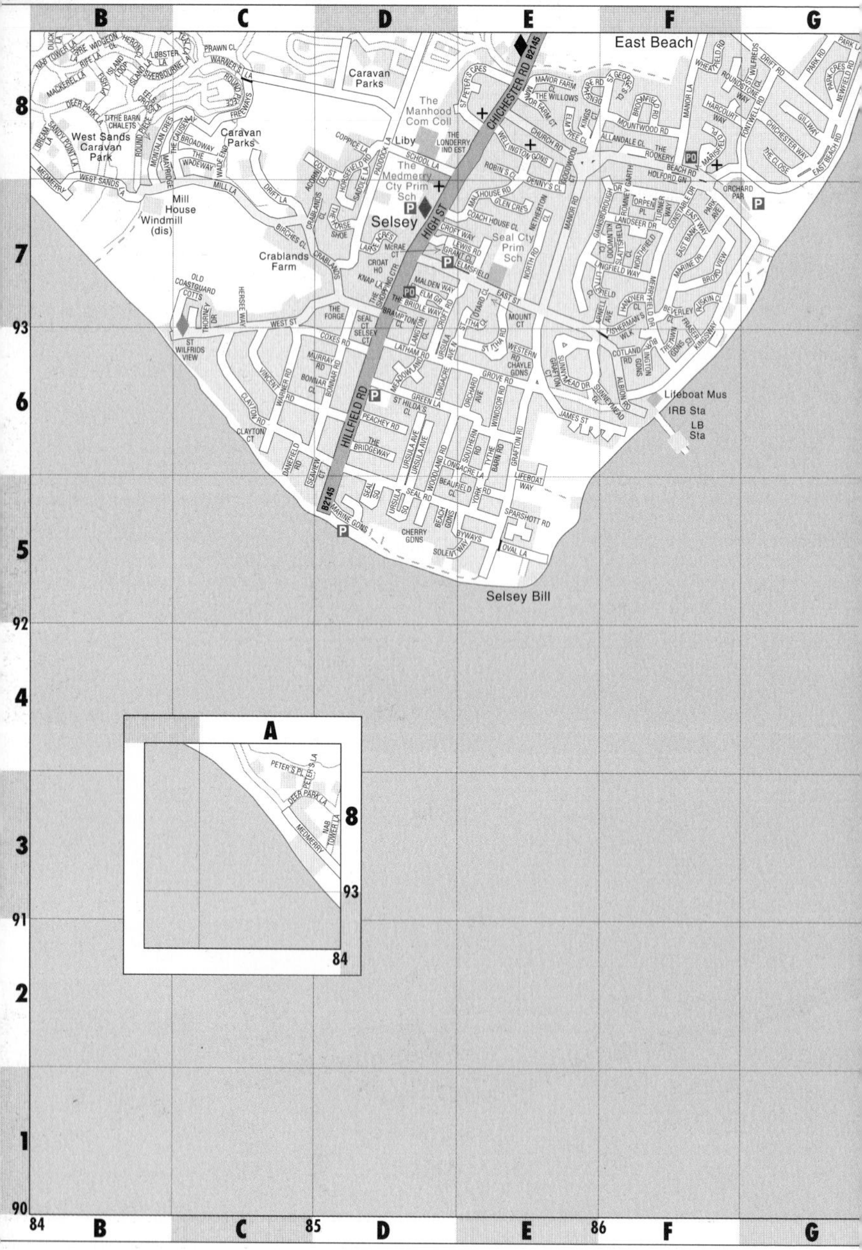

East Beach

West Sands
Caravan
Park

Caravan
Parks

Caravan
Parks

Mill
House
Windmill
(dis)

The Manhood
Com Coll

The
Medmerry
City Prim
Sch

Selsey

Crablands
Farm

Seal City
Prim Sch

Old
Coastguard
Cotts

St
Wilfrids
View

The
Forge

Lifeboat Mus
IRB Sta
LB
Sta

Selsey Bill

Peter's La
Deer Park La
Medmerry

84 85 86

90 91 92 93

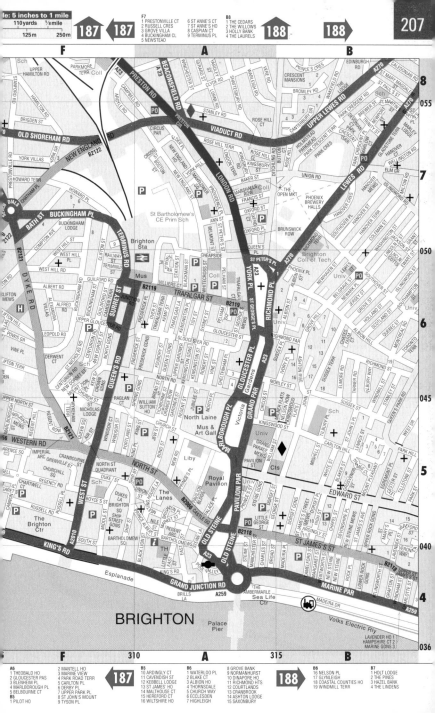

F7
1 PRESTONVILLE CT
2 RUSSELL CRES
3 GROVE VILLA
4 BUCKINGHAM CL
5 NEWSTEAD

6 ST ANNE'S CT
7 ST ANNE'S HO
8 CASPIAN CT
9 TERMINUS PL

B8
1 THE CEDARS
2 THE WILLOWS
3 HOLLY BANK
4 THE LAURELS

BRIGHTON

A6
1 THEOBALD HO
2 GLOUCESTER PAS
3 BLENHEIM PL
4 MARLBOROUGH PL
5 BELBOURNE CT

B5
1 PILOT HO

2 MANTELL HO
3 MARINE VIEW
4 PARK ROAD TERR
5 CARLTON PL
6 DERBY PL
7 UPPER PARK PL
8 ST JOHN'S MOUNT
9 TYSON PL

B5
10 ARDINGLY CT
11 CAVENDISH ST
12 KEBBELL LODGE
13 ST JAMES' HO
14 MALTHOUSE CT
15 HEREFORD CT
16 WILTSHIRE HO

B6
1 WATERLOO PL
2 BLAKE CT
3 ALBION HO
4 THORNSDALE
5 CHURCH WAY
6 ECCLESDEN
7 HIGHLEIGH

8 GROVE BANK
9 NORMANHURST
10 DINAPORE HO
11 RICHMOND HTS
12 COURTLANDS
13 CRANBROOK
14 ASHTON LODGE
15 SAXONBURY

B6
16 NELSON PL
17 GLYNLEIGH
18 COASTAL COUNTIES HO
19 WINDMILL TERR

B7
1 HOLT LODGE
2 THE PINES
3 HAZEL BANK
4 THE LINDENS

LAVENDER HO 1
HAMPSHIRE CT 2
MARINE GDNS 3

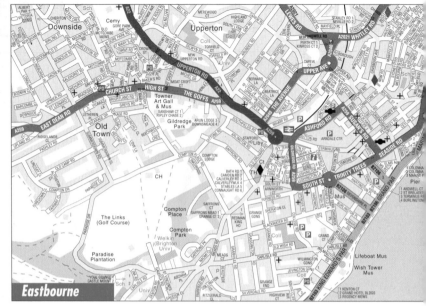

Eastbourne

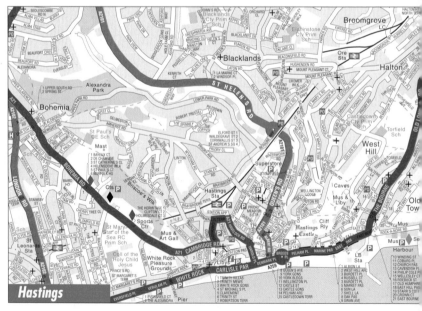

Hastings

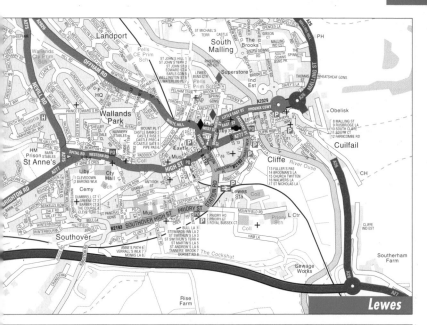

Lewes

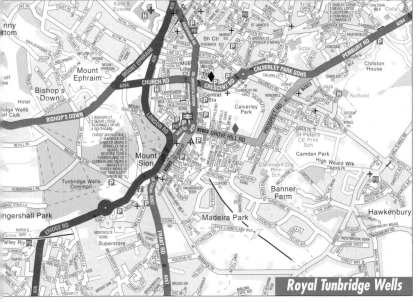

Royal Tunbridge Wells

Index

Street names are listed alphabetically and show the locality, the Postcode District, the page number and a reference to the square in which the name falls on the map page

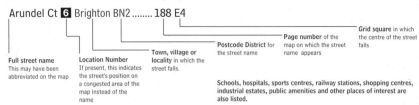

Arundel Ct **6** Brighton BN2 .... 188 E4

Full street name
This may have been abbreviated on the map

Location Number
If present, this indicates the street's position on a congested area of the map instead of the name

Town, village or locality in which the street falls.

Postcode District for the street name

Page number of the map on which the street name appears

Grid square in which the centre of the street falls

Schools, hospitals, sports centres, railway stations, shopping centres, industrial estates, public amenities and other places of interest are also listed.

Abbreviations used in the index

App	Approach	Cl	Close	Ent	Enterprise	La	Lane	Rdbt	Roundabout

App **Approach**
Arc **Arcade**
Ave **Avenue**
Bvd **Boulevard**
Bldgs **Buildings**
Bsns Pk **Business Park**
Bsns Ctr **Business Centre**
Bglws **Bungalows**
Cswy **Causeway**
Ctr **Centre**
Cir **Circus**

Cl **Close**
Comm **Common**
Cnr **Corner**
Cotts **Cottages**
Ct **Court**
Ctyd **Courtyard**
Cres **Crescent**
Dr **Drive**
Dro **Drove**
E **East**
Emb **Embankment**

Ent **Enterprise**
Espl **Esplanade**
Est **Estate**
Gdns **Gardens**
Gn **Green**
Gr **Grove**
Hts **Heights**
Ho **House**
Ind Est **Industrial Estate**
Intc **Interchange**
Junc **Junction**

La **Lane**
N **North**
Orch **Orchard**
Par **Parade**
Pk **Park**
Pas **Passage**
Pl **Place**
Prec **Precinct**
Prom **Promenade**
Ret Pk **Retail Park**
Rd **Road**

Rdbt **Roundabout**
S **South**
Sq **Square**
Strs **Stairs**
Stps **Steps**
St **Street, Saint**
Terr **Terrace**
Trad Est **Trading Estate**
Wlk **Walk**
W **West**
Yd **Yard**

A'becket Gdns BN13 .... 181 F6
A'becket's Ave PO21 .... 194 B1
Abberton Field BN6 .... 126 E5
Abbey Church
  The Brighton RH10 .... 20 B1
Abbey Cl BN15 .... 184 B6
Abbey Ho RH20 .... 140 D8
Abbey Rd Brighton BN2 ... 188 D4
  Lancing BN15 .... 183 C7
  Steyning BN44 .... 143 E4
  Worthing BN11 .... 182 B1
Abbots Cl BN6 .... 126 E4
Abbots Leigh RH13 .... 80 A8
Abbotsbury Ct RH13 .... 36 E3
Abbotsfield Rd RH11 .... 17 D4
Abbotsford Sch RH15 .... 106 E6
Abbotswood Wlk BN16 ... 199 C4
Abbotts Cl BN15 .... 187 E5
Abbotts Cl BN11 .... 182 D2
Abbotts View BN15 .... 183 C8
Abbotts Way BN15 .... 183 F6
Abbottsbury PO21 .... 205 A8
Aberdeen Rd BN2 .... 188 C8
Abergavenny Rd BN1 .. 187 D6
Abigail Ho **10** RH16 .... 85 E4
Abingdon Wlk BN13 .... 181 D5
Abinger Cotts RH13 .... 80 F5
Abinger Rd BN41 .... 186 B8
Abrahams Rd RH11 .... 18 A1
Acacia Ave Hove BN3 ...... 166 F1
  Worthing BN13 .... 181 D1
Acacia Ct BN1 .... 167 F2
Acorn Ave RH13 .... 81 F1
Acorn Cl Angmering BN16 . 179 F4
  East Grinstead RH19 .... 22 E8
  Horley RH6 .... 2 C4
  Selsey PO20 .... 206 D8
Acorn End PO21 .... 194 D2
Acorns RH13 .... 37 A4
Acorns The Crawley RH11 .. 18 B1
  Sayers Common BN6 ... 105 D2
Acre Cl
  Haywards Heath RH16 ...... 85 D2
  Rustington BN16 .... 199 B6
Acre Cl The BN11 .... 182 B1
Acre St PO20 .... 190 F2
Adams Cl BN1 .... 168 B2
Adamson Ct **6** RH11 .... 18 B1
Adastra Ave BN1 .... 127 A4
Adderbury Ave PO10 ... 149 B3
Addison Cl BN15 .... 183 E6
Addison Rd BN1, BN3, BN41 . 187 E7
Addison Way PO22 .... 195 C7

Adelaide Cl Crawley RH11 .... 5 D1
  Horsham RH12 .... 36 F4
  Worthing BN13 .... 181 C7
Adelaide Cres BN3 .... 187 C5
Adelaide Ho GU29 .... 92 E6
Adelaide Rd PO19 .... 173 B7
Adelaide Sq BN43 .... 185 B7
Adelphi Cl RH16 .... 19 D4
Admers Cres GU30 .... 25 C2
Admiral Rd RH11 .... 18 A3
Admiral's Bridge La RH19 .. 22 C2
Admirals Wlk
  Funtington PO18 .... 151 A5
  Littlehampton BN16 ...... 199 A6
  1 Shoreham-by-Sea
  BN43 .... 184 F6
Admiralty Ct PO20 .... 201 F7
Admiralty Gdns PO22 ... 195 F3
Admiralty Rd PO22 .... 195 F4
Admiralty Row PO20 ...... 201 F7
Adrian Ct RH11 .... 18 B1
Adur Ave
  Shoreham-by-Sea BN43 .. 164 E1
  Worthing BN13 .... 181 C8
Adur Cl **6** BN15 .... 184 C5
Adur Ct
  5 Shoreham-by-Sea
  BN15 .... 184 C5
  10 Shoreham-by-Sea
  BN43 .... 185 C8
Adur Dr BN43 .... 185 A7
Adur Rd Burgess Hill RH15 107 C4
  Shoreham-by-Sea BN43 ... 184 E8
Adur Valley Ct BN44 ...... 144 B2
Adur View BN44 .... 144 A2
Adversane Ct RH12 ...... 36 D4
Adversane La RH14 .... 77 D2
Adversane Rd BN14 ...... 182 B5
Agate La RH12 .... 36 F5
Aglaia Rd BN11 .... 181 F1
Agnes St BN2 .... 188 C7
Aigburth Ave PO21 ...... 194 D3
Ailsa Cl RH11 .... 18 B3
Ainsdale Cl BN13 .... 181 D6
Ainsdale Rd BN13 .... 181 D6
Ainsworth Ho **1** BN2 ... 188 C7
Aintree Rd RH10 .... 19 A4
Air St BN1 .... 207 F5
Airedale Ct **8** BN41 ...... 187 B2
Airport Way RH6 .... 6 B8
Airport Way Rdbt W RH6 .... 5 F8
Aitken Ho GU27 .... 27 C7
Ajax Pl PO22 .... 196 C5

Akehurst Cl RH10 .... 7 B3
Alan Way BN2 .... 188 F5
Alandale Rd Birdham PO20 191 F4
  Sompting BN15 .... 163 C1
Albany Cl BN11 .... 182 A1
Albany Mews BN3 .... 187 B6
Albany Rd RH11 .... 18 C6
Albany Villas
  Cuckfield RH17 .... 85 A6
  Hove BN3 .... 187 B6
Albert Cl RH16 .... 86 A4
Albert Crane Ct RH11 ...... 18 A8
Albert Dr RH15 .... 106 E2
Albert Mews **24** BN3 ...... 187 C6
Albert Rd
  Bognor Regis PO21 ... 195 D3
  Brighton BN2 .... 207 F6
  Fishbourne PO19 ...... 172 C6
  Horley RH6 .... 2 A3
  Littlehampton BN17 ... 198 D5
  Rustington BN16 .... 199 C6
  Southwick BN42 .... 185 D7
Alberta Rd BN13 .... 181 D6
Alberta Wlk BN13 .... 181 D6
Albery Cl RH12 .... 36 B4
Albion Cl RH10 .... 19 D5
Albion Ct RH15 .... 106 F2
Albion Hall BN41 .... 207 B6
Albion Ho
  3 Brighton BN2 .... 207 B6
  Southwick BN42 .... 185 F7
Albion Rd PO20 .... 206 F6
Albion St Brighton BN2 ... 207 B6
  Portslade-by-Sea BN41 ... 186 B7
  Southwick BN42 .... 185 E7
Albion Way RH12 .... 36 C2
Albourne Way PO21 ... 194 D2
Albourne CE (C) Prim Sch
  BN6 .... 125 C6
Albourne Cl BN2 .... 188 F7
Albourne Rd Henfield BN5 124 A8
  Hurstpierpoint BN6 ...... 125 E6
Albury Keep RH6 .... 2 B4
Aldbourne Dr PO21 ...... 194 D2
Alder Cl
  Crawley Down RH10 ...... 21 B8
  Worthing BN13 .... 181 C5
Alder Copse RH12 .... 57 F8
Alder Way PO22 .... 196 E6
Aldermoor Ave RH20 ... 119 E3
Alderney Rd BN12 .... 200 F4
Alders Ave RH19 .... 9 E3
Alders View Dr RH19 ...... 9 E3

Aldingbourne Cl RH11 ...... 17 F7
Aldingbourne Ctry Ctr
  PO18 .... 155 C3
Aldingbourne Cty
  Prim Sch PO20 .... 175 D6
Aldingbourne Dr
  PO18, PO20 .... 155 B3
Aldingbourne Ho
  Crockerhill PO18 .... 155 B3
  Littlehampton BN17 ... 178 B3
Aldingbourne Pk PO20 ... 175 D5
Aldrich Cl BN2 .... 188 F6
Aldrington Ave BN3 ...... 187 A8
Aldrington CE Fst Sch
  BN3 .... 186 F7
Aldrington CE Prim Sch
  BN3 .... 167 A2
Aldrington Cl BN3 .... 186 D7
Aldrington House (Hospl)
  BN3 .... 186 F6
Aldrington Pl BN3 .... 186 D8
Aldrington Sta BN3 ...... 187 A8
Aldsworth Ave BN12 ...... 181 B1
Aldsworth Ct BN12 .... 181 B2
Aldwick Ave PO21 .... 194 F2
Aldwick Cl **1** BN16 ...... 199 B3
Aldwick Cres BN14 ...... 162 A1
Aldwick Felds PO21 ...... 194 F2
Aldwick Gdns PO21 ...... 194 F3
Aldwick Grange PO21 ... 194 E2
Aldwick Ho BN17 .... 178 B3
Aldwick Hundred PO21 · 194 F1
Aldwick Pl PO21 .... 194 F2
Aldwick Rd PO21 .... 195 B2
Aldwick St PO21 .... 194 E2
Aldwych Cl RH10 .... 19 D4
Alexander Cl PO21 ...... 194 E2
Alexandra Ct
  10 Crawley RH11 ...... 18 D5
  Worthing BN12 .... 181 C3
Alexandra Ho PO22 ...... 195 E4
Alexandra Rd
  Burgess Hill RH15 ...... 107 C2
  Chichester PO19 .... 173 B7
  Lancing BN15 .... 183 F5
  Worthing BN11 .... 182 F2
Alexandra Terr **13** PO21 ... 195 D3
Alexandra Villas BN1 ...... 207 F6
Alfold By-Pass GU6 ...... 11 A5
Alfold La GU6 .... 11 A7
Alfold Rd GU6 .... 11 B7
Alford Cl BN14 .... 182 A7
Alfred Cl RH10 .... 19 E5

Alfred Pl BN11 .... 182 E2
Alfred Rd BN1 .... 207 F6
Alfrey Cl PO10 .... 169 E8
Alfriston Cl
  Bognor Regis PO22 ... 196 C6
  Brighton BN2 .... 188 F6
  Worthing BN14 .... 182 B5
Alfriston Ho **2** BN14 ... 182 D5
Alfriston Rd BN14 .... 182 B5
Alice St BN3 .... 187 D5
Alicia Ave Ashington RH20 121 A5
  Crawley RH10 .... 19 C6
Alicks Hill RH14 .... 77 D8
Alinora Ave BN12 .... 181 D1
Alinora Cl BN12 .... 181 D1
Alinora Cres BN12 .... 181 D1
Alinora Dr BN12 .... 181 D1
Allandale Cl PO20 .... 206 F8
Allangate Dr BN16 ...... 199 D6
Allcard Cl RH12 .... 36 D4
Allcot Cl RH11 .... 17 E3
Allee Dr GU30 .... 25 B5
Allen Rd RH16 .... 86 A4
Allen's Cl RH19 .... 23 D6
Allendale RH13 .... 57 F3
Allendale Ave
  New Brighton PO10 ...... 149 A3
  Worthing BN14 .... 162 A1
Alley The Amberley BN18 .. 138 D7
  Stedham GU29 .... 70 A1
Alleyne Way PO22 ...... 197 B5
Allfreys Wharf RH20 ...... 98 B2
Allingham Gdns RH12 ... 37 B5
Allington Rd BN14 .... 182 E7
Allman Bsns Pk PO20 ... 192 B6
Allyington Way RH10 ...... 19 D5
Alma Rd RH16 .... 86 B8
Alma St BN15 .... 183 E4
Almodington La PO20 ... 202 FB
Almond Cl RH11 .... 18 A5
Almshouses The PO18 ... 154 D4
Alperton Cl PO21 .... 194 C1
Alpha Cotts RH20 .... 98 D2
Alpha Ct BN17 .... 198 C5
Alpha Rd RH11 .... 18 C6
Alpine Rd BN3 .... 186 F8
Alston Way RH13 .... 181 D5
Alverstone Rd BN11 ...... 182 F3
Amadeus Ho BN16 ...... 200 B6
Ambassadors The **6** BN3 187 C6
Amber Ct **17** Hove BN3 ... 187 C6
  8 Hove BN3 .... 187 D7
Amber Glade RH13 .... 57 F1

Amberley CE (C) Sch
BN18 .... 138 E7
Amberley CI
  Burgess Hill RH15 .... 107 A5
  Crawley RH10 .... 19 C6
  Haywards Heath RH16 .... 85 D4
  Horsham RH12 .... 37 A6
  Hove BN3 .... 166 E3
  Littlehampton BN17 .... 198 E6
  Shoreham-by-Sea BN43 ... 164 F1
Amberley Ct Lancing BN15 183 F6
  🗓 Worthing BN11 .... 181 F2
Amberley Dr
  Bognor Regis PO21 .... 195 A4
  Hove BN3 .... 166 E3
  Worthing BN12 .... 181 B1
Amberley Gate RH20 .... 119 B1
Amberley Lodge BN2 .... 207 A7
Amberley Mus BN18 .... 138 D5
Amberley Rd RH20 .... 140 A8
  Horsham RH12 .... 37 A6
  Littlehampton BN16 .... 199 C4
Amberley Sta BN18 .... 138 D4
Ambermale The BN2 .... 207 A4
Ambersham Cres BN16 ... 179 F3
Ambleside
  Bognor Regis PO22 .... 196 B6
  Crawley RH10 .... 17 D5
Ambleside Rd BN15 .... 183 C6
Ambrose Hill RH17 .... 105 B7
Ambrose PI BN11 .... 182 D2
Amelia Rd BN11 .... 182 C2
Amenic Cl 🗓 BN17 .... 198 E5
America La RH16 .... 86 A5
Amesbury Cres BN3 .... 186 F7
Amherst Cres BN3 .... 186 F8
Amstel Ct 🗓 BN17 .... 198 F4
Amundsen Rd RH12 .... 36 D6
Anchor Hill RH17 .... 87 A2
Anchor Springs 🗓 BN17 .. 198 D5
Ancren Cl BN12 .... 180 F3
Ancton Cl PO22 .... 196 F5
Ancton Dr PO22 .... 197 A6
Ancton La PO22 .... 196 F6
Ancton Lodge La PO22 ... 197 A5
Ancton Way PO22 .... 197 A6
Andlers Ash Rd GU33 .... 45 A3
Andrew Ave PO22 .... 196 C5
Andrew Cl
  Rustington BN16 .... 199 B6
  Steyning BN44 .... 143 D2
Andrew's La RH13 .... 57 F1
Andrews Cotts RH13 .... 79 F7
Andrews La GU29 .... 91 F7
Andrews Rd RH13 .... 79 F7
Andromeda Cl RH11 .... 17 E4
Angel St GU28 .... 95 F8
Angell Est PO19 .... 173 D5
Anglesea St BN11 .... 182 C3
Anglesey Cl RH11 .... 18 C2
Angmering Ct BN1 .... 168 F5
Angmering La BN16 .... 199 E5
Angmering Sch The BN16 179 F3
Angmering Sta BN16 .... 199 F6
Angmering Way BN16 ...... 179 E2
Angola Rd BN14 .... 182 F4
Angus Cl RH12 .... 36 D4
Angus Rd BN12 .... 181 E2
Ann Cl BN6 .... 127 A5
Ann St Brighton BN1 .... 207 A7
  Worthing BN11 .... 182 E2
Annandale Ave PO21 .... 195 C6
Anne Howard Gdns BN18 158 A3
Annington Commercial Ctr
  BN44 .... 163 D8
Annington Gdns 🗓 BN43 164 F1
Annington Rd BN44, BN15 163 F8
Annweir Ave BN15 .... 183 E6
Anscombe 🗓 RH16 .... 85 D6
Anscombe Cl BN11 .... 181 F1
Anscombe Rd BN11 .... 181 F1
Ansisters Rd BN12 .... 200 E5
Anson Ct BN12 .... 181 C4
Anson Rd
  Bognor Regis PO21 .... 194 B2
  Worthing BN12 .... 181 C4
Ansty Cl BN2 .... 188 E5
Answorth Cl PO19 .... 153 B1
Antlands La RH6 .... 7 B6
Antlands La E RH6 .... 6 F5
Antlands La W RH6 .... 6 E6
Antonia Ct 🗓 BN17 .... 198 D5
Anvil Cl Billingshurst RH14 .. 77 C8
  Portslade-by-Sea BN41 ... 166 B2
  Southwater RH13 .... 57 F1
Apple Gr
  Bognor Regis PO21 .... 194 B1
  Hermitage PO10 .... 169 D8
Apple Tree Wlk BN17 .... 177 D1
Appledore Ct RH16 .... 86 A7
Appledore Gdns RH16 ...... 86 A6

Appledore Rd BN2 .... 168 F4
Appledram La N
  PO19, PO20 .... 172 C6
Appledram La S PO20 ...... 172 C4
Applefield RH10 .... 18 E7
Applesham Ave BN3 .... 166 E2
Applesham Way BN41 ...... 166 A1
Appletree Dr PO22 .... 176 B6
Appletrees BN16 .... 200 B4
Approach The
  🗓 Brighton BN1 .... 167 E3
  Dormansland RH19 .... 9 F6
April Cl Horsham RH12 ...... 36 C4
  Kingston Gorse BN12 .... 200 E4
Apsley Ct RH11 .... 17 C4
Apsley Way BN13 .... 181 B5
Aquarius Ct RH11 .... 17 E4
Arbor Ct 🗓 RH16 .... 85 E5
Arcade Rd BN17 .... 198 D5
Arcade The
  🗓 Bognor Regis PO21 ... 195 D3
  🗓 Littlehampton BN17 ... 198 D5
Archers Ct RH11 .... 18 D8
Archibald Rd RH13 .... 183 A3
Arcturus Rd RH17 .... 17 E3
Ardale Cl BN11 .... 181 F2
Arden Rd RH10 .... 18 F4
Ardingly Cl RH11 .... 18 B8
Ardingly Coll RH17 .... 64 A6
Ardingly Ct 🗓 BN20 .... 207 B5
Ardingly Dr BN12 .... 181 B3
Ardingly Rd RH17 .... 84 F7
Ardingly St BN2 .... 207 B5
Ardings Ct RH17 .... 64 B7
Ardmore Sch BN11 .... 182 D2
Ardsheal Cl BN14 .... 182 C5
Ardsheal Rd BN14 .... 182 C6
Argus Wlk RH11 .... 18 A3
Argyle Ct 🗓 PO21 .... 195 C3
Argyle Rd
  Bognor Regis PO21 .... 195 C3
  Brighton BN1 .... 207 F8
Ariadne Rd BN11 .... 182 B1
Ariel Ct BN15 .... 183 D4
Arkendale RH19 .... 9 A4
Arlington Ave BN12 .... 181 B1
Arlington Cl BN12 .... 181 B1
Arlington Cres
  Brighton BN1 .... 168 E5
  East Preston BN16 .... 180 B3
Armada Ct PO20 .... 202 B5
Armada Way BN16 .... 199 A6
Armadale Rd RH10 .... 173 C7
Armdale Rd BN17 .... 198 B6
Arne Cl RH11 .... 17 F3
Arne Gr RH6 .... 1 E5
Arnell Ave PO20 .... 206 E7
Arnfield Cl RH11 .... 17 E5
Arnhem Rd PO21 .... 195 B5
Arnold St BN2 .... 188 C7
Arnold Way PO18 .... 171 C7
Arnside Cl RH15 .... 183 C5
Arran Cl RH11 .... 18 B3
Arran Gate RH12 .... 195 E3
Arrancourt RH12 .... 36 B2
Arrivals Rd RH6 .... 5 F8
Artel Croft RH10 .... 19 A6
Artex Ave BN16 .... 179 C3
Arthur Bliss Ho RH16 .... 86 A8
Arthur Rd Crawley RH11 ... 17 E6
  Arun Bsns Pk PO22 .... 195 E5
Arun Cl Amberley BN18 ... 138 E7
  Lancing BN15 .... 183 C7
  Rustington BN16 .... 199 C6
  Worthing BN13 .... 181 C7
Arun Ct
  East Preston BN16 .... 200 A5
  Littlehampton BN17 .... 178 D3
  🗓 Pulborough RH20 .... 98 C2
  🗓 Shoreham-by-Sea
  BN43 .... 185 C8
Arun La Ctr PO22 .... 195 F5
Arun Par BN17 .... 198 D3
Arun Prospect RH20 .... 98 A1
Arun Rd Billingshurst RH14 . 55 C1
  Bognor Regis PO21 .... 195 A4
  Arun Ret Pk PO22 .... 195 E6
Arun St BN18 .... 158 B2
Arun Terr BN18 .... 158 A2
Arun Vale RH20 .... 117 C5
Arun Vale Cty Inf Sch
  BN17 .... 198 D5
Arun Way
  Bognor Regis PO21 .... 205 B8
  Horsham RH13 .... 36 E1
Arundale Sch RH20 .... 98 D2
Arundel By-Pass BN18 ..... 158 B2
Arundel Castle BN18 .... 158 B3

Arundel CE (A) Prim Sch
  BN18 .... 157 F2
Arundel Cl
  Bognor Regis PO21 .... 195 A4
  Conford GU30 .... 24 D8
  Crawley RH10 .... 19 C6
  Shoreham-by-Sea BN43 ... 185 C8
  Southwater BN13 .... 58 A1
Arundel Ct
  🗓 Brighton BN2 .... 188 E4
  Burgess Hill RH15 .... 106 F4
  Ferring BN12 .... 200 F4
  🗓 Shoreham-by-Sea
  BN43 .... 185 C8
  🗓 Worthing BN11 .... 181 F2
Arundel & District Hospl
  BN18 .... 158 A3
Arundel Dr BN17 .... 178 C5
Arundel Gdn 🗓 BN16 ...... 199 C5
Arundel Mews 🗓 BN2 ..... 188 E4
Arundel PI BN2 .... 188 E3
Arundel Rd
  Angmering BN16 .... 179 F6
  Brighton BN2 .... 188 E4
  Fontwell BN18, PO20 .... 155 F3
  Littlehampton BN17 .... 198 D6
  Selden BN13, BN16 .... 180 C8
  Walberton BN18 .... 156 D2
  Worthing BN13 .... 181 D8
Arundel St BN2 .... 188 E3
Arundel Sta BN18 .... 158 C1
Arundel Terr 🗓 BN2 .... 188 E3
Arundel Villas GU30 .... 24 D8
Arundel Way PO22 .... 197 B5
Arundel Wildfowl Reserve
  BN18 .... 158 C5
Arunside RH12 .... 36 A1
Arunside Cty Prim Sch
  RH12 .... 36 A2
Arunside Ind Est BN17 .... 198 C6
Ascot Ct PO18 .... 201 F8
Ascot Way BN16 .... 199 E6
Ash Cl
  Crawley Down RH10 .... 21 C8
  Findon RH11 .... 161 E6
  Hove BN3 .... 167 C3
  Ash Ct BN42 .... 165 F1
Ash Gr Bognor Regis PO22 195 C6
  Fernhurst GU27 .... 49 A6
  Haywards Heath RH16 ...... 85 D2
  Liphook GU30 .... 25 D3
  Ash Grove Snd Pk PO22 195 D7
  Ro RH14 .... 55 C1
Ash Keys RH10 .... 18 E5
Ash La BN16 .... 199 C5
Ash Rd Crawley RH10 .... 19 A8
  Southwater RH13 .... 57 E1
Ashacre La BN13 .... 182 A7
Ashacre Mews BN13 .... 181 F7
Ashacre Way BN13 .... 182 A6
Ashburnham Cl
  Brighton BN1 .... 168 E5
  Chichester PO19 .... 172 D7
  Worthing BN13 .... 181 B5
Ashburnham Dr BN1 .... 168 E5
Ashburnham Rd RH10 ...... 19 A4
Ashby Ct RH13 .... 36 E1
Ashcroft 🗓 BN43 .... 185 D7
Ashcroft Cl BN43 .... 185 D8
Ashcroft La PO8 .... 128 F6
Ashcroft Way PO21 .... 205 A8
Ashdown 🗓 BN13 .... 187 C6
Ashdown Cl
  Angmering BN16 .... 179 F4
  Haywards Heath RH16 ...... 86 A4
Ashdown Dr RH10 .... 18 E3
Ashdown Gate RH19 .... 1 E7
Ashdown Hospl The RH16 . 85 D6
Ashdown Llama Farm
  RH18 .... 44 E4
Ashdown Rd
  🗓 Brighton BN2 .... 188 B8
  Forest Row RH18 .... 23 F2
  Worthing BN12 .... 182 D3
Ashdown View RH17 .... 22 C4
Ashenground Cl 🗓 RH16 . 85 E3
Ashenground Rd RH16 ..... 85 E3
Ashfield Cl GU29 .... 92 E8
Ashfield Rd GU29 .... 92 E7
Ashfold Ave BN14 .... 162 A1
Ashfold Crossways RH17 .. 60 D6
Ashford Rd BN1 .... 168 A2
Ashington Ce (C) Prim Sch
  RH20 .... 120 F5
Ashington Ct Brighton BN2 188 F6
  🗓 Worthing BN14 .... 182 D5
Ashleigh Cl
  Angmering BN16 .... 180 A6
  Horley RH6 .... 1 F3
Ashleigh Rd RH12 .... 36 C4

Ashley Cl BN11 .... 167 E7
Ashley Ct BN3 .... 187 C5
Ashlings Way Hove BN2 ... 166 E2
  Shoreham-by-Sea BN43 ... 165 B1
Ashmere Gdns PO22 .... 196 D5
Ashmere La PO22 .... 196 D5
Ashmore Ho RH11 .... 5 D1
Ashmore La RH12 .... 16 C6
Ashton Gdns BN16 .... 199 C4
Ashton Lodge 🗓 BN2 ...... 207 B6
Ashton Rise BN2 .... 207 B6
Ashurst CE (A) Prim Sch
  BN44 .... 122 D5
Ashurst Cl
  Bognor Regis PO21 .... 195 A6
  Horsham RH12 .... 37 A5
  Worthing BN12 .... 181 B1
Ashurst Cotts RH19 .... 42 F4
Ashurst Dr Crawley RH10 .. 19 D6
  Worthing BN12 .... 181 B1
Ashurst Rd BN2 .... 168 F5
Ashurst Way BN16 .... 180 A3
Ashurstwood Abbey RH19 23 E6
Ashurstwood Cty Prim Sch
  RH19 .... 23 E6
Ashway RH15 .... 107 A2
Ashwood 🗓 RH11 .... 18 D5
Ashwood Cl BN13 .... 182 F4
Ashwood Ct BN16 .... 199 C5
Ashwyn Bsns Ctr RH15 ... 106 F5
Aspen Cl RH6 .... 86 B4
Aspen Way Horsham RH12 . 36 E4
  Middleton-on-Sea PO22 .. 196 E6
Aspen Wlk RH6 .... 86 B4
Aston Cl
  🗓 Bognor Regis PO21 ... 195 D3
  Crawley RH10 .... 18 B1
Aston Ho 🗓 BN43 .... 184 E7
Aston Rise BN2 .... 98 C3
Astra Bsns Ctr RH1 .... 2 A7
Astra Cl PO18 .... 171 C5
Astra Ho 🗓 RH11 .... 187 E5
Athelstan Cl RH10 .... 19 E6
Athelstan Rd BN13, BN14 . 182 A4
Athelstan Way RH13 .... 58 E8
Athenaeum The 🗓 BN3 .. 187 C6
Atkinson Ct RH1 .... 2 B2
Atkinson Rd RH10 .... 19 C4
Atlantic Cl 🗓 BN43 .... 184 F6
Atlingworth St BN2 .... 207 B4
Attlee Ho 🗓 RH11 .... 18 B2
Attree Ct 🗓 BN2 .... 188 C6
Attree Dr BN2 .... 188 C6
Auchinleck Ct RH10 .... 21 B7
Auckland Cl RH11 .... 5 D1
Auckland Dr RH11 .... 18 B2
Audrey Cl BN1 .... 167 E5
Augusta Ct 🗓 PO19 .... 153 A2
Augusta Ho 🗓 BN11 .... 182 D1
Augusta PI BN11 .... 182 D1
Augustines Way RH16 ...... 85 F4
Aurum Cl RH6 .... 2 B2
Austen Ct RH19 .... 9 B1
Austens GU29 .... 113 C8
Avalon Ct PO10 .... 149 B2
Avalon Way BN13 .... 181 D6
Avebury Cl
  Bracklesham PO20 .... 202 C5
  Horsham RH12 .... 37 A7
Aveling Cl RH10 .... 19 C4
Avenals The RH10 .... 180 A5
Avenue App PO19 .... 172 F7
Avenue Ct GU30 .... 25 B2
Avenue Ct 🗓 BN3 .... 187 C6
Avenue De Chartres PO19 172 F6
Avenue Gdns RH6 .... 2 C2
Avenue The
  Bognor Regis PO21 .... 195 B3
  Brighton BN1 .... 168 E1
  Chichester PO19 .... 153 A2
  Dormansland RH19 .... 10 B6
  Funtington PO18 .... 150 E7
  Hambrook PO18 .... 150 D1
  Haslemere GU27 .... 26 F7
  Horley RH6 .... 1 F2
  Horsham RH13 .... 57 D5
  Liphook GU30 .... 25 B4
  Shoreham-by-Sea BN43 ... 164 E1
  Worthing BN12 .... 181 C4
Avery Cl BN1 .... 165 F4
Aviary Way RH10 .... 8 C1
Avila Ho 🗓 BN11 .... 182 C2
Avisford Park Rd BN18 .... 156 F1
Avisford Terr PO21 .... 194 D3
Avocet Quay PO10 .... 169 C7
Avocet Trad Est RH15 ...... 106 F2
Avon Cl
  Bognor Regis PO22 .... 196 D5
  Lancing BN15 .... 183 B6
  Avon Ct BN15 .... 183 B6
Avon Rd BN17 .... 198 D5

Avon Wlk RH11 .... 17 F5
Avondale Cl Horley RH6 ...... 2 A5
  Worthing BN12 .... 181 D3
Avondale Rd BN3 .... 187 D7
Avonhurst RH15 .... 107 B3
Awbrook Cl RH17 .... 86 F3
Aylesbury BN3 .... 187 E6
Aylwin Pl PO20 .... 173 C1
Aymer Ho 🗓 BN3 .... 187 A6
Aymer Rd BN3 .... 187 A6
Aynsley Cl BN2 .... 187 C8
Aythe Court Dr RH13 .... 36 E3
Azalea Dr GU27 .... 26 F8
Azara Par PO20 .... 202 B6

Babsham La PO21 .... 194 F8
Back La
  Balcombe Lane
  RH10, RH17 .... 41 C7
  Plaistow RH14 .... 30 E2
Backwoods Cl RH16 .... 86 B6
Backwoods La RH16 .... 86 B6
Baden Dr RH6 .... 1 E4
Baden Rd BN2 .... 168 D1
Badger Cl BN41 .... 166 B2
Badger Dr RH16 .... 85 C5
Badger Way BN1 .... 168 E6
Badgers Cl RH12 .... 36 F6
Badgers Holt RH20 .... 120 B1
Badgers Way
  East Grinstead RH19 .... 9 F2
  Loxwood RH14 .... 32 A4
Badgers Wlk
  Angmering BN16 .... 179 F4
  Burgess Hill RH15 .... 107 D2
Badgers Wood RH20 .... 119 D6
Baffin's La PO19 .... 173 A6
Bailey Cl Horsham RH12 ... 36 F7
  Littlehampton BN16 .... 179 A3
Bailing Hill RH12 .... 35 E7
Baird Cl RH10 .... 6 A1
Bakehouse Barn Cl RH12 . 36 E7
Bakehouse Rd RH6 .... 2 A5
Baker Cl RH10 .... 18 D4
Baker St BN1, BN2 .... 207 A7
Baker's La RH13 .... 79 B4
Bakerfield GU29 .... 113 C8
Bakers Arms Hill BN18 ... 158 B3
Bakers Cl RH13 .... 57 F1
Bakers Ct RH10 .... 19 E5
Bakers Mews RH13 .... 60 A3
Bala Cres PO21 .... 195 C2
Balchins Cl RH14 .... 76 B8
Balcombe Ave BN14 .... 182 C5
Balcombe CE (C) Prim Sch
  RH17 .... 40 F2
Balcombe Ct Crawley RH10 19 D7
  🗓 Worthing BN11 .... 182 B1
Balcombe Gdns Rd 2 C2
Balcombe La Ardingly RH17 . 63 F8
  Sharpthorne RH17, RH17 .. 43 E2
Balcombe Rd
  Balcombe Lane
  RH10, RH17 .... 40 F8
  Crawley RH10 .... 19 D5
  Haywards Heath
  RH16, RH17 .... 85 D7
  Horley RH6 .... 2 B2
  Tinsley Green RH10, RH6 ... 6 D5
Balcombe Sta RH17 .... 40 F1
Baldwin Cl Crawley RH10 .. 19 C3
  Middleton-on-Sea PO22 .. 196 D6
Baldwins Hill Cty Prim Sch
  RH19 .... 9 D3
Balfour Cl
  Bognor Regis PO21 .... 194 E4
  Crawley RH10 .... 6 D1
Balmoral Ho 🗓 23 A8
Balmoral Cl
  Bognor Regis PO21 .... 194 E2
  Chichester PO19 .... 173 D6
Balmoral Ct
  🗓 Crawley RH11 .... 18 B2
  Hove BN3 .... 167 A3
  Worthing BN12 .... 182 A2
Baltimore Ct 🗓 BN3 .... 187 C7
Bamborough Cl RH13 .... 58 A1
Bampfield St BN41 .... 186 B8
Bancroft Rd RH10 .... 19 D5
Banfield Ct RH10 .... 198 E3
Banjo Rd BN17 .... 198 E3
Bank La RH11 .... 18 D6

Bank Pas Steyning BN44 ...... 143 D3
Worthing **9** BN11 .... 182 D2
Banks Croft RH20 .... 119 E2
Banks Rd Crawley RH10 ...... 19 C5
Scaynes Hill BN8 .... 87 F1
Bankside Bolney RH17 .... 83 C2
Brighton BN1 .... 167 C5
Hassocks BN6 .... 126 F5
Singleton PO18 .... 133 E7
Bankview Cl **2** PO21 .... 195 D4
Bannister Gdns RH20 .... 119 E3
Bannister Way RH16 .... 85 D6
Banstead Cl BN2 .... 181 C1
Bar La RH13 .... 80 B5
Baranscraig Ave BN1 .... 168 A7
Barbary La BN12 .... 200 E5
Barber Cl RH10 .... 19 C2
Barclay Ho **2** BN2 .... 188 C7
Barclays Ct **2** RH20 .... 98 C2
Barcombe Pl BN1 .... 168 F5
Barcombe Rd BN1 .... 168 E4
Barfield Pk BN15 .... 183 F6
Barford Rd PO19 .... 173 A5
Barkdale RH15 .... 107 D5
Barker Cl PO18 .... 172 A7
Barkworth Way RH20 .... 119 C7
Barlavington Way GU29 ...... 92 E5
Barley Cl RH10 .... 18 D5
Barley Dr BN6 .... 106 D4
Barleycroft
Albourne Green BN6 .... 125 C6
Cowfold RH13 .... 81 E1
Barleymead RH6 .... 2 B4
Barlow Rd
Chichester PO19 .... 172 E8
Crawley RH11 .... 17 E3
Barn Cl
Albourne Green BN6 .... 125 C6
Littlehampton BN17 .... 178 E4
Pease Pottage RH11 .... 39 B7
Worthing BN13 .... 181 F7
Barn Cottage La RH16 .... 86 A5
Barn Elm PO18 .... 154 D3
Barn End BN5 .... 123 F5
Barn Field PO22 .... 195 F4
Barn Field Gdns **8** BN2 .... 188 C6
Barn House La RH20 .... 98 C2
Barn La PO22 .... 175 D1
Barn Plat GU29 .... 92 D8
Barn Rd PO20 .... 201 F7
Barn Rise Barnham PO22 .... 176 C5
Brighton BN1 .... 167 D5
Barn Wlk PO20 .... 201 F6
Barnard Gate RH16 .... 85 E7
Barncroft Cl PO22 .... 154 C1
Barnes Rd BN41 .... 186 B8
Barnet Way Hove BN3 .... 166 E3
Worthing BN13 .... 181 D5
Barnett Cl PO20 .... 175 E8
Barnett Rd BN1 .... 168 B2
Barnett's Field PO20 .... 175 D7
Barnfield Ct PO10 .... 150 A1
Barnfield Cotts BN18 .... 156 A2
Barnfield Dr PO19 .... 173 C8
Barnfield Gdns BN1 .... 127 E3
Barnfield Rd RH10, RH11 ... 18 E7
Barnham Cty Prim Sch
Barnham PO22 .... 176 C5
West Barnham PO22 .... 176 B6
Barnham La BN18, PO22 ..... 176 C7
Barnham Rd PO20, PO22 .... 176 A6
Barnhouse Cl **7** RH20 ...... 98 C2
Barnmead RH16 .... 85 D7
Barns Farm La RH20 .... 141 B7
Barnsfold La RH12, RH14 ... 32 E6
Barnside PO18 .... 171 D7
Barnside Ave RH15 .... 107 D1
Barnside Way GU33 .... 45 B3
Barnsite Cl BN16 .... 199 B6
Barnsite Gdns BN16 .... 199 B6
Barnsnap Cl RH12 .... 36 D6
Barnum Sta PO22 .... 176 B5
Barnwood Cl RH10 .... 19 C7
Baron Cl PO20 .... 201 E7
Barons Ct RH15 .... 107 B2
Barons Mead PO21 .... 205 A8
Barque Cl RH11 .... 199 A6
Barrack La PO21 .... 194 D2
Barrhill Ave BN1 .... 167 F7
Barrington Cl
Haywards Heath RH16 .... 85 F8
Worthing BN12 .... 181 C2
Barrington Rd
Crawley RH10 .... 18 D3
Haywards Heath RH16 .... 86 A8
Horsham RH13 .... 36 E2
Worthing BN12 .... 181 C2
Worthing BN12 .... 181 E3

Barrington Wood RH16 ...... 85 F8
Barrow Cl BN1 .... 168 C2
Barrow Hill Brighton BN1 .. 168 C2
Henfield BN5 .... 123 F3
Barrowfield RH17 .... 84 F7
Barrowfield Cl BN3 .... 167 C3
Barrowfield Dr BN3 .... 167 D2
Barrowfield Lodge BN3 ..... 167 C2
Barry Cl RH10 .... 18 E3
Barry Wlk BN2 .... 188 C6
Bartholomew Cl GU27 .... 27 D8
Bartholomew Sq BN1 .... 207 A5
Bartholomew Way RH12 .... 37 A7
Bartholomews BN1 .... 207 A5
Barton Cl
Bognor Regis PO21 .... 194 A1
Worthing BN13 .... 182 A5
Barton Cres RH19 .... 23 A8
Barton Ct BN16 .... 199 B5
Barton La GU28 .... 95 F8
Barton Rd
Bognor Regis PO22 .... 195 A7
Chichester PO19 .... 172 E7
Barton Way PO20 .... 202 B6
Barton Wlk RH10 .... 19 B4
Bartons Cty Inf Sch
PO22 .... 195 B6
Bartteloi Rd RH12 .... 36 D2
Barwell Gr PO10 .... 149 A3
Bashford Way RH10 .... 19 D8
Bashfords La BN14 .... 182 D4
Bashurst Copse RH12 .... 56 F8
Bashurst Hill RH13 .... 56 E6
Basildon Way RH11 .... 17 E2
Basin Rd PO19 .... 173 A5
Basin Rd N BN41 .... 186 B6
Basin Rd S BN3, BN41 ...... 186 B6
Bassing Hill RH20, RH13 ... 121 C7
Bassets La RH13 .... 102 B5
Bassett Rd PO21 .... 195 C3
Batchmere Est PO20 ...... 191 F1
Batchmere Rd PO20 .... 192 A2
Batemans Cl BN13 .... 181 B5
Batemans Ct RH10 .... 19 A3
Bates Rd BN1 .... 167 F2
Bath Ct BN3 .... 187 A5
Bath Pl BN11 .... 182 D2
Bath Rd Emsworth PO10 .... 169 B8
Worthing BN11 .... 182 B1
Bath St BN1 .... 207 F7
Batts Dr BN5 .... 123 D5
Batts La RH20 .... 98 F1
Batworthpark Ho BN18 ...... 158 E1
Bavant Rd BN1 .... 167 E2
Baxter Cl RH10 .... 19 B4
Baxter St BN2 .... 188 C7
Baxters La RH17 .... 66 C6
Bay Cl RH6 .... 1 E6
Bay Ct PO21 .... 205 B8
Bay Tree Cl BN43 .... 165 C1
Bay Tree Cetts BN18 .... 156 D1
Bay Tree Gdn BN16 .... 199 F5
Bay Trees Cl BN16 .... 199 F5
Bay Wlk PO21 .... 205 C8
Baycombe La BN16 .... 156 D6
Bayfield Rd RH6 .... 1 E4
Bayford Rd BN12 .... 198 D4
Bayhams Field RH19 .... 42 F6
Bayhorne La RH6 .... 2 C1
Bayley Rd PO20 .... 154 C1
Baylis Cres RH15 .... 106 D4
Baylis Wlk RH11 .... 18 B1
Baynards Rd RH12 .... 12 A2
Bayton Ct PO19 .... 173 B6
Baytree Cl PO19 .... 152 F3
Beach Cl PO21 .... 194 C1
Beach Ct
5 Rustington BN16 .... 199 B4
10 Shoreham-by-Sea
BN43 .... 185 A6
Beach Gdns PO20 .... 206 D5
Beach Gn BN43 .... 184 E6
Beach Mews **3** BN17 ...... 198 F4
Beach Par BN11 .... 182 F2
Beach Rd
Bognor Regis PO21 .... 205 A7
Emsworth PO10 .... 169 A8
Littlehampton BN17 .... 198 E4
Selsey PO20 .... 206 F8
Shoreham-by-Sea BN43 ...... 184 E6
Beachcroft Pl BN15 .... 183 F4
Beachside Cl BN12 .... 181 E1
Beachy Rd RH11 .... 18 A1
Beacon Cl RH13 .... 37 A4

Beacon The RH19 .... 42 E7
Beacon Way BN17 .... 199 A6
Beaconsfield Cl PO22 .... 196 E5
Beaconsfield Cotts RH17 ... 86 F3
Beaconsfield Rd
Brighton BN1 .... 188 A8
Chelwood Gate RH17 .... 66 D8
Littlehampton BN17 .... 178 D3
Portslade-by-Sea BN41 ...... 186 B8
Beaconsfield Villas BN1 ..... 167 F1
Beaconsville Ct BN1 .... 167 F1
Beagle Dr BN18 .... 177 B2
Beal Cres BN1 .... 168 B2
Beale Cl RH11 .... 18 A3
Beale St RH15 .... 106 F1
Bear Rd BN2 .... 188 D8
Bearsden Way RH12 .... 35 D3
Beatrice Ho PO22 .... 195 E4
Beatty Ave BN1 .... 168 D6
Beatty Rd PO21 .... 195 C4
Beaufield Cl PO20 .... 206 D5
Beaufield Gate GU27 .... 27 D7
Beaufort Ct **4** BN16 .... 199 A6
Beaufort Terr BN2 .... 188 C6
Beaumont Cl RH11 .... 17 E5
Beaumont Ct BN16 .... 199 F6
Beaumont Pk BN16, BN17 . 199 A5
Beaumont Rd BN14 .... 182 D5
Beauvale Cl PO22 .... 206 B5
Beaver Ct Fishbourne PO19 172 B6
Horsham RH12 .... 36 F6
Beaver Ind Est GU30 .... 25 C3
Beaver Units PO19 .... 173 D5
Beccles Rd BN11 .... 182 B2
Beckenham Terr PO10 .... 149 D4
Becket Rd BN14 .... 182 B3
Beckett La RH11 .... 5 D1
Beckett Way **11** RH19 ..... 22 F8
Beckley Ct BN2 .... 188 E5
Beckworth Cl
Haywards Heath RH16 .... 86 A6
Worthing BN13 .... 181 B5
Beckworth La RH16 .... 86 A6
Bedale Cl RH11 .... 18 C4
Bedales BN16 .... 86 D4
Bedales Cnr RH16 .... 86 D4
Bedales Hill RH16 .... 86 D4
Bedelands Cl RH15 .... 107 B5
Bedelands Farm
Nature Reserve RH15 .... 107 B6
Bedenscroft PO21 .... 195 A3
Bedford Ave PO21 .... 195 A6
Bedford Pl BN1 .... 187 E5
Bedford Rd RH13 .... 36 D1
Bedford Row BN11 .... 182 E2
Bedford Sq BN1 .... 187 E5
Bedford St
Bognor Regis PO21 .... 195 D3
Brighton BN2 .... 188 C4
Bedford Towers **18** BN1 . 187 E5
Bedham La RH20 .... 97 B5
Beech Ave
Bracklesham PO20 .... 202 B6
Chichester PO19 .... 172 E6
Beech Cl Findon BN14 .... 161 E7
Portslade-by-Sea BN41 ...... 165 F3
Westergate BN18 .... 175 D7
Worthing BN13 .... 9 F3
Beech Gdns
Crawley Down RH10 .... 21 A8
3 Worthing BN14 .... 182 C4
Beech Gr Brighton BN2 ...... 168 E3
Midhurst GU29 .... 92 E6
Storrington RH20 .... 119 F3
Beech Hill RH16 .... 86 B4
Beech Rd RH14 .... 77 C8
Beech Holme RH10 .... 21 B8
Beech Hurst Cl RH16 .... 85 D4
Beech Rd Findon BN14 ...... 161 E7
Haslemere GU27 .... 27 D8
Horsham RH12 .... 37 B5
Beech Tree Cl RH11 .... 18 D7
Beech View BN16 .... 180 A6
Beech Wood BN5 .... 144 F7
Beechcroft Cl GU30 .... 24 D3
Beechers Rd BN14 .... 165 F3
Beeches Ave BN14 .... 182 D7
Beeches Cres RH10 .... 18 E7
Beeches Head RH19 .... 10 F5
Beeches La RH19 .... 23 D6
Beeches The BN1, BN3 ...... 167 D3
Beechey Cl RH10 .... 7 B3
Beechey Way RH10 .... 7 B3
Beechfield Cotts GU28 .... 72 B3
Beeching Way RH19 .... 9 E1
Beechings BN5 .... 123 D5
Beechlands Cl BN16 .... 200 A5
Beechlands Cl BN16 .... 200 A5
Beechside RH10 .... 18 E5
Beechwood
9 Brighton BN1 .... 167 E3
Southwater RH13 .... 79 F8

Beechwood Ave
Brighton BN1 .... 167 F4
Worthing BN13 .... 181 F7
Beechwood Cl BN1 .... 167 F4
Beechwood Gdn GU33 .... 45 C6
Beechwood La GU28 .... 115 B5
Beechwood Villas RH1 .... 2 A7
Beechwoods RH15 .... 107 A1
Beeding Ave BN3 .... 166 F3
Beeding Cl
Bognor Regis PO22 .... 195 E7
Horsham RH12 .... 37 A5
Lancing BN15 .... 183 D8
Beeding Ct **4** BN43 .... 185 B8
Beedingwood Dr RH12 .... 37 F6
Beeechfield Pk PO20 .... 175 C5
Beehive La BN12 .... 200 F5
Beehive La BN12 .... 200 F5
Beehive Ring Rd RH10, RH6 .. 6 B4
Beehive Rd RH10 .... 181 A2
Beeding Cl GU29 .... 92 E6
Beeken Rd PO22 .... 195 C6
Beethorpe Rd PO22 .... 195 C6
Beerweeke Rd PO22 .... 196 A4
Bergamot Cres BN43 .... 165 C1
Berghestede Rd PO22 .... 195 C6
Berkeley Cl RH11 .... 17 E2
Berkeley Ct
Bognor Regis PO21 .... 195 D2
2 Hove BN3 .... 187 E4
9 Littlehampton BN17 .. 198 E4
Berkeley Sq BN11 .... 182 A2
Berkshire Cl BN12 .... 181 B3
Bermuda Cl **2** BN16 .... 199 A6
Bernard Deegan Ho
2 PO21 .... 195 C3
Bernard Pl BN2 .... 188 C7
Bernard Rd Arundel BN18 . 157 F2
Brighton BN2 .... 188 C7
Worthing BN11 .... 181 F1
Berriedale Ave BN3 .... 186 E6
Berriedale Cl BN15 .... 183 C7
Berriedale Dr BN15 .... 183 C7
Berriedale Ho BN3 .... 186 E6
Berry Cl RH15 .... 107 A5
Berry La Ardingly RH17 .. 64 C7
Bognor Regis PO22 .... 195 A7
Littlehampton BN17 .... 198 E5
Berrybarn La PO20 .... 201 B8
Berryfields GU33 .... 45 C7
Berrymeade Wlk RH11 .... 17 E5
Berrymill Cl **6** PO21 ...... 195 D4
Berstead Wlk **1** RH11 ..... 17 F3
Bersted Mews PO22 .... 195 C6
Bersted St
Bognor Regis PO21, PO22 195 C5
Bognor Regis PO22 .... 195 D5
Bessborough Terr BN15 ..... 183 D4
Betchley Cl RH19 .... 9 E3
Betchworth Works RH6 .... 4 D6
Bethune Cl RH10 .... 19 D5
Bethune Rd RH13 .... 36 E1
Bethwines Cl PO18 .... 172 A7
Betts Way RH11 .... 5 D2
Bevan Ct RH11 .... 18 B1
Bevendean Cres BN2 .... 168 E2
Bevendean Prim Sch BN2 . 168 F1
Bevendean Rd BN2 .... 168 D1
Beverley Cl PO20 .... 206 F7
Beverley Ct
5 Pulborough RH20 .... 98 C2
Southwick BN3 .... 186 D7
3 Worthing BN11 .... 182 B1
Beverley Gdns BN16 .... 179 C3
Beverley Ho **5** BN15 .... 183 E5
Bewbush Dr RH11 .... 17 F3
Bewbush Fst Sch RH11 ...... 17 F3
Bewbush Manor RH11 .... 17 E2
Bewbush Mid Sch RH11 .... 17 F3
Bewley Rd BN16 .... 179 F6
Bex La GU29 .... 92 E2
Bickley Cl RH11 .... 18 A3
Biddens Cl **1** PO21 .... 195 B2
Bigglns Cl **1** BN11 .... 18 C4
Bignor Cl Horsham RH12 ... 37 A7
Rustington BN16 .... 199 D6
Bignor Park Rd RH20 .... 116 E5
Bigwood Ave BN3 .... 187 D8
Bilberry Cl RH11 .... 18 B3
Bilbets RH12 .... 36 C3
Billinghurst Rd PO21 .... 120 F8
Billingshurst Inf Sch RH14 . 77 D8
Billingshurst Jun Sch RH14 77 D7
Billingshurst Rd RH12 .... 35 D3
Billingshurst Sta RH14 ...... 77 D7
Billinton Dr RH10 .... 19 B5
Bilsham Cnr BN18 .... 196 F8
Bilsham Ct BN18 .... 176 F2
Bilsham La BN18 .... 176 E1
Bilsham Rd BN18 .... 176 E1
Binderton La PO18 .... 132 D2
Binney Ct RH10 .... 6 L1
Binstead Ave PO22 .... 196 A5
Binstead Cl RH11 .... 18 B4
Binsted Cl BN16 .... 199 B4
Binsted La BN18 .... 177 B7

Birch Ave RH16 .... 86 A3
Birch Cl Angmering BN16 ... 179 F4
  Arundel BN18 .... 157 E1
  Bognor Regis PO21 .... 194 D3
  Crawley Down RH10 .... 21 C8
  Haywards Heath RH16 ..... 86 B3
  Lancing BN15 .... 183 D4
  Liss GU33 .... 45 C4
Birch Ct BN42 .... 166 A1
Birch Dr RH14 .... 77 D7
Birch End RH20 .... 119 D7
Birch Gr RH20 .... 119 D5
Birch Grove Cres BN1 ..... 168 A5
Birch Lea RH10 .... 6 A1
Birch Tree Cl PO11 .... 149 B4
Birch Tree Ct BN11 .... 182 E3
Birch Tree Dr PO10 .... 149 B4
Birch Tree La RH20 .... 119 E6
Birch Way
  Haywards Heath RH16 ...... 86 A2
  Heath Common RH20 ..... 120 B3
Birchen La RH16 .... 85 F8
Birches Cl Selsey PO20 .... 206 C7
  Worthing BN13 .... 181 C5
Birches End Est RH19 .... 9 A3
Birches Rd RH12 .... 37 B5
Birches The Crawley RH10 ... 19 A7
  Mannings Heath RH13 .... 59 C7
  West Chiltington Common
  RH20 .... 119 C8
Birchgrove La RH17 .... 44 A1
Birchgrove Rd RH17 .... 65 E7
Bircholt Rd GU30 .... 24 D4
Birchwood Cl Crawley RH10 19 D3
  Horley RH6 .... 2 B4
Birchwood Grove Cty
  Prim Sch RH11 .... 107 C1
Birchwood Grove Rd
  RH15 .... 107 C1
Birdham CE (C) Prim Sch
  PO20 .... 191 E5
Birdham Cl
  Bognor Regis PO21 .... 194 F5
  Crawley RH11 .... 18 B8
Birdham Pl BN2 .... 168 E3
Birdham Rd
  Apuldram PO19, PO20 ... 172 D2
  Brighton BN2 .... 168 F3
  South Hayling PO11 ...... 189 A2
Birkdale Cl BN13 .... 181 D6
Birkdale Dr RH11 .... 17 D5
Birkdale Rd BN13 .... 181 D6
Birling Cl BN2 .... 168 D1
Birthday Ho GU29 .... 71 B2
Biscay Cl BN16 .... 199 B6
Bishearne Gdns GU33 .... 45 A5
Bishop Bell Mid Sch RH10 ... 18 F3
Bishop Luffa CE Sch (A)
  PO19 .... 172 D7
Bishop Luffa Cl PO19 ...... 172 D7
Bishop Tufnell CE (A)
  Inf Sch PO22 .... 196 C5
Bishop Tufnell CE (A)
  Jun Sch PO22 .... 196 C5
Bishop's Cl BN6 .... 126 A7
Bishopric RH12 .... 36 B2
Bishopric CI RH12 .... 36 B2
Bishops Cl
  Bognor Regis PO21 .... 205 A8
  Fernhurst GU27 .... 49 A6
  Henfield BN5 .... 123 E5
  Worthing BN13 .... 182 A4
Bishops Ctyd PO19 .... 173 B6
Bishops Ho RH20 .... 140 D8
Bishops Rd Hove BN3 ..... 167 C1
  Tangmere PO20 .... 154 D2
Bishopsgate Wlk PO19 ... 173 B7
Bishopstone La
  BN6, RH17 .... 106 A7
Bishopstone Wlk RH11 .... 18 C1
Bitmead Cl RH11 .... 17 E5
Bittern Cl RH11 .... 17 D5
Black Dog Wlk RH10 .... 18 E8
Black Lake La RH20 .... 98 D7
Black Hill RH16 .... 86 A7
Black Horse Way RH12 .... 36 C2
Black Lion St BN1 .... 207 A4
Black Swan Cl RH11 .... 39 B7
Blackberry La
  Chichester PO19 .... 173 C6
  Felcourt RH7 .... 9 D8
Blackberry Rd RH19, RH7 ... 9 D8
Blackbird Cl RH6 .... 106 D3
Blackboy La PO18 .... 172 A7
Blackbridge Ct RH12 .... 36 B2
Blackbridge La RH12 .... 36 A1
Blackbrook La RH14 .... 79 D7
Blackcap Cl Crawley RH11 ... 18 C4
  Red Hill PO9 .... 128 C1
Blackdown Rd BN13 .... 181 F7
Blackdown Rural Ind Est GU27 27 E4

Blackfold Rd RH10 .... 19 A5
Blackgate La BN5 .... 123 E4
Blackheath RH10 .... 19 D8
Blackhouse La
  Burgess Hill RH15 .... 107 B4
  Faygate RH12 .... 74 D5
Blackhouse Rd RH12, RH13 38 D5
Blacklands Cres RH18 ...... 23 F2
Blackman St BN1 .... 207 A6
Blackman Way PO20 .... 173 B1
Blackmill La PO18, PO20 ... 155 C3
Blackpatch Gr **6** BN43 ... 164 F1
Blacksmith's Cnr BN18 ... 176 F8
Blacksmiths Cl RH20 .... 121 A4
Blacksmiths Cres RH15 .... 183 B6
Blackstone La
  Blackstone BN5 .... 124 E6
  Woodmancote BN5 .... 124 D3
Blackstone Rise BN5 ...... 124 E5
Blackstone St BN5 .... 124 E5
Blackstone Way RH15 ..... 107 A5
Blackthorn Cl
  Brighton BN1 .... 167 D3
  Crawley RH11 .... 5 C1
Blackthorn La RH11 .... 37 A2
Portslade-by-Sea BN41 ... 166 B2
Blackthorns
  Haywards Heath RH16 ..... 86 A7
  Hurstpierpoint BN6 .... 125 F7
Blackthorns Cl RH16 .... 86 A6
Blackthorns Cty Prim Sch
  RH16 .... 86 A6
Blackthorns The RH15 .... 107 B5
Blackwater La RH10 .... 19 D6
Blackwell Cty Prim Sch
  RH19 .... 9 F3
Blackwell Farm Rd RH19 ... 9 F3
Blackwell Hollow RH19 ...... 9 F2
Blackwell Rd RH19 .... 9 F2
Blake Cl RH10 .... 18 F2
Blake Cotts PO18 .... 172 A6
Blake Ct **2** BN2 .... 207 B6
Blakehurst La BN18 .... 159 B3
Blakehurst Way BN17 ..... 198 D6
Blakemyle PO21 .... 194 F2
Blaker St BN2 .... 207 B5
Blakes Farm Rd RH13 ...... 58 A3
Blakes Rd PO22 .... 196 A4
Blanches Rd RH13 .... 103 A3
Blanches Wlk RH13 .... 103 A3
Blanford Rd RH20 .... 173 C8
Blatchen The BN17 .... 198 F4
Blatchford Cl RH13 .... 36 F3
Blatchford Rd RH13 .... 36 F3
Blatchington Mill Sch BN3 166 F2
Blatchington Rd BN3 ...... 187 B7
Bleach's Yard Ind Est GU30 25 B2
Blendworth CE Inf Sch
  PO8 .... 128 A8
Blendworth La PO8 .... 128 A7
Blenheim Ave BN13 .... 181 E5
Blenheim Cl
  East Grinstead RH19 .... 10 A3
  Littlehampton BN16 .... 179 B3
Blenheim Ct
  Bognor Regis PO21 .... 194 E4
  1 Hove BN3 .... 187 A6
Blenheim Dr BN16 .... 179 B3
Blenheim Fields RH18 ...... 23 E3
Blenheim Gdns PO19 ...... 173 C6
Blenheim Pl **3** BN1 ..... 207 A6
Blenheim Rd
  Horsham RH12 .... 36 D4
  Lancing BN15 .... 183 D4
  Yapton BN18 .... 176 F2
Bletchley Cl BN1 .... 188 A8
Bligh Cl RH10 .... 18 F4
Blindley Rd RH10 .... 6 D1
Blomfield Dr PO19 .... 153 A1
Blondell Dr PO21 .... 194 D2
Bloomsbury Pl **17** BN2 . 188 C4
Bloomsbury St **18** BN2 .. 188 C4
Bloor Cl RH12 .... 36 D7
Blount Ave RH19 .... 9 F2
Blue Cedars Cl BN16 ...... 179 E4
Bluebell Cl Crawley RH11 ... 18 B3
  East Grinstead RH19 .... 9 F1
  Haywards Heath RH16 ..... 85 F4
  Horsham RH12 .... 36 E5
Bluebell Rly
  RH17, RH19, TN22 .... 43 A5
Blueberry Hill RH20 .... 120 B1
Bluebird Ct **10** BN3 ..... 187 A6
Blundell Ave RH6 .... 1 F4
Blunden Dr RH17 .... 84 F8
Blunts Way RH12 .... 36 C3
Blunts Wood Cres RH17 ... 85 B6
Blunts Wood Rd RH17 ..... 85 C6
Blytons The RH19 .... 9 D7
Boath Mus of Natural History
  BN1 .... 187 E8

Bob La RH17 .... 104 E6
Boddingtons La BN6 .... 127 D3
Bodiam Ave BN12 .... 181 B2
Bodiam Cl Crawley RH10 ... 19 C6
  Southwater RH13 .... 58 A2
Bodiam Ct **2** RH16 .... 85 E5
Bodmin Cl BN13 .... 181 D8
Bodmin Rd BN13 .... 181 D8
Bognor Rd
  Chichester PO19, PO20 ... 173 C5
  Warnham RH12, RH5 ...... 14 D4
Bognor Regis Com Coll
  Bognor Regis PO21 .... 194 F4
  Bognor Regis PO22 .... 195 A5
  Bognor Regis Sta PO21 ... 195 C3
Bohunt Com Sch GU30 .... 25 B4
Bolding Way RH16 .... 85 E2
Boleyn Dr PO21 .... 194 B1
Bolney CE (C) Prim Sch
  RH17 .... 83 C2
Bolney Chapel Rd RH17 ... 105 B7
Bolney Crossways RH17 ... 83 D1
Bolney Ct RH11 .... 17 F3
Bolney Grange Ind Est
  RH17 .... 105 F6
Bolney Lodge La RH17 ...... 83 B3
Bolney Rd RH20 .... 168 F4
Bolney St RH17 .... 83 C3
Bolnore RH16 .... 85 B4
Bolnore Rd RH16 .... 85 C4
Bolsover Rd Hove BN3 .... 186 E8
  Worthing BN13 .... 181 E3
Bolters Rd RH6 .... 2 A5
Bolters Rd S RH6 .... 1 F6
Bolton Rd BN1 .... 19 C2
Boltro Rd RH16 .... 85 D5
Bonchurch Rd BN2 .... 188 C7
Bond St Arundel BN18 .... 158 A3
  Brighton BN1 .... 207 A5
Bonehurst Rd RH1, RH6 ..... 2 A7
Bonfire La RH17 .... 65 D5
Bonnar Cl PO20 .... 206 D6
Bonnar Cl RH20 .... 206 D6
Bonnetts La RH11, RH6 ...... 5 A3
Bonny Wood Rd BN6 ...... 126 E3
Bookers La PO20 .... 206 D8
Booth Rd RH11 .... 17 E3
Borage Cl RH11 .... 18 A3
Borde Hill Gdns RH17 ...... 63 C2
Bordehill La RH16, RH17 ... 63 D3
Borden La GU30 .... 69 A6
Border Chase RH10 .... 7 A2
Border End GU27 .... 26 D6
Border Rd GU27 .... 26 D6
Borers Arms Rd RH10 ...... 7 C3
Borers Yard Ind Est RH10 ... 7 C3
Borough Ho GU29 .... 92 F8
Borough St BN1 .... 187 E6
Borrow King Cl BN2 .... 188 D8
Borrowdale Cl RH11 .... 18 B4
Bosham Cty Prim Sch
  PO18 .... 171 A5
Bosham La PO18 .... 171 B5
Bosham Rd PO18 .... 19 C3
Bosham Sta PO18 .... 171 C7
Bosham Gdns PO10 .... 149 B1
Bosmere Rd PO11 .... 189 A2
Bost Hill BN13, BN14 ...... 161 E3
Bostal Rd BN44 .... 143 C1
Bostal The BN44 .... 144 C1
Bostock Ave RH12 .... 37 A5
Boston Ct RH16 .... 86 A5
Boston St BN1 .... 207 A7
Boswell Rd RH10 .... 18 E3
Botany Cl BN16 .... 199 E4
Bough Beeches RH15 ..... 107 C1
Boulevard The
  Crawley RH10, RH11 ...... 18 E6
  Worthing BN12, BN13 ... 181 E4
Boundary Cl
  Crawley RH10 .... 18 E6
  Worthing BN11 .... 182 B1
Boundary Pas **6** BN3 ... 187 E6
Boundary Rd
  Balcombe RH17 .... 41 B4
  Brighton BN2 .... 188 F4
  Crawley RH10 .... 18 E7
  Portslade-by-Sea
  BN3, BN41 .... 186 C7
  Shoreham-by-Sea BN15 ... 184 B5
  Worthing BN11 .... 182 B1
Boundary Way RH16 ...... 200 B6
Boundstone Cl BN15 ...... 183 D7
Boundstone Com Coll
  BN15 .... 183 D7
Bourg-De-Peage Ave RH19 10 A1
Bourne Cl PO19 .... 172 A7
Bourne Com Coll The
  PO10 .... 149 F1

Bourne Ct
  Bracklesham PO20 .... 202 A6
  Brighton BN1 .... 167 D4
Bourne The BN6 .... 126 E5
Bourne View Cl PO10 ...... 149 F2
Bourne Way GU29 .... 92 E6
Bourns Ct RH13 .... 36 E3
Bowater Rd RH10 .... 19 C3
Bowden Cl **4** BN3 .... 187 C6
Bower Ho RH15 .... 119 D6
Bower Rd BN2 .... 188 F5
Bower The RH16 .... 85 D5
Bowerhill Cotts RH19 .... 43 F6
Bowers Pl RH10 .... 21 B8
Bowes Hill PO9 .... 128 E3
Bowhill La PO18 .... 151 D7
Bowley La PO20 .... 193 E5
Bowling Green Cl PO21 ... 194 B1
Bowling Green La RH12 ... 36 D3
Bowman Ct RH11 .... 18 D7
Bowman Rd BN44 .... 143 D4
Bowness Ave BN15 .... 183 C5
Bowness Cl **7** RH11 ...... 17 D5
Bowring Way BN2 .... 188 D4
Box Cl RH11 .... 18 C1
Box La RH19 .... 22 C4
Box Tree Ave BN16 .... 199 B5
Box's La RH17 .... 66 C6
Boxall Wlk RH13 .... 36 D1
Boxes La RH17 .... 65 C5
Boxgrove BN12 .... 181 B4
Boxgrove CE Prim Sch
  PO18 .... 154 D4
Boxgrove Cl BN15 .... 183 F8
Boxgrove Gdns PO21 ..... 194 D2
Boxgrove Ho
  Boxgrove PO18 .... 154 D3
  Littlehampton BN17 .... 178 B3
Boxham La PO20 .... 192 D3
Boyce's St BN1 .... 207 F5
Bracken Cl Copthorne RH10 ... 7 B2
  Crawley RH10 .... 18 F8
  Heath Common RH20 .... 120 B2
Bracken Gr RH12 .... 37 B5
Bracken La RH10 .... 120 B2
Brackenbury Cl BN41 ...... 166 B2
Brackensdale RH4 .... 2 A4
Bracklesham Cl PO20 ..... 202 B6
Bracklesham La PO20 ..... 202 B6
Bracklesham Rd PO11 .... 189 B2
Bracknell Wlk RH11 .... 17 E3
Bradbury Rd RH10 .... 19 C3
Brading Rd BN2 .... 188 C7
Bradlond Cl PO21 .... 195 A3
Bradshaw Rd PO19 .... 173 C8
Braemar Ho **5** BN1 ...... 187 E6
Braemar Rd PO21 .... 194 F7
Braemore Cl BN3 .... 186 E6
Braemore Rd BN3 .... 186 E6
Braeside Ave BN13 .... 168 A7
Braeside Cl GU27 .... 26 F8
Brainsmead RH17 .... 84 F7
Brainsmead Cl RH17 .... 84 F7
Bramber Ave Hove BN3 ... 166 F3
  Shoreham-by-Sea
  BN43 .... 185 B8
  2 Worthing BN11 ...... 181 F2
Bramber Cty Fst Sch
  BN14 .... 182 F6
Bramber Rd
  Chichester PO19 .... 173 B5
  Steyning BN44 .... 143 D2
  Worthing BN14 .... 182 E6
Bramber Sq BN16 .... 199 C6
Bramber Way RH15 .... 107 A4
Bramble Cl Copthorne RH10 ... 7 B3
  Worthing BN13 .... 181 D8
Bramble Cres RH13 .... 106 D4
Bramble Gdns RH15 .... 106 D4
Bramble Hill RH17 .... 40 F2
Bramble La BN13 .... 181 D7
Bramble Mead RH17 .... 40 F1
Bramble Rise RH11 .... 167 C5
Bramble Twitten RH19 ..... 10 A1
Bramble Way BN1 .... 168 C6
Brambledean Rd BN41 ... 186 B7
Brambles BN6 .... 126 F5
Brambles The RH17 .... 85 A6
Brambletye Rd RH10 .... 19 A5
Brambletye Sch RH19 ..... 23 C5
Brambletyne Cl BN16 ..... 180 A6
Brambling Cl RH13 .... 37 A1

Brambling La GU29 .... 70 C3
Brambling Rd
  Horsham RH13 .... 37 A1
  Red Hill PO9 .... 128 D1
Bramblings The BN16 ..... 199 D5
Bramfield Rd PO22 .... 196 C4
Bramlands La BN5 .... 145 D8
Bramley Cl Crawley RH10 ... 18 F6
  Worthing BN14 .... 182 D6
Bramley Gdns
  Bognor Regis PO22 .... 195 B7
  Hermitage PO10 .... 169 D8
Bramley Rd BN14 .... 182 D6
Bramley Wlk RH6 .... 2 C3
Brampton Cl PO20 .... 206 D7
Brandy Hole La PO19 ...... 152 E2
Brangwyn Ave BN1 .... 167 E5
Brangwyn Cres BN1 .... 167 E6
Brangwyn Dr BN1 .... 167 E5
Brangwyn Way BN1 .... 167 E5
Brantridge La RH17 .... 62 B6
Brantridge Rd RH10 .... 18 F4
Brantridge Sch RH17 .... 62 A8
Brasslands Dr RH14 .... 165 F1
Braybon Ave BN1 .... 167 E4
Braybon Bsns Pk RH15 ... 106 E2
Braypool La BN1 .... 167 D7
Brazwick Ave PO21 .... 194 F7
Breach Ave PO10 .... 150 A2
Breach Cl BN44 .... 143 D4
Bread La BN17 .... 197 F6
Bread St BN1 .... 207 A6
Bream La PO20 .... 206 B8
Brecon Cl BN13 .... 181 F7
Brecon Ct **6** BN3 .... 187 C7
Brede Cl BN2 .... 188 F5
Breezehurst Dr RH11 .... 17 F3
Bremner Ave RH6 .... 1 F4
Brendon Rd BN13 .... 181 E7
Brendon Way BN16 .... 199 B6
Brent Cl PO10 .... 169 A8
Brent Rd PO21 .... 195 A4
Brentwood Cl RH11 .... 168 B3
Brentwood Cres RH11 .... 168 B3
Brentwood Rd RH11 .... 168 B3
Brettingham Cl RH11 .... 17 E3
Bretton RH15 .... 106 E5
Brewells La GU33 .... 46 A5
Brewer Rd RH10 .... 18 E4
Brewer St BN2 .... 207 B7
Brewers Yd RH20 .... 119 D1
Brewery Hill BN18 .... 158 B2
Brewhurst La RH14 .... 32 A2
Breydon Wlk RH10 .... 19 B4
Briar Ave PO20 .... 190 F1
Briar Cl Angmering BN16 ... 179 F4
  Oving PO20 .... 174 C6
  Yapton BN18 .... 176 F3
Briar Wood GU33 .... 45 C7
Briars Wood RH6 .... 2 C4
Brickfield Cl PO21 .... 195 B5
Bricklands RH10 .... 21 B7
Brickyard La RH10 .... 21 B8
Brideake Cl RH11 .... 18 A3
Bridge Cl PO19 .... 172 E8
Bridge Cl
  Burgess Hill RH15 .... 106 F4
  Lancing BN15 .... 183 E5
  Worthing BN12 .... 181 C4
Bridge Meadows GU33 ..... 45 B4
Bridge Rd
  Chichester PO19 .... 173 C7
  Emsworth PO10 .... 149 B1
  Haslemere GU27 .... 27 C7
  Haywards Heath RH16 ..... 85 F6
  Littlehampton BN17 .... 198 B6
  Rudgwick RH12 .... 33 D7
  Worthing BN14 .... 182 D3
Bridge Road Bsns Pk RH16 85 F7
Bridgefield Cl GU20 .... 92 E6
Bridgefoot Path PO10 .... 169 B8
Bridgelands RH10 .... 7 A3
Bridgermill RH16 .... 85 D6
Bridges Ct RH12 .... 37 A5
Bridgeway The PO20 ...... 206 D6
Bridgnorth Cl BN13 .... 181 B5
Bridle Cl BN44 .... 143 B2
Bridle Rd BN18 .... 156 D4
Bridle Way RH10 .... 19 D7
Bridle Way The PO20 ..... 206 D7
Bridorley Cl PO21 .... 194 B2
Brierley Gdns BN15 .... 183 F6
Brigden St BN1 .... 207 F7
Brigham Pl PO22 .... 196 D4

Brighton Coll BN2 .... 188 C5
Brighton Coll of Tech
 Brighton BN1 .... 207 A6
 Brighton BN2 .... 207 B7
 Brighton BN1 .... 207 F8
Brighton Ctr The BN1 ...... 207 F5
Brighton General Hospl
 BN2 .... 188 D7
Brighton & Hove Golf Course
 BN41 .... 166 D6
Brighton & Hove High Sch for
 Girls BN3 .... 187 E6
Brighton & Hove Stad
 BN3 .... 167 B1
Brighton, Hove & Sussex
 Sixth Form Coll BN3 .... 187 E8
Brighton Marina BN2 ...... 188 F2
Brighton Marina Village
 BN2 .... 188 F3
Brighton Mus & Art Gall
 BN1 .... 207 A5
Brighton Pl BN1 .... 207 A5
Brighton Race Course
 BN2 .... 188 E7
Brighton Rd
 Crawley RH11 .... 18 D4
 Handcross RH17 .... 61 C8
 Horley RH6 .... 1 F2
 Hornbrook Hill RH13 .... 58 F3
 Hurstpierpoint BN6 ..... 125 F3
 Lancing BN43 .... 183 C3
 Mannings Heath RH13 .. 59 C6
 Pease Pottage
  RH10, RH11 .... 39 B4
 Shoreham-by-Sea BN43 . 185 B7
 Woodmancote BN5 ...... 124 A3
 Worthing
  BN11, BN15, BN43 ..... 183 C3
Brighton Rd
 (Pease Pottage Hill)
 RH11 .... 39 C8
Brighton Sea Life Ctr BN1 207 A4
Brighton Sq BN1 .... 207 A5
Brighton Sta BN1 .... 207 A6
Brills La BN1, BN2 .... 207 A4
Brinfast La PO20 .... 192 F4
Brinsbury Coll of Agriculture &
 Horticulture RH20 ...... 76 F1
Brisbane Cl Crawley RH11 .. 5 D1
 Worthing BN13 .... 181 C6
Brisbane Ho GU29 .... 92 E6
Bristol Ave BN15 .... 184 B5
Bristol Cl RH10 .... 6 D1
Bristol Gate BN2 .... 188 D4
Bristol Gdns
 Brighton BN2 .... 188 E4
 Chichester PO19 .... 152 F2
Bristol Mews 3 BN2 ...... 188 E4
Bristol Pl BN2 .... 188 E4
Bristol Rd BN2 .... 188 C4
Bristol St BN2 .... 188 E4
Britannia Ct PO18 .... 171 A5
British Engineerium (Mus)
 BN3 .... 167 B2
Briton's Croft BN44 ...... 143 C3
Brittany Ct BN3 .... 186 D7
Brittany Rd
 Hove BN3, BN41 .... 186 D6
 Worthing BN14 .... 182 C4
Britten Cl RH11 .... 17 F3
Britten's La
 BN18, PO18, PO20 ...... 155 E4
Broad Croft PO9 .... 128 E3
Broad Green Ave RH15 .. 107 C2
Broad Meadow PO18 ..... 170 D8
Broad Piece BN17 .... 198 B6
Broad Rd PO18 .... 150 D2
Broad Rig Ave BN3 ...... 166 D3
Broad St Brighton BN2 .. 207 A4
 Cuckfield RH17 .... 85 A6
Broad Strand BN16 ...... 199 D3
Broad View PO20 .... 206 F7
Broad Wlk
 Crawley RH10, RH11 .... 18 D6
 Heysham PO18 .... 113 D5
Broad Wlk The PO18 .... 151 C6
Broadbridge Cotts RH20 .. 121 A4
Broadbridge Ct PO18 .... 171 C7
Broadbridge Dr PO18 .... 171 C7
Broadbridge Heath Rd
 RH12 .... 35 D4
Broadbridge La RH6 ...... 7 B8
Broadbridge Mill PO18 .. 171 C7
Broadbridge Ret Pk RH12 .. 35 E3
Broadfield RH19 .... 42 E7
Broadfield Barton 4 RH11 . 18 B3

Broadfield East Cty Fst Sch
 RH11 .... 18 C2
Broadfield East Cty Mid Sch
 RH11 .... 18 C2
Broadfield North Cty
 Fst & Mid Sch RH11 .... 18 B2
Broadfield Pl RH11 .... 18 B2
Broadfields BN2 .... 168 E3
Broadfields Rd BN2 ...... 168 E3
Bradford Bridge Rd RH20 . 99 E4
Broadlands Horw RH6 .... 2 C4
 Hurstpierpoint RH15 .... 127 B8
Broadmark Ave BN16 .... 199 C4
Broadmark Beach BN16 .. 199 C3
Broadmark Ho 4 BN16 .. 199 C5
Broadmark Par 2 BN16 .. 199 C5
Broadmark La BN16 ...... 199 C4
Broadmark Way BN16 ... 199 C4
Broadmead RH6 .... 2 C4
Broadview Gdns BN13 ... 181 E8
Broadwater Bvd BN14 ... 182 D5
Broadwater CE (A)
 Prim Sch BN14 .... 182 C5
Broadwater Hall BN14 ... 182 C4
Broadwater Ind Est BN14 182 F5
Broadwater La RH13 ..... 58 D2
Broadwater Manor Sch
 BN14 .... 182 D5
Broadwater Rd
 BN11, BN14 .... 182 D4
Broadwater St E BN14 .. 182 D5
Broadwater St W BN14 .. 182 C6
Broadwater Way BN14 .. 182 D6
Broadway PO20 .... 206 C8
Broadway The 11 BN43 .. 185 C8
Broadway The
 Chichester PO19 .... 153 A2
 Crawley RH10 .... 18 D6
 Haywards Heath RH16 .. 85 D4
 Shoreham-by-Sea BN15 . 184 B5
Broadwood Cl RH12 ..... 37 A5
Broadwood Rise RH11 ... 18 A2
Brock End RH17 .... 84 E8
Brock Rd RH11 .... 5 B1
Brockhurst BN2 .... 188 F7
Brockhurst Cl RH12 ...... 35 F1
Brockhurst Farm RH20 .. 117 B5
Brockley Cl BN14 .... 182 C4
Bromley Cl BN6 .... 127 E4
Bromley Rd BN2 .... 207 B8
Brompton Cl BN1 .... 167 E6
Brontes The RH19 .... 9 D1
Bronze Cl PO22 .... 195 C7
Brook Ave Bosham RH17 . 171 B5
 Hassocks BN6 .... 126 F3
Brook Barn Way BN12 .. 181 E1
Brook Cl
 Bognor Regis PO21 ..... 194 F4
 East Grinstead RH19 ... 10 B1
 Storrington RH20 .... 119 F3
 Worthing BN11 .... 183 A4
Brook Cotts PO10 .... 149 D3
Brook Gdns PO10 .... 169 A8
Brook Gn RH17 .... 62 E1
Brook Hill RH13 .... 81 E3
Brook Ho 5 RH20 .... 98 C2
Brook La
 Coldwaltham RH20 ...... 117 C5
 Faygate RH12 .... 37 C8
 Ferring BN12 .... 200 E6
 Haywards Heath RH16 .. 85 F8
Brook Rd RH12 .... 36 E6
Brook St RH17 .... 62 F2
Brook The RH13 .... 58 A2
Brook Way BN15 .... 183 F5
Brookdean Rd RH11 ..... 183 B3
Brookenbee Cl BN16 .... 179 B3
Brooker Pl BN3 .... 187 A7
Brooker Rd BN3 .... 187 A7
Brooker's Rd RH14 ...... 77 E6
Brookfield La River GU28 .. 72 D1
 Upperton GU28 .... 72 F2
Brookfield Way RH14 ... 77 D6
Brookham Sch GU30 .... 25 E2
Brookhill Cl RH11 .... 7 A3
Brookhill Rd RH11 .... 7 A3
Brookhouse Bottom
 RH17 .... 66 C4
Brookland Way RH20 .... 117 C5
Brooklands
 Bognor Regis PO21 ..... 194 A1
 Shoreham-by-Sea BN15 . 184 C6
Brooklands Cotts PO18 .. 130 E2
Brooklands Pleasure Grounds
 The BN11 .... 183 C4
Brooklands Rd RH11 .... 18 C1
Brooklands Trad Est
 BN14 .... 182 C3
Brooklyn Ave RH11 ...... 181 F2
Brooklyn Ct 4 BN11 .... 181 F2

Brooks La
 Bognor Regis PO22 ..... 195 E4
 Bognor Regis PO22 ..... 195 E5
 Broadbridge PO18 ...... 171 D7
Brooks La W PO22 .... 195 D5
Brooks The RH15 .... 106 E5
Brooks Way RH20 .... 98 C2
Brookside Ashington BN17 . 121 A4
 Copthorne RH10 .... 7 A2
 Crawley RH10 .... 18 F7
 Runcton PO20 .... 173 E1
Brookside Ave BN16 .... 179 C3
Brookside Cl Ferring BN12 180 E3
 Runcton PO20 .... 173 E1
Brookside Ind Est BN16 . 179 C3
Brookside BN12, BN16 .. 200 D4
Brooksmead PO22 ...... 195 E4
Brookview
 Coldwaltham RH20 ...... 117 C5
 Copthorne RH10 .... 7 A3
Brookway
 Burgess Hill RH15 ...... 107 C3
 Haywards Heath RH16 .. 86 A8
Brookwood RH6 .... 2 B4
Brookwood Ho RH6 ...... 2 B6
Broomcroft Rd PO22 .... 196 C4
Broomdashers Rd RH10 . 18 F7
Broome Cl RH12 .... 36 D5
Broomers Hill La RH20 .. 98 E4
Broomers Hill Pk RH20 .. 98 D5
Broomers La PO20 ...... 191 F6
Broomfield Ave
 BN13, BN14 .... 182 B5
Broomfield Dr
 Billingshurst RH14 ...... 77 E8
 Portslade-by-Sea BN41 . 166 A3
Broomfield Gdns BN5 ... 123 E5
Broomfield Rd
 Henfield BN5 .... 123 E5
 Selsey PO20 .... 206 F8
Broomfields Cl BN16 .... 200 B5
Brougham Ct 10 BN11 .. 183 B3
Brougham Rd BN11 ..... 183 B3
Brougham Wlk 11 BN11 . 183 B3
Brow Cl RH20 .... 119 B1
Brow The RH15 .... 107 A2
Brown's La RH20 .... 119 D1
Browning Cl RH10 .... 19 C7
Browning Rd
 Lancing BN15 .... 183 E8
 Worthing BN11 .... 182 B3
Browning's Hill RH13 ... 81 C2
Brownings The 1 RH19 .. 9 C1
Browns Wood RH19 ...... 9 E4
Broxmead La Bolney RH17 . 83 D4
 Slough Green RH17 .... 84 A5
Broyle Cl PO19 .... 152 F1
Broyle Rd PO19 .... 173 A8
Bruce Ave BN11 .... 181 F3
Bruce Cl RH16 .... 85 E3
Bruce Way BN11 .... 181 F3
Brunel Ctr RH10 .... 5 F2
Brunel Pl RH10 .... 18 E5
Brunswick Cl
 Bognor Regis PO22 ..... 196 A5
 Crawley RH10 .... 19 A4
Brunswick Ct RH10 ...... 19 A4
Brunswick Mews BN3 .. 187 D5
Brunswick Pl BN3 .... 187 D6
Brunswick Rd Hove BN3 . 187 D6
 Shoreham-by-Sea BN43 . 184 F7
 Worthing BN11 .... 182 C1
Brunswick Row BN1 .... 207 A7
Brunswick Sq BN3 ...... 187 D5
Brunswick St E BN3 .... 187 D5
Brunswick St W BN3 ... 187 D5
Brunswick Terr
 BN1, BN3 .... 187 D5
Brushes La RH16 .... 86 B8
Brushwood Rd RH12 ... 37 B6
Bryce Cl RH12 .... 37 A5
Buchans Lawn RH11 .... 18 B2
Buci Cres BN43 .... 165 C1
Buck Barn Bglws RH13 .. 80 A2
Buckburn Crossroads
 RH13 .... 80 B2
Buckhurst Cl RH19 .... 9 C3
Buckhurst Mead RH19 .. 9 C4
Buckhurst Way RH19 ... 9 C3
Buckingham Ave BN43 .. 164 E1
Buckingham Cl
 4 Brighton BN1 .... 207 F7
 Shoreham-by-Sea BN43 . 185 A8
Buckingham Ct
 Crawley RH11 .... 18 B2
 Worthing BN11 .... 182 B7
Buckingham Cty Mid Sch
 BN43 .... 184 F8
Buckingham Dr
 Chichester PO19 .... 173 D6
 East Grinstead RH19 ... 23 A8

Buckingham Gate RH6 .... 6 C7
Buckingham Lodge BN1 .. 207 F7
Buckingham Mews 16
 BN43 .... 164 F1
Buckingham Pl BN1 ..... 207 F7
Buckingham Rd
 Brighton BN1 .... 207 F6
 Shoreham-by-Sea BN43 . 184 F8
 Worthing BN11 .... 182 D2
Buckingham St
 Brighton BN1 .... 207 F6
 Shoreham-by-Sea BN43 . 184 E7
Buckland Dr PO21 .... 194 B2
Buckler St BN41 .... 186 B8
Buckley Cl BN3 .... 166 E4
Buckley Pl RH10 .... 21 A8
Buckmans Rd RH11 ..... 18 D6
Bucknor Cl PO21 .... 194 C2
Bucks Green Sch RH12 .. 33 B7
Bucksham Ave PO21 .... 194 F7
Buckshead Hill RH13 ... 59 F7
Buckswood Dr RH11 .... 18 A4
Budgen Cl RH10 .... 6 D1
Buffbeards La GU27 .... 26 E6
Bugshill La GU29 .... 91 D1
Bulbeck Cl RH15 .... 106 E1
Bulkington Ave RH14 ... 182 B4
Bull Hill GU33 .... 46 A4
Bull's La RH11, RH12 ... 82 D4
Bulldogs Bank RH19 .... 42 F5
Buller Rd BN2 .... 168 D1
Bullfinch Cl Horley RH6 .. 1 E4
 Horsham RH12 .... 36 C7
Bunbury Cl RH20 .... 120 B2
Bunch La GU27 .... 27 B8
Bunch Way GU27 .... 27 A6
Buncton Crossways BN44 142 C7
Buncton La RH17 .... 83 E3
Bungalows The BN18 ... 156 D1
Bunting Cl RH13 .... 36 F3
Bunyan Cl RH11 .... 17 E3
Burbeach Cl RH11 .... 18 B3
Burch Gr BN18 .... 156 D1
Burchell Cl BN15 .... 183 F7
Burchens The BN14 .... 182 C6
Burchett Wlk PO21 ..... 194 F5
Burchetts Cl RH16 ...... 85 E2
Burdock Cl RH11 .... 18 A2
Burdocks Dr RH15 ...... 107 D1
Burford Cl BN13, BN14 .. 182 A7
Burford Rd RH13 .... 36 E2
Burgess Hill Sch RH15 .. 107 B2
Burgess Hill Sta RH15 .. 107 B2
Burgh Cl RH10 .... 6 D1
Burgh Hill Rd GU30 ..... 25 A7
Burlands RH11 .... 5 A1
Burleigh Cl RH10 .... 21 B8
Burleigh Ct 4 BN11 .... 182 C1
Burleigh Cty Inf Sch RH10 . 21 B8
Burleigh La RH10 .... 21 C7
Burleigh Way RH10 ..... 21 B8
Burley Cl Lancing BN15 . 183 E6
 Loxwood RH14 .... 32 A4
Burley Rd PO22 .... 196 D4
Burleys Rd RH10 .... 19 C6
Burlington Ct BN11 ..... 181 F1
Burlington Gdns
 Portslade-by-Sea BN41 . 166 C1
 Selsey PO20 .... 206 F6
Burlington Rd BN12 .... 181 D3
Burlington St BN2 .... 188 C4
Burlow Cl Birdham PO20 . 191 D4
 Brighton BN2 .... 188 E5
Burma Cl RH16 .... 86 C4
Burmill Cl RH16 .... 179 E3
Burndell Rd BN18 .... 177 A2
Burners Cl RH15 .... 107 D1
Burney Ct 5 RH11 ...... 18 A3
Burngreave Ct PO21 .... 195 B3
Burnham Ave PO21 ..... 195 C3
Burnham Gdns PO21 ... 195 C3
Burnham Pl RH13 .... 36 D1
Burnham Rd BN13 ...... 181 E6
Burns Cl RH12 .... 36 E7
Burns Gdns PO22 .... 196 D6
Burns Rd RH10 .... 19 C8
Burns Way Crawley RH10 . 17 C1
 East Grinstead RH19 ... 9 C1
Burnside Cres BN15 .... 183 C5
Burnt House La RH12 .. 17 A7
Burnthouse Bostall BN5 . 148 C8
Burnthouse La RH13 ... 81 C4
Burrell Ave BN15 .... 183 D5
Burrell Bldgs RH15 ..... 183 D5
Burrell Cl RH13 .... 103 A3
Burrell Cotts RH17 ...... 84 E8
Burrell Rd RH17 .... 17 F4
Burrell Gn RH17 .... 84 F8

Burrell Rd RH16 .... 85 D6
Burrells The BN43 .... 185 B6
Bursledon Cl PO21 ...... 196 A5
Burstead Cl BN1 .... 168 B3
Burston Gdns RH19 ..... 9 D4
Burstow Ho RH6 .... 2 B6
Burstowhill La RH17 .... 64 D6
Burton Cl PO22 .... 2 A2
Burton Villas BN3 .... 187 D8
Burtons Ct RH12 .... 36 C2
Burwash Cl RH16 .... 180 B3
Burwash Lodge 1 BN1 . 168 C1
Burwash Rd Crawley RH11 . 19 A5
 Hove BN3 .... 166 F3
Bury CE (A) Prim Sch
 RH20 .... 137 F7
Bury Common Cotts RH20 116 F1
Bury Dr BN12 .... 181 B2
Bury Hill BN18, RH20 ... 137 F6
Bury Ho 3 BN14 .... 182 D5
Bury Rd RH20 .... 116 F3
Bush Farm Dr BN41 .... 166 C3
Bushby Ave BN16 .... 199 D5
Bushby Cl BN15 .... 183 C5
Bushfield RH14 .... 30 F2
Busticle La BN15 .... 183 C7
Bute St BN2 .... 188 D5
Butler's Green Ho RH16 . 85 B4
Butlers Green Rd RH16 . 85 C4
Butlers Rd RH13 .... 37 B4
Butt La BN18 .... 156 C6
Butterbox La BN8, RH17 . 87 D4
Buttercup Wlk BN1 ..... 168 B7
Butterfield RH19 .... 9 B3
Buttermere Cl RH12 .... 37 B6
Buttermere Way BN16 . 179 A3
Butternere Dr BN1 ...... 207 B7
Butts Cl RH11 .... 18 B7
Butts Meadow RH14 .... 54 B1
Butts Rd BN42 .... 185 E7
Buxshalls Hill RH16 ..... 64 C2
Buxted Rise BN1 .... 168 B5
Buxton Rd BN1 .... 207 E7
By Sunte RH16 .... 85 F8
Bycroft Way RH10 .... 19 B8
Bye Way The PO21 ..... 205 C8
Byerley Cl PO10 .... 149 D5
Byerley Way RH10 ...... 19 E2
Byeway The PO20 .... 190 C1
Byfield Pl PO22 .... 195 D6
Byfleets La RH12 .... 35 D6
Bylands 3 BN2 .... 188 F5
Bylanes Cl RH17 .... 84 F7
Bylanes Cres RH17 ..... 84 F8
Byne Cl RH20 .... 119 E1
Byrd Rd RH11 .... 17 F3
Byron Cl
 Bognor Regis PO22 ..... 196 D6
 Crawley RH10 .... 19 B7
 Horsham RH12 .... 36 E6
Byron Ct 1 RH16 .... 85 D5
Byron Gr 2 RH19 .... 9 C1
Byron Rd
 Littlehampton BN16 .... 199 A5
 Worthing BN11 .... 182 C1
Byron St BN3 .... 187 A7
Bywater Way PO19, PO20 . 172 F4
Bywaves PO20 .... 202 C4
Byway The Brighton BN1 . 148 B8
Byway The Brighton PO22 . 196 E5
 Middleton-on-Sea PO22 . 196 E5
Byworth PO20 .... 206 E5
Byworth Cl RH13 .... 188 F6

Caburn Ct RH11 .... 18 C4
Caburn Hts RH11 .... 18 C4
Caburn Rd BN3 .... 187 E7
Cackstones The RH10 .. 19 D7
Caedwalla Dr PO20 ..... 154 C2
Caernarvon Rd PO19 ... 173 D6
Caffins Cl RH10 .... 18 E8
Cagefoot La BN5 .... 123 E4
Caister's Cl BN3 .... 187 C8
Caius Ct 16 BN43 .... 185 C8
Cakeham Rd
 East Wittering PO20 .... 201 D8
 East Wittering PO20 .... 201 F7
Cakeham Way PO20 .... 201 F7
Calbourne Rd PO21 .... 195 B5
Caldbeck Ho 7 RH11 ... 17 F3
Calderdale Cl RH11 ..... 18 B4
Caledon Ave PO22 ...... 196 D5
Caledonia Ho RH11 ..... 18 D8
Caledonian Pl 1 BN11 . 182 D1
Caledonian Rd
 Brighton BN2 .... 207 B8
 Chichester PO19 .... 173 B6
Callosa Way RH6 .... 6 B8
Callisto Cl RH11 .... 17 E3
Calluna Dr RH12 .... 7 A3
Calvecroft GU30 .... 25 C4
Calvin Wlk RH11 .... 17 E3

Camargue Ct 5 BN11 182 A3
Camber Cl Brighton BN2 188 F5
Crawley RH10 19 C6
Cambourne Ct 4 BN11 182 C2
Cambrai Ave PO19 173 B5
Cambria Cl PO18 171 C5
Cambridge Ave PO20 201 E8
Cambridge Dr PO21 194 F4
Cambridge Gr BN3 187 C7
Cambridge Rd
Horsham RH13 36 D2
Hove BN3 187 D6
Worthing BN11 182 D3
Cambridge Wlk PO21 194 F4
Camden St BN41 186 C6
Camden Terr BN1 207 F6
Camelford St BN2 207 B4
Camelot Cl RH13 58 A2
Camelot Ct RH11 17 E6
Camelsdale Cty Fst Sch GU27 26 F5
Camelsdale Rd GU27 26 F5
Campbell Cres RH19 9 B1
Campbell Dr BN16 199 B6
Campbell Rd
Bognor Regis PO21 195 D3
Brighton BN1 207 F8
Crawley RH10 19 C5
Tangmere PO20 154 B1
Campion Rd RH12 36 E5
Canada Cnr GU31 89 B6
Canada Cotts GU29 71 A3
Canada Gr
Bognor Regis PO21 195 C3
Easebourne GU29 71 A2
Canada Rd BN18 157 F3
Canal Rd BN18 176 F3
Canal Wharf PO19 172 F5
Canal Wharf Rd PO19 172 F5
Canberra Cl Crawley RH11 5 D1
Horsham RH12 36 F4
Canberra Pl Horsham RH12 36 F5
Tangmere PO20 154 D2
Canberra Rd
Thorney Island PO10 169 C3
Worthing BN13 181 C6
Candleford Gate GU30 25 C4
Canfield Cl BN2 168 D1
Canfield Rd BN2 168 D1
Canhouse La
GU30, GU31, GU33 46 C3
Canning Rd PO22 195 F3
Canning St BN2 188 D5
Cannon Pl BN1 207 F5
Canon La PO19 172 F6
Canon's Cl PO21 194 D1
Canonbury Cotts RH12 16 F6
Canons Way BN44 143 E4
Cansiron La RH19 23 F6
Cantelupe Rd RH19 9 F1
Canter The RH10 19 E7
Canterbury Cl
Bognor Regis PO21 194 A1
Chichester PO19 172 F8
Canterbury Ct BN13 181 F3
Canterbury Dr 5 BN2 207 B7
Canterbury Rd
Crawley RH10 18 E2
Rustington BN16 199 E6
Worthing BN13, BN14 182 A3
Canton 3 RH16 85 D6
Cants Cl RH15 107 C3
Cants La RH15 107 C3
Canute Rd PO18 171 B5
Canvey Cl RH11 18 C3
Cape Copse RH12 33 D7
Cape The BN16, BN17 199 A5
Capel La RH11 17 F5
Capel Rd RH12 16 A8
Capelia Ho BN11 182 A1
Capenors RH15 106 F1
Capricorn Cl RH11 17 E4
Capsey Rd RH11 17 E6
Capstan Dr BN16 179 A3
Caraway Cl RH11 18 B2
Card Hill RH18 23 F1
Carden Ave BN1 168 B6
Carden Cl BN1 168 A6
Carden Cres BN1 168 A6
Carden Cty Inf Sch BN1 168 B6
Carden Cty Jun Sch BN1 168 B6
Carden Hill BN1 168 B5
Cardew Rd GU33 45 C3
Cardinal Ct 4 BN11 182 A1
Cardinal Newman Sch BN3 187 D8
Cardinal's Dr PO21 194 B1
Carey Ho RH11 18 C6
Carfax RH12 36 C2
Cargo Forecourt Rd RH6 5 D7
Cargo Rd RH6 5 D7
Carisbrooke Cl BN15 183 E8
Carisbrooke Dr BN13 181 B5
Carisbrooke Rd BN2 188 D7
Carleton Rd PO19 172 E8
Carlingford Ct PO21 195 C4
Carlisle Gdns PO19 152 F1
Carlisle Rd BN3 186 F6
Carlton Ave PO21 194 C3
Carlton Ct Horley RH6 2 A5
Portslade-by-Sea BN3 186 C8
Carlton Hill BN2 207 B5
Carlton Hill Cty Prim Sch BN2 207 B5
Carlton Ho
11 Brighton BN1 167 E2
Worthing BN13 182 A6
Carlton Mews BN11 182 A2
Carlton Pl 5 BN2 207 B5
Carlton Terr BN3 186 C8
Carlton Tye RH6 2 C3
Carlyle Ave BN2 168 D1
Carlyle St BN2 188 C7
Carman Wlk RH11 18 B1
Carnegie Cl BN14 182 C5
Carnegie Gdns BN14 182 D5
Carnegie Ho BN13 181 F6
Carnegie Rd BN14 182 C5
Carnforth Rd BN15 183 C5
Carol Cl BN1 167 F6
Caroline Ct RH11 18 D4
Carolyn Ho BN13 181 E5
Caron Cl BN15 183 E5
Carousel Ct PO21, PO22 195 B5
Carpenters RH14 77 D8
Carpenters Meadow RH20 98 C2
Carron La GU29 92 E7
Carter Rd RH10 19 D3
Carters Way RH14 76 B8
Cartersland GU30 47 B3
Carterslodge La RH17 60 E7
Cartersmead Cl RH6 2 B4
Carvel Way BN16, BN17 199 A6
Carylls Cotts RH12 16 F1
Casher Rd RH10 19 C3
Cashman Lodge BN1 168 A5
Caspian Ct 8 BN1 207 F7
Cassells Rd 2 PO19 153 A2
Cassidy Pl RH20 119 B1
Castle Cl Bramber BN44 143 E2
Worthing BN13 181 F4
Castle Ct BN13 181 F4
Castle Dr RH6 2 C2
Castle Gdns BN18 158 A3
Castle Goring Mews BN13 181 A8
Castle La Bramber BN44 143 E2
West Grinstead RH13 101 F7
Castle Rd
Broadridge Heath RH12 35 D3
Red Hill PO9 128 D1
Worthing BN13 181 F4
Castle Sq BN1 207 A5
Castle St BN1 187 E5
Castle The RH12 36 E7
Castle Way
Bramber BN44 143 E3
Worthing BN13 181 F4
Castledean Sch BN2 168 C2
Castlegate RH20 119 B7
Castleman Rd PO19 173 C8
Castlereagh Gn PO22 196 A5
Castlewood Prim Sch RH13 58 A2
Castlewood Rd RH13 58 A2
Caterways RH12 36 A3
Cathedral of Our Lady & St Philip Howard BN18 158 B3
Cathedral Way PO19 172 E5
Catherington Sch RH11 5 D2
Catkin Way RH16 86 B4
Catslands La BN5 145 C8
Causeway Ct BN18 158 C2
Causeway The
Arundel BN18 158 C2
Bognor Regis PO21 205 A8
Brighton BN2 188 D6
Horsham RH12 36 C1
Partridge Green RH13 103 A3
Selsey PO20 206 C8
Westlands PO20 191 F6
Worthing BN12 181 E3
Cavalier Cl GU29 92 E7
Cavalier Way RH19 22 F7
Cavell Rd RH10 19 C5
Cavendish Cl
Horsham RH12 36 D7
Worthing BN12 181 D3
Cavendish Ho
Bognor Regis PO21 195 D2
12 Hove BN1 187 E5
Cavendish Pl BN1 187 E5
Cavendish Rd PO21 195 C3
Cavendish St
11 Brighton BN2 207 B5
Chichester PO19 172 F7
Cawley Rd PO19 173 A5
Caxton Cl RH10 18 E3
Caxton Ct 4 BN14 182 D4
Caxton Way 15 RH16 85 E4
Cecil Norris Ho 3 BN43 184 F7
Cecil Pashley Way BN43 184 D8
Cecil Rd BN15 183 E4
Cecilian Ave BN14 182 D4
Cedar Ave BN13 181 F6
Cedar Cl
Bognor Regis PO21 194 D3
Burgess Hill RH15 107 B5
Crawley RH11 5 C1
Ferring BN12 200 E5
Horsham RH12 36 C3
Lancing BN15 183 D4
Worthing BN13 181 F6
Cedar Cl E PO21 194 D3
Cedar Ct Haslemere GU27 27 B6
Petworth GU28 95 E7
Cedar Dr Chichester PO19 172 E7
Southwater RH13 58 A1
Cedar Lodge RH11 18 D4
Cedar Way
Haywards Heath RH16 86 B4
Henfield BN5 123 F4
Cedars Farm Cl RH14 77 C8
Cedars Gdns BN1 167 E3
Cedars The
1 Brighton BN1 167 E3
1 Brighton BN2 207 B8
Haywards Heath RH16 85 D7
Rustington BN16 199 E6
Cedarwood 6 BN1 167 E3
Celandine Cl 1 RH11 18 B2
Cemetery La
Tillington GU28 73 C1
Westbourne PO10 149 F3
Centenary Ho 9 BN1 167 E2
Centenary Ind Est 6 BN2 188 B8
Central Ave
Bognor Regis PO21 195 A6
Littlehampton BN16 199 C4
Worthing BN14 161 F3
Central Bldgs 2 PO21 195 D3
Central CE (A) Jun Sch PO19 172 F7
Central Dr
Bognor Regis PO21 195 A6
Middleton-on-Sea PO22 197 A5
Centrecourt Cl 5 BN14 182 C4
Centrecourt Rd BN14 182 C4
Centurion Rd BN1 207 F6
Ceres Pl PO22 196 D4
Chadborn Cl BN2 188 D5
Chadds Cotts RH17 39 C1
Chadwick Cl RH11 18 B1
Chaffer La PO20 191 D4
Chaffinch Cl
Burgess Hill RH15 106 D4
Crawley RH11 18 D8
Horsham RH12 36 D7
Worthing BN13 181 C5
Chaffinch Way RH6 1 E4
Chailey Cl 2 RH11 18 A3
Chailey Ct 2 RH16 85 F3
Chailey Heritage Craft Sch & Hospl New Heritage BN8 87 E1
Chailey Rd BN1 168 E4
Chainbridge La PO20 203 C1
Chalcraft Cl GU30 25 A4
Chalcraft La PO21, PO22 194 F5
Chalder La PO20 192 F3
Chaldon Rd RH11 18 C1
Chalet Cl BN12 200 E4
Chalet Gdns BN12 200 F4
Chalet Rd BN12 200 E4
Chalfont Cl PO22 196 E5
Chalfont Dr BN3 167 C3
Chalfont Way BN13 181 D6
Chalk La PO20 203 E7
Chalk Rd
Goodwood Park PO18 134 A4
Ifold RH14 31 C3
Chalkdock La PO20 191 A5
Chalkers La BN6 126 B8
Chalkpit La PO18 153 B7
Chalky Rd BN41 166 A3
Challen Cl PO20 174 C6
Challen Ct RH12 36 B3
Challoners RH17 65 C4
Challow Cl BN6 126 E4
Chalmers Ct RH6 4 E6
Chaloner Cl RH16 86 B7
Chaloner Rd RH16 86 B7
Chalvington Cl BN1 168 E6
Champion's Gate RH13 81 A2
Chancellors Pk BN6 126 F4
Chancton Cl
Heath Common RH20 120 B3
Worthing BN11 181 F3
Chancton View Rd BN11 181 F3
Chanctonbury Cl RH20 141 E6
Chanctonbury Dr BN43 164 F1
Chanctonbury L Ctr RH20 119 C2
Chanctonbury Rd
Burgess Hill RH15 107 A1
Hove BN3 187 E7
Littlehampton BN16 199 B4
Chanctonbury Ring Rd BN44 142 D6
Chanctonbury View BN5 123 D4
Chanctonbury Way RH11 18 C4
Chanctonbury Wlk RH20 119 D1
Chandler Cl RH10, RH11 18 D4
Chandler Rd PO19 172 E5
Chandlers Reach PO20 191 A7
Chandlers Way BN44 143 C2
Chandos Rd BN11 182 D2
Channel Ct BN15 183 E4
Channel Keep 11 BN17 198 E4
Channel View
Bognor Regis PO21 205 A8
13 Southwick BN42 185 E7
Chantlers Cl RH19 9 C2
Chantrey Rd RH10 18 E3
Chantry Cl Henfield BN5 123 E6
Horley RH6 1 F4
Storrington RH20 119 E1
Chantry Est The RH20 140 E8
Chantry La BN13, RH20 140 E6
Chantry Rd BN13 182 A6
Chantryfield Rd BN16 179 F6
Chapel Cl
Burgess Hill RH15 106 F4
Littlehampton BN17 198 C6
Chapel La
Ashurst Wood RH19 23 D6
Cootham RH20 119 A1
Copthorne RH10 7 F4
East Ashling PO18 152 A3
Forest Row RH18 23 F2
Horsted Keynes RH17 65 C5
West Wittering PO20 190 F2
Chapel Mews BN3 187 D5
Chapel Pl BN41 186 B7
Chapel Rd
Barns Green RH13 56 F2
Charlwood RH6 4 F7
Southwick BN41 186 A7
Worthing BN11 182 D3
Chapel Row
East Dean PO18 134 C6
West Hoathly RH19 42 E7
Chapel St
Bognor Regis PO21 195 C2
Brighton BN2 207 B5
Chichester PO19 172 F6
Chapel Terr 2 BN2 188 D4
Chapel Wlk BN16 179 F5
Chapelfields RH17 84 F8
Chapman Ct BN13 181 F6
Chapman Rd RH10 19 C2
Chapman's La
East Grinstead RH19 9 B1
East Grinstead RH19 9 D1
Chappell Cl GU30 25 C4
Chappell Croft 2 BN11 182 B2
Charis Ct 18 BN3 187 C7
Charlecote Rd BN11 182 E2
Charles Ave
Burgess Hill RH15 106 D2
Chichester PO19 173 D6
Charles Bennett Ct RH16 86 A4
Charles Cl BN3 167 A3
Charles Ct BN11 182 C3
Charles Ho BN12 181 D2
Charles St BN2 207 A4
Charlesfield Rd RH6 1 F4
Charleston Ct RH10 19 B3
Charlesworth Pk RH16 86 C4
Charlmead PO20 201 F6
Charlock Cl RH11 18 A2
Charlock Way RH13 58 A3
Charlotte Ct RH11 18 C6
Charlotte Ho PO22 195 E4
Charlotte St BN2 207 B4
Charlton Mill Way PO18 133 F6
Charlton Rd PO18 134 B6
Charlton St BN44 143 C3
Charltons The BN1 168 D6
Charlwood Cty Fst Sch RH6 4 F7
Charlwood Gdns RH15 107 C5
Charlwood La RH5 4 A5
Charlwood Rd
Burgess Hill RH15 107 D6
Charlwood RH11, RH6 4 E2
Crawley RH6 5 C4
Charlwood Rd
Hookwood RH6 5 C8
Charlwood St PO21 195 B2
Charlwood Wlk RH11 5 B1
Charlwoods Bsns Ctr RH19 9 D2
Charlwoods Pl RH19 9 E3
Charlwoods Rd RH19 9 E3
Charm Cl RH6 1 E4
Charmandean La BN14 182 D8
Charmandean Rd BN14 182 D6
Charmans Cl RH12 37 B5
Charnwood Rd PO22 195 B6
Charrington Way RH12 35 C3
Chartfield BN3 167 A2
Chartfield Way BN3 167 B2
Chartwell Ct BN1 207 F5
Chartwell Rd BN15 183 D5
Chase Cl GU33 45 C4
Chase La GU27 27 E3
Chase Rd GU33 45 C4
Chase The Crawley RH10 19 A5
Nepcote BN14 161 E5
Chatelet Cl RH6 2 B4
Chates Farm Ct BN2 207 B6
Chatfield Rd
Chichester PO19 173 C8
Cuckfield RH17 85 A6
Chatfield's Farm RH13 81 E6
Chatfields RH11 18 B4
Chatham Pl BN1 207 F7
Chatham Rd BN11 183 A3
Chatsmore Cath High Sch (A) BN12 181 A3
Chatsmore Cres BN12 181 B3
Chatsmore Ho BN12 181 A2
Chatsworth Ave GU27 27 C8
Chatsworth Cl BN16 179 B3
Chatsworth Ct 5 BN43 184 F6
Chatsworth Dr BN16 179 B3
Chatsworth Rd
Brighton BN1 187 E8
Chichester PO19 173 D6
Worthing BN11 182 D2
Chaucer Ave 3 RH19 9 C1
Chaucer Ct 2 RH16 85 D5
Chaucer Rd Crawley RH10 19 C8
Worthing BN11 182 B3
Chaucer Way PO22 196 D6
Chaucher Ave BN16 199 B5
Chawkmare Coppice PO21 194 F2
Chayle Gdns PO20 206 E6
Cheal Cl BN43 184 F6
Cheam Rd BN16 199 D4
Cheapside BN1 207 A6
Cheeleys RH17 65 C5
Cheesemans La PO18 150 E4
Chelsea Arc RH16 85 E4
Chelston Ave BN3 186 D7
Cheltenham Pl BN1 207 A6
Chelwood Ave BN12 181 C1
Chelwood Cl
Brighton BN1 168 C6
Crawley RH10 18 F4
Chelwood Ct RH15 107 A4
Chelwood Gate Rd RH17 66 F7
Chennells Way RH12 36 E5
Chepstow Cl RH10 19 E6
Chepstow Ct BN1 168 F5
Chequer Grange RH18 23 E1
Chequer La PO18 171 D6
Chequer Rd RH19 9 F1
Chequers Cl RH6 2 A4
Chequers Ct RH13 36 E2
Chequers Dr RH6 2 A4
Chequers Quay PO10 169 C8
Cherington Cl BN6 126 B5
Chermont Ct BN16 199 F6
Cherrimans Orch GU27 26 F6
Cherry Ave BN18 177 A2
Cherry Cl
Bognor Regis PO21 194 E2
Burgess Hill RH15 106 E3
Cherry Croft BN17 178 D3
Cherry Ct RH13 36 D1
Cherry Gdns Selsey PO20 206 D5
Worthing BN13 161 D1
Cherry La Birdham PO20 191 F5
Bolney RH17 83 C3
Brook Street RH17 62 F5
Crawley RH11 5 C1
Cherry Orchard Rd PO19 173 B5
Cherry Tree Ave GU27 26 F7
Cherry Tree Cl
Billingshurst RH14 55 C1
Crawley RH10 19 D8
Worthing BN13 161 D1
Cherry Tree Dr PO20 175 F8

Cherry Tree Lodge 🏠
BN15 .... 183 D6
Cherry Tree Wlk
Horsham RH12 .... 37 B6
Petworth GU28 .... 95 E7
Cherry Trees RH17 .... 84 E8
Cherry Wlk BN13 .... 161 E1
Cherrytree Cotts PO22 ... 176 C5
Cherrywood 🏠 BN1 .... 167 E3
Cherwell Rd BN13 .... 181 C8
Cherwell Wlk RH11 .... 17 F5
Chesham Cl BN12 .... 181 E2
Chesham Pl BN2 .... 188 D4
Chesham Rd BN2 .... 188 D4
Chesham St BN2 .... 188 D4
Cheshire Cl PO21 .... 195 D4
Cheshire Cres PO20 .... 154 C1
Cheshire Way PO10 .... 150 A2
Chesholt Cl GU27 .... 49 B6
Chesley Cl BN13 .... 181 C6
Chess Brook Gn BN5 ...... 123 F7
Chesswood Ave PO22 ..... 196 C6
Chesswood Cl BN11 .... 182 F4
Chesswood Cty Mid Sch
BN14 .... 182 E4
Chesswood Rd BN11 .... 182 F4
Chester Ave Lancing BN15 183 E4
Worthing BN11 .... 183 A3
Chester Cl 🏠 BN3 .... 187 E7
Chester Lodge 🏠 BN1 ..... 182 A2
Chester Terr BN1 .... 168 A1
Chesterfield Cl RH10 ...... 8 C4
Chesterfield Rd BN12 ..... 181 D3
Chesters RH6 .... 1 E5
Chesterton Cl RH19 .... 22 F7
Chesterton Ct RH13 .... 37 A4
Chestnut Ave
Chichester PO19 .... 152 F3
Haslemere GU27 .... 27 C7
Chestnut Cl
Angmering BN16 .... 179 F4
Burgess Hill RH15 .... 107 B5
East Grinstead RH19 ...... 10 A1
Heath Common RH20 ...... 120 B3
Liphook GU30 .... 25 D3
Midhurst GU29 .... 92 E5
Chestnut Ct
East Preston BN16 .... 200 A5
Horsham RH13 .... 36 E2
Chestnut End BN5 .... 123 E5
Chestnut Gdns RH12 ...... 36 C5
Chestnut Gr
Bognor Regis PO22 .... 195 C6
Hurstpierpoint BN6 .... 125 F7
Chestnut Rd
Billingshurst RH14 .... 77 D7
Horley RH6 .... 2 B5
Chestnut Way BN5 .... 123 E5
Chestnut Wlk Crawley RH11 . 5 C1
Felcourt RH19 .... 9 C8
Pulborough RH20 .... 98 B2
Tangmere PO20 .... 154 C1
Worthing BN13 .... 181 C5
Chestnuts Cl RH16 .... 86 A7
Chestnuts The
Haywards Heath RH16 ..... 85 F7
Horley RH6 .... 2 A5
Hunston PO20 .... 193 A8
Sayers Common BN6 ...... 105 D1
Chesworth Cl RH13 .... 58 C8
Chesworth Cres RH13 ..... 36 C1
Chesworth Gdns RH13 .... 36 C1
Chesworth Jun Sch RH13 . 36 C1
Chesworth La RH12, RH13 . 36 C1
Chet Nole RH19 .... 9 D2
Chetwood Rd RH11 .... 17 D2
Cheveley Gdns PO21 ...... 194 E2
Chevening Cl RH11 .... 18 C1
Cheviot Cl
East Preston BN16 .... 200 A6
Worthing BN13 .... 181 E8
Cheviot Rd BN13 .... 181 E8
Cheviot Wlk RH11 .... 18 B6
Cheyne Ct BN43 .... 185 C7
Cheyne Wlk RH6 .... 2 A1
Cheynell Wlk RH11 .... 17 F4
Chichester By-Pass
Chichester PO20 .... 173 D5
Stockbridge PO19 .... 172 F4
Chichester Cath PO19 .... 172 F6
Chichester Ct
8 Rustington BN16 .... 199 C5

Chichester Ct
1 Worthing BN11 .... 182 A1
Chichester Dr PO20 .... 154 D1
Chichester
Festival Theatre PO19 .. 173 A8
Chichester High Sch
for Boys PO19 .... 173 A5
Chichester High Sch
for Girls PO19 .... 172 F5
Chichester Inst of
Higher Ed PO19 .... 173 A8
Chichester Mus PO19 ..... 173 A6
Chichester Pl BN2 .... 188 D4
Chichester Rd
Arundel BN18 .... 157 E3
Bognor Regis
PO21, PO22 .... 195 B5
East Beach PO20 .... 203 F1
Midhurst GU29 .... 92 F5
Selsey PO20 .... 206 E8
Street End PO20 .... 192 E5
Chichester Sta PO19 ...... 172 F5
Chichester Terr
16 Brighton BN2 .... 188 D4
Horsham RH12 .... 36 D2
Chichester Tutorial Unit
PO20 .... 173 C1
Chichester Way
Burgess Hill RH15 .... 107 C5
Selsey PO20 .... 206 G8
Chiddingley Cl BN2 .... 188 F5
Chiddingly Cl RH10 .... 19 B5
Chidham La PO18 .... 170 E6
Chidholm Parochial (C)
Prim Sch PO18 .... 170 E6
Chilcomb RH15 .... 107 C1
Chilcroft La GU27 .... 27 B1
Chilcroft Rd GU27 .... 26 F7
Chilcrofts Rd GU27 .... 27 A1
Chilgrove Cl BN12 .... 181 B3
Chillis Wood Rd RH16 .... 85 C5
Chiltern Cl Crawley RH11 . 18 B6
East Preston BN16 .... 200 A6
Haslemere GU27 .... 27 B5
Shoreham-by-Sea BN43 . 185 C8
Chiltern Cres BN13 .... 181 E7
Chiltington Cl
Burgess Hill RH15 .... 106 F5
West Chiltington Common
RH20 .... 119 C7
Chiltington Ct RH12 .... 36 D4
Chiltlee Cl GU30 .... 25 C4
Chiltlee Manor GU30 ..... 25 C3
Chiltley La GU30 .... 25 D2
Chiltley Way GU30 .... 25 C2
Chine The BN17 .... 199 A4
Chipley Ct PO21 .... 195 A4
Chippendale Rd RH11 .... 18 B1
Chippers Cl BN13 .... 181 F4
Chippers Rd BN13 .... 181 F4
Chippers Wlk BN13 .... 181 F4
Chithurst La
Chithurst
GU29, GU30, GU31 .... 69 C4
Domewood RH6, RH7 ..... 7 F7
Chownes Mead La
RH16, RH17 .... 85 B4
Chrisdory Rd BN41 .... 165 F3
Christ's Hospital Rd
Horsham RH13 .... 57 E6
Itchingfield RH13 .... 57 C6
Christ's Hospital (Sch)
RH13 .... 57 D5
Christ's Hospital Sta (West
Horsham) RH13 .... 57 D7
Christchurch Cres PO21 . 194 E3
Christchurch Rd BN11 .... 182 D3
Christie Pl PO22 .... 195 D6
Christies RH19 .... 22 D8
Christopher Rd RH19 ..... 9 E1
Christopher Way PO10 ... 149 B2
Church App 1 BN17 .... 198 E4
Church Ave RH16 .... 85 E6
Church Cl Brighton BN1 . 167 F5
Burgess Hill RH15 .... 107 A3
Clapham BN13 .... 160 F1
Lancing BN15 .... 183 E8
Lower Beeding RH13 ...... 60 A3
Pagham PO21 .... 204 E7
Shipley RH13 .... 101 D8
Upper Beeding BN44 ...... 144 A3
Church Cotts PO20 .... 202 D6
Church Ct
3 Haywards Heath RH16 . 85 E4
Hove BN3 .... 166 F1
Church Farm Ct PO20 .... 202 A8
Church Farm La PO20 .... 202 A8
Church Farm Wlk BN44 . 144 A3
Church Gn BN43 .... 185 C7
Church Gr RH20 .... 99 D1

Church Hill Brighton BN1 . 167 E7
Midhurst GU29 .... 92 F8
Pulborough RH20 .... 98 B2
Pyecombe BN45 .... 147 C6
Slindon BN18 .... 156 C5
Church Ho BN17 .... 198 D4
Church House Cl BN42 ... 165 F1
Church La Albourne BN6 . 125 B5
Ardingly RH17 .... 63 F8
Ashington RH20 .... 121 A4
Ashurst BN44, RH13 ...... 122 D5
Barnham PO22 .... 176 B4
Birdham PO20 .... 191 E5
Bognor Regis PO22 .... 195 C5
Boxgrove PO18 .... 158 D3
Bramshott GU30 .... 25 C6
Broadridge Heath RH12 .. 35 D3
Burgess Hill RH16, RH17 . 107 F6
Burstow RH6 .... 6 F7
Bury RH20 .... 138 A7
Climping BN17, BN18 ..... 177 E1
Cocking GU29 .... 112 D7
Coldwaltham RH20 .... 117 C6
Copthorne RH10 .... 7 B3
Danehill RH17 .... 66 A3
Ditchling BN6 .... 127 D3
East Grinstead RH19 ...... 9 F1
Eastergate PO20 .... 175 E8
Ferring BN12 .... 200 E6
Funtington PO18 .... 151 A5
Haslemere GU27 .... 27 D7
Henfield BN5 .... 123 E5
Horsted Keynes RH17 .... 65 C5
Hunston PO20 .... 193 A8
Lancing BN15 .... 183 A8
Lodsworth GU28 .... 72 C2
Lower Beeding RH13 ...... 60 D5
Oving PO20 .... 174 C7
Pagham PO21 .... 204 E8
Partridge Green RH13 .... 102 F3
Poynings BN45, BN6 ...... 146 E7
Pyecombe BN45 .... 147 C6
Southwater RH13 .... 57 E1
Southwick BN42, BN43 .. 185 D7
Steyning BN44 .... 143 D4
Street End PO20 .... 192 E3
Tangmere PO20 .... 154 C1
Upper Beeding BN44 ...... 144 A2
Yapton BN18 .... 181 E8
Church Mead Keymer BN6 . 127 B3
Steyning BN44 .... 143 E3
Church Meadow PO18 .... 171 B5
Church Mews PO20 .... 173 D1
Church Path 3 PO10 ...... 169 B8
Church Pl Brighton BN2 .. 188 E4
Church Platt RH17 .... 84 E5

Church St Henfield BN5 .. 123 E5
Liss GU33 .... 45 A6
Littlehampton BN17 .... 198 E5
Petworth GU28 .... 95 F8
Portslade-by-Sea BN41 .. 186 B7
Rudgwick RH12 .... 33 E8
Shoreham-by-Sea BN43 . 184 F7
Steyning BN44 .... 143 D3
Storrington RH20 .... 119 D1
Warnham RH12 .... 35 F8
West Chiltington BN20 ... 99 E1
Church Terr Cowfold RH13 . 81 E2
Henfield BN5 .... 123 E5
Church View PO10 .... 149 D3
Church View Cl RH6 ...... 1 F2
Church Way
Bognor Regis PO21 .... 194 A1
5 Brighton BN2 .... 207 B6
Singleton PO18 .... 133 D7
Worthing BN13 .... 182 A5
Church Way Cl BN13 ...... 182 A5
Church Wlk
Burgess Hill RH15 .... 107 A3
Horley RH6 .... 1 F2
Worthing BN11 .... 182 F2
Church Wood RH20 .... 97 B4
Churcher Rd PO10 .... 149 D4
Churcharm La PO20 .... 192 F2
Churchfield RH20 .... 97 A3
Churchfield Ct GU30 ...... 25 B3
Churchill Ave
Bognor Regis PO21 .... 194 E4
Horsham RH12 .... 36 B3
Churchill Ct Crawley RH10 . 6 A1
1 Rustington BN16 .... 199 C5
Churchill Dr PO10 .... 149 B4
Churchill Ho
Barnham PO22 .... 176 C5
Hove BN3 .... 166 E2
Churchill Ind Est BN15 .. 183 C4
Churchill Par BN16 .... 199 C5
Churchill Sq BN1 .... 204 A2
Churchill Way RH15 .... 107 C2
Churchill Wlk PO21 .... 205 A8
Churchmead Cl PO18 .... 152 F6
Churchside PO19 .... 173 A7
Churchwood Dr PO20 .... 154 D1
Chute Ave BN13 .... 161 E1
Chute Way BN13 .... 181 E8
Cidermill Rd
Cudworth RH12, RH6 ..... 3 F3
Newdigate RH5, RH12 .... 3 F3
Cinder Hill RH19 .... 43 B1
Circle The BN16 .... 200 A4
Circus St BN2 .... 207 A7
Circus St BN2 .... 207 A5
Cissbury Ave BN14 .... 161 F2
Cissbury Cl RH12 .... 37 A6
Cissbury Dr BN14 .... 161 F3
Cissbury Gdns BN14 ...... 162 A2
Cissbury Hill RH11 .... 18 C4
Cissbury Rd
Ferring BN12 .... 200 E3
Hove BN3 .... 187 E7
Worthing BN14 .... 162 C6
Cissbury Way 5 BN43 .... 164 F1
City Bsns Ctr
Chichester PO19 .... 172 F5
Horsham RH13 .... 36 D1
City Fields Way PO20 ..... 154 D2
City Fields Way PO20 ..... 154 D2
Civic Way RH15 .... 107 A3
Claigmar Rd BN16 .... 199 C5
Clair Ct 1 RH16 .... 85 E5
Clair Rd RH16 .... 85 E5
Clammer Hill GU27 .... 27 F8
Clapgate La RH13 .... 34 C5
Clapham Cl BN13 .... 160 F1
Clapham Comm BN13 .... 180 E8
Clapham & Patching CE (C)
Prim Sch BN13 .... 160 E1
Clappers Gate
RH10, RH11 .... 18 D7
Clappers La
Bracklesham PO20 .... 202 C6
Fulking BN5 .... 145 F5
Clappers Meadow GU6 ... 11 A3
Clare Ct RH10 .... 6 C1
Clare Lodge 2 BN16 ...... 199 B5
Clare Wlk BN2 .... 188 D5
Claremont Ct 15 PO21 ... 195 D3
Claremont Way GU29 ..... 92 E7
Clarence Ave BN17 .... 178 C3
Clarence Ct Horley RH6 .. 2 D4
3 Worthing BN11 .... 182 F2
Clarence Dr
2 East Grinstead RH19 . 22 F7
East Preston BN16 .... 199 F6
Clarence Gate 10 PO21 .. 195 D3

Clarence Rd
Bognor Regis PO21 .... 195 D3
Horsham RH11 .... 36 E1
Clarence Sq BN1 .... 207 F5
Clarence Way RH6 .... 2 D4
Clarendon Ho 2 BN3 ...... 187 B7
Clarendon Pl
15 Brighton BN2 .... 188 C4
Portslade-by-Sea BN41 .. 186 C6
Clarendon Rd Hove BN3 . 187 B7
Southwick BN42, BN43 .. 185 D8
Worthing BN14 .... 182 E6
Clarendon Terr 16 BN2 .. 188 D4
Clarendon Villas BN3 ..... 187 B7
Clark Rd RH11 .... 18 A1
Clarke Ave BN3 .... 166 F3
Clarke Ct BN41 .... 186 F6
Clarks Ind Est BN3 .... 187 B8
Clay Hall La RH10 .... 7 C4
Clay La Crossbush BN18 . 158 F1
Fishbourne PO18, PO19 . 172 B7
Storrington RH20 .... 119 A1
West Ashling PO18 .... 151 D1
Claypit La PO18 .... 153 D2
Clays Cl RH19 .... 22 E8
Clays Rd BN44 .... 143 E2
Clayton Ave BN6 .... 126 F3
Clayton Ct PO20 .... 206 C6
Clayton Dr RH15 .... 106 F1
Clayton Hill Crawley RH11 . 18 C4
Pyecombe BN45, BN6 .... 147 D7
Clayton La PO20 .... 202 B7
Clayton Pk BN6 .... 126 E4
Clayton Rd Brighton BN2 . 188 D7
Ditchling BN6 .... 127 C3
Selsey PO20 .... 206 C6
Clayton Way BN3 .... 166 F3
Clayton Wlk BN13 .... 181 D5
Claytons Cnr PO20 .... 191 E5
Clearwater La RH17 .... 87 A3
Clearwaters La RH15 ..... 107 D8
Cleaver's La RH17 .... 62 B2
Clement's Ct 1 BN43 ..... 184 F7
Clerks Acre BN6 .... 124 A4
Clermont Cl 5 BN1 .... 167 E2
Clermont Rd BN1 .... 167 E2
Clermont Terr BN1 .... 167 E2
Cleve Way RH14 .... 77 D8
Cleveland Cl BN13 .... 181 F8
Cleveland Gdns RH15 .... 107 B2
Cleveland Rd
Brighton BN1 .... 168 A1
Chichester PO19 .... 173 B5
Worthing BN13 .... 181 F7
Clevelands
Billingshurst RH14 .... 77 D8
Haywards Heath RH16 ... 85 E6
Clevets The PO21 .... 194 C1
Cliff App BN2 .... 188 F4
Cliff Rd BN2 .... 188 F4
Cliff The BN2 .... 188 F4
Clifton Cl
Chichester PO19 .... 173 B5
4 Worthing BN11 .... 182 C3
Clifton Gdns RH11 .... 182 C3
Clifton Hill BN1 .... 207 F6
Clifton Mews BN1 .... 207 F6
Clifton Pl BN1 .... 187 E6
Clifton Rd
Bognor Regis PO21 .... 195 C4
Brighton BN1 .... 207 F6
Burgess Hill RH15 .... 106 D5
Crawley RH10 .... 19 C5
Littlehampton BN17 .... 198 D4
Worthing BN11 .... 182 C3
Clifton Sq BN1 .... 207 F7
Clifton Terr BN1 .... 207 F6
Cliftonville Ct 6 BN3 ..... 187 B7
Climping Cl BN13 .... 85 D3
Climping Ct 2 BN16 ...... 199 B3
Climping Rd RH11 .... 18 B8
Climping St RH17 .... 197 E7
Clinton Hill RH7 .... 14 E6
Clitheroe Gdns RH10 ..... 18 E5
Clive Ave BN12 .... 181 D2
Clive Way RH10 .... 19 C6
Clivedale BN44 .... 143 D3
Clivedale Gdns BN44 ..... 143 E3
Cliveden Ct BN1 .... 167 E3
Clock Ho PO21 .... 194 E1
Clock Pt BN42 .... 195 E6
Clock Wlk 9 PO21 .... 195 D3
Close The Ardingly RH17 . 64 A8
Ashington RH20 .... 121 A5
Bognor Regis PO21 .... 194 C1
Boxgrove PO18 .... 154 D3
Brighton BN1 .... 167 E5
Burgess Hill RH15 .... 107 C4
East Grinstead RH19 ..... 22 D8
Hassocks BN6 .... 126 F4
Horley RH6 .... 2 C1

Close The Ifold RH14 .... 31 D3
Lancing BN15 .... 183 F4
Liphook GU30 .... 25 C2
Littlehampton BN16 .... 199 D4
Mid Lavant PO18 .... 152 F5
Middleton-on-Sea BN22 ...... 197 A5
Selsey PO20 .... 206 G8
Shoreham-by-Sea BN43 .... 184 FB
Closewalks GU29 .... 92 F7
Clothalls La RH13 .... 102 B5
Clovelly Ave PO22 .... 196 B5
Clovelly Rd Breach PO10 .... 149 F1
Emsworth PO10 .... 169 A8
Clover Ct **2** RH16 .... 85 E4
Clover Field RH12 .... 34 D4
Clover La BN12 .... 200 E5
Clover Way BN41 .... 166 B2
Cloverlands RH10 .... 18 F8
Clovers Cotts RH12 .... 16 F1
Clovers End
  Brighton BN2 .... 168 B7
  Horsham RH12 .... 37 A5
Clovers Way RH12 .... 37 D7
Club Wlk BN16 .... 200 A4
Clun Rd BN17 .... 198 C6
Clyde Cl BN13 .... 181 C8
Clyde Rd
  Bognor Regis PO22 .... 195 F3
  Brighton BN1 .... 207 A8
  Worthing BN13 .... 181 C8
Clydesdale Ave PO19 .... 173 B5
Clydesdale Gdns PO22 ...... 195 A7
Coach & Horses La RH17 .... 66 C6
Coach House Cl PO20 .... 206 E7
Coach House Mews BN11 .. 182 C2
Coach La RH17 .... 66 C6
Coach Rd
  Gatwick Airport,
    North Terminal RH6 .... 5 F8
  Gatwick Airport,
    South Terminal RH6 .... 6 B7
  Shopwyke PO20 .... 173 F7
  Westhampnett
    PO18, PO20 .... 153 E1
Coachmans Dr RH11 .... 18 B2
Coastal Counties Ho **18**
  BN2 .... 207 B6
Coastal Rd BN16 .... 200 C4
Coastguard Cotts BN16 .... 200 A4
Coastguard La PO20 .... 190 A1
Coastguard Par PO21 .... 194 D1
Coastguard Rd BN17 .... 198 D3
Coastguards Cotts PO20 .. 190 A1
Coates Ct **11** BN42 .... 185 E7
Coates La RH20 .... 116 D8
Cob Cl RH10 .... 21 C8
Cob Cl RH11 .... 42 B1
Cob Wlk RH11 .... 18 A6
Cobbett Cl RH10 .... 19 C8
Cobbetts Mead RH16 .... 86 B3
Cobblers RH12 .... 34 D4
Cobbles Cres RH10 .... 18 E7
Cobblewood PO10 .... 149 B3
Cobden Ho GU29 .... 92 E6
Cobden La GU27 .... 27 D7
Cobden Rd Brighton BN2 .... 92 E7
  Midhurst GU29 .... 92 E7
  Worthing BN11 .... 182 C2
Cobham Cl BN18 .... 176 F2
Cobham Way RH10 .... 6 B4
Cobnor Cl RH11 .... 17 F4
Cobton Dr BN3 .... 167 A3
Cockhaise Cotts RH16 .... 87 A8
Cocking Hill GU29, PO18 .. 112 C5
Cohen Cl PO20 .... 175 D5
Cokeham Ct BN15 .... 183 C7
Cokeham Gdns BN15 .... 183 C6
Cokeham La BN15 .... 183 C6
Cokeham Rd BN15 .... 183 C6
Colbourne Ave BN3 .... 168 D2
Colbourne Rd BN3 .... 187 E7
Colchester Vale RH18 .... 23 E2
Colchins RH15 .... 106 F1
Coldean Cty Inf Sch BN1 .. 168 D6
Coldean Cty Jun Sch
  BN1 .... 168 D6
Coldean La BN1 .... 168 E6
Coldharbour Farm Rd
  PO10 .... 149 B2
Coldharbour La BN13 .... 160 D1
Coldwaltham La RH15 ...... 107 D2
Cole Cl RH11 .... 18 B1
Colebrook Cl BN11 .... 182 F3
Colebrook La RH20 .... 117 B5
Colebrook Rd
  Brighton BN2 .... 167 D4
  Littlehampton BN17 .... 178 C3
  Southwick BN42 .... 185 F7
Coleman Ave BN3 .... 186 E7
Coleman St BN2 .... 207 B7
Colemans Hatch Rd RH18 .. 44 E5

Coleridge Cl
  Horsham RH12 .... 36 E6
  Worthing BN12 .... 181 B3
Coleridge Cres BN12 .... 181 A3
Coleridge Rd BN12 .... 181 B3
Coleridge St BN3 .... 187 A8
Colet Rd RH10 .... 18 D3
Colgate Cl Brighton BN2 .. 188 F6
  Crawley RH11 .... 18 B8
Colgate Cty Prim Sch
  RH13 .... 38 C6
Colhook Ind Pk GU28 .... 51 D1
Colindale Rd BN12 .... 200 E6
Colindale Rd N BN12 .... 200 E6
Coll of St Barnabas RH7 ...... 9 FB
Coll of Tech Three Bridges
  CE (C) Prim Sch PO18 .. 109 B2
Compass Brow La RH13 .... 37 A3
Compass La RH12, RH13 .. 36 F3
Conbar Ave BN16 .... 199 C6
Concorde Cl RH20 .... 119 F3
Condor Way RH15 .... 106 E3
Conduit Mead PO19 .... 173 C8
Coney Cl Crawley RH11 ...... 18 B8
  East Wittering PO20 .... 201 F6
Coney Croft RH12 .... 37 B5
Coney Rd PO20 .... 201 F6
Coney Six PO20 .... 201 F6
Coneyhurst Rd RH14 .... 77 FB
Congreve Rd BN14 .... 182 E4
Conifer Dr PO18 .... 150 E2
Conifer Cl RH12 .... 37 B6
Conifers Sch GU29 .... 71 A1
Conigar Rd PO10 .... 149 B3
Coniston Cl
  Bognor Regis PO22 .... 196 B6
  Crawley RH11 .... 17 D4
  Horsham RH12 .... 37 B6
  Lancing BN15 .... 183 C6
Coniston Ct **9** BN3 .... 187 D7
Coniston Rd BN16 .... 181 C4
Coniston Way BN16 .... 179 A3
Connaught Ave BN43 ...... 184 E8
Connaught Cty Jun Sch
  BN17 .... 198 D5
Connaught Gdns RH11 .... 18 D8
Connaught Ho **6** PO21 .. 195 C2
Connaught Rd Hove BN1 .. 187 A6
  Littlehampton BN17 .... 198 D5
Connaught Ctr Brighton
  Coll of Tech & F Ed
  BN3 .... 187 A6
Connaught Terr BN3 .... 187 B7
Consort Way
  Burgess Hill RH15 .... 106 E2
  Horley RH6 .... 2 A3
Consort Way E RH6 .... 2 B2
Constable Dr PO20 .... 206 F7
Constable Rd RH10 .... 18 F2
Control Tower Rd RH6 .... 5 D6
Convent Ct PO10 .... 169 A8
Convent La PO10 .... 169 B8
Conway Ct **1** BN3 .... 187 B7
Conway Dr BN12 .... 205 A8
Conway Pl BN3 .... 187 B7
Conway St BN3 .... 187 B8
Cook Rd Crawley RH10 ...... 18 F4
  Horsham RH12 .... 36 D6
Cook's Pond Rd GU30 .... 69 A7
Cooks Cl RH12 .... 33 A8
Cooks La
  Breach PO10, PO18 .... 150 A1
  Walderton PO18 .... 130 D2
Cooks Mead RH12 .... 16 D7
Cooks Meadow RH12 .... 16 D7
Cooksbridge Rd BN2 .... 188 E6
Coolham La PO10 .... 17 F6
Coolham Dr BN2 .... 188 E7
Coolham Rd RH13, RH20 .. 100 C5
Coolhurst La RH13 .... 37 A1
Coombe Cl
  Billingshurst RH14 .... 55 D1
  Crawley RH11 .... 5 D1
Coombe Cres RH20 .... 138 A7
Coombe Dr BN44 .... 143 D2
Coombe Hall La RH19 ...... 22 D6
Coombe Hill RH14 .... 55 D1
Coombe Hill Rd RH19 ...... 22 D6
Coombe La BN18 .... 159 B7
Coombe Lea **22** BN3 ...... 187 C6
Coombe Rd Brighton BN2 .. 168 D1
  Steyning BN44 .... 143 C2
Coombe Rise BN14 .... 162 A2
Coombe Road Cty Prim Sch
  BN2 .... 168 D1
Coombe Terr BN2 .... 168 C1
Coombelands La RH20 ...... 98 A5
Coombers RH17 .... 41 A1
Coombes Rd BN15 .... 86 B5
Coombes Rd BN15 .... 164 B4

Coomes Way BN17 .... 178 D4
Cooper Row RH10 .... 18 B3
Cooper St PO19 .... 173 A6
Coopers Cl RH15 .... 107 C5
Coopers Cl The RH15 .... 56 D4
Coopers La RH12 .... 123 F4
Coopers Wood RH17 .... 39 C3
Coos La RH17 .... 61 A6
Cootes Ave RH10 .... 36 A3
Cootes Cotts RH20 .... 116 D2
Coots La PO22 .... 196 F5
Cootham Rd RH20 .... 119 B2
Copeland Rd PO22 .... 196 A4
Copestake Dr RH15 .... 107 D3
Copnall Way RH12 .... 36 C2
Copper Cl BN6 .... 106 C4
Copper Hall Cl **4** BN16 .. 199 E6
Copperfield RH12 .... 36 B4
Copperfields RH13 .... 59 B8
Copperfields Manor RH13 .. 59 B8
Coppets Wood **6** BN16 .. 199 B4
Coppice La PO20 .... 206 D8
Coppice Way RH16 .... 85 D3
Coppice Wlk RH10 .... 19 A7
Coppins Ct PO22 .... 196 F5
Copsale Rd RH13 .... 80 D6
Copse The
  Crawley Down RH10 .... 21 BB
  East Grinstead RH19 .... 10 A3
  East Liss GU33 .... 45 C4
  Horsham RH12 .... 36 F6
Copse Cres RH11 .... 18 C7
Copse Hill BN1 .... 167 D5
Copse La Horley RH6 .... 2 D4
  Walberton BN18 .... 156 D2
Copse Rd GU27 .... 26 D5
Copse The
  Chichester PO19 .... 173 A8
  Haywards Heath RH16 ...... 86 B5
  Southwater RH13 .... 57 F2
Copse View BN16 .... 199 F6
Copthorne Bank RH10 ...... 7 C4
Copthorne CE (C) Sch
  RH10 .... 7 B3
Copthorne Cl BN13 .... 182 A8
Copthorne Common Rd
  RH10 .... 7 C5
Copthorne Ct **2** BN3 ...... 187 C6
Copthorne Hill BN13 .... 181 F7
Copthorne Rd
  Copthorne RH10 .... 6 F1
  Felbridge RH10, RH19 ...... 8 D4
Copthorne Sch Trust Ltd
  RH10 .... 7 E3
Copthorne Way
  Bognor Regis PO21 .... 194 D4
  Copthorne RH10 .... 6 F2
Copyhold Hill GU27 .... 49 C8
Copyhold La
  Cuckfield RH17 .... 85 A4
  Haywards Heath RH16 ...... 63 E2
Copyhold Rd RH19 .... 22 D8
Copthorne Ho RH14 .... 55 E6
Corbishley Gn PO22 .... 195 C6
Corbishley Rd PO22 .... 195 C6
Corby Cl RH11 .... 17 E3
Corfe Cl Southwater RH13 .. 58 A1
  Worthing BN13 .... 181 B5
Cormorant Way PO20 ...... 202 A6
Corner Garth BN12 .... 200 F5
Cornfield Cl BN17 .... 178 E3
Cornfield Sch BN17 .... 178 E3
Cornford Cl RH15 .... 106 E5
Cornwall Ct **2** BN3 .... 187 C7
Cornwall Gdns
  Brighton BN1 .... 167 E2
  6 East Grinstead RH19 .. 22 F8
  Littlehampton BN17 .... 198 D6
Cornwall Ho BN1 .... 167 E2
Cornwall Rd BN16 .... 198 D6
Coronation Bldgs BN11 .. 183 A3
Coronation Homelets **9**
  BN11 .... 183 B3
Coronation Rd
  East Grinstead RH19 .... 22 E7
  South Hayling PO11 .... 189 A1
Coronation St **7** BN2 .... 188 C7
Coronet Cl RH11 .... 19 E7
Coronet The RH6 .... 2 C1
Corsletts Ave RH12 .... 35 D3
Cortis Ave BN14 .... 182 C5
Corunna Rd RH13 .... 36 F2
Cosstick Rd BN11 .... 182 B7
Costells Edge RH17 .... 86 F3
Cot La PO18 .... 170 D6

Cote St BN13 .... 161 C1
Cotland Rd PO20 .... 206 F6
Cotsford RH11 .... 39 B7
Cotswold Cl Crawley RH11 .. 18 B6
  Worthing BN13 .... 181 E8
Cotswold Ct RH11 .... 36 E2
Cotswold Pl **7** BN2 ...... 188 F5
Cotswold Rd BN13 .... 181 E7
Cotswold Way BN16 .... 200 A6
Cotswolds The BN42 .... 185 E7
Cottage Bush Cl RH14 .... 166 C2
Cottage Cl
  Bognor Regis PO21 .... 194 C2
  Horsham RH12 .... 37 B8
Cottage Homes BN6 .... 127 E6
Cottage Pl RH10 .... 7 E3
Cottenham Rd BN11 .... 182 F3
Cottesmore Golf Club
  RH11 .... 38 E7
Cottesmore Sch RH11 ...... 19 F8
Cottesmore St Mary's RC
  Prim Sch BN2 .... 187 D8
Cottingham Ave RH12 ...... 36 D7
Cotton Dr PO10 .... 149 A3
Cotton Wlk RH11 .... 18 A1
Cottrells The BN16 .... 179 F5
Coulstock Rd BN16 .... 106 C4
Council Cotts
  Charlwood RH6 .... 4 C6
  Clapham BN13 .... 160 E1
  Crosspost RH17 .... 83 B1
  High Cross BN6 .... 125 A7
  Loxwood RH14 .... 32 A2
  Plaistow RH14 .... 30 D3
  Sayers Common BN6 ...... 105 E3
  Southwater RH13 .... 79 F7
  Sutton RH20 .... 115 F3
  Twineham Green RH17 .... 105 B6
  Warningcamp BN18 .... 158 F2
  Wepham BN18 .... 159 A5
Countisbury Cl PO21 .... 194 F3
Countryman La RH13 ...... 101 B7
County Hall RH10 .... 18 E5
County Oak Ave BN1 .... 168 B6
County Oak La RH11 .... 5 D3
County Oak Ret Pk RH11 .. 5 D2
County Oak Way RH11 ...... 5 D3
Courcels BN2 .... 188 E3
Court Barn La PO20 .... 191 E6
Court Cl Brighton BN1 .... 167 E7
  East Grinstead RH19 .... 9 F1
Court Cres RH19 .... 9 F1
Court Est The **8** BN11 .. 183 B3
Court Farm Rd BN3 .... 167 A2
Court Lodge Cty Fst Sch RH6 1 F3
Court Lodge Rd RH6 .... 1 F3
Court Meadow Sch RH17 .. 85 A8
Court Ordge PO21 .... 194 A1
Court The PO21 .... 194 A1
Courtfields Ho **4** PO21 .. 195 B3
Courtfields RH15 .... 183 D5
Courtlands
  12 Haywards Heath RH16 .. 207 B6
  Haywards Heath RH16 .... 85 E3
Courtlands Cl BN12 .... 181 E1
Courtlands Way
  Bognor Regis PO22 .... 196 C6
  Worthing BN11, BN12 .... 181 F1
Courtmead Rd RH17 .... 84 F6
Courtney Gate BN3 .... 187 B5
Courtney King Ct **8** BN2 .. 188 C5
Courtney King Ho **1** BN2 .. 188 D4
Courts Hill Rd GU27 .... 27 B6
Courts Mount Rd GU27 .... 27 B6
Courtup Hill RH13 .... 80 E6
Courtwick La BN17 .... 178 C4
Courtwick Rd BN17 .... 178 C3
Courtyard The
  Bognor Regis PO21 .... 194 F2
  Chichester PO19 .... 172 F4
  Crawley RH11 .... 37 E4
  East Grinstead RH19 .... 10 B1
  Haywards Heath RH16 .... 64 C3
  1 Horsham RH10 .... 18 D5
  Worthing BN13 .... 180 A5
  Worthing BN13 .... 182 B3
Cousins Way RH20 .... 98 C3
Cove Rd BN16 .... 199 B4
Coventry Cl PO21 .... 194 D4
Coventry St BN1 .... 187 E8
Coverdale Ct RH19 .... 9 C3
Coverdale Ct RH10 .... 18 E7
Covert Mead RH17 .... 61 B7
Covey The RH10 .... 19 E8
Covington Rd PO10 .... 149 D5
Cow La Sidlesham PO20 .. 203 D7
Cow Sharting GU31 .... 89 C3
Cowdens Cl BN3 .... 166 D4

Cowdown La PO18 .... 108 F4
Cowdray GU29 .... 93 A8
Cowdray Cl Crawley RH10 .. 19 C5
  Rustington BN16 .... 179 B3
  Worthing BN12 .... 181 D1
Cowdray Ct **1** BN3 .... 187 D7
Cowdray Dr
  Rustington BN16 .... 179 B3
  Worthing BN12 .... 181 D1
Cowdray Park Golf Course
  GU29 .... 71 D2
Cowdray Rd GU29 .... 71 A2
Cowfold Cl RH11 .... 17 F3
Cowfold Rd Brighton BN2 .. 188 E5
  Cowfold RH13 .... 80 D2
Cowley Dr **1** BN15 .... 183 F5
Cowper Rd BN11 .... 182 B2
Cowper St BN3 .... 187 A7
Cox Gr RH15 .... 106 E5
Cox Green Rd RH12 .... 12 C2
Cox Ho RH12 .... 36 B2
Coxcomb Wlk RH11 .... 18 A4
Coxes Rd PO20 .... 206 D6
Coxham La BN44 .... 143 C4
Crabbet Rd RH10 .... 19 B2
Crabden La PO8 .... 128 A8
Crablands PO20 .... 206 D7
Crablands Cl PO20 .... 206 C7
Crabtree Ave RH11 .... 168 B5
Crabtree Gate RH13 ...... 81 F5
Crabtree La BN15 .... 183 D6
Crabtree Lodge **2** BN15 . 183 D6
Crabtree Rd RH11 .... 18 C7
Cradock Pl BN13 .... 181 E8
Craggits La BN5 .... 123 E5
Craigans RH11 .... 18 A5
Craignair Ave RH11 .... 167 F7
Craigweil La PO21 .... 194 E2
Craigwell La PO21 .... 194 E2
Craigwell Manor PO21 .... 194 D1
Cranborne Wlk RH10 ..... 18 F4
Cranbourne Cl RH6 .... 2 B5
Cranbourne St BN1 .... 207 F5
Cranbrook **13** BN2 .... 207 B6
Crane St PO19 .... 173 A6
Cranford Gdns PO21 ...... 195 C4
Cranleigh Ct **6** BN12 ..... 182 C2
Cranleigh Rd BN14 .... 182 C5
Cranley Ct BN3 .... 186 D7
Cranmer Ave BN3 .... 166 F1
Cranmer Rd BN3 .... 182 A3
Cranmer Wlk RH10 .... 19 C5
Cranston Rd RH19 .... 9 F2
Cranworth Rd BN11 .... 182 B3
Craven Rd Brighton BN2 . 188 D6
  Crawley RH10 .... 19 B5
Crawford Gdns RH13 ..... 36 E4
Crawford Way RH19 ...... 9 F3
Crawley Ave Crawley RH10 .. 6 C1
  Crawley RH10, RH11 ..... 18 A6
Crawley Coll of Tech RH10 . 18 E6
Crawley Coll (West Green
  Annexe) RH11 .... 18 C7
Crawley Down CE (C)
  Prim Sch RH10 .... 21 B8
Crawley Down Rd RH19 .. 8 F4
Crawley Hospl (General)
  RH11 .... 18 C6
Crawley La Balcombe RH17 . 40 E4
  Crawley RH10 .... 19 C7
Crawley Rd Brighton BN1 . 168 D6
  Crawley RH11 .... 17 B1
  Horsham RH12 .... 37 B5
Crawley Sta RH10 .... 18 E5
Crawters Cl RH10 .... 18 F3
Cray La RH20 .... 98 D5
Cray's La PO20 .... 120 C8
Crayford Rd BN2 .... 168 D1
Creasys Dr RH11 .... 18 B1
Crede Cl PO18 .... 171 C5
Crede La PO18 .... 171 C5
Creek End Emsworth PO10 . 169 B7
  Fishbourne PO19 .... 172 B6
Crescent Cl RH15 .... 107 B3
Crescent Mansions BN2 .. 207 B8
Crescent Pl BN2 .... 188 C4
Crescent Rd
  Bognor Regis PO21 ...... 195 C3
  Brighton BN2 .... 188 B8
  Burgess Hill RH15 .... 107 B3
  East Grinstead RH19 .... 9 D1
  Worthing BN11 .... 182 C2
Crescent Rise RH20 ...... 120 A3
Crescent The
  Bognor Regis PO22 ...... 196 A4
  Bognor Regis PO21 ...... 205 A8
  Brighton BN2 .... 168 E2
  Cootham RH20 .... 119 A2

Crescent The
  East Wittering PO20 ..... 201 E7
  Felcourt RH19 .... 9 C8
  Horley RH6 .... 6 B8
  Horsham RH12 .... 36 A2
  Keymer BN6 .... 127 B3
  Lancing BN15 .... 183 E5
  Littlehampton BN16 ..... 199 B5
  Southbourne PO10 ...... 169 F8
  Southwick BN42 .... 185 F8
  Steyning BN44 .... 143 D2
  West Kingston BN16 .... 200 A4
Crescent Way
  Burgess Hill RH15 ...... 107 A3
  Horley RH6 .... 2 A1
Crescenta Wlk PO21 ..... 195 A3
Crespin Way BN1 .... 168 C2
Cressey Way PO19 .... 153 A1
Crest Way BN1 .... 166 B3
Crestway Par **1** BN1 .... 168 C2
Crestway The BN1 .... 168 C2
Crewdson Rd RH6 .... 2 B3
Cricket Ct RH19 .... 9 E3
Cricket Field Rd RH12 ... 36 B1
Cricketers Par BN14 ..... 182 D6
Crimbourne La RH14 ..... 75 D3
Cripland Cl RH16 .... 86 B6
Cripplecrutch Hill GU8 .. 28 F5
Cripplegate La RH13 ..... 80 A8
Cripps Ho RH11 .... 18 A2
Cripps La BN44 .... 143 E3
Critchel's La PO20 .... 192 C1
Critchfield Rd PO18 ...... 171 B5
Critchmere Dr PO20 ..... 175 F7
Critchmere Hill GU27 .... 26 E7
Critchmere La GU27 ..... 26 E6
Critchmere Vale GU27 ... 26 E6
Croat Ho PO20 .... 206 D7
Crockford Rd PO10 ...... 149 D4
Crockham Cl RH11 .... 18 C4
Crockhurst Hill
  BN13, BN14 .... 181 F8
Croft Ave BN42 .... 185 F7
Croft Cl BN41 .... 166 A3
Croft La BN5 .... 123 E4
Croft Mead PO19 .... 153 A2
Croft Rd Brighton BN1 .. 167 D4
  Selsey PO20 .... 206 D7
Croft The
  Bognor Regis PO21 .... 194 F5
  Cocking GU29 .... 112 D8
  Crawley RH11 .... 18 A6
  East Preston BN16 ..... 200 A5
  Hassocks BN6 .... 126 F5
  Lodsworth GU28 .... 72 B3
  Southwick BN42 .... 185 E8
  Yapton BN18 .... 176 F4
Croft Villas BN5 .... 123 E5
Croft Way
  Bognor Regis PO22 .... 196 C6
  Horsham RH12 .... 36 A3
  Selsey PO20 .... 206 D7
Crofters Wood BN44 .... 143 F2
Cromleigh Way BN42 ... 165 E2
Crompton Fields RH10 .. 5 E1
Crompton Way RH10 ... 5 E1
Cromwell Cl **8** BN3 ..... 187 D7
Cromwell Ct **1** RH19 ... 22 F7
Cromwell Rd
  Burgess Hill RH15 ..... 106 F3
  Hove BN3 .... 187 C7
Cromwell St BN2 .... 188 C7
Crooked La PO20 .... 191 E4
Crookthorn La BN17 ... 197 E8
Crosbie Cl PO19 .... 172 F3
Crosby Cl BN13 .... 181 D6
Croshaw Cl BN15 .... 183 D5
Cross Colwood La RH17 . 82 F5
Cross Gates BN18 ...... 139 A7
Cross Keys RH10, RH11 . 19 B6
Cross La Barns Green RH13 . 57 A1
  Burstow RH6 .... 2 E4
  Findon BN14 .... 161 E5
Cross Oak La RH1, RH6 . 2 C7
Cross Rd
  Rustington BN16 .... 199 E5
  Southwick BN42 .... 185 D8
Cross St Brighton BN1 .. 207 A7
  Hove BN1, BN3 .... 187 D5
  Worthing BN11 .... 182 C3
Crossbush La BN18 ..... 158 E1
Crossbush Rd
  Bognor Regis PO22 .... 196 C4
  Brighton BN2 .... 188 E6
Crossfield GU27 .... 49 B5
Crossman Ct RH11 ..... 18 B1
Crosspath RH10 .... 18 E7
Crosspost RH17 .... 83 B1
Crosspost Ind Pk RH17 . 83 B1
Crossroad Cl BN42 .... 185 D8

Crossway RH6 .... 5 F8
Crossway The
  Brighton BN1 .... 168 B2
  Portslade-by-Sea BN41 . 166 A2
Crossways Crawley RH10 . 19 A7
  Easebourne GU29 ...... 71 A2
  East Preston BN16 ..... 180 B3
  Littlehampton BN17 ... 172 C3
  Middleton-on-Sea PO22 . 196 F5
  Navant Hill GU38 ...... 50 E4
  West Chiltington Common
    RH20 .... 119 D7
  Littlehampton BN17 ... 178 C3
Crossways Ave
  East Grinstead RH19 .. 9 C1
  Worthing BN11 .... 181 B4
Crossways Cl RH10 ..... 18 F7
Crossways Cotts
  Alfold Crossways GU6 . 11 A3
  Poynings BN45 .... 146 C6
  Tisman's Common RH12 . 32 F6
Crossways Ct GU27 ..... 49 B6
Crossways Pk RH20 .... 119 D7
Crossways The
  Hassocks BN6 .... 126 C4
  Littlehampton BN17 ... 178 C3
Crouch Cross La PO18 .. 154 D3
Crouch Hill BN5 .... 123 F7
Crouchlands Farm RH17 . 84 E8
Crowberry Cl RH11 ..... 18 A2
Crowborough Dr BN12 . 181 B2
Crowhurst Cl RH10 ..... 19 E6
Crowhurst Keep RH10 . 19 E6
Crowhurst Rd BN11 .... 168 C7
Crown Bldgs BN15 ..... 183 C4
Crown Ct BN16 .... 200 A4
Crown Gdns BN1 .... 207 F5
Crown Hill **4** BN2 ...... 188 C6
Crown Point Ho BN6 ... 126 F4
Crown Rd
  Portslade-by-Sea BN41 . 186 A8
  Shoreham-by-Sea BN43 . 185 B8
Crown St BN1 .... 207 F5
Crowsbury Cl PO10 .... 149 A3
Croxton La RH16 .... 86 B6
Croy Cl PO19 .... 172 E4
Crundens Cnr **5** BN16 . 199 E6
Crutchfield La RH6 ..... 1 B5
Crypt La GU29 .... 77 A2
Cuckfield Ct RH11 ..... 17 F3
Cuckfield Cres BN13 ... 181 F6
Cuckfield La RH17 ..... 61 B1
Cuckfield Rd
  Burgess Hill RH15, RH17 . 106 E7
  Goddards' Gn BN6, RH17 . 106 A4
  Slough Green RH17 .... 62 A2
Cuckmere Cres RH11 .. 17 F5
Cuckmere Way BN1 ... 168 C5
Cudlow Ave BN16 ..... 199 C5
Cudlow Gdn
  Rustington BN16 ...... 199 C4
  Rustington BN16 ...... 199 C5
Cudworth La RH5 ...... 3 E8
Cuffs Hill RH10 .... 19 E2
Culimore Cl PO20 ..... 201 E7
Culimore Rd PO20 .... 201 E7
Culpepper RH15 .... 106 E4
Culpepper Cl BN2 ..... 168 D2
Culross Ave BN16 ..... 85 D5
Culver Ct RH15 .... 183 E6
Culver Rd
  Bognor Regis PO22 ... 196 A4
  Lancing BN15 .... 183 E6
Culvers GU31 .... 89 D3
Cumberland Ave
  New Brighton PO10 ... 149 B4
  Worthing BN11 .... 181 D5
Cumberland Cres BN16 . 179 F5
Cumberland Dr BN1 .. 167 E2
Cumberland Lodge
  8 BN1 .... 167 E2
Cumberland Rd
  Angmering BN16 ...... 180 A6
  Brighton BN1 .... 167 E2
Cumbernauld Wlk RH12 . 17 E2
Cumbrian Cl BN13 .... 181 E7
Cumnor House Sch RH17 . 66 B5
Cunliffe Cl PO20 .... 190 C2
Cunningham Gdns PO22 . 196 C5
Curbey Cl RH20 .... 99 D1
Curlescroft PO21 ...... 194 F2
Curlew Cl PO10 .... 169 A7
Curlews The BN43 .... 185 A8
Curteys Wlk RH11 .... 18 A3
Curvins Way BN15 .... 183 F7
Curwen Pl BN1 .... 167 E3
Curzon Ave RH12 ..... 36 B3
Curzon Cl BN13 .... 181 F6
Cutfield Cl PO19 ...... 172 F3
Cuthbert Rd BN2 ..... 188 C5
Cuttinglye La RH10 ... 8 A1

Cuttinglye Rd RH10 ... 8 C2
Cygnet Wlk PO22 ..... 195 B6
Cygnets The BN43 .... 184 F8
Cylinders The GU27 ... 49 B5
Cymens Ora PO20 .... 203 D8
Cypress Ave BN12, BN13 . 181 C5
Cypress Cl **12** BN43 ... 164 F1
Cypress Way PO21 ... 194 D1
Cyprus Rd RH11 ...... 107 A3
D'Aubigny Rd BN2 .... 188 B8
Dacre Gdns BN3 ...... 164 B7
Dagbrook La BN5 ..... 123 E3
Dagmar St BN11 ...... 182 E3
Dairy Farm BN12 ..... 181 A3
Dairy La
  Maudlin PO18, PO20 . 153 F1
  Walberton BN18 ...... 156 D1
Dairyfields RH11 ...... 18 A5
Daisycroft The BN5 .. 123 F4
Dakin Cl RH10 .... 19 C2
Dakins The RH19 .... 22 E8
Dale Ave Brighton BN1 . 167 F5
  Keymer BN6 .... 127 A3
Dale Cl RH12 .... 36 F5
Dale Copse GU27 ... 49 B6
Dale Cres BN1 .... 167 F6
Dale Dr BN1 .... 168 A6
Dale Hill BN45 .... 172 A8
Dale Rd Forest Row RH18 . 23 F1
  Worthing BN11 .... 183 B4
Dale View Haslemere GU27 . 26 F5
  Hove BN3 .... 166 D2
Dale View Gdns BN13 . 181 C5
Dalewood Gdns
  Burgess Hill RH15 .... 107 C2
  Crawley RH10 .... 18 F8
Dallaway Gdns RH19 . 9 E1
Dallaway Rd PO19 ... 173 B4
Dallington Rd BN3 ... 186 F8
Dalloway Rd BN18 ... 157 F1
Dalton Cl RH11 ...... 18 B1
Daltons Pl BN18 .... 158 A2
Dame School Ct PO18 . 153 A5
Damer's Bridge GU28 . 95 F8
Damian Way BN6 .... 127 B4
Dampier Wlk RH11 .. 18 B1
Danby Ct PO10 ...... 149 C2
Danefield Rd PO20 .. 206 C6
Danehill CE Prim Sch
  RH17 .... 66 B4
Danehill Rd RH15 ... 65 E5
Danehill Rd BN2 .... 188 F5
Danehurst **6** PO21 . 195 B3
Danehurst Cres RH13 . 36 F2
Daniel Cl BN15 ...... 183 F7
Dankton Gdns BN15 . 183 B7
Dankton La BN15 ... 183 B7
Danley La GU27 .... 26 A3
Danny Sheldon Ho **14**
  BN2 .... 188 C4
Danworth La BN6 ... 106 B3
Dapper's La BN16 .. 180 A7
Darcey Dr BN1 ...... 168 A6
Darenth Way RH6 .. 1 F6
Dark La PO21 .... 194 F1
Darleydale RH11 ... 18 C3
Dart Cl BN13 .... 181 D8
Dart Ct RH19 .... 10 A3
Dartmouth Cl BN2 . 188 F8
Dartmouth Cres BN2 . 168 F1
Darwin Cl RH12 .... 36 F4
Daux Ave RH14 .... 77 D6
Daux Hill RH12 .... 36 B6
Daux Rd RH14 ..... 77 D7
Dauxwood Cl RH14 . 77 D6
Davenport Cl **5** BN11 . 181 F2
Davenport Rd PO22 . 196 B4
Davey Dr BN1 ...... 168 B1
Davids Cl PO21 .... 194 F5
Davies Cl **11** BN11 . 182 A1
Davigdor Cty Inf Sch BN3 . 187 D6
Davigdor Rd BN3 .. 187 E7
Davis Cl RH11 ..... 18 A1
Davison CE Girls' High Sch
  BN11 .... 182 F4
Davits Dr BN17 .... 199 A6
Davys Ct PO18 .... 151 A5
Dawes Ave BN11 .. 182 F3
Dawes Cl BN11 .... 182 F3
Dawlish Cl BN2 .... 188 F1
Dawn Cl BN44 ..... 144 B1
Dawn Cres BN44 .. 144 A1
Dawson Terr BN2 . 188 C6
Dawtrey Cl BN16 .. 199 E6
Dawtrey Rd GU28 . 95 F7
Daynes Way RH15 . 106 E1
Days La PO18 ...... 155 F3
De Braose Way BN44 . 143 E2
De Courcel Rd BN2 . 188 E3
De La Warr Rd RH19 . 9 F1

De Montfort Rd BN2 .. 188 C7
Deacon Trad Est RH14 . 182 F5
Deacon Way BN14 ... 182 F5
Deacons Dr BN41 ... 166 C2
Deacons Way BN44 . 144 B2
Deak's La RH17 ..... 84 B6
Dean Cl
  Littlehampton BN17 . 178 C3
  Portslade-by-Sea BN41 . 166 C2
Dean Gdns BN41 ... 166 C2
Dean La
  Finchdean PO8, PO9 . 128 F5
  Upperton GU28 ...... 73 A1
Dean St BN1 .... 187 E5
Dean Way RH20 ... 119 C2
Deanland Rd RH17 . 41 A1
Deanway BN3 ...... 167 B3
Decoy Dr BN16 .... 179 F7
Decoy Rd BN14 .... 182 F5
Dedisham Cl RH10 . 19 A5
Dedisham Sch RH12 . 34 C6
Deep Dene GU27 .. 26 E6
Deepdene Cl PO22 . 197 A5
Deepdene Sch BN3 . 186 D7
Deepfields RH6 .... 1 F5
Deer Park La PO20 . 206 B8
Deer Pk BN5 .... 123 E6
Deerswood Cl
  Crawley RH11 ...... 18 B7
  Worthing BN13 .... 181 B5
Deerswood Ct RH11 . 18 A7
Deerswood Lower Sch
  RH11 .... 18 A6
Deerswood Rd RH11 . 18 A6
Deerswood Upper Sch
  RH11 .... 18 A6
Deeside Ave PO19 . 172 B7
Deeside The BN1 .. 168 A7
Defiance Pl PO22 .. 196 C4
Delfryn BN41 ...... 165 F3
Dell Cl GU27 .... 27 A2
Dell La RH14 ...... 179 F4
Dell La RH14 ..... 77 D8
Dell Quay Rd PO20 . 172 B2
Dell The
  Bognor Regis PO22 . 195 A6
  East Grinstead RH19 . 10 B3
  Haywards Heath RH16 . 85 C5
  Horley RH6 .... 2 A4
  Wrays RH6 .... 1 C6
Delling Cl PO18 ... 171 B6
Delling La PO18 ... 171 C6
Dellney Ave RH16 . 85 F3
Delta Bglws RH6 . 2 A1
Delta Dr RH6 ..... 2 A1
Delta Ho RH6 .... 2 A1
Dempsey Rd **3** PO19 . 153 A2
Den Ave PO20 ... 195 D3
Denbigh Rd GU27 . 27 D5
Denchers Plat RH11 . 5 D1
Dene Cl Haslemere GU27 . 27 C6
  Horley RH6 .... 1 E5
Dene The Hove BN3 . 166 D3
  Southwater RH13 . 58 A2
Dene Tye RH10 ... 19 D2
Dene Vale BN1 ... 167 D5
Denecroft BN1 ... 167 D5
Deneside BN1 ... 167 D5
Deneway The
  Brighton BN1 .... 167 D4
  Lancing BN15 ... 183 C6
Denham Cl PO22 . 196 E5
Denham Rd BN6, RH15 . 106 D3
Denison Ct **3** PO19 . 172 F3
Denman's Cl RH16 . 86 A6
Denman's La RH16 . 86 A7
Denmans RH10 ... 19 D7
Denmans Gdns BN18, PO20 . 155 C9
Denmans La BN18, PO20 . 155 E2
Denmark Rd BN41 . 186 C7
Denmark Terr BN1 . 187 E6
Denmark Villas BN3 . 187 B2
Denne Par RH12, RH13 . 36 C1
Denne Rd Crawley RH11 . 18 D5
  Horsham RH12 ... 36 C1
Dennis Ct RH20 .. 98 C2
Dennis Hobden Cl BN2 . 168 E1
Dennis Way GU33 . 45 C8
Denny's Cl PO20 . 206 E8
Denshare Rd PO20 . 206 E8
Denshire Dr RH20 . 119 E3
Denshale PO21 ... 195 A3
Denton Cl BN12 .. 181 B3
Denton Dr BN1 ... 168 A6
Departures Rd RH6 . 5 FB
Depot Rd Crawley RH11 . 5 D1
  Horsham RH13 ... 36 C1
Derby Ct **3** BN3 .. 187 E7
Derby Pl **6** BN2 .. 207 B5
Derby Rd GU27 ... 27 B7
Derek Ave BN3, BN41 . 186 D6

Derek Ho BN3 ..... 186 F6
Derek Rd BN15 ..... 183 E8
Derwent CI Crawley RH11 ... 17 F5
Horsham RH12 ..... 37 B6
Lancing BN15 ..... 183 C5
Littlehampton BN16 ..... 179 A3
Tangmere PO20 ..... 154 D2
Derwent Ct BN2 ..... 207 F6
Derwent Dr BN12, BN13 .. 181 D5
Der wr PO22 ..... 196 B6
Desmond Anderson Cty
Fst Sch RH10 ..... 18 E2
Desmond Anderson Cty
Mid Sch RH10 ..... 18 E2
Desmond Way BN2 ..... 188 F6
Detling Rd RH11 ..... 18 C1
*Devil's Dyke BN45 ..... 146 C3
Devil's Dyke Rd BN45 .. 146 C1
Devils La GU30 ..... 25 E3
Devonian Ct BN2 ..... 207 B7
Devonport PI BN11 ..... 183 A3
Devonport Rd BN11 ..... 183 A2
Devonshire Ct 1 BN3 ... 187 C7
Devonshire Lodge 12
BN11 ..... 181 F2
Devonshire PI
3 Bognor Regis PO21 . 195 C3
Brighton BN2 ..... 207 B5
Devonshire Rd
Bognor Regis PO21 ... 195 C3
Horsham RH12 ..... 36 D2
Dewar CI RH11 ..... 17 E5
Dewe Rd BN2 ..... 168 C1
Dexter Dr RH19 ..... 22 E8
Dial CI PO22 ..... 176 C5
Diamond Cotts RH17 .. 83 B1
Dickens CI RH19 ..... 9 C1
Dickens Rd RH10 ..... 18 E3
Dickins Way RH13 ..... 58 F8
Dickinson PI PO22 ..... 195 D6
Diggers The BN1 ..... 168 B3
Dinapore Ho 10 BN2 .. 207 B6
Dingemans BN44 ..... 143 D5
Dingle The RH11 ..... 18 B6
Dingley Rd BN16 ..... 199 C5
Dinsdale Gdns BN16 .. 199 C6
Divine Wlk RH11 ..... 17 E4
Dirty La RH19 ..... 23 E7
Discovery Pk RH10 ..... 6 A2
Ditcham Park Sch GU31 .. 108 B8
Ditchfield Ct PO22 ..... 196 D6
Ditchling Beacon
Nature Reserve BN6 .. 148 D7
Ditchling Bostall BN6 .. 148 D7
Ditchling Ct BN12 ..... 181 B4
Ditchling Common Cntry Pk
BN6 ..... 107 F1
Ditchling Cres BN1 ..... 168 C5
Ditchling Ct 4 BN1 ..... 188 B8
Ditchling Gdns BN1 ..... 168 B1
Ditchling Hill RH11 ..... 18 C4
Ditchling Mus BN6 ..... 127 C3
Ditchling Rd
Brighton BN1, BN2 ..... 168 B4
Westmeston BN1, BN6 .. 148 D4
Ditchling Rise BN1 ..... 188 A8
Ditton Place Sch RH17 .. 62 A8
Dobbins PI RH11 ..... 17 E5
Dobson Rd RH11 ..... 5 D1
Dodsley Gr GU29 ..... 70 F2
Dodsley La GU29 ..... 71 A2
Dog Kennels GU28 ..... 115 B3
Dog La BN44 ..... 143 D3
Dolby Terr RH6 ..... 4 E6
Dollis CI RH10 ..... 19 C5
Dolphin CI
Fishbourne PO19 ..... 172 B6
Haslemere GU27 ..... 26 E6
Dolphin Ct
4 Bognor Regis PO21 .. 195 C2
5 Hove BN3 ..... 187 A6
Rustington BN16 ..... 199 D4
Dolphin Ind Est BN43 .. 185 B7
Dolphin L Ctr The RH16 .. 85 D6
Dolphin Lodge 12 BN11 .. 182 A1
Dolphin Mews PO19 .. 172 D6
Dolphin Rd
Haywards Heath RH16 .. 85 D4
Shoreham-by-Sea BN43 .. 185 B7
Dolphin Way
Littlehampton BN16 .. 199 D4
Shoreham-by-Sea BN43 .. 185 B7
Dominion Bldgs BN14 .. 182 F4
Dominion CI BN14 ..... 182 E5
Dominion Rd BN14 ..... 182 F5
Dominion Way
Rustington BN16 ..... 179 C3
Worthing BN14 ..... 182 F5
Dominion Way W BN14 .. 182 F5
Donald Hall Rd BN2 .. 188 D5
Doncaster Wlk RH10 .. 19 A4

Donegal Rd PO19 ..... 152 F1
Donkey La RH6 ..... 6 D7
Donkey Mews BN3 ..... 187 D5
Donne CI RH10 ..... 19 B8
Donnington Ct 2 RH11 .. 17 F3
Donnington Pk PO20 .. 172 D3
Donnington PI 2 BN16 .. 199 C6
Doomsday Gdn RH13 .. 37 A1
Dorcale Dene BN12 ..... 200 F4
Dorchester Gdns BN11 .. 182 A2
Dorking Rd RH12, RH5 .. 15 B4
Dorman's CI RH7 ..... 10 A8
Dormans RH11 ..... 18 A5
Dormans Gdns RH19 ..... 9 E6
Dormans High St RH7 .. 10 A8
Dormans Park Rd
Dormans Park RH19 ..... 9 E6
East Grinstead RH19 ..... 9 D3
Dormans Sta RH7 ..... 9 F6
Dormans Station Rd RH7 ... 9 F7
Dormansland Prim Sch
RH7 ..... 10 A8
Dorothy Rd BN3 ..... 186 D8
Dorothy Stringer Sch
BN1 ..... 167 F3
Dorset Ave RH19 ..... 9 C3
Dorset CI BN17 ..... 198 E5
Dorset Ct BN41 ..... 186 F6
Dorset Gdns Brighton BN2 . 207 B5
East Grinstead RH19 ..... 9 C3
Dorset Ho RH14 ..... 78 E2
Dorset House Sch RH20 .. 138 B7
Dorset PI Brighton BN2 .. 207 B5
4 Worthing BN13 ..... 182 A5
Dorset Rd PO21 ..... 195 C5
Dorset St BN2 ..... 207 A5
Dorsten Sq RH11 ..... 17 F3
Doubledays RH15 ..... 107 B2
Douglas Ave BN11 ..... 181 F2
Douglas CI Burndell BN18 .. 177 B2
Worthing BN11 ..... 181 F2
Douglas Martin Rd PO19 .. 173 B7
Dove CI RH11 ..... 18 D8
Dove Ct PO22 ..... 195 B5
Dovecote Mews BN15 .. 183 C8
Dovedale Cres RH11 .. 18 B4
Dover CI RH13 ..... 57 F2
Dover Rd Brighton BN1 .. 168 A2
Worthing BN11 ..... 182 A1
Dovercourt PO22 ..... 195 A6
Dower Wlk RH11 ..... 18 A5
Dowlands La RH10, RH6 .. 7 D7
Down CI GU29 ..... 113 C8
Down Cotts PO18 ..... 130 A8
Down St PO18 ..... 151 B3
Down Terr BN12 ..... 188 C6
Down The BN14 ..... 166 D4
Down View Rd BN11 .. 182 A2
Downash Ct BN2 ..... 188 E6
Downe CI RH6 ..... 1 E5
Downe Wlk BN13 ..... 181 D5
Downe Ct 9 BN43 ..... 185 C8
Downing Cl PO21 ..... 194 E4
Downland Ave BN42 .. 165 E1
Downland CI Findon BN14 .. 161 E6
Southwick BN42 ..... 165 D1
Downland Cres BN3 .. 166 F3
Downland Ct
Chichester PO19 ..... 172 F8
Crawley RH11 ..... 18 C4
Portslade-by-Sea BN41 .. 166 A2
Downland Dr
Crawley RH11 ..... 18 C3
Hove BN3 ..... 166 F3
Downland PI RH11 ..... 18 C4
Downland Rd BN44 ..... 144 B2
Downlands
Partridge Green RH13 .. 102 F3
Pulborough RH20 ..... 98 D2
Worthing BN13 ..... 161 E2
Downlands Ave BN14 .. 182 D6
Downlands Bsns Pk BN14 .. 182 E8
Downlands CI
Bognor Regis PO21 .. 194 A2
Lancing BN15 ..... 183 C7
Downlands Gdns BN14 .. 182 E7
Downlands La RH6 ..... 7 D7
Downlands Pk RH14 .. 182 E7
Downlands Ret Ctr BN14 .. 182 E7
Downlands Sch BN6 .. 126 F3
Downs Cl BN15 ..... 184 B6
Downs Cty Inf Sch BN1 .. 207 B8
Downs Cty Jun Sch BN1 .. 168 A1
Downs Mead BN15 ..... 183 C8
Downs Park Sch BN41 .. 166 B2
Downs Rd
Burgess Hill RH15 .. 106 E4
West Stoke PO18 ..... 151 D6
Downs View Rd BN16 .. 126 F3
Downs Way BN16 ..... 179 F3

Downsbrook Mid Sch
BN14 ..... 182 E5
Downsbrook Trad Est
BN14 ..... 182 E6
Downscroft
Burgess Hill RH15 .. 107 D6
Upper Beeding BN44 .. 144 B1
Downside Brighton BN1 .. 167 D5
Hove BN3 ..... 167 B3
Shoreham-by-Sea BN43 .. 165 A1
Downside Ave BN14 .. 161 F3
Downside CI
Shoreham-by-Sea BN43 .. 164 F1
Worthing BN14 ..... 161 F3
Downside Ct 6 BN16 .. 199 B3
Downsman Ct RH10 .. 18 D3
Downsview Hove BN3 .. 166 D3
Hurstpierpoint BN6 .. 126 A5
Small Dole BN5 ..... 144 F7
Downsview Ave RH20 .. 119 E2
Downsview Cotts RH14 ... 77 C8
Downsview Dr GU29 .. 92 E5
Downsview Rd
Horsham RH12 ..... 37 B6
Kingston Gorse BN16 .. 200 D4
Portslade-by-Sea BN41 .. 166 A2
Seaview Terr BN5 ..... 123 D5
Downsway
Shoreham-by-Sea BN43 .. 164 F1
Southwick BN42 ..... 165 F1
Downview Ave BN43 .. 180 E3
Downview CI
Burndell BN18 ..... 177 A3
East Wittering PO20 .. 202 A6
Mid Lavant PO18 ..... 152 E6
Downview Ct 7 Cty Prim Sch
PO22 ..... 195 F6
Downview Rd
Bognor Regis PO21 .. 196 A5
Burndell BN18 ..... 177 A3
Ferring BN12 ..... 180 E3
Findon BN14 ..... 161 E7
West Barnham PO22 .. 176 A7
Downview Way BN18 .. 177 A3
Dragons Green Council Cotts
RH13 ..... 79 C3
Dragons Green Rd RH13 .. 79 C5
Dragons La
Dragons Green RH13 ..... 79 C3
Little Parkminster RH13 .. 103 E7
Drake Ave BN12 ..... 181 D4
Drake CI RH12 ..... 36 E6
Drake Gr BN10 ..... 177 B2
Drake Pk PO22 ..... 196 C5
Drake Rd Crawley RH10 .. 18 E3
Horley RH6 ..... 1 E3
Drakeleys Field GU30 .. 47 B2
Drakes CI BN15 ..... 184 B6
Draxmont Way BN1 .. 167 F3
Draycliff CI BN12 ..... 200 E5
Drayman's Mews PO19 .. 173 B6
Drayton La PO20 ..... 174 A5
Drewitts Mews PO20 .. 174 C7
Drift La Nutbourne PO18 .. 170 E8
Selsey PO20 ..... 206 C7
Drift Rd
Bognor Regis PO21 .. 194 B2
Selsey PO20 ..... 206 G8
Drift The PO9 ..... 128 D1
Driftway
The Rustington BN16 .. 179 B3
Upper Beeding BN44 .. 144 B3
Drive Lodge 10 BN6 .. 187 C7
Drive The
Bognor Regis PO21 .. 194 D1
Bosham PO18 ..... 171 C4
Burgess Hill RH15 .. 107 B4
Chichester PO19 ..... 153 A3
Copthorne RH10 ..... 7 C3
East Lavington GU28 .. 114 E5
Horley RH6 ..... 2 B1
Hove BN3 ..... 187 C7
Ifold RH14 ..... 31 D2
Lancing BN15 ..... 183 D4
North Lancing BN15 .. 184 B3
Shoreham-by-Sea BN43 .. 164 F1
Southbourne PO10 .. 169 F8
Southwick BN42 ..... 165 E1
West Kingston BN16 .. 200 B4
Worthing BN13 ..... 181 F3
Driveway The BN43 .. 164 F1
Droke La PO18 ..... 134 E6
Dropping Holms BN5 .. 123 D4
Drove Cres BN41 ..... 166 A2
Drove La Earnley PO20 .. 202 D5
Yapton BN18, PO22 .. 176 D2
Drove Rd BN41 ..... 166 A1
Drove The BN1 ..... 167 D1
Drovers RH17 ..... 83 C3

Drovers CI BN41 ..... 166 C2
Drovers Way RH15 ..... 107 C1
Droveway The
Haywards Heath
RH16, RH17 ..... 85 C6
Hove BN3 ..... 167 B2
Hove BN3 ..... 167 C1
Drummond CI RH16 .. 85 D4
Drummond Ct RH16 .. 85 D5
Drummond Rd
Crawley RH11 ..... 17 E5
Worthing BN12 ..... 181 E1
Drungewick La RH14 .. 32 D2
Drury CI RH19 ..... 19 D4
Dryad Way PO22 ..... 196 D4
Dryad Wlk PO22 ..... 196 D4
Dryden Way GU30 ..... 25 A5
Drygrounds La PO22 .. 195 F5
Duck La Midhurst GU29 .. 92 F7
Selsey PO20 ..... 206 B8
Duckmead La GU33 .. 45 D5
Dudeney Lodge BN1 .. 168 B1
Dudley Rd BN1 ..... 168 B1
Dudley Terr GU33 ..... 45 C5
Duffield La PO10 ..... 150 A3
Duke CI RH10 ..... 19 C2
Duke St Brighton BN1 .. 207 F5
Littlehampton BN17 .. 199 D5
Duke's CI
Chichester PO19 ..... 173 D5
2 Littlehampton BN17 .. 198 D5
Duke's Dr RH5 ..... 3 D6
Duke's Hill RH20 ..... 120 A8
Duke's Mound BN2 .. 188 D4
Duke's Rd BN18 ..... 155 F4
Dukes Barn Ct RH16 .. 86 B7
Dukes CI BN18 ..... 157 F2
Dukes La Brighton BN1 .. 207 F5
Steyning BN44 ..... 143 D4
Dukes Meadow PO21 .. 194 B3
Dukes Rd RH16 ..... 86 B8
Dukes Row RH20 ..... 119 A2
Dukes St BN44 ..... 143 D3
Dumbrells Court Rd BN6 .. 127 D4
Dumbrells Ct BN6 ..... 127 D4
Dumbrills CI RH15 ..... 107 A5
Dumpford La GU31 ..... 90 D8
Duncan Rd PO19 ..... 172 F8
Duncton CE (C) Prim Sch
GU28 ..... 115 B7
Duncton CI
Bognor Regis PO22 .. 196 B4
Haywards Heath RH16 .. 85 D4
Duncton High St GU28 .. 115 B6
Duncton Ho BN6 ..... 126 E4
Duncton Rd BN16 ..... 199 C6
Dunes The PO21 ..... 205 C8
Dunford Hollow GU29 .. 93 A3
Dunning's Rd RH19 ..... 10 A5
Dunnings Mill L Complex
RH19 ..... 10 A4
Dunsfold CI RH11 ..... 18 A5
Dunsfold Rd GU8, RH14 .. 30 D4
Dunstall Ave RH15 ..... 106 E4
Dunstall Farm Rd RH15 .. 106 F4
Dunstan CI PO19 ..... 153 A3
Dunster CI BN1 ..... 168 B1
Durban Pk PO22 ..... 195 D5
Durban Rd PO22 ..... 195 D6
Durbans Rd RH14 ..... 54 C2
Durfold Rd RH12 ..... 36 D7
Durfold Wood RH14 .. 30 D5
Durham CI
Bognor Regis PO21 .. 205 A8
Crawley RH11 ..... 18 E2
Durham Ct BN3 ..... 187 B6
Durham Gdns PO19 .. 152 F1
Durkins Rd RH19 ..... 9 D3
Durleston Dr PO22 .. 195 B6
Durlston Par PO22 ..... 195 B6
Durnford CI PO19 ..... 172 E7
Durrington Cty Fst Sch
BN13 ..... 181 D6
Durrington Cty Mid Sch
BN13 ..... 181 E7
Durrington High Sch
BN13 ..... 181 E5
Durrington Hill BN13 .. 181 D7
Durrington La
BN12, BN13 ..... 181 D6
Durrington-on-Sea Sta
BN12 ..... 181 E3
Dutchells Copse RH12 ... 36 E7
Duxhurst La RH6 ..... 1 B7
Dyall CI RH15 ..... 106 E4
Dyers Almshouses RH10 .. 18 D7
Dyers La BN18 ..... 156 C5
Dyke CI Hove BN3 ..... 167 B4
Poynings BN45 ..... 146 C4

Dyke Golf Course BN1 .. 146 D1
Dyke Rd BN1, BN3 ..... 187 E7
Dyke Road Ave BN1, BN3 . 167 C4
Dyke Road Dr BN1 ..... 187 F8
Dyke Road PI BN1, BN3 .. 167 C3
Dymock's Farm Ho 127 D3
Dymoke St PO10 ..... 149 A4
Dyson Wlk RH11 ..... 18 B1

Eady CI RH13 ..... 36 F2
Eagle Est RH14 ..... 77 D7
Eagle Ho 10 PO21 ..... 195 B2
Eagles Chase RH17 ..... 78 D4
Earles Meadow RH12 ..... 37 B6
Earlswood CI RH13 ..... 37 A4
Early Commons RH10 ..... 18 F7
Earnley Manor CI PO20 .. 202 D7
Earnley Rd Earnley PO20 .. 202 D7
South Hayling PO11 ..... 189 B2
Eartham Ho (Great
Ballard Sch) PO18 ..... 155 D7
Earwig La RH17 ..... 82 E6
Easebourne La GU29 ..... 71 A1
Easebourne St GU28, GU29 .. 71 D5
East Ave
Middleton-on-Sea PO22 .. 196 F6
Worthing BN12 ..... 181 F1
East Bank North End BN18 .. 177 A5
Selsey PO20 ..... 206 F7
East Bank Wlk BN17 ..... 199 A4
East Beach Rd PO20 ..... 206 G8
East Bracklesham Dr
PO20 ..... 202 B5
East CI PO22 ..... 196 E5
East Court Way BN16 ..... 199 E6
East Dean PO20 ..... 195 D5
East Dr Angmering BN16 .. 179 F2
Brighton BN2 ..... 188 C5
Middleton-on-Sea PO22 .. 197 A5
East Field CI PO10 ..... 150 A2
East Front Rd PO21 ..... 205 A7
East Gdns BN6 ..... 127 D3
East Grinstead Sta RH19 . 9 D1
East Gun Copse Rd RH13 .. 57 D5
East Ham Rd BN17 ..... 198 D5
East Hampnett La PO20 .. 154 F2
East Harting St GU31 ..... 89 F3
East Hill RH19 ..... 9 E2
East Hill Ct 1 BN11 ..... 182 D6
East Hill Dr GU33 ..... 45 C3
East Hill La RH10 ..... 7 D5
East Lake PO21 ..... 195 D4
East Lodge Lancing BN15 .. 183 E4
Rogate GU31 ..... 68 B4
East Mascalls Rd RH16 .. 86 E6
East Mead
Bognor Regis PO21 .. 205 A8
Ferring BN12 ..... 200 F5
East Meadway BN43 .. 185 A6
East Onslow CI BN12 .. 200 E5
East Pallant PO19 ..... 173 A6
East Park La RH7 ..... 8 C8
East Pk RH10, RH11 .. 18 D5
East Point 8 BN16 ..... 201 F5
East Preston Cty Inf Sch
BN16 ..... 200 A6
East Preston Cty Jun Sch
BN16 ..... 200 A6
East Row PO19 ..... 173 A6
East Row Mews 9 PO19 . 173 A6
East St Amberley BN18 .. 138 E7
Billingshurst RH14 ..... 77 D8
Brighton BN1 ..... 207 A4
Chichester PO19 ..... 173 A6
Horsham RH12 ..... 36 C1
Lancing BN15 ..... 183 E4
Littlehampton BN17 .. 198 E5
Petworth GU28 ..... 95 F8
Portslade-by-Sea BN41 .. 186 C7
Rusper RH12 ..... 16 E7
Selsey PO20 ..... 206 E7
Shoreham-by-Sea BN43 .. 184 F7
West Chiltington BN13 .. 99 E1
Westbourne PO10 ..... 149 D3
East Strand PO20 ..... 201 C8
East Tyne BN13 ..... 181 D6
East View CI PO18 ..... 152 F7
East Walls PO19 ..... 173 A6
East Walls CI 2 PO19 .. 173 A6
East Way PO20 ..... 206 F7
East Wick Bsns Ctr
PO20 ..... 202 A8
East Wittering Cty Prim Sch
PO20 ..... 201 F7
East Worthing Ind Est
BN14 ..... 182 F5

East Worthing Sta BN11 .... 182 F4
Eastbank BN42 .... 165 F1
Eastbourne Rd
  Brighton BN2 .... 168 D1
  Felbridge RH7 .... 8 E8
Eastbrook Rd BN41 .... 186 B7
Eastbrook Way BN42 .... 186 A7
Eastcourt Rd BN14 .... 182 D4
Eastcroft Mews RH12 .... 35 F1
Eastdale Rd RH15 .... 107 D4
Eastdean Hill PO18 .... 134 C5
Easteds La RH13 .... 58 A2
Eastend La BN6 .... 127 D3
Eastergate CE (C) Prim Sch
  PO20 .... 175 E7
Eastergate Cl BN12 .... 180 F3
Eastergate Gn **6** BN16 .... 199 C5
Eastergate La BN18, PO20 156 B1
Eastergate Rd BN2 .... 168 F4
Eastern Ave BN43 .... 185 A7
Eastern Cl
  East Preston BN16 .... 200 B6
  Shoreham-by-Sea BN43 .. 185 A7
Eastern Cotts RH15 .... 86 B7
Eastern Pl BN2 .... 188 E4
Eastern Rd Brighton BN2 .. 188 D4
  Haywards Heath RH16 .... 85 F3
  Haywards Heath RH16 .... 86 C7
Eastern Terr **10** BN2 ...... 188 D4
Eastern Terrace Mews **9**
  BN2 .... 188 D4
Eastfield Cres BN1 .... 168 A4
Eastfield La GU31 .... 90 A4
Eastgate Ct PO19 .... 173 B6
Eastgate Sq PO19 .... 173 A6
Easthill Dr BN41 .... 166 B2
Easthill Way BN41 .... 166 B1
Easting Cl BN14 .... 182 F5
Eastland Rd PO19 .... 173 B5
Eastlands Cotts RH13 ...... 81 F1
Eastmead Ind Est PO18 .... 152 E7
Eastoke Ave PO11 .... 209 A2
Easton Cres RH14 .... 77 E8
Easton La PO20 .... 203 A6
Eastover Way PO22 .... 195 F4
Eastshaw La GU29 .... 70 C4
Eastway RH6 .... 6 B7
Eastwick Cl BN1 .... 168 B7
Eastwood RH10 .... 18 F6
Eaton Ct **9** Hove BN3 .... 187 B7
  Worthing BN14 .... 182 B6
Eaton Gardens Mansions **20**
  BN3 .... 187 C7
Eaton Gate **17** BN3 ...... 187 C7
Eaton Gdns BN3 .... 187 C7
Eaton Gr BN3 .... 187 C7
Eaton Hall **11** BN3 .... 187 C7
Eaton Manor **11** BN3 .... 187 C7
Eaton Pl BN2 .... 188 D4
Eaton Rd BN3 .... 187 C7
Eaton Villas BN3 .... 187 B7
Ecclesden **6** BN2 .... 207 B6
Edburton Ave BN1 .... 168 A1
Edburton Dro BN5 .... 145 D6
Edburton Gdns BN43 .... 164 F1
Eddington Hill RH11 .... 18 B1
Eden Rd RH11 .... 17 F4
Eden Vale RH19 .... 9 E5
Edgar Ct RH10 .... 19 E5
Edgehill Cl BN13 .... 181 F7
Edgehill Way BN41 .... 165 F2
Edgell Rd PO10 .... 149 D4
Edgewood Ct GU33 .... 45 D2
Edinburgh Cl
  Bognor Regis PO21 .... 194 E2
  Southwater RH13 .... 58 A1
Edinburgh Cotts **3** BN11 182 C1
Edinburgh Rd BN2 .... 188 B8
Edinburgh Sq GU29 .... 92 F7
Edinburgh Way RH19 .... 22 F7
Edith Cotts PO18 .... 151 A2
Edmonton Rd BN13 .... 181 D6
Edrich Rd RH11 .... 18 A1
Edward Ave BN3 .... 167 A3
Edward Bryant Cty
  Prim Sch PO21 .... 195 D4
Edward Cl BN3 .... 167 A3
Edward Ho BN3 .... 186 F6
Edward Rd RH16 .... 85 E2
Edward St BN2 .... 207 B5
Edward Way RH15 .... 106 D2
Edwards Ave PO20 .... 154 C2
Edwards Way BN17 .... 178 C4
Edwen Cl PO21 .... 194 B3
Edwin Cl BN15 .... 183 C6
Eels Cross PO20 .... 206 B8
Effingham La RH10 .... 7 E4
Effingham Rd RH10, RH6 ...... 7 D6

Eggington Rd BN2 .... 168 F5
Egmont Ho GU29 .... 71 A1
Egmont Rd
  Easebourne GU29 .... 71 A1
  Hove BN3 .... 166 D1
Egremont Pl Brighton BN2 207 B5
Eighth Ave BN15 .... 183 E7
Eirene Ave BN12 .... 181 F1
Eirene Rd BN11, BN12 ...... 181 F1
Elanor Cl GU30 .... 24 D8
Elbridge Cres PO21 .... 194 C2
Elder Cl BN41 .... 166 B2
Elder Pl BN1 .... 207 A7
Elderfield Cl PO10 .... 149 C3
Eldon Rd BN11 .... 182 F3
Eldon Way BN17 .... 198 B6
Eldred Ave BN1 .... 167 D5
Eleanor Cl **1** BN11 .... 181 F2
Eleanor Gdns PO22 .... 196 D5
Elfin Gr PO21 .... 195 B3
Elfn Mews **1** PO21 .... 195 B3
Elger Way RH10 .... 7 A4
Elgin Cl RH13 .... 36 F3
Elgin Ct PO19 .... 173 A5
Elgin Rd PO20 .... 181 D2
Eliot Dr GU27 .... 26 E6
Eliot Ho **4** RH16 .... 85 E3
Elizabeth Ave
  Bognor Regis PO21 .... 194 D4
  Hove BN3 .... 167 A3
Elizabeth Cl
  Bognor Regis PO21 .... 194 C3
  Hove BN3 .... 167 A3
Elizabeth Cres RH19 .... 9 F3
Elizabeth Ct
  5 Bognor Regis PO21 .. 195 B2
  Horley RH6 .... 2 A3
  7 Hove BN3 .... 187 C7
  7 Worthing BN11 .... 181 F2
Elizabeth Ho
  Bognor Regis PO22 .... 195 E4
  1 Worthing BN13 .... 182 A5
Elizabeth Pl BN15 .... 183 C5
Elizabeth Rd
  Chichester PO19 .... 173 E7
  Shoreham-by-Sea BN43 .. 185 C8
  Worthing BN11 .... 182 C2
Elizabethan Way RH10 ...... 19 C5
Elkham Cnr GU28 .... 52 C1
Ella Cl PO20 .... 201 E7
Ellanore La PO20 .... 190 B2
Ellasdale Rd PO21 .... 195 B2
Ellen Ho **3** BN3 .... 187 B7
Ellen St Hove BN3 .... 187 B7
  Portslade-by-Sea BN41 .. 186 C7
Ellesmere Orch PO10 .... 149 D5
Elliot Cl RH10 .... 19 C4
Ellis Ave BN13 .... 161 E1
Ellis Cl BN18 .... 157 F2
Ellis Way PO21 .... 205 A8
Ellman Rd RH11 .... 17 F4
Ellson Cl RH10 .... 19 C4
Elm Ave BN16 .... 200 B6
Elm Cl Bognor Regis PO21 194 A1
  Bracklesham PO20 .... 202 B6
  Hove BN3 .... 167 C2
  Shoreham-by-Sea BN41 .. 164 F1
Elm Ct
  1 Bognor Regis PO21 .. 195 C2
  Brighton BN1 .... 187 E8
  Southwick BN41 .... 186 B8
Elm Dale PO22 .... 176 A6
Elm Dr
  East Grinstead RH19 .... 10 A1
  Hove BN3 .... 166 E1
  Middleton-on-Sea PO22 .. 197 B5
Elm Gr
  Bognor Regis PO21 .... 195 A3
  Brighton BN2 .... 188 C7
  Cowfold RH13 .... 81 E2
  Horsham RH13 .... 36 E1
  Lancing BN15 .... 183 D5
  Runcton PO20 .... 173 E1
  Selsey PO20 .... 206 D7
  West Barnham PO22 ...... 176 B7
  Worthing BN11 .... 181 F2
Elm Gr S PO22 .... 176 A6
Elm Grove Cty Fst Sch
  BN11 .... 181 F2
Elm Grove Cty Inf Sch
  BN17 .... 198 E6
Elm Grove Cty Prim Sch
  BN2 .... 188 C7
Elm Grove La BN44 .... 143 D3
Elm Ho RH14 .... 77 C8
Elm Pk Bosham PO18 ...... 171 C6
  Ferring BN12 .... 180 F3
Elm Pl BN16 .... 199 D6
Elm Rd
  Portslade-by-Sea BN41 .. 186 B8
  Westergate PO20 .... 175 E7

Elm Rd Worthing BN11 ...... 182 E2
Elm Rise BN14 .... 161 E6
Elm Terr BN44 .... 143 D3
Elm Tree Cl PO20 .... 206 E8
Elmcroft Pl PO20 .... 175 D6
Elmdene Ct PO20 .... 202 B5
Elmeigh Ct GU29 .... 92 E8
Elmer Cl PO22 .... 197 B5
Elmer Ct PO22 .... 197 C5
Elmer Rd PO22 .... 196 F5
Elmgrove Rd BN17 .... 198 F6
Elmhurst Cl BN16 .... 180 A6
Elmhurst La RH13 .... 56 C6
Elmleigh GU29 .... 92 D8
Elmore Rd BN2 .... 207 B6
Elms Dr BN15 .... 183 D6
Elms La PO20 .... 190 D1
Elms Lea Ave BN1 .... 167 E3
Elms Rde PO20 .... 190 C1
Elms Way PO20 .... 190 C2
Elmsfield PO20 .... 206 E7
Elmstead RH19 .... 22 E8
Elmstead Gdns PO20 .... 190 C2
Elmstead Park Rd PO20 .... 190 C2
Elmstead Rd BN15 .... 183 D6
Elmwood Ave PO22 .... 195 D5
Elrington Rd BN3 .... 167 C1
Elsay Ct PO19 .... 173 A5
Elsie Rd BN11 .... 182 B1
Elsted Cl RH11 .... 18 B8
Elsted Cres BN1 .... 168 C6
Elsted Rd GU29 .... 91 C7
Elverlands Cl BN12 .... 200 F4
Elwood Cl RH15 .... 106 F1
Ely Cl Crawley RH10 .... 18 F2
  East Wittering PO20 ...... 201 F8
  Worthing BN13 .... 181 F4
Ely Gdns PO21 .... 194 D3
Ely Rd BN13 .... 181 F4
Embassy Ct BN3 .... 187 D5
Emberwood RH11 .... 18 D8
Emerald Quay BN43 .... 185 A6
Emlyn Rd RH6 .... 1 E4
Emmabrook Ct BN16 ...... 199 A3
Emms La RH13 .... 78 F7
Empire Villas RH1 .... 2 B7
Emsbrook Dr PO10 .... 149 B2
Emsworth Cl PO10 .... 149 C6
Emsworth Common Rd
  PO10, PO9 .... 149 C6
Emsworth House Cl PO10 149 A1
Emsworth Prim Sch PO10 149 A1
Emsworth Rd PO10 .... 169 D2
End Cotts BN18 .... 138 E6
End La BN5 .... 123 A5
Enfield Cl GU30 .... 25 D3
Enfield Rd RH11 .... 18 C2
Engalee RH19 .... 9 C2
Englefield RH12 .... 35 F2
English Cl BN2 .... 186 E8
English Martyrs RC (A) Sch
  BN12 .... 181 D5
Ennerdale Cl RH11 .... 18 B4
Ennerdale Dr BN15 .... 183 B5
Ensign Way BN1 .... 199 E6
Enterprise Ct BN12 .... 181 C3
Enterprise Est BN1 .... 168 C7
Epping Wlk RH10 .... 18 F4
Epsom Gdns BN16 .... 199 E6
Epsom Rd RH10 .... 19 A4
Erica Way Copthorne RH10 .. 7 A2
  Horsham RH12 .... 36 D5
Eridge Cl RH10 .... 19 C6
Eridge Rd BN3 .... 167 A2
Erin Way RH15 .... 106 E3
Eriskay Ct BN13 .... 181 B6
Eriswell Rd BN11 .... 182 C1
Erles Rd GU30 .... 25 C4
Ernest Cl PO10 .... 149 B1
Erringham Rd BN43 .... 164 E1
Erroll Rd BN3, BN41 .... 186 C6
Erskine Cl RH11 .... 17 E2
Esher Cl PO21 .... 194 B2
Esher Dr BN17 .... 198 F5
Eskbank Ave BN1 .... 168 A7
Esmond Cl PO10 .... 169 B8
Esmonde Cl BN17 .... 198 F6
Esplanade The
  Bognor Regis, Felpham
  PO22 .... 195 F3
  Worthing BN11 .... 182 F2
Essex Ct BN11 .... 182 A2
Essex Pl **3** BN2 .... 188 C4
Essex Rd PO21 .... 195 C5
Essex Rd PO21 .... 195 C5
Estcots Cty Prim Sch RH19 10 A1
Estcots Dr RH19 .... 10 A1
Estuary The BN17 .... 198 F5
Ethel St BN3 .... 187 B7
Ethelred Rd BN13, BN14 .. 182 A4

Ethelwulf Rd BN13, BN14 . 182 A4
Eton Cl PO21 .... 194 E4
Eton Dr PO20 .... 201 F8
Eton Rd BN11 .... 182 A3
Ettrick Cl PO19 .... 173 B5
Ettrick Rd PO19 .... 173 B5
Eurythmy Sch RH19 .... 22 G6
Evans Cl RH10 .... 19 D5
Evans Gdns **1** BN17 .... 198 D5
Evans Pl PO22 .... 195 D6
Evelyn Ave BN16 .... 199 D4
Evelyn Cl BN41 .... 186 A8
Evelyn Glennie Ct **7** BN2 188 C5
Evelyn Rd BN14 .... 182 D4
Evelyn Terr BN2 .... 188 C5
Everest Ho **2** BN3 .... 186 F7
Eversfield RH13 .... 58 B1
Eversfield Rd RH13 .... 36 E1
Eversleigh Ct GU29 .... 71 A2
Ewart St BN2 .... 207 B6
Ewelands RH6 .... 2 C4
Ewens Gdns PO20 .... 176 A7
Ewhurst Cl RH11 .... 18 C6
Ewhurst Rd Brighton BN2 . 168 C1
  Crawley RH11 .... 18 C7
Excalibur Cl RH11 .... 17 E5
Exchange Rd RH10 .... 18 E6
Exeat Cl BN12 .... 188 E6
Exeter Cl
  Bognor Regis PO21 .... 194 F3
  Crawley RH10 .... 18 E2
  New Brighton PO10 .... 149 B2
Exeter Ct **2** BN11 .... 182 A1
Exeter Rd PO19 .... 152 E1
Exeter St BN1 .... 187 E8
Exford Wlk BN13 .... 181 D5
Exmoor Cl BN13 .... 181 E7
Exmoor Cres BN13 .... 181 E7
Exmoor Ct BN13 .... 181 E7
Exmoor Dr BN13 .... 181 E7
Exton Rd PO19 .... 173 A4
Eyles Cl BN12 .... 36 B4

Fabians Way BN5 .... 123 D5
Fair View RH12 .... 36 A3
Fairbanks RH16 .... 85 E4
Fairbridge Way RH15 ...... 106 F5
Faircox La BN5 .... 123 D5
Fairdene BN42 .... 165 F1
Fairfield Ave RH6 .... 2 A1
Fairfield Cl Ardingly RH17 .. 64 A8
  Bosham PO18 .... 171 C5
Fairfield Cl
  Burgess Hill RH15 .... 106 F4
  New Brighton PO10 .... 149 B2
  Shoreham-by-Sea BN43 .. 165 C1
Fairfield Cotts RH13 .... 81 E2
Fairfield Cres BN6 .... 126 A6
Fairfield Ct RH13 .... 81 E2
Fairfield Gdns
  Burgess Hill RH15 .... 106 F4
  Portslade-by-Sea BN41 .. 166 B1
Fairfield Rd
  Ashington BN13 .... 121 A4
  Bosham PO18 .... 171 B5
  Burgess Hill RH15 .... 106 F4
  East Grinstead RH19 .... 22 F8
Fairfield Rise GU28 .... 95 F7
Fairfield Way
  Ashington BN13 .... 121 A4
  Haywards Heath RH16 .... 85 D8
Fairfields **2** BN14 .... 182 D4
Fairlands Horley RH6 .... 2 B2
  6 Hove BN3 .... 187 A6
  Shoreham-by-Sea BN43 .. 185 A8
  Southwick BN41 .... 186 F6
Fairlea Cl RH15 .... 106 F4
Fairlea Rd PO10 .... 149 B3
Fairlead BN17 .... 198 F4
Fairlie Gdns BN1 .... 167 E3
Fairlight Cty Prim Sch
  BN2 .... 188 C8
Fairlight Pl **4** BN2 .... 188 C8
Fairmead Cl RH20 .... 97 A3
Fairmile Bottom BN18 ...... 157 B7
Fairmile Bottom Nature Trail
  BN18 .... 157 C8
Fairoak **3** BN13 .... 182 A5

Fairstone Ct RH6 .... 2 B4
Fairview Ave BN12 .... 181 C1
Fairview Cotts RH13 .... 58 B3
Fairview Rd BN15 .... 183 E8
Fairview Rise BN1 .... 167 D5
Fairway Copthorne RH10 .... 7 B2
  Crawley RH11 .... 17 D4
  Littlehampton
  BN16, BN17 .... 199 A4
Fairway Cl Copthorne RH10 .. 7 A2
  Liphook GU30 .... 24 D3
Fairway Cres BN41 .... 166 C2
Fairway Cty Inf Sch RH10 .. 7 A3
Fairway The
  Bognor Regis PO21 .... 205 B8
  Midhurst GU29 .... 92 E6
  Rowland's Castle PO9 .... 128 E2
Fairway Trad Est BN2 ...... 168 E4
Fairways BN1 .... 187 E8
Faithfull Cres RH20 .... 119 B2
Falcon Cl Crawley RH11 .... 18 D8
  Shoreham-by-Sea BN43 .. 185 C6
Falcon Gdns BN17 .... 178 C4
Falkland Ave BN12 .... 198 F6
Falklands Cl PO22 .... 195 D5
Falklands Rd BN13 .... 37 B4
Fallow Deer Cl RH13 .... 37 B4
Fallowfield Cl BN3 .... 166 F2
Fallowfield Dres BN3 ...... 166 F2
Fallowfield Way RH6 .... 2 B4
Falmer Ave BN12 .... 181 B1
Falmer Cl Crawley RH11 .. 18 D4
  Worthing BN11 .... 181 C1
Faraday Ave BN9 .... 22 F6
Faraday Cl BN13 .... 181 C5
Faraday Rd RH10 .... 5 F2
Faresmead PO21 .... 194 F2
Farhalls Cres RH12 .... 36 F6
Farlington Ave RH16 .... 85 F5
Farlington Cl RH16 .... 85 F5
Farlington Sch RH12 .... 35 B6
Farm Ave RH12 .... 36 B3
Farm Cl Barns Green RH13 .. 56 F2
  Crawley RH10 .... 19 A7
  East Grinstead RH19 .... 23 B8
  Hassocks BN6 .... 126 E4
  Henfield BN5 .... 123 E5
  Loxwood RH14 .... 32 A3
  Middleton-on-Sea PO22 .. 197 B5
  Portslade-by-Sea BN41 .. 166 A2
  Warnham RH12 .... 35 F7
Farm Cnr PO22 .... 197 A5
Farm Cotts PO20 .... 190 F6
Farm Ct Ditchling BN6 .... 123 E3
  Nutbourne PO18 .... 170 B7
Farm Mews **8** BN3 ...... 187 D6
Farm Rd
  Bracklesham PO20 .... 202 B5
  Hove BN3 .... 187 D6
  Farm View PO10 .... 149 B3
Farm Way
  Burgess Hill RH15 .... 107 D1
  Rustington BN16 .... 200 B6
  Southwick BN42 .... 186 A7
Farmfield Dr RH6 .... 5 B8
Farmfield Hospl RH6 .... 1 B1
Farmleigh Cl RH10 .... 19 C8
Farmway Cl BN3 .... 166 D2
Farncombe Rd BN11 .... 182 F2
Farndell Cl PO19 .... 173 C7
Farne Cl PO20 .... 191 E4
Farne La PO20 .... 191 E4
Farney Close Sch
  Bolney Court RH17 .... 83 D2
Farnfold Rd BN44 .... 143 D4
Farnham Ave BN6 .... 127 A5
Farnham Cl RH11 .... 39 C8
Farnham La GU27 .... 27 A7
Farnham Rd GU33 .... 45 A3
Farnhurst Rd PO22 .... 176 B6
Farnlea RH15 .... 107 D5
Faroes The BN17 .... 199 A6
Farr Cl RH17 .... 84 F8
Farriers Cl RH14 .... 77 C7
Fastnet Way BN16, BN17 .. 199 A6
Faulkners Way RH15 .... 107 A5
Fay Rd RH12 .... 36 C5
Faygate Bsns Ctr RH12 .... 16 F1
Faygate Ct BN2 .... 168 A4
Faygate La RH12 .... 16 F4
Faygate Sta RH12 .... 16 F1
Felbridge Ave RH10 .... 19 D7
Felbridge Cl RH19 .... 9 C3
Felbridge Ct RH19 .... 9 A4
Felbridge Ctr The RH19 .... 9 A3
Felbridge Cty Prim Sch RH19 8 F4
Felbridge Rd RH19 .... 8 D3
Felcot Rd RH10 .... 8 B3
Felcourt Cotts RH19 .... 9 C8
Felcourt La RH19, RH7 ...... 9 C8
Felcourt Rd RH19, RH7 ...... 9 C7

Fellcott Way RH12 .... 35 F1
Felpham Com Coll PO22 ... 195 F5
Felpham Gdns PO22 .... 196 B5
Felpham Ho BN17 .... 178 B3
Felpham Rd PO22 .... 195 F4
Felpham Way PO22 .... 196 A5
Felride RH16 .... 85 E3
Felwater Ct RH19 .... 9 A3
Fenchurch Rd RH10 .... 19 B4
Fender Ho RH12 .... 36 B2
Fenhurst Cl RH12 .... 35 F1
Fennel Cres RH11 .... 18 B2
Fennel Wlk BN43 .... 165 B1
Fereday Cl BN15 .... 183 E6
Fermandy La RH10 .... 8 A1
Fern Rd RH20 .... 119 C1
Fern Way RH12 .... 36 D5

Ferndale Rd
   Burgess Hill RH15 .... 107 C2
   Chichester PO19 .... 153 A3
   Hove BN3 .... 187 D7
Ferndale Wlk BN16 .... 180 A6
Fernden La GU27 .... 27 C2
Fernden Sch GU27 .... 27 B2
Ferndown Cranley RH10 ...... 6 D2
   Horley RH6 .... 2 A5
Ferndown Gdns PO22 .... 196 A5
Fernhill Cl RH10 .... 8 B1
Fernhill Rd RH6 .... 6 D7
Fernhurst Cl Brighton BN1 . 168 B6
   Crawley RH11 .... 18 B8
Fernhurst Cres BN1 .... 168 B5
Fernhurst Ct BN11 .... 181 F1
Fernhurst Cty Prim Sch
   GU27 .... 49 B6
Fernhurst Dr BN12 .... 181 A2
Fernhurst Gdns PO21 .... 194 D2
Fernhurst Gn GU27 .... 49 B6
Fernwood Rise BN1 .... 167 D5
Feroners Cl RH10 .... 19 A4
Ferring CE (C) Prim Sch
   BN12 .... 200 F6
Ferring Cl Crawley RH11 .... 18 B8
   Ferring BN12 .... 200 E4
Ferring Ct BN1 .... 168 F5
Ferring Gdns PO22 .... 196 A5
Ferring Grange Gdns
   BN12 .... 200 E3
Ferring La BN12 .... 180 F3
Ferring Marine BN12 .... 200 F4
Ferring St BN12 .... 200 E6
Ferringham La BN12 .... 200 E5
Ferringham Way BN12 ...... 200 E4
Feroners Ct RH10 .... 19 A4
Ferry Rd
   Littlehampton BN17 .... 198 B4
   Shoreham-by-Sea BN43 ... 184 F6
Festival Ct PO19 .... 173 A7
Fetherston Rd BN15 .... 183 E7
Feversham Cl BN43 .... 185 B6
Fidlers Copse GU27 .... 49 A6
Field Cl Burgess Hill RH15 . 106 E4
   Lancing BN15 .... 183 D6
   Walberton BN18 .... 156 D1
Field End RH20 .... 119 E2
Field Ho
   Bognor Regis PO21 .... 195 E3
   East Preston BN16 .... 199 F6
Field Pl Liphook GU30 .... 25 C3
   Littlehampton BN17 .... 198 D5
Field Rd PO20 .... 202 A7
Field Row **6** BN11 .... 182 D2
Field Sch The BN3 .... 186 D7
Fieldend RH12 .... 37 B5
Fieldgate Cl RH13 .... 59 C4
Fieldings Cotts RH14 .... 55 F5
Fieldings The Horley RH6 ..... 2 C4
   Southwater RH13 .... 79 F7
Fields End Cl RH16 .... 85 F4
Fieldview RH6 .... 2 B4
Fieldway Ditchling BN6 ..... 127 D3
   Haslemere GU27 .... 27 C7
   Haywards Heath RH16 ..... 85 F8
Fifth Ave Lancing BN15 .... 183 E7
   Worthing BN14 .... 182 C8
Filbert Cres RH11 .... 18 A6
Filey Cl RH11 .... 17 F4
Filton Wlk BN13 .... 181 D6
Finch Gdns PO21 .... 195 B7
Fincham Cl BN16 .... 199 F5
Fincham Ct BN16 .... 199 F5
Finchdean Rd PO9 .... 128 F3
Finches Cl Lancing BN15 .. 183 D5
   Littlehampton BN17 .... 178 C4
   Partridge Green RH13 .... 103 A3
Finches Ct RH14 .... 64 A1
Finches Gdns RH16 .... 86 A8
Finches La
   Haywards Heath RH16 .... 86 A8
   West Chiltington Common
   RH20 .... 119 C8

Finches Park Rd RH16 .... 86 A8
Finches The BN43 .... 185 A8
Findon By-Pass BN14 .... 161 D6
Findon Cl BN3 .... 166 F3
Findon Dr PO22 .... 196 D6
Findon Rd Brighton BN2 ... 188 F5
   Crawley RH11 .... 18 B8
   Worthing BN14 .... 161 F3
Findon Way RH12 .... 35 D3
Finians Field RH13 .... 56 F2
Finisterre Way BN17 .... 199 A4
Finsbury Cl RH11 .... 18 C2
Finsbury Lodge **1** BN2 .. 188 C6
Fir Tree Ave GU27 .... 26 D6
Fir Tree Cl Crawley RH11 ..... 5 B1
   Lower Beeding RH13 .... 60 A3
   West Chiltington Common
   RH20 .... 119 D6
Fir Tree La RH20 .... 119 D6
Fir Tree Way RH6 .... 127 A4
Firbank Cotts RH6 .... 7 C7
Fircroft Ave BN15 .... 183 E8
Fircroft Cl Brighton BN1 ... 167 E3
   Worthing BN13 .... 181 F6
Fircroft Cres BN16 .... 179 D3
Firlands
   Haywards Heath RH16 ..... 85 F4
   Horley RH6 .... 2 B4
Firle Cl RH10 .... 18 E8
Firle Rd Brighton BN2 ...... 188 D6
   North Lancing BN15 ...... 163 E1
Firs Ave PO22 .... 196 B5
Firs Ave W PO22 .... 196 B5
Firsdown Cl BN13 .... 161 E2
Firsdown Rd BN13 .... 161 E2
Firsland Park Ind Est
   BN5 .... 124 F8
First Ave
   Almodington BN20 .... 191 F2
   Bognor Regis PO22 .... 196 B4
   Bracklesham PO20 .... 202 B5
   Hove BN3 .... 187 C6
   Lancing BN15 .... 183 E7
   Middleton-on-Sea PO22 . 196 F6
   Southbourne PO10 .... 169 F8
   Worthing BN14 .... 182 C7
Firtoft Cl RH15 .... 107 B3
Firview GU30 .... 25 B3

Fish La
   Bognor Regis PO21 .... 194 F2
   Selsey PO20 .... 206 B8
Fishbourne CE (C)
   Prim Sch PO19 .... 172 B6
Fishbourne Rd W
   PO19,PO20 .... 172 C6
Fishbourne Rd E PO19 ..... 172 D6
Fishbourne Roman Palace
   PO19 .... 172 B6
Fishbourne Sta PO19 .... 172 B7
Fisher Cl RH10 .... 18 E4
Fisher La Plaistow GU8 ...... 30 B7
   South Nutbourne PO20 . 193 C7
Fisherman's Wlk
   Bognor Regis PO21 .... 194 D1
   Selsey PO20 .... 206 F7
Fishermans The PO10 ...... 169 C8
Fishermans Wlk
   Shoreham-by-Sea BN43 .. 184 D5
   South Hayling PO11 ...... 189 A2
Fishers Cl BN15 .... 199 A4
Fishers Ct RH12 .... 36 C4
Fishersgate Cty Fst Sch
   BN41 .... 186 A7
Fishersgate Sta BN41 .... 186 C8
Fishersgate Terr
   BN41,BN42 .... 186 A7
Fitch Dr BN2 .... 168 F1
Fitchet Cl RH11 .... 18 B8
Fitzalan CE (C) Fst Sch
   RH20 .... 97 A3
Fittleworth Cl BN12 .... 181 B4
Fittleworth Dr PO22 .... 196 C7
Fittleworth Gdn **7** BN16 . 199 C5
Fittleworth Rd RH14 .... 75 F5
Fitzalan Ct
   Littlehampton BN17 ...... 198 E4
   4 Rustington BN16 ... 199 B3
Fitzalan Mews BN18 .... 158 B2
Fitzalan Rd
   Arundel BN18 .... 158 B2
   Horsham RH12,RH13 ..... 37 A4
   Littlehampton BN17 ..... 198 F4
Fitzherbert Dr BN2 .... 188 D8
Fitzjohn Ct BN6 .... 126 F3
Fitzleet Ho **9** PO21 ...... 195 C3
Fitzroy Ct BN17 .... 198 E5
Fitzwilliam Cl PO21 .... 194 F4
Five Acres Crawley RH10 ... 18 E8
   Funtington PO18 .... 151 A5
Five Oaks Rd RH13,RH14 ... 56 D7

Fixcroft Cotts BN5 .... 104 D4
Flag Ct BN3 .... 187 B5
Flag Sq BN43 .... 184 F6
Flamsteed Hts RH11 .... 18 B1
Flansham La PO22 .... 196 C6
Flansham Pk PO22 .... 196 D6
Flatt Rd PO18 .... 170 D8
Flax Mean PO22 .... 196 B5
Flax Mean Ho PO22 .... 196 B5
Flaxman Ave PO19 .... 172 D6
Fleet The RH20 .... 97 B3
Fleming Ct PO21 .... 194 A1
Fleming Way RH10,RH11 ... 5 F2
Fletcher Cl
   Bognor Regis PO21 .... 195 C3
   Crawley RH10 .... 18 E4
   North Mundham PO20 ... 173 D1
Fletcher Ho PO20 .... 173 C1
Fletcher Pl PO20 .... 173 C1
Fletcher Rd BN14 .... 182 E5
Fletcher Way BN16 .... 179 F6
Fletcher's Croft PO20 ...... 119 D2
Fletcher's La PO18 .... 171 D1
Fletchers RH13 .... 57 F3
Fletchers Cl RH13 .... 36 E1
Fletchers Est PO20 .... 192 D2
Fletchers Field GL30 .... 25 C3
Fletchers Ho GU30 .... 25 B3
Fletchers La PO20 .... 192 D3
Fletching Cl BN2 .... 188 F6
Flimwell Cl BN2 .... 188 E5
Flint Cl Crawley RH10 .... 19 B3
   Portslade-by-Sea BN41 .. 166 B2
Flint Cotts BN18 .... 158 A3
Flint Ho **2** PO21 .... 195 C3
Flint Pk RH6 .... 199 C4
Flora McDonald Cty
   Jun Sch BN17 .... 198 C6
Floral Dean Ct BN14 .... 162 A1
Florence Ave BN3 .... 186 D8
Florence Cl PO20 .... 191 D4
Florence Ct BN1 .... 167 F2
Florence Pl BN1 .... 168 B1
Florence Rd
   Brighton BN1 .... 188 A8
   Chichester PO19 .... 173 C6
Florets The BN44 .... 144 B1
Florida Cl BN12 .... 200 F4
Florida Gdns BN12 .... 200 F4
Florida Rd BN12 .... 200 F4
Florlandia Cl BN13 .... 183 B6
Flower Farm Cl BN5 .... 123 D5
Foamcourt Waye BN12 .... 200 D5
Folders Cl RH15 .... 107 D1
Folders La BN6,RH15 .... 107 D1
Follett Cl PO21 .... 194 E2
Follis Gdns PO19 .... 172 B8
Folly La GU28,RH20 .... 115 E3
Fontwell Ave BN18,PO20 . 155 F1
Fontwell Cl
   Fontwell BN18 .... 156 A2
   Littlehampton BN16 ..... 199 B4
   Worthing BN14 .... 182 A8
Fontwell Dr BN14 .... 182 A8
Fontwell Park Race Course
   BN18 .... 155 F2
Fontwell Rd Crawley RH10 . 19 A3
   East Beach PO20 .... 206 G8
Ford Airfield Ind Est
   BN18 .... 177 C3
Ford La
   Ashurst BN44,RH13 ...... 122 D7
   Ford BN18 .... 177 C4
Ford Rd Arundel BN18 ..... 158 A2
   Ford BN18 .... 177 E3
   Tortington BN18 .... 177 F7
Fordingbridge Cl RH12 ..... 36 C1
Fordingbridge Ind Site
   PO22 .... 176 A7
Fordwater Gdns BN18 ..... 177 B2
Fordwater La PO19 .... 153 A2
Fordwater Rd
   Chichester PO18, PO19 . 153 A3
   East Lavant PO19 .... 153 A5
Foredown Ctry Pk PO20 . 172 B8
Foredown Cl BN41 .... 166 B2
Foredown Dr BN41 .... 166 C1
Foredown Rd
   Portslade Village BN41 . 166 B4
   Portslade-by-Sea BN41 .. 166 B2
Forest Cnr GU33 .... 45 C7
Forest Com Sch RH13 ...... 36 F1
Forest Lane Cl GU30 .... 25 A4
Forest Lodge **2** RH19 ... 22 F8
Forest Oaks RH13 .... 37 B4

Forest Rd Brighton BN1 ... 168 E6
   Colgate RH12 .... 38 D6
   Liss Forest GU33 .... 45 C7
   Midhurst GU29 .... 92 D6
   Worthing BN14 .... 182 D6
Forest Ridge RH19 .... 43 A5
Forest Rise GU33 .... 45 C6
Forest Row Bsns Pk RH18 . 23 F4
Forest Row CE Inf Sch
   RH18 .... 23 F2
Forest View RH10 .... 19 A3
Forest View Rd RH19 .... 22 E6
Forester Rd RH10 .... 18 E4
Forestfield Crawley RH10 ... 19 B3
   Horsham RH13 .... 37 A3
Forge Cl
   Broadridge Heath RH12 ... 35 D4
   East Preston BN16 .... 199 F6
   Portslade-by-Sea BN41 .. 166 B2
   Stockbridge PO19 .... 172 F3
Forge La
   Broadridge Heath RH12 ... 35 D4
   Crawley RH10 .... 6 D3
Forge Wood Ind Est RH10 .. 6 B3
Forge Rd RH10 .... 19 A7
Forge The Handcross RH17 . 61 C8
Selsey PO20 .... 206 D7
   Southwater RH13 .... 57 F1
   Warnham RH12 .... 35 E7
Forge Way
   Billingshurst RH14 .... 77 C8
   Burgess Hill RH15 .... 107 A4
Forge Wood RH10 .... 6 D3
Forge Wood Ind Est RH10 .. 6 B3
Forsters Yd BN17 .... 198 B5
Fort Haven BN43 .... 185 C6
Fort Rd BN17 .... 198 C6
Forty Acre La GU31 .... 108 E3
Fosters Cl BN16 .... 199 E4
Foundry Cl RH13 .... 36 E4
Foundry Cotts GU29 .... 93 C3
Foundry La RH13 .... 107 B3
Foundry La
   Haslemere GU27 .... 27 A6
   Horsham RH12,RH13 ..... 36 E3
Foundry St BN1 .... 207 A6
Fountains Cl
   Brighton BN1 .... 168 C2
   Crawley RH11 .... 18 A4
Fourth Ave
   Bognor Regis PO22 .... 196 C4
   Hove BN3 .... 187 B6
   Lancing BN15 .... 183 E7
   Worthing BN14 .... 182 D7
Fowey Cl BN43 .... 185 B6
Fowler Cl RH10 .... 19 C4
Fox Cl Burgess Hill RH15 .. 106 F1
   Crawley RH11 .... 5 B1
Fox Ct PO20 .... 119 B1
Fox Dell RH20 .... 119 B1
Fox Hill CI RH16 .... 85 E1
Fox Hill RH16 .... 85 F1
Fox Hill Village RH16 .... 85 E1
Fox Lea BN14 .... 161 E5
Fox Rd Easebourne GU29 .. 71 A2
   Haslemere GU27 .... 26 E6
Foxbridge La RH14 .... 31 C1
Foxbush La PO10 .... 149 E4
Foxdale Dr BN16 .... 179 F4
Foxes Cl RH13 .... 79 F7
Foxes Croft PO22 .... 176 C6
Foxfield Cotts RH13 .... 79 F7
Foxfields RH10 .... 119 C8
Foxglove Ave RH12 .... 36 E6
Foxglove Wlk RH11 .... 18 B3
Foxhill Ct **3** BN15 .... 183 E5
Foxhole La RH17 .... 83 B2
Foxholes RH12 .... 33 D8
Foxhunters Rd BN41 .... 165 F3
Foxleigh Chase RH12 .... 36 F5
Foxley La BN13 .... 181 F8
Foxoven Rd RH16 .... 85 C5
Foxwarren Cl PO20 .... 201 F7
Foxwells RH17 .... 41 A1
Framed **11** BN2 .... 188 F5
Framfield Cl Brighton BN1 . 168 E6
   Crawley RH11 .... 18 A8
Frampton Cl BN12 .... 181 C2
Framptons The BN16 .... 200 B5
France La BN13 .... 160 D1
Francis Edwards Way
   RH11 .... 17 E2
Francis Rd RH16 .... 86 B8
Francis St BN1,BN2 .... 207 A7
Franciscan Way BN17 ..... 198 D5
Francisclea RH16 .... 85 D6
Francome Ho BN15 .... 183 D3
Frandor Rd PO21 .... 194 F5
Frankland Mead RH20 .... 141 E6
Frankland Terr **2** PO10 . 169 C8

Franklands Cl
   Burgess Hill RH15 .... 107 B1
   Worthing BN14 .... 162 A1
Franklands Gdns RH15 .... 127 A8
Franklands Way RH15 ..... 127 A8
Franklin Pl PO19 .... 173 A7
Franklin Rd Brighton BN2 . 188 C7
   Crawley RH10 .... 19 C5
   Portslade-by-Sea BN43 . 165 D1
   Shoreham-by-Sea BN43 . 165 D1
   Worthing BN13 .... 181 E7
Franklin St BN2 .... 188 C8
Franklynn Rd RH16 .... 85 F3
Frankton Ave RH16 .... 86 A3
Frant Rd BN3 .... 167 A2
Frarydene PO10 .... 169 F8
Fraser Cl PO20 .... 206 F6
Fraser Ct **2** BN43 .... 185 C8
Fraser Gdns PO10 .... 150 A2
Fred Emery Ct **10** BN1 . 187 E5
Frederick Cotts RH16 .... 86 B7
Frederick Gdns BN1 .... 207 A6
Frederick Pl BN1 .... 207 A6
Frederick Rd PO19 .... 172 C7
Frederick St BN1 .... 207 A6
Freehold St BN43 .... 184 F7
Freehold Terr **1** BN2 .... 188 C8
Freek's La RH15 .... 107 A5
Freeman Cl BN18,PO20 .... 156 B3
Freeman Rd RH12 .... 35 F8
Freemans Cl RH14 .... 77 C8
Freemans Rd BN41 .... 186 A8
Freeways PO20 .... 206 C8
French Gdns RH16 .... 86 A6
Frenches RH10 .... 119 D2
Frenches Mead RH14 .... 77 C8
Freshbrook Cl BN15 .... 183 E5
Freshbrook Ct **3** BN15 . 183 E5
Freshbrook Cty Fst Sch
   BN15 .... 183 E6
Freshbrook Rd BN15 .... 183 F5
Freshfield Bank RH18 .... 23 E2
Freshfield Cl RH10 .... 19 A5
Freshfield Halt RH17 .... 87 B8
Freshfield La RH17 .... 65 E2
Freshfield Pl BN2 .... 188 C5
Freshfield Rd BN2 .... 188 D6
Freshfield St BN2 .... 188 D6
Freshfield Way BN2 .... 188 C5
Freshfields Dr RH15 .... 183 D6
Freshfields Dr RH15 .... 183 D6
Friar Cl BN1 .... 168 A4
Friar Cres BN1 .... 168 A3
Friar Rd BN1 .... 168 A3
Friar Wlk BN1 .... 167 F4
Friars Cl BN6 .... 126 E4
Friars Oak Rd BN6 .... 126 E5
Friars Rookery RH10 .... 18 F6
Friars Wlk BN3 .... 181 F3
Friary La PO19 .... 173 A6
Friary La PO19 .... 173 A6
Friary Way RH10 .... 18 E5
Friday St Faygate RH12 .... 15 E6
   Warnham RH12 .... 35 E7
Friends Cl RH11 .... 5 D1
Friston Cl BN2 .... 168 F4
Friston Wlk BN13 .... 181 A7
Frith Pk RH19 .... 9 E3
Frith Rd
   Bognor Regis PO21 .... 195 A4
   Hove BN3 .... 187 A8
Frobisher Cl BN12 .... 181 D4
Frobisher Rd PO21 .... 194 C2
Frobisher Way
   Littlehampton BN16 ..... 199 E4
   Worthing BN12 .... 181 D4
Fry Cl RH11 .... 18 B1
Fry Cres RH15 .... 106 E5
Fryern Cl RH20 .... 119 D3
Fryern Rd RH20 .... 119 D3
Fryland La BN5, RH13 ..... 104 B4
Fuel Farm Rd RH6 .... 5 E8
Fulfords Hill RH13 .... 57 A7
Fulham Cl RH11 .... 18 B2
Fullers Wlk RH17 .... 178 D5
Fulmar Cl **1** Crawley RH11 17 D5
   Hove BN3 .... 167 D1
Fulmar Dr RH19 .... 10 B3
Fulmar Way PO20 .... 154 E1
Fulmer Cl **1** BN1 .... 182 B1
Funtington Cty Prim Sch
   PO18 .... 151 A3
Funtington Ho BN17 .... 178 B3
Furlong Way RH6 .... 5 F8
Furlonge Ho PO10 .... 149 A1
Furnace Dr RH10 .... 18 E4
Furnace Farm Rd RH10 .... 19 A4

Furnace Par RH10 .... 19 A4
Furnace PI RH10 .... 19 A4
Furnace Rd RH10, RH19 ...... 8 C3
Furners La BN15 .... 124 A5
Furners Mead BN5 .... 123 F4
Furnston Gr PO10 .... 150 A1
Furse Feld PO21 .... 195 A2
Furze CI BN13 .... 161 D2
Furze Common Rd RH20 ... 120 A6
Furze Croft BN3 .... 187 D6
Furze Hill BN3 .... 187 D6
Furze Hill Ct BN3 .... 187 E6
Furze Hill Ho BN3 .... 187 E6
Furze La RH19 .... 9 A4
Furze Meadow GU31 .... 90 A8
Furze Rd Rudgwick RH12 ... 33 D8
Worthing BN13 .... 161 E2
Furze View RH14 .... 56 B6
Furzedene BN3 .... 187 D6
Furzedown BN17 .... 198 E4
Furzefield Crawley RH11 .... 18 C7
East Wittering PO20 .... 190 F1
Furzefield Chase RH19 .... 9 E6
Furzefield La RH14 .... 179 F7
Furzefield Rd
East Grinstead RH19 .... 9 D4
Horsham RH12 .... 37 B5
Furzeholme BN13 .... 161 E2
Furzeland Way BN6 .... 125 D8
Furzen La RH12, RH5 .... 13 B4
Fyning La GU31 .... 68 C5

Gables The Copthorne RH10 .. 7 B3
Cowfold RH13 .... 81 E1
Horsham RH12 .... 36 D4
Southwater RH13 .... 79 F8
Gableson Ave BN1 .... 167 B4
Gabriel Rd RH10 .... 19 C2
Gage CI RH10 .... 8 C1
Gage Ridge RH18 .... 23 E2
Gaggle Wood RH13 .... 59 C6
Gainsboro Rd PO21 .... 195 C3
Gainsborough Ave BN14 .. 182 E7
Gainsborough Dr PO20 ... 206 F7
Gainsborough Ho 18 BN3 .. 187 D7
Gainsborough Lodge 1
BN14 .... 182 C4
Gainsborough Rd RH10 ... 18 F3
Gaisford CI BN14 .... 182 C4
Gaisford Rd BN14 .... 182 B4
Galahad Rd RH11 .... 17 E6
Gales Dr RH10 .... 18 F6
Gales PI RH10 .... 18 F6
Galliers CI BN1 .... 168 B6
Galsworthy CI BN12 .... 181 B3
Galsworthy Rd BN12 .... 181 B3
Gamecock Terr PO20 .... 154 D1
Gander CI RH15 .... 107 A5
Gander Gn RH16 .... 85 F7
Gander Hill RH16 .... 85 F7
Ganders CI BN15 .... 123 D5
Gandersgate La RH14 ...... 75 A7
Gannet Ho BN1 .... 167 B1
Gannon Rd BN11 .... 182 F3
Ganymede Ct RH11 .... 17 E3
Garbitts La GU31 .... 68 B4
Garcia Trad Est BN13 ...... 181 F3
Garden Ave PO20 .... 202 B6
Garden CI
Angmering BN16 .... 180 A7
East Grinstead RH19 .... 22 F7
Lancing BN15 .... 183 C6
Portslade-by-Sea BN41 .. 186 C8
Shoreham-by-Sea BN43 ... 165 B1
Storrington RH20 .... 119 D2
Garden Cres PO22 .... 176 C5
Garden Ct PO21 .... 194 E2
Garden Head RH19 .... 42 E6
Garden Ho PO19 .... 152 F2
Garden Ho The BN1 .... 207 F6
Garden House La RH19 .... 22 F7
Gardens The
Fittleworth RH20 .... 97 A3
Southwick BN42 .... 185 F7
Gardner La RH11 .... 21 A8
Gardner Rd BN41, BN42 .. 186 A7
Gardner St BN1 .... 207 A5
Garland Ave PO10 .... 149 B3

Garland CI PO19 .... 173 B5
Garland Rd RH19 .... 9 D2
Garland Sq PO20 .... 154 D2
Garnet Ho 18 BN2 .... 188 C4
Garrett CI RH10 .... 19 C4
Garrick Rd BN14 .... 182 E4
Garrick Wlk RH10 .... 18 E3
Garrats The RH10 .... 19 E7
Garsons Rd PO10 .... 169 F8
Garton CI RH11 .... 17 E5
Gaskyns CI RH11 .... 33 D7
Gasson Wood Rd RH11 .... 17 E4
Gaston Way PO18 .... 152 E7
Gatcombe CI BN13 .... 181 B5
Gateford Dr RH12 .... 36 F6
Gatehouse La
Burgess Hill BN6, RH15 .. 106 C4
Trotton GU31 .... 69 A4
Gates CI RH10 .... 19 C2
Gatesmead RH16 .... 85 F8
Gateway Lodge PO22 ...... 195 F4
Gatwick Terr BN44 .... 143 D3
Gattons Cty Inf Sch The
RH15 .... 106 E3
Gattons The RH15 .... 106 D3
Gatwick Airport Sta RH6 ... 6 B7
Gatwick Airport-London
RH6 .... 1 C2
Gatwick Gate RH6 .... 5 E5
Gatwick Metro Ctr RH6 ..... 2 B4
Gatwick Park Hospl RH6 .... 1 E2
Gatwick Rd RH10, RH6 .... 6 A3
Gatwick Way RH6 .... 5 F8
Gatwick Zoo RH6 .... 4 C6
Gaugemaster Way BN18 .. 177 E5
Gay St RH20 .... 99 C4
Gay Street La RH20 .... 99 A6
Gaywood Wlk BN13 .... 181 D5
Gemini CI RH11 .... 17 E4
Genistos The BN6 .... 126 E4
Genoa CI BN16 .... 199 A6
George Denyer CI GU27 ... 27 C7
George IV Wlk PO22 .... 196 A5
George Pinion Ct RH12 ..... 36 B3
George Pringle Sch BN12 . 181 D5
George St Brighton BN2 .. 207 A5
Chichester PO19 .... 173 A7
Hove BN3 .... 187 B6
Portslade-by-Sea BN41 .. 186 C7
Southwick BN41 .... 186 A7
George V Ave
Shoreham-by-Sea BN15 .. 184 B5
Worthing BN11, BN12 .... 181 F2
Georges La RH20 .... 120 C1
Georgia Ave BN14 .... 182 D4
Georgian CI RH10 .... 19 D5
Georgian Gardens Cty
Prim Sch BN16 .... 199 E6
Georgian Gdns BN16 ...... 199 E6
Gerald CI RH15 .... 107 D3
Gerald Ct RH13 .... 36 E2
Gerald Rd BN11 .... 181 F1
Gerard St BN1 .... 207 A8
Gerrard House Bsns Ctr
RH16 .... 199 F6
Ghyll Cres RH13 .... 58 B7
Ghyll Ct RH13 .... 57 F1
Ghyllside BN2 .... 168 E1
Gibbons Ct RH10 .... 19 C3
Giblets La RH12 .... 36 F7
Giblets Way RH12 .... 36 E7
Gibson Rd RH10 .... 154 C2
Gibson Way PO21 .... 195 D4
Giffards CI RH19 .... 9 F1
Gifford Rd PO18 .... 171 C7
Gilbert Rd PO19 .... 172 E8
Gilberts The BN16 .... 199 B3
Giles CI BN18 .... 176 F2
Gilham La RH18 .... 23 E2
Gillett CI RH13 .... 37 B4
Gillett Ho RH13 .... 37 B4
Gillham's La GU27 .... 26 A5
Gilligan CI RH12 .... 36 B2
Gilligans The RH15 .... 106 F5
Gillmans Ind Est RH14 .... 77 D6
Gilway PO20 .... 206 G8
Gilmore Rd PO19 .... 173 C6
Gilpin CI PO19 .... 173 C6
Gilwynes PO21 .... 194 F2
Gilwynes Ct PO21 .... 194 F2
Ginhams Rd RH11 .... 18 B6
Girton Ho BN41 .... 186 F6
Glade Cty Inf Sch The
PO22 .... 195 A5
Glade The
Bognor Regis PO21 .... 205 A8
Crawley RH10 .... 19 A4
Horsham RH13 .... 37 A3
Gladepoint 7 RH16 .... 85 E5
Glades The RH10 .... 10 B1
Gladonian Rd BN17 .... 178 D3

Gladstone PI BN2 .... 188 C8
Gladstone Rd
Burgess Hill RH15 .... 107 C4
Horsham RH13 .... 36 D3
Portslade-by-Sea BN41 .. 186 B7
Yapton BN18 .... 176 F2
Gladstone Terr
Brighton BN2 .... 207 B7
Littlehampton BN17 ...... 178 D3
Gladys Rd BN3 .... 186 D8
Glamis Ct PO21 .... 195 D3
Glamis St PO21 .... 195 D3
Glanville Wlk 7 RH11 .... 18 A3
Glaseby La RH20 .... 141 D4
Glasshouse La GU28, RH14 .. 74 F3
Glastonbury Rd BN3 .... 186 D6
Glatting La RH20 .... 115 E1
Glaziers La GU29 .... 71 B2
Gleave CI RH19 .... 10 A2
Glebe CI Crawley RH10 .... 18 E7
Lancing BN15 .... 183 E7
Norton PO20 .... 155 B1
Southwick BN42 .... 185 F7
Glebe Cty Mid Sch BN42 . 185 D7
Glebe Field Rd PO20 ...... 191 A5
Glebe Rd Cuckfield RH17 .. 84 F6
Fernhurst GU27 .... 49 B5
Worthing BN13 .... 161 D4
Glebe The Copthorne RH10 .. 7 B3
Felbridge RH19 .... 9 A4
Haywards Heath RH16 ... 86 A8
Horley RH6 .... 1 E3
Hurstpierpoint BN6 ...... 126 A6
Tangmere PO20 .... 154 C1
Glebe Twitten RH17 .... 84 F6
Glebe View RH17 .... 41 A1
Glebe Villas Hove BN3 ... 186 D7
Petworth GU28 .... 73 F1
Glebe Way Lancing BN15 . 183 E7
Wisborough Green RH14 ... 76 C8
Glebelands
Crawley Down RH10 .... 21 A7
Loxwood RH14 .... 31 F4
Pulborough RH20 .... 98 D2
Glebelands CI BN43 .... 185 B8
Glebeside Ave RH14 .... 182 A5
Glebeside CI BN14 .... 182 B5
Glebe Cres PO20 .... 206 E7
Glen Dale PO9 .... 128 F1
Glen Gdns BN12 .... 200 F6
Glen Rise BN1 .... 167 B5
Glen Rise BN1 .... 167 B5
Glen The Southwater RH13 .. 58 A2
Worthing BN13 .... 182 A7
Glen Vue RH19 .... 9 E1
Glenbarrie Way BN12 ...... 180 E3
Glencathara Rd PO21 ..... 195 B3
Glendale CI RH12 .... 37 A6
Glendale Rd
Burgess Hill RH15 .... 107 B2
Hove BN3 .... 187 D7
Glendon Ho 9 RH11 .... 18 D5
Glendor Rd BN3 .... 186 E6
Glendyne Ct RH19 .... 23 A8
Glendyne Way RH19 .... 23 A8
Gleneagles Ct
Crawley RH10, RH11 ...... 18 D5
10 Haywards Heath RH16 .. 85 E4
Glenelg Ct PO21 .... 194 F6
Glenfalls Ave BN1 .... 168 A7
Glenfield Cotts RH6 .... 4 D7
Glenham Ct RH19 .... 43 A5
Glenlea Hollow
GU26, GU27 .... 26 E8
Glenmore St 13 BN17 .... 198 E4
Glenview CI RH10 .... 18 F8
Glenville Rd BN16 .... 199 D4
Glenway PO22 .... 195 A4
Glenwood Ave PO22 .... 195 A4
Glenwood Rd PO10 .... 150 A1
Gleton Ave BN3 .... 166 D2
Globe PI BN17 .... 178 D3
Gloster Dr PO21 .... 194 B2
Gloucester CI RH12 .... 23 A8
Gloucester CI BN12 .... 181 F1
Gloucester La BN17 .... 198 D5
Gloucester Pas 2 BN1 .... 207 A6
Gloucester PI
Brighton BN1, BN2 .... 207 A6
Littlehampton BN17 ...... 198 D5
Gloucester Rd
Bognor Regis PO21 .... 195 E3
Brighton BN1, BN2 .... 207 A6
Burgess Hill RH15 .... 106 F3
Crawley RH10 .... 18 E2
Littlehampton BN17 ...... 198 C5
Gloucester St BN1, BN2 .. 207 A6
Gloucester Terr PO18 ..... 171 B4
Gloucester Way PO19 .... 152 F1
Glover's Rd RH6 .... 4 D7
Glovers Field GU27 .... 26 F6

Glynde Ave BN12 .... 181 A2
Glynde CI BN2 .... 200 F6
Glynde Cres PO22 .... 196 A5
Glynde Ho BN3 .... 187 D6
Glynde PI RH12 .... 36 C2
Glynde Rd BN2 .... 188 D6
Glyndebourne Ct 9
BN43 .... 184 F7
Glynleigh 17 BN2 .... 207 B6
Glyns Mead RH7 .... 198 E5
Goddard CI RH10 .... 19 B3
Goddards Green Hospl
(Cuckfield Hospl Annexe)
BN6 .... 106 B5
Godman CI PO21 .... 194 D2
Godmans Ct RH13 .... 81 E1
Godolphin CI RH10, RH11 .. 18 D5
Godstalls La BN44 .... 143 C2
Godstrode La GU8 .... 29 A6
Godwin CI PO10 .... 149 A3
Godwin Rd BN3 .... 166 D1
Godwin Way PO18 .... 172 A8
Goffs CI RH11 .... 18 C5
Goffs La RH13 .... 122 E6
Goffs Park Rd RH11 .... 18 C4
Goldcrest Ave BN17 .... 178 C4
Goldcrest CI RH6 .... 1 E4
Golden Acre
Bognor Regis PO21 .... 205 A8
West Kingston BN16 ..... 200 B4
Golden Ave BN16 .... 200 B5
Golden Avenue CI BN16 . 200 B5
Golden Fields GU30 .... 25 D3
Golden Hill RH15 .... 107 D3
Golden La RH13 .... 122 E6
Golden Sq Henfield BN5 . 123 E4
Petworth GU28 .... 95 F8
Goldfinch CI Crawley RH11 . 18 D8
Horsham RH12 .... 36 C7
Golding Barn Farm (Works)
BN5 .... 144 E2
Golding La RH13 .... 59 D7
Goldsmid Rd BN1, BN3 .. 187 E7
Goldsmith Rd BN14 .... 182 E4
Goldstone CI BN3 .... 167 A2
Goldstone Cres BN3 ...... 167 B2
Goldstone Ct BN3 .... 167 A3
Goldstone Cty Jun Sch
BN3 .... 166 E1
Goldstone Ho 4 BN3 ..... 187 B7
Goldstone La BN3 .... 187 B8
Goldstone Rd BN3 .... 187 B7
Goldstone St BN3 .... 187 B7
Goldstone Villas BN3 .... 187 B7
Goldstone Way BN3 ...... 167 A2
Golf Club La RH20 .... 118 F7
Golf Dr BN1 .... 168 B3
Golf Links La PO20 .... 203 E1
Golf Links Rd PO22 .... 196 A6
Golfers La BN16 .... 179 D3
Goodacres PO22 .... 176 C5
Goodhew Dr BN18 .... 177 A3
Goodwin CI RH11 .... 17 F3
Goodwins CI RH19 .... 9 D3
Goodwood Ave PO22 ..... 195 F5
Goodwood CI
Crawley RH10 .... 19 A3
Midhurst GU29 .... 92 E5
Rustington BN16 .... 199 E6
Goodwood Ct
2 Hove BN3 .... 187 D7
Selsey PO20 .... 206 E8
Southbourne PO10 .... 170 A8
Goodwood Ctry Pk PO18 . 134 A4
Goodwood Gdns PO20 .. 173 E1
Goodwood Ho PO18 ..... 153 F6
Goodwood Rd
BN13, BN14 .... 182 A7
Goodwood Way BN2 ..... 168 F3
Goose Green CI RH12 ...... 36 D5
Goosegreen La RH20 .... 100 C2
Gooserye Ct GU30 .... 25 B3
Gorden Rd BN15 .... 183 D6
Gordon Ave
1 Bognor Regis PO21 .... 195 D4
Bognor Regis PO22 .... 195 C4
Shoreham-by-Sea BN43 . 185 A7
Stockbridge PO19 .... 172 E3
Selsey W PO22 .... 195 D5
Gordon CI RH16 .... 85 E6
Gordon Ho
8 Bognor Regis PO21 .... 195 C3
Burgess Hill RH15 .... 107 C4
Gordon Rd Brighton BN1 . 167 F2
Burgess Hill RH15 .... 107 C4
Haywards Heath RH16 ... 85 E6
Hermitage PO10 .... 169 D8
Horsham RH12 .... 36 D4
Portslade-by-Sea BN41 .. 186 C7
Shoreham-by-Sea BN43 . 185 A7
Southwick BN41 .... 186 A7

Gordon Rd
Worthing BN11 .... 182 D3
Gordon Terr PO18 .... 171 B6
Goreside La RH17 .... 84 F8
Goring Chase BN12 .... 181 A4
Goring Crossways BN12 .. 181 A4
Goring Ct BN1 .... 168 F5
Goring Hall Hospl (private)
BN12 .... 181 B1
Goring Rd Steyning BN44 . 143 E2
Worthing BN11, BN12 .... 181 D2
Goring St BN12 .... 181 A3
Goring Way
Partridge Green RH13 ... 103 A3
Worthing BN12 .... 181 A2
Goring's Mead RH13 .... 36 D1
Goring-by-Sea CE (A)
Fst Sch BN12 .... 181 C2
Goring-by-Sea Sta BN12 . 181 A3
Gorling CI RH11 .... 17 E5
Gorringe CI BN43 .... 185 D7
Gorringes Brook RH12 .... 36 D6
Gorse Ave
Bognor Regis PO22 .... 196 D6
Kingston Gorse
BN12, BN16 .... 200 D4
Worthing BN14 .... 182 B6
Gorse Bank CI RH20 ...... 120 C3
Gorse CI Copthorne RH10 .. 7 B2
Crawley RH11 .... 18 B1
Portslade-by-Sea BN41 .. 165 F4
Gorse Cotts GU27 .... 26 C8
Gorse End RH12 .... 36 D5
Gorse La BN13 .... 161 E2
Gorse Terr PO20 .... 192 D4
Gorselands RH14 .... 77 E8
Gosden CI RH10 .... 19 A5
Gosden Rd BN17 .... 198 F6
Gospond Rd PO22 .... 176 B5
Gossamer La PO21 .... 194 D3
Gossops Dr RH11 .... 18 A5
Gossops Green Cty Fst Sch
RH11 .... 18 A5
Gossops Green Cty Mid Sch
RH11 .... 18 A5
Gossops Green La RH11 ... 18 A5
Gossops Par RH11 .... 17 F5
Goudhurst CI RH10 .... 19 E6
Goudhurst Keep RH10 .... 19 E6
Gower Rd
Haywards Heath RH16 ... 85 E3
Horley RH6 .... 1 E3
Gowers CI RH17 .... 64 B8
Grace Ct BN6 .... 126 E5
Grace Rd RH11 .... 18 A1
Graffham CI Brighton BN2 . 188 C6
Chichester PO19 .... 153 A3
Crawley RH11 .... 18 B8
Graffham Cty Prim Sch
GU28 .... 114 B6
Grafton Ave PO22 .... 196 C6
Grafton CI BN16 .... 199 C6
Grafton Ct PO20 .... 206 E6
Grafton Dr BN15 .... 183 C6
Grafton Gdns BN15 .... 183 C6
Grafton PI 5 BN11 .... 182 D2
Grafton Rd Selsey PO20 .. 206 E6
Worthing BN11 .... 182 D2
Graham Ave
Brighton BN1 .... 167 F5
Portslade-by-Sea BN41 .. 165 F4
Graham CI BN41 .... 165 F4
Graham Cres BN41 .... 165 F4
Graham Rd
Worthing BN11 .... 182 D2
Yapton BN18 .... 176 F1
Graham's Cotts RH16 ...... 64 B1
Grailands CI GU27 .... 49 C6
Granary CI RH6 .... 2 A5
Granary Way
Horsham RH11 .... 36 A1
Littlehampton BN17 ...... 178 D4
Grand Ave Hassocks BN6 . 126 F4
Hove BN3 .... 187 C6
Lancing BN15 .... 183 E7
Littlehampton BN11 ...... 178 C3
Worthing BN11 .... 182 A2
Grand Avenue Mansions 2
BN3 .... 187 C6
Grand Junction Rd
BN1, BN2 .... 207 A4
Grand Par Brighton BN2 .. 207 A5
Crawley RH11 .... 18 D6
Grand Parade Mews BN2 . 207 A5
Grange CI Brighton BN1 .. 167 E1
Burgess Hill RH15 .... 107 C5
Crawley RH10 .... 19 A8
Ferring BN12 .... 200 E5
Grange Cres RH10 .... 21 B7

Grange Ct
Bognor Regis PO21 .... 194 E1
Middleton-on-Sea PO22 ... 196 F5
9 Southwick BN42 .... 185 E7
Grange Field Way PO21 ... 194 D2
Grange Ind Est The
BN42 .... 185 D7
Grange La PO20 .... 204 B2
Grange Park Rd BN12 ..... 200 E5
Grange Rd
Crawley Down RH10 .... 21 A7
Hove BN3 .... 186 E8
Midhurst GU29 .... 92 F7
Southwick BN42 .... 185 E7
Grange The RH6 .... 2 A6
Grange Way RH13 .... 57 F2
Grangeway The BN16 ...... 199 C5
Grangeways BN1 .... 167 E5
Grangewood Dr PO21 ..... 194 D2
Granston Way RH10 .... 21 C8
Grant CI PO20 .... 206 D7
Grant St BN2 .... 207 B7
Grantham Rd BN1 .... 168 A1
Grantsmead BN15 .... 183 E8
Granville Ct **10** BN3 ...... 187 B7
Granville Rd Hove BN3 .... 187 E7
Littlehampton BN17 .... 198 E4
Graperies The **3** BN2 ... 188 C5
Grasmere Ave BN15 .... 183 B6
Grasmere Gdns RH12 .... 37 B6
Grassmere RH6 .... 2 C4
Grassmere CI
Bognor Regis PO22 .... 195 F4
Littlehampton BN17 .... 179 A3
Grassmere Par PO22 .... 195 F4
Gratten La
Twineham BN5, RH17 ...... 105 A3
Wineham BN5 .... 104 D3
Grattons Dr RH10 .... 6 C1
Grattons The RH13 .... 34 E3
Gratwicke CI RH14 .... 77 D8
Gratwicke Rd BN11 .... 182 C2
Gravel La PO19 .... 173 C5
Gravelly Cres BN15 .... 183 F6
Gravelpit Cnr RH17 .... 39 C1
Gravelye CI RH16 .... 86 B5
Gravelye La
Haywards Heath RH16 ...... 86 A4
Haywards Heath RH16 ...... 86 B6
Graveney Rd RH10 .... 19 C5
Gravett Ct RH15 .... 106 F2
Gravetye CI RH10 .... 19 A4
Gravits La PO21 .... 195 B4
Graydon Ave PO19 .... 172 E4
Graylingwell Hospl PO19 . 153 B1
Grays CI GU27 .... 27 E8
Grays Wood RH6 .... 2 C3
Graywood Ave PO20 .... 202 B6
Graywood PI GU27 .... 27 E8
Graywood Rd GU27 .... 27 D8
Great College St BN2 ...... 188 C4
Great Heathmead RH16 .... 85 D6
Great House Ct **4** RH19 .. 22 F8
Great Walstead Sch RH16 . 86 F6
Greatfield Way PO9 .... 128 D3
Greatham CI BN1 .... 167 E6
Greatham Rd
Crawley RH10 .... 19 C3
Worthing BN14 .... 162 A1
Greatlake CI RH6 .... 2 B4
Greatpin Croft RH20 .... 97 A3
Grebe Cres RH13 .... 37 A1
Green Bushes CI BN16 ..... 199 B4
Green CI Southwater RH13 . 57 F3
4 Southwick BN42 .... 185 E7
Green Cross RH17 .... 84 C3
Green Ct
East Wittering PO20 .... 201 F7
3 Southwick BN42 .... 185 E7
Green Field CI BN42 .... 185 E8
Green Hedges Ave RH19 .... 9 D2
Green Hedges CI RH19 .... 9 D2
Green La Bosham PO18 .... 171 C6
Broadbridge PO18 .... 171 A8
Burstow RH6 .... 6 F6
Chichester PO19 .... 173 B6
Copthorne RH10 .... 7 F4
Crawley RH10 .... 18 E8
Crawley, Worth RH10 ...... 19 D6
Faygate RH12 .... 15 F4
Fernhurst GU27 .... 27 B4
Merston PO20 .... 173 F4
Newdigate RH5 .... 3 D2
Runcton PO20 .... 173 F2
Selsey PO20 .... 206 D6
Sidlesham PO20 .... 203 C8
Street End PO20 .... 192 E6
West Grinstead RH13 ...... 102 B8
Green Lane CI BN18 .... 157 F2
Green Meadows RH16 .... 86 B8
Green Pk BN12 .... 180 F3

Green Ridge BN1 .... 167 B5
Green The
Bognor Regis PO21 .... 205 A8
Broadbridge Heath RH12 ... 35 D4
Copthorne RH10 .... 7 B3
Crawley RH11 .... 18 C7
East Lavington GU28 .... 114 E5
Henfield BN5 .... 123 E4
Hove BN3 .... 167 C2
Liss GU33 .... 45 A5
Pulborough RH20 .... 98 C4
Southwick BN42 .... 185 E7
Storrington RH20 .... 119 F2
Green View RH15 .... 106 E3
Green Way PO22 .... 196 F5
Green Way The BN12 ...... 181 B4
Green Wlk RH10 .... 18 E8
Greena CI **7** BN11 .... 182 C2
Greenacre CI RH20 .... 119 B1
Greenacres
Ashington BN13 .... 121 A6
Brighton BN1 .... 167 F1
Crawley RH10 .... 19 A5
Horsham RH12 .... 36 C4
Shoreham-by-Sea BN43 ... 184 E8
Steyning BN44 .... 143 D2
Westlands PO20 .... 191 D6
Greenacres Ring BN16 .... 180 A6
Greenbank PO22 .... 176 C5
Greencourt Dr PO21 .... 195 A5
Greenfield Cres BN1 .... 167 F3
Greenfield CI
Brighton BN1 .... 168 A5
Liphook GU30 .... 25 C5
Greenfield Cres BN1 .... 167 F3
Greenfield Rd
Chichester PO19 .... 173 C7
Slinfold RH13 .... 34 D3
Greenfield Way RH20 ..... 119 E2
Greenfields CI Liss GU33 ... 45 C4
Littlehampton BN17 .... 178 B3
Nyewood GU31 .... 90 A7
Greenfields CI Horley RH6 ... 1 E5
Horsham RH12 .... 37 A6
Nyewood GU31 .... 90 A8
Greenfields Rd Horley RH6 ... 1 E5
Horsham RH12 .... 37 A5
Greenfields Sch RH18 ...... 23 C1
Greenfields Way RH12 ..... 37 A6
Greenfinch Way RH12 ...... 36 D7
Greengates GU28 .... 50 D2
Greenhill Pk RH16 .... 86 A2
Greenhill Way RH16 .... 86 A2
Greenhurst La RH20 .... 119 E4
Greenland CI BN13 .... 181 E7
Greenland Rd BN13 .... 181 E7
Greenland Wlk BN13 .... 181 E7
Greenlands CI BN15 .... 181 E7
Greenlands Dr RH15 .... 122 B8
Greenlea Ave PO21 .... 194 B2
Greenleas BN3 .... 166 D2
Greenoaks BN15 .... 183 E8
Greenside BN17 .... 198 C6
Greenstede Ave RH19 .... 9 F2
Greentree La RH13 .... 140 F4
Greentrees Lancing BN15 ... 183 C6
5 Worthing BN13 .... 182 B2
Greentrees Ct BN15 .... 183 C6
Greentrees Cres BN15 .... 183 C6
Greenway RH12 .... 36 B3
Greenway Cty Prim Sch
RH12 .... 36 B3
Greenway The PO10 .... 149 B4
Greenways
Bognor Regis PO21 .... 194 B1
Haywards Heath RH16 ...... 85 F6
Henfield BN5 .... 123 D5
Portslade-by-Sea BN41 ... 166 B1
Southwick BN42 .... 165 F1
Greenways Cres
Ferring BN12 .... 200 F5
Shoreham-by-Sea BN43 ... 165 A1
Greenwich CI RH11 .... 18 D2
Greenwood Ave PO22 ...... 195 B6
Greenwood CI GU27 .... 26 C5
Greenwood Dr **2** RH11 .. 18 B1
Greenwood Dr BN16 .... 179 F4
Great Red BN15 .... 183 D7
Gregory CI RH10 .... 19 C2
Gregsons RH12 .... 35 E8
Grendon CI RH6 .... 1 F5
Grenfield Ct PO10 .... 149 B3
Grenville Ave GU28 .... 181 D3
Grenville CI
Liphook GU30 .... 25 C4
Worthing BN12 .... 181 B3
Grenville Gdns PO19 ...... 172 F4
Grenville St BN1 .... 207 F5
Gresham Gdns RH10 .... 18 E3
Gresham PI BN5 .... 123 D5
Gresham Wlk RH10 .... 18 E3

Grevatt's La
BN17, BN18, PO22 .... 197 B8
Grevatt's La W
BN18, BN17 .... 196 F8
Greville Gn PO10 .... 149 A3
Grey Alders RH16 .... 86 B6
Greyfriars BN3 .... 187 D8
Greyfriars CI
Bognor Regis PO21 .... 194 F3
Worthing BN13 .... 182 A6
Greyfriars La PO20 .... 140 C8
Greyhound Slip RH10 ...... 19 D7
Greylink CI PO21 .... 194 C2
Greypoint Ho BN14 .... 161 E6
Greystoke Mews BN12 .... 200 E6
Greystoke Rd BN12 .... 200 E6
Greystone Ave
Bognor Regis PO21 .... 194 F7
Worthing BN13 .... 181 F5
Gribble La PO20 .... 174 B7
Grier CI RH11 .... 17 E5
Griffin Cres BN17 .... 178 D4
Griffith's Ave BN15 .... 183 D8
Grinstead Ave BN15 .... 183 E6
Grinstead La Lancing BN15 183 E6
Sharpthorne RH19 .... 43 C7
Grinstead Mount 6 BN2 . 188 F5
Grisedale CI RH11 .... 18 C4
Groombridge Way RH12 ... 35 F1
Grooms The RH10 .... 19 D8
Groomsland Dr RH14 .... 77 C6
Grosvenor Ct BN1 .... 167 C3
Grosvenor Gdns PO21 .... 194 C3
Grosvenor Rd
East Grinstead RH19 .... 9 D1
Stockbridge PO19 .... 172 F3
3 Worthing BN11 .... 182 D2
Grosvenor St BN2 .... 207 B8
Grosvenor Way PO21 ...... 194 C3
Grouse Rd
Barnsnap RH11, RH13 ...... 38 D3
Mannings Heath RH13 ...... 59 F7
Grove **8** BN2 .... 207 B6
Grove Cres BN17 .... 198 F6
Grove CI **5** BN3 .... 187 C6
Grove Hill **2** BN2 .... 207 B6
Grove La Petworth GU28 .... 96 A6
West Chiltington Common
PO20 .... 119 E5
Grove Pk PO19 .... 172 D6
Grove Rd
Burgess Hill RH15 .... 107 B3
Chichester PO19 .... 173 B5
Horley RH6 .... 1 C2
Selsey PO20 .... 206 E6
Worthing BN14 .... 182 C6
Grove St Brighton BN2 .... 207 B6
Petworth GU28 .... 95 F7
Grove The
Bognor Regis PO22 .... 196 A4
Crawley RH11 .... 18 C6
Ferring BN12 .... 200 E6
Haywards Heath RH16 ...... 86 B3
Horley RH6 .... 2 B2
Worthing BN14 .... 182 C6
Grove Villa 8 BN1 .... 207 F7
Grovelands RH6 .... 2 B2
Grovelands CI RH15 .... 106 F1
Grovelands The BN15 ...... 183 B4
Grover Ave BN15 .... 183 D7
Guardian CI BN13 .... 182 A6
Guernsey CI RH11 .... 18 A2
Guernsey Farm La PO22 .. 196 D5
Guernsey Rd BN12 .... 200 F4
Guildbourne Ctr The BN11 182 D2
Guilden Rd PO19 .... 173 B6
Guildford Cl Breach PO10 . 150 A1
Worthing BN14 .... 182 A3
Guildford PI PO19 .... 152 F1
Guildford Rd
Portslade-by-Sea BN41 ... 166 A3
Stedham GU31 .... 69 F1
Worthing BN14 .... 182 E5
Rowhook RH12 .... 34 C7
Rudgwick RH12 .... 33 C6
Rustington BN16 .... 199 E6
Strood Green RH12 .... 35 B6
Worthing BN14 .... 182 A3
Guildford St BN1 .... 207 F6
Guildhall St PO19 .... 173 A7
Guilford Rd BN1 .... 207 F6
Guildalls Oak GU29 .... 92 E7
Guillemot Path **2** RH11 .. 17 D5
Guillods Cotts GU28 .... 114 B7
Guinevere Rd RH11 .... 17 E6
Guinness St RH11 .... 18 D2
Gunning CI RH11 .... 18 A3
Gunns Farm GU30 .... 25 C2
Gunwin Ct PO21 .... 194 D2
Guyhurst Spinney RH20 ... 21 C6
Gwydyr Mansions **4** BN3 187 D6
Gwynne Gdns RH19 .... 9 C2

Habin Hill GU31 .... 68 B3
Hackenden CI RH19 .... 9 E3
Hackenden La RH19 .... 9 E3
Haddington CI BN3 .... 187 B6
Haddington St **11** BN3 .... 187 B7
Hadley Ave BN14 .... 182 D6
Hadley CI PO22 .... 196 E6
Hadlow CI BN2 .... 188 D6
Hadlow Way BN15 .... 183 F6
Hadmans CI RH12 .... 36 C1
Hadrian Ave BN42 .... 186 A8
Haglands Copse RH20 .... 119 D7
Haglands CI PO21 .... 194 C2
Haglands La RH20 .... 119 D7
Haig Ave BN1 .... 168 D6
Haigh CI BN15 .... 184 B6
Hailsham CI BN16 .... 180 B3
Hailsham Rd BN11 .... 181 F1
Hale CI PO20 .... 202 B6
Hales Field GU27 .... 27 C6
Halewick CI BN15 .... 183 C8
Halewick La BN15 .... 183 C8
Haleybridge Wlk PO20 ... 154 D1
Half Moon Hill GU27 .... 27 C6
Half Moon La BN13 .... 181 F7
Halfrey CI PO18 .... 172 F2
Halfrey Rd PO18, PO19 ... 172 B7
Halifax CI RH10 .... 6 E1
Halifax Dr BN13 .... 181 C6
Hall Ave BN14 .... 182 B7
Hall CI BN14 .... 182 A7
Halland CI RH10 .... 19 A7
Halland Rd BN2 .... 188 C7
Halleighs RH17 .... 84 E8
Hallett Rd BN2 .... 188 D7
Halley CI RH11 .... 18 B1
Halley's Ct PO19 .... 173 C6
Halliford Dr PO22 .... 176 C6
Halliwick Gdns PO22 ...... 196 B4
Hallsland RH10 .... 21 C8
Hallyburton Rd BN3 .... 186 D8
Halnaker Barn La PO18 ... 155 B4
Halnaker Gdns PO21 ...... 194 C2
Halnaker Wlk **8** RH11 .... 17 F3
Halsbury CI BN11 .... 182 F3
Halsbury Rd BN11 .... 182 F3
Halsford Croft RH19 .... 9 B3
Halsford Gn RH19 .... 9 B3
Halsford La RH19 .... 9 C3
Halsford Park Cty Prim Sch
RH19 .... 9 C3
Halsford Park Rd RH19 ..... 9 C2
Halson CI PO21 .... 195 C4
Halton Shaws BN6 .... 126 B5
Ham Bridge Trad Est
BN14 .... 183 A4
Ham Bsns Ctr BN43 .... 185 A7
Ham CI BN11, BN14 .... 183 A4
Ham La Oving PO20 .... 174 D7
Prinsted PO10 .... 169 F7
Scaynes Hill RH17 .... 86 E3
Ham Manor CI BN16 .... 179 E4
Ham Manor Farm Cotts
BN16 .... 179 E4
Ham Manor Way BN16 .... 179 E4
Ham Rd
Shoreham-by-Sea BN43 ... 184 F7
Sidlesham PO20 .... 203 C5
Worthing BN11, BN14 ..... 183 A3
Ham Way BN11 .... 183 A4
Hamble Gdns BN13 .... 181 B5
Hamble Rd BN15 .... 183 B6
Hamble Way BN13 .... 181 C7
Hambledon PI PO21 .... 195 B3
Hambleton Ct RH11 .... 18 C4
Hambleton Hill RH11 .... 18 C4
Hambrook HI5 .... 107 C1
Hambrook Hill N PO18 .... 150 D3
Hambrook Hill S PO18 .... 150 D2
Hamilton CI
Portslade-by-Sea BN41 ... 166 A3
Stedham GU31 .... 69 F1
Worthing BN14 .... 182 E5
Hamilton Ct BN11 .... 181 D4
Hamilton Gdns PO21 ...... 194 D2
Hamilton Lodge Sch BN2 . 188 D5
Hamilton Mansions BN3 . 187 B1
Hamilton Mews BN15 ..... 183 C6
Hamilton Rd Brighton BN1 . 207 F7
Horsham RH12 .... 36 B3
Lancing BN15 .... 183 D7
Hamlet The PO22 .... 195 C6
Hamlin's Cnr BN6 .... 106 A6
Hammer Hill Hammer GU27 . 26 C6
Stapleford RH17 .... 62 A3
Hammer La
Chithurst GU29, GU31 ...... 69 D4
Hammer GU27, GU30 .... 26 B6
Haslemere GU26 .... 26 C5
Hammer Vale GU26 .... 26 C6

Hammer Yd RH11 .... 18 D5
Hammerpond Rd
Ashford Crossways
RH13, RH17 .... 60 B6
Doomsday Green RH13 ..... 59 C8
Hammerwood Copse GU27 26 D5
Hammerwood Rd RH19 ..... 23 E6
Hammingden La
RH17, RH19 .... 42 E3
Hammond Dr BN13 .... 181 E8
Hammond PI **2** RH20 .... 119 D1
Hammonds Ridge RH15 ... 106 F1
Hammy CI BN43 .... 185 C8
Hammy La BN43 .... 185 B8
Hammy Way BN43 .... 185 B8
Hampden CI Crawley RH10 .. 6 E1
Middleton-on-Sea PO22 ... 196 F5
Hampden PI PO20 .... 154 D2
Hampden Rd BN2 .... 188 C7
Hamper's La RH13 .... 37 A2
Hampers Common Ind Est
GU28 .... 73 F2
Hampers Ct RH13 .... 36 D2
Hampers Gn GU28 .... 73 E2
Hampers La RH20 .... 120 B2
Hampshire Ave PO21 ...... 195 B5
Hampshire Ct BN2 .... 207 B4
Hampshire Ho GU30 .... 25 B7
Hampstead Rd BN1 .... 167 D2
Hampton Cotts RH13 ...... 180 B6
Hampton Ct
Bognor Regis PO21 .... 194 F4
8 Littlehampton BN17 ... 198 D5
Hampton Fields **8** BN17 . 198 D6
Hampton Lodge RH6 .... 2 A2
Hampton PI BN1 .... 187 E5
Hampton St 14 BN1 ...... 187 E5
Hampton Way RH10 .... 22 F7
Hamsey CI BN2 .... 188 F5
Hamsey Rd RH19 .... 43 A6
Hamshire Hill RH17 .... 60 F5
Hamsland RH17 .... 65 C4
Hamstead Meadow PO18 . 170 F2
Hanbury La RH16 .... 86 A5
Hanbury Park Sports Stad
RH16 .... 86 A5
Hanbury Rd RH11 .... 17 E5
Handcross Cty Prim Sch
RH17 .... 39 C2
Handcross Park Sch RH17 . 39 C2
Handcross Rd
Balcombe RH17 .... 40 D3
Lower Beeding RH13, RH17 60 C5
Handford Way RH17 .... 60 D6
Handsworth Ho **8** RH11 .. 18 D5
Hangleton CI Brighton BN1 . 166 D2
Hangleton Gdns BN3 ...... 166 E1
Hangleton Grange BN12 .. 180 E1
Hangleton La
Hangleton BN12 .... 180 D4
Hove BN3, BN41 .... 166 C4
Portslade-by-Sea BN41 ... 166 B2
Hangleton Manor CI BN3 . 166 D2
Hangleton Valley Dr BN3 . 166 D4
Hangleton Way BN3 .... 166 D3
Hanlye La RH17 .... 85 B8
Hannah Sq PO19 .... 172 D7
Hannington PI BN6 .... 126 A7
Hanover CI Bury PO20 .... 138 A7
Crawley RH10 .... 18 F3
Selsey PO20 .... 206 F7
Hanover Cres BN2 .... 207 B7
Hanover Ct Brighton BN2 . 207 B7
Haywards Heath RH16 ...... 85 F6
Horsham RH13 .... 36 F3
Liphook GU30 .... 25 B5
Worthing BN14 .... 182 C6
Hanover Mews BN2 .... 207 B7
Hanover St BN2 .... 207 B7
Hanover Terr BN2 .... 207 B7
Hanover Wlk RH20 .... 119 D1
Hanover Cres PO19 .... 153 A3
Harbeldown Ho PO10 ...... 100 A5
Harbolets Rd RH14, RH20 100 A5
Harborough Cl RH20 .... 119 B8
Harborough Dr RH20 ...... 119 B8
Harborough Gorse RH20 .. 119 B8
Harborough Hill RH20 ..... 119 B8
Harborough Meadow
RH20 .... 119 B8
Harbour Cotts PO18 .... 171 A4
Harbour Ct Bosham PO18 . 171 C5
Southwick BN42 .... 185 F7
Harbour Rd
Bognor Regis PO21 .... 204 F6
Bosham PO18 .... 171 B4

Harbour View Rd PO21 .... 205 A8
Harbour Way
 Bosham PO18 .... 171 C4
 Chidham PO18 .... 170 F5
 Emsworth PO10 .... 169 C8
 Shoreham-by-Sea BN43 ... 185 B6
Harcourt Way PO20 .... 206 F8
Hard The PO22 .... 197 C5
Hard's Hill RH13 .... 58 D5
Hardbarrow Woods
 RH20 .... 120 A6
Hardham Cl Crawley RH11 . 18 A8
 Rustington BN16 .... 199 B4
Hardham Rd PO19 .... 173 B5
Hardwick Rd BN3 .... 166 E3
Hardwick Way BN3 .... 166 E3
Hardy Cl
 Bognor Regis PO22 .... 196 D5
 Crawley RH10 .... 19 C7
 Horley RH6 1
 Horsham RH12 .... 36 B4
 Shoreham-by-Sea BN43 ... 184 F6
Hare La Crawley RH11 ..... 18 B8
 Selsey PO20 .... 206 B8
Harebell Dr BN41 .... 166 A3
Harefield Ave BN13 .... 181 F4
Harefield Gdns PO22 ...... 196 F5
Harefield Rd PO22 .... 196 F6
Hares La PO18 .... 150 E6
Haresfield Terr PO20 ...... 154 D1
Haresfoot Cl PO18 .... 150 F5
Harewood Cl RH10 .... 6 A1
Harewood Ct **B** BN3 ..... 187 C6
Harfield Ct **B** PO21 .... 195 D3
Harlands Cl RH16, RH17 ... 85 C6
Harlands Cty Prim Sch
 RH16 .... 85 D7
Harlands Rd RH16, RH17 ... 85 D6
Harlech Cl BN13 .... 181 B5
Harley Ct **B** BN11 .... 182 B2
Harmans Dr RH19 .... 10 B1
Harmans Mead RH19 ...... 10 C8
Harmony Cl RH11 .... 17 E4
Harmony Dr PO20 .... 202 B5
Harmsworth Cres BN3 .... 166 E3
Harold Rd Crawley RH10 .. 19 E5
 Westbourne PO10 .... 149 D4
Harold Terr PO10 .... 149 B1
Haroldslea RH6 .... 2 E2
Haroldslea Cl RH6 .... 2 C1
Haroldslea Dr RH6 .... 2 D1
Harper Dr RH10 .... 19 C2
Harrier Ct RH10 .... 6 C1
Harrington Ct **B** BN1 ...... 167 E2
Harrington Mansions **B**
 BN1 .... 167 E2
Harrington Pl BN1 .... 168 B2
Harrington Rd BN1 .... 167 E2
Harrington Villas BN1 ..... 167 F2
Harriot's Hill RH13 .... 81 A8
Harriots Cl RH13 .... 59 A1
Harris Cl RH11 .... 18 B3
Harris La PO8 .... 108 A5
Harrison Cl BN14 .... 182 E5
Harrison Rd BN14 .... 182 F5
Harrow Dr PO20 .... 201 F7
Harrow Rd BN11 .... 182 B3
Harrows The GU28 .... 95 B8
Harrowsley Ct RH6 .... 2 B4
Harsfold Cl BN16 .... 199 B4
Harsfold Rd BN16 .... 199 B4
Hartfield Ave BN1 .... 168 A5
Hartfield Rd RH18 .... 23 F2
Harting Cl BN12 .... 181 B4
Harting Cl RH11 .... 17 F3
Harting Rd BN17 .... 178 D3
Hartings The PO22 .... 196 D6
Hartington Pl BN2 .... 188 C8
Hartington Rd BN2 .... 188 C8
Hartington Terr BN2 .... 188 C8
Hartington Villas BN3 ..... 187 B8
Hartland Ct PO10 .... 149 F1
Harvest Cl RH16 .... 86 B7
Harvest Hill Ansty RH17 .. 84 D2
 East Grinstead RH19 ...... 22 E8
Harvest Rd RH10 .... 19 C4
Harvesters
 Hayward Heath RH16 ..... 86 B7
 Horsham RH12 .... 36 D5
Harvestside RH6 .... 2 C4
Harvey Cl Crawley RH11 ... 18 A1
 Sayers Common BN6 ..... 105 D1
Harvey Rd BN12 .... 181 E1
Harvey Villas GU30 .... 24 A8
Harwarden Cl RH10 .... 21 C8
Harwood Ave BN12 .... 181 D4
Harwood Pk RH1 .... 2 A8

Harwood Rd
 Horsham RH12, RH13 ...... 37 A3
 Littlehampton BN17 .... 198 C6
Harwood Road Ent Units
 BN17 .... 198 C6
Harwoods Cl **B** RH19 ...... 22 E7
Harwoods La RH19 .... 22 F7
Hascombe Ct RH11 .... 18 A5
Hasle Dr GU27 .... 27 B6
Haslemere & District Hospl
 GU27 .... 27 D7
Haslemere Gdns PO11 .... 189 B2
Haslemere Prep Sch GU27 . 27 D5
Haslemere Rd
 Breach PO10 .... 149 F2
 Fernhurst GU27 .... 49 B7
 Liphook GU27, GU30 ..... 25 D4
Haslemere Sta GU27 ...... 27 B6
Hasler's La PO18 .... 132 E5
Haslett Ave E RH10 .... 19 A6
Haslett Ave W RH10, RH11 . 18 D5
Haslingbourne La GU28 .... 95 F5
Hassocks Cl **B** RH11 ...... 17 F3
Hassocks Cty Inf Sch
 BN6 .... 126 F3
Hassocks Lodge BN6 ...... 126 F3
Hassocks Rd BN6 .... 126 B5
Hassocks Sta BN6 .... 126 E4
Haste Hill GU27 .... 27 D5
Hastings Cl PO21 .... 194 F4
Hastings Ct **B** BN11 ...... 182 A1
Hastings Rd
 Brighton BN2 .... 188 C8
 Crawley RH10 .... 19 C6
 Worthing BN11 .... 182 A1
Hatch Cl GU6 .... 11 A3
Hatch End RH18 .... 23 F2
Hatch Hill GU27 .... 27 B1
Hatch La East Liss GU33 ... 45 C4
 Kingsley Green GU27 ..... 27 B2
Hatchetts Dr GU27 .... 26 B7
Hatchgate RH6 .... 1 F2
Hatchgate Cl RH17 .... 85 A6
Hatchgate La RH17 .... 85 A6
Hatchlands RH17 .... 84 F6
Hatfield Ct **B** BN3 .... 187 C6
Hatfield Wlk
 Crawley RH11 .... 17 E2
 Worthing BN13 .... 181 D5
Hatherleigh Cl PO21 ...... 195 A5
Hatherleigh Gdns PO21 ... 195 A5
Hathersham La RH1, RH6 ... 2 F6
Havant Rd PO10 .... 169 A8
Havelock Cl PO22 .... 195 F3
Havelock Rd
 Bognor Regis PO21 .... 195 C4
 Brighton BN1 .... 167 F1
Haven Cotts PO22 .... 195 D5
Haven Ct PO20 .... 201 F7
Haven Gdns RH10 .... 8 B1
Haven Rd
 Rudgwick RH12, RH14 .... 33 D3
 South Hayling PO11 ...... 189 A1
 The Lancing BN15 .... 183 F4
 Rustington BN16 .... 199 C4
Havengate RH12 .... 36 F5
Havenside BN43 .... 184 E6
Havenstoke Cl PO19 ...... 153 A1
Havenwood Cvn Pk BN18 . 157 B3
Haversham Cl RH10 .... 18 F6
Haversham Ho RH6 .... 2 B5
Hawke Cl BN16 .... 199 E5
Hawkesbourne Rd RH12 .. 36 F5
Hawkesmoor Rd RH11 .... 17 E4
Hawkhurst Pl BN1 .... 168 D6
Hawkhurst Rd BN1 .... 168 D6
Hawkhurst Wlk RH10 ..... 19 B4
Hawkins Cl
 Bognor Regis PO21 .... 194 B2
 Shoreham-by-Sea BN43 .. 165 D1
Hawkins Cres BN43 .... 165 D2
Hawkins Rd Crawley RH10 . 18 E4
 Shoreham-by-Sea BN43 .. 165 D1
Hawkley Rd GU33 .... 45 A5
Hawkridge RH12 .... 12 E1
Hawks Mead GU33 .... 45 A5
Hawks Pl PO22 .... 195 B6
Hawksfold La E GU27 ..... 49 A6
Hawksfold La W GU27 .... 49 A6
Hawkshaw Cl GU30 .... 26 C5
Hawley Rd BN16 .... 199 B4
Hawmead RH10 .... 21 C8
Hawth (Arts Ctr) The RH10 . 18 F5
Hawth Ave RH10 .... 18 F5
Hawth Cl RH10 .... 18 E4
Hawthorn Bank BN2 ...... 168 F4
Hawthorn Cl
 Burgess Hill RH15 .... 107 D5
 Chichester PO19 .... 172 F7
 Crawley RH11 .... 5 C1
 Horsham RH12 .... 36 C4

Hawthorn Cl
 Midhurst GU29 .... 92 D6
 B Rustington BN16 .... 199 C4
Hawthorn Cres BN14 ..... 182 D6
Hawthorn Gdns BN14 .... 182 D6
Hawthorn Rd
 Bognor Regis PO21, PO22 . 195 B4
 Littlehampton BN17 ...... 178 D3
 Worthing BN14 .... 182 D6
Hawthorn Way
 Portslade-by-Sea BN41 .. 166 A3
 Storrington RH20 .... 119 D2
Hawthorne Cotts RH6 .... 7 C7
Hawthorns Cty Fst Sch
 BN13 .... 181 C5
Hawthorns The
 Bognor Regis PO21 .... 195 C4
 Burgess Hill RH15 .... 107 A5
 West Chiltington Common
 RH20 .... 119 E7
Hay Rd PO19 .... 173 B4
Haybarn Dr RH12 .... 36 E7
Haybourne Cl BN2 .... 188 E7
Haybourne Rd BN2 .... 188 E7
Haydon Cl PO21 .... 194 C1
Hayes Cl Mid Lavant PO18 . 152 E7
 Portslade-by-Sea BN41 .. 186 C8
Hayes La RH13 .... 34 D2
Hayes Wood Rd RH14 .... 55 F5
Hayfields RH6 .... 2 C4
Hayley Rd BN15 .... 183 F7
Hayley's Gdns PO22 ...... 196 A4
Haylind Rd RH16 .... 86 B5
Hayling Ct RH11 .... 18 C3
Hayling Gdns BN13 .... 161 E1
Hayling Rise BN13 .... 161 E1
Haynes Rd BN13, BN14 ... 182 B4
Haynes Way BN14 .... 182 B4
Haystacks GU29 .... 113 C8
Hayton Ct BN13 .... 181 B5
Haywards RH10 .... 6 D1
Haywards Cl PO22 .... 196 B5
Haywards Heath Coll RH16 . 85 D5
Haywards Heath Golf Course
 RH16 .... 63 F1
Haywards Heath Hospl
 RH16 .... 85 C4
Haywards Heath Rd RH17 . 41 A1
Haywards Heath Sta RH16 . 85 E6
Haywards Rd
 Brighton BN1 .... 168 A6
 Haywards Heath RH16 ... 85 E5
Hazel Bank **B** 207 B7
Hazel Cl Crawley RH11 ... 5 C1
 Crawley Down RH10 ..... 21 C8
 Portslade-by-Sea BN41 .. 166 C3
 Southwater RH13 .... 55 E4
Hazel Gr Arundel BN18 ... 157 E2
 Bognor Regis PO21 .... 194 D3
 Burgess Hill RH15 .... 107 B1
Hazel Rd PO22 .... 195 B6
Hazel Way RH10 .... 21 C8
Hazelbank Cl GU30 .... 25 D4
Hazeldean Dr PO9 .... 128 D1
Hazeldene Meads BN1 ... 167 D2
Hazeldene Rd GU30 ...... 24 D4
Hazelgrove Gdns **B** RH16 . 85 E4
Hazelgrove Rd RH16 ...... 85 E4
Hazelhurst Cres BN14 .... 21 C8
Hazelhurst Cres
 Horsham RH12 .... 35 F1
 Worthing BN14 .... 161 F3
Hazelhurst Dr RH10 ...... 19 C8
Hazelmead Dr BN16 ...... 200 A5
Hazelwick Ave RH10 ..... 19 B8
Hazelwick Mill La RH10 .. 19 A8
Hazelwick Rd RH10 .... 19 A7
Hazelwick Sch RH10 ..... 19 A8
Hazelwood Brighton BN1 . 167 D3
 Crawley RH11 .... 18 A5
Hazelwood Cl
 Crawley RH10 .... 20 F8
 Easebourne GU29 .... 71 A3
 Heath Common RH20 ... 120 B2
 Worthing BN14 .... 182 F4
Hazelwood Cotts GU16 .. 54 C8
Hazelwood Lodge **B**
 BN15 .... 183 F5
Hazelwood Rd RH13 ..... 103 E3
Hazelwood Trad Est BN14 . 182 F5
Headborough Ct BN15 ... 183 E4 (Hazelen Cross RH19 .. 22 B6)
Headborough Gdns BN15 . 183 E4
Headlands Cotts RH17 ... 39 C2
Headley Cl RH10 .... 19 B2
Headley Rd GU30 .... 25 B5
Hearn Cl PO20 .... 154 C1
Hearnfield Rd BN17 ...... 178 D4
Heath Cl
 Broadridge Heath RH12 .. 35 E3
 B Haywards Heath RH16 . 85 E4

Heath Cl Hunston PO20 ... 193 A8
 Mannings Heath RH13 .... 59 D6
 Sayers Common BN6 .... 105 D1
Heath Ct
 Broadridge Heath RH12 .. 35 E3
 B Haywards Heath RH16 . 85 E5
Heath Hill Ave BN2 .... 168 F1
Heath Pl PO22 .... 195 D7
Heath Rd Hammer GU27 .. 26 D5
 Haywards Heath RH16 ... 85 E5
Heath Sq RH16 .... 85 D5
Heath Way RH12 .... 36 D5
Heathcote Dr RH19 .... 9 C2
Heathcourt BN12 .... 198 F5
Heather Bank RH16 ...... 85 C5
Heather Rd
 Horsham RH12 .... 36 D5
 West Ashling PO18 .... 151 C3
Heather Ct
 Chichester PO19 .... 172 F5
 B Hove BN1 .... 187 E6
Heather Ho BN15 .... 183 F7
Heather La
 West Chiltington Common
 RH20 .... 119 C6
 Worthing BN13 .... 161 E2
Heather Way RH20 .... 119 F1
Heathfield Ave BN11 ..... 18 B3
Heather Wlk RH11 .... 18 D3
Heatherlands Horley RH6 . 2 B4
 Storrington RH20 .... 119 F2
Heatherstone Rd BN11 .. 183 B2
Heatherton Mews PO10 . 149 B3
Heatherway RH19, RH7 ... 8 F7
Heathfield GU29 .... 92 E8
Heathfield RH10 .... 19 D8
Heathfield Ave BN16 ..... 179 F3
Heathfield Cl
 B Midhurst GU29 .... 92 D6
 Worthing BN13 .... 181 F5
Heathfield Copse RH41 .. 165 F3
Heathfield Cres BN41 .... 165 F4
Heathfield Ct BN41 .... 165 F4
Heathfield Gate **B** GU29 . 92 E7
Heathfield Gdns GU29 ... 92 E7
Heathfield Gn GU29 ...... 92 E7
Heathfield Pk GU29 ...... 92 E7
Heaven Farm Mus RH17 . 66 B1
Hebe Rd BN43 .... 184 E7
Hechle Wood PO21 ...... 194 F2
Hedge End Rd PO22 ..... 176 C6
Hedgehog La GU27 ...... 27 B5
Hedgerow Gdns PO10 ... 149 B3
Hedgers Hill BN18 .... 156 F2
Hedgeside RH11 .... 18 C1
Hedgeway PO22 .... 196 D5
Hedingham Cl RH6 .... 2 C4
Heene CE Fst (A) Prim Sch
 BN11 .... 182 C3
Heene Pl BN11 .... 182 C1
Heene Rd BN11 .... 182 B2
Heene Terr BN11 .... 182 B2
Heene Way BN11 .... 182 B2
Heghbrok Way PO21 ..... 195 A2
Heights The Brighton BN1 . 167 B5
 B Haywards Heath RH16 . 85 E4
 Worthing BN14 .... 162 A1
Helen Ct **B** BN11 .... 181 F2
Helena Cl BN41 .... 166 D2
Helicon Ho RH11 .... 18 C5
Hellingly Cl BN2 .... 188 F5
Helston Dr PO10 .... 149 B3
Helyer's Gn RH17 .... 198 C6
Hemsby Wlk RH10 .... 19 B4
Henbane Ct **B** RH11 .... 18 B2
Henderson Rd RH11 ..... 57 F8
Henderson Way RH12 .... 57 F8
Henderson Wlk BN44 .... 143 D4
Hendon Ave BN16 .... 199 A3
Hendon St BN2 .... 188 D5
Henfield Bsns Pk BN5 .... 124 A1
Henfield Cl Brighton BN2 . 188 F5
 Worthing BN12 .... 181 B4
Henfield Rd
 Albourne Green BN6 ..... 125 E7
 Upper Beeding
 BN44, BN5 .... 144 D3
Henfield Way
 Bognor Regis PO22 ...... 196 D6
 Hove BN3 .... 185 C2
Henge Way BN41 .... 166 B2
Hengist Cl RH12 .... 36 A1
Henley Cl BN2 .... 188 F4
Henley Dr RH19 .... 10 E1
Henry Ave BN16 .... 199 B5
Henry Burt Way RH15 ... 106 F1
Henry Cl PO19 .... 173 D6
Henryson St RH11 .... 17 F4
Henshaw Cl RH11 .... 17 F4
Henson Rd RH10 .... 19 B7
Henty Cl Crawley RH11 .. 17 E3
 Walberton BN18 .... 176 E8

Henty Cl
 4 Worthing BN14 .... 182 C
Henty Gdns PO19 .... 172 F
Henty Rd Ferring BN12 ... 200 F
 Worthing BN14 .... 182 C
Heo Gn BN17 .... 178 B
Hepplewhite Cl RH11 .... 18 B
Herald Dr PO19 .... 173 A
Herbert Rd Brighton BN1 . 167 F
 North Lancing BN15 ..... 163 B
Herbert Shiner Sch GU28 . 95 F
Hercules Pl PO22 .... 196 D
Hereford Cl
 Chichester PO19 .... 152 F
 Crawley RH10 .... 18 C
Hereford Ct
 15 Brighton BN2 .... 207 B
 16 Hove BN3 .... 187 C
Hereford St BN2 .... 188 C
Herington Rd BN18 ...... 157 F
Heritage Lawn RH6 ...... 2 C
Herm Cl RH11 .... 18 A
Herm Rd BN12 .... 200 F
Hermione Cl BN12 .... 180 E
Hermit Terr BN14 .... 161 E
Hermitage Cl PO20 ...... 173 D
Hermitage La RH11 ...... 22 F
Hermitage Rd RH19 ...... 1 B
Hermitage The PO20 .... 173 D
Hermits Rd RH10 .... 18 F
Hermonger La RH12 ..... 12 F
Herndon Dr RH13 .... 58 E
Herne Gdns BN16 .... 199 D
Herne La BN16 .... 199 D
Heron Cl
 Bognor Regis PO22 ...... 195 B
 Crawley RH11 .... 18 C
 Mid Lavant PO18 .... 152 B
 Selsey PO20 .... 206 B
Heron Ct PO19 .... 173 C
Heron Mead PO21 .... 204 F
Heron Pl RH19 .... 22 F
Heron Quay PO10 .... 169 C
Heron Way RH13 .... 37 A
Heron Way Cty Prim Sch
 RH13 .... 37 A
Heron's Ct Cl **3** BN16 . 199 C
Heron's Rye BN20 .... 98 C
Heron's Tye BN6 .... 125 B
Herondale GU27 .... 26 E
Herondean PO19 .... 152 B
Herons Cl Domewood RH10 . 8 B
 Kirdford RH14 .... 53 B
Herons Dale Sch BN43 .. 165 C
Herons Lea RH10 .... 8 A
Herons The BN43 .... 185 A
Herons Wood Ct RH6 .... 2 E
Heronrye Dr RH19 .... 23 A
Herrick Cl RH10 .... 19 C
Herschel Wlk **9** RH11 . 18 E
Hersee Way PO20 .... 206 C
Hertford Cl PO21 194
Hertford Cty Inf Sch BN1 . 168 C
Hertford Cty Jun Sch BN2 . 168 C
Hertford Rd Brighton BN1 . 168 C
 Worthing BN14 .... 182 C
Heston Ave BN1 .... 167 F
Heston Gr PO21 .... 194 C
Hevers Ave RH6 .... 2 A
Hewart's La PO22 .... 194 C
Hewitts BN5 .... 123 E
Hewitts End BN5 .... 123 E
Hewshott Gr GU30 ...... 25 B
Hewshott La GU30 ...... 25 B
Hexham Cl RH10 .... 19 E
Heyshott Cl RH15 .... 183 H
Heyworth Cty Prim Sch
 RH16 .... 85 C
Hickling Wlk RH10 .... 19 B
Hickman's Cl RH16 ...... 86 D
Hickman's La RH16 ...... 86 A
Hickstead Int Arena
 RH17 .... 105 C
Hickstead La RH17 ...... 105 C
Hickstead Pk BN6 .... 105 D
Hide Gdns BN16 .... 199 B
High Bank PO20 192
High Bar La RH20 .... 120 C
High Beach La RH16 63
High Beeches Cotts RH17 . 39
High Beeches Gdns The
 RH17 39
High Beeches La RH17 .. 39 B
High Cl BN41 .... 166 A
High La GU27 27
High Meadow GU29 ..... 112 D
High Oaks RH11 .... 18 A
High Park Ave BN3 ...... 166 B
High Pines RH11 182
High Point RH16 85
High Ridge Cl BN18 157

High Seat Gdns RH14 .... 55 D1
High Spinney RH20 .... 119 E5
High St Amberley BN18 ..... 138 E7
Angmering BN16 .... 180 A5
Ardingly RH17 .... 64 B8
Arundel BN18 .... 138 B3
Balcombe RH17 .... 40 C5
Billingshurst RH14 .... 55 D1
Bognor Regis PO21 .... 195 D3
Bosham PO18 .... 171 A4
Brighton BN2 .... 207 B5
Chichester PO19 .... 172 F7
Crawley RH11 .... 18 D6
Cuckfield RH17 .... 84 E6
Ditchling BN6 .... 127 D3
East Grinstead RH19 .... 22 F8
Emsworth PO10 .... 169 B8
Findon BN14 .... 161 E6
Handcross RH17 .... 61 C8
Haslemere GU27 .... 27 D7
Haywards Heath RH16 ...... 86 B8
Henfield BN5 .... 123 F4
Horley RH6 .... 2 B3
Hurstpierpoint BN6 .... 126 A5
Littlehampton BN17 .... 198 D5
Oving PO20 .... 174 C6
Partridge Green RH13 ..... 103 A3
Petworth GU28 .... 95 FB
Portslade-by-Sea BN41 .... 166 A1
Rusper RH12 .... 16 D7
Selsey PO20 .... 206 D7
Shoreham-by-Sea BN43 .. 184 E7
Steyning BN44 .... 143 D3
Storrington BN20 .... 119 D1
Upper Beeding BN44 .... 144 A2
Worthing BN11 .... 182 E2
Worthing BN11 .... 182 E3
Worthing, West Tarring
BN13 .... 182 A5
High Titten BN18 .... 138 E5
High Trees
Bognor Regis PO21 .... 194 F2
Haywards Heath RH16 .... 85 F5
Hunston PO20 .... 173 A1
High Trees Ct RH6 .... 1 A4
High View BN13 .... 9 E6
Highams Hill RH11 .... 17 F5
Highbank BN1 .... 167 C5
Highbarn BN14 .... 161 E7
Highbirch Cl RH12 .... 37 B5
Highbrook Cl BN2 .... 168 D3
Highbury Cotts RH17 .... 61 B8
Highbury Gr GU27 .... 27 C8
Highclere Way BN13 .... 181 B5
Highcroft Ave PO22 .... 195 D5
Highcroft Cl PO22 .... 195 E5
Highcroft Cres PO22 .... 195 E5
Highcroft Dr RH12 .... 12 E1
Highcroft Lodge BN1 ..... 167 E1
Highcroft Rd RH19 .... 43 A6
Highcroft Villas BN1, BN3 187 E8
Highden 2 BN2 .... 188 C6
Highdown BN1, BN42 ..... 165 F1
Highdown Ave BN13 .... 182 A5
Highdown Cl Ferring BN12 180 E3
Southwick BN41, BN42 ... 165 F1
Highdown Ct
Brighton BN2 .... 167 E3
Crawley RH10 .... 19 B3
Highdown Dr BN17 .... 198 D6
Highdown Rd BN1, BN1 .. 187 E7
Highdown Sch BN13 .... 181 D5
Highdown Way
Ferring BN12 .... 180 E3
Horsham RH12 .... 36 F6
Highercombe Rd GU27 .... 27 E8
Highfield
Horsted Keynes RH17 ...... 65 C4
Littlehampton BN17 .... 178 B3
Highfield Cl
Angmering BN16 .... 180 A5
Easebourne GU29 .... 71 A2
Highfield Cres BN1 .... 168 A5
Highfield Ct 7 RH16 .... 85 E4
Highfield Dr BN18 .... 126 C5
Highfield Gdns
Bognor Regis PO22 .... 195 D5
Liss GU33 .... 45 D4
1 Rustington BN16 .... 199 B5
Highfield La
Liphook GU27, GU30 .... 25 E3
Oving PO20 .... 174 C7
Highfield Rd
Bognor Regis PO22 .... 195 D5
East Grinstead RH19 .... 9 D3
Worthing BN13 .... 182 A6
Highfield Sch GU30 .... 25 E2
Highfields Brighton BN1 .. 168 E5
Forest Row RH18 .... 23 F2
Highgate Ct RH11 .... 18 C2
Highgate Dr PO21 .... 194 F6

Highgate Rd RH18 .... 23 F1
Highground La PO22 .... 176 B4
Highgrove Gdns BN11 .... 182 B2
Highland Ave PO21 .... 195 B4
Highland Cl PO10 .... 169 A8
Highland Croft BN44 ...... 143 D3
Highland Ct RH16 .... 85 E4
Highland Rd
Chichester PO19 .... 153 A2
Emsworth PO10 .... 149 A1
Haywards Heath RH16 .... 85 F3
Highlands Ave RH13 .... 36 E2
Highlands Cl
Keymer BN6 .... 127 A3
Worthing BN13 .... 161 E1
Highlands Cotts RH17 ..... 84 F8
Highlands Cres RH13 .... 36 E2
Highlands Dr RH15 .... 107 A4
Highlands Rd
Horsham RH13 .... 36 F2
Portslade-by-Sea BN41 ... 166 B1
Highlands The RH17 .... 84 F8
Highleigh 7 BN2 .... 207 B6
Highleigh Rd PO20 .... 192 C2
Highstanding La GU29 .... 72 A8
Highstead La GU28 .... 72 A8
Highview BN15 .... 163 D1
Highview Ave N BN1 ...... 167 E6
Highview Ave S BN1 .... 167 E6
Highview Rd Brighton BN1 167 E6
Eastergate PO20 .... 175 F7
Highview Way BN1 .... 167 E6
Highway Cl BN2 .... 168 D2
Highway The BN2 .... 168 D2
Highways BN41 .... 166 B2
Hilary Lodge 2 BN2 ...... 188 C5
Hilary Rd PO19 .... 172 E7
Hildon Cl BN13 .... 181 D5
Hill Barn Golf Course
BN14 .... 182 B8
Hill Barn La BN14 .... 182 B8
Hill Brow BN3 .... 167 B3
Hill Brow Cl PO9 .... 128 D1
Hill Brow Rd GU33 .... 45 C3
Hill Cotts GU29 .... 113 C8
Hill Crest RH19 .... 9 E6
Hill Ct GU27 .... 27 B6
Hill Dr BN3 .... 167 B3
Hill Farm La PO20 .... 98 B5
Hill Farm Way BN42, BN43 165 E2
Hill House Cl RH10 .... 21 A5
Hill House Hill GU30 .... 25 A6
Hill La Barnham PO22 .... 176 C4
South Harting GU31 .... 89 E2
Hill Manor RH12 .... 36 A2
Hill Mead RH12 .... 36 B3
Hill Pl RH11 .... 18 C5
Hill Rd Haslemere GU27 .. 27 C6
Littlehampton BN17 .... 198 F6
Hill Top BN1 .... 167 B5
Hill Top Rd BN41 .... 165 F2
Hill View Elsted GU29 ...... 90 D4
Small Dole BN5 .... 144 F7
Hillary Cl RH19 .... 10 A3
Hillbank Cl BN41 .... 165 F3
Hillbarn Ave BN15 .... 163 D1
Hillbarn La GU29, PO18 .. 112 D6
Hillbarn Par BN15 .... 183 C8
Hillbrow Cl RH17 .... 67 D4
Hillbrow Rd BN1 .... 167 C5
Hillcrest Cl
Ashington RH20 .... 121 A5
Crawley RH10 .... 19 D6
Scaynes Hill RH17 .... 86 F3
Hillcrest Ct RH17 .... 167 C5
Hillcrest Dr RH20 .... 121 A5
Hillcrest La RH17 .... 86 F3
Hillcroft BN41 .... 165 F2
Hillfield Rd PO20 .... 206 D6
Hillhouse La RH12, RH14 .. 11 F1
Hillingdale RH11 .... 18 C1
Hillmead RH11 .... 17 F6
Hillrise Ave BN15 .... 183 D8
Hills Farm La RH12 .... 35 F1
Hills Pl RH12 .... 36 A2
Hills Rd BN44 .... 143 C2
Hillsboro Rd PO21 .... 195 C4
Hillside Brighton BN2 .... 168 E2
Crawley Down RH10 .... 21 B8
Forest Row RH18 .... 23 E3
Horsham RH12 .... 36 A2
Portslade-by-Sea BN41 ... 166 C1
Southwick BN42 .... 165 F1
Hillside Ave BN14 .... 183 B7
Hillside Cl Crawley RH11 .. 18 B4
East Grinstead RH19 .... 9 E3
Hillside Cotts
Clapham BN13 .... 160 E1
East Marden PO18 .... 110 B1
West Stoke PO18 .... 152 A5
Hillside Cres BN16 .... 180 A5

Hillside La BN5 .... 144 E5
Hillside Rd
Camelsdale GU27 .... 26 F5
Heath Common RH20 .... 120 A2
Sompting BN15 .... 163 C1
Hillside Sch BN41 .... 166 B2
Hillside Scout Camp BN5 .. 144 E5
Hillside Terr BN44 .... 143 D3
Hillside Way
Brighton, Moulsecoomb
BN2 .... 168 E2
Brighton, Westdene BN1 .. 167 C4
Hillside Wlk
Haywards Heath RH17 .... 85 C6
Heath Common RH20 .... 120 A2
Hilltop Rd RH19 .... 42 E6
Hillview Cres BN16 .... 200 A6
Hillview Gdns RH11 .... 39 C8
Hillview Rd BN14 .... 161 F2
Hillview Rise BN41 .... 161 F1
Hillyard Rd RH11 .... 4 C1
Hilton Ct RH6 .... 2 C4
Hilton Pk PO20 .... 202 A8
Hinde Rd PO22 .... 196 C4
Hindhead Cl RH11 .... 18 C4
Hindhead Rd GU26, GU27 .. 26 E7
Hindle Cl RH20 .... 119 D7
Hindleap Warren
Activity Ctr RH18 .... 44 D5
Hinton Cl BN1 .... 168 C2
Hislop Wlk 12 PO21 .... 195 D3
Hoadly La RH16, RH17 .... 64 D4
Hoathly Hill RH19 .... 42 F5
Hobart Cl BN13 .... 181 C7
Hobbs Ind Est RH7 .... 8 D7
Hobbs Rd RH11 .... 18 A2
Hobbs Way BN16 .... 199 C5
Hobdens La RH17 .... 64 B7
Hoblands RH16 .... 86 B4
Hobs Acre BN44 .... 144 E1
Hocken Mead RH10 .... 19 D8
Hodshrove La BN2 .... 168 E3
Hodshrove Pl BN2 .... 168 E3
Hodshrove Rd BN2 .... 168 E3
Hoe Ct
North Lancing BN15 .... 163 F1
Shoreham-by-Sea BN15 .. 184 A8
Hoe La Bosham PO18 .... 171 C1
Flansham PO22 .... 196 B7
Walberton BN18 .... 177 C7
Hoefield La PO18 .... 112 C5
Hoewood BN5 .... 144 F7
Hogarth Rd Crawley RH10 .. 18 F3
Hove BN3 .... 186 F7
Hogspudding La RH5 .... 3 C8
Hogwood Rd RH14 .... 31 C3
Holbein Rd RH10 .... 18 F3
Holbrook CE Prim Sch
RH12 .... 36 E7
Holbrook School La RH12 .. 36 E7
Holdens The PO18 .... 171 A5
Holder Rd RH10 .... 19 B3
Holders BN6 .... 125 C6
Holdfast La GU27 .... 27 F8
Hole St BN44, RH20 .... 121 B2
Holford Gn PO20 .... 206 F8
Holktham Cotts BN18 .... 177 A3
Holland Cl PO21 .... 194 F5
Holland Mews BN3 .... 187 D5
Holland Rd Hove BN3 .... 187 D6
Steyning BN44 .... 143 E3
Hollands Rd BN1 .... 207 B6
Hollands La RH5 .... 123 C4
Hollands Rd BN5 .... 123 D5
Hollands Rd RH15 .... 115 C7
Hollands Way
East Grinstead RH19 .... 10 A4
Warnham RH12 .... 35 F8
Hollies The PO21 .... 194 F5
Hollin Ct RH10, RH11 .... 5 E1
Hollingbourne Cres RH11 .. 39 C8
Hollingbourne Ct 8 BN2 .. 188 E4
Hollingbury Copse BN1 .. 168 A4
Hollingbury Court Sch
RH17 .... 61 A1
Hollingbury Cres BN1 .... 168 B2
Hollingbury Gdns BN14 .. 162 A2
Hollingbury La BN1, BN7 .. 168 C7
Hollingbury Park Ave
BN1 .... 168 A2
Hollingbury Park Golf Course
BN1 .... 168 B4
Hollingbury Pl BN1 .... 168 B2
Hollingbury Rd BN1 .... 168 B2
Hollingbury Rise BN1 .... 168 B2
Hollingbury Rise W BN1 .. 168 A3
Hollingbury Terr BN1 ..... 168 A2
Hollingdean La BN1, BN2 .. 188 B8
Hollingdean St BN1 .... 168 B1

Hollingdean Terr BN1 .... 168 B2
Hollist La
Easebourne GU29 .... 70 E2
South Harting GU31 .... 89 F4
Hollow La RH19, RH7 ...... 10 D6
Hollow The Bury RH20 .. 138 A8
Crawley RH11 .... 17 F5
Haywards Heath RH16 .... 86 B5
Washington RH20 .... 141 FB
West Chiltington RH20 .... 99 D1
West Hoathly RH19 .... 42 F6
Holly Bank 3 BN2 .... 207 B8
Holly Cl Brighton BN1 .... 167 E3
Crawley RH10 .... 19 A8
Horsham RH12 .... 37 B5
Storrington RH20 .... 119 C1
West Chiltington RH20 .... 99 D2
Worthing BN13 .... 181 C5
Holly Ct
Bognor Regis PO22 .... 195 D4
Storrington RH20 .... 119 C2
Holly Dr BN17 .... 178 E4
Holly Rd RH16 .... 86 A3
Hollybank La PO10 .... 149 B4
Hollybush Rd RH10 .... 18 E8
Hollycombe Cl GU30 ...... 25 C5
Hollycombe Ctr Prim Sch
GU30 .... 47 D4
Hollycombe Steam Collection
GU30 .... 47 E7
Hollyridge GU27 .... 27 B6
Hollywater Rd GU30, GU35 .. 24 C8
Hollywood CI RH16 .... 85 E5
Holman CI RH11 .... 39 B8
Holmans CI RH17 .... 14 C4
Holmbush Cl
Haywards Heath RH16 .... 85 E2
Horsham RH12 .... 36 D6
Shoreham-by-Sea BN43 .. 165 D2
Holmbush Ct 8 BN43 .... 165 D8
Holmbush Cty Fst Sch
BN43 .... 165 D1
Holmbush Ind Est GU29 .. 92 E6
Holmbush La BN5 .... 145 F8
Holme Ct
Midhurst GU29 .... 92 E6
Southwick BN42, BN43 .. 165 E1
Holmcroft RH10 .... 18 E5
Holmcroft Gdns BN14 ... 161 E6
Holmes Ave BN3 .... 166 F1
Holmes Foundation BN18 158 B2
Holmesdale Rd RH15 ..... 107 A1
Holmfield Cl BN16 .... 199 B6
Holmgarth BN5 .... 123 F5
Holming Ho RH12 .... 37 B3
Holmstead BN2 .... 207 B7
Holmsted Hill RH17 .... 62 A1
Holmwood Cl PO20 .... 190 C1
Holmwood Ct BN6 .... 126 F4
Holt Gdns PO9 .... 128 D3
Holt Lodge 1 BN2 .... 207 B7
Holt The
Burgess Hill RH15 .... 107 C2
Washington RH20 .... 141 E6
Holtye Ave RH19 .... 10 A3
Holtye Rd RH19 .... 10 B3
Holtye Wlk RH10 .... 19 B3
Holy Cross Hospl GU27 .. 26 F7
Holy Trinity CE (A) Prim Sch
RH17 .... 84 F6
Holy Trinity CE (C) Prim Sch
RH13 .... 60 A3
Holyrood RH19 .... 23 E8
Holyroyd Pl RH11 .... 18 B2
Home CI RH10 .... 19 C8
Home Farm Bsns Ctr BN1 168 D3
Home Farm Ct RH17 .... 65 C5
Home Farm Rd BN1 .... 168 D3
Home Platt RH19 .... 43 A6
Homecroft Ho 6 PO21 .. 195 B3
Homedrive Ho BN3 .... 187 C8
Homefield Ave PO22 ..... 196 C6
Homefield CI RH6 .... 2 B4
Homefield Cotts GU33 .... 45 A5
Homefield Cres BN18 .... 156 D1
Homefield Rd
Portslade-by-Sea PO10 .. 149 D4
Worthing BN13 .... 182 E3
Homegreen Ho GU27 ...... 27 A6
Homehaven Ct 2 BN43 .. 165 E7
Homelands Ave BN16 .... 200 A4
Homelands Copse GU27 .. 49 F8
Homeleigh BN1 .... 167 E5
Homepier Ho 7 BN11 .... 182 B4
Homesearle Ho BN12 .... 181 C2
Homestall Rd RH19 .... 23 E8

Homestead The BN16 ... 200 A5
Homesteyne Ho 3 BN14 . 182 D4
Homewood BN14 .... 161 E7
Homing Gdns PO22 .... 195 B7
Honer La PO20 .... 193 D3
Honey Croft BN3 .... 166 D4
Honey La BN16 .... 180 A5
Honeybridge La
Ashurst
BN44, RH13, RH20 .... 122 A6
Dial Post RH13 .... 101 E3
Honeysuckle Cl Horley RH6 .. 2 C4
North Lancing BN15 ...... 163 D1
Honeysuckle La
Crawley RH11 .... 5 C1
Worthing BN13 .... 161 C3
Honeysuckle Wlk RH12 .. 37 A5
Honeywood La RH5 .... 13 F5
Honeywood Rd RH13 ...... 37 A4
Hooe Farm Ind Est BN18 . 156 D2
Hooe The BN17 .... 199 A5
Hook La
Bognor Regis PO21, PO22 195 E4
Bognor Regis, Rose Green
PO21 .... 194 B3
Bosham PO18 .... 171 F2
West Hoathly RH17, RH19 .. 42 D4
Woodgate PO20 .... 175 C6
Hooklands La RH13, RH20 101 B3
Hooks The BN5 .... 123 E4
Hop Garden La PO20 ..... 193 D8
Hop Garden The GU31 ... 89 D3
Hope Cotts BN42 .... 185 E8
Hope St BN1 .... 18 B1
Hopedene Ct 5 BN11 .... 182 C2
Hopgarton The PO21 .... 194 E3
Hophurst Cl RH10 .... 21 B8
Hophurst Dr RH10 .... 21 B8
Hophurst Hill RH10, RH19 .. 8 D2
Hophurst La RH10 .... 8 B1
Hordens The RH13 .... 56 F2
Hordern Ho RH12 .... 36 A4
Horley Cty Fst Sch RH6 .... 2 A3
Horley Lodge La RH1 .... 1 A8
Horley Pl RH10 .... 188 E6
Horley Rd RH6 .... 5 B7
Horley Row RH6 .... 2 A4
Horley Sta RH6 .... 2 B2
Hormare Cres RH20 .... 119 C2
Horn La BN5 .... 124 B1
Hornbeam Cl
Bognor Regis PO21 .... 194 F1
Horsham RH13 .... 36 F1
Hornbeam Way GU29 .... 92 D5
Hornbrook Copse RH13 .. 58 F8
Hornby Rd BN2 .... 168 F1
Horndean Ho 6 BN14 ...... 6 D2
Horndean Rd PO10 .... 149 A3
Hornet Ent Ctr PO19 ..... 173 B6
Hornet Pl PO10 .... 169 C3
Hornet The PO19 .... 173 B6
Horns La PO21 .... 193 F1
Hornshill La RH12 .... 32 F7
Horse Hill RH6 .... 1 B4
Horse Shoe The PO20 ... 206 D7
Horsebridge Hill RH14 .... 75 E2
Horsed Keynes Sta RH17 .. 65 A7
Horsefield Rd PO20 .... 206 D8
Horsemere Green La
BN17 .... 179 D7
Horseshoe Cl RH10 .... 19 D7
Horsgate Ho RH17 .... 85 A8
Horsgate La RH17 .... 85 A6
Horsham Bsns Pk RH12 .. 15 C4
Horsham Cl BN2 .... 188 C3
Horsham Com Hospl RH12 36 C3
Horsham Golf Course
RH13 .... 58 A6
Horsham Rd
Alfold Crossways
GU6, RH14 .... 11 C1
Ashurst BN44 .... 143 C7
Cranleigh RH12 .... 12 B8
Crawley RH11 .... 18 B4
Findon BN14 .... 161 D8
Five Oaks RH14 .... 56 A6
Handcross RH17 .... 61 B7
Kingsfold RH5 .... 15 C8
Littlehampton BN17 ...... 198 F6
Pease Pottage RH11 .... 39 B6
Petworth GU28 .... 74 B2
Rowhook RH5, RH12 ...... 13 D5
Rusper RH12 .... 16 B5
Steyning BN44 .... 143 C4
Wallis Wood RH5 .... 13 D8
Horsham Rd W BN17 ..... 198 F6
Horsham Sta RH13 .... 36 D2

Horsted Ho **1** RH16 .... 85 F3
Horsted Keynes Ind Est
RH17
Horsted Keynes Sta RH17 .... 65 A7
Horsted La Danehill RH17 .... 66 A4
Sharpthorne RH19 .... 43 B3
Horton Rd BN1 .... 168 B1
Hoskins PI RH19 .... 10 A4
Hospital Villas **5** RH16 ..... 205 F3
Hotham Gdns PO22 .... 195 E4
Hotham Way PO21, PO22 .. 195 D4
Houghton Bridge BN18 ...... 138 D4
Houghton Ho BN17 .... 178 B3
Houghton La BN18, RH20 .. 138 A6
Houghton Rd RH10 .... 19 C3
Hova Villas BN3 .... 187 B6
Hove Bsns Ctr BN3 .... 187 B8
Hove Ent Ctr BN41 .... 186 C6
Hove General Hospl BN3 .... 187 A7
Hove Manor **7** BN3 .... 187 A6
Hove Mus & Art Gall BN3 .. 187 B6
Hove Park Gdns Hove BN3 . 167 B1
Hove BN3 .... 186 F8
Hove Park Rd BN1, BN3 ...... 167 C1
Hove Park Sch (Lower)
BN3 .... 166 D2
Hove Park Sch (Upper)
BN3 .... 167 A1
Hove Park Villas BN3 .... 187 B8
Hove Park Way BN1 .... 167 C1
Hove PI BN3 .... 187 B5
Hove St BN3 .... 187 A6
Hove Sta BN3 .... 187 B8
Hovedene BN3 .... 187 C7
Howard Ave
Burgess Hill RH15 .... 106 E6
East Wittering PO20 .... 201 D7
Howard Ct BN3 .... 167 A2
Howard Ho PO21 .... 202 F8
Howard PI Brighton BN1 ..... 207 F7
Howard Rd Arundel BN18 .. 158 A2
Brighton BN2 .... 188 C7
Crawley RH11 .... 17 D2
Horsham RH13 .... 37 A4
Littlehampton BN17 .... 198 C5
Sompting BN15 .... 163 C1
Howard St BN11 .... 182 C3
Howards Way BN16 .... 199 B3
Hoylake CI RH11 .... 17 D5
Hoyle La GU29 .... 93 D2
Huddlestones BN16 .... 179 F6
Hudson CI BN13 .... 181 D6
Hudson Dr BN16 .... 199 E4
Hudson Rd RH10 .... 19 C2
Huffwood Trad Est
Billingshurst RH14 .... 77 D7
Partridge Green RH13 ...... 103 A3
Hughes CI PO21 .... 194 F4
Hughes Rd BN2 .... 188 B8
Hugo Platt GU31 .... 68 A4
Humber Ave BN13 .... 181 C7
Humber CI
Littlehampton BN17 .... 198 F4
Worthing BN13 .... 181 C7
Humphrey Lodge RH15 ...... 107 D3
Humphrey's Gap BN43 .... 185 A7
Humphrys Rd **4** BN1 ...... 182 D2
Hundredsteddle La PO20 ... 191 D2
Hungers La GU28 .... 96 A1
Hunston CI RH11 .... 17 D5
Hunt's Gate BN8 .... 87 E3
Hunter Ho RH10 .... 18 D3
Hunter Rd
Crawley RH10, RH11 .... 18 D4
Thorney Island PO10 .... 169 C3
Hunter's Mead BN6 .... 125 C6
Hunters Chase GU20 .... 25 B5
Hunters CI PO21 .... 194 C1
Hunters Mead RH13 .... 103 A3
Hunters Race PO19 .... 152 E3
Hunters Way PO19 .... 152 F3
Hunterscroft Gdns RH13 ..... 81 E1
Huntingdon Way RH15 .... 107 D5
Huntsbottom La GU33 .... 45 D3
Hurley Rd BN13 .... 181 E6
Hurst Ave Horsham RH12 ..... 36 D3
Worthing BN11 .... 181 F2
Hurst CI Amberley BN18 .... 138 E7
Crawley RH11 .... 17 F4
Hurst CI Liphook GU30 .... 215 A5
Hurst Cotts BN18 .... 138 E7
Hurst Cres BN41 .... 186 B8
Hurst Ct RH12 .... 36 D3
Hurst Farm Rd RH19 .... 22 D7
Hurst Gdns BN6 .... 125 F7
Hurst Hill BN1 .... 168 C5

Hurst Rd Hassocks BN6 ...... 126 D4
Horley RH6 .... 1 E4
Horsham RH12 .... 36 D3
Rustington BN16 .... 199 E6
Hurst Wickham CI BN6 .... 126 C5
Hurstfield BN15 .... 183 D5
Hurstfield CI RH16 .... 86 A2
Hurstlands RH14 .... 77 C7
Hurston CI BN14 .... 182 A8
Hurston Gr RH20 .... 119 B3
Hurston La RH20 .... 119 B3
Hurstpierpoint Coll BN6 ... 126 B8
Hurstwood **6** BN2 .... 188 F5
Hurstwood Ave PO10 .... 150 A1
Hurstwood Ct GU29 .... 92 E5
Hurstwood La
Haywards Heath RH16 ...... 86 A2
Sharpthorne RH17, RH19 .. 43 D1
Hutchins Way RH16 .... 1 F5
Hutton Rd BN1 .... 168 B3
Huxley's Experience Bird of
Prey Ctr RH13 .... 58 F8
Hyde Dr RH11 .... 17 E5
Hyde Heath Ct RH10 .... 19 D8
Hyde La BN44 .... 144 B2
Hyde Sq BN44 .... 144 B2
Hyde St BN44 .... 144 B1
Hyde The BN2 .... 188 F8
Hylands CI RH10 .... 19 A5
Hylters's La PO18 .... 132 B7
Hyperion Ct RH11 .... 17 E4
Hyperion Wlk RH6 .... 2 B1
Hythe CI BN11 .... 182 A1
Hythe Rd Brighton BN1 ..... 168 A2
Worthing BN11 .... 182 A1

Icarus Way PO22 .... 196 C5
Icklesham Ho **9** RH11 .... 17 F3
Iden CI BN2 .... 188 E5
Iden Hurst BN6 .... 126 A7
Idsworth CI PO8 .... 128 A8
Iford Ave RH11 .... 18 C7
Ifield Com Sch RH11 .... 18 A7
Ifield Cty Jun Sch RH11 ...... 18 A6
Ifield Cty Mid Sch RH11 ..... 18 A6
Ifield Fst Sch RH11 .... 18 A8
Ifield Gn RH11 .... 5 A1
Ifield Rd Charlwood RH6 ...... 4 E5
Crawley RH11 .... 18 C6
Ifield St RH11 .... 17 F8
Ifield Sta RH11 .... 18 A6
Ifield Wood RH11 .... 4 E1
Ifold Bridge La RH14 .... 31 D4
Ifoldhurst RH14 .... 31 C2
Ilex CI BN16 .... 199 C4
Ilex Ct
Portslade-by-Sea BN42 .... 166 A1
Worthing BN12 .... 181 B2
Ilex Ho **1** BN6 .... 126 A7
Ilex Way
Middleton-on-Sea PO22 ... 196 E6
Worthing BN12 .... 181 B2
Image Cross Flats RH19 ...... 43 A5
Imberhorne La RH19 .... 9 B2
Imberhorne Lower Sch RH19 9 B3
Imberhorne Sch RH19 .... 9 B3
Imberhorne Way RH19 .... 9 B3
Imperial Arc BN1 .... 207 F5
Independent Bsns Pk The
RH19 .... 10 A3
Infirmary Dr RH13 .... 57 E6
Infirmary Terr PO19 .... 172 F8
Ingfield Manor Sch RH14 ... 55 D6
Ingham Dr BN1 .... 168 D6
Ingle Green CI BN12 .... 200 E4
Inglecroft Ct **4** BN15 ... 183 C7
Inglenook RH11 .... 79 F7
Ingleside Cres BN15 .... 183 F5
Ingleside Rd BN15 .... 183 E5
Inglewood CI PO21 .... 194 C1
Inglewood Dr PO21 .... 194 B2
Ingram CI Horsham RH12 ... 36 A2
Rustington BN16 .... 199 B5
Steyning BN44 .... 143 D2
Ingram Cres E BN3 .... 186 B8
Ingram Cres W BN3 .... 186 B8
Ingram Ct BN3 .... 186 B7
Ingram Rd BN44 .... 143 D2
Ingram's Green La GU29 ..... 91 C4
Inholmes CI RH15 .... 107 C3
Inholmes Cotts RH17 .... 84 A4
Inholmes Park Rd RH15 .... 107 B3
Ink Pen La RH18 .... 23 E1
Inlands Rd PO18 .... 170 B8
Innerwyke CI PO22 .... 196 B5
Innes Rd RH12 .... 36 F4
Inval Hill GU27 .... 27 C8
Inverness Rd BN1 .... 188 C8
Inwood Cres BN1 .... 167 E1
Inwood Rd GU33 .... 45 C3
Iona CI RH11 .... 18 B3

Iona Way **12** RH16 .... 85 E4
Iping La GU29 .... 69 E4
Irene Ave BN15 .... 183 D7
Irons Bottom Rd RH6 .... 1 A6
Irvine Rd BN17 .... 198 E4
Irving Wlk RH10 .... 18 E3
Irwin Dr RH12 .... 23 A6
Isaac's La
Burgess Hill RH15 .... 106 F6
Haywards Heath
RH16, RH15 .... 85 A2
Isabel Cres BN3 .... 186 E8
Isfield Rd BN1 .... 168 C2
Island CI BN17 .... 206 B8
Island Lo PO20 .... 206 B8
Island Loop PO20 .... 206 B8
Isle of Thorns
(Univ of Sussex) RH17 ...... 44 D1
Islingword PI BN2 .... 188 C6
Islingword Rd BN2 .... 188 C7
Islingword St BN2 .... 207 B6
Itchenor Rd
Shipton Green PO20 .... 191 A4
South Hayling PO11 .... 189 B2
Itchingfield Cty Prim Sch
Barns Green RH13 .... 56 F3
Itchingfield RH13 .... 57 A6
Ithaca Terr PO22 .... 195 F3
Ivanhoe CI RH11 .... 5 D1
Ivanhoe PI PO22 .... 196 C5
Iveagh CI RH11 .... 18 C1
Ivory PI BN2 .... 207 B6
Ivory Wlk RH11 .... 17 E3
Ivy Arch CI BN14 .... 161 F6
Ivy Arch Rd BN14 .... 182 D3
Ivy CI Ashington RH20 ...... 121 A5
Southwater RH13 .... 57 F1
Westergate PO20 .... 175 D7
Ivy Cotts RH17 .... 84 E8
Ivy Cres PO22 .... 195 D5
Ivy Dene La RH19 .... 23 D6
Ivy La Bognor Regis PO22 . 195 D5
Westergate PO20 .... 175 E7
Ivy PI Hove BN1, BN3 .... 187 D5
Worthing BN12 .... 182 B1
Ivydale Rd PO21 .... 195 A4
Ivydene Cres PO18 .... 170 D7
Ivydore Ave BN13 .... 181 D8
Ivydore CI BN13 .... 181 D7

Jackdaw CI RH11 .... 18 C8
Jackdaw La RH12 .... 36 E6
Jacket's Hill RH20 .... 120 A5
Jackrells La RH13 .... 58 B2
Jackson Rd RH10 .... 39 B8
Jackson St BN2 .... 207 B7
Jacobean CI RH10 .... 19 C5
Jacqueline Du Pre Ct **6**
BN2 .... 188 C5
James CI BN13 .... 181 F6
James St BN2 .... 206 E6
James Watt Way RH10 .... 1 C3
Jane Murray Way
Burgess Hill BN6, RH15 .. 106 D5
Burgess Hill RH15 .... 106 E1
Jane's La RH15 .... 107 E4
Janes La
Burgess Hill RH15 .... 107 D4
River GU28 .... 72 E3
Janeston Ct **4** BN3 .... 187 C7
Japonica CI BN43 .... 165 B1
Jarvis CI RH11 .... 39 B8
Jarvis Cotts BN44 .... 143 D3
Jarvis La BN44 .... 143 D3
Jarvis Rd BN18 .... 157 F2
Jasmine Ct Brighton BN1 .. 167 C5
Horsham RH12 .... 36 C2
Javelin CI RH10 .... 6 D1
Javelin Rd PO10 .... 169 C3
Jay CI RH13 .... 58 A2
Jay's La GU27 .... 28 C8
Jays CI BN17 .... 198 D6
Jays The RH15 .... 106 F4
Jeans CI **10** RH11 .... 18 B1
Jefferies RH17 .... 65 C4
Jefferies La BN12 .... 181 C1
Jeffreys Ave PO19 .... 153 A1
Jengers Mead RH14 .... 55 D1
Jenner Rd RH10 .... 5 F3
Jeremy's La RH17 .... 83 C6
Jerrard Rd PO20 .... 154 D2
Jersey Rd Crawley RH11 .... 18 A2
Ferring BN12 .... 200 F4
Jersey St BN2 .... 207 B6
Jervis Ave BN16 .... 199 D5
Jesmond CI BN3 .... 186 E7
Jesmond Rd BN3 .... 186 E7
Jessie Younghusband Cty
Prim Sch PO19 .... 172 F8
Jesters RH15 .... 107 C7
Jetty The PO22 .... 197 A5

Jevington CI BN13 .... 181 B5
Jevington Ct
Shoreham-by-Sea BN43 .. 185 D6
Worthing BN13 .... 181 B5
Jevington Dr BN2 .... 168 D1
Jew St BN1 .... 207 A5
Jib CI BN16 .... 179 A3
Jireh Ct **4** RH16 .... 85 E5
Joan Nightingale Ho RH16 85 C4
Job's Cnr RH10 .... 105 E5
Job's La BN6, RH17 .... 105 F5
Jobes RH17 .... 40 F1
Jobson's La GU27 .... 28 D2
Jockey Mead RH12 .... 36 A1
John Arundel Rd PO19 ...... 172 C7
John Horniman Sch BN11 182 E2
John King Shipyard PO10 169 C8
John Pounds Ho RH11 .... 18 D4
John Selden Cty Fst Sch
BN12 .... 181 D4
John Selden Mid Sch
BN12 .... 181 D4
John St
Bognor Regis PO21 .... 195 D3
Brighton BN2 .... 207 B6
Shoreham-by-Sea BN43 .. 184 E7
John Whittle Lodge **4**
BN2 .... 168 C1
Johnson Bank **4** BN2 ... 188 C7
Johnson Dr RH15 .... 107 D3
Johnson Way BN18 .... 177 B2
Johnson Wlk RH10 .... 18 E3
Jolesfield Crawley RH11 .... 17 F3
Partridge Green RH13 ...... 102 F4
Jolesfield CE (C) Prim Sch
RH13 .... 103 A4
Jolliffe Rd PO20 .... 201 D7
Jordan Ct BN3 .... 186 E8
Jordans CI RH11 .... 18 D8
Jordans Cres RH11 .... 5 D1
Jordans The RH19 .... 22 E8
Joy Wlk **3** PO19 .... 173 A6
Joyce CI BN17 .... 198 C2
Joys Croft PO19 .... 173 B7
Joys Croft Cty PO19 .... 173 B7
Jubilee Ave BN16 .... 199 C6
Jubilee CI RH16 .... 86 A4
Jubilee Ct BN2 .... 168 E2
Jubilee Ho
Crockerhill PO18 .... 155 B3
Emsworth PO10 .... 149 A1
Jubilee Rd
Burgess Hill RH15 .... 107 C4
Chichester PO19 .... 173 A7
Portslade-by-Sea BN41 ... 186 A8
Rudgwick RH12 .... 33 D8
Jubilee St BN1 .... 207 A6
Jubilee Terr
Chichester PO19 .... 173 A7
Westbourne PO10 .... 149 D3
Jubilee Way PO20 .... 119 F3
Jubilee Wlk KO10 .... 19 A6
Judge's Terr RH19 .... 22 E8
Juggs La RH20 .... 99 E1
Juggs The RH20 .... 99 E1
Julian Ct **5** BN43 .... 185 C8
Julian Rd BN3 .... 187 E7
Junction CI
Burgess Hill RH15 .... 107 C4
Burndell BN18 .... 177 B2
Junction PI GU27 .... 26 F6
Junction Rd Brighton BN1 207 F6
Burgess Hill RH15 .... 107 C4
June Ct PO21 .... 204 F8
June La GU29 .... 92 E8
June Meadows GU29 .... 92 E8
June Rise GU29 .... 92 E8
Juniper CI
Middleton-on-Sea PO22 ... 196 E6
Portslade-by-Sea BN41 ... 166 B3
Worthing BN13 .... 181 D5
Juniper Rd RH11 .... 5 C1
Juniper Wlk BN43 .... 165 C1
Jupp's La BN12 .... 181 C3
Jura CI RH11 .... 18 B3
Jury La PO20 .... 192 D5
Juxon CI Chichester PO19 . 173 A5
Crawley RH11 .... 17 F4

Kaithwood Ho RH12 .... 37 B5
Karenza Ct BN1 .... 188 A8
Kearsley Dr BN14 .... 162 A1
Keats CI RH12 .... 36 F7
Keats PI RH19 .... 9 D1
Keats Wlk PO21 .... 195 B3
Kebbell Lodge **12** BN2 . 207 B5
Keble CI
Bognor Regis PO21 .... 194 F3
Crawley RH10 .... 6 D1
Keelson Way BN16 .... 199 A6
Keepers Wood PO19 .... 152 F3

Keir Hardie Ho **7** RH11 .. 18 B1
Kelly Rd BN3 .... 167 D1
Kelsey Ave PO10 .... 150 A1
Kelsey CI East Liss GU33 ... 45 C5
Horley RH6 .... 1 F3
Kelsey Ct RH15 .... 107 D3
Kelso CI Crawley RH10 .... 19 E7
Lancing BN15 .... 183 B7
Worthing BN13 .... 181 E4
Kelvin Bsns Ctr RH10 .... 5 F2
Kelvin La RH10 .... 5 F2
Kelvin Way RH10 .... 5 F2
Kemnal Pk GU27 .... 27 D7
Kemp Ct BN2 .... 188 E4
Kemp St BN1 .... 207 A6
Kemp Town PI **18** BN2 . 188 D4
Kemps BN2 .... 125 F7
Kempshott Rd RH12 .... 36 B4
Kempton Mews **1** BN2 . 188 E4
Kendal CI BN16, BN17 .... 179 A3
Kendal Rd Hove BN3 .... 186 F8
Lancing BN15 .... 183 C6
Kenhurst BN16 .... 200 A5
Kenilworth Ct RH11 .... 18 B2
Kenilworth Rd PO21 .... 195 B4
Kenlegh PO21 .... 194 F2
Kenmara CI RH10 .... 6 A1
Kenmara Ct RH10 .... 6 A2
Kenmure Ave BN1 .... 168 A7
Kennard Ct RH18 .... 23 E3
Kennedy Ave RH19 .... 9 D3
Kennedy Rd RH13 .... 36 D1
Kennel Hill PO18 .... 133 E1
Kennel La Hookwood RH6 .... 1 D2
Maplehurst RH13 .... 80 E2
Kennet CI Crawley RH11 .... 17 F5
Worthing BN13 .... 181 D7
Kensett's Cnr RH20 .... 121 A3
Kensington CI RH20 .... 119 C7
Kensington Gdns BN1 .... 207 A6
Kensington PI BN1 .... 207 A6
Kensington Rd
Chichester PO19 .... 173 D6
Crawley RH11 .... 18 C2
Kensington St BN1 .... 207 A6
Kent CI BN43 .... 185 C7
Kent Rd Chichester PO19 .. 173 B7
Littlehampton BN17 .... 198 D6
Kent St RH13, RH17 .... 104 C6
Kenton Rd BN3 .... 186 D7
Kents Rd RH16 .... 85 F3
Kentstreet La RH13 .... 82 C3
Kentwyns Dr RH13 .... 58 E8
Kenwards BN1 .... 168 D7
Kenya Ct Horley RH6 .... 1 F4
Kerdale CI RH10 .... 19 C2
Kerrison Mews BN1 .... 187 D5
Kerves La RH13 .... 58 D6
Kestrel CI
Bracklesham PO20 .... 202 A6
Crawley RH11 .... 18 C6
Horsham RH12 .... 36 E5
Hove BN3 .... 187 D6
Kestrel Ct
Bognor Regis PO21 .... 204 F7
Chichester PO19 .... 173 D7
Kestrel Way BN17 .... 178 C4
Kestrels The BN43 .... 185 A8
Keswick CI Crawley RH11 ... 17 D4
Worthing BN12 .... 181 D5
Ketch Rd BN16, BN17 .... 199 A4
Ketche's La RH17 .... 87 E7
Kew Gdns PO21 .... 194 F5
Kewell's Cnr PO20 .... 191 E5
Keymer Cres BN12 .... 181 D1
Keymer Ct RH15 .... 107 B2
Keymer Gdns RH15 .... 107 B3
Keymer Par RH15 .... 107 B2
Keymer Rd Brighton BN1 .. 168 B6
Burgess Hill RH15 .... 107 B2
Crawley RH11 .... 18 D4
Keymer Bns 127 B3
Keymer Way BN12 .... 181 C1
Keynor La PO20 .... 203 E8
Keysford La RH16, RH17 .... 64 E3
Kidborough Rd RH11 .... 17 F4
Kidbrook RH16 .... 86 B6
Kidbrooke Park (Michael Hall
Sch) RH18 .... 23 D3
Kidbrooke Rise RH18 .... 23 E2
Kidders La BN15 .... 123 D8
Kidmans CI RH12 .... 36 B5
Kidworth CI RH16 .... 1 F5
Kilbarn Ct RH16 .... 85 D2
Kilbarn Way RH16 .... 85 D2
Killinghurst La GU8 .... 28 D8
Kilmore CI BN14 .... 161 E6
Kiln Field GU33 .... 45 A5

Kiln Fields GU27 .... 27 C8
Kiln La
　Haywards Heath RH16 ...... 86 B5
　Horley RH6 .... 2 A5
Kiln Rd RH10 .... 21 B7
Kiln The RH15 .... 107 C3
Kilnfield Rd RH12 .... 33 D8
Kilnmead RH10, RH11 .... 18 E7
Kilnmead CI RH10 .... 18 E7
Kilnwood CI PO20 .... 206 F7
Kilnwood La RH12 .... 17 B3
Kilwich CI PO22 .... 196 D6
Kimber CI BN15 .... 183 D5
Kimberley CI RH6 .... 1 E3
Kimberley Rd
　Brighton BN2 .... 168 D1
　Crawley RH10 .... 19 B7
Kimbridge Pk PO20 .... 202 A6
Kimbridge Rd PO20 .... 202 A6
Kindersley CI RH19 .... 10 B3
Kinfauns Dr BN3 .... 161 D2
King Alfred CI BN44 .... 143 D3
King Alfred (Swimming
　Pool & Sports Ctr) BN3 187 E4
King Bsns Ctr BN6 .... 105 C1
King Charles Pl 3 BN43 .... 185 A6
King Edward Ave BN14 .... 182 E4
King Edward CI
　Horsham RH13 .... 57 D6
　Worthing BN14 .... 182 E4
King Edward Rd RH13 .... 57 D6
King Edward VII Hospl
　GU29 .... 70 E6
King George Ave RH19 .... 9 C3
King George Rd BN43 .... 185 D8
King George VI Ave
　BN1, BN3 .... 167 A3
King George VI Dr BN3 ...... 167 A4
King George VI Mansions
　BN3 .... 166 F2
King James La BN5 .... 123 E4
King John CI 4 BN43 .... 185 A6
King PI BN1 .... 207 F5
King St Arundel BN18 .... 158 A3
　Brighton BN1 .... 207 A5
　East Grinstead RH19 .... 9 E1
Emsworth PO10 .... 169 C8
Westbourne PO10 .... 149 D3
Worthing BN14 .... 182 D4
King's Arms Hill BN18 .... 158 B3
King's Ave PO19 .... 172 F4
King's Barn La BN44 .... 143 F4
King's Barn Villas BN44 ...... 143 E3
King's Ct PO21 .... 195 E3
King's Dr GU29 .... 70 F7
King's Espl BN3 .... 187 A5
King's Gdns BN3 .... 187 B5
King's La RH13 .... 104 B8
King's Manor Sch BN3 .... 185 D8
King's Par PO21 .... 195 A2
King's Rd
　Brighton BN1, BN3 .... 187 E5
Emsworth PO10 .... 169 A8
Haslemere GU27 .... 27 A6
Haywards Heath RH16 .... 85 F3
Horsham RH12, RH13 .... 36 E3
King's Stone Ave BN44 .... 143 F3
King's Terr 6 PO10 .... 169 B8
Kingfisher CI
　Crawley RH10 .... 6 A1
Rowland's Castle PO9 ...... 128 D1
　Worthing BN13 .... 181 C5
Kingfisher Ct PO22 .... 196 F5
Kingfisher Par PO20 .... 201 F7
Kingfisher Rise RH19 .... 22 F8
Kingfisher Way RH12 .... 36 C5
Kingley Vale Nature Reserve
　PO18 .... 131 E2
Kingmere 10 BN17 .... 198 E4
Kings Barn End BN44 .... 143 F3
Kings CI Burndell BN18 ...... 177 A3
　Lancing BN15 .... 183 F5
　Red Hill PO9 .... 128 C1
Kings Copse 8 RH19 .... 22 F8
Kings Cres BN43 .... 185 D7
Kings Ct Horsham RH13 ...... 36 E3
　Lancing BN15 .... 183 F4
　Selsey PO20 .... 206 E8
　Shoreham-by-Sea BN43 .... 184 D5
Kings Dr
　Bognor Regis PO21 .... 205 B8
Hassocks BN6 .... 126 F4
Kings Dr
　Shoreham-by-Sea BN43 .... 184 D5
Kings Gap BN43 .... 184 D5
Kings Gate BN3 .... 187 C8
Kings La
　Coldwaltham RH20 .... 117 C6
　Marehill RH20 .... 98 F1
　Southwater Street RH13 ...... 58 A4

Kings Mews BN3 .... 187 B6
Kings Par BN1 .... 168 A2
Kings Platt RH13 .... 101 D8
Kings Rd Horley RH6 .... 2 A3
　Lancing BN15 .... 183 F5
　Southwick BN42 .... 165 E1
Kings Ride RH15 .... 107 D1
Kings Way
　Burgess Hill RH15 .... 107 D2
　Red Hill PO9 .... 128 C1
Kings Wlk BN43 .... 184 D5
Kingsbridge Mews BN13 .... 181 D7
Kingsbury Rd BN1 .... 207 A7
Kingsbury St BN1, BN2 ...... 207 A7
KIngscliffe Sch BN2 .... 188 C5
Kingscote Hill RH11 .... 18 B4
Kingscote Lodge BN1 .... 168 F5
Kingscote Sta RH19 .... 21 F4
Kingsdene BN1 .... 182 B2
Kingsey Ave PO10 .... 169 A8
Kingsfield Henfield BN5 ...... 123 E5
　Storrington RH20 .... 119 E2
Kingsfield CI BN42 .... 185 E8
Kingsfold 2 BN2 .... 188 F5
Kingsfold CI RH14 .... 77 D6
Kingsfold La PO22 .... 15 B5
Kingsham Ave PO19 .... 173 B5
Kingsham Cty Prim Sch
　PO19 .... 173 B4
Kingsham Rd PO19 .... 173 A5
Kingsland RH5 .... 3 A8
Kingsland CI
　Shoreham-by-Sea BN43 .... 185 B7
　Storrington RH20 .... 119 E2
Kingsland Cotts BN6 .... 105 C1
Kingsland Rd BN14 .... 182 D6
Kingslea RH13 .... 36 E3
Kingsley CI Horley RH6 .... 1 F5
　Worthing BN14 .... 182 F4
Kingsley Ct 11 BN1 .... 187 E5
Kingsley Rd Brighton BN1 . 167 D1
　Crawley RH11 .... 18 A3
　Horley RH6 .... 1 F5
Kingsmead
　Bognor Regis PO22 .... 195 F3
　Brighton BN1 .... 168 B3
　Littlehampton BN17 .... 178 C5
Kingsmead CI
　Horsham RH12 .... 37 B6
　Steyning BN44 .... 143 D1
Kingsmead Gdns PO22 ...... 197 A6
Kingsmead PI RH12 .... 35 C3
Kingsmead Rd
　Ancton PO22 .... 197 A5
　Broadridge Heath RH12 ..... 35 D3
Kingsmere BN1 .... 167 E2
Kingsmill Rd PO22 .... 176 C6
Kingspit La GU28 .... 96 D8
Kingsthorpe Rd BN3 .... 186 F8
Kingston Bay Rd BN43 .... 185 C6
Kingston Broadway
　BN42, BN43 .... 165 D1
Kingston Buci Cty Fst Sch
　BN43 .... 185 B8
Kingston CI Brighton BN1 . 168 E6
　Hove BN3 .... 166 E2
　Shoreham-by-Sea BN43 .... 185 C8
Kingston Ct 17 BN43 .... 185 C8
Kingston La East Preston
　BN16 .... 200 B5
　Southwick
　BN41, BN42, BN43 .... 185 D7
Kingston Way BN42, BN43 165 D1
Kingsway
　Bognor Regis PO21 .... 194 D1
　Hove BN3 .... 187 B5
　Selsey PO20 .... 206 F6
　Worthing BN12 .... 181 F2
Kingsway Ct BN3 .... 187 C5
Kingsway Sch The BN18 .... 176 F3
Kingswood RH20 .... 119 C7
Kingswood CI RH11 .... 39 C8
Kingswood Flats BN2 .... 207 B5
Kingswood St BN2 .... 207 A5
Kinnell CI PO10 .... 169 B8
Kinrara Ho 10 PO21 .... 195 C3
Kinsale CI BN3 .... 167 D7
Kipling Ave BN12 .... 181 B3
Kipling CI RH10 .... 19 C8
Kipling Ct
　3 Haywards Heath RH16 . 85 D5
　Horsham RH11 .... 37 A4
Kipling Way RH19 .... 9 C1
Kirby La RH13 .... 80 B2
Kirdford CI
　Burgess Hill RH15 .... 107 C1
　Crawley RH11 .... 18 A8
Kirdford CI 3 Littlehampton BN16 ..... 199 B5
Kirdford Cty Jun Sch RH14 53 B2
Kirdford Rd BN18 .... 158 A2
Kirkby CI PO18 .... 154 D3
Kirkland CI RH16 .... 199 B5

Kites CI RH11 .... 18 C6
Kithurst CI Crawley RH11 .... 18 D4
　Littlehampton BN16 .... 199 F4
　Worthing BN12 .... 181 B4
Kithurst Cres BN12 .... 181 B4
Kithurst Farm Rd RH20 ..... 140 B8
Kithurst La RH20 .... 119 C1
Kithurst Rd PO20 .... 119 B1
Kitlear Ct 5 BN3 .... 187 D6
Kitsmead RH10 .... 7 A2
Kittiwake CI RH11 .... 17 D4
Knap La PO20 .... 206 D7
Knepp CI Brighton BN2 ...... 168 F2
　Crawley RH10 .... 19 C6
Knight's Hill PO18 .... 133 E5
Knighton CI RH10 .... 6 D2
Knights Cotts PO18 .... 151 B3
Knightscroft Ave BN16 ...... 199 C4
Knightscroft Ct 4 BN16 .... 199 B4
Knob Hill RH12 .... 15 A1
Knockhundred Row GU29 ... 92 F8
Knole CI RH10 .... 19 D7
Knole Gr RH19 .... 9 C3
Knoll Bsns Ctr The BN3 ..... 186 D8
Knoll CI BN3 .... 166 D1
Knoll Cty Inf Sch BN3 .... 166 D1
Knowle CI RH10 .... 7 C3
Knowle Dr RH10 .... 7 B3
Knowle La GU6, RH10 .... 11 D4
Knowle The RH17 .... 84 E7
Knowles CI BN5 .... 123 E5
Knowles Meadow GU33 ...... 45 D1
Knoyle Rd BN1 .... 167 E2
Knyveton Ct RH15 .... 107 B3
Kymer Gdns BN6 .... 127 A3
Kynon Gdns PO22 .... 196 D6
Kyoto Ct PO21 .... 195 B3

Laburnum Ave BN3 .... 166 E1
Laburnum CI
　Ferring BN12 .... 200 F5
　Lancing BN15 .... 183 D4
Laburnum Gr
　Bognor Regis PO22 .... 195 C6
　Brighton BN1 .... 168 B3
　Southwater PO22 .... 173 A5
Laburnum Grove Cty
　Jun Sch The PO22 .... 195 C6
Laburnum Way RH16 .... 86 B4
Laburnum Wlk BN16 .... 199 C6
Lacey Ho PO19 .... 172 F5
Lackenhurst La RH13 .... 79 A6
Ladbroke Rd RH6 .... 2 B5
Ladies Mile BN1 .... 168 B7
Ladies Mile CI BN1 .... 167 F6
Ladies' Mile CI BN1 .... 167 E6
Lady Bee Ind Est BN42 ...... 185 E6
Lady Margaret Rd RH11 ..... 18 A7
Lady Margaret Wlk RH11 ... 18 A7
Laddyell Rd BN11 .... 182 F3
Ladymead RH15 .... 107 C5
Ladymead Cl RH10 .... 19 C3
Ladysmith Rd BN2 .... 188 D8
Lagoon Rd PO21 .... 206 F7
Lagwood CI BN6 .... 126 F3
Laine CI BN1 .... 167 E3
Laines Rd BN44 .... 143 C2
Lake Cotts PO22 .... 176 D6
Lake La
　Barnham BN18, PO22 .... 176 D6
　Horley RH1, RH6 .... 2 C6
　Lake Rd PO19 .... 173 C6
Lake View
　Bognor Regis PO21 .... 194 A1
　1 Brighton BN2 .... 188 C5
Lake View Rd
　Dormans Park RH19 .... 9 F5
　Furnace Wood RH10 .... 8 C4
Lakers La RH14 .... 31 F1
Lakers Meadow RH14 .... 77 D8
Lakeside Horsham RH12 ...... 36 C5
　Midhurst PO22 .... 92 E6
　Shoreham-by-Sea BN3 ..... 184 B5
Lakeside Wlk RH10 .... 19 A5
Lambert's La GU29 .... 92 F8
Lambeth CI RH11 .... 18 B2
Lambleys La RH14 .... 182 F8
Lambourn CI RH19 .... 9 E3
Lambourne CI
　Brighton BN2 .... 168 C2
　Crawley RH10 .... 18 F4
Lambourne La GU29, GU30 47 E2
Lambourne Rd BN1 .... 168 C2
Lambs Cres RH12 .... 36 F5
Lambs Farm CI RH12 .... 37 A5
Lambs Green Rd RH12 .... 16 F6
Lambs Lease GU33 .... 45 D3
Lambyn Croft RH6 .... 2 C4
Lammas CI BN17 .... 178 E3

Lamorna Gdns
　Ferring BN12 .... 200 F4
　Westergate PO20 .... 175 D6
Lanara Gr BN14 .... 182 C6
Lanark CI RH13 .... 36 E2
Lancaster CI RH10 .... 6 D1
Lancaster Ct 10 BN3 .... 187 A6
Lancaster Dr RH19 .... 10 A3
Lancaster Pl PO22 .... 195 C6
Lancaster Rd
　Brighton BN1 .... 207 F7
　Worthing BN12 .... 181 E2
Lancasterian Grange
　PO19 .... 172 F6
Lancastrian Cty Inf Sch
　PO19 .... 172 F7
Lancelot CI RH11 .... 17 E6
Lancing CI Crawley RH11 .... 18 A8
　Lancing BN15 .... 183 D6
Lancing Coll BN15 .... 164 A2
Lancing Ct
　5 Brighton BN2 .... 188 F5
　Horsham RH12 .... 37 A4
Lancing Manor L Ctr BN15 183 F8
Lancing Sq BN15 .... 183 D4
Lancing Sta BN15 .... 183 E5
Landen Pk RH6 .... 1 A5
Landseer Dr PO20 .... 206 F7
Landseer Rd BN3 .... 187 A8
Lane End Dr PO10 .... 169 B8
Lane End Rd PO22 .... 197 A5
Lane Ho RH13 .... 36 D2
Lane The Chichester PO19 . 153 A2
　Ifold RH14 .... 31 C4
Lanercost Rd RH11 .... 18 C5
Lanfranc Rd BN14 .... 182 B4
Langbury CI BN12 .... 180 D3
Langbury La BN12 .... 180 E3
Langdale Ave PO19, PO20 173 C4
Langdale CI BN15 .... 183 C5
Langdale Ct BN41 .... 186 F6
Langdale Gdns BN3 .... 186 F6
Langdale Rd Crawley RH11 . 17 D4
　Hove BN3 .... 186 F6
Langham CI 4 BN11 .... 182 A2
Langham Gdns BN11 .... 182 A2
Langham La RH11 .... 15 E4
Langhurst La RH12 .... 17 A8
Langhurstwood Rd RH12 ... 15 D3
Langley Dr RH11 .... 18 D8
Langley Gr PO21 .... 194 C1
Langley Green Cty Fst Sch
　RH11 .... 5 D1
Langley Green Cty Mid Sch
　RH11 .... 18 C8
Langley La RH11 .... 18 A8
Langley Par RH11 .... 5 C1
Langley Pl RH11 .... 5 C1
Langley Wlk RH11 .... 5 B1
Langmead CI BN17 .... 197 E8
Langridge Dr
　East Grinstead RH19 .... 22 E8
　Portslade-by-Sea BN41 ... 166 B3
Langridge Ho RH10 .... 36 B2
Langridge La RH16 .... 86 A6
Langridge Way RH15 .... 106 E5
Langshott RH6 .... 2 D4
Langshott La RH6 .... 2 C4
Langshott Sch RH6 .... 2 C3
Langstone CI RH10 .... 19 C3
Langstone PO20 .... 206 D6
Langton La BN6 .... 125 E7
Langton Pl 4 RH20 .... 119 D1
Langton Rd
　Chichester PO19 .... 172 E7
　Worthing BN14 .... 182 D4
Lanka CI PO20 .... 201 E7
Lansbury Rd RH11 .... 18 B1
Lansdown CI RH12 .... 37 B6
Lansdown Terr PO10 .... 149 D5
Lansdowne CI
　Angmering BN16 .... 179 F6
　Worthing BN11 .... 182 A3
Lansdowne CI BN11 .... 182 A2
Lansdowne Mews 9 BN3 187 D6
Lansdowne Rd
　Angmering BN16 .... 179 F6
　Hove BN3, BN3 .... 187 D6
　Littlehampton BN17 .... 178 D3
　Worthing BN11 .... 182 A2
Lansdowne Sq BN3 .... 187 D5
Lansdowne St BN3 .... 187 D6
Lansdowne Way BN11 .... 182 A2
Lanyards BN16 .... 179 A3
Lanyon CI RH13 .... 37 A6
Lanyon Mews RH12 .... 36 E3
Lapwing CI RH13 .... 36 F3
Larch CI
　Bognor Regis PO22 .... 195 C7
　Chichester PO19 .... 152 F2

Larch CI Liphook GU30 .... 25 B3
　Rustington BN16 .... 199 D5
Larch End Horsham RH12 ... 36 B4
　West Chiltington Common
　RH20 .... 119 D7
Larch Way RH16 .... 86 B4
Larches The RH12 .... 37 C6
Larches Way RH10 .... 21 C8
Larchfield CI PO21 .... 194 D1
Large Acres PO20 .... 206 D7
Lark Hill BN3 .... 166 E3
Lark Rise Crawley RH11 .... 18 C8
　Liphook GU30 .... 25 A5
Larkbeck BN14 .... 185 C7
Larkfield CI BN15 .... 183 F5
Larkfield Way BN1 .... 168 A4
Larkins Rd RH6 .... 5 D7
Larkspur Way RH13 .... 58 A3
Lashmar Rd BN16 .... 200 A6
Lashmere RH10 .... 7 D3
Laski Ct RH11 .... 18 B1
Latham Rd PO20 .... 206 D6
Latimer CI RH11 .... 5 D1
Latimer Rd BN1 .... 181 F1
Laud Dr RH10 .... 19 D5
Lauder CI PO10 .... 149 F2
Laughton Rd RH12 .... 36 F5
Laundry La RH17 .... 44 D1
Laurel 2
　4 RH2 .... 85 D6
Laurel CI
　Burgess Hill RH15 .... 107 D5
　Crawley RH10 .... 19 A3
　Worthing BN13 .... 181 C5
Laurel Dene RH19 .... 9 F1
Laurel Gr PO22 .... 195 C6
Laurel Mount RH20 .... 98 C2
Laurel Wlk RH13 .... 36 E3
Laurels Cty Fst Sch The
　BN3 .... 181 B6
Laurels The
　4 Brighton BN1 .... 207 B8
　Crawley RH10 .... 6 A1
Henfield BN5 .... 123 E5
　Southwater RH13 .... 57 F2
Lavant Cl
　Crawley RH10 .... 6 A1
　Lauriston Rd BN1 .... 167 E2
Lavant Ce (C) Prim Sch
　PO18 .... 152 E6
Lavant CI Crawley RH11 ...... 17 F5
　Worthing BN11 .... 181 A4
Lavant Down Rd PO18 .... 152 E7
Lavant Ho (Rosemead Sch)
　PO18 .... 152 E5
Lavant Rd PO18, PO19 ...... 152 F3
Lavender Ct BN15 .... 165 B1
Lavender Ho BN2 .... 207 B4
Lavender St BN2 .... 207 B4
Lavington CI RH11 .... 18 A7
Lavington Rd BN14 .... 182 B6
Lavinia CI
　Bognor Regis PO21 .... 194 F4
　Worthing BN12 .... 181 C3
Lavinia Way BN16 .... 200 A2
Lawn The PO21 .... 194 C2
Lawns Rd RH12 .... 12 A3
Lawns The Lancing BN15 ... 183 C8
Lawns The West Kingston BN16 ..... 200 A4
Lawrence Ave BN16 .... 199 D6
Lawrence Rd BN3 .... 186 F7
Lawrie Ct BN2 .... 207 C8
Lawrie La RH16 .... 86 B5
Laws CI RH11 .... 18 B1
Lawson-Hunt Ind Pk RH12 35 C4
Lawyer's La BN5 .... 123 C4
Laylands CI BN41 .... 186 A7
Laylands Rd BN41 .... 186 A7
Layne The PO22 .... 197 A5
Layzy Acre PO10 .... 169 F8
Le May CI RH6 .... 2 A4
Lea CI RH11 .... 17 F5
Lea Farm La RH20 .... 97 C2
Lea Ho PO22 .... 195 A6
Leach CI BN2 .... 188 C5
Leahurst Court Rd BN1 ...... 167 E3
Leahurst Ct 2 BN1 .... 167 E3
Leamon CI PO22 .... 196 F5
Leander Rd PO18 .... 171 C5
Leas CI PO22 .... 195 C5
Leas The Angmering BN16 . 179 E3
Burgess Hill RH15 .... 106 F4
Leatherbottle La PO19 ...... 173 C6
Lechford Rd RH6 .... 2 A1
Leconfield Rd BN15 .... 183 C5
Ledbury Way PO21 .... 194 B2
Ledgers Meadow RH17 .... 84 F6
Ledra Dr PO21 .... 205 B8
Lee St RH6 .... 1 E4
Leechpond Hill RH13 .... 59 F2
Leechpool La RH12, RH13 .. 37 A4

Leechpool Lane Cty
 Prim Sch RH13 .... 37 A4
Leechwood & Owlbeech Wood
 Nature Reserve RH13 .... 37 B3
Leecroft PO21 .... 194 E2
Leeds Cl Southwater RH13 . 58 A2
 Worthing BN13 .... 181 B5
Leemark Ho **4** BN17 .... 198 E4
Lees Cnr BN16 .... 185 F5
Leeward Ct BN13 .... 181 F5
Leeward Rd
 Littlehampton
 BN16, BN17 .... 199 A5
 Worthing BN13 .... 181 F5
Legion Way PO20 .... 202 A6
Legsheath La RH18, RH19 . 43 F8
Leicester St BN2 .... 207 B5
Leicester Villas BN3 ... 186 D7
Leigh Ct PO20 .... 202 C4
Leigh Rd Chichester PO19 172 F5
 Worthing BN13 .... 182 D6
Leighlands RH10 .... 19 C8
Leighton Ave BN14 ..... 182 E6
Leighton Rd
 Horsted Keynes RH17 ... 65 C5
 Hove BN3 .... 187 A8
Leighton Villas RH17 ... 65 C5
Leinster Gdns PO22 .... 196 D4
Leith View Rd RH12 .... 37 A5
Lemmington Way RH12 .. 37 A7
Lenhurst Way BN13 ..... 181 F4
Lennox Rd
 Chichester PO19 ...... 173 B7
 Hove BN3 .... 186 F8
 Shoreham-by-Sea BN43 . 185 B8
 Worthing BN11 .... 182 D3
Lennox St
 Bognor Regis PO21 .... 195 D2
 Brighton BN2 .... 207 B5
Leonardslee Ct RH10 ... 19 B3
Leonardslee Gardens RH13 82 A8
Leonora Dr PO21 .... 194 B2
Leopold Cl PO22 .... 196 A5
Leopold Rd Brighton BN1 207 F6
 Crawley RH11 .... 18 C6
Lesser Foxholes BN43 .. 164 D1
Letchworth Cl BN12 .... 200 E5
Letchworth Ct RH11 .... 17 E3
Level Mare La PO20 .... 155 E2
Leveret La RH11 .... 18 B8
Leverton Ave PO22 ..... 196 D4
Levine Ct **4** PO21 ... 195 D4
Lewes Cl
 Bognor Regis PO21 .... 194 F4
 Crawley RH10 .... 19 C6
Lewes Cres BN2 .... 188 E4
Lewes Rd
 Ashurst Wood RH19 .... 23 C6
 Brighton BN1, BN2 .... 168 E3
 Chelwood Gate
 RH17, RH18 .... 44 C1
 Danehill RH17 .... 66 B3
 Ditchling BN6 .... 127 F2
 Forest Row RH18 ...... 23 E2
 Haywards Heath RH16 .. 86 B7
 Horsted Keynes RH17 .. 65 C5
 Scaynes Hill RH16, RH17 86 D4
Lewes St BN2 .... 207 B6
Lewin Cl BN15 .... 183 F7
Lewis Ct **2** Brighton BN2 188 C8
 Worthing BN13 .... 181 B5
Lewis La BN18 .... 177 B2
Lewis Rd Chichester PO19 173 B7
 Lancing BN15 .... 183 D8
 New Brighton PO10 .... 149 C3
 Selsey PO20 .... 206 E7
Lewisham Cl RH11 ...... 18 C2
Ley Rd PO22 .... 196 B4
Leybourne Cl RH11 .... 18 C1
Leyfield BN6 .... 125 D5
Leylands Pk RH15 ..... 107 B5
Leylands Rd RH15 ..... 107 B4
Leys The Fernhurst GU27 . 49 A5
 Singleton PO18 .... 133 D7
Leythorne Cotts PO20 .. 173 E3
Leyton Lea RH17 ...... 84 E6
Library Pl BN11 .... 182 E1
Lichfield Ct
 10 Brighton BN2 ... 188 F5
 3 Worthing BN11 ... 182 A1
Lichfield Gdns PO21 ... 194 E3
Lidsey Rd PO20, PO22 .. 175 D4
Lifeboat Way PO20 ..... 206 E5
Lilac Cl
 Middleton-on-Sea PO22 196 E6
 Worthing BN13 .... 181 B5
Lillywhite Cl RH15 ... 106 F5
Limbourne La RH20 ..... 97 B3

Limbrick Cl BN12 ...... 181 C3
Limbrick La BN12 ...... 181 C4
Limbrick Way BN12 .... 181 C4
Lime Ave RH12 .... 37 A4
Lime Chase RH20 ...... 119 D2
Lime Cl Chichester PO19 173 B7
 Copthorne RH10 .... 7 B3
 Crawley RH11 .... 5 C1
Lime Gr BN16 .... 179 F4
Lime Kiln Rd RH13 .... 59 D6
Lime Rd BN14 .... 161 E6
Lime Tree Ave BN14 ... 161 F2
Lime Tree Cl BN14 .... 199 F6
Lime Tree Gr RH16 .... 86 C7
Lime Ave RH6 .... 2 B1
Limes Cl Bramshott GU30 25 C7
 Liss GU33 .... 45 B4
Limes The
 East Grinstead RH19 .. 9 A5
 Yapton BN18 .... 177 A3
Limmard Way PO22 .... 196 C4
Limmer La PO22 ...... 196 B4
Limney Rd BN2 .... 188 E7
Linacre Dr GU6, RH12 . 12 C4
Lincett Ave BN13 .... 181 F4
Lincett Cl BN13 ..... 181 F4
Lincett Dr BN13 ..... 181 F3
Linch Rd GU29, GU27 . 70 B7
Linchmere BN2 .... 188 F7
Linchmere Pl RH11 ... 18 A7
Linchmere Rd
 Hammer GU27 .... 26 D5
 Linchmere GU27 ...... 26 C4
Lincoln Ave PO21 .... 194 C4
Lincoln Cl Crawley RH10 18 E3
 Horley RH6 .... 2 A2
Lincoln Cotts BN2 ... 207 B6
Lincoln Ct Hove BN3 . 187 C8
 Liphook GU30 .... 25 C4
Lincoln Gn PO19 ..... 152 F1
Lincoln Rd
 Portslade-by-Sea BN41 186 B7
 Worthing BN13 .... 181 F4
Lincoln St BN2 ...... 207 B7
Lincoln Wood RH16, RH17 85 C5
Lindale Pl **5** RH20 . 119 D1
Linden Ave RH19 ..... 9 C2
Linden Cl Crawley RH10 19 A3
 Horsham RH12 .... 36 E4
Linden Ct
 1 Bognor Regis PO21 195 C3
 Petworth GU28 .... 95 E7
Linden Dr GU33 ...... 45 B4
Linden Gr RH16 ...... 86 B7
Linden Pk BN17 ...... 198 C5
Linden Rd
 Bognor Regis PO21 ... 195 C4
 Littlehampton BN17 . 198 C5
Lindens Cl PO10 ..... 149 B2
Lindens The
 4 Brighton BN2 ... 207 B7
 Copthorne RH10 ...... 7 B3
Lindfield BN41 ...... 166 A1
Lindfield Ct **2** BN1 168 C2
Lindfield Cty Inf Sch RH16 86 A7
Lindfield Cty Jun Sch RH16 86 B7
Lindfield Ent Pk RH16 66 C6
Lindfield Rd RH17 ... 66 C6
Lindgren Wlk RH11 ... 18 B1
Lindsey Ct PO22 ..... 196 A6
Lindum Rd BN13 ...... 181 F5
Lindum Way BN13 .... 181 F5
Lineside Ind Est BN17 198 B6
Lineside Way BN17 ... 198 B6
Linfield Copse RH20 . 119 F6
Linfield Cl BN13 .... 181 F6
Linfield Dr RH10 .... 19 E7
Linfield Rd RH19 .... 9 D3
Linfield Way PO20 ... 206 F7
Link Hill RH20 ...... 119 B1
Link La RH20 .... 98 C2
Link The RH11 .... 18 D6
Link Way PO21 .... 194 A1
Links Ave PO22 ...... 195 F4
Links Cl
 Portslade-by-Sea BN41 186 C8
 Red Hill PO9 .... 128 D1
Links La PO9 .... 128 D2
Links Rd Lancing BN15 183 F6
 Portslade-by-Sea BN41 186 C8
 Worthing BN14 .... 182 A8
Linkway RH6 .... 6 C7
Linkway The
 Brighton BN1 .... 168 B1
 Worthing BN11 .... 182 C3
Linton Ho GU28 ...... 73 C1
Linton Rd BN3 .... 186 F8
Lintott Gdns RH13 ... 36 E3
Lion Cl GU27 .... 26 F7
Lion Ct PO21 .... 194 B2
Lion Gn GU27 .... 26 F6

Lion La Haslemere GU27 26 F7
 Turners Hill RH10 ... 21 A4
Lion Mead GU27 ...... 26 F6
Lion Mews **4** BN3 .. 186 F7
Lion Rd PO21 .... 194 A2
Lion Rd PO19 .... 173 A6
Lionel Ave PO22 ..... 196 C6
Lions Ct BN2 .... 188 E5
Lions Gdns BN1 ...... 167 D4
Lions Gdns BN1 ...... 167 D2
Liphook CE (C) Jun Sch
 GU30 .... 25 B4
Liphook Cl BN1 ...... 168 C1
Liphook Cty Inf Sch GU30 25 B4
Liphook Golf Course GU30 47 A7
Liphook Rd
 Haslemere GU27 ..... 26 F6
 Hollywater GU35 .... 24 A8
 Linchmere GU27 ..... 26 B4
Liphook Sta GU30 ... 25 C2
Lisher Rd BN15 ..... 183 F7
Lisle Way PO10 ..... 149 A3
Lismore Cres RH11 . 18 B3
Liss Inf Sch GU33 . 45 C3
Liss Jun Sch GU33 . 45 C3
Liss Ave RH19 ...... 22 F6
Listers RH17 .... 60 F1
Listen Terr PO19 ... 173 A7
Little Ashfield GU29 92 E8
Little Babbsham PO21 194 E2
Little Barn Pl GU33 45 D4
Little Bentswood RH16 85 F5
Little Bentswood Cl RH16 85 F5
Little Black Hill RH16 86 B7
Little Boultons PO20 193 A8
Little Breach PO19 . 172 F8
Little Bridges Cl RH13 57 F1
Little Cl RH13 ..... 79 F7
Little Comptons RH13 36 F2
Little Copse Rd BN6 126 E4
Little Court Rd GU29 92 D8
Little Crabtree RH11 18 C7
Little Dipper's RH20 98 C2
Little Dro BN44 .... 143 D2
Little East St
 Billingshurst RH14 . 55 D1
 Brighton BN2 .... 207 A4
Little Finches RH13 103 A3
Little Gables BN13 . 181 F6
Little George St BN2 207 A4
Little Grebe RH12 .. 36 C5
Little Haven La RH12 36 F5
Little Hayes Cotts RH14 55 F5
Little High St
 Shoreham-by-Sea BN43 184 E7
 Worthing BN11 ...... 182 D3
Little Hill RH20 ... 119 C8
Little King St RH19 9 E1
Little London PO19 . 173 A6
Little London Mews **5**
 PO19 .... 173 A6
Little Oak RH13 .... 103 A3
Little Paddocks BN12 200 E5
Little Paddocks Way PO20 200 F5
Little Park Enterprises RH6 4 E3
Little Pembrokes BN11 182 A3
Little Preston St BN1 187 E5
Little Western St **1** BN1 187 E5
Littlecote GU28 .... 95 F7
Littledrove Cotts PO18 133 D7
Littlefield Cl PO20 206 E7
Littlefield Rd PO19 173 B5
Littlefield Sch GU30 25 D2
Littlegreen Sch PO18 109 A4
Littlehampton Com Sch The
 BN17 .... 198 E6
Littlehampton Hospl BN17 198 E5
Littlehampton Marina
 BN17 .... 198 B5
Littlehampton Rd
 Ferring BN12, BN16 . 180 D3
 Worthing BN12, BN13 181 D5
Littlehampton Sta BN17 198 D5
Littlehaven Sch RH12 36 F5
Littleheath Rd BN18 155 E4
Littlemead Gram Sch
 PO20 .... 174 A7
Littlestone Rd BN13 181 E6
Littleworth La RH13 103 A6
Liverpool Bldgs **7** BN11 182 D2
Liverpool Gdns BN11 182 D2
Liverpool Rd BN11 .. 182 D2
Liverpool Terr BN11 182 D2
Livesay Cres BN14 . 182 D4
Livingstone Ho **5** BN3 187 B7
Livingstone Rd
 Burgess Hill RH15 . 106 F3
 Crawley RH10 ...... 18 E4
 Horsham RH13 ...... 36 D1
 Hove BN3 .... 187 B7

Livingstone St BN14 188 D5
Lizzard Head BN17 . 199 A6
Lloyd Cl BN13 ..... 187 C8
Lloyd Goring Cl BN16 179 F6
Lloyd Rd BN3 ...... 187 C8
Lloyds Ct RH10 .... 5 E1
Lucas La PO21, PO22 194 F7
Lobs Wood La RH20 . 119 D2
Lobster La PO20 ... 206 B8
Lock La PO20 ...... 191 F6
Locke Rd GU30 ..... 25 C4
Lockgate Rd PO20 . 192 C4
Locks Cres BN41 .. 166 B1
Locks Ct **10** BN42 185 E7
Locks Hill BN41 .. 166 B1
Lockash Cl PO20 .. 190 C2
Lockash La PO18 .. 130 C7
Lockwood Cl RH12 . 37 A5
Lockwood Ct RH10 . 18 F8
Loddon Cl BN13 ... 181 C8
Loder Gdns BN14 .. 182 C5
Loder Pl BN1 ..... 167 F2
Loder Rd BN1 ..... 167 F2
Loders RH17 ...... 64 B8
Lodge Cl Crawley RH11 18 C6
 East Grinstead RH19 . 9 D1
Lodge Ct
 Bognor Regis PO21 . 194 E2
 Shoreham-by-Sea BN43 164 E1
Lodge Hill La BN6 127 C4
Lodge La Forestside PO9 129 F6
 Horley RH6 .... 1 E8
 Keymer BN6 .... 127 B2
Lodge The BN2 .... 207 B8
Lodgebury Cl PO10 170 A8
Lodgelands RH17 .. 64 B6
Lodsworth Cl RH10 18 F7
Lodsworth Rd PO21 194 B3
Lombard St GU28 .. 95 F8
Lomond Ave BN1 ... 168 B7
Londerry Ind Est The
 PO20 .... 206 D8
London Fields Ho RH11 18 C2
London La RH17 ... 84 F6
London Meed Cty Prim Sch
 RH15 .... 107 A1
London Rd Arundel BN18 157 E6
 Arundel BN18 ..... 158 A3
 Ashington RH20 ... 121 A4
 Balcombe RH17 .... 40 F2
 Bognor Regis PO21 195 D3
 Brighton BN1 ..... 207 A7
 Brighton, Withdene BN1 167 D4
 Burgess Hill RH15 106 F5
 Clayton BN1, BN45 147 C4
 Coldwaltham RH20 . 117 D6
 Crawley RH11 ..... 5 E3
 Cuckfield RH17 ... 84 F7
 Danehill RH17 .... 66 A4
 East Grinstead RH19 9 C3
 Fontwell BN18 .... 156 A3
 Forest Row RH18 .. 23 E4
 Hassocks BN6, RH15 126 E6
 Heath Common RH20 120 E2
 Henfield BN5 ..... 123 F6
 Hill Brow GU31, GU33 67 B8
 Horsham RH12 ..... 36 C2
 Hurstpierpoint BN6 125 E2
 Liphook GU30 ..... 25 C5
 Pyecombe BN45, BN6 146 F7
London Road Cotts BN18 158 A4
London Road Sta BN1 188 A8
London St BN11 ... 182 C3
London Terr BN1 .. 207 A7
Lonesome La RH6 .. 1 D8
Loney Ct **1** BN43 185 C8
Long Acre RH10 ... 21 A8
Long Cl RH10 ..... 19 D6
Long Copse Ct PO10 149 B4
Long Copse La PO10 149 C4
Long Furlong BN13, BN14 161 B5
Long Hill RH13 ... 81 F8
Long La Arundel BN18 157 D4
 East Marden PO18 . 110 A3
Long Mead BN18 .. 156 D1
Long Meadow BN14 162 A3
Long Park Cnr BN6 127 D2
Long Wlk RH10 ... 86 B4
Longacre Liss GU33 45 C4
 Selsey PO20 ..... 206 D6
Longacre Cres RH17 84 F8
Longacre Pk BN18 206 E6
Longbridge Gate RH6 5 E8
Longbridge Rd Crawley RH6 5 F8
 Horley RH6 ...... 1 F1
Longbridge Rdbt RH6 1 E2
Longbridge Wlk RH6 1 F1
Longbrook PO22 .. 195 F3

Longchamp Cl RH6 . 2 C3
Longcroft **4** BN43 184 E7
Longdene Rd GU27 27 B6
Longfellow Cl RH12 36 E7
Longfellow Rd BN11 182 B3
Longfield Rd
 New Brighton PO10 149 B3
 Tower Hill RH12 . 58 A8
Longford Rd PO21 195 C4
Longfurlong La BN13 160 E4
Longhurst
 9 Brighton BN2 188 E4
 Burgess Hill RH15 107 D2
Longhurst Rd RH11 18 A1
Longland Ave RH20 119 C2
Longlands BN14 .. 182 D8
Longlands Glade BN14 182 D8
Longlands Rd
 East Wittering PO20 201 F6
 Southbourne PO10 169 F8
Longlands Spinney BN14 182 D8
Longmead GU33 .. 45 B4
Longmeadow Gdns PO20 191 E4
Longmere Rd RH11 181 C8
Longmoor Dr GU30 24 D4
Longmoor Rd GU30 24 E4
Longport Rd PO22 196 B4
Longships BN16 .. 199 A6
Longwood View RH10 19 A3
Longyard Ho RH6 . 2 B5
Loop The PO22 ... 196 C5
Loose La BN15 ... 183 B6
Loppets Rd RH10 18 F3
Lordings La RH20 119 D7
Lordings Rd RH14 77 A6
Loriners RH10 ... 18 D8
Loriners Ct BN3 . 186 D8
Lorna Rd BN3 .... 187 D7
Lorne Rd BN2 .... 207 A8
Lorraine Ct **7** BN3 187 E7
Lotts La BN13 ... 183 C6
Loudoun Rd BN17 198 C5
Lourier Cl **1** BN14 182 D4
Love La RH20 .... 119 D2
Lovegrove Ct BN3 186 E8
Loveletts RH11 .. 18 A5
Lovells Cl PO21 . 194 B2
Lover's Wlk BN1 . 187 F8
Lovett Ct BN12 .. 181 C4
Loveys Rd BN18 .. 176 F2
Lowdells Cl RH19 9 C4
Lowdells Dr RH19 9 D4
Lowdells La RH19 9 C3
Lower Cl RH11 ... 39 B8
Lower Barn Cl RH12 36 F5
Lower Beach Rd BN43 184 F6
Lower Bevendean Ave
 BN2 .... 168 E1
Lower Bognor Rd
 PO20, PO21 ..... 194 D5
Lower Chalvington Pl BN2 188 E5
Lower Church Rd RH15 106 F3
Lower Dene RH19 . 10 A1
Lower Dr BN42 ... 165 C1
Lower Faircox BN5 123 D5
Lower Forecourt RH6 6 B7
Lower Hanger GU27 26 D6
Lower Hone La PO18 171 A2
Lower Market St BN3 187 D5
Lower Mere RH19 22 F8
Lower Rd
 East Lavant PO18 153 A5
 Forest Row RH18 . 23 F3
Lower Rock Gdns BN2 207 B4
Lower Sq RH18 ... 23 E3
Lower St Fittleworth RH20 97 A2
 Haslemere GU27 . 27 C6
 Pulborough RH20 . 98 C2
Lower Station Rd
 Billingshurst RH14 77 D6
 Henfield BN5 .... 123 D4
Lower Tanbridge Way
 RH12 .... 36 B2
Lowestoft Wlk RH10 19 B4
Lowfield Heath Rd RH6 4 F5
Lowfield Rd
 Haywards Heath RH16 85 F3
 Slinfold RH13 ... 34 D3
Lowfield Way RH6 5 E5
Lowlands Rd RH15 107 B5
Lowther Rd Brighton BN1 168 A2
 Worthing BN13 .. 181 F7
Loxdale (The Swedish Folk
 High Sch) BN1 .. 166 B1
Loxley Gdns **2** BN14 182 C4
Loxwood BN16 ... 180 B3
Loxwood Ave BN14 182 D8
Loxwood Cty Prim Sch
 RH14 .... 32 A4
Loxwood Rd
 Alfold Crossways GU6 11 A3

Loxwood Rd
Bucks Green RH12 ... 33 A6
Ifold RH14 ... 31 A2
Loxwood RH12, RH14 ... 32 D4
Loxwood Wlk RH11 ... 18 A8
Lucas RH17 ... 65 D5
Lucas Cl RH19 ... 10 A1
Lucas Field GU27 ... 26 E6
Lucas Grange RH16 ... 85 D5
Lucas Rd RH12 ... 35 F8
Lucas Way RH16 ... 85 C5
Lucastes Ave RH16, RH17 ... 85 D6
Lucastes La RH16, RH17 ... 85 C6
Lucastes Rd RH16 ... 85 C5
Lucerne Cl BN41 ... 166 B1
Lucerne Ct PO21 ... 194 E2
Lucerne Dr RH10 ... 19 D4
Lucerne Rd BN1 ... 168 A1
Lucking La PO22 ... 196 F5
Lucraft Rd BN2 ... 168 F5
Ludlow Cl PO21 ... 194 E2
Luffs Meadow GU28 ... 51 A7
Lullington Ave BN3 ... 186 F8
Lumley Ct RH6 ... 2 A4
Lumley Gdns PO10 ... 169 C8
Lumley Rd Horley RH6 ... 2 A3
Lumley PO10 ... 149 C1
Lumley Terr PO10 ... 149 C1
Lunce's Hill RH16, RH17 ... 107 F8
Lundy Cl Crawley RH11 ... 18 C3
Littlehampton BN16 ... 199 A4
Lurgashall RH15 ... 107 C1
Lutener Rd GU29 ... 71 A1
Luth The
Wisborough Green RH14 ... 54 B1
Wisborough Green RH14 ... 76 A8
Luther St BN2 ... 188 C7
Lutman St PO10 ... 149 A4
Lutyens Cl RH11 ... 17 E4
Luxford Cl RH12 ... 36 F5
Luxford Rd RH16 ... 86 B7
Luxford's La RH19 ... 23 B6
Lychgates The BN18 ... 176 F4
Lydon Ho RH11 ... 5 D1
Lye La East Ashling PO18 ... 151 F4
West Stoke PO18 ... 151 F5
Lyminster Ave BN1 ... 168 A5
Lyminster Cty Inf Sch
BN17 ... 178 D3
Lyminster Gate BN17 ... 178 D4
Lyminster Rd
Crossbush BN18 ... 158 D1
Littlehampton
BN17, BN18 ... 178 D6
Lyn Rd BN13 ... 181 C6
Lynch Down PO18 ... 151 A6
Lynchborough Rd GU30 ... 24 D8
Lynchet Cl BN1 ... 168 C3
Lynchet Down BN1 ... 168 C2
Lynchet Wlk BN1 ... 168 C2
Lynchets Cres BN3 ... 166 D3
Lynchette The BN43 ... 164 F1
Lynchmere Ave BN15 ... 183 D8
Lynchpole Wlk BN12 ... 181 B3
Lynden Ct [6] BN1 ... 167 E2
Lyndhurst Cl RH11 ... 18 D5
Lyndhurst Ct BN3 ... 187 D7
Lyndhurst Cty Fst Sch
BN11 ... 182 F3
Lyndhurst Farm Cl RH19 ... 8 D4
Lyndhurst Rd
Chichester PO19 ... 173 B5
Hove BN3 ... 187 D7
Worthing BN11 ... 182 F3
Lynton Cl
East Grinstead RH19 ... 10 A2
Hurstpierpoint BN6 ... 126 B5
Lynton Park Ave RH19 ... 10 A2
Lynton St BN2 ... 188 C7
Lynwick St RH12 ... 33 C8
Lynwood Ct RH12 ... 36 C3
Lyon Cl Crawley RH10 ... 19 C2
Hove BN3 ... 187 D7
Lyon Ct
[1] Bognor Regis PO21 ... 195 D3
Horsham RH13 ... 36 E2
Lyon St PO21 ... 195 D3
Lyon St W PO21 ... 195 D3
Lyons Cl RH13 ... 34 D3
Lyons Farm Ret Pk BN14 ... 182 E8
Lyons Rd RH13 ... 34 E3
Lyons Way BN14 ... 182 E7
Lyoth La RH16 ... 86 C4
Lyoth Villas RH16 ... 86 C4
Lyric Cl RH10 ... 19 D4
Lysander Ho RH20 ... 119 E1
Lysander Way PO20 ... 154 D1
Lytton Dr RH10 ... 19 D7
M'tongue Ave PO18 ... 171 C7
Mackerel La PO20 ... 206 B8
Mackie Ave Brighton BN1 ... 168 A7
Keymer BN6 ... 127 A5
Mackley's Ind Est BN5 ... 144 F6
Macklin Rd PO22 ... 195 E4
Macleod Rd RH13 ... 36 F1
Madehurst Cl
Brighton BN2 ... 188 D5
Littlehampton BN16 ... 199 F4
Madehurst Ct
Crawley RH11 ... 17 F3
[6] Littlehampton BN17 ... 198 D5
Madehurst Way BN17 ... 198 D6
Madeira Ave
Bognor Regis PO22 ... 195 E5
Horsham RH12 ... 36 C2
Worthing BN11 ... 182 E2
Madeira Dr BN2 ... 188 C4
Madeira Par PO22 ... 195 E5
Madeira Pl BN2 ... 207 B4
Madgwick La PO18 ... 153 D1
Mafeking Rd BN2 ... 168 D1
Magdalene Cl RH10 ... 6 C1
Magellan Terr RH10 ... 6 A2
Magnolia Cl BN13 ... 181 B5
Magnolia Ct RH6 ... 2 A3
Magpie Cotts PO9 ... 128 E4
Magpie La Horsham RH13 ... 58 F6
Selsey PO20 ... 203 C1
Magpie Rd PO8 ... 128 E5
Magpie Wlk RH10 ... 18 F8
Maiden La RH11 ... 18 C8
Maidenbower Cty Fst Sch
RH10 ... 19 C4
Maidenbower Dr RH10 ... 19 D4
Maidenbower La RH10 ... 19 C4
Maidenbower Pl RH10 ... 19 C4
Maidenbower Sq RH10 ... 19 C4
Maidment Cl BN5 ... 123 F6
Main Dr PO22 ... 196 F5
Main Rd Birdham PO20 ... 191 E4
Broadbridge PO18, PO19 ... 171 D7
East Dean PO18 ... 134 C6
Nutbourne PO10, PO18 ... 170 B7
Yapton BN18 ... 176 F3
Maines Farm Rd BN44 ... 144 C1
Mainstone Rd [1] BN3 ... 186 F7
Maizecroft RH6 ... 2 C4
Major Cl BN1 ... 168 B1
Major's Hill RH10 ... 20 C5
Malcolm Cl BN12 ... 200 E5
Malcolm Gdns RH6 ... 1 D1
Malcolm Rd
Tangmere PO20 ... 154 C1
Tangmere PO20 ... 154 C2
Malden Pl [3] RH20 ... 119 D1
Malden Way PO20 ... 206 D7
Maldon Rd BN1 ... 167 D2
Malham Cl RH10 ... 19 C3
Malin Rd BN16 ... 199 A5
Malla Way BN5 ... 123 E6
Mallard Cl Haslemere GU27 ... 26 E6
Horley RH6 ... 2 A5
Horsham RH12 ... 36 C5
Mallard Cres PO21 ... 204 F7
Mallard Pl RH19 ... 22 F8
Mallard Rd PO9 ... 128 D1
Mallion's La RH17 ... 61 E2
Mallon Dene BN16 ... 199 D4
Mallory Rd BN3 ... 167 C2
Mallow Cl RH12 ... 36 E6
Malmayne Ct PO21 ... 194 E3
Malt House Trad Est BN43 ... 185 B7
Malthouse Cl
Arundel BN18 ... 158 A2
Lancing BN15 ... 183 B7
Malthouse Cotts
Cocking GU29 ... 112 D7
West Ashling PO18 ... 151 B3
West Wittering PO20 ... 190 D3
Worthing BN12 ... 181 C1
Malthouse Ct [14] BN2 ... 207 B5
Malthouse La
Burgess Hill BN6, RH15 ... 106 C2
West Ashling PO18 ... 151 B3
Malthouse Meadows GU30 ... 25 C4
Malthouse Pas [3] BN17 ... 198 D6
Malthouse Rd
Crawley RH10, RH11 ... 18 D4
Selsey PO20 ... 206 E7
Malthouse Trad Est BN43 ... 185 B7
Maltings Gn BN44 ... 143 D2
Maltings The
Burgess Hill BN6 ... 106 D4
Chichester PO19 ... 172 F6
Liphook GU30 ... 25 D4
Maltravers Ct [2] BN17 ... 198 E4
Maltravers Dr BN17 ... 198 E4
Maltravers Rd BN17 ... 198 E4
Maltravers St BN18 ... 158 B3
Malvern Cl BN11 ... 183 B3
Malvern Mews PO10 ... 149 B1
Malvern Rd Crawley RH11 ... 18 C5
Hill Brow GU33 ... 45 D2
Malvern St [12] BN3 ... 187 B7
Malvern Way PO21 ... 194 B1
Manaton Cl RH16 ... 85 F4
Manchester St BN2 ... 207 A4
Manchester Terr PO10 ... 149 D4
Mandalay Ct BN1 ... 167 D4
Manet Sq PO22 ... 195 B6
Manhattan Ct BN1 ... 167 D4
Manhood Com Coll The
PO20 ... 206 D8
Manhood Cotts PO20 ... 202 F7
Manhood La PO20 ... 203 F8
Manitoba Way BN13 ... 181 C6
Manley's Hill RH20 ... 119 E1
Manning Cl RH19 ... 9 D2
Manning Rd
Chichester PO19 ... 173 C7
Littlehampton BN17 ... 198 C6
Mannings [8] BN43 ... 184 F7
Mannings Cl RH10 ... 6 D1
Mannings Heath Golf Course
RH13 ... 59 F6
Mannock Rd PO20 ... 154 B1
Manor Ave BN6 ... 127 A5
Manor Cl
Bognor Regis PO22 ... 196 A4
Brighton BN2 ... 188 E5
Burgess Hill RH15 ... 107 D4
East Preston BN16 ... 199 F5
Haslemere GU27 ... 26 E6
Henfield BN5 ... 123 F5
Horley RH6 ... 1 F3
Lancing BN15 ... 183 F7
Shoreham-by-Sea BN15 ... 184 B6
Southwick BN42 ... 186 A8
Stockbridge PO19 ... 172 F3
Storrington RH20 ... 119 D1
Worthing BN11 ... 182 B2
Manor Cotts BN6 ... 125 F5
Manor Cres Brighton BN2 ... 188 E5
Haslemere GU27 ... 26 E6
Manor Ct Elmer PO22 ... 197 B5
Horsham RH12 ... 37 A5
North Lancing BN15 ... 183 D8
Rustington BN16 ... 199 B6
Southwick BN42 ... 186 A7
Worthing BN11 ... 182 B1
Manor Dr Cuckfield RH17 ... 84 E7
Horley RH6 ... 1 F3
Manor Farm Cl PO20 ... 206 E8
Manor Farm Ct PO20 ... 206 E8
Manor Field Ct BN14 ... 182 D5
Manor Fields
Horsham RH12, RH13 ... 37 A4
Liphook GU30 ... 25 D4
Manor Gdns Breach PO10 ... 149 F1
Brighton BN2 ... 188 E5
Hurstpierpoint BN6 ... 125 F6
Rustington BN16 ... 199 B5
Manor Gn BN2 ... 188 E5
Manor Hall Cty Fst Sch
BN42 ... 185 F7
Manor Hall Cty Mid Sch
BN42 ... 185 F8
Manor Hall Rd BN42 ... 185 F8
Manor Hill BN2 ... 188 E6
Manor Ho BN11 ... 182 B2
Manor House Pl BN15 ... 183 F8
Manor La East Beach PO20 ... 206 F8
South Mundham PO20 ... 193 D6
Manor Lea Haslemere GU27 ... 26 E6
Worthing BN11 ... 182 B1
Manor Lodge Rd PO9 ... 128 C1
Manor Paddock BN2 ... 188 E4
Manor Par BN13 ... 181 D7
Manor Pk PO21 ... 194 A1
Manor Pl
Bognor Regis PO21 ... 195 C2
Brighton BN2 ... 188 E4
Manor Rd Breach PO10 ... 149 F1
Brighton BN2 ... 188 E5
Burgess Hill RH15 ... 107 D4
East Grinstead RH19 ... 9 C2
Horsham RH12 ... 37 A5
Hurstpierpoint BN6 ... 125 F6
Lancing BN15 ... 183 E8
Portslade-by-Sea BN41 ... 166 B1
Rustington BN16 ... 199 B6
Selsey PO20 ... 206 E7
Upper Beeding BN44 ... 144 B2
West Kingston BN16 ... 200 A4
Worthing BN11 ... 182 B2
Manor Royal RH10, RH11 ... 5 E1
Manor The [3] BN11 ... 182 B2
Manor View Ct BN14 ... 182 D5
Manor Villas PO18 ... 171 C5
Manor Way
Bognor Regis PO21 ... 194 C1
Breach PO10 ... 149 F1
Manor Way Brighton BN2 ... 188 E5
Henfield BN5 ... 123 F6
Lancing BN15 ... 183 F7
Middleton-on-Sea PO22 ... 197 B5
Manorfields RH11 ... 17 D2
Mansell Ct RH15 ... 107 B3
Mansell Rd BN43 ... 185 B8
Manser Rd BN18 ... 156 F1
Mansfield Cl BN11 ... 183 A4
Mansfield Cotts PO18 ... 170 D7
Mansfield Rd
Bognor Regis PO21, PO22 ... 195 B6
Hove BN3 ... 186 E7
Worthing BN11 ... 183 A4
Mansion Cl RH15 ... 107 D3
Mant Cl RH20 ... 119 D1
Mant Rd GU28 ... 95 F7
Mantell Ho [2] BN2 ... 207 B5
Mantling Rd BN17 ... 198 D5
Manton Rd BN2 ... 168 E1
Mants Farm Ct PO21 ... 194 C3
Maple Cl
Billingshurst RH14 ... 55 D1
Burgess Hill RH15 ... 107 B5
Crawley RH11 ... 5 C1
Haywards Heath RH16 ... 86 B3
Horsham RH12 ... 37 A5
Middleton-on-Sea PO22 ... 196 E6
New Brighton PO10 ... 149 B2
Worthing BN13 ... 161 E1
Maple Ct [6] BN11 ... 181 F2
Maple Dr
Burgess Hill RH15 ... 107 A5
East Grinstead RH19 ... 10 A1
Maple Gdns
Bognor Regis PO22 ... 195 C7
Hove BN3 ... 166 F1
Maple Ho BN12 ... 181 A4
Maple Leaf RH20 ... 117 D6
Maple Par BN18 ... 176 E8
Maple Rd
Billingshurst RH14 ... 77 D7
Walberton BN18 ... 176 E8
Maple Wlk Lancing BN15 ... 183 B7
Rustington BN16 ... 199 C6
Mapledown Cl RH13 ... 57 F2
Maplehurst Rd
Chichester PO19 ... 153 B2
Maplehurst RH13 ... 81 A3
Portslade-by-Sea BN41 ... 166 A1
Maples The
[3] Bognor Regis PO21 ... 195 B3
Ferring BN12 ... 200 F4
Maplewood [7] BN1 ... 167 E3
Mapsons La PO20 ... 192 B3
Marama Gdns BN16 ... 199 B3
March CE Prim Sch The
PO18 ... 153 E1
Marchants Cl BN6 ... 126 A6
Marchants Rd BN6 ... 126 A6
Marchants Way RH15 ... 106 F5
Marches Rd RH12 ... 14 E4
Marchwell Ind Unit PO19 ... 153 B1
Marchwood PO19 ... 153 A3
Marcuse Fields PO18 ... 171 B6
Mardale Rd BN13 ... 181 F6
Marden Ave PO19 ... 172 E3
Marden Ho Barnham PO22 ... 176 C6
Littlehampton BN17 ... 178 B3
Mardens The RH11 ... 18 B7
Mardyke BN43 ... 184 D6
Mare Hill Rd RH20 ... 98 E1
Maresfield Rd BN2 ... 188 E5
Margaret Cl PO21 ... 194 E3
Margaret Cotts RH13 ... 81 E2
Margaret Ho PO22 ... 195 E4
Margaret St BN2 ... 207 B4
Margery Rd BN3 ... 186 D8
Marian Way PO21 ... 195 E3
Marigolds Lodge [2] BN16 ... 199 B4
Marina Cl PO10 ... 169 C7
Marina Way BN2 ... 188 F3
Marine Ave BN3 ... 186 E6
Marine Cl
East Wittering PO20 ... 201 E6
Worthing BN11 ... 182 A1
Marine Cres BN12 ... 181 D1
Marine Ct BN43 ... 184 D5
Marine Dr Brighton BN2 ... 188 F3
East Wittering PO20 ... 201 E7
Selsey PO20 ... 206 F7
Worthing BN12 ... 181 B1
Marine Dr W
Bognor Regis PO21 ... 195 A2
East Wittering PO20 ... 201 D7
Marine Gdns Brighton BN2 ... 207 B4
Selsey PO20 ... 206 D5
Marine Par
Bognor Regis PO21 ... 195 B2
Brighton BN2 ... 188 C4
Worthing BN11 ... 182 D1
Marine Pk [3] PO21 ... 195 B2
Marine Pl BN11 ... 182 D1
Marine Point [13] BN11 ... 182 A1
Marine Sq BN2 ... 188 C4
Marine Terrace Mews [7]
BN2 ... 188 C4
Marine View [3] BN2 ... 207 B5
Mariners Cl BN43 ... 184 D5
Mariners Quay BN2 ... 188 F3
Mariners Terr PO18 ... 171 B4
Mariners The BN15 ... 183 D3
Mariners Wlk BN16 ... 199 D4
Marineside PO20 ... 202 B5
Marion Rd RH10 ... 19 B3
Marisfield Pl PO20 ... 206 F8
Marjoram Pl BN43 ... 165 B1
Market Ave PO19 ... 173 A5
Market Cl PO22 ... 176 B6
Market Field BN44 ... 143 E3
Market Pl
Burgess Hill RH15 ... 107 A2
Haywards Heath RH16 ... 85 E6
Market Rd PO19 ... 173 A6
Market Sq Horsham RH12 ... 36 C1
Midhurst GU29 ... 92 F7
Petworth GU28 ... 95 F8
Market St
Bognor Regis PO21 ... 195 C2
Brighton BN1 ... 207 A5
[10] Worthing BN11 ... 182 D2
Markfield PO22 ... 195 B6
Markwick Mews BN11 ... 182 E3
Marlborough Bsns Ctr
BN15 ... 183 C4
Marlborough Cl
Chichester PO19 ... 173 D6
Crawley RH11 ... 18 C2
Horsham RH12 ... 36 D5
Marlborough Ct
Bognor Regis PO21 ... 194 F5
Burgess Hill RH15 ... 106 E3
[1] Hove BN3 ... 187 C6
Marlborough Dr RH15 ... 107 C2
Marlborough Mews BN1 ... 207 F5
Marlborough Pl BN1, BN2 ... 207 A6
Marlborough Rd
Lancing BN15 ... 183 D4
Worthing BN12 ... 181 D2
Marlborough St BN1 ... 207 F5
Marlborough Way BN12 ... 181 D2
Marle Ave RH15 ... 107 A4
Marles La RH14 ... 55 C8
Marley Combe Rd GU27 ... 26 F4
Marley Hanger GU27 ... 27 A3
Marley La GU27 ... 26 E4
Marley Lodge BN2 ... 207 B7
Marley Way RH20 ... 119 E2
Marlinspike The BN43 ... 185 A6
Marlow Ct Brighton BN2 ... 207 B7
Crawley RH10, RH11 ... 18 D7
Marlow Dr RH16 ... 86 C4
Marlow Rd BN2 ... 188 F4
Marlowe Cl PO22 ... 196 D6
Marlowe Rd BN14 ... 182 E5
Marlpit Cl RH19 ... 9 E4
Marlpit La Oving PO20 ... 174 B7
Woodmancote PO10 ... 150 C4
Marlpit Rd RH19 ... 43 A6
Marlpost Rd RH13 ... 57 C1
Marmion Rd BN3 ... 186 F7
Marquis Way PO21 ... 194 E1
Marringdean Rd RH14 ... 77 E4
Marsh Barns PO20 ... 173 F2
Marsh Ct RH11 ... 18 B1
Marsh Ho [3] BN43 ... 185 D7
Marsh La Chidham PO18 ... 170 C4
Crockerhill PO20 ... 155 A2
Merston PO20 ... 174 A2
Mid Lavant PO18 ... 152 F6
Marshall Ave
Bognor Regis PO21 ... 195 B4
Worthing BN14 ... 161 F3
Marshall Cl PO22 ... 176 B5
Marshall Rd RH10 ... 19 C4
Marshalls Row BN1 ... 207 A7
Marston Ct [6] BN3 ... 187 E7
Marston Rd BN14 ... 182 E4
Martello Ent Ctr BN17 ... 178 C4
Martha Gunn Cl BN2 ... 168 E1
Martin Cl RH11 ... 18 D8
Martin Rd BN3 ... 166 D1
Martins La PO20 ... 191 F5
Martins The RH10 ... 21 C8
Martlet Cl PO19 ... 173 A5
Martlet Cnr RH12 ... 33 D7
Martlet Ho BN1 ... 188 A8
Martlet Rd GU28 ... 95 E7
Martlet The BN3 ... 167 D1

Martlet Way PO21 .... 204 F7
Martlets RH20 .... 119 D8
Martlets CI RH12 .... 36 C5
Martlets Ct BN18 .... 158 B2
Martlets The
  Burgess Hill RH15 .... 107 A3
  Crawley RH10 .... 18 E6
  Lancing BN15 .... 183 C6
  Littlehampton BN16 .... 199 A4
  Shoreham-by-Sea BN43 .. 184 F8
Martlets Trad Est BN12 .. 181 C3
Martlets Way BN12 .... 181 C3
Marts The RH12 .... 33 D7
Martyn CI BN5 .... 123 E5
Martyns PI RH19 .... 23 A8
Martyrs Ave RH11 .... 5 D1
Marvell CI RH10 .... 19 C8
Marylands RH16 .... 85 F5
Marylands Cres PO22 .... 195 E5
Masefield Rd RH11 .... 17 E3
Mash Barn La BN15 .... 184 A7
Mason CI RH19 .... 9 E2
Mason Rd RH10 .... 18 E4
Masons Field RH13 .... 59 C6
Masons Way RH20 .... 98 D5
Massetts Rd RH6 .... 2 A2
Matlock Rd BN1, BN3 .... 167 D2
Matthew Dr RH10 .... 19 C3
Matthey PI RH10 .... 6 D1
Maudlin La BN44 .... 143 E1
Maudlyn CI BN44 .... 143 E1
Maudlyn Parkway BN44 .. 143 D1
Maudlyn Pk RH44 .... 143 D1
Mauldmare CI PO21 .... 194 F2
Maunsell Pk RH10 .... 19 B6
Maxton Wlk RH11 .... 18 B2
Maxwell Rd Arundel BN18 . 157 F1
  Littlehampton BN17 ...... 198 C5
Maxwell Way RH10 .... 6 A1
May CI Bognor Regis PO22 .. 195 E5
  Sidlesham PO20 .... 203 F8
  Worthing BN12 .... 181 C4
May Rd BN2 .... 188 D7
May Tree Ave BN14 .... 161 F3
Maybridge Cres BN12 .... 181 C3
Maybridge Sq BN12 .... 181 C4
Maybush Dr PO18 .... 170 D7
Maydwell Ave RH13 .... 34 C2
Mayes CI RH10 .... 19 C5
Mayes La RH12 .... 14 F3
Mayfair Ct PO19 .... 172 F7
Mayfield Crawley RH10 .... 19 D6
  East Preston BN16 .... 180 B3
Mayfield CI
  Bognor Regis PO21 .... 194 B3
  Brighton BN1 .... 168 A5
  Worthing BN14 .... 162 A1
Mayfield Cres BN1 .... 167 F5
Mayfield Rd RH15 .... 107 B3
Mayfield Rd PO21 .... 195 A4
Mayflower CI RH10 .... 19 D5
Mayflower Ct
  Haywards Heath RH16 .... 85 F4
  9 Shoreham-by-Sea
  BN43 .... 185 A6
Mayflower Rd RH16 .... 85 F4
Mayflower Sq BN1 .... 207 A7
Mayflower Way BN16 .... 180 A3
Mayhouse Rd RH15 .... 106 F1
Mayo Ct **5** BN2 .... 188 B8
Mayo Rd BN2 .... 188 B8
Maypole La BN18 .... 176 F5
Maypole Pk BN18 .... 176 F5
Maypole Rd
  Ashurst Wood RH19 .... 23 E6
  East Grinstead RH19 .... 9 D2
Mayridge PO20 .... 206 B8
Maytree CI
  Angmering BN16 .... 179 F4
  Lancing BN15 .... 183 B6
Maytree Wlk BN3 .... 166 E1
McKerchar CI BN15 .... 183 F7
McIndoe Rd RH19 .... 9 D3
McIver CI RH19 .... 30 A7
McRae Ct PO20 .... 206 D7
Mead La
  Bognor Regis PO21, PO22 195 E4
  Storrington RH20 .... 119 E2
Mead Rd RH10 .... 18 F7
Mead Sway BN18 .... 156 D4
Mead The Liphook GU30 .. 25 B5
  Liss GU33 .... 45 B4
Mead Way GU29 .... 92 E6
Meadow App RH10 .... 7 A3
Meadow Brook Ind Ctr
  RH10 .... 7 A3
Meadow CI Balcombe RH17 . 41 A1
  Copthorne RH10 .... 7 A3

Meadow CI
  Horsham RH12 .... 37 A5
  Hove BN3 .... 167 B3
  Hunston PO20 .... 193 A8
  Liphook GU30 .... 25 C4
  Portslade-by-Sea BN41 .. 166 B2
  Southwick BN42 .... 186 A8
  Worthing BN11 .... 183 B3
Meadow Court Est **2**
  BN11 .... 183 B3
Meadow Cres BN11 .... 183 A3
Meadow Croft CI RH6 .... 6 C8
Meadow Ct
  4 Emsworth PO10 .. 169 B8
  Middleton-on-Sea PO22 .. 196 D6
Meadow Dr RH16 .... 86 B6
Meadow End GU30 .... 25 C5
Meadow Farm La RH12 .... 36 F7
Meadow La
  Burgess Hill RH15 .... 106 F1
  Haywards Heath RH16 .... 86 B6
  Lancing BN15 .... 183 E5
  West Wittering PO20 .... 190 D2
Meadow Rd BN11 .... 183 B3
Meadow Road Ind Est
  BN11 .... 183 B4
Meadow Sweet CI BN13 .. 181 A5
Meadow The RH10 .... 7 A3
Meadow Vale GU27 .... 27 A6
Meadow Way
  Bognor Regis PO21 .... 194 B1
  Bognor Regis PO22 .... 195 A6
  Ferring BN12 .... 200 E6
  Liphook GU30 .... 25 C5
  Littlehampton BN17 .... 198 F5
  Petworth GU28 .... 95 E7
  Tangmere PO20 .... 154 D2
  Westergate PO20 .... 175 D6
Meadow Wlk Liss GU33 .... 45 B4
  Middleton-on-Sea PO22 .. 197 A5
Meadowbank RH14 .... 76 B8
Meadowcroft CI
  Crawley RH11 .... 17 F5
  East Grinstead RH19 .... 9 C2
Meadowfield Dr PO19 .... 173 B7
Meadowland PO20 .... 206 D6
Meadowlands
  Crawley RH11 .... 18 C6
  Rowland's Castle PO9 .... 128 E3
Meadows BN6 .... 126 F5
Meadows Rd PO20 .... 202 A7
Meadows The
  East Preston BN16 .... 200 A5
  Hove BN3 .... 166 C3
  Walberton BN18 .... 176 E8
Meadowside
  Angmering BN16 .... 180 A6
  Horley RH6 .... 2 B4
  Storrington RH20 .... 119 D1
Meadowside Ct BN12 .... 181 A2
Meadowview BN2 .... 168 E1
Meadowview Rd BN15 .... 183 D8
Meads Ave BN3 .... 166 C3
Meads CI BN3 .... 166 C3
Meads Cty Prim Sch The
  RH19 .... 22 E7
Meads The Brighton BN1 .. 168 D5
  East Grinstead RH19 .... 22 E7
  Fulking BN5 .... 145 F4
  Haslemere GU27 .... 26 F6
  South Harting GU31 .... 89 D4
Meadvale RH12 .... 35 D7
Meadway Haslemere GU27 .. 26 F6
  Rustington BN16 .... 199 D5
Meadway Cres BN3 .... 166 F2
Meadway Ct
  Southwick BN42, BN43 .. 185 D8
  Worthing BN13 .... 181 E4
Meadway The
  Brighton BN2 .... 188 F5
  Horley RH6 .... 2 C3
  Shoreham-by-Sea BN43 .. 185 A6
Measham CI BN12 .... 200 F5
Meath Green Ave RH6 .... 1 F5
Meath Green Cty Fst Sch
  RH6 .... 1 F5
Meath Green Cty Jun Sch
  RH6 .... 1 F5
Meath Green La RH1, RH6 .... 1 E6
Medina PI BN3 .... 187 B6
Medina Terr BN3 .... 187 B5
Medina Villas BN3 .... 187 B6
Medlar CI RH11 .... 5 C1
Medmerry PO20 .... 206 A8
Medmerry Cty Prim Sch The
  PO20 .... 206 D7
Medmerry Hill BN2 .... 168 E2
Medway RH10 .... 21 A5
Medway CI BN13 .... 181 D7
Medway Cotts BN18 .... 176 F2
Medway Ct RH12 .... 37 B5

Medway Dr
  East Grinstead RH19 .... 22 D6
  Forest Row RH18 .... 23 F2
Medway Rd RH11 .... 17 F5
Medwyn Wlk RH12 .... 36 C2
Meeds Rd RH15 .... 107 A2
Meeting House La BN1 .... 207 A5
Melanie's Gdns **10** PO21 .. 195 D4
Melbourne Ave BN12 .... 181 C2
Melbourne Rd
  Chichester PO19 .... 173 B7
  Worthing BN12 .... 181 D2
Melbourne St BN2 .... 188 C8
Melbourne Way
  Horsham RH12 .... 36 F5
  Worthing BN12 .... 181 C2
Melksham CI RH13 .... 36 E1
Melrose Ave
  Portslade-by-Sea BN41 .. 166 A1
  Worthing BN13 .... 181 A4
Melrose CI Brighton BN1 .. 168 D7
  Worthing BN13 .... 181 A4
Melrose PI RH20 .... 120 C3
Melton Ave RH20 .... 119 D3
Melton CI RH20 .... 119 E3
Melton Dr RH20 .... 119 E3
Melville Rd BN3 .... 187 E7
Melville Way BN12 .... 181 C4
Mendip CI BN16 .... 200 A6
Mendip Cres BN13 .... 181 E7
Mendip CI **1** BN6 .... 199 E5
Mendip Rd BN13 .... 181 E7
Mendip Wlk RH11 .... 18 B6
Mercer CI RH10 .... 19 C3
Mercer Rd RH12 .... 36 C8
Mercers Mead RH13 .... 81 E1
Merchant St PO21 .... 195 C3
Mercury CI RH11 .... 17 E3
Meredith Rd BN14 .... 182 F4
Merevale BN1 .... 168 B2
Mereworth Dr RH10 .... 19 D8
Meridian Gr RH6 .... 2 C4
Meridian Way RH19 .... 9 F3
Merle Way GU27 .... 49 A6
Merlin CI Crawley RH11 .... 17 E6
  Hove BN3 .... 187 D8
Merlin Ct BN13 .... 181 F6
Merlin Ctr RH11 .... 5 D2
Merlin Way
  East Grinstead RH19 .... 10 A3
  Middleton-on-Sea PO22 .. 196 C6
Merrion Ave PO21, PO22 . 195 B5
Merrivale Ct PO10 .... 149 F1
Merry End PO22 .... 196 D5
Merryfield Cres BN16 .... 180 A6
Merryfield Dr
  Horsham RH12 .... 36 A3
  Selsey PO20 .... 206 F7
Merryfield Rd PO20 .... 119 D2
Merryfield Way RH20 .... 119 D2
Merryhills La RH14 .... 32 A5
Merryweather Rd PO18 .. 171 B5
Merrywood Ho RH20 .... 120 B3
Merrywood La RH20 .... 120 B4
Mersey CI BN13 .... 181 C7
Mersey Rd BN13 .... 181 C7
Mersham Gdns BN12 .... 181 C2
Merton Ave BN16 .... 199 D4
Merton CI PO21 .... 194 E4
Merton Dr **1** BN17 .... 198 D6
Merton Rd BN11 .... 182 E7
Metcalf Way RH11 .... 5 B2
Meteor Rd PO10 .... 169 C3
Metropole CI **19** BN1 .. 187 E5
Mews Ct RH19 .... 22 F6
Mews The
  14 Bognor Regis PO21 .. 195 C3
  Bognor Regis PO22 .... 195 E4
  Brighton BN1 .... 167 E2
  Broadridge Heath RH12 .. 35 D4
  Pulborough RH20 .... 98 D2
Meyers Wood RH13 .... 103 A2
Meyners CI BN3 .... 166 C3
Michael Ayres Cty
  Jun Sch The PO22 .... 195 A5
Michael Cres RH6 .... 2 A1
Michael Fields RH18 .... 23 E2
Michel Gr BN16 .... 199 F5
Michelbourne CI RH15 .. 106 C6
Michelgrove Cotts BN13 .. 160 C5
Michell CI RH12 .... 36 A2
Micklam CI PO21 .... 194 C2
Middle Mead
  Littlehampton BN17 .... 199 A5
  Steyning BN44 .... 143 D4
Middle Meadow GU33 .... 45 C4
Middle Onslow CI BN12 .. 180 E3
Middle Rd Brighton BN1 .. 167 E1
  Lancing BN15 .... 183 D5
  Partridge Green BN5 .... 103 A3
  Shoreham-by-Sea BN43 .. 185 B7

Middle Row **1** RH19 .... 22 F8
Middle St Brighton BN1 .. 207 F5
  Horsham RH12 .... 36 C2
  Petworth GU28 .... 95 F8
  Portslade-by-Sea BN41 .. 186 B6
  Shoreham-by-Sea BN43 .. 184 F7
Middle Street Cty Prim Sch
  BN1 .... 207 F5
Middle Tyne BN13 .... 181 D5
Middle Way
  Burgess Hill RH15 .... 107 B3
  Kingston Gorse BN16 .... 200 D4
Middlefield Horley RH6 .... 2 C4
  West Wittering PO20 .... 190 C1
Middlefield La PO18 .... 153 C7
Middleton Ave BN3 .... 186 D6
Middleton Bsns Pk PO22 .. 196 E6
Middleton CI PO20 .... 202 B6
Middleton Gdns PO20 .... 154 D2
Middleton Rd
  Horsham RH12 .... 36 A2
  Middleton-on-Sea PO22 .. 196 D5
  Middleton Rise BN1 .... 168 E5
  Middleton Way RH11 .... 17 E5
Midfields CI RH15 .... 107 B3
Midfields Rd RH15 .... 107 B3
Midfields Wlk RH15 .... 107 B4
Midgley Rd RH10 .... 18 F8
Midholme BN16 .... 199 F5
Midhurst CE (C) Prim Sch
  GU29 .... 92 E7
Midhurst Dr Crawley RH11 .. 18 A7
  Ferring BN12 .... 200 F6
Midhurst Cottage Hospl
  GU29 .... 70 F1
Midhurst Dr BN12 .... 181 A4
Midhurst Gram Sch GU29 .. 70 F1
Midhurst Gram Sch (C)
  GU29 .... 92 F8
Midhurst Rd Fernhurst GU27 49 A4
  Haslemere GU27 .... 27 B5
  Haslemere GU27 .... 27 B5
  Liphook GU30 .... 25 C2
  Petworth GU28 .... 95 E7
Midhurst Rise BN1 .... 168 B6
Midhurst Wlk BN3 .... 166 F3
Midway The PO22 .... 196 A4
Mighell St BN2 .... 207 B5
Milborne Rd RH10 .... 19 C2
Milbury CI BN12 .... 200 F4
Milcote Ave BN3 .... 186 F8
Mile End Cotts BN1 .... 167 C6
Mile End La PO20 .... 172 C2
Mile Oak Cres BN42 .... 165 F1
Mile Oak Cty Prim Sch
  BN41 .... 165 F3
Mile Oak Gdns BN41 .... 166 A1
Mile Oak Rd
  Portslade-by-Sea BN41 .. 166 C1
  Southwick BN41, BN42 .. 165 F1
Miles CI BN18 .... 177 B2
Miles Cotts PO18 .... 171 A5
Milford Ct BN15 .... 183 D3
Mill Ave BN43 .... 164 F1
Mill Bay La RH12 .... 36 B1
Mill CI Crabtree RH13 .... 82 A7
  East Grinstead RH19 .... 22 E7
  Fishbourne PO19, PO20 .. 172 B6
  Haslemere GU27 .... 26 E6
  Rustington BN16 .... 199 D6
Mill Copse Rd GU27 .... 27 B4
Mill Cotts
  East Grinstead RH19 .... 22 E7
  Rudgwick RH12 .... 33 D5
Mill CI BN45 .... 146 C5
Mill Dr Henfield BN5 .... 123 F4
  Hove BN3 .... 167 A5
Mill End Hermitage PO10 .. 169 D8
  West Chiltington Common
  RH20 .... 119 C8
Mill Gdns PO20 .... 201 F7
Mill Green Rd RH16 .... 85 E6
Mill Hill BN43 .... 164 E3
Mill Hill CI
  Haywards Heath RH16 .... 85 E7
  Shoreham-by-Sea BN43 .. 164 E1
Mill Hill Dr BN43 .... 164 E1
Mill Hill Gdns BN43 .... 164 E1
Mill Ho **4** BN1 .... 183 B3
Mill House Gdns BN11 .. 182 A2
Mill La Amberley BN18 .. 138 E6
  Arundel BN18 .... 158 B3
  Ashington RH20 .... 120 F4
  Balcombe RH17 .... 41 C1
  Clayton BN45, BN6 .... 147 E7
  Cocking GU29 .... 112 D8
  Coolham RH13 .... 78 D3

Mill La Copthorne RH10 .... 7 E3
  Crabtree RH13 .... 82 B7
  Crawley RH11 .... 18 A8
  Dumpford GU31 .... 69 A1
  Dumpford GU31 .... 90 F8
  Felbridge RH19 .... 8 E5
  Felcourt RH7 .... 9 F8
  Fernhurst GU27 .... 27 C3
  Fishbourne PO19 .... 172 B6
  Goddards' Green BN6 .... 106 A3
  Heyshott Green GU29 .... 93 A2
  Hookwood RH6 .... 1 D3
  Littlehampton BN17 .... 178 D5
  Littleworth RH13 .... 102 F5
  Portslade-by-Sea BN41 .. 166 B1
  Poynings BN45 .... 146 C5
  Runcton PO20 .... 173 E1
  Rustington BN16 .... 179 D3
  Sayers Common
  BN6, RH17 .... 105 E2
  Selsey PO20 .... 206 C7
  Shoreham-by-Sea BN43 .. 184 F8
  Sidlesham PO20 .... 203 F7
  Slindon BN18 .... 156 C6
  South Harting GU31 .... 89 D4
  Stedham GU29 .... 70 A2
  Storrington RH20 .... 119 D2
  Walberton BN18 .... 156 D1
  West Chiltington Common
  RH20 .... 119 C8
  Westbourne PO10 .... 149 D3
  Worthing BN13 .... 161 F1
Mill Lodge PO21 .... 194 A2
Mill Mead RH20 .... 121 A4
Mill Park Rd PO21 .... 194 B2
Mill Pk RH15 .... 107 B3
Mill Quay PO10 .... 169 C7
Mill Race BN6 .... 126 E8
Mill Rd Angmering BN16 .. 179 F5
  Arundel BN18 .... 158 C3
  Brighton BN1 .... 167 C6
  Burgess Hill RH15 .... 107 B3
  Crawley RH10 .... 19 B7
  Lancing BN15 .... 183 E8
  Liss GU33 .... 45 C4
  Southwick BN41 .... 186 B7
  Steyning BN44 .... 143 C3
  Walberton BN18 .... 156 D3
  West Ashling PO18 .... 151 A3
  West Chiltington Common
  RH20 .... 119 C8
  Westbourne PO10 .... 149 D4
  Worthing BN11 .... 182 A2
Mill Rd Ind Est BN41 .... 186 B7
Mill Rise BN1 .... 167 C5
Mill Road Ave BN16 .... 179 F5
Mill Stream Meadow RH16 85 D7
Mill Vale Meadows GU30 .. 47 B3
Mill View Rd BN18 .... 176 F2
Mill Way Billingshurst RH14 55 C3
  Billingshurst RH14 .... 55 D3
  East Grinstead RH19 .... 22 E7
Mill Wood RH15 .... 107 B3
Millais RH13 .... 37 A3
Millais CI RH13 .... 17 F2
Millais Rd RH13 .... 37 A4
Millais Sch RH13 .... 36 F2
Millais Sch Lower Sch
  RH13 .... 36 F2
Milland La GU30 .... 47 A5
Milland Rd GU30, GU29 .. 47 C2
Millars Ct PO21 .... 194 B1
Millbank RH15 .... 107 B4
Millbank The RH11 .... 17 F6
Millbrook CI GU33 .... 45 C4
Millcroft BN1 .... 167 C5
Millcroft Ave BN42 .... 165 E3
Millcroft Gdns BN42 .... 165 E3
Millcross Rd BN41 .... 166 B1
Miller's Rd BN1 .... 167 E1
Millers CI BN16 .... 199 D6
Millers Gate RH12 .... 36 DE
Millers The BN18 .... 176 F2
Millers Way RH15 .... 107 B4
Millfield Lancing BN15 .. 183 C7
  Southwater RH13 .... 80 A7
Millfield CI
  Chichester PO19 .... 173 C8
  Littlehampton BN16 .... 199 B3
Millfield Cotts **8** BN2 .. 188 D4
Millpond La PO18 .... 151 B3
Millstream The GU27 .... 26 E5
Millthorpe Rd RH12 .... 36 F4
Millwood RH19 .... 21 E5
Milne CI RH11 .... 17 E3
Milner Flats BN2 .... 207 B5
Milner Rd BN2 .... 168 D1
Milnthorpe Rd BN3 .... 186 F8
Milnwood Rd RH12 .... 36 C3
Milton Ave BN16 .... 199 B5

Milton Ct Lancing BN15 .... 183 F5
Rustington BN16 .... 199 B5
Milton Cres RH19 .... 22 C8
Milton Ct
6 Haywards Heath RH16 .. 85 D5
2 Worthing BN11 .... 182 C1
Milton Dr BN42 .... 185 F8
Milton Mount RH10 .... 6 D1
Milton Mount Ave RH10 ...... 19 D8
Milton Mount Fst & Mid Sch
RH10 .... 19 C8
Milton Rd Brighton BN2 ...... 207 B7
Crawley RH10 .... 19 C7
Haywards Heath RH16 .. 85 D6
Horsham RH12 .... 36 C2
Worthing BN11 .... 182 C1
Milton St BN11 .... 182 C1
Milward Ct **3** BN43 .... 185 C8
Milwood Ct PO19 .... 172 F7
Mimmack Cl BN44 .... 143 D4
Mimosa Ct BN1 .... 168 B3
Mindleheim Ave RH19 .... 10 B2
Minnels The BN6 .... 127 A3
Minsted Rd GU29 .... 91 F7
Minster Ct BN17 .... 178 C4
Mint Rd GU33 .... 45 D6
Minton Rd PO22 .... 196 B4
Miranda Wlk RH11 .... 17 E4
Mitchamer Cotts PO18 ..... 130 F2
Mitchell Gdns RH13 .... 34 E3
Mitchells Rd RH10 .... 18 F6
Mitford Wlk **10** BN1 .... 18 A3
Mitre Ho **18** BN1 .... 187 E5
Moat La RH20 .... 98 D2
Moat Rd RH19 .... 9 E2
Moat The RH20 .... 98 C2
Moat Way BN12 .... 181 E1
Moat Wlk RH10 .... 19 C7
Moatfield La RH13 .... 104 A8
Mocatta Way RH15 .... 106 D5
Model Buildings Cotts
RH13 .... 80 B2
Modena Rd BN3 .... 186 F7
Mole Cl RH11 .... 18 B8
Mole The BN7 .... 199 A5
Molecomb Broadwalk
PO18 .... 134 A2
Molesworth St BN3 .... 186 F8
Molins Ct **4** RH11 .... 18 A3
Monarch Cl RH11 .... 18 A3
Monastery La RH20 .... 119 C1
Monk Cl BN1 .... 168 E6
Monk's Hill PO10 .... 149 C5
Monkmead Copse RH20 .... 119 C6
Monkmead La RH20 .... 119 B6
Monks Ave BN15 .... 183 F6
Monks Cl BN15 .... 183 F6
Monks Cl BN15 .... 183 E6
Monks La RH5 .... 13 F5
Monks Wlk BN44 .... 144 B2
Monksfield RH10 .... 18 F7
Monmouth St **13** BN3 ... 187 B7
Mons Ave PO21 .... 195 B5
Montagu Ct PO19 .... 172 E8
Montague Cl BN43 .... 185 D7
Montague Ct
6 Brighton BN2 .... 188 C4
Lancing BN15 .... 183 B7
2 Shoreham-by-Sea
BN43 .... 185 D7
Montague Ctr **8** BN11 ... 182 D2
Montague Pl
Brighton BN2 .... 188 C4
Worthing BN11 .... 182 D1
Montague Rd GU29 .... 71 A2
Montague St
4 Brighton BN2 .... 188 C4
Worthing BN11 .... 182 C1
Montalan Cres PO20 .... 206 B8
Montefiore Rd BN3 .... 187 E7
Monterey Ct BN1 .... 167 E3
Montes Hill RH16 .... 86 F8
Monteswood La
RH16, RH17 .... 87 B8
Montford Cl BN43 .... 185 D8
Montfort Rise RH6 .... 1 F8
Montgomery Dr PO22 .... 196 D6
Montgomery St BN3 .... 187 A7
Montpelier Cotts BN1 ...... 141 E8
Montpelier Cres BN1 .... 187 E6
Montpelier Gdns BN1 .... 141 E8
Montpelier Lodge **8** BN1 187 E6
Montpelier Pl **7** BN1 ..... 187 E6
Montpelier Rd
Brighton BN1 .... 187 E5
East Preston BN16 .... 200 A5
Montpelier St BN1 .... 187 E6
Montpelier Terr **10** BN1 .. 187 E6
Montpelier Villas BN1 ...... 187 E6
Montreal Rd BN2 .... 207 B6
Montreal Way BN13 .... 181 C6

Montreux Ct RH11 .... 18 B6
Montrose Cl BN12 .... 181 C2
Monument La PO18 .... 150 B7
Monument View BN2 .... 188 D6
Moon's La RH19, RH7, TN8 . 10 E8
Moons La RH13 .... 36 E1
Moor Park Cres RH11 .... 17 D5
Moor Pl RH19 .... 9 D2
Moor Rd GU27 .... 26 C5
Moorcroft Cl RH11 .... 18 B7
Moore Ct RH12 .... 36 A1
Moorfield GU27 .... 26 F5
Moorfoot Rd BN13 .... 181 F7
Moorhead Rd RH17 .... 37 B5
Moorhen Way PO22 .... 195 B6
Moorhouse La GU29 .... 69 D6
Moorings The
East Grinstead RH19 .... 9 A3
Lancing BN15 .... 183 F8
5 Littlehampton BN16 . 199 A6
Shoreham-by-Sea BN43 . 185 C6
Moorland Cl RH10 .... 19 C3
Moraunt Dr PO22 .... 196 E6
Morecambe Cl RH11 .... 17 F4
Morecambe Rd RH11 .... 168 A6
Moreton Rd PO18 .... 171 B5
Morland Ave BN14 .... 182 E7
Morley St BN2 .... 207 B6
Morleys RH20 .... 121 A4
Mornington Cres
Bognor Regis PO21 .... 195 A5
Hove BN3 .... 186 D7
Mornington Mansions
BN3 .... 186 D7
Morrell Ave RH11 .... 36 F6
Morris Way RH20 .... 119 C7
Morrison St **5** RH11 ...... 18 B1
Mortimer Rd BN3 .... 187 A8
Morton Cl RH11 .... 39 B8
Morton Rd RH19 .... 22 E7
Mosdell Rd PO10 .... 170 A8
Mosford Cl RH6 .... 1 F5
Moss Cl GU33 .... 45 C4
Mosse Gdns PO19 .... 172 B7
Moulsecoomb Cty Inf Sch
BN2 .... 168 E3
Moulsecoomb Cty Jun Sch
BN2 .... 168 E3
Moulsecoomb Sta BN2 ..... 168 D2
Moulsecoomb Way BN2 ... 168 F4
Mount Cl RH10 .... 19 D7
Mount Cl PO20 .... 206 E7
Mount La Chichester PO19 172 F6
Turners Hill RH10 .... 12 A4
Mount Noddy RH17 .... 84 C3
Mount Pk BN44 .... 143 D1
Mount Pleasant
Arundel BN18 .... 158 A3
Brighton BN2 .... 207 B5
Mount The
Lambs Green RH12 .... 17 B8
Rusper RH11, RH12 .... 4 B1
Mount Way BN15 .... 163 E1
Mount Zion Pl BN1 .... 207 F6
Mountbatten Cl RH11 .... 18 C2
Mountbatten Ct
Bognor Regis PO21 .... 195 D2
Hove BN3 .... 186 E8
7 Littlehampton BN16 . 199 A6
Mountfields BN1 .... 168 C2
Mountview Rd BN15 .... 163 C1
Mountwood Rd
Breach PO10 .... 149 F1
Selsey PO20 .... 206 F8
Mouse La BN44 .... 142 E6
Mouthey's La PO18 .... 151 E2
Mowbray Dr RH11 .... 17 F4
Mowden Sch BN1 .... 167 D1
Moyne Cl BN1 .... 166 E1
Moyne Rd RH11 .... 18 C2
Mudberry La PO18 .... 171 A8
Muggeridge's Hill
RH5, RH12 .... 15 E8
Muirfield Cl Crawley RH11 . 17 D5
Worthing BN13 .... 181 E6
Muirfield Ct **16** RH6 ..... 85 E4
Muirfield Rd BN13 .... 181 E6
Mulberry Cl Brighton BN1 . 167 F3
Ferring BN12 .... 200 E6
Horsham RH12 .... 36 C5
Lancing BN15 .... 183 E6
Shoreham-by-Sea BN43 .. 165 D1
Worthing BN13 .... 181 C3
Mulberry Ct
Bognor Regis PO21 .... 205 A7
Petworth GU28 .... 95 E7
Worthing BN12 .... 181 C2
Mulberry Gdns BN12 .... 181 C2
Mulberry La Ditchling BN6 127 D3
Worthing BN12 .... 181 C2
Mulberry Rd RH11 .... 5 B1

Mullein Wlk RH11 .... 18 A2
Mumford PO19 .... 172 B8
Munmere Way **3** BN16 . 199 E6
Munnion Rd RH17 .... 64 B7
Munns Dr RH15 .... 107 B4
Muntham Dr RH13 .... 56 E7
Muntham House Sch RH13 56 E4
Murina Ave PO21 .... 195 C5
Murray Ct Crawley RH11 ... 18 A1
Horsham RH13 .... 37 B4
Murray Rd PO20 .... 206 D6
Museum Hill GU27 .... 27 D6
Musgrave Ave RH19 .... 22 E8
Mustang Cl BN18 .... 177 B2
Muster Ct RH16 .... 85 D4
Muster Gn N RH16 .... 85 D4
Muster Gn S RH16 .... 85 D4
Mutton Hill RH10 .... 10 B7
Mutton's La BN18 .... 120 D3
Myrtle Cres BN15 .... 183 D5
Myrtle Gr BN16 .... 199 F5
Myrtle La RH14 .... 77 D7
Myrtle Rd BN15 .... 183 D5
Mytchett Ho **1** PO19 .... 153 A2
Mytten Bank RH17 .... 84 F6
Mytten Cl RH17 .... 84 F6

Nab Tower La PO20 .... 206 B8
Nab Wlk PO20 .... 201 F6
Nagels Cl PO22 .... 202 A6
Naiad Ave PO22 .... 196 D5
Naldrett Cl RH12 .... 36 F4
Naldretts La RH12 .... 33 D5
Namrik Mews BN3 .... 187 A6
Nanson Rd BN1 .... 168 D6
Napier Ho **3** BN2 .... 188 C7
Napier Way RH10 .... 6 A1
Nappers Wood GU27 .... 49 A6
Nash La RH17 .... 87 B4
Nash Rd RH10 .... 18 E3
Nash Way BN18 .... 156 D1
Natal Rd BN2 .... 168 D1
Natts La RH14 .... 77 D6
Naunton Rd PO19 .... 153 B1
Navarino Rd BN11 .... 183 A2
Neale Cl RH19 .... 9 B3
Need's Hill RH13 .... 102 F6
Needlemakers PO19 .... 173 B6
Needles Cl RH11 .... 36 B1
Nell Ball RH14 .... 30 E2
Nelson Cl Crawley RH10 ... 19 C5
Lancing BN15 .... 183 D8
Tangmere PO20 .... 154 D2
Nelson Ct BN43 .... 184 D5
Nelson Pl **10** BN2 .... 207 B6
Nelson Rd
Bognor Regis PO21 .... 195 A3
Horsham RH12 .... 36 C3
Worthing BN11 .... 181 D4
Nelson Row Brighton BN2 . 207 B5
Ford BN18 .... 177 E3
Nep Cl BN5 .... 123 E4
Nep Town Rd BN5 .... 123 E4
Nepcote La BN14 .... 161 F5
Nepcote Par BN14 .... 161 E6
Nepfield Cl RH14 .... 161 F5
Neptune Cl RH11 .... 17 E4
Neptune Ct PO22 .... 196 D4
Neptune Way BN16 .... 199 A4
Nesbit Ct RH11 .... 17 E3
Nesbitt Rd BN2 .... 168 D1
Nestor Ct BN1 .... 167 E1
Netherton Cl Selsey PO20 . 207 A5
Southwater RH13 .... 57 F4
Netherwood RH11 .... 18 B4
Netherwoods Rd RH13 ...... 79 B6
Netley Cl RH11 .... 39 C8
Nettleton Ave PO20 .... 154 C2
Nettleton Ct BN1 .... 168 B1
Nevile Cl RH11 .... 18 A3
Nevill Ave BN3 .... 166 F1
Nevill Cl BN3 .... 167 A2
Nevill Cotts BN6 .... 127 D2
Nevill Ct BN3 .... 167 A1
Nevill Gdns BN3 .... 167 A2
Nevill Pl BN3 .... 167 A2
Nevill Rd BN3 .... 167 A2
Neville Gdns PO10 .... 149 A3
Neville Rd
Bognor Regis PO22 .... 195 D4
Chichester PO19 .... 172 D7
New Barn Cl
Portslade-by-Sea BN41 .. 166 B2
Shoreham-by-Sea BN43 . 165 B1
New Barn Hill PO18 .... 154 B7
New Barn La RH20 .... 119 B8
New Barn Rd
Amberley BN18 .... 138 D5
Shoreham-by-Sea BN43 . 165 B1
New Brighton Rd PO10 ..... 149 B2

New Broadway BN14 .... 182 A3
New Church Rd
BN3, BN41 .... 186 E7
New Cotts
Scaynes Hill RH17 .... 86 F1
Turners Hill RH10 .... 21 A4
Washington RH20 .... 141 E6
New Courtwick La BN17 .. 178 C4
New Cut BN18 .... 158 B3
New Dorset St BN1 .... 207 F6
New England Coll BN18 ... 177 E7
New England Ho BN1 .... 207 A7
New England Rd
Brighton BN1 .... 207 F7
Haywards Heath RH16 .... 85 F4
New England Rise BN41 ... 166 A4
New England St BN1 .... 207 A7
New Farthingdale RH7 ...... 10 B8
New Hall La BN5 .... 144 E7
New House La RH11 .... 2 E8
New La GU31 .... 89 D2
New Life Sch RH19 .... 9 D2
New Moorhead Dr RH12 ... 37 C6
New Par
East Wittering PO20 .... 201 E7
Worthing BN11 .... 182 F2
New Park Rd PO19 .... 173 A7
New Place RH20 .... 98 C3
New Rd Billingshurst RH14 .. 56 B2
Brighton BN1 .... 207 A5
Camelsdale GU27 .... 26 F5
East Dean RH18 .... 138 C8
Keymer BN6 .... 127 B2
Littlehampton BN17 .... 198 D4
Midhurst GU29 .... 92 E6
Rustington BN16 .... 179 E3
Shoreham-by-Sea BN43 . 184 F7
South Ambersham GU29 . 93 E4
Southbourne PO10 .... 170 A8
Southwater RH13 .... 57 F4
Upper Beeding BN44 ...... 144 B1
Upperton GU28 .... 73 A2
Westbourne PO10 .... 149 D3
Westerton PO18 .... 153 D4
Worthing BN13 .... 181 C7
New Row BN44 .... 144 C3
New Salts Farm Rd BN43 .. 184 C6
New St Crawley RH10 .... 19 A7
Horsham RH13 .... 36 D2
Petworth GU28 .... 95 FB
2 Worthing BN11 .... 182 D1
New Steine BN2 .... 207 B4
New Steine Mews BN2 ..... 207 B5
New Sussex Hospl BN3 .... 187 E6
New Town
16 Chichester PO19 .. 173 A6
Copthorne RH10 .... 7 B3
New Town Rd RH20 .... 119 B1
New Way La BN6 .... 126 B2
Newark Pl BN2 .... 207 B6
Newark Rd RH10 .... 18 F8
Newbarn La
Bognor Regis, Felpham
PO22 .... 196 B6
Bognor Regis, North Bersted
PO21 .... 194 F6
Henfield BN5 .... 123 F2
Walderton BN5 .... 150 B8
Newbridge Cl RH12 .... 35 C3
Newbridge Rd RH14 .... 77 B8
Newbury La RH17 .... 84 E5
Newdigate Rd RH12 .... 16 C8
Newells La
Broadbridge RH18 .... 171 A7
Monk's Gate RH13 .... 59 D2
West Ashling PO18 .... 150 F1
Newfield Rd
Liss Forest GU33 .... 45 C6
Selsey PO20 .... 206 G8
Newhall Cl PO21 .... 194 F3
Newham Cl BN44 .... 143 C3
Newham La BN44 .... 143 C2
Newhaven St BN2 .... 207 B6
Newhouse La
East Dean PO18 .... 134 D8
Heath Common RH20 ..... 120 C3
Newick House Sch RH17 .. 107 C1
Newick Rd BN1 .... 168 E4
Newland Rd
Upper Beeding BN44 ...... 144 B2
Worthing BN11 .... 182 D3
Newland St BN11 .... 182 D3
Newlands Cl RH17 .... 40 F1
Newlands Cl Horley RH6 ... 1 F5
Keymer BN6 .... 127 B3
Newlands Cres RH19 .... 9 D2
Newlands La PO19 .... 172 D8
Newlands Pk RH20 .... 7 E3
Newlands Rd RH18 .... 23 F3
Newlands Rd Crawley RH18 . 15 C5
Horsham RH12 .... 36 C4

Newling Way BN13 .... 161 E1
Newman Cl RH10 .... 19 C4
Newman's Gdns BN15 ..... 183 B7
Newmarket Rd
Brighton BN2 .... 188 C8
Crawley RH10 .... 19 A4
Newmarket Terr **8** BN2 . 188 C8
Newport Dr PO18, PO19 .. 172 B7
Newport Mews BN11 .... 183 B3
Newport Rd RH15 .... 106 F3
Newport St BN2 .... 207 B7
Newpound RH14 .... 54 E3
Newpound La RH14 .... 54 D1
Newstead **5** BN11 .... 207 F7
Newtimber Ave BN12 ...... 181 B3
Newtimber Dr BN41 .... 166 A1
Newtimber Gdns BN43 .... 164 F1
Newton Ave RH19 .... 22 F6
Newton Cl RH16 .... 86 B7
Newton Ct **3** RH16 .... 85 E5
Newton Rd Crawley RH10 ... 5 F2
Haywards Heath RH16 ..... 86 C7
Newtown Ave
PO21, PO22 .... 195 A6
Newtown Ct RH13 .... 36 E1
Newtown Rd Hove BN3 ... 187 B8
Liphook GU30 .... 25 C3
Nicholsfield RH14 .... 31 F4
Nicolson Dr BN43 .... 184 F8
Nightingale Cl
Crawley RH11 .... 18 C8
East Grinstead RH19 .... 22 D7
Red Hill PO9 .... 128 C1
Storrington RH20 .... 119 E1
Nightingale Ct PO22 .... 196 F5
Nightingale La
Burgess Hill RH15 .... 126 F8
Hambrook PO18 .... 150 D3
Storrington RH20 .... 119 E1
Nightingale Pk RH20 .... 119 E1
Nightingale Rd RH12 .... 36 D3
Nightingale Wlk RH14 ...... 77 E8
Nightingales Findon BN14 161 E7
West Chiltington Common
RH20 .... 119 D7
Nightingales Bsns Pk RH20 98 C5
Nile St Brighton BN1 .... 207 A5
Emsworth PO10 .... 169 B8
Nimbus Cl RH17 .... 199 A6
Nimrod Ct RH10 .... 6 D1
Nine Acres GU29 .... 92 D8
Ninfield Cl PO22 .... 188 E7
Ninfield Ct RH10 .... 19 D5
Nizells Ave BN3 .... 187 E7
Noah's Ct RH10 .... 21 A4
Noah's Farm Yard
Nature Trail GU28 .... 94 E8
Noahs Ark La RH16 .... 86 C7
Noel Gn RH15 .... 107 B4
Noel Rise RH15 .... 107 B4
Nonnington La GU28 .... 94 B1
Nookery The BN16 .... 200 A5
Nor'bren Ave PO21 .... 195 A5
Norbury Cl BN15 .... 183 F8
Norbury Dr BN15 .... 183 F8
Nordester Lodge **1** BN16 199 B4
Nore Down Way PO18 ...... 130 A8
Norfolk Bldgs **2** BN1 ... 187 E5
Norfolk Cl
5 Bognor Regis PO21 195 C2
Crawley RH11 .... 17 E2
Horley RH6 .... 2 A2
Norfolk Cotts Bury PO20 . 138 A7
Steyning BN44 .... 143 D3
Norfolk Ct Horsham RH12 .. 37 B5
8 Rustington BN16 .... 199 B4
1 Worthing BN11 .... 182 C3
Norfolk Gdns BN17 .... 198 F4
Norfolk Ho PO22 .... 195 F4
Norfolk Mews
3 Hove BN1 .... 187 E5
Littlehampton BN17 .... 198 F4
Norfolk Pl BN17 .... 198 F4
Norfolk Rd
Horsham RH12, RH13 .... 36 D2
Hove BN1 .... 187 E6
Norfolk Sq
2 Bognor Regis PO21 195 C2
4 Hove BN1 .... 187 E5
Worthing BN11 .... 182 C3
Norfolk Terr
Horsham RH12, RH13 .... 36 D2
Hove BN1 .... 187 E6

Norfolk Way PO22 .... 197 B5
Norman Cl BN17 .... 198 F5
Norman Cres **9** BN43 ...... 164 F1
Norman Rd
  Burgess Hill RH15 .... 107 A3
  Hove BN3 .... 186 E6
Norman Way BN44 .... 143 D4
Norman's Dr PO22 .... 196 B6
Normandy RH12 .... 36 C1
Normandy Cl
  Crawley RH10 .... 19 C4
  7 East Grinstead RH19 ... 22 F8
Normandy Ct **5** BN11 ..... 182 B1
Normandy Dr BN16 .... 200 A4
Normandy Gdns RH12 ...... 36 C1
Normandy Ho **3** BN3 ..... 187 C6
Normandy La BN16 .... 200 A4
Normandy Rd BN14 .... 182 C4
Normanhurst
  9 Brighton BN2 .... 207 B6
  4 Shoreham-by-Sea
  BN43 .... 184 F7
Normanhurst Cl
  Crawley RH10 .... 18 F6
  Rustington BN16 .... 199 C4
Normanscourt **3** BN43 .. 164 F1
Normanton Ave PO21 ...... 195 B3
Normanton St **8** BN2 ... 188 C7
Norris The BN16 .... 200 B5
North Ash RH12 .... 36 C4
North Ave
  Middleton-on-Sea PO22 ... 196 F5
  Worthing BN12 .... 181 E1
North Ave E PO22 .... 197 A5
North Ave S PO22 .... 197 A5
North Bank BN6 .... 126 E4
North Bay PO10 .... 169 C3
North Bersted St PO22 ... 195 A7
North Cl Chichester PO19 . 173 A7
  Crawley RH10 .... 18 F7
  Portslade-by-Sea BN41 ... 166 A2
North Ct BN6 .... 126 E4
North Dr Angmering BN16 . 179 F4
  Brighton BN2 .... 188 C6
North End BN6 .... 127 D4
North End Cl GU28 .... 73 F1
North End Cotts BN14 ..... 161 E8
North End Rd BN18 .... 176 F4
North Farm Cotts BN14 ... 141 D2
North Farm Ct BN15 .... 183 E6
North Farm Rd BN15 .... 183 F6
North Gdns BN1 .... 207 F6
North Ham Rd BN17 .... 198 D6
North Heath Cl RH12 .... 36 D5
North Heath Cty Prim Sch
  RH12 .... 36 D5
North Heath Est RH12 ..... 36 D6
North Heath La RH12 .... 36 E6
North Holmes Cl RH12 ..... 37 B5
North La Buriton GU31 ..... 88 A5
  Charlton PO18 .... 134 A7
  East Preston BN16 .... 200 B6
  Littlehampton BN16 .... 199 B6
  Portslade-by-Sea BN41 ... 166 A3
  South Harting GU31 .... 89 D4
  West Hoathly RH19 .... 42 E6
  Wiston BN44 .... 121 C2
North Lancing Cty Fst &
  Mid Sch BN15 .... 183 E8
North Lodge PO21 .... 194 A2
North Mead PO10 .... 18 E8
North Mundham Cty
  Prim Sch PO20 .... 173 D1
North Pallant PO19 .... 173 A6
North Par RH12 .... 36 C3
North Pl Brighton BN1 ..... 207 A5
  14 Littlehampton BN17 . 198 E4
North Point **1** BN43 .... 185 A6
North Pound BN18 .... 156 D1
North Rd Brighton BN1 .... 207 A6
  Brighton, Preston BN1 .... 167 E1
  Broadbridge PO18 .... 171 C7
  Crawley RH10 .... 19 A7
  Haywards Heath RH16 ..... 86 A4
  Lancing BN15 .... 183 E6
  Portslade-by-Sea BN41 .... 166 A2
  Selsey PO20 .... 206 E7
North St Brighton BN1 ..... 207 A5
  Chichester PO19 .... 173 A7
  Emsworth PO10 .... 149 B1
  Horsham RH12, RH13 ...... 36 D3
  Littlehampton BN17 .... 178 D3
  Midhurst GU29 .... 92 F8
  Petworth GU28 .... 73 F1
  Portslade-by-Sea BN41 .... 186 C7
  Shoreham-by-Sea BN43 ... 184 E7
  Storrington RH20 .... 119 D1
  Turners Hill RH10 .... 21 A4

North St
  Westbourne PO10 .... 149 D4
  Worthing BN11 .... 182 D3
North Terminal App RH6 .... 5 F8
North View BN5 .... 124 E5
North Walls
  Chichester PO19 .... 172 F6
  Chichester PO19 .... 172 F7
North Way
  Bognor Regis PO22 .... 195 F4
  Petworth GU28 .... 95 E7
Northbourne Cl BN43 ...... 184 F8
Northbrook Cl BN14 .... 182 E6
Northbrook Coll
  Worthing, Goring-by-Sea
  BN13 .... 181 B4
  Worthing,West Worthing
  BN11 .... 182 D2
Northbrook Coll
  Design & Tech BN14 ...... 182 D5
Northbrook Coll of
  Design & Tech RH12 .... 36 C4
Northbrook Rd BN14 .... 182 E6
Northbrook Trad Est
  BN14 .... 182 E6
Northchapel Cty Prim Sch
  GU28 .... 51 A7
Northcliffe Rd PO22 .... 195 E4
Northcote Rd PO21 .... 195 A4
Northcourt Cl BN16 .... 199 E6
Northcourt Rd BN14 .... 182 C4
Northcroft BN5 .... 123 E5
Northdown Cl RH12 .... 36 F4
Northdown Terr RH19 .... 9 D3
Northease Cl BN3 .... 166 D2
Northease Dr BN3 .... 166 E3
Northease Gdns BN3 .... 166 E3
Northend La BN6 .... 105 F3
Northerlea BN41 .... 166 A1
Northern Breach RH17 ...... 84 E6
Northern Cres PO20 .... 201 F7
Northfield PO20 .... 206 F7
Northfield Rd BN13 .... 182 A6
Northfield Rise BN3 .... 166 D4
Northfield Way BN1 .... 168 A4
Northfields La PO20 .... 155 D1
Northgate PO19 .... 173 A7
Northgate Ave RH10 .... 18 F7
Northgate Cl BN15 .... 183 C6
Northgate Cty Fst Sch
  RH10 .... 18 E7
Northgate Cty Mid Sch
  RH10 .... 18 E7
Northgate Pl RH10 .... 18 E7
Northgate Rd
  Crawley RH10, RH11 .... 18 D6
  Gatwick Airport RH6 .... 5 F8
Northlands PO19 .... 152 B1
Northlands Ave RH16 ...... 86 B4
Northlands La RH20 .... 119 E4
Northlands Rd RH12 .... 14 D2
Northlands Wood Cty
  Prim Sch RH16 .... 86 B4
Northmead GU28 .... 73 F1
Northside PO18 .... 152 E7
Northview Terr BN14 .... 161 E6
Northway
  Burgess Hill RH15 .... 107 C4
  Gatwick Airport RH6 .... 5 F8
Northway Rd BN17 .... 178 D4
Northwood Pk RH10 .... 6 A2
Northwyke Cl PO22 .... 196 C5
Northwyke Rd PO22 .... 196 C5
Norton La PO20 .... 155 B1
Norton Rd Hove BN3 .... 187 B6
  Lancing BN15 .... 183 D5
Norway La BN17 .... 178 F3
Norway St BN41 .... 186 C7
Norwich Cres BN2 .... 168 F2
Norwich Dr BN2 .... 168 F2
Norwich Rd
  Chichester PO19 .... 152 F1
  Crawley RH10 .... 19 B5
Norwood BN1 .... 168 A4
Norwood La N GU28 .... 114 E6
Norwood La S GU28 .... 114 E5
Norwoodhill Rd RH6 .... 4 E8
Notre Dame Int Sch
  RH10 .... 19 D6
Nowhurst La RH12 .... 35 A5
Nuffield Cl RH10 .... 194 E3
Nursery Cl
  Haywards Heath RH16 ..... 85 D5
  Hurstpierpoint BN6 .... 125 F7
  Lancing BN15 .... 183 D7
  New Brighton BN41 .... 149 B3
  Portslade-by-Sea BN41 ... 165 E4
  Shoreham-by-Sea BN43 ... 185 B8
  West Barnham PO22 ...... 176 B6
  West Kingston BN16 .... 200 A4

Nursery Field GU33 .... 45 A3
Nursery Gdns BN17 .... 178 D3
Nursery La
  Fishbourne PO18, PO19 ... 172 B7
  Hookwood RH6 .... 1 D2
  Worthing BN11 .... 182 C1
Nursery The RH15 .... 107 C4
Nurserylands RH11 .... 18 A6
Nutbourne Halt PO18 ...... 170 D8
Nutbourne La RH20 .... 99 A4
Nutbourne Manor Vineyard
  RH20 .... 99 B2
Nutbourne Rd
  Nutbourne Common RH20 . 99 A1
  South Hayling PO11 .... 189 A1
  Worthing BN14 .... 182 B4
Nutcombe La GU26, GU27 . 26 E8
Nutcroft RH20 .... 98 C3
Nutham La RH13 .... 58 A1
Nuthatch Cl PO09 .... 128 D1
Nuthatch Way RH12 .... 36 D7
Nuthurst Cl Brighton BN2 . 188 F6
  Crawley RH11 .... 18 A7
Nuthurst Pl BN2 .... 188 F5
Nuthurst Rd
  Maplehurst RH13 .... 80 F6
  Monk's Gate RH13 .... 59 B3
Nuthurst St RH13 .... 59 A2
Nutley Ave BN12 .... 181 C1
Nutley Cl Hove BN3 .... 166 F3
  Worthing BN12 .... 181 C1
Nutley Cres BN12 .... 181 C1
Nutley La RH20 .... 74 A8
Nye La Ditchling BN6 ...... 127 D1
  Westmeston BN6 .... 148 D8
Nye Rd RH15 .... 107 C3
Nyes Cl BN5 .... 123 F5
Nyes La RH13 .... 57 F3
Nyetimber Cl
  Bognor Regis PO21 .... 194 B2
  West Chiltington Common
  RH20 .... 119 C6
Nyetimber Copse RH20 ... 119 C7
Nyetimber Cres PO21 ...... 194 B2
Nyetimber Hill BN2 .... 168 E2
Nyetimber La
  Bognor Regis PO21 .... 194 B2
  West Chiltington Common
  RH20 .... 119 C7
Nyetimber Mill PO21 ...... 194 A2
Nyetimbers The PO21 ..... 194 A2
Nyewood CE Inf (A) Sch
  PO21 .... 195 A4
Nyewood CE Jun (A) Sch
  PO21 .... 195 A3
Nyewood Gdns **2** PO21 . 195 B3
Nyewood La PO21 .... 195 B3
Nyewood Pl PO21 .... 195 B2
Nymans Cl RH17 .... 37 A7
Nymans Cotts RH17 .... 61 C7
Nymans Ct RH10 .... 19 B3
Nymans (NT) RH17 .... 61 D7
Nyton Rd PO20 .... 175 C8

Oak Ave Chichester PO19 . 172 E7
  Heath Common RH20 ...... 120 B3
Oak Bank RH6 .... 85 F7
Oak Cl Bognor Regis PO22 . 195 C6
  Brighton BN1 .... 167 E3
  Chichester PO19 .... 172 E7
  Worthing BN14 .... 183 A4
Oakleigh Ct
  2 Bognor Regis PO21 .. 195 B2
  Southwater RH13 .... 80 A7
  Worthing BN14 .... 183 A4
Oakleigh Rd Horsham RH12 . 36 F4
  Worthing BN11, BN14 ..... 183 A4
Oakley Cl RH19 .... 23 B7
Oakley Cres RH17 .... 64 F1
Oakley Ct RH19 .... 23 B7
Oakley Gdns BN16 .... 200 A5
Oakleys Way PO09 .... 173 A7
Oakmead RH15 .... 106 F1
Oakmeadow Cl PO10 ...... 149 C3
Oakmeeds Com Sch
  RH15 .... 107 A2
Oaks Cl Horsham RH12 ..... 37 B6
  Westergate PO20 .... 175 D6
Oaks The
  Burgess Hill BN6 .... 106 C4
  East Grinstead RH19 .... 23 B8
  Haywards Heath RH16 ..... 86 A4
  Haywards Heath RH16 ..... 86 C4
  Rustington BN16 .... 199 E5
  Small Dole BN5 .... 144 E6
  Southwater RH13 .... 57 F2
Oakside Ct RH6 .... 2 C4
Oakside La RH6 .... 2 C4
Oaktree Cotts BN18 .... 176 C8
Oakway RH13 .... 59 C6
Oakwood
  Haywards Heath RH16 ..... 85 D4
  Partridge Green RH13 ..... 103 A3

Oak Way RH10 .... 18 E8
Oak Wlk RH12 .... 16 F1
Oakapple Cl Cowfold RH13 . 81 E1
  Crawley RH11 .... 18 B1
Oakapple Rd BN42 .... 165 E1
Oakcroft Gdns BN17 .... 178 F3
Oakdale Rd **6** RH16 ...... 85 F3
Oakdene Brighton BN2 .... 168 F4
  7 Haywards Heath RH16 . 85 D5
Oakdene Ave BN41 .... 165 E3
Oakdene Cl BN41 .... 165 E3
Oakdene Cres BN41 .... 165 E3
Oakdene Gdns BN41 .... 165 E3
Oakdene Rise BN41 .... 165 E4
Oakdene Way BN41 .... 165 E4
Oakenden RH13 .... 82 B1
Oakenfield RH15 .... 107 A5
Oakfield Lodsworth GU28 . 72 B3
  Plaistow RH14 .... 30 E2
Oakfield Ave PO20 .... 201 F7
Oakfield Cl RH16 .... 86 A7
Oakfield Cty Mid Sch
  BN15 .... 183 E7
Oakfield Rd Cowfold RH13 . 81 F1
  East Wittering PO20 ...... 201 F7
Oakfield Way RH19 .... 9 F3
Oakfields Crawley RH10 ... 19 D7
  Wallis Wood RH5 .... 13 D8
Oakhaven RH10, RH11 ..... 18 D4
Oakhill Rd BN43 .... 81 E1
Oakhurst RH13 .... 36 E2
Oakhurst
  Haywards Heath RH16 ..... 85 D8
  Henfield BN5 .... 123 F6
  Midhurst GU29 .... 92 D7
  Sayers Common BN6 ...... 105 D2
Oakhurst Gdns
  East Grinstead RH19 .... 9 C2
  Rustington BN16 .... 199 E6
Oakhurst La
  Haywards Heath RH16 ..... 85 D8
  Loxwood RH14 .... 31 E7
Oakhurst Mews RH13 .... 37 B4
Oakland Ct
  Bognor Regis PO22 .... 196 A4
  Bognor Regis, Nyetimber
  PO21 .... 194 A1
  7 Littlehampton BN17 . 198 E4
  5 Shoreham-by-Sea
  BN43 .... 184 F7
  Worthing, Goring-by-Sea
  BN12 .... 181 A1
  2 Worthing, West Worthing
  BN11 .... 182 C2
Oaklands Ardingly RH17 ... 44 B8
  Billingshurst RH14 .... 77 D7
  Haslemere GU27 .... 27 C7
  Horley RH6 .... 2 C3
  Horsham RH13 .... 36 E2
  2 Lancing BN15 .... 183 F5
Oaklands Bsns Ctr BN11 . 181 F3
Oaklands Ct PO19 .... 172 F8
Oaklands La GU29 .... 92 F5
Oaklands Rd RH16 .... 85 D5
Oaklands Way PO09 .... 173 A7
Oakleigh Annexe (Queen
  Victoria Hospl) RH19 ...... 23 C7
Oakleigh Cl BN11 .... 183 A4

Oakwood Cl
  Burgess Hill RH15 .... 107 B2
  Midhurst GU29 .... 92 E7
  Tangmere PO20 .... 154 D2
Oakwood Ct GU28 .... 95 E7
Oakwood Gdns PO21 ...... 195 C4
Oakwood Ind Pk RH10 ..... 6 A2
Oakwood Pk RH18 .... 23 F2
Oakwood Rd
  Burgess Hill RH15 .... 107 B2
  Haywards Heath RH16 .... 85 D4
  Horley RH6 .... 2 B4
Oakwood Sch
  East Ashling PO18 .... 151 F2
  Horley RH6 .... 2 C3
Oates Wlk RH10 .... 18 F3
Oathall Ave RH16 .... 85 F6
Oathall Com Coll RH16 .... 85 F6
Oathall Rd RH16 .... 85 E5
Oatlands Crawley RH11 ... 18 A5
  Horley RH6 .... 2 C4
Oberon Way RH11 .... 17 E3
Ocean Cl BN12 .... 200 E4
Ocean Dr BN12 .... 200 E4
Ocean Par BN12 .... 200 E4
Ockenden La RH17 .... 84 E6
Ockenden Way BN6 .... 126 E3
Ockley Cl PO21 .... 195 C3
Ockley Hill BN6, RH15 ..... 127 B6
Ockley La
  Burgess Hill RH15 .... 127 B7
  Keymer BN6 .... 127 B7
Ockley Rd PO21 .... 195 C3
Ockley Way BN6 .... 127 A5
Octagon The BN2 .... 188 F3
Offington Ave BN13, BN14 . 182 B6
Offington Cnr BN13 .... 182 A8
Offington Ct BN14 .... 182 C6
Offington Dr BN14 .... 182 B7
Offington Gdns BN14 ..... 182 A6
Offington La BN13, BN14 . 182 A7
Okehurst La RH14 .... 55 D4
Okehurst Rd RH14 .... 55 A6
Old Barn Ct RH16 .... 85 D2
Old Barn Way BN42 .... 186 A7
Old Boat Cnr BN1 .... 168 C7
Old Boat Wlk BN1 .... 168 B7
Old Bridge Rd PO18 .... 171 C7
Old Bridge St PO18 .... 171 C7
Old Brighton Rd N RH11 ... 39 C7
Old Brighton Rd S
  Crawley RH11, RH6 .... 5 E5
  Pease Pottage RH11 .... 39 B6
Old Broyle Rd PO19 .... 152 D2
Old Buddington La GU29 ... 70 E3
Old Church Ho The PO21 . 195 A6
Old Coastguard Cotts
  PO20 .... 206 C7
Old Coastguards PO22 ... 195 F3
Old Control Rd RH6 .... 5 D6
Old Convent The RH19 ...... 9 E2
Old Cottage Cl PO20 ...... 154 C1
Old Cotts BN1 .... 161 E7
Old Court Cl BN1 .... 167 F4
Old Crawley Rd RH12 .... 37 C7
Old Denne Gdns RH12 ..... 36 C1
Old Farm Cl PO21 .... 194 D2
Old Farm Ct BN15 .... 184 C6
Old Farm La PO10 .... 149 E3
Old Farm Rd BN1 .... 167 F5
Old Fort Rd BN43 .... 185 B6
Old Glebe GU27 .... 49 B6
Old Granary The PO18 .... 154 D4
Old Guildford Rd RH12 .... 35 E4
Old Haslemere Rd GU27 .. 27 C5
Old Holbrook Faygate RH12 . 15 F2
  Horsham RH12 .... 36 E7
Old Horsham Rd RH11 ..... 18 B4
Old London Rd
  Brighton BN1 .... 167 E6
  Coldwaltham RH20 .... 117 D6
  Washington RH20 .... 141 E8
Old Manor Cl RH11 .... 18 A8
Old Manor House Gdns
  PO22 .... 196 B5
Old Manor Rd BN16 .... 199 B6
Old Market Ave **9** PO19 . 173 A6
Old Market Sq BN44 ...... 143 E3
Old Martyrs RH11 .... 5 D1
Old Mead Rd BN17 .... 178 C5
Old Mill Cl Brighton BN1 .. 167 E5
  Southwick BN41 .... 186 A7
Old Mill Dr PO20 .... 191 D5
Old Mill Rd PO20 .... 98 D1
Old Mill Sq PO20 .... 119 D1
Old Mill The PO19 .... 173 A7
Old Millmeads RH12 .... 36 C5
Old Museum Ct GU27 ..... 27 D6
Old Orchards RH10 .... 19 E6
Old Park Cl RH17 .... 85 A6
Old Park La PO18 .... 171 E5

Old – Pat 233

Old Patcham Mews BN1 167 E6
Old Pl PO21 194 E3
Old Point PO22 196 E4
Old Quarry The GU27 26 F4
Old Rd RH19 9 F1
Old Rectory Cl PO10 149 D3
Old Rectory Dr PO20 175 E7
Old Rectory Flats PO22 196 A4
Old Rectory Gdns
Bognor Regis PO22 196 A4
Southwick BN43 185 D8
Old Rectory The PO22 196 A4
Old Salts Farm Rd BN15 184 A5
Old School Cl PO20 191 E4
Old School Mews PO22 196 A5
Old School Pl RH15 106 F2
Old School Rd GU33 45 B4
Old School The RH20 97 A2
Old Shoreham Rd
North Lancing BN15 184 A8
Portslade-by-Sea
BN1, BN3, BN41, BN42 186 C8
Shoreham-by-Sea BN43 184 E8
Old Stables The PO22 195 F4
Old Station Cl RH10 21 B7
Old Steine BN1, BN2 207 A5
Old Thorns Golf Course
GU30 24 D3
Old Viaduct Ct 6 BN2 188 C8
Old Wickham La RH16 85 E7
Old Wickhurst La RH12 35 D2
Old Worthing Rd BN16 180 B3
Older Way BN16 179 F6
Oldfield Cres BN42 185 E8
Oldfield Rd RH6 1 F1
Oldhouse La
Balls Green RH14 78 B3
Broadford Bridge
RH14, RH20 100 A7
Sidlesham PO20 203 C7
West Marden PO18, PO9 130 A6
Oldlands Ave
Balcombe RH17 41 A1
Keymer BN6 127 A4
Oldlands Way PO22 195 E7
Oldwick Meadows PO18 152 F5
Olive Rd BN3 186 D8
Oliver Cl BN2 188 C5
Oliver Ho BN3 187 B5
Oliver Rd RH12 36 A1
Oliver Whitby Rd PO19 172 E7
Olivers Meadow PO20 175 D7
Olivier Ct PO21 195 A6
Olivier Rd RH10 19 D5
Onslow Ct 7 BN11 183 B3
Onslow Dr BN12 200 E6
Onslow Rd BN3 167 C2
Ontario Cl BN13 181 C6
Ontario Gdns BN13 181 C6
Open Mkt The BN1 207 A7
Ophir Rd BN11 183 A3
Orange Row Brighton BN1 207 A5
Emsworth PO10 169 B8
Orchard Ave
Chichester PO19 172 F7
Hove BN3 167 A1
Lancing BN15 183 E7
Selsey PO20 206 E6
Worthing BN14 182 B5
Orchard Bsns Ctr The RH1 2 A8
Orchard Cl
Bognor Regis PO21 195 B3
East Harting GU31 90 A4
Elsted GU29 90 D4
Ferring BN12 180 E3
Haywards Heath RH16 85 D8
Horley RH6 1 F4
Petworth GU28 95 F7
Scaynes Hill RH17 86 F3
Shoreham-by-Sea BN43 184 E8
Small Dole BN5 144 F6
Southwick BN42 185 F8
Worthing BN14 182 B5
Orchard Cnr RH16 86 B5
Orchard Cott RH17 84 F6
Orchard Cotts
Charlwood RH6 4 F7
Fishbourne PO18 172 A8
Woodgate PO20 175 D5
Orchard Cres BN18 156 A3
Orchard Dell RH20 99 E2
Orchard Gdns
Chichester PO19 172 F7
Hove BN3 167 B1
Rustington BN16 199 D6
Woodgate PO20 175 D5
Orchard Hill RH12 33 C7
Orchard Ho BN15 183 E6
Orchard La Ditchling BN6 127 D4
Hassocks BN6 126 F4
Hermitage PO10 169 D8
Orchard Par PO20 206 F8
Orchard Pl BN18 158 B3
Orchard Rd
Burgess Hill RH15 106 E3
East Preston BN16 200 A6
Horsham RH13 36 E2
Hove BN3 167 B1
West Itchenor PO20 191 A7
Orchard Side PO20 193 A8
Orchard St
Chichester PO19 172 F7
Crawley RH11 18 D6
Orchard The
Bognor Regis PO21 194 C1
Haslemere GU27 26 F5
Hassocks BN6 126 F3
Orchard Way
Barnham PO22 176 B6
Bognor Regis PO22 195 C5
Bolney RH17 83 D8
Burgess Hill RH15 106 F3
East Grinstead RH19 9 E1
Fontwell BN18 156 A3
Haywards Heath RH16 85 D8
Hurstpierpoint BN6 125 F6
Lancing BN15 183 E7
Midhurst GU29 92 F8
Pulborough RH20 98 C3
Orchards The
Brighton BN2 168 E3
4 Crawley RH11 17 D5
11 Haywards Heath RH16 85 E4
Horsham RH12 36 F5
Orchid Pk RH16 86 C4
Orchid View BN1 168 C6
Orde Cl RH10 6 D1
Oriel Cl Crawley RH10 6 C1
West Barnham PO22 176 B6
Orient Rd BN15 184 C5
Oriental Pl BN1 187 E5
Orion Ct RH11 17 D4
Orion Par BN6 126 F3
Orkney Ct BN13 181 B5
Orltons La RH12 3 F2
Orme Cotts BN16 179 F6
Orme Rd BN11 182 C3
Ormerod Ct 5 RH16 85 E5
Ormesby Cres PO22 196 A6
Ormesby Wlk RH10 19 B4
Ormonde Ave PO19 173 B6
Ormonde Way BN43 184 D6
Orpen Pl PO20 206 F7
Orpen Rd BN3 167 D1
Osborn Cres PO19 153 A1
Osborne Cl BN15 183 C6
Osborne Cres PO19 173 D6
Osborne Ct Crawley RH11 18 B2
7 Shoreham-by-Sea
BN43 185 C8
Osborne Dr BN15 183 C6
Osborne Rd BN1 168 A2
Osborne Villas BN3 187 B6
Osmond Rd BN3 187 E7
Osmonde Cl BN14 182 C4
Osmund Cl RH10 19 E6
Osmunda Bank RH19 9 E6
Osney Cl RH11 18 C5
Osprey Cl BN17 178 D4
Osprey Gdns PO22 195 C7
Osprey Ho 8 BN1 187 E5
Osprey Quay PO10 169 C7
Ostlers View RH14 77 C7
Otard Cl PO20 206 E7
Otford Cl RH11 39 C8
Ottafield Ct RH16 85 F6
Otter Cl PO19 172 E8
Otway Cl RH11 17 F4
Otway Rd PO19 153 A2
Oulton Wlk RH10 19 B4
Our Lady of Sion RC
Jun Sch BN11 182 D2
Our Lady of Sion Sch
BN11 182 C2
Our Lady Queen of Heaven
RC (A) Prim Sch RH11 18 B8
Outerwyke Ave PO22 196 A6
Outerwyke Gdns PO22 196 B6
Outerwyke Rd PO22 196 A6
Outram Ho PO22 195 F3
Outram Rd PO22 195 F3
Oval La PO20 206 E5
Oval The Findon BN14 161 E7
Liss GU33 45 B4
Worthing BN13 182 A5
Oval Waye BN12 200 E4
Over St BN1 207 A6
Overdene Dr RH11 18 A6
Overdown Rd PO22 196 B5
Overdown Rise BN41 165 F4
Overhill BN42 165 E1
Overhill Dr BN1 167 E5
Overhill Gdns BN1 167 E5
Overhill Way BN1 167 E6
Overmead BN43 184 E8
Overstrand Ave BN16 199 C4
Overton Rd PO10 150 A1
Overton Shaw RH19 9 E4
Oving Ct PO19 173 C6
Oving Rd Chichester PO19 173 C6
Oving PO20 174 B7
Oving Terr PO19 173 C6
Owen Cl RH15 106 F1
Owers Way PO20 201 E7
Owlbeech Ct RH13 37 B4
Owlbeech Pl RH13 37 B4
Owlbeech Way RH13 37 B4
Owletts RH10 19 D7
Owlscastle Cl RH12 36 D5
Oxen Ave BN43 184 F8
Oxen Ct BN43 184 F8
Oxford Cl PO20 201 F7
Oxford Ct Brighton BN1 207 A7
5 Midhurst GU29 92 E7
Oxford Dr PO21 194 F3
Oxford Mews BN3 187 C7
Oxford Pl BN1 207 A7
Oxford Rd Crawley RH10 18 F2
Horsham RH13 36 E2
Worthing BN11 182 C3
Oxford St
Bognor Regis PO21 195 B2
Brighton BN1, BN2 207 A7
Oxford Terr BN44 143 D3

Pacific Ct 3 BN43 184 F6
Packer Cl RH19 10 A3
Packham Way RH15 106 F4
Paddock Cl GU27 49 B5
Paddock Ct BN41 165 F3
Paddock Gdns RH19 22 E7
Paddock Gn BN16 199 E6
Paddock La PO20 206 D8
Paddock The
Bognor Regis PO22 195 C5
Crawley RH10 19 D7
Haslemere GU27 27 A8
Hove BN3 167 C1
Littlehampton BN17 178 C6
Shoreham-by-Sea BN43 164 D1
Paddock Way
Findon BN14 161 E6
Liphook GU30 25 C5
Paddockhall Rd RH16 85 D5
Paddockhurst La RH17 41 D3
Paddockhurst Rd
Crawley RH11 18 A5
Turners Hill RH10 20 C2
Paddocks PO22 176 B6
Paddocks The
Lancing BN15 183 F5
Upper Beeding BN44 144 B3
Padstow Wlk RH11 17 F4
Padwick Rd RH13 37 A2
Page Ct RH13 36 D1
Pages Cnr BN11 183 A3
Pages La BN11 183 A4
Paget Cl RH13 58 E8
Pagham Cl PO10 169 C8
Pagham Gdns PO11 189 B2
Pagham Harbour
Nature Reserve
PO20,PO21 204 C6
Pagham Ho BN17 178 B3
Pagham Rd
Bognor Regis
PO20, PO21 194 A3
Runcton PO20 173 E1
Pain's Flat RH15, RH17 106 D8
Palace Pl BN1 207 A5
Palace Yd PO19 172 F6
Palatine Rd BN12, BN13 181 D4
Palings Way GU27 49 A5
Pallant The BN12 181 B4
Pallingham Dr RH10 19 C3
Pallingham La RH14 75 F2
Palm Court Cotts BN16 200 A4
Palm Ct BN13 181 E7
Palmeira Ave BN3 187 D6
Palmeira Ct 20 BN3 187 C6
Palmeira Ho 6 BN3 187 D7
Palmeira Mansions 18
BN3 187 C6
Palmeira Pl BN3 187 D7
Palmeira Sq BN3 187 C6
Palmer Cl Horley RH6 1 F5
Storrington RH20 119 F2
Palmer Pl PO20 173 D1
Palmer Rd
Angmering BN16 179 F7
Crawley RH10 19 C3
Palmer's Rd PO10 149 B1
Palmers Way BN13 161 D1
Palmerston Ave BN12 181 C2
Pangdean La BN6 106 C4
Pangdene Cl RH15 106 F1
Pankhurst Ave BN2 188 D6
Pankhurst Ct 11 RH11 18 B1
Pannell Cl RH19 9 D1
Pannett RH15 106 E4
Pantiles The BN12 200 E5
Panton Cl PO10 149 A3
Parade Mansions BN16 200 A4
Parade The
Bognor Regis PO21 205 A7
East Wittering PO20 201 F7
Hove BN3 166 E2
West Kingston BN16 200 A4
Paradise La PO10 149 D4
Parchment St PO19 172 F7
Parham Cl Brighton BN2 188 D5
Littlehampton, Rustington
BN16 199 B4
Littlehampton, Wick BN17 198 D6
Worthing BN14 161 F1
Parham Ct 3 BN11 182 A2
Parham Ho RH20 118 D1
Parham Rd Crawley RH11 17 F7
Worthing BN14 161 F1
Parish Ho 6 RH11 18 D5
Parish La RH10 39 E6
Park Ave Hove BN3 186 E7
Keymer BN6 127 A2
Selsey PO20 206 F7
Shoreham-by-Sea BN43 185 A8
Worthing BN11 182 E3
Park Cl Brighton BN1 168 E5
Burgess Hill RH15 106 F4
Hove BN3 166 E3
Hurstpierpoint BN6 126 A6
Portslade-by-Sea BN41 166 B1
Worthing BN14 182 A7
Park Copse PO20 204 C1
Park Cotts BN6 125 F6
Park Cres Brighton BN2 207 B7
Emsworth PO10 149 A1
Midhurst GU29 92 E8
Portslade-by-Sea BN41 186 A8
Selsey PO20 206 G8
Worthing BN11 182 C2
Park Crescent Pl BN2 207 B7
Park Crescent Rd BN2 207 B7
Park Crescent Terr BN2 207 B7
Park Ct
Brighton, Patcham BN1 167 E6
Brighton, Preston BN1 167 F1
Burgess Hill RH15 107 A3
4 Haywards Heath RH16 85 E4
Park Dr Bognor Regis
PO22 196 D5
Burndell BN18 177 A2
Ferring BN12 200 F6
Rustington BN16 199 D6
Park Farm Cl RH12 36 D7
Park Farm Rd RH12 36 D7
Park Gate BN3 187 D6
Park Hill BN2 207 B5
Park Ho 3 BN11 183 B3
Park La Aldingbourne PO20 175 B7
Aldsworth PO10, PO18 149 E8
Ashurst Wood RH19 23 D6
Bosham PO18 171 D2
East Beach PO20 204 A1
Fernhurst GU27 49 B6
Halnaker PO18 154 D5
Haywards Heath RH16 64 D2
Maplehurst RH13 81 B6
Slindon BN18 156 C4
Southwick BN42, BN43 185 D7
Warminghurst RH20 120 D5
West Grinstead RH13 102 D8
Park Lodge BN3 187 D8
Park Manor BN1 167 D4
Park Pl Arundel BN18 158 A3
Horsham RH12 36 C1
Park Rd Barnham PO22 176 D6
Breach PO10 149 F1
Brighton BN1 168 E5
Burgess Hill RH15 107 A3
Burndell BN18 177 A2
Dormans Park RH19 9 F6
East Grinstead RH19 9 D1
Faygate RH12 16 F1
Forest Row RH18 23 F2
Goodwood Park PO18 153 F8
Handcross RH17 61 B6
Haslemere GU27 27 C5
Haywards Heath RH16 85 E4
Henfield BN5 123 E4
Petworth GU28 95 F8
Selsey PO20 206 G8
Shoreham-by-Sea BN43 185 A8
Slinfold RH13 34 D3
Worthing BN11 182 E3
Park Rise Horsham RH12 36 B4
Hove BN3 166 E3
Petworth GU28 95 E7
Park Road Terr 4 BN2 207 B5
Park Royal BN1 187 E6
Park St Brighton BN2 207 B5
Horsham RH12 36 D2
Park Street RH13 34 C3
Park Terr
Bognor Regis PO21 195 B2
Tillington GU28 73 C1
Park Terr E RH13 36 D1
Park Terr W RH13 36 D1
Park View Brighton BN1 187 E8
Brighton BN2 188 C6
Haywards Heath RH16 85 E6
Park View Horley RH6 2 A3
Park View Ct BN16 199 C6
Park View Rd BN3 167 B1
Park View Terr BN1 187 E8
Park Way Crawley RH10 19 C7
Easebourne GU29 71 B2
Horsham RH12 36 C2
Southwick BN42 185 F8
Park Way Cl BN42 185 F8
Parker Cl RH10 19 D5
Parker Ct BN41 166 B2
Parker's Cotts PO18 153 A6
Parkers RH13 56 F3
Parkfield RH12 36 C3
Parkfield Ave PO21 194 D3
Parkfield Cl RH11 17 F6
Parkfield Ct BN13 182 A4
Parkfield Rd BN13 182 A4
Parkhurst Gr RH6 1 F4
Parkhurst Rd RH6 1 E4
Parklands BN43 185 C8
Parklands Ave
Bognor Regis PO21 195 B4
Worthing BN12 181 D1
Parklands Ct BN12 181 D2
Parklands Cty Prim Sch
PO19 172 E7
Parklands Rd
Chichester PO19 172 F7
Hassocks BN6 126 F3
Parklawn Ave RH6 1 F5
Parkmead BN2 207 B7
Parkmore Terr BN1 207 F8
Parkside
8 Bognor Regis PO21 195 D4
Burgess Hill RH15 106 F3
Crawley RH10 18 E6
East Grinstead RH19 9 C1
Keymer BN6 127 A4
Shoreham-by-Sea BN43 165 A1
Worthing BN11 182 E3
Parkside Ave BN17 198 F5
Parkside Ct BN17 198 F5
Parkside Mews RH12 36 D2
Parkview BN6 126 A5
Parkway
Bognor Regis PO21 195 A3
Horley RH6 2 A3
Parkway The BN16 199 D5
Parnell Cl RH10 19 D4
Parry Dr BN16 199 B5
Parson's Hill BN18 158 B3
Parsonage Bsns Pk RH12 36 E4
Parsonage Est GU31 68 B4
Parsonage Rd
Henfield BN5 123 E6
Horsham RH12, RH13 36 E4
Parsonage Way RH12 36 E4
Parsons Cl Haslemere GU27 27 C8
Horley RH6 1 E4
Parsons Gn GU27 27 C8
Parsons Wlk Horsham RH12 57 F8
Walberton BN18 176 E8
Parthings La RH12, RH13 57 F8
Pascoe Ct 2 PO19 172 F7
Pashley Ct 10 BN43 184 F7
Passfield Ent Ctr GU30 24 D8
Passfield Rd GU30 24 E8
Paston Pl BN2 188 D4
Pasture Hill Rd RH16 85 D6
Pasture The RH10 19 C6
Patcham By-Pass BN1 167 E6
Patcham Cty Inf Sch BN1 167 E6
Patcham Cty Jun Sch BN1 167 F6
Patcham High Sch BN1 167 F6
Patcham House Sch BN1 167 E6
Patchdean BN1 167 F5
Patching Cl Crawley RH11 17 F7
Worthing BN12 181 B4
Patching Lodge 5 BN2 188 C5
Patchings RH13 36 F3
Paterson Wilson Rd BN17 198 E6

Path Link RH10 .... 18 E7
Pathfield CI RH12 .... 33 D7
Pathfield Rd RH12 .... 33 D7
Pathfields CI GU27 .... 27 D7
Patnore PO18 .... 152 E7
Patricia Ave BN12 .... 181 D1
Patricia CI BN12 .... 181 D1
Patrick's CI GU33 .... 45 C4
Patrick's Copse Rd GU33 ... 45 C4
Patrington CI RH11 .... 18 A3
Patterdale CI RH11 .... 18 C4
Paulus Ct **1** PO19 .... 172 F7
Pavilion Bldgs BN1 .... 207 A5
Pavilion CI BN6 .... 126 E5
Pavilion Ct **11** BN1 .... 187 E7
Pavilion Par BN2 .... 207 A5
Pavilion Rd BN14 .... 182 B3
Pavilion Ret Pk BN2 .... 168 C1
Pavilion St BN2 .... 207 A5
Pavilion Way RH19 .... 22 E8
Pax CI RH11 .... 17 E4
Paxhill Park Golf Course
RH16 .... 86 E8
Paxmead Cres BN14 .... 182 F6
Payne Ave BN3 .... 186 F8
Payne CI
Bognor Regis PO21 .... 205 A8
Crawley RH10 .... 19 D8
Payne Terr BN1 .... 168 B1
Paynesfield RH17 .... 83 C3
Paythorne CI BN42 .... 165 D1
Paythorne Dro BN5 .... 145 D4
Payton Dr RH15 .... 106 E2
Payton Ho RH15 .... 107 D3
Peace CI BN1 .... 168 C1
Peacemaker CI RH11 .... 17 E4
Peacheries The PO19 .... 173 C5
Peachey Rd PO20 .... 206 D6
Peacock End Est BN3 ...... 187 D7
Peacock La BN1 .... 167 E4
Peacock Wlk **8** RH11 ... 18 A3
Peacock's Hill RH13 .... 81 D6
Peacocks La RH20 .... 100 C1
Peak La BN16 .... 200 C4
Peak The PO9 .... 128 E2
Pear Tree Hill RH1 .... 2 A8
Pearson Rd Arundel BN18 . 157 F2
Crawley RH10 .... 19 C6
Pearsons Retreat BN11 .... 183 B3
Peartree CI RH15 .... 106 E3
Peartree Cnr RH13 .... 81 C2
Peary CI RH12 .... 36 D6
Pease Croft GU31 .... 89 D3
Pease Pottage Service Area
RH10 .... 39 C5
Pebble Ct PO22 .... 195 C5
Pebble Wlk BN16 .... 179 A3
Peckhams Copse La PO20 173 D3
Peeks Brook La Fernhill RH6 .. 6 E7
Horley RH6 .... 2 F2
Peel CI BN17 .... 198 C6
Peel Ctr The PO22 .... 195 D7
Peel Rd BN2 .... 188 F4
Peerley Rd PO20 .... 202 A6
Peerley Rd PO20 .... 202 A6
Pegasus CI GU27 .... 26 D5
Pegasus Ct RH11 .... 17 E4
Pegasus Way RH19 .... 10 B3
Pegwell CI RH11 .... 17 F4
Pelham Ct Crawley RH11 .. 18 B2
Horsham RH12 .... 36 B2
2 Worthing BN13 .... 182 A5
Pelham Dr RH11 .... 18 A2
Pelham PI RH11 .... 18 B2
Pelham Place Cotts RH16 . 86 A7
Pelham Rd
Haywards Heath RH16 ..... 86 A6
Worthing BN13 .... 182 A5
Pelham Sq BN1 .... 207 A6
Pelham Terr
Brighton BN2 .... 168 C1
Lumley PO10 .... 169 C8
Pelleys La PO19 .... 172 F1
Pemberton CI BN15 .... 183 E7
Pembley Gn RH10 .... 7 E3
Pembroke Ave Hove BN3 . 187 A7
Worthing BN11 .... 181 F2
Pembroke Cres BN3 .... 187 A7
Pembroke Ct **2** BN3 .... 187 A6
Pembroke Gdns BN3 .... 187 A6
Pembroke Rd RH10 .... 6 C1
Pembroke Way PO21 .... 194 E4
Pembury CI
Haywards Heath RH16 .... 86 B3
Worthing BN14 .... 182 D4
Pembury Rd BN14 .... 182 D4
Pempeys Terr BN44 .... 143 C4

Penarth Gdns BN17 .... 178 D5
Pende CI BN15 .... 183 D8
Pendean RH15 .... 107 C1
Pendine Ave BN11 .... 183 A3
Pendragon Ct BN3 .... 187 A8
Penfold La BN16 .... 179 C3
Penfold Rd Crawley RH10 .. 19 B2
Worthing BN14 .... 182 E5
Penfolds Way BN44 .... 143 D2
Penfolds PI BN18 .... 158 A2
Penhill Rd BN15 .... 183 E5
Penhurst Ct
Worthing BN13 .... 181 B5
Worthing, Broadwater
BN14 .... 182 C6
Penhurst PI BN2 .... 188 F6
Penland CI RH16 .... 85 D7
Penland La BN44 .... 123 C2
Penland Rd RH16, RH17 .. 85 D7
Penland's Dr BN44 .... 123 C2
Penlands Rise BN44 .... 143 C2
Penlands Vale BN44 .... 143 C2
Penlands Way BN44 .... 143 C2
Penleigh CI BN15 .... 183 F5
Penn CI Crawley RH11 ...... 5 D1
Middleton-on-Sea PO22 .. 196 E5
Penn Cres RH16 .... 86 A5
Penn Gdns RH20 .... 120 E5
Pennells CI GU30 .... 47 B2
Pennine CI RH11 .... 18 B6
Pennington Ho RH16 ...... 86 A3
Penns Ct BN44 .... 143 C4
Penny La PO10 .... 169 D8
Pennycress Ave
BN12, BN13 .... 181 A5
Pennyfields PO22 .... 196 C5
Penrith CI BN14 .... 182 D5
Pensfold La RH12, RH13 .. 33 E5
Penshurst CI RH10 .... 19 D7
Penstone CI BN15 .... 183 F5
Penstone CI **4** BN43 .. 185 C8
Penstone Pk BN15 .... 183 E6
Penthorpe Sch RH12 ...... 33 C7
Pentland Rd BN13 .... 181 E8
Penwarden Way PO18 .... 171 C7
Penwith Dr GU27 .... 26 E5
Peperham Ho GU27 .... 27 C7
Peperham Rd GU27 .... 27 C8
Pepper Ct BN17 .... 198 C5
Pepper Dr RH15 .... 106 F1
Pepper's La BN44 .... 122 C5
Peppering La BN18 .... 159 A7
Pepperscoombe La BN44 144 B2
Perche CI GU27 .... 92 D6
Perching Dro BN5 .... 145 E4
Percival Terr **14** BN2 .. 188 D4
Percy Rd BN2 .... 36 B3
Percy Row GU28 .... 95 F8
Peregrine Rd BN17 .... 198 F6
Perimeter Rd E RH6 .... 6 B6
Perimeter Rd N RH6 .... 5 D7
Perimeter Rd S RH6 .... 5 E5
Perkstead Ct **6** RH11 .. 18 A3
Perrots La BN44 .... 143 C2
Perry Ave RH19 .... 9 E3
Perryfield Ho **7** RH11 . 18 D5
Perryfield La RH13 .... 82 C6
Perryfield Rd RH11 .... 18 D5
Perryfields RH15 .... 106 E4
Perrylands RH6 .... 4 F7
Perrylands La RH6 .... 2 F2
Perryman's La RH17 .... 66 D3
Perrymount Rd RH16 ..... 85 E5
Perth CI RH11 .... 5 D1
Perth Ho GU29 .... 92 E6
Perth Way RH12 .... 36 F4
Pescott's CI PO20 .... 191 E5
Peskett CI RH13 .... 56 F3
Peter Gladwin Cty Prim Sch
BN1 .... 166 B2
Peter Rd BN15 .... 183 C4
Peter Weston PI PO19 .... 173 B6
Peter's La PO20 .... 206 A8
Peter's PI PO20 .... 206 A8
Peterborough Rd RH10 ... 18 E2
Peterhouse CI PO21 .... 194 F4
Peterhouse Par RH10 .... 6 C1
Peterlee Wlk RH11 .... 17 E2
Petersfield Rd GU29 .... 92 E8
Petlands Gdns **4** RH16 . 85 F3
Petlands Rd RH16 .... 85 E3
Pett CI BN2 .... 188 F6
Petworth Ave BN12 .... 181 C1
Petworth CE (C) Prim Sch
GU28 .... 95 F7
Petworth Ct Crawley RH11 . 17 F3
Haslemere GU27 .... 27 D6
5 Rustington BN16 .... 199 B3
Petworth Dr
Burgess Hill RH15 .... 107 A4
Horsham RH12 .... 36 F7

Petworth Pk
GU28 .... 73 D2
Petworth Rd
Ansteadbrook GU27, GU8 .. 28 B6
Brighton BN1 .... 168 B6
Pevensey CI RH10 .... 19 C5
Pevensey Gdn BN11 .... 182 A1
Pevensey Rd
Bognor Regis PO21 .... 195 A4
3 Brighton BN2 .... 188 C8
Southwater RH13 .... 58 A2
Worthing BN11 .... 182 A1
Peverel Rd Crawley RH11 .. 17 E5
Worthing BN13 .... 182 A4
Peveril CI BN15 .... 183 A6
Peveril Dr BN15 .... 183 B6
Pharos Quay BN17 .... 198 C5
Pheasant Cotts PO18 ..... 132 F6
Philip Ct **8** BN3 .... 187 C7
Phillips Bsns Ctr PO19 ... 172 E5
Philliswood La PO18 ...... 110 D3
Philpots Manor Sch RH19 . 42 C5
Phoenix Brewery Halls
BN2 .... 207 B7
Phoenix CI PO19 .... 173 A5
Phoenix Cres BN42 ....-185 D8
Phoenix La RH19 .... 23 E6
Phoenix PI BN2 .... 207 B6
Phoenix Way BN42 .... 185 D8
Phrosso Rd BN11 .... 181 F1
Pickers Gn RH16 .... 86 A8
Picketts La RH1 .... 2 C8
Pickhurst La PO20 .... 189 B6
Pickwell La RH17 .... 83 F4
Picton St BN2 .... 188 C7
Picts Hill RH13 .... 58 A7
Picts La RH13 .... 82 A4
Pier Rd BN17 .... 198 D4
Pierpoint CI BN6 .... 125 F6
Pigeonhouse La BN16 .... 199 E4
Piggery Hall La PO20 ..... 190 F1
Piggott Ct RH12 .... 36 E1
Piggott's Bsns Pk
BN1 .... 182 C3
Pike The RH20 .... 141 E7
Pilgrim Ct RH16 .... 86 A5
Pilgrims CI **1** BN14 .... 182 B3
Pilgrims Terr BN13 .... 182 A3
Pilgrims Way PO21 .... 194 B1
Pilgrims Wlk BN13 .... 182 A3
Pilot Ho **1** BN2 .... 207 B5
Piltdown Rd BN2 .... 188 F6
Pine CI Billingshurst RH14 . 55 C1
Crawley RH11 .... 5 C1
Heath Common PO20 ..... 120 B3
Midhurst GU29 .... 92 F5
Pine Cotts GU33 .... 45 C7
Pine Ct PO10 .... 149 B4
Pine Gdns RH6 .... 2 A2
Pine Gr Chichester PO19 . 152 C1
East Grinstead RH19 .... 9 B3
Pine Shaw RH10 .... 19 D7
Pine Tree CI BN6 .... 126 B5
Pine Trees BN16 .... 179 F7
Pine Trees St BN6 .... 126 D4
Pine View CI GU27 .... 27 C8
Pine Way CI RH19 .... 22 E7
Pine Wlk
Bognor Regis PO21 .... 194 D4
Liss Forest GU33 .... 45 C6
Pineham Copse RH16 ...... 85 F4
Pinehurst
Burgess Hill RH15 .... 107 A1
Horsham RH12 .... 36 C4
Pinehurst Pk PO21 .... 194 A4
Pines Ave BN14 .... 182 D7
Pines Rd GU30 .... 24 E4
Pines The
Angmering BN16 .... 179 F4
2 Brighton BN2 .... 207 B7
Haywards Heath RH16 ..... 86 B4
Horsham RH12 .... 37 C5
Hove BN3 .... 187 E6
Yapton BN18 .... 176 F3
Pinetrees CI RH10 .... 7 B3
Pinewood **6** BN1 .... 167 E3
Pinewood **4** RH6 .... 85 D6
Pinewood CI RH13 .... 35 A2
Pinewood Ct PO20 .... 191 D3
Pinks La PO20 .... 191 D3
Pinland Rd RH13 .... 102 F1

Pipers CI Hove BN3 .... 166 C3
Southwater RH13 .... 57 F1
Pipers End RH13 .... 34 E3
Pipers La Ebernoe GU28 .. 52 A4
Northchapel GU28 .... 51 A7
Pirles PI RH12 .... 36 C2
Pit Rd BN6 .... 126 A5
Pitcroft La GU31 .... 88 B5
Pitcroft The PO19 .... 173 C8
Pitfold Ave GU27 .... 26 D6
Pitfold Rd GU27 .... 26 D6
Pitfold CI GU27 .... 26 C6
Pitsham La GU29 .... 92 D5
Pitsham Wood GU29 .... 92 D6
Plainfields Ave BN11 ...... 168 A7
Plainwood CI PO19 .... 152 F2
Plaistow CI BN2 .... 188 F6
Plaistow Cty Inf Sch RH14 . 30 F3
Plaistow Rd Ifold RH14 ... 31 D1
Kirdford RH14 .... 53 B5
Plantain Cres RH11 .... 18 A2
Plantation CI BN13 .... 181 F7
Plantation Rd GU33 .... 45 D2
Plantation Rise BN13 ..... 182 A7
Plantation The
East Preston BN16 .... 200 A5
Storrington RH20 .... 119 B1
Worthing BN13, BN14 .... 182 A7
Plantation Way
Storrington RH20 .... 119 C1
Worthing BN13 .... 181 F7
Plat The RH12 .... 36 A3
Platt The
Dormansland RH7 .... 10 A8
Handcross RH17 .... 61 C8
Haywards Heath RH16 .... 86 B5
Plaw Hatch La RH18, RH19 . 43 E5
Playden CI **1** BN2 ...... 188 E4
Playden Ct **3** RH11 .... 18 A3
Pleasant La PO10 .... 169 F1
Plough CI RH11 .... 17 F8
Plough La RH12 .... 36 E5
Plover CI
Bognor Regis PO21 .... 195 C7
Bracklesham PO20 .... 202 A6
Crawley RH11 .... 18 C8
Plovers Rd RH13 .... 36 F3
Plovers The BN15 .... 184 A5
Plumb Pudding Cnr RH20 . 96 D6
Plummerden La RH16 ...... 64 F2
Plumpton Rd BN2 .... 188 D6
Plumtree Cross RH13 ...... 57 A5
Plumtree Cross La RH13 .. 57 A5
Plymouth Ave RH10 .... 168 F1
Polecat La RH13 .... 88 C8
Poles La RH1, RH6 .... 5 C3
Polestub La RH17 .... 84 F7
Poling CI BN12 .... 181 B4
Poling St BN18 .... 179 B7
Pollard Ct BN1 .... 187 A3
Pollard's Hill RH13 .... 80 A6
Pollards RH11 .... 18 A5
Pollards Dr RH13 .... 36 F2
Polperro CI BN12 .... 200 E5
Pomper La BN6 .... 106 A2
Pond CI RH14 .... 31 F4
Pond Copse La RH14 ...... 31 F5
Pond Farm CI RH13 .... 57 F4
Pond Farm La BN13 .... 181 D7
Pond Mews BN13 .... 181 D7
Pond Rd
Bracklesham PO20 .... 202 B6
Shoreham-by-Sea BN43 .. 184 F7
Pond Rise RH20 .... 99 E1
Pond Way RH19 .... 10 B1
Pond Wood Rd RH10 ...... 19 A8
Pondcroft Rd RH16 .... 86 B7
Pondfield Rd RH12 .... 33 D8
Pondtail CI RH12 .... 36 D6
Pondtail Dr RH12 .... 36 D7
Pondtail Rd RH12 .... 36 D6
Pony Farm BN14 .... 161 F6
Pook La PO18 .... 153 A5
Pookbourne La BN6, RH17 105 E4
Pool Valley BN2 .... 207 A4
Popes Mead GU27 .... 27 C7
Poplar Ave RH6 .... 166 E3
Poplar CI Brighton BN1 .. 167 F2
Crawley RH11 .... 5 C1
Hove BN3 .... 166 E3
Poplar Ct RH20 .... 98 A2
Poplar Rd BN13 .... 181 C5
Poplar Way GU29 .... 92 E5
Poplars The
Burndell BN18 .... 177 A3
Ferring BN12 .... 200 E4
Horsham RH13 .... 36 E3
Keymer BN6 .... 127 A3
Poppy CI RH13 .... 58 A3
Porchester CI RH13 .... 58 A2
Port Hall Ave BN1 .... 187 E8
Port Hall Mews BN1 .... 187 E8

Port Hall PI BN1 .... 187 E8
Port Hall Rd BN1 .... 187 E8
Port Hall St BN1 .... 187 E8
Portfield Ave BN1 .... 168 A6
Portfield Ret Pk PO19 .... 173 D7
Portfield Way
PO19, PO20 .... 173 D8
Portland Ave BN3 .... 186 E7
Portland CI BN16 .... 199 A6
Portland Gate BN1 .... 186 E7
Portland CI RH19 .... 22 F8
Portland PI **18** BN2 ... 188 C4
Portland Rd
Burgess Hill RH15 .... 106 F3
Portland Rd
East Grinstead RH19 ...... 22 F8
Hove BN3 .... 186 E7
Worthing BN11 .... 182 D2
Portland Road Trad Est
BN3 .... 186 D8
Portland Sq GU33 .... 45 B4
Portland St BN1 .... 207 F5
Portland Villas BN3 .... 186 D7
Portside BN42 .... 186 F3
Portside Com Coll
(Lower) BN41 .... 166 A3
Portside Com Coll
(Sixth Form) BN41 .... 166 A1
Portslade Cty Inf Sch
BN41 .... 186 B8
Portslade Sta BN3 .... 186 B8
Portslade La RH16 .... 85 F8
Portsmouth Rd
Bramshott GU30 .... 25 E6
Liphook GU30 .... 25 B2
Portsmouth Wood RH16 .. 85 F8
Portsmouth Wood CI
RH16 .... 85 F8
Portway BN44 .... 143 C2
Post Office La PO20 .... 173 C1
Post View RH20 .... 140 E8
Potters CI BN13 .... 36 E2
Potters Field GU33 .... 45 C4
Potters Gn RH13 .... 81 E2
Potters La RH15 .... 106 F1
Potters Mead BN17 .... 178 C3
Pottersfield RH10 .... 18 D7
Pottingfield La PO18 ..... 170 D8
Poulner CI PO22 .... 196 A5
Poulter's Cnr BN13 .... 182 A6
Poulter's La BN13, BN14 . 182 B6
Pound CI Loxwood RH14 .. 31 F5
Petworth GU28 .... 95 F7
Pound Cnr RH13 .... 101 D7
Pound Farm Rd PO19 .... 173 C6
Pound Gate BN6 .... 126 D3
Pound Hill Cty Fst &
Mid Schs RH10 .... 19 C7
Pound Hill Par RH10 ...... 19 C7
Pound Hill PI RH10 .... 19 C6
Pound La
Little Parkminster RH13 .. 103 D8
Mannings Heath RH13 .... 59 C6
Shipley RH13 .... 79 D2
Upper Beeding BN44 ..... 144 B2
Pound Rd
Walberton BN18 .... 156 D1
West Wittering PO20 ..... 190 B2
Pound St GU28 .... 95 F8
Pound The
Bognor Regis PO21 .... 194 E2
Burgess Hill RH15 .... 106 F4
Poundfield La RH14 .... 31 B3
Povey Cross Rd RH6 .... 1 E1
Poveys CI RH11 .... 106 D3
Powell CI RH6 .... 1 E4
Powis Gr BN1 .... 207 F6
Powis Rd BN1 .... 187 E6
Powis Sq BN1 .... 187 E6
Powis Villas BN1 .... 207 F6
Poynes Rd RH6 .... 1 E5
Poynings Crossways
BN45 .... 125 B1
Poynings Dr BN3 .... 166 F3
Poynings Rd RH11 .... 17 E5
Poynter Rd BN3 .... 187 A8
Poyntz CI PO19 .... 172 F3
Pratton Ave BN15 .... 183 D7
Prawn CI PO20 .... 206 C8
Prebendal Sch The PO19 . 172 F6
Precinct The PO21 .... 194 F4
Prescott Gdns RH15 ..... 107 A3
Preston Ave RH16 .... 199 D5
Preston Cir BN1 .... 207 A7
Preston Dro BN1 .... 167 F2
Preston Grange BN1 ...... 167 E1
Preston Manor (Mus) BN1 167 E1
Preston Paddock BN16 .. 199 E5
Preston Park Ave BN1 .... 167 F1
Preston Park Sta BN1 .... 167 D2
Preston Rd BN1 .... 187 F6

Preston BN1 .... 187 E5
Prestonville La 1 BN1 .... 207 F7
Prestonville Rd BN1, BN3 . 207 F7
Prestwick Cl RH11 .... 17 D5
Prestwood Cl RH11 .... 5 B1
Prestwood La
 RH11, RH12, RH6 .... 4 C3
Pretoria Ave GU29 .... 92 E7
Pretoria Rd GU29 .... 92 E7
Price Way RH17 .... 64 B7
Pricehollm RH17 .... 64 B7
Priest Croft Cl RH11 .... 18 A6
Priestley Way Crawley RH10 6 A3
 Middleton-on-Sea PO22 ... 196 D5
Prime Cl BN18 .... 176 E8
Primrose Ave RH6 .... 2 B1
Primrose Cl RH11 .... 18 B3
Primrose Copse RH12 .... 36 E7
Primrose La GU33 .... 45 F4
Prince Albert St BN1 .... 207 A5
Prince Ave BN15 .... 184 B5
Prince Charles Cl
 BN41, BN42 .... 166 A1
Prince Of Wales Cl BN41 . 186 F6
Prince Regent's Cl BN2 ... 188 E4
Prince Regent's Ct 2
 BN2 .... 188 E4
Prince William Cl BN14 ... 182 A8
Prince William Ct 4
 PO21 .... 195 D3
Prince's Cres BN2 .... 207 B8
Prince's Dr PO18 .... 133 E1
Prince's Pl BN1 .... 207 A5
Prince's Rd BN1, BN2 ..... 188 B8
Prince's St BN2 .... 207 A5
Prince's Terr BN2 .... 188 E4
Princes Ave BN3 .... 187 A6
Princes Cres BN1 .... 187 A6
Princes Croft PO21 .... 194 A1
Princes Ct 6 BN3 .... 187 A6
Princes Gate BN11 .... 181 F2
Princes Sq BN3 .... 187 A6
Princess Anne Rd RH12 ... 33 D6
Princess Ave
 Bognor Regis PO21 .... 195 A2
 Worthing BN13 .... 181 F4
Princess Cl BN13 .... 181 F3
Princess Margaret Rd
 RH12 .... 33 D7
Princess Rd RH11 .... 18 C6
Princess Royal Hospl The
 RH16 .... 85 F2
Prings La RH13 .... 81 C8
Prinsep Rd BN3 .... 187 A8
Prinsted La PO10 .... 169 F7
Priors Acre PO18 .... 154 D3
Priors Cl Breach PO10 .... 150 A1
Upper Beeding BN44 ...... 144 A2
Priors Leaze La PO18 ..... 150 C1
Priors Waye PO21 .... 194 A2
Priors Wlk RH10 .... 18 F6
Priors Wood GU27 .... 26 F6
Priory Cl
 Bognor Regis PO21 .... 205 B8
 Boxgrove PO18 .... 154 D3
 Horley RH6 .... 1 F4
 Lancing BN15 .... 183 B7
 Worthing BN13 .... 182 A4
Priory Ct 14
 Bognor Regis PO21 .... 195 D3
 Brighton BN1 .... 187 F8
Priory Field BN44 .... 144 A2
Priory Gate BN15 .... 183 E6
Priory Lanes PO19 .... 173 A7
Priory Rd Arundel BN18 ... 157 F2
 Burgess Hill RH15 .... 107 A1
 Chichester PO19 .... 173 A7
 Forest Row RH18 .... 23 D2
 Hassocks BN6 .... 126 E5
 Rustington BN16 .... 199 B6
Priory The Brighton BN1 .. 167 D5
 Hove BN3 .... 187 B5
Priory Way RH16 .... 85 F4
Proctor Cl RH10 .... 19 C4
Promenade The
 Emsworth PO10 .... 169 B7
 Littlehampton BN17 ...... 198 E3
Pronger's Cnr RH13 .... 59 E3
Prospect Pl Crawley RH11 . 18 C6
 3 Worthing BN11 .... 182 D1
Providence Pl
 Brighton BN1 .... 207 A7
 6 Chichester PO19 ...... 172 F7
Providence Terr BN11 ..... 182 E2
Providence The 5 PO19 .. 172 F7
Pruetts La GU31, GU33 .... 45 B1
Pryors Gn PO21 .... 194 C2
Pryors La PO21 .... 194 C1
Puckshott Way GU27 ...... 27 D8
Pudding La RH6 .... 4 E7
Puffin Rd RH11 .... 17 D5

Pulborough Cl BN2 .... 188 F7
Pulborough Rd RH20 ...... 119 B2
Pulborough Sta RH20 ..... 98 A2
Pulborough Way PO22 .... 196 D6
Pump Ho The BN3 .... 186 D8
Punch Copse Rd RH10 .... 18 F7
Punches La PO20 .... 193 D5
Punnetts Ct RH11 .... 17 F2
Purbeck Pl BN17 .... 198 C5
Purcell Rd RH11 .... 17 F3
Purton Rd RH12 .... 36 B4
Putmans La GU31 .... 89 B7
Puttock Cl GU27 .... 26 D5
Pyecombe Ct 4 RH11 ..... 17 F3
Pyecombe Golf Course
 BN45 .... 147 E6
Pyecombe St BN45 .... 147 A6
Pyrford Cl PO21 .... 194 B2

Quadrangle The BN14 ..... 161 E4
Quadrant BN1 .... 207 F5
Quadrant The
 Keymer BN6 .... 127 A4
 Worthing BN12 .... 181 C3
Quail Cl RH12 .... 36 D7
Quakers La RH16 .... 86 A5
Quantock Cl Crawley RH11 . 18 B6
 Worthing BN13 .... 181 F8
Quantock Rd BN13 .... 181 F7
Quantocks 2 BN17 .... 198 D6
Quarries The RH13 .... 59 D6
Quarry Bank Rd BN1 ...... 168 B2
Quarry Cl
 Burgess Hill RH15 .... 107 D3
 Horsham RH12 .... 36 F6
Quarry Hill RH17 .... 85 C6
Quarry La PO19 .... 173 C5
Quarry Lane Ind Est
 PO19 .... 173 C5
Quarry Rise RH19 .... 10 A3
Quarry Way RH13 .... 57 F2
Quarterbrass Farm Rd
 RH12 .... 36 D7
Quashetts The
 Worthing BN14 .... 182 D4
 Worthing BN15 .... 182 D5
Quay Ct BN43 .... 185 B6
Quay The 5 BN43 .... 185 A6
Quayside BN17 .... 198 B5
Quebec St BN2 .... 207 B6
Queen Alexandra Ave
 BN3 .... 167 A3
Queen Caroline Ct BN3 ... 167 A3
Queen Elizabeth Ave
 RH15 .... 67 A6
Queen Elizabeth II Jubilee
 Sch The RH13 .... 36 F1
Queen Elizabeth Rd RH12 . 33 D7
Queen Mary Ave BN3 ..... 167 A3
Queen Sq BN1 .... 207 F5
Queen St Arundel BN18 ... 158 B2
 Emsworth PO10 .... 169 C8
 Horsham RH11 .... 36 D1
 Littlehampton BN17 ...... 198 D5
 Worthing BN14 .... 182 C4
Queen Victoria Ave RH3 .. 167 A3
Queen Victoria Hospl The
 RH19 .... 9 F3
Queen's Ave PO19 .... 172 F4
Queen's Ct RH16 .... 85 F6
Queen's Gdns
 Brighton BN1 .... 207 A6
 Hove BN3 .... 187 C5
 Stockbridge PO19 .... 172 F4
Queen's Par BN3 .... 166 E2
Queen's Park City Prim Sch
 BN2 .... 188 C5
Queen's Park Rd BN2 ..... 188 C6
Queen's Park Rise BN2 ... 188 C6
Queen's Park Terr BN2 ... 188 C6
Queen's Pl Brighton BN1 .. 207 A7
 Hove BN3 .... 187 C6
 Shoreham-by-Sea BN43 .. 184 F7
 East Grinstead RH19 ..... 9 E1
 Horley RH6 .... 2 A3
 Worthing BN11 .... 182 C1
Queen's Sq PO21 .... 195 D3
Queens Cres RH15 .... 107 A2
Queens Dr BN6 .... 126 F4
Queens Fields E PO21 .... 194 F4
Queens Fields W PO21 ... 194 F4
Queens Fields Wlk PO21 .. 194 F4
Queens Gate RH6 .... 6 48
Queens La BN18 .... 158 B2
Queens Rd
 Haywards Heath RH16 .... 85 E6
 Lancing BN15 .... 183 F5
 Liphook GU30 .... 24 C3
 Southwick BN42 .... 165 E1
Queens Sq RH10 .... 18 D6

Queens St GU29 .... 70 A2
Queensborough Ct 6
 BN11 .... 182 A3
Queensbury Mews BN11 .. 187 E5
Queensdown Sch BN1 ..... 168 C3
Queensdown School Rd
 BN1, BN2 .... 168 D2
Queensmead PO21 .... 204 F8
Queensway
 Bognor Regis PO21 .... 195 A5
 Bognor Regis, Aldwick
 PO21 .... 194 E1
 Brighton BN2 .... 188 D6
 Crawley RH10 .... 18 E6
 East Grinstead RH19 ..... 9 E1
 Horsham RH11 .... 36 C1
 Lancing BN15 .... 183 E6
Queensway Ho 7 PO21 ... 195 C3
Quell Farm Ind Est RH20 . 117 E4
Querneby Cl BN43 .... 185 D7
Quest Cl PO19 .... 173 B6

Racecourse Rd RH6 .... 5 F8
Racecourse Way RH6 ..... 5 F8
Rackfield GU27 .... 26 D7
Rackham Cl Crawley RH11 . 18 D4
 Worthing BN13 .... 181 F5
Rackham Rd
 Amberley BN18 .... 138 F7
 3 Littlehampton BN16 ... 199 B3
 Worthing BN13 .... 181 F5
Rackham St
 Amberley BN18 .... 139 A8
 Rackham BN18, RH20 .... 139 C8
Racton Rd PO10 .... 149 C3
Radford Rd
 Bognor Regis PO21, PO22 195 B5
 Tinsley Green RH10, RH6 . 6 C4
Radinden Dr BN3 .... 167 D1
Radinden Manor Rd BN3 .. 187 D8
Radnor Cl BN3 .... 181 F4
Radnor Rd BN3 .... 181 F4
Raglan Ave BN13 .... 181 E5
Raglan Ct Brighton BN1 .. 207 F5
 2 Worthing BN11 .... 182 A2
Raglan Terr PO10 .... 149 C1
Railey Rd RH10 .... 18 E7
Railway App
 East Grinstead RH19 ..... 9 E1
 Worthing BN11 .... 182 D3
Railway Cotts
 Cinder Hill RH19 .... 65 A8
 Maplehurst RH13 .... 80 E2
Railway St BN1 .... 207 F6
Railway Terr GU27 .... 92 D7
Rainbow Way RH20 .... 119 F3
Rake Bsns Pk GU33 .... 46 B4
Rake CE (C) Prim Sch GU33 46 B5
Rake Rd Liss GU33 .... 45 D4
 Milland GU30 .... 47 A2
Rakers Ridge RH12 .... 36 D5
Raleigh Cl BN43 .... 184 F6
Raleigh Cres BN12 .... 181 D3
Raleigh Ho PO21 .... 195 D3
Raleigh Rd PO21 .... 194 C3
Raleigh Way BN13 .... 181 C3
Raleigh Wlk RH10 .... 18 E4
Rambledown La RH20 .... 119 C6
Ramblers Way RH11 .... 39 B8
Ramillies Gdns PO22 ..... 196 C5
Ramsey Cl Horley RH6 .... 1 F3
 Horsham RH12 .... 36 D5
Ramsey 17 RH11 .... 18 B1
Randall Schofield Ct
 RH10 .... 19 A7
Randdilles Cl BN6 .... 126 B4
Ranelagh Villas BN3 ..... 187 B8
Ranmore Cl RH11 .... 39 C8
Ransome Cl RH11 .... 17 E3
Ranville Ct GU28 .... 95 E7
Ranworth Cl PO22 .... 195 F5
Rapeland Hill RH12 .... 15 F2
Raphael Rd BN3 .... 186 F7
Rapley Ave PO21 .... 194 B2
Rascals Cl RH13 .... 79 F7
Rascals Ct RH15 .... 106 F1
Rathan La
 Broadbridge PO18 .... 171 C8
 West Ashling PO18 .... 151 C1
Rathbone Ho RH11 .... 18 B1
Rathlin Rd RH11 .... 18 B3
Raughmere Ct PO18 ...... 152 F4
Raughmere Dr
 PO18, PO19 .... 152 F4
Raven Cl RH12 .... 36 E6
Raven La RH11 .... 18 C8
Raven's Rd BN43 .... 184 F7
Ravendene Ct 3 RH11 ... 18 D5
Ravens Croft 7 BN16 .... 199 C4
Ravens Way PO22 .... 195 B6
Ravensbourne Ave BN43 . 164 F1

Ravensbourne Cl 11
 BN43 .... 164 F1
Ravenscroft RH20 .... 140 D8
Ravenscroft Ct RH12 ..... 36 C3
Ravenswood BN6 .... 126 E4
Ravenswood Cl BN13 ..... 180 A4
Ravenswood Rd RH15 .... 107 B3
Ravenwood Ct PO21 ...... 194 E2
Rawarth Cl RH10 .... 19 C4
Rawson Villas BN16 ...... 199 C6
Raycroft Cl PO21 .... 194 F2
Rayden Cl BN17 .... 198 E5
Raymer Wlk RH6 .... 2 C4
Rayner Ct BN5 .... 123 E4
Reading Rd BN2 .... 188 F4
Reapers Cl RH12 .... 36 D5
Record Rd PO10 .... 149 A1
Rectory Cl
 Ashington RH20 .... 121 A5
 Hove BN3 .... 186 D7
 Pulborough RH20 .... 98 C2
 Southwick BN43 .... 185 D7
 Storrington RH20 .... 119 D1
Rectory Ct 15 BN43 ...... 185 C8
Rectory Farm Rd BN15 ... 183 B7
Rectory Gdns BN14 .... 182 C5
Rectory La
 Angmering BN16 .... 179 F5
 Bramshott GU30 .... 25 D7
 Charlwood RH6 .... 4 D7
 Church Norton PO20 ..... 204 B3
 Crawley RH11 .... 17 F8
 Pulborough RH20 .... 98 C2
 Warminghurst RH20 ...... 120 E6
Rectory Rd
 Southwick BN43 .... 185 D7
 Storrington RH20 .... 119 D1
 Worthing BN13, BN14 .... 182 A5
Rectory Wlk Lancing BN15 183 C7
 Storrington RH20 .... 119 D1
Red Admiral St RH12 ..... 36 E5
Red Deer Cl RH13 .... 37 B4
Red House Ct GU31 ...... 68 B4
Red La RH13 .... 79 D1
Red Lion St GU29 .... 92 F7
Red Oak Ct GU29 .... 71 A2
Red Ridges PO21 .... 195 A2
Red River Ct RH12 .... 36 B5
Redcotts 1 BN11 .... 182 B2
Redditch Cl RH11 .... 17 E2
Redford Ave RH12 .... 36 B4
Redgarth Ct RH19 .... 9 B3
Redgrave Dr RH10 .... 19 D5
Redhill Cl BN1 .... 167 C5
Redhill Distribution Ctr RH1 2 A8
Redhill Dr BN1 .... 167 C5
Redhill PO9 .... 128 D1
Redhouse Mews GU30 .... 25 C2
Redkiln Cl RH13 .... 36 F4
Redkiln Way RH12, RH13 . 36 F3
Redlands La
 New Brighton PO10 ...... 149 B4
 New Brighton PO10 ...... 149 C4
 Shipton Green PO20 ..... 190 F3
Redmoor PO21 .... 191 E4
Redshank Ct 5 RH11 .... 17 D5
Redvers Rd PO22 .... 168 D1
Redwing Cl Horsham RH13 . 36 F3
 Littlehampton BN17 ...... 178 C4
Redwood Cl Crawley RH10 . 18 E8
 Worthing BN13 .... 181 C5
Redwood Ct BN17 .... 198 F5
Redwood Dr RH6 .... 85 D3
Redwood Manor GU27 .... 27 C7
Redwood Pl PO21 .... 194 E2
Reed Cl RH11 .... 19 C1
Reed Pond Wlk RH16 ..... 86 A4
Reed's La BN6 .... 125 B8
Reedings RH11 .... 17 D4
Reeds La Liss Forest GU33 .. 45 F6
 Southwater Street RH13 .. 58 B3
Reef Cl BN17 .... 198 F4
Regal Dr 10 RH19 .... 22 F8
Regency Cl BN13 .... 182 A6
Regency Mews 18 BN1 ... 187 E5
Regency Sq BN1 .... 207 F5
Regency Sq BN1 .... 187 E5
Regent Arc BN1 .... 207 A5
Regent Bsns Pk RH15 .... 106 E2
Regent Hill BN1 .... 207 A5
Regent Row BN1 .... 207 A5
Regents Cl RH13 .... 18 C2
Regents Way PO21 .... 194 F4
Regis Ave PO21 .... 205 B8
Regis Ct
 Bognor Regis PO21 .... 195 D3
 Worthing BN11 .... 182 A1

Reigate Ct 2 .... 6 D1
Reigate Ct BN11 .... 181 F2
Reigate Rd Brighton BN1 . 167 D1
 Hookwood RH6 .... 1 C4
 Worthing BN11 .... 181 F3
Renoir Ct PO22 .... 195 A6
Renoir Mews PO21 .... 195 A6
Renton Cl RH14 .... 77 D8
Rew La PO19 .... 152 F3
Reynard Cl RH12 .... 37 B5
Reynolds La BN18 .... 156 D4
Reynolds Pl RH11 .... 18 C7
Reynolds Rd Crawley RH11 18 C7
 Hove BN3 .... 186 F7
Rhodes Way RH10 .... 18 F3
Ribbetts Ho BN6 .... 126 A5
Ribbetts The BN6 .... 126 A5
Rices Hill RH19 .... 9 E1
Richard Allen Ct 2 BN2 .. 168 C1
Richardson Ct 16
 Crawley RH11 .... 18 B1
 5 Hove BN3 .... 186 F7
Richardson Rd BN3 .... 186 F7
Richmond Ave
 Bognor Regis PO21 .... 195 B2
 Chichester PO19 .... 153 A1
Richmond Ave W PO21 ... 195 A3
Richmond Cl 1 BN16 ..... 199 E6
Richmond Ct 5 Hove BN3 187 E7
 3 Rustington BN16 ...... 199 B5
 Worthing BN11 .... 182 C2
Richmond Ho W PO21 .... 195 C3
Richmond Par BN2 .... 207 B6
Richmond Pl BN2 .... 207 A6
Richmond Rd 16
 Bognor Regis PO21 .... 195 C3
 Brighton BN2 .... 188 B8
 Horsham RH12 .... 36 A4
 Westerton PO18 .... 153 F3
 Worthing BN11 .... 182 C2
Richmond Rd N 5 PO21 . 195 C4
Richmond Sq RH19 .... 9 D2
Richmond St BN2 .... 207 B6
Richmond Terr BN2 .... 207 B7
Richmond Villas PO21 .... 195 F3
Richmond Way RH19 ..... 22 F8
Rickfield RH11 .... 18 A5
Rickman's La RH14 .... 31 B2
Rickwood RH6 .... 2 C4
Riddens The RH12 .... 33 A6
Ride The Brighton BN1 ... 167 F1
 Ifold RH14 .... 31 C2
Ridge Cl BN41 .... 166 A4
Ridge View BN1 .... 168 E5
Ridge Way RH16 .... 86 B2
Ridgdale RH10 .... 21 B8
Ridgehurst Dr RH11 ...... 35 F1
Ridge RH16 .... 18 F6
Ridgeside Ave BN1 .... 167 E5
Ridgeway
 East Grinstead RH19 ..... 22 E7
 Shoreham-by-Sea
 BN41, BN42 .... 165 F1
Ridgeway Cl BN42 .... 165 F1
Ridgeway The
 Burgess Hill RH15 .... 107 B4
 Chichester PO19 .... 172 E7
 Fernhurst GU27 .... 49 B6
 Horley RH6 .... 2 A1
 Worthing BN13 .... 143 D1
Ridgway The PO22 .... 196 B4
Ridings The
 Bognor Regis PO21 .... 194 C1
 Burgess Hill RH15 .... 107 C2
 Crawley RH10 .... 19 D7
 Liss GU33 .... 45 D4
 Littlehampton BN16 ...... 199 F4
 Steyning BN44 .... 143 D1
Ridleys RH19 .... 42 E6
Rife La PO20 .... 206 B8
Rife Way
 Bognor Regis PO22 .... 195 F4
 Ferring BN12 .... 200 E6
Rifeside Gdns BN12 ...... 180 E3
Rigden Rd BN3 .... 167 C1
Rikkyo Sch in England
 RH14 .... 32 D8
Riley Rd BN2 .... 168 C1
Rill Wlk RH19 .... 10 B1
Rillside RH10 .... 19 A3
Rimmer Cl RH11 .... 39 B8
Ring Rd BN15 .... 163 F1
Ring Rd N RH6 .... 6 C8
Ring Rd S RH6 .... 6 C7
Ringley Ave RH6 .... 2 A2
Ringley Oak RH12 .... 36 F4
Ringley Rd RH12 .... 36 E4

236 Rin – St C

Ringmer Cl BN1 168 E4
Ringmer Rd
Brighton BN1 168 E4
Brighton BN1 168 F4
Worthing BN13 181 E5
Ringwood Cl RH10 18 E4
Ripley Rd BN11 181 F3
Ripon Gdns PO21 194 E3
Rise The Crawley RH10 19 D6
East Grinstead RH19 22 F8
Haywards Heath RH16 86 B5
Partridge Green RH13 103 A4
Portslade-by-Sea BN41 165 F2
Rissom Ct BN1 167 E2
River Cl BN43 184 E6
River La River GU28 72 E3
Watersfield RH20 117 B4
River Mead Crawley RH11 5 A1
Horsham RH12 36 B1
River Rd Arundel BN18 158 B2
Littlehampton BN17 198 C5
River St PO10 149 D4
River's Rd RH16 63 D3
Riverhill La GU28, RH20 96 E7
Rivermead RH20 98 D1
Rivermead Ct PO10 149 C3
Riverside Chichester PO19 173 B7
Forest Row RH18 23 E3
Horley RH6 2 A1
Horsham RH12 36 A2
Littlehampton BN17 198 C4
Shoreham-by-Sea BN43 184 F6
Southwick BN42 185 E7
Storrington RH20 119 D2
Upper Beeding BN44 144 A2
Riverside Bsns Ctr 11
BN43 184 F7
Riverside Cl GU33 45 B4
Riverside Ct RH20 98 A1
Riverside Ind Est BN17 198 B5
Riverside Rd BN43 184 F6
Rixons Cl RH17 65 C5
Rixons Orch RH17 65 C5
Robell Way RH20 119 F3
Robert Lodge BN2 188 F4
Robert May Cty Fst Sch The
RH10 18 F4
Robert St BN1 207 A6
Robert Way RH12 36 F7
Roberts Cl RH13 57 F4
Roberts Rd BN15 183 E4
Robertson Rd BN1 167 D1
Robin Cl Crawley RH11 18 C8
East Grinstead RH19 9 F2
Littlehampton BN17 178 C4
Southwater RH13 58 A2
Robin Davis Cl BN2 168 E1
Robin Dene BN2 188 E4
Robin Hood La RH12 35 F5
Robin Rd BN6 106 D2
Robin's Cl PO20 206 E8
Robinia Lodge 1 BN1 167 E2
Robins Dr PO21 194 D3
Robins La GU29 69 D7
Robins Row BN41 166 A1
Robinson Cl BN15 183 E6
Robinson Rd RH11 18 D5
Robinswood Ct RH12 36 F4
Robson Rd BN11, BN12 181 E2
Rochester Cl
Chichester PO19 152 F1
2 Hove BN3 187 D6
Worthing BN13 181 B5
Rochester Ct 3 BN3 187 D6
Rochester Gdns BN3 187 D6
Rochester St BN2 188 D5
Rochester Way PO21 194 E3
Rock Cl 12 BN42 185 E7
Rock Gdns PO21 195 C2
Rock Gr BN2 188 E4
Rock La RH20 120 E1
Rock Pl BN2 207 B4
Rock Rd RH20 120 C2
Rock St BN2 188 E4
Rockall Cl BN16 179 A3
Rockingham Cl BN13 181 E6
Rockpit Cotts GU33 45 D4
Rocks La RH17 40 F1
Rocks The RH19 23 D6
Rocky La RH16, RH15 85 D1
Rodgate La GU8 28 E5
Rodmell Pl BN1 168 A6
Rodmell Rd BN13 181 E5
Rodney Cl PO21 194 C3
Rodney Cres BN18 177 D4
Roebuck Cl RH13 37 B4
Roedale Rd BN1 168 B1
Roedean Ct BN2 188 F4
Roedean Rd Brighton BN2 188 F4
Worthing BN13 181 E6
Roedeer Copse GU27 26 E6
Roffey Cl RH6 1 F3
Roffey Cnr RH12 37 B4
Roffey Ct RH13 37 A4
Roffey's Cl RH10 7 A4
Rogate CE (C) Prim Sch
GU31 68 B4
Rogate Cl Lancing BN15 183 B7
Worthing BN13 182 A6
Rogate Rd BN13 182 A6
Roger's La BN14 161 E4
Rolfe Dr RH15 107 D3
Rollaston Pk BN18 177 C2
Romaine Cl RH15 107 D5
Roman Acre BN17 198 C6
Roman Cres BN42 185 E8
Roman Landing PO20 190 B2
Roman Rd Bramber BN44 143 E3
Hove BN3 186 D6
Southwick BN42 185 E8
Roman Way
Billingshurst RH14 55 D1
Fishbourne PO19 172 B6
Southwick BN42 185 E8
Roman Wlk BN15 183 B7
Romany Cl BN41 186 B8
Romany Rd BN13 181 B5
Romney Broadwalk PO22 195 B6
Romney Ct BN11 181 F1
Romney Garth PO20 206 F7
Romney Rd BN11 181 F1
Romsey Cl BN1 168 C2
Rona Cl RH11 18 B3
Rook Way RH12 36 F6
Rookcross La RH13 102 A4
Rookery La PO20 203 F8
Rookery The Lumley PO10 149 C1
Selsey PO20 206 F8
Rookery Way RH16 85 E1
Rookwood La PO20 190 D4
Rookwood Pk RH12 35 F3
Rookwood Rd PO20 190 C2
Rope Wlk
Littlehampton BN17 198 C4
Shoreham-by-Sea BN43 184 F7
Ropeland Way RH12 36 E7
Ropes La GU27 49 C5
Ropetackle BN43 184 E7
Rosamund Rd RH10 19 B3
Rosary Ct RH15 107 B2
Rose Ave PO22 196 F5
Rose Cottage La RH17 62 A5
Rose Cotts RH17 66 A4
Rose Ct
Bognor Regis PO21 194 D3
Chichester PO19 173 A7
Hassocks BN6 126 E4
7 Littlehampton BN17 198 D5
Rose Green Cty Inf Sch
PO21 194 C2
Rose Green CtyJun Sch
PO21 194 C3
Rose Green Rd PO21 194 C3
Rose Hill BN2 207 B7
Rose Hill Cl BN1, BN2 207 A7
Rose Hill Ct BN1 207 A7
Rose Hill Terr BN1 207 A7
Rose Wlk BN11, BN12 181 E1
Rosebarn Cl RH15 107 C1
Rosebery Ave BN12 181 E2
Rosecroft Cl BN15 183 E5
Rosedale Cl RH11 18 A4
Rosehill RH14 55 D1
Roseleigh Gdns RH17 86 F3
Rosemary Ave BN44 143 E3
Rosemary Cl
Bramber BN44 143 E3
Haywards Heath RH17 85 B6
Petworth GU28 95 F8
Storrington RH20 119 D1
Rosemary Ct
Haslemere GU27 27 C7
Horley RH6 1 E4
Rosemary Dr BN43 165 C1
Rosemary La Charlwood RH6 4 E7
Horley RH6 2 B3
Petworth GU28 95 F8
Rosier Commercial Ctr
RH14 77 F7
Rosier Way RH14 77 E6
Roslan Ct RH6 2 B2
Ross Cl
Bognor Regis PO21 194 B2
Crawley RH10 18 F3
Rossalyn Cl PO21 194 B3
Rossiter Rd BN15 183 E8
Rosslyn Ave BN43 185 A7
Rosslyn Ct BN43 184 F7
Rosslyn Rd BN43 184 F7
Rossmore Cl RH10 6 D2
Rostock Ct PO20 202 B6
Rotary Ho BN15 183 E4
Rotary Lodge BN1 168 E6
Rotary Point BN41 166 B1
Rothbury Rd BN3 186 D7
Rother Cl RH20 119 F3
Rother Cres RH11 17 F5
Rother Ho GU33 45 B3
Rother La GU31 69 A1
Rotherbank Farm La GU33 45 C6
Rotherbridge La GU28 95 E5
Rotherfield Cl BN1 168 B6
Rotherfield Cres BN1 168 B5
Rothermead GU28 95 E7
Rothervale RH6 1 F5
Rothesay Cl BN13 181 E4
Rothley Chase RH16 85 F4
Rotten Row PO20 192 E3
Rough Field RH19 9 D4
Rough Way RH12 36 F5
Round Hill Rd 2
BN1, BN2 188 B8
Round Hill St 3 BN2 188 B8
Round Piece PO20 206 C8
Round Piece La PO20 206 B8
Roundabout Copse RH20 119 D5
Roundabout Cotts RH12 33 C5
Roundabout La RH20 119 D6
Roundabouts The GU33 45 C5
Roundhill Cres BN2 188 B8
Roundhouse Meadow
PO10 169 C7
Roundle Ave PO22 196 C6
Roundle Rd PO22 196 C5
Roundle Sq PO22 196 B5
Roundle Square Rd PO22 196 B5
Roundstone By-Pass Rd
BN16 180 A3
Roundstone Cres BN16 200 A6
Roundstone Dr BN16 200 A6
Roundstone La BN16 180 A4
Roundstone Way PO20 206 F8
Roundway BN1 168 E5
Roundway Ct RH11 18 D8
Roundway The BN16 199 D4
Roundwood La RH16 85 F8
Row Hill La RH17 62 E7
Rowan Ave BN3 166 E1
Rowan Cl Crawley RH10 18 F6
Haywards Heath RH16 86 B4
Horsham RH12 37 B5
Portslade-by-Sea BN41 166 A1
Storrington RH20 119 F2
Rowan Ct RH14 55 D1
Rowan Dr RH14 55 D1
Rowan Ho BN12 181 A4
Rowan Tree Cl GU33 45 C4
Rowan Way
Bognor Regis PO22 195 C7
Horsham RH12 37 C5
Rowena Ho RH11 5 D1
Rowens The BN11 182 A2
Rowfant Bsns Ctr RH10 20 E6
Rowhook Hill RH12 34 F8
Rowhook Rd Rowhook RH12 13 E1
Slinfold RH12 35 A8
Rowland Cl RH10 7 E5
Rowlands Castle Rd PO8 128 B6
Rowlands Castle Sta PO9 128 E2
Rowlands Rd
Horsham RH12 37 A6
Worthing BN11 182 B1
Rowner Rd RH14 55 A2
Rowplatt La RH19 8 E4
Roxburgh Cl BN13 181 F7
Royal Alexandra Hospl for
Sick Children The BN1 207 F6
Royal Ashdown Forest
Golf Course RH18 44 F8
Royal Bldgs BN15 183 C4
Royal Cl PO19 173 C6
Royal Cres BN2 188 C4
Royal Crescent Mansions 10
BN2 188 C4
Royal Crescent Mews 8
BN2 188 C4
Royal Gdns PO9 128 C1
Royal George Par BN43 165 C1
Royal George Rd RH15 106 E3
Royal Oak Cotts BN45 146 C5
Royal Oak Ho RH10 21 B7
Royal Par PO21 195 A6
Royal Pavilion BN1 207 A5
Royal Sussex Cty Hospl
(General) BN2 188 D4
Royal West Sussex Hospl
PO19 172 F8
Royce Cl PO20 190 C1
Royce Rd RH10 6 A3
Royce Way PO20 190 C1
Royston Cl RH10 6 A2
Roystons The BN16 199 F4
Ruckmans La RH5 14 B7
Rucrofts Cl PO21 194 F3
Rudford Ind Est BN18 177 D2
Rudgwick Ave BN12 181 A2
Rudgwick Cl BN16 199 B4
Rudgwick Cty Prim Sch
RH12 33 D7
Rudgwick Rd RH11 17 F7
Rudwick Way PO22 196 C4
Rudwick's Cl PO22 196 C4
Rufwood RH10 21 A8
Rugby Ct 5 Brighton BN2 188 E4
3 Worthing BN11 182 A3
Rugby Pl BN2 188 E4
Rugby Rd Brighton BN1 168 A1
Worthing BN11 182 A3
Ruislip Gdns PO21 194 C2
Rumbolds Cl PO19 173 C5
Rumbolds Hill GU29 92 F7
Rumbolds La RH16 85 D2
Rumboldswyke CE (C)
Prim Sch PO19 173 C5
Runcorn Cl RH11 17 E2
Runcton La PO20 193 E7
Runnymede Ct PO21 194 F5
Runshooke Ct 9 RH11 18 A3
Rusbridge Cl PO21 194 D4
Rushams Rd RH12 36 B3
Rushes The RH16 86 C4
Rushetts Pl RH11 5 C1
Rushetts Rd RH11 5 B1
Rushfield Rd GU33 45 B3
Rushlake Cl BN1 168 E5
Rushlake Rd BN1 168 E5
Rushwood Cl RH16 86 B4
Ruskin Cl Crawley RH10 6 C1
Selsey PO20 206 F7
Ruskin Rd Hove BN3 186 F8
Worthing BN14 182 F4
Rusper Cty Prim Sch RH12 16 C7
Rusper Rd Brighton BN1 168 D6
Crawley RH11, RH12 17 D7
Crawley RH11 17 E6
Faygate RH12 16 A1
Horsham RH12 36 F6
Newdigate RH12, RH5 3 C4
Rusper RH5 15 E8
Worthing BN13 181 E5
Rusper Rd S BN13 181 F5
Ruspers RH15 107 D2
Ruspers Keep RH11 17 F7
Russ Hill RH5, RH6 4 C5
Russell Cl BN14 182 E5
Russell Cres 2 BN1, BN3 207 F7
Russell Ct 4 BN15 183 E5
Russell Mews 17 BN1 187 E5
Russell Pl 7
Bognor Regis PO21 195 D3
Brighton BN1 207 F5
Russell Rd Brighton BN1 207 F5
East Wittering PO20 201 E7
Russell Sq BN1 207 F5
Russell St PO19 173 C6
Russell Way RH10 19 A5
Russell's Cl BN16 200 B6
Russells Cres RH6 2 A2
Russells Dr BN15 183 E5
Russet Cl RH6 2 C3
Russet Ct GU27 49 B5
Rustington Cty Prim Sch
BN16 199 B6
Rustington Rd BN1 168 A5
Rustington Trad Est BN16 179 F3
Rustlings Cl RH16 86 B5
Ruston Ave BN16 199 D5
Ruston Cl RH10 19 C3
Ruston Pk BN16 199 E5
Rutherford Way RH10 6 A3
Rutherwick Cl RH6 1 F3
Rutland Ct BN3 186 F6
Rutland Gdns BN3 186 F7
Rutland Rd BN3 187 A7
Rutland Way PO18, PO20 173 D8
Rycroft Cl BN12 181 C1
Rydal Cl Crawley RH11 17 D4
Littlehampton BN16 179 A3
Ryde Ct BN3 166 D1
Ryde Rd BN2 188 D7
Ryders Way RH12 36 F7
Rydon Com Sch The
RH20 120 A2
Rye Ash RH10 19 A7
Rye Cl BN11 182 A1
Rye Farm La RH13 57 A2
Ryecroft 12 Brighton BN2 188 F5
Haywards Heath RH16 85 E3
Ryecroft Dr RH12 36 A3
Ryecroft Gdns BN12 181 C2
Ryecroft La RH20 119 D1
Ryecroft Meadow RH13 59 C6
Ryecroft Rd RH17 83 C3
Ryelands Crawley RH11 18 A5
Horley RH6 2 C4
Ryelands Dr BN2 168 D3

Sabre Rd PO10 169 C3
Sack La PO22 175 E2
Sackville Cl RH19 9 C3
Sackville Coll RH19 9 F1
Sackville Cres BN14 182 E4
Sackville Ct 3 RH19 22 F8
Sackville Gdns
East Grinstead RH19 9 C3
Hove BN3 186 F6
Sackville La RH19 9 C3
Sackville Rd Hove BN3 187 A7
Worthing BN14 182 E4
Sackville Sch RH19 10 A1
Sackville Trad Est BN3 187 B8
Sackville Way BN14 182 E4
Saddle La PO20 206 D8
Saddler Row RH10 18 D3
Saddler's Row GU28 95 F8
Saddlers Cl RH15 107 D1
Sadler St PO21 195 C2
Sadler Way BN2 188 F6
Sadlers Wlk 4
Chichester PO19 173 A6
Lumley PO10 169 C8
Saffron Cl Crawley RH11 18 A3
Shoreham-by-Sea BN43 165 C1
Saffron Ct BN13 182 A3
Saffrons The RH15 106 F5
Saint Hill Rd RH19 22 C5
St Agnes Rd RH19 9 E2
St Andrew's CE (A) Prim Sch
BN3 187 B6
St Andrew's CE Boys High Sch
BN14 182 E4
St Andrew's CE (C) Prim Sch
BN44 143 D4
St Andrew's CE Fst & Mid Sch
RH10 19 A4
St Andrew's Cl
Ferring BN12 200 E6
Oving PO20 174 C6
St Andrew's Gdns BN13 182 A4
St Andrew's Prim Sch (CE)
RH13 59 A1
St Andrew's Rd
Brighton BN1 168 A1
Portslade-by-Sea BN41 186 C7
Worthing BN13 181 F4
St Andrews Rd
Burgess Hill RH15 107 D3
Crawley RH11 17 D5
St Ann's Ct 12 BN3 187 D7
St Ann's Hill GU29 92 F7
St Anne's Ct
9 Brighton BN2 188 C4
6 Brighton BN1 207 F7
East Wittering PO20 201 F7
St Anne's Gdns BN6 127 A3
St Anne's Ho 7 BN1 207 F7
St Anne's Rd RH10 6 C2
St Annes Well Ho 7 BN3 187 D6
St Anselm's Rd BN14 182 B4
St Anthony's Sch PO19 172 F8
St Anthony's Way 1
BN16 199 D6
St Anthony's Wlk PO21 194 D3
St Aubin Cl RH11 17 F2
St Aubins Ct BN12 200 F4
St Aubins Rd BN12 200 F4
St Aubyn's Cres BN41 186 B7
St Aubyn's Rd
Portslade-by-Sea BN41 186 C7
Southwick BN41 186 A7
St Aubyns BN3 187 B6
St Aubyns S BN3 187 A5
St Augustine Cl RH17 86 F3
St Augustine Rd 12 BN17 198 E4
St Barnabas Ct RH10 19 C7
St Bartholomew CE Prim Sch
GU27 27 C7
St Bartholomew's CE Prim Sch
BN1 207 A7
St Bartholomews Cl PO19 172 E6
St Bernadette's RC Prim Sch
BN1 167 E2
St Bernards Ct BN15 183 E5
St Blaises Rd PO18 154 C4
St Botolph's Rd BN11 182 B3
St Botolphs Ct 2 BN11 182 B3
St Brelades Rd RH11 17 F2
St Catherine's RC (A)
Prim Sch BN17 198 D6
St Catherine's Rd BN17 198 D4
St Catherines Ct BN17 198 D4
St Catherines Rd RH10 6 D1

St Christopher's Cl
Fishbourne PO19 .... 172 C6
Haslemere GU27 .... 27 A6
St Christopher's Gn GU27 .. 27 A6
St Christopher's Rd
Haslemere GU27 .... 27 A6
Hurstpierpoint BN6 .... 126 A6
St Christopher's Sch BN3 187 A6
St Christophers Cl RH12 ...... 36 D4
St Christophers Day Hospl
RH12 .... 36 D3
St Clement Rd RH11 .... 17 F2
St Cuthman's BN44 .... 143 D4
St Cuthman's Sch GU29 ...... 70 A6
St Cuthmans Cl BN2 .... 188 F6
St Cyriacs PO19 .... 173 A7
St David's Gate ⬛ BN15 .. 183 D6
St Dunstan's Rd
BN13, BN14 .... 182 A3
St Edmund Cl RH11 .... 5 D1
St Edmund's Rd RH16 .... 85 F3
St Edward's Cl RH19 .... 9 C1
St Elmo Rd BN14 .... 182 B4
St Flora's Rd BN17 .... 198 F5
St Francis Cl RH16 .... 85 F2
St Francis of Assisi RC (A)
Prim Sch RH10 .... 18 E4
St Francis Wlk RH11 .... 17 E4
St Gabriels Rd RH14 .... 77 B8
St George's CE Prim Sch PO20 206 F8
St George's Dr PO19 .... 172 F3
St George's Gdns
Horsham RH13 .... 36 E4
⬛ BN11 .... 182 F2
St George's La BN6 .... 126 B5
St George's Mews BN1 .... 207 A6
St George's Pl
Brighton BN1 .... 207 A6
Hurstpierpoint BN6 .... 126 B5
St George's Rd
Brighton BN2 .... 188 D4
Worthing BN11 .... 182 F2
St George's Terr ⬛ BN2 .. 188 D4
St Georges Ct RH6 .... 2 B3
St Georges Ct
Crawley RH11 .... 18 D8
East Grinstead RH19 .... 9 C3
St Georges Wlk PO20 .... 175 F7
St Giles CE Prim Sch RH17 65 C6
St Giles Cl BN43 .... 185 B8
St Helen's Cres BN3 .... 166 D3
St Helen's Dr BN3 .... 166 D3
St Helen's Rd BN2 .... 188 D7
St Helier Cl RH11 .... 18 A2
St Helier Ct BN12 .... 200 F4
St Helier Rd BN12 .... 200 F4
St Heliers Ave BN3 .... 186 E7
St Hilda's Cl Crawley RH10 .. 6 C1
Horley RH6 .... 2 B3
Selsey PO20 .... 206 E6
St Hugh's Cl RH10 .... 6 C1
St Itha Cl PO20 .... 206 E7
St Itha Rd PO20 .... 206 E6
St Ives RH10 .... 19 C7
St Ives Sch GU27 .... 27 E8
St James Ave BN15 .... 183 E8
St James CE Prim Sch
PO10 .... 149 B2
St James Ct PO19 .... 173 B7
St James Wlk RH11 .... 18 C2
St James' CE (C) Prim Sch
RH20 .... 117 C6
St James' Cty Prim Sch
PO19 .... 173 C7
St James' Ho ⬛ BN2 ..... 207 B5
St James' Ind Est PO19 ... 173 C7
St James' Rd
Chichester PO19 .... 173 C7
Emsworth PO10 .... 149 B1
St James's Ave BN2 .... 207 B5
St James's Cl PO20 .... 191 E5
St James's Rd RH19 .... 9 D1
St James's Sq PO19 .... 173 C7
St James's St BN2 .... 207 B5
St James's Street Mews
BN2 .... 207 B5
St Joan Cl RH11 .... 5 D1
St John Baptist (A)
Prim Sch BN14 .... 161 E6
St John Cl RH13 .... 36 E1
St John's Ave
Bognor Regis PO21 .... 194 F4
East Grinstead RH19 .... 9 C2
Midhurst GU29 .... 92 E7
Worthing BN12 .... 181 D1
St John's Cl
Fishbourne PO19 .... 172 C6
Haslemere GU27 .... 27 A6

St John's Cres RH12 .... 35 E3
St John's Ct BN15 .... 183 D6
St John's Mews Cotts ⬛
BN43 .... 184 E7
St John's Mount ⬛ BN2 .. 207 B5
St John's Pl Brighton BN2 . 207 B5
⬛ Hove BN3 .... 185 A8
St John's RC Prim Sch
RH12 .... 36 A1
St John's Rd Breach PO10 149 F1
Crawley RH11 .... 18 C6
East Grinstead RH19 .... 9 E2
Haywards Heath RH16 ...... 85 E2
Hove BN3 .... 187 C5
St Johns Sch BN2 .... 188 D5
St Johns St PO19 .... 173 A6
St Johns Ch PO20 .... 175 D5
St Johns Ct RH15 .... 107 A3
St Johns Rd RH15 .... 107 A3
St Joseph's Cl BN3 .... 187 A8
St Joseph's Dominican Sch
BN20 .... 140 D8
St Joseph's RC (A) Cty
Prim Sch BN2 .... 168 C1
St Joseph's RC (A) Prim Sch
RH16 .... 212 B5
St Joseph's Trad Est
BN3 .... 187 A8
St Josephs Way RH16 ...... 85 E4
St Julian's La BN43 .... 185 D7
St Julians Cl BN43 .... 185 C7
St Keyna Ave BN3, BN41 . 186 D6
St Lawrence Ave BN14 .... 182 B4
St Lawrence CE (A) Prim Sch
BN6 .... 126 A6
St Lawrence Way BN6 ..... 126 A7
St Leodegar's Way PO20 . 173 A1
St Leonard's Ave
BN3, BN41 .... 186 C7
St Leonard's Gdns
BN3, BN41 .... 186 D7
St Leonard's Rd
⬛ Brighton BN2 .... 188 C8
Hove BN3, BN41 .... 186 C7
St Leonards Cty Inf Sch
RH13 .... 36 E2
St Leonards Dr RH10 .... 19 A4
St Leonards Pk RH19 .... 9 E1
St Leonards Rd RH13 .... 37 A1
St Louie Cl BN42 .... 186 A8
St Luke's Cl BN11 .... 183 B4
St Luke's Inf Sch
BN2 .... 188 C6
St Luke's Cty Jun Sch
BN2 .... 188 C6
St Luke's Rd BN2 .... 188 C6
St Luke's Terr BN2 .... 188 C6
St Lukes Ct RH15 .... 107 A3
St Mald Ct BN12 .... 200 F4
St Malo Cl BN12 .... 200 F4
St Margaret CE Prim Sch
BN6 .... 127 D3
St Margaret's Ave RH19 .... 9 F6
St Margaret's CE (A) Prim Sch
Angmering BN16 .... 179 F7
Crawley RH11 .... 18 B7
St Margaret's Cotts GU27 .. 49 B6
St Margaret's Ct BN16 .... 179 F6
St Margaret's Pl BN1 ...... 207 F5
St Margaret's Rd RH19 ...... 9 F5
St Margaret's Sch GU29 ... 92 E8
St Margarets Ct RH12 ...... 35 F7
St Mark's CE (C) Prim Sch
RH17 .... 61 F5
St Mark's CE Prim Sch
BN2 .... 188 E5
St Mark's Cres BN11 .... 183 B4
St Mark's La RH12 .... 36 E6
St Mark's Rd BN42 .... 186 C8
St Martin's Flats ⬛ BN2 . 188 C7
St Martin's La ⬛ BN17 .. 198 D5
St Martin's Pl BN2 .... 188 C7
St Martin's Sch PO19 ...... 173 A7
St Martin's St
Brighton BN2 .... 207 B8
Chichester PO19 .... 173 A6
St Martins CE Prim Sch
BN2 .... 188 C8
St Martins Rd BN17 .... 198 D5
St Mary Magdalen RC
Prim Sch BN1 .... 186 F4
St Mary Magdalene St
BN2 .... 207 B8
St Mary & St Paul CE (C)
Fst Sch GU31 .... 89 D3
St Mary's Cl Chidham
Clmping BN17 .... 197 E8
East Grinstead RH19 .... 9 D2
Pulborough RH20 .... 98 C3
St Mary's CE Fst Sch
BN12 .... 181 C2

St Mary's CE Prim Sch
RH20 .... 141 D6
St Mary's Ct
Billingshurst RH14 .... 77 D8
Littlehampton BN17 .... 198 E5
Mid Lavant PO18 .... 152 E7
Pulborough RH20 .... 98 C2
Shoreham-by-Sea BN43 .. 184 F7
St Mary's Ct
Bramber BN44 .... 143 F2
Worthing BN11 .... 185 D6
St Mary's Dr Crawley RH10 . 19 B8
Rustington BN16 .... 199 F5
St Mary's Gdns
Horsham RH12 .... 36 C1
⬛ Littlehampton BN17 ... 198 E5
St Mary's RC High Sch
Horsham RH12 36 C1
St Mary's Ho Horsham RH12 36 C1
Bramber BN44 .... 143 F2
St Mary's Lodge ⬛ PO19 . 173 A6
St Mary's Pl BN2 .... 207 B5
St Mary's RC (A) Prim Sch
PO21 .... 195 D3
St Mary's RC Prim Sch
Portslade-by-Sea BN41 ... 186 B7
Worthing BN11 .... 182 C2
St Mary's Rd
Boxgrove PO18 .... 154 C4
Burgess Hill RH15 .... 106 F4
Liss GU33 .... 45 B4
Shoreham-by-Sea BN43 .. 184 F7
St Mary's Rd W RH15 ..... 106 E4
St Mary's Sch RH10 .... 19 A4
St Mary's Sq ⬛ BN2 ..... 188 D4
St Mary's Terr ⬛ BN43 .. 184 E7
St Mary's Way BN17 .... 198 E5
St Marys Cl
Bognor Regis PO22 .... 195 D5
Lancing BN15 .... 183 B7
St Marys Meadow BN18 .. 176 F4
St Marys Pl ⬛ BN43 ..... 185 A6
St Matthew's Rd BN11 .... 182 C3
St Matthews Ct BN2 .... 188 C5
St Maur's Rd BN12 .... 200 E6
St Michael's Ct BN11 ...... 182 B2
St Michael's Pl BN1 .... 187 E6
St Michael's Rd
Portslade-by-Sea BN41 ... 186 B7
Worthing BN11 .... 182 B2
St Michaels Cl GU28 .... 51 A7
St Michaels Way RH13 .... 103 A3
St Nicholas' CE Jun Sch
BN41 .... 186 B8
St Nicholas Ct
Crawley RH10 .... 19 C7
Haywards Heath RH16 ..... 86 A6
Middleton-on-Sea PO22 .. 196 E5
St Nicholas' Cl
⬛ Lancing BN15 .... 183 D6
Middleton-on-Sea PO22 .. 196 E5
St Nicholas' La PO22 ...... 196 F5
St Nicholas Lodge BN1 ... 207 F5
St Nicholas Pl ⬛ BN21 .. 185 A6
St Nicholas Rd
Brighton BN1 .... 207 F6
Mid Lavant PO18 .... 152 E6
Portslade-by-Sea BN41 ... 186 B7
St Nicolas Cl BN43 .... 184 D8
St Nicolas La BN43 .... 184 D8
St Nicolas & St Mary CE (A)
Prim Sch BN43 .... 185 A8
St Osmund Rd BN12 .... 200 E6
St Pancras PO19 .... 173 B7
St Pancras Ct PO19 .... 173 B6
St Patrick's La GU33 .... 45 F5
St Patrick's Rd BN3 .... 187 A7
St Paul's Ave
BN11, BN15 .... 183 B4
St Paul's CE Prim Sch
BN1 .... 207 F6
St Paul's Cl RH16 .... 85 F5
St Paul's Gdns PO19 .... 172 F7
St Paul's RC (A) Sec Sch
RH16 .... 85 F5
St Paul's Rd PO19 .... 172 F8
St Paul's Rd PO20 .... 207 B8
St Paul's St PO19 .... 173 A7
St Peter's CE (A) Prim Sch
Cowfold RH13 .... 81 E2
Henfield BN5 .... 123 D5
St Peter's CE (C) Prim Sch
RH17 .... 64 A8
St Peter's Cl Cowfold RH13 . 81 E1
Hove BN3 .... 166 F2
St Peter's Cres PO20 ...... 206 E8
St Peter's Cty Inf Sch
BN41 .... 186 B7
St Peter's Pl
Brighton BN1, BN2 .... 207 A6
Lancing BN15 .... 183 C4

St Peter's RC (A) Prim Sch
East Grinstead RH19 .... 9 C1
Shoreham-by-Sea BN43 .. 185 A8
St Peter's Rd Crawley RH11 18 C6
Portslade-by-Sea BN41 ... 186 B7
St Peter's RH15 .... 107 A4
St Peter's Sq ⬛ PO10 ... 169 B8
St Peter's St BN1 .... 207 A7
St Peters Ct PO21 .... 194 E4
St Peters Ct ⬛ PO10 ..... 169 C8
St Peters Rd RH15 .... 107 A4
St Peters View BN5 .... 123 E6
St Philip Howard
High Sch The PO22 .... 176 A6
St. Philip's RC (A) Prim Sch
BN18 .... 158 A3
St Philips Mews ⬛ BN3 . 186 F7
St Raphael's Rd BN11 ..... 181 F2
St Richard's Cotts GU31 .. 90 A4
St Richard's Cl BN3 .... 166 D1
St Richard's Dr PO21 ...... 194 D3
St Richard's Flats BN41 .. 186 B7
St Richard's Hospl PO19 . 173 B8
St Richard's Mews RH10 . 18 F6
St Richard's RC Prim Sch
PO19 .... 173 A5
St Richard's Rd BN41 ...... 186 B7
St Richard's Way PO21 ... 194 D3
St Richard's Wlk PO19 .... 172 F6
St Richards GU29 .... 92 D8
St Richards Cotts
Codmore Hill RH20 .... 98 D6
Lower Fittleworth RH20 ... 97 A2
St Richards Rd PO20 ...... 175 E7
St Robert Southwell RC
Prim Sch RH12 .... 35 F8
St Robert's Lodge ⬛
BN15 .... 183 E5
St Roche's Cl PO18 .... 152 F7
St Sampson Rd RH11 .... 17 F2
St Saviours Ct ⬛ BN1 ... 188 B8
St Stephen's Cl GU27 ...... 26 F6
St Stephens Cl GU27 .... 27 C7
St Swithun's Cl RH19 .... 9 F1
St Thomas Ct PO21 .... 205 A8
St Thomas Dr PO21 .... 204 F8
St Thomas's Rd BN14 ..... 182 B4
St Valerie Rd BN11 .... 182 A1
St Vincent Cl RH10 .... 19 D5
St Wilfred's Ct ⬛ RH16 .. 85 E4
St Wilfred's Rd BN14 ...... 182 D4
St Wilfreds Ct PO20 .... 206 G8
St Wilfreds Rd RH15 .... 107 B4
St Wilfrid Rd PO19 .... 172 D7
St Wilfrid's CE (A) Prim Sch
RH16 .... 85 F4
St Wilfrid's RC (A) Prim Sch
Angmering BN16 .... 179 F6
Crawley RH11 .... 18 B5
St Wilfrid's Way RH16 ..... 85 E4
St Wilfrids RC (A) Prim Sch
RH15 .... 106 F2
St Wilfrids View PO20 ..... 206 C6
St Winefride's Rd BN17 ... 198 E4
St Winifred's Cl PO21 ..... 195 B2
Sake Ride La BN5 .... 104 C1
Salbrook Rd RH1 .... 2 A8
Salehurst Rd RH10 .... 19 E6
Salisbury Rd Crawley RH10 . 18 F2
Hove BN3 .... 187 C6
Tower Hill RH12, RH13 ..... 58 A8
Worthing BN11 .... 182 D2
Salisbury Way PO19 .... 152 F1
Salt Box Cl RH13 .... 56 F2
Saltdean Cl RH10, RH11 .. 18 D3
Saltdean Dr BN2 .... 190 C3
Saltham La PO20 .... 173 E1
Salthill La PO19 .... 172 C8
Salthill Rd PO19 .... 172 B7
Saltings
The Birdham PO20 .... 191 E4
Lancing BN15 .... 183 F5
Littlehampton BN16 .... 199 A6
Shoreham-by-Sea BN43 .. 184 D6
Saltings Way BN44 .... 144 A2
Salvington Cl BN13 .... 181 D7
Salvington Ct BN13 .... 161 F2
Salvington Gdns BN13 .... 181 F6
Salvington Hill BN13 .... 161 E1
Salvington Rd Crawley RH11 17 F3
Worthing BN13 .... 181 E7
Samaritan Cl RH11 .... 17 E4
Samphire Cl RH11 .... 18 A3
Samphire Dr BN13 .... 181 A5
Sampsons Dr PO20 .... 174 C7
San Feliu Cl RH19 .... 10 B2
Sanctuary La RH20 .... 120 C1
Sandbrook BN6 .... 126 F3
Sandcroft PO20 .... 175 D7
Sandeman Way RH13 ...... 58 F8
Sanders Ho BN3 .... 186 E8

Sanderstead ⬛ BN2 ...... 188 F5
Sandfield Ave BN17 .... 178 D4
Sandgate La RH20 .... 120 A2
Sandgate Rd BN1 .... 168 A2
Sandhawes Hill RH19 ...... 10 A4
Sandhill La
Crawley Down RH10 .... 21 B7
Washington BN20 .... 141 E7
Sandhills Rd RH13 .... 56 F3
Sandhurst Sch BN11 .... 182 F2
Sandown Ave BN12 .... 181 C1
Sandown Cl BN12 .... 181 C1
Sandown Ct Hove BN3 .... 166 D1
⬛ Worthing BN11 .... 182 C1
Sandown Rd Brighton BN2 188 D7
Southwick BN42 .... 185 E8
Sandpiper Cl RH11 .... 17 D4
Sandpiper Ct PO20 .... 202 A6
Sandridge La RH16 .... 63 F1
Sandringham Cl
Bracklesham PO20 .... 202 B5
East Grinstead RH19 .... 23 A8
Hove BN3 .... 167 A3
Sandringham Dr BN3 ...... 167 A3
Sandringham Lodge ⬛
BN3 .... 187 C6
Sandringham Mews
Worthing BN13 .... 181 D7
Worthing BN13 .... 182 D6
Sandringham Rd
Chichester PO19 .... 173 C6
Crawley RH11 .... 18 B2
Sandringham Way PO21 . 195 B4
Sandrock Haslemere GU27 . 27 C6
Midhurst GU29 .... 92 D8
Sandrock Cotts GU28 ...... 51 A7
Sandrocks Way RH16 .... 85 E2
Sands La BN5 .... 144 F6
Sandwich Rd BN11 .... 181 F1
Sandy Beach Est PO11 ... 189 B1
Sandy La
Crawley Down RH10 .... 21 A8
East Ashling PO18 .... 151 D4
East Grinstead RH19 .... 9 F1
Fittleworth RH20 .... 97 A2
Haslemere GU26, GU27 ... 26 C7
Heath Common RH20 ..... 120 C1
Henfield BN5 .... 123 D4
Midhurst GU29 .... 92 D8
Rake GU33 .... 46 A4
Watersfield RH20 .... 117 A5
West Hoathly RH19 .... 42 E6
Sandy Point La PO20 ...... 206 B8
Sandy Point Rd PO11 ..... 189 A1
Sandy Rd PO21 .... 205 A7
Sandy Vale RH16 .... 85 E2
Sandygate La RH13 .... 59 F3
Sandymount Ave PO22 ... 195 B5
Sandymount Cl PO22 ...... 195 C6
Sangers Cty Jun Sch RH6 .. 1 F3
Sangers Dr RH6 .... 1 F3
Sanyhils Ave BN1 .... 167 F7
Sarel Way RH6 .... 2 B5
Sargent Cl RH10 .... 18 F2
Sarisbury Cl PO22 .... 196 A5
Sark Cl RH11 .... 18 A2
Sark Gdns BN12 .... 200 F4
Satellite Bsns Village The
RH10 .... 5 E2
Satinwood Cl PO22 .... 196 E6
Saturn Cl RH11 .... 17 E4
Saucelands Rd RH13 ...... 100 E7
Saunders Cl RH10 .... 19 B7
Saunders Hill BN1 .... 168 C7
Saunders Park Rise ⬛
BN2 .... 168 C1
Saunders Park View BN2 . 168 C1
Savernake Wlk RH10 .... 18 F3
Savill Rd RH16 .... 86 A8
Saville Ct RH14 .... 77 D7
Saville Gdns RH14 .... 77 D7
Sawyers Cl RH15 .... 107 D1
Saxby Rd RH15 .... 106 D4
Saxifrage Way
BN12, BN13 .... 181 A5
Saxley RH6 .... 2 C4
Saxon Cl
Bognor Regis PO21 .... 204 F8
East Preston BN16 .... 180 B3
Saxon Cres RH17 .... 36 B4
Saxon Ct BN3 .... 186 D6
Saxon Meadow PO20 ...... 154 C1
Saxon Rd Bramber BN44 . 143 F3
Crawley RH10 .... 19 E5
Hove BN3 .... 186 D6
Saxonbury ⬛ BN2 .... 207 B6
Saxons BN43 .... 164 F1

Saxony Rd BN14 .... 182 C4
Sayers The **5** RH19 .... 9 C1
Scallows Cl RH10 .... 19 A7
Scallows Rd RH10 .... 19 A7
Scamps Hill RH16 .... 86 C6
Scant Rd E PO18 .... 150 F2
Scant Rd W PO18 .... 150 E2
Scarborough Rd BN1 .... 167 D1
Scaynes Hill CE (C)
  Prim Sch RH17 .... 86 F3
Sceptre **2** BN1 .... 167 E2
Scholars Ct RH10 .... 21 A8
School Cl
  Burgess Hill RH15 .... 106 F2
  Fittleworth RH20 .... 97 A3
  Horsham RH12 .... 37 A6
  1 Southwick BN42 .... 185 E7
School Dell PO18 .... 151 A4
School Hill Findon BN14 .... 161 E6
  Slindon BN18 .... 156 C5
  Storrington RH20 .... 119 E1
  Warnham RH12 .... 35 F8
School La Arundel BN18 .... 158 A2
  Ashurst BN44 .... 122 D5
  Ashurst Wood RH19 .... 23 E6
  Bosham PO18 .... 171 C5
  Compton PO18 .... 109 B2
  Danehill RH17 .... 66 B5
  Eastergate PO20 .... 175 F7
  Emsworth PO10 .... 169 B8
  Fittleworth RH20 .... 97 A3
  Liss GU33 .... 45 B4
  Lodsworth GU28 .... 72 B4
  North Mundham PO20 ...... 173 D2
  Nutbourne PO18 .... 170 B7
  Pyecombe BN45 .... 147 C6
  Selsey PO20 .... 206 D8
  Shipley BN11 .... 79 C1
  Stedham GU29 .... 69 F1
  Steyning BN44 .... 143 D3
  Storrington RH20 .... 119 C1
  Sutton RH20 .... 115 F4
  Washington RH20 .... 141 E7
  Westbourne PO10 .... 149 D5
School Rd Amberley BN18 138 E7
  Camelsdale GU27 .... 26 F5
  Hove BN3 .... 186 F8
  Upper Beeding BN44 ...... 144 B2
School Rise BN2 .... 188 E6
Schooner Ct **3** BN16 ...... 199 A6
Scolliers Crossways RH13 .. 79 B3
Scory Cl RH11 .... 18 A3
Scotland La GU27 .... 27 C5
Scotland St BN2 .... 207 B6
Scotlands Cl GU27 .... 27 B5
Scotlands Dr GU27 .... 27 C5
Scotney Cl BN13 .... 181 B5
Scott Cl PO21 .... 195 C2
Scott Rd Crawley RH10 .... 18 F3
  Hove BN3 .... 186 F7
Scott St PO21 .... 195 C2
Scrace Hill Terr RH16 ...... 107 F8
Scrase Lodge RH15 .... 107 D3
Scratchings La GU28 .... 52 C6
Sea Ave BN16 .... 199 D5
Sea Cl
  Middleton-on-Sea PO22 .. 196 E5
  Worthing BN12 .... 181 E2
Sea Dr Bognor Regis PO22 196 D4
  Ferring BN12 .... 200 F4
Sea Ho **14** BN42 .... 185 E7
Sea La Bognor Regis PO21 204 F7
  Ferring BN12 .... 200 F5
  Kingston Gorse BN16 ...... 200 D4
  East Preston BN16 .... 199 F4
  Middleton-on-Sea PO22 .. 196 E5
  Rustington BN16 .... 199 B4
  Worthing BN12 .... 181 C1
Sea Lane Cl
  East Preston BN16 .... 199 F5
  Ferring BN12 .... 200 F6
Sea Lane Gdns BN12 .... 200 F5
Sea Pl BN12 .... 181 E1
Sea Rd Bognor Regis PO22 195 F3
  Littlehampton
    BN16, BN17 .... 199 A3
  West Kingston BN16 ...... 200 A5
Sea View Cotts PO10 .... 169 B8
Sea View Rd BN11 .... 182 B1
Sea Way
  Bognor Regis PO21 .... 204 F8
  Elmer PO22 .... 197 B5
  Middleton-on-Sea PO22 .. 196 E4
Seabright **6** BN11 .... 182 B1
Seabrook Ct BN15 .... 183 E4
Seacourt Cl PO21 .... 194 D2
Seafarers Wlk PO11 .... 189 B1
Seafield Ave BN12 .... 181 D1
Seafield Ct
  East Wittering PO20 ...... 202 A6
  Littlehampton BN16 ...... 199 C4
Seafield Rd Hove BN3 ...... 187 B6
  Littlehampton BN16 ...... 199 C4
  West Kingston BN16 ...... 200 A4
Seafield Terr **4** PO21 .. 195 B2
Seafield Way PO20 .... 202 A6
Seafields
  Bracklesham PO20 .... 202 C5
  Emsworth PO10 .... 169 B8
  Shoreham-by-Sea BN43 .. 184 F8
Seaford Coll GU28 .... 114 C5
Seaford Rd Crawley RH11 .. 18 A2
  Hove BN3, BN41 .... 186 C6
Seagate Ct PO20 .... 201 E6
Seagate Wlk BN17 .... 199 A4
Seagull La PO10 .... 149 B1
Seahaven Gdns BN43 ...... 184 D5
Seal Ct PO20 .... 206 D7
Seal Cty Prim Sch PO20 .. 206 E7
Seal Rd PO20 .... 206 D6
Seal Sq PO20 .... 206 D5
Seaman Ct **5** BN11 ...... 183 B3
Seamill Park Ave BN11 .... 183 B3
Seamill Park Cres BN11 .. 183 B3
Seamill Way BN11 .... 183 B3
Searle's View RH12 .... 36 E5
Seasaw Way BN2 .... 188 F7
Seaside Ave BN15 .... 183 F5
Seaside Cl BN15 .... 183 F5
Seaside Rd BN15 .... 183 F5
Seaton Cl BN17 .... 178 D4
Seaton La BN17 .... 178 D4
Seaton Park Cotts BN17 .. 178 D4
Seaton Pk BN17 .... 178 D4
Seaton Rd BN17 .... 178 D4
Seaview Ave
  Kingston Gorse BN16 .... 200 D4
  West Kingston BN16 ...... 200 A4
Seaview Ct
  2 Bognor Regis PO21 .. 195 C2
  Lancing BN15 .... 183 D4
  Selsey PO20 .... 206 D6
  4 Worthing BN11 ...... 182 B1
Seaview Est BN42 .... 185 F7
Seaview Gdns **5** BN16 .. 199 C4
Seaview Rd BN16 .... 200 A4
Seaward Ct **6** PO21 .... 195 C3
Seaward Dr PO20 .... 190 C1
Seawaves Cl BN16 .... 200 A5
Seawood Ho PO20 .... 201 F7
Second Ave
  Almodington PO20 .... 191 F1
  Bognor Regis PO22 ...... 196 B4
  Hove BN3 .... 187 C6
  Lancing BN15 .... 183 E7
  Southbourne PO10 .... 169 F8
  Worthing BN14 .... 182 D7
Sedbury Rd BN15 .... 183 C8
Sedborn Cl RH11 .... 18 B1
Sedgefield Cl RH10 .... 19 E7
Sedgewick Cl RH10 .... 19 C6
Sedgwick La RH13 .... 58 E4
Sefter Rd PO21 .... 194 B3
Sefton Ave PO21 .... 194 D3
Sefton Cl BN13 .... 181 D6
Sefton Rd BN41 .... 165 F3
Selba Dr BN2 .... 168 E3
Selborne Pl BN3 .... 187 C7
Selborne Rd Hove BN3 .... 187 C6
  Littlehampton BN17 ...... 198 E4
  Worthing BN13 .... 182 F3
Selborne Way BN16 .... 199 F4
Selbourne Cl RH10 .... 6 D2
Selby Ct RH16 .... 85 E3
Selden La
  Hammerpot BN13 .... 160 B1
  Worthing BN13 .... 182 F2
Selden Rd BN11 .... 182 F2
Selden's Mews BN13 ...... 181 F6
Selden's Way RH13 .... 181 F7
Sele Gdns BN44 .... 144 B2
Selham Cl Brighton BN1 .. 168 D6
  Chichester PO19 .... 153 A3
  Crawley RH11 .... 18 A7
Selham Dr BN1 .... 168 D6
Selham Pl BN1 .... 168 D6
Selham Rd GU29 .... 93 C6
Selhurst Cl BN16 .... 199 F5
Selhurstpark Rd PO18 .... 135 B4
Selkirk Cl BN13 .... 181 E4
Selmeston Pl BN2 .... 188 F6
Selmestone Rd BN2 ...... 188 F5
Selsey Ave PO21 .... 195 A2
Selsey Cl Brighton BN1 .. 168 E6
  South Hayling PO11 ...... 189 B2
Selsey Ct **3** Crawley RH11 18 B2
  6 Rustington BN16 .. 199 B4
Selsey Ct Selsey PO20 .... 206 D6
Selsey Rd Crawley RH11 .. 18 A2
  Sidlesham PO20 .... 203 F7
  Stockbridge PO19 .... 172 E3
  Street End PO20, PO19 .. 192 D7
Selsfield Dr BN2 .... 168 D3
Selsfield Rd
  Little London RH17, RH19 .. 42 A4
  West Hoathly RH19 .... 42 C7
Selway La BN17 .... 198 F6
Selwyn Ave BN17 .... 178 D3
Selwyn Cl
  Bognor Regis PO21 ...... 194 F4
  Crawley RH10 .... 6 C1
Semley Rd Brighton BN1 .. 168 A1
  Hassocks BN6 .... 126 E4
Senator Gdns PO19 .... 172 A7
Sequoia Pk RH11 .... 18 D4
Sergison Cl RH16 .... 85 D5
Sergison Rd RH16 .... 85 D5
Serrin Way RH12 .... 36 E5
Service Rd
  Gatwick Airport, North Terminal
    RH6 .... 5 F8
  Gatwick Airport, South Terminal
    RH6 .... 6 B7
Servite Ct PO21 .... 195 B4
Servite Ho PO21 .... 195 B4
Sevelands Cl BN2 .... 188 F7
Seven Dials BN1 .... 207 F7
Sevenfields BN6 .... 106 D4
Seventh Ave BN15 .... 183 E8
Severals Rd GU29 .... 92 C7
Severn Rd RH10 .... 19 C5
Seville St BN2 .... 188 C7
Sewill Cl RH6 .... 4 F7
Sextant Ct **6** BN16 .... 199 A6
Seymour Pl **12** PO21 .. 195 C3
Seymour Ho **5** BN2 .. 188 D4
Seymour Rd RH11 .... 18 B2
Seymour Sq **3** BN2 .. 188 D4
Seymour St **4** BN2 .. 188 D4
Shackleton Rd RH10 ...... 18 F3
Shadwells Cl BN15 .... 183 F7
Shadwells Ct BN15 .... 183 F7
Shadwells Rd BN15 .... 183 F7
Shaftesbury Ave
  BN11, BN12, BN13 ...... 181 E3
Shaftesbury Ct **4** BN16 .. 199 C4
Shaftesbury Pl BN11 .... 188 A8
Shaftesbury Rd
  Brighton BN1 .... 207 A8
  Crawley RH10 .... 19 D4
  Littlehampton BN16 ...... 199 C4
Shakespeare Rd BN11 .. 182 C3
Shakespeare St BN3 ...... 187 A8
Shalbourne Cres PO20 .. 202 C5
Shalesbrook La RH18 .... 23 F1
Shamrock Cl
  Bosham PO18 .... 171 C5
  Chichester PO19 .... 173 B8
Shandon Gdns BN14 .... 182 D6
Shandon Rd BN14 .... 182 D6
Shandon Way BN14 ...... 182 D6
Shands BN6 .... 126 F3
Shandys Ct RH12 .... 36 A1
Shanklin Ct
  7 Brighton BN2 ...... 188 C8
  Hove BN3 .... 166 D1
Shanklin Rd BN2 .... 188 C8
Shannon Cl BN16 .... 199 A4
Shardelows Rd BN16 .... 179 F6
Sharon Cl RH10 .... 19 A4
Sharpthorne Cl RH11 .... 17 F6
Sharpthorne Cres BN41 .. 166 C1
Sharrow Cl **9** RH16 .... 85 E5
Shaves Wood La BN6 .... 125 A2
Shaw Cl PO22 .... 196 F5
Shaw's La RH13 .... 57 D1
Shawcross Ho **10** BN1 .. 167 E2
Shaw Rd RH10 .... 18 F7
Shearwater Cl **6** RH11 .. 17 D5
Shearwater Dr PO22 .... 195 C6
Sheddingdean Bsns Ctr
  RH15 .... 106 F5
Sheddingdean Cl RH15 .. 107 A4
Sheddingdean Cty Inf Sch
  RH15 .... 107 A5
Sheddingdean Cty Prim Sch
  RH15 .... 107 A5
Sheep Fold Ave RH10 .... 199 E6
Sheep La GU29 .... 92 FB
Sheep Pen La BN44 ...... 143 D3
Sheepbell Cl BN41 ...... 166 B3
Sheepdown Cl GU28 .... 96 A7
Sheepdown Dr GU28 .... 96 A7
Sheepwash La
  East Lavant PO18 .... 152 F5
  Shipton Green PO20 .... 190 E4
Sheffield Cl RH10 .... 19 B4
Shelby Rd BN13 .... 181 C6
Sheldon Cl RH10 .... 19 D5
Sheldon Ct BN11 .... 182 B1
Shell La RH17 .... 41 C1
Shellbridge Rd BN18 .... 156 E3
Shelldale Ave BN41 ...... 186 B7
Shelldale Cres BN41 .... 186 B7
Shelldale Rd BN41 ...... 186 B8
Shelley Cl RH10 .... 19 C8
Shelley Ct **4** RH16 .... 85 D5
Shelley Rd BN12 .... 35 C3
Shelley Rd
  Bognor Regis PO21 ...... 195 B3
  East Grinstead RH19 .... 9 D1
  Horsham RH12 .... 36 B3
  Hove BN3 .... 186 F7
  Worthing BN11 .... 182 C2
Shelley Wood BN6 .... 106 D4
Shelly Cty Prim Sch RH12 .. 35 E3
Shellys Ct RH13 .... 37 A3
Shenfield Way BN1 ...... 168 B3
Shenstone RH16 .... 86 B8
Shepherd Cl RH10 .... 18 E3
Shepherd's Hill GU27 .. 27 C6
Shepherd's Hill Bglws
  GU27 .... 27 C6
Shepherds Croft
  Brighton BN1 .... 167 C4
  Findon BN14 .... 161 E6
Shepherds La GU28 ...... 72 B3
Shepherds Mead
  Burgess Hill RH15 ...... 106 F4
  Worthing BN14 .... 162 A2
Shepherds Way
  Horsham RH12 .... 37 A5
  Liphook GU30 .... 25 D3
Shepherds Wlk BN6 .... 126 F5
Shepherdsgrove La RH19 .. 10 F5
Sheppard Way BN41 .... 166 A3
Sheppey Cl RH11 .... 18 C3
Sheppeys RH16 .... 85 D2
Sherston Wlk **12** RH11 .. 18 B1
Sherborne Rd PO19 ...... 172 E7
Sherbourne Cl BN13 .... 166 D3
Sherbourne La RH13 .... 187 D5
Sherbourne Rd BN13 .... 166 D3
Sherbourne Way BN13 .. 166 D3
Sherbrooke Cl BN13 .... 181 D6
Sherburne Hospl The
  PO19 .... 152 F1
Sheridan Cl RH11 .... 9 C1
Sheridan Mansions BN3 .. 187 A8
Sheridan Rd BN14 ...... 182 E5
Sheridan Terr BN3 ...... 187 A8
Sherlock Ave PO19 ...... 172 E7
Shermanbury Cl
  t Horsham RH12 .... 36 D4
  Lancing BN15 .... 183 C5
Shermanbury Dr RH20 .. 119 C2
Shermanbury Rd RH14 .. 182 B4
Sherston Ct RH10 .... 119 E2
Sherwood Cl
  Bognor Regis PO22 ...... 195 B6
  Liss Forest GU33 .... 45 C7
Sherwood Dr RH16 ...... 85 C5
Sherwood Rd PO22 ...... 195 B6
Sherwood Wlk RH10 .... 18 F3
Shetland Cl RH10 .... 19 E7
Shetland Ct BN13 .... 181 B5
Shillinglee Park Golf Course
  GU8 .... 29 D6
Shilpey CE (C) Prim Sch
  RH13 .... 79 B1
Shingle Rd BN41 .... 185 A6
Shingle Wlk PO20 .... 201 F6
Shinwell Wlk **3** RH11 .. 18 B1
Ship St Brighton BN1 .... 207 F5
  East Grinstead RH19 .... 22 E8
  Shoreham-by-Sea BN43 .. 184 E7
Ship Street Gdns BN1 .. 207 F5
Shipfield PO21 .... 194 F2
Shipley Bridge La RH10 .. 7 A3
Shipley Cl GU30 .... 25 C3
Shipley Rd Crawley RH11 .. 18 A6
  Southwater RH13 .... 79 E5
Shipleybridge La
  RH10 .... 6 F4
Shipton Green La PO20 .. 191 B4
Shire Pair Rd RH10 ...... 19 D7
Shirlands Cl **2** BN16 .. 199 D6
Shirley Ave BN3 .... 167 B2
Shirley Cl
  Bognor Regis PO21 ...... 205 A8
  Crawley RH11 .... 17 E2
  Littlehampton BN16 ...... 199 D4
  Southwick BN43 .... 185 D8
  Worthing BN14 .... 182 B7
Shirley Dr
  Bognor Regis PO22 ...... 196 A6
  Hove BN3 .... 167 C2
  Worthing BN14 .... 182 B6
Shirley Rd BN3 .... 187 C8
Shirley St BN3 .... 187 B7
Shirley Ho 127 E2
Shirleys Gdn PO22 ...... 196 B5
Shooting Field BN44 .... 143 D4
Shop La PO18 .... 153 A5
Shopfield Cl BN16 ...... 199 C6
Shopping Ctr The PO20 .. 206 D7
Shopsdam Rd BN15 .... 183 F4
Shopwhyke Ind Ctr PO20 173 D7
Shopwhyke Rd
  PO19, PO20 .... 173 E7
Shore Rd Bosham PO18 .. 171 B3
Bosham PO18 .... 171 B4
East Wittering PO20 ...... 201 E7
Shorecroft PO21 .... 194 F1
Shoreham Airport
  BN15, BN43 .... 184 C8
Shoreham Beach Cty
  Fst Sch BN43 .... 185 A6
Shoreham By-Pass
  BN41, BN42, BN43, BN15 165 D2
Shoreham Coll BN43 .... 185 D7
Shoreham Cty Fst Sch
  BN43 .... 184 E8
Shoreham Rd Crawley RH10 19 C3
  Small Dole BN5 .... 144 F8
  Upper Beeding
    BN43, BN44 .... 164 B7
Shoreham-by-Sea Sta
  BN43 .... 184 F7
Short Cl RH11 .... 18 D8
Short Furlong BN17 ...... 198 F5
Short Gallop RH10 ...... 19 D7
Shortgate Rd BN2 ...... 168 F4
Shortsfield Cl RH12 .... 36 C5
Shotford PO20 .... 203 F8
Shotterfield Terr GU33 .. 45 B4
Shottermill RH12 .... 37 A7
Shottermill Cty Fst Sch
  GU27 .... 26 F7
Shottermill Cty Jun Sch
  GU27 .... 26 F7
Shottermill Rd GU27 .... 26 E5
Shotters RH15 .... 106 E1
Shovelstrode La RH19 .. 23 D8
Shripney La PO22 .... 175 C1
Shripney Rd
  Bognor Regis PO22 ...... 195 D5
  Bognor Regis PO22 ...... 195 D5
Shrubbs Dr PO22 .... 196 E5
Sickle Rd GU27 .... 27 A5
Sidehill Dr BN41 .... 165 F2
Sidings The RH12 .... 33 D7
Sidlesham Cl PO11 ...... 189 B2
Sidlesham Cty Prim Sch
  PO20 .... 203 D8
Sidlesham La PO20 ...... 192 A4
Silchester Dr RH11 ...... 18 B4
Silkin Wlk **8** RH11 .. 18 B1
Sillwood Cl **6** BN1 .. 187 E5
Sillwood Hall **5** BN1 .. 187 E5
Sillwood Pl **9** BN1 .. 187 E5
Sillwood Rd BN1 .... 187 E5
Sillwood St BN1 .... 187 E5
Silver Birch Cl GU33 .... 45 C4
Silver Birch Dr
  Middleton-on-Sea PO22 .. 196 E6
  Worthing BN13 .... 181 C5
Silver Birches
  Haywards Heath RH16 .. 86 A4
  Small Dole BN5 .... 144 F7
Silver Glade RH20 ...... 119 E6
Silver La RH14 .... 77 D8
Silver Way PO20 .... 202 C4
Silver Wood RH20 ...... 119 B7
Silver Wood Copse RH20 .. 119 B7
Silverdale
  Coldwaltham PO20 ...... 117 C5
  Keymer BN6 .... 127 B3
Silverdale Ave BN3 ...... 187 D7
Silverdale Cl PO21 ...... 205 A8
Silverdale Ct BN13 ...... 183 C5
Silverdale Ind Est BN11 .. 183 B3
Silverdale Rd
  Burgess Hill RH15 ...... 107 C2
  Hove BN3 .... 187 D7
Silverlea Gdns RH6 ...... 2 C2
Silverlock Pl PO10 ...... 149 D5
Silverston Ave PO21 .... 195 A2
Silvertrees PO10 .... 149 B2
Simcor Ct **13** PO21 .. 195 C3
Sinclair Cl RH10 .... 19 C4
Sinclair La BN13 .... 100 D6
Singing Hills Golf Course
  BN6 .... 125 B4
Singleton CE (C) Prim Sch
  PO18 .... 133 D7
Singleton Cl PO21 ...... 194 C1
Singleton Cres BN12 .... 200 F6

Singleton Cres W BN12 ..... 180 F3
Singleton Ho BN17 .... 178 B3
Singleton Rd
  Brighton BN1 .... 168 A6
  Broadridge Heath RH12 .... 35 D3
Singleton Way RH15 .... 107 C1
Sinnocks RH20 .... 99 E1
Sir George's PI BN44 .... 143 C3
Sir Robert Peel Ct **[11]**
  PO21 .... 195 D4
Siskin Cl RH12 .... 36 E5
Sissinghurst Cl RH10 .... 19 D7
Six Acres Cl RH13 .... 56 F2
Skelmersdale Wlk RH11 ..... 17 E2
Skeyne Dr **[4]** RH20 .... 98 C2
Skiff La RH14 .... 53 F5
Skipton Way RH10 .... 2 B5
Skye Cluan Cl PO22 .... 176 B6
Skylark View RH12 .... 36 D7
Slade La GU31 .... 67 F5
Slattsfield Cl PO20 .... 206 F7
Slaugham Cl RH11 .... 17 F3
Slaugham La RH17 .... 61 A2
Sleets Rd RH12 .... 35 E3
Slider's La
  Furner's Green RH17 .... 66 B1
  Furner's Green TN22 .... 87 F6
Slimbridge Rd RH15 .... 106 F3
Slindon Bottom Rd BN18 . 156 A4
Slindon CE (C) Prim Sch
  BN18 .... 156 D4
Slindon Cl BN14 .... 182 D6
Slindon Coll BN18 .... 156 B5
Slindon La BN18 .... 182 D6
Slindon CE (C) Sch RH12 . 34 D4
Slinfold Park (Golf & Ctry Pk)
  RH12 .... 34 A2
Slinfold Wlk RH11 .... 18 A6
Slinfold Cl BN2 .... 188 D5
Slipper Rd PO10 .... 169 C8
Sloane Ct **[4]** BN2 .... 188 C5
Slonk Hill Rd BN43 .... 165 A1
Sloughbrook Cl RH12 .... 36 F6
Sloughgreen La RH17 .... 61 E1
Slugwash La RH16, RH17 .. 86 D2
Small's La RH11 .... 18 C6
Smallcroft Cl RH17 .... 198 C5
Smallcuts Ave PO10 .... 149 F1
Smallfield Rd RH6 .... 2 D3
Smallmead RH6 .... 2 B3
Smalls Mead RH11 .... 18 C6
Smith Cl RH10 .... 18 D3
Smith La PO10 .... 169 F1
Smith's Cross RH13 .... 82 C3
Smithbarn RH13 .... 37 A2
Smithbarn Cl RH6 .... 2 B4
Smithers Cotts RH14 .... 33 F7
Smithers Hill La RH13 .... 79 B2
Smithy The RH13 .... 81 E1
Smock Alley RH20 .... 119 E7
Smokejack Hill RH5 .... 13 D7
Smokyhouse La GU28 .... 94 B5
Smolletts RH19 .... 22 C8
Smugglers La PO18 .... 171 B1
Smugglers' La
  Barns Green RH13 .... 56 D3
  Barns Green RH13 .... 56 F3
  Paynes Green RH12, RH5 . 14 E7
Smugglers Way RH15 .... 56 F2
Smugglers Wlk BN12 .... 181 E1
Snapes Rd RH20 .... 119 F3
Snell Hatch RH11 .... 18 B6
Snipe La GU27 .... 27 A1
Snow Hill RH10 .... 8 A4
Snow Hill Bsns Ctr RH10 ... 8 A4
Snowdrop Cl RH11 .... 18 A2
Snowdrop La RH16 .... 86 C4
Snowflakes La RH16 .... 86 D6
Snowhill La RH10 .... 7 F5
Soames Ct RH15 .... 106 F4
Soane Cl RH11 .... 17 E4
Solent Cl BN16 .... 179 A3
Solent Rd PO20 .... 201 F6
Solent Way PO20 .... 206 E5
Solway Ave BN1 .... 167 F7
Solway Cl BN17 .... 199 A5
Somergate RH12 .... 35 F2
Somerhill Ave BN3 .... 187 D7
Somerhill Ct **[10]** BN3 .. 187 D7
Somerhill Cty Jun Sch
  BN3 .... 187 D7
Somerhill Lodge **[6]** BN3 . 187 D6
Somerhill Rd BN3 .... 187 D6
Somerley La PO20 .... 191 E1
Somersbury La GU6, RH12 . 12 F7
Somerset Cl BN13 .... 182 A5
Somerset Ct **[3]** BN3 .... 187 C7
Somerset Gdns
  PO21, PO22 .... 195 C5
Somerset Hospl GU28 .... 95 F8
Somerset Point **[1]** BN2 . 188 C4

Somerset Rd
  East Preston BN16 .... 200 B6
  Ferring BN12 .... 200 F4
Somerset St BN2 .... 188 C5
Somerstown PO19 .... 172 F8
Somerton Gn PO22 .... 195 F5
Somerville Dr RH10 .... 6 C1
Somping Rd BN14 .... 182 E7
Sompting Abbotts Sch
  BN15 .... 183 A8
Sompting Ave BN14 .... 182 D5
Sompting By-Pass BN14 ... 182 E7
Sompting Cl **[3]** BN43 .. 188 B8
Sompting Rd
  Lancing BN15 .... 183 D5
  Worthing BN14 .... 182 E6
Sopers La BN44 .... 163 C7
Sorrel Cl RH11 .... 18 A2
Sorrel Rd RH12 .... 36 E5
South Acre GU31 .... 89 D3
South Ash BN44 .... 143 D4
South Ave
  Bognor Regis PO21 .... 194 F3
  Brighton BN2 .... 188 C5
  Hurstpierpoint BN6 .... 126 A5
  Worthing BN11 .... 181 E1
South Bank Hassocks BN6 . 126 E3
  Stockbridge PO19 .... 172 F4
South Bank Cl BN15 .... 184 A4
South Bay PO10 .... 169 C3
South Beach **[6]** BN15 . 184 F6
South Bersted CE (C)
  Prim Sch PO22 .... 195 D5
South Bersted Ind Est
  PO22 .... 195 D6
South Cl Burgess Hill RH15 106 E3
  Crawley RH10 .... 18 F7
South Dr Angmering BN16 179 E3
  Bognor Regis PO22 .... 196 C5
  Burgess Hill RH15 .... 106 E3
  Ferring BN12 .... 200 E4
  South Farm Innds BN14 . 182 C5
South Farm Rd
  BN11, BN14 .... 182 C5
South Gr Horsham RH13 .... 36 D1
  Petworth GU28 .... 95 F7
South Holmes Rd RH13 ..... 37 B4
South La Breach PO10 ...... 150 A2
  Houghton BN18 .... 138 B3
  Tillington GU28 .... 94 F7
  Woodmancote PO10 ...... 150 A3
South Lodge
  Bognor Regis PO21 .... 194 A2
  [9] Brighton BN2 ...... 188 F5
  [1] Lancing BN15 ...... 183 C7
South Lodge Cl RH15 .... 106 F4
South Pallant PO19 .... 173 A6
South Par RH6 .... 1 F4
South Pas BN17 .... 198 E4
South Point RH6 .... 6 B7
South Point **[7]** BN43 .. 185 A6
South Terr
  Bognor Regis PO22 .... 195 D5
  Brighton BN1 .... 167 E1
  Hayward Heath RH16 ..... 85 E4
  Liphook GU30 .... 25 D1
South St Brighton BN1 ..... 207 F5
  Chichester PO19 .... 173 A6
  Cuckfield RH17 .... 84 E6
  Ditchling BN6 .... 127 D3
  Emsworth PO10 .... 169 B8
  Horsham RH12 .... 36 C2
  Lancing BN15 .... 183 E4
  Midhurst GU29 .... 92 F7
  Partridge Green RH13 ... 103 A3
  Portslade-by-Sea BN41 . 166 A1
  Worthing BN11 .... 185 D1
  Worthing, West Tarring
  BN11, BN13, BN14 .... 182 A4
South Strand BN16 .... 200 A4
South Strand BN16 .... 200 A4
South View Copthorne RH10 . 7 E3
  Ditchling BN6 .... 127 E5
  West Kingston BN16 ...... 200 B4
South View Terr BN5 .... 123 E4
South Way BN15 .... 195 A5
South Wlk PO22 .... 196 E5
South Woodlands BN1 ..... 167 E5
Southall Ave BN2 .... 168 D2
Southampton St BN2 .... 207 B6
Southan View RH5 .... 183 C3
Southbourne Ave PO10 .... 169 D8
Southbourne Cty Inf Sch
  PO10 .... 170 A8
Southbourne Cty Jun Sch
  PO10 .... 170 A8
Southbourne Halt PO10 ... 170 A8

Southbrook RH11 .... 18 C1
Southbrook Rd
  West Ashling PO18 .... 151 B2
  West Ashling PO18 .... 151 C3
Southcote Ave PO20 .... 201 E7
Southcourt Cl BN16 .... 179 E6
Southcourt Rd BN14 .... 182 C3
Southdean Cl PO22 .... 196 C5
Southdean Dr PO22 .... 196 F5
Southdown Ave
  Brighton BN1 .... 168 A1
  Portslade-by-Sea BN41 . 186 C8
Southdown Cl
  Haywards Heath RH16 .... 85 D2
  Horsham RH12 .... 37 A5
  Midhurst GU29 .... 92 D6
Southdown Ct PO20 .... 202 A7
Southdown Ho BN12 .... 181 D2
Southdown Pl BN1 .... 168 A1
Southdown Rd
  Bognor Regis PO21 .... 195 C3
  Brighton BN1 .... 168 A1
  Portslade-by-Sea BN41 . 166 A2
  Shoreham-by-Sea BN43 . 184 F7
  Southwick BN42 .... 185 E7
Southdown Sch BN44 ...... 143 D3
Southdown Terr BN44 ..... 143 E3
Southdown View Cl BN14 182 F5
Southdown View Rd BN14 182 F5
Southdown View Way
  BN14 .... 182 E6
Southdown Way RH20 ..... 119 F3
Southern Cross Ind Est
  PO22 .... 195 C8
Southern L Ctr PO20 .... 173 D3
Southern Rd PO20 .... 206 E6
Southey Rd BN11 .... 182 C1
Southfield Ind Pk PO18 ... 171 B6
Southfield Rd BN14 .... 182 D6
Southfields Cl PO19 .... 172 F3
Southfields Rd RH17, BN16 198 F5
Southgate PO19 .... 172 F5
Southgate Ave RH10, BN14 18 E4
Southgate Cty Fst &
  Mid Sch RH10 .... 18 D4
Southgate Cty West Fst &
  Mid Sch RH10 .... 18 C4
Southgate Dr RH10, RH11 . 18 E4
Southgate Par RH10 .... 18 D4
Southgate Rd RH10, RH11 . 18 D4
Southlands
  East Grinstead RH19 ..... 22 E7
  Horley RH6 .... 1 F3
Southlands Ave RH6 .... 2 A4
Southlands Cl **[1]** BN43 . 185 B8
Southlands General Hospl
  BN43 .... 185 B8
Southlands La RH10 .... 119 E8
Southlands Pk GU29 .... 92 E5
Southleigh Rd PO10, PO9 . 149 B2
Southleys GU27 .... 49 A5
Southmount BN1 .... 168 B1
Southon Cl BN41 .... 165 F3
Southover Pl BN2 .... 207 B7
Southover Rd PO21 .... 195 C3
Southover St BN2 .... 207 B6
Southover Way PO20 .... 173 A1
Southsea Ave BN12 .... 181 E1
Southside RH20 .... 98 D2
Southview
  Scaynes Hill RH17 .... 86 F3
  Small Dole BN5 .... 144 F6
Southview Cl RH17 .... 165 E1
Southview Dr BN11 .... 182 A2
Southview Gdns BN11 ..... 182 A2
Southview Rd
  Bognor Regis PO22 .... 196 B4
  Findon BN14 .... 161 E6
  Southwick BN42 .... 185 E7
Southwark Cl RH11 .... 18 B2
Southwark Wlk PO21 ...... 194 E4
Southwater Bsns Pk RH13 . 57 F1
Southwater Cl
  Brighton BN2 .... 188 D6
  Worthing BN12 .... 181 B3
Southwater Cty Inf Sch
  RH13 .... 57 F2
Southwater Cty Jun Sch
  RH13 .... 57 F2
Southwater St RH13 .... 58 A4
Southway
  Burgess Hill RH15 .... 106 D3
  Littlehampton BN17 ...... 198 F4
Southway Cty Jun Sch
  RH15 .... 106 D3
Southways Ave BN14 ...... 182 E6
Southways Pk RH11 .... 5 D3
Southwick Cl BN19 .... 9 D2
Southwick Ho RH19 .... 9 D2
Southwick Sq BN42 .... 185 E7
Southwick St BN42 .... 185 E8

Southwick Sta **[2]** BN42 . 185 E7
Southwold Cl BN13 .... 161 E1
Southwood Rd PO11 .... 189 A1
Sovereign Ct **[16]** PO21 195 D3
Sovereign Rd PO22 .... 196 C5
Spa Ct BN3 .... 187 B5
Spanish Ct RH15 .... 107 B4
Spark's La RH17 .... 62 E2
Sparks Ct BN17 .... 198 D5
Sparrow Way BN6 .... 106 D3
Sparshott Rd PO20 .... 206 E5
Spartan Cl PO10 .... 169 C3
Spatham La BN6 .... 127 F4
Spear Hill RH20 .... 121 A7
Speedwell Cl BN13 .... 181 A5
Speedwell Way RH12 .... 36 E5
Spencer Ave BN3 .... 166 D3
Spencer Rd Lancing BN15 . 183 D5
  New Brighton PO10 ...... 149 A4
Spencer St PO21 .... 195 D4
Spencer's Rd RH12 .... 36 B3
Spencers La RH6 .... 1 A2
Spencers Pl RH12 .... 36 B4
Spencers Rd BN11 .... 181 D5
Spey Cl BN13 .... 181 B8
Spicers Cl RH15 .... 106 F5
Spierbridge Rd RH20 ...... 119 C2
Spiers Way RH6 .... 2 B1
Spindle Way RH10 .... 2 C6
Spinnaker Cl BN16, BN17 . 199 A5
Spinnals Gn BN42 .... 185 D7
Spinney Cl
  Crawley Down RH10 ...... 21 C8
  Horsham RH12 .... 37 B6
  Hurstpierpoint BN6 ..... 126 C5
Spinney La
  West Chiltington Common
  RH20 .... 119 D5
  West Itchenor PO20 ..... 191 A6
Spinney North RH20 .... 98 D2
Spinney The
  Bognor Regis PO21 .... 194 E3
  Burgess Hill RH15 .... 107 B5
  Crawley RH11 .... 18 B4
  Haslemere GU27 .... 27 F2
  Hassocks BN6 .... 126 F5
  Haywards Heath
  RH16, RH17 .... 85 D8
  Horley RH6 .... 167 C3
  Hove BN3 .... 167 C3
  Pulborough RH20 .... 98 D2
  West Itchenor PO20 ..... 191 B5
  West Kingston BN16 ..... 200 A4
Spinney Wlk PO22 .... 196 B6
Spitalfield La PO19 .... 173 B7
Spitfire Ct PO20 .... 154 D2
Spithandle La BN44 .... 122 B3
Spooners Rd RH12 .... 37 A4
Spring Copse
  Copthorne RH10 .... 7 C3
  East Grinstead RH19 .... 9 D3
Spring Gdns Brighton BN1 207 A5
  Copthorne RH10 .... 7 C3
Emsworth PO10 .... 169 C8
Heath Common RH20 .... 120 E2
[6] Southwick BN42 . 185 E7
Spring Hill Wildfowl Pk
  RH18 .... 23 A1
Spring La Clayton BN6 .... 147 E8
  Haywards Heath RH16 .... 64 B1
  Slinfold RH13 .... 34 C3
Spring Meadow RH18 .... 23 F1
Spring Meadows GU29 .... 92 C6
Spring Plat RH10 .... 19 C6
Spring Plat Ct RH10 .... 19 C6
Spring St BN1 .... 187 E5
Spring Way RH19 .... 10 A4
Springate Rd BN42 .... 185 F8
Springbank PO19 .... 152 F1
Springfarm Rd GU27 .... 26 E5
Springfield
  Bognor Regis PO22 .... 194 A2
  East Grinstead RH19 ...... 9 D4
  Liss GU33 .... 45 B4
Springfield Cl
  Birdham PO20 .... 191 F5
  Bolney RH17 .... 83 C4
  Mid Leavant PO18 .... 152 F7
  Rustington BN16 .... 199 E5
Springfield Cotts RH17 ..... 83 C4
Springfield Cres RH12 ..... 36 B2
Springfield Dr RH12 .... 36 B2
Springfield Fst Sch BN14 . 182 E4
Springfield Gdns BN11 ... 182 A7
Springfield La RH12, RH13 . 38 B5
Springfield Park Rd RH12 . 36 B2
Springfield Rd
  Brighton BN1 .... 188 A8
  Crawley RH11 .... 18 D5
  Horsham RH12 .... 36 C2
Springfields Farm Ind Est
  RH17 .... 107 F5

Springhead Farm Cotts
  BN18 .... 139 E7
Springhills BN5 .... 123 E4
Spronkett's La RH17 .... 82 E3
Sproule Cl BN18 .... 177 B2
Sproutes La RH13 .... 100 D8
Spur Rd PO19 .... 173 D5
Spurgeon Cl RH11 .... 18 C7
Spy La RH14 .... 32 A4
Square Dr Fernhurst GU27 . 49 B7
  Marley Heights GU27 .... 27 B1
Square The Brighton BN1 . 167 E6
  Crawley RH11 .... 18 D6
  Findon BN14 .... 161 E6
  Prinsted PO10 .... 169 F7
  South Harting GU31 .... 89 D4
  Storrington RH20 .... 119 D1
  Washington BN14 .... 143 C3
  West Barnham PO22 .... 176 B5
  Westbourne PO10 .... 169 D3
Squire Way BN5 .... 123 E4
Squires Cl RH11 .... 21 A8
Squires Cotts RH20 .... 138 A7
Squirrel Cl RH11 .... 5 B1
Squirrels Copse RH20 .... 120 C3

Stable Cotts Crawley RH11 . 39 A8
  Shopwyke PO20 .... 173 F7
Stable Field PO22 .... 197 B5
Stable Flats RH11 .... 39 A8
Stable La BN14 .... 161 E6
Stace Way RH10 .... 19 E8
Stackfield Rd RH11 .... 17 E5
Stafford House F Ed Ctr
  BN6 .... 127 A3
Stafford Rd Brighton BN1 . 187 E8
  Crawley RH11 .... 1 B1
Stafford Way BN6 .... 127 A3
Staffords Cl BN13 .... 199 B6
Staffords Pl RH6 .... 2 B2
Stag Cl BN5 .... 123 E6
Stagelands RH11 .... 18 C8
Stagelands Ct RH11 .... 18 C8
Stairbridge La RH17 .... 105 E7
Stakers La RH13 .... 80 A8
Stalham Way PO22 .... 196 A6
Stall House La RH20 .... 99 A8
Stamford **[6]** RH6 .... 85 D6
Stamford Lodge **[7]** BN1 . 167 E2
Stammerham Bsns Ctr
  RH5 .... 15 E7
Stammers Hill BN5 .... 145 F3
Stan Hill RH6 .... 4 D8
Stanbridge Cl RH11 .... 17 E6
Stanbridge Way RH17 ..... 64 B7
Standard Cl PO21 .... 194 E3
Stanbury Cl PO18 .... 171 C7
Standean Cl BN1 .... 168 D6
Standen Cl RH19 .... 9 A4
Standen St BN44 .... 144 B2
Standen (NT) RH19 .... 22 D4
Standen Pl RH12 .... 37 A7
Standgrove Pl RH17 .... 64 A6
Standinghall La RH10 .... 20 A3
Stane St
  Billingshurst RH14, RH20 . 77 B4
  Codmore Hill RH20 .... 98 D6
  Five Oaks RH14, RH13 ... 55 E4
  Park Street RH12, RH13 . 34 C4
  Strettington PO18 .... 154 B3
Stane Street Cl RH20 .... 98 C4
Stanford Ave
  Brighton BN1 .... 168 A1
  Brighton BN6 .... 126 E4
Stanford Cl
  Bognor Regis PO22 .... 195 E5
  Hassocks BN6 .... 126 E4
  Hove BN3 .... 167 C1
Stanford Ct BN1 .... 187 F8
Stanford Cty Jun Sch BN1 187 F8
Stanford Orch RH12 .... 35 F8
Stanford Rd BN1 .... 187 F8
Stanford Sq BN11 .... 182 E4
Stanford Terr BN6 .... 126 E4
Stanford Way RH12 .... 35 D3
Stanhope Rd
  Littlehampton BN17 ..... 198 E5
  Worthing BN11 .... 182 D3
Stanley Ave BN41 .... 165 F3
Stanley Cl
  Bognor Regis PO21 .... 195 D4
  Crawley RH10 .... 18 E4
Stanley Ctr RH10 .... 5 F2
Stanley Deason L Ctr BN2 188 F5

Stanley Deason Sch BN2 .... 188 F5
Stanley Rd Brighton BN1 ... 207 A7
  Emsworth PO10 .... 169 C8
  Littlehampton BN17 .... 178 D3
  Portslade-by-Sea BN41 .... 186 A8
  Worthing BN11 .... 182 D3
Stanley St BN2 .... 207 B6
Stanley Wlk RH13 .... 36 D2
Stanmer BN1 .... 168 F8
Stanmer Park Rd BN1 .... 168 B2
Stanmer St BN1 .... 168 B2
Stanmer Villas BN1 .... 168 B2
Stanmere Gdns PO21 .... 194 E2
Stanover La PO22 .... 196 B7
Stansfield St BN16 .... 196 D6
Stanstead CI PO9 .... 128 E2
Stansted Ho PO9 .... 129 E1
Stanton Dr PO19 .... 153 A3
Statwater La GU29 .... 69 F3
Staple La PO18 .... 152 F8
Staplecross CI 1 RH11 .... 18 A3
Staplefield Dr BN3 .... 168 F3
Staplefield Place Sch RH17 61 E5
Staplefield Rd
  Cuckfield RH17 .... 84 C8
  Stapleford RH17 .... 61 E4
Staples Barn BN5 .... 123 D5
Staples Barn La BN5 .... 123 D5
Staples Hill RH13 .... 102 F4
Stapleton Ct PO21 .... 194 D2
Stapley CI BN3 .... 186 D8
Stapley Rd BN3 .... 166 D1
Star Rd RH13 .... 103 A2
Starboard Ct BN2 .... 188 E5
Starboard Wlk 9 BN17 ...... 198 F4
Starborough Cotts RH7 .... 9 F7
Station App
  Haslemere GU27 .... 27 B6
  Hassocks BN6 .... 126 F4
  Horley RH6 .... 2 B2
  Horsted Keynes RH17 .... 65 A7
  Hove BN3 .... 187 B8
Station Approach Rd RH6 ..... 6 A7
Station CI RH13 .... 36 D2
Station Cotts
  Hassocks BN6 .... 126 E4
  Horsham RH13 .... 57 D7
Station Hill RH10 .... 19 B7
Station Par
  1 Lancing BN15 .... 183 E5
  6 Rustington BN16 .... 199 E6
  1 Worthing BN11 .... 182 A3
Station Rd
  Angmering BN16 .... 179 F4
  Billingshurst RH14 .... 77 D7
  15 Bognor Regis PO21 ... 195 C3
  Brighton BN1 .... 167 D3
  Broadbridge PO18 .... 171 C7
  Burgess Hill RH15 .... 187 B2
  Cowfold RH13 .... 81 B2
  Cranleigh RH12 .... 12 C3
  Crawley RH10, RH11 .... 18 D5
  Crawley Down RH10 .... 21 B8
  Crossbush BN18 .... 158 D1
  East Grinstead RH19 .... 9 D1
  Ford BN18 .... 177 E4
  Forest Row RH18 .... 23 F3
  Henfield BN5 .... 123 D5
  Horley RH6 .... 2 B3
  Horsham RH13 .... 36 D2
  Horsted Keynes RH17 .... 65 C5
  Liphook GU30 .... 215 C2
  Liss GU33 .... 45 B4
  Littlehampton BN16 .... 199 E5
  Loxwood RH14 .... 32 A3
  Midhurst GU29 .... 92 D7
  Petworth GU28 .... 95 E5
  Portslade-by-Sea
  BN3, BN41 .... 186 C7
  Pulborough RH20 .... 98 A2
  Rudgwick RH12 .... 33 D7
  Sharpthorne RH19 .... 43 A6
  Southwater RH13 .... 57 F1
  7 Southwick BN42 .... 186 E5
  Steyning BN44 .... 143 E3
  Tower Hill RH13 .... 57 D7
  Warnham RH12 .... 36 B8
  Worthing BN11 .... 182 E3
Station St BN1 .... 207 A6
Station Way RH10, RH11 ... 18 D5
Staunton Ctry Pk PO9 ...... 128 A2
Stavely Gdns PO19 .... 152 F3
Stean Furlong BN17 .... 178 C3
Stedham Cty Prim Sch
  GU29 .... 69 F1
Stedham La GU29 .... 70 A3
Steeds Cnr RH13 .... 80 D6
Steele CI RH20 .... 99 E1

Steels La PO18 .... 170 E5
Steep CI BN14 .... 161 E5
Steep La BN14 .... 161 E5
Steepdown Rd BN15 .... 183 C8
Steeple View BN13 .... 182 A5
Steeres Hill RH12 .... 16 C6
Steers La RH10 .... 6 C4
Stein Rd PO10 .... 149 F2
Steine Gdns BN2 .... 207 A5
Steine CI BN1, BN2 .... 207 A5
Steine St BN2 .... 207 A4
Stemp Dr RH14 .... 77 C8
Stempswoop Way PO22 ... 176 C6
Stephen CI RH11 .... 5 D1
Stephens Rd BN1 .... 168 B8
Stephenson Dr RH19 .... 22 F7
Stephenson PI RH10 .... 19 B6
Stephenson Way RH10 ...... 19 B6
Stepney CI RH10 .... 19 C4
Sterling Bldgs RH12 .... 36 C2
Sterling Par 1 BN16 .... 199 C5
Sternway BN17 .... 199 A5
Stevenage Rd RH11 .... 17 E3
Stevens CI BN3 .... 186 E7
Stevenson Rd BN2 .... 188 C5
Stewards Rise BN18 .... 157 F1
Steyne Gdns BN11 .... 182 E2
Steyne St PO21 .... 195 C3
Steyne The
  Bognor Regis PO21 .... 195 C2
  Worthing BN11 .... 182 E2
Steyning Ave BN1 .... 166 F3
Steyning By-Pass BN44 ... 143 E3
Steyning CI Crawley RH10 .. 18 E8
  Lancing BN15 .... 183 D8
  Worthing BN12 .... 181 B3
Steyning Cres RH20 .... 119 C2
Steyning CI 7 BN3 .... 187 B7
Steyning Gram Sch
  BN44 .... 143 D3
  Steyning BN44 .... 143 D3
Steyning Ho 1 BN14 .... 182 D5
Steyning Mus BN44 .... 143 E3
Steyning Rd
  Shoreham-by-Sea BN43 .. 164 C4
  Shoreham-by-Sea, Mill Hill
  BN43 .... 164 D1
  West Grinstead RH13 ...... 102 C7
Steyning Way PO22 .... 195 E7
Stile Gdns GU27 .... 26 F6
Stipenhooks BN5 .... 123 F4
Stirling CI
  Burgess Hill RH15 .... 107 C4
  Crawley RH10 .... 19 C5
Stirling Court Rd RH15 .... 107 C4
Stirling Ct 5 BN3 .... 187 B7
Stirling PI BN3 .... 187 A6
Stirling Rd PO19 .... 173 A5
Stirling Way
  Bognor Regis PO21 .... 194 E2
  East Grinstead RH19 .... 10 B3
  Horsham RH13 .... 36 E3
Stirrup Way RH10 .... 19 D7
Stoatley Hollow GU27 ...... 27 A8
Stoatley Rise GU27 .... 27 A8
Stock Ho BN15 .... 183 A7
Stockbridge Gdns PO19 .. 172 F4
Stockbridge PI PO19 .... 172 F4
Stockbridge Rd PO19 ...... 172 F4
Stockcroft Rd RH17 .... 41 A1
Stocker Rd PO21 .... 195 B2
Stockfield RH6 .... 2 B4
Stocklands CI RH17 .... 84 F8
Stocks CI RH6 .... 2 B2
Stocks Field BN44 .... 121 D1
Stocks La
  Bracklesham PO20 .... 202 A6
  Chichester PO18 .... 153 C3
Stocks Mead RH10 .... 141 E6
Stockwell Ct
  Burgess Hill RH15 .... 106 F3
  1 Haywards Heath RH16 .. 85 E3
Stockwell Rd RH13 .... 36 C2
Stockwell Works RH10 ..... 19 A6
Stodham La
  Hill Side GU33 .... 45 C2
  Prince's Marsh
  GU33, GU31 .... 45 B1
Stoke Abbott Ct 2 BN11 . 182 D2
Stoke Abbott Rd 3 BN11 . 182 D2
Stoke Brunswick Sch RH19 23 E7
Stoke Rd BN18 .... 138 D3
Stokes CI RH10 .... 19 C3
Stone CI BN13 .... 181 F6
Stone Cross RH16 .... 64 D3
Stone Ct GU29 .... 92 D8
Stone Hatch GU6 .... 11 A3
Stone La BN13 .... 181 F6
Stone Quarry Rd RH17 ...... 66 D7
Stone St BN1 .... 187 E5
Stoneage CI PO22 .... 195 C7

Stonebridge Ct
  Crawley RH11 .... 18 C2
  Horsham RH11 .... 36 A2
Stonecourt CI RH6 .... 2 C3
Stonecourt Cotts RH17 ...... 62 A5
Stonecroft BN44 .... 143 D3
Stonecross La BN18 .... 166 E4
Stonecrop CI BN13 .... 18 B3
Stonecross La RH16 .... 64 E3
Stonecross Rd BN2 .... 168 F4
Stonefield CI RH10, RH11 .. 18 D5
Stonefield Way RH15 ...... 106 F5
Stonefields BN10 .... 199 D5
Stonehall La RH17 .... 63 C6
Stonehill Rd BN3 .... 186 F7
Stonehill Cres PO21 .... 194 B3
Stonehouse La RH13 .... 81 B1
Stonehouse Rd GU30 .... 25 D4
Stonehurst Ct BN2 .... 188 C6
Stonehurst La RH17 .... 66 B6
Stoneleigh Ave BN1 .... 167 F6
Stoneleigh CI Brighton BN1 167 F6
  East Grinstead RH19 .... 9 F1
Stonepit La BN5 .... 123 F5
Stonepound Crossroads
  BN6 .... 126 D4
Stonepound Rd BN6 .... 126 E4
Stoners CI RH6 .... 5 E7
Stonery CI BN41 .... 166 A2
Stonery Rd BN41 .... 166 A2
Stoney La
  Balcombe Lane RH11 .... 41 B5
  Bracklesham PO20 .... 202 D4
  Shoreham-by-Sea BN43 .. 185 C8
  Storey CI Stile PO21 ...... 194 C2
  Stoney Stile La PO21 ..... 194 C1
Stoneybrook RH12 .... 35 F1
Stoneycroft Wlk 3 RH11 .. 17 D5
Stoneyfield Cotts PO20 ... 156 B1
Stoneywish Ctry Pk BN6 . 127 E3
Stopham CI BN14 .... 182 A5
Stopham Rd Crawley RH11 . 19 C3
  Stopham RH20 .... 97 E1
Stor Meadow RH20 .... 119 D2
Storrington CI
  Fishbourne PO18, PO19 .. 172 B7
  Hove BN3 .... 166 E2
Storrington Cty Prim Sch
  RH20 .... 119 C2
Storrington Rd Heath Common
  RH20 .... 120 A5
  Washington RH20 .... 141 C8
Storrington Rise RH14 ..... 161 F4
Story Rd PO19 .... 173 C1
Stour CI BN13 .... 181 C8
Stour Rd BN13 .... 181 C8
Strachey CI 1 RH11 .... 18 B1
Strand CI RH10 .... 19 D4
Strand Par BN12 .... 181 E3
Strand The Brighton BN2 .. 188 F7
  Ferring BN12 .... 200 E4
  Worthing BN11 .... 181 C3
Strand Way PO22 .... 196 B4
Strange Gdn PO21 .... 194 E1
Strathfield CI RH16 .... 85 F4
Strathmoor Gdns GU29 ... 70 F1
Strathmore CI BN13 .... 181 C1
Strathmore Rd
  Crawley RH11 .... 5 A1
  Worthing BN11, BN13 ... 181 C1
Stratton Ct PO22 .... 195 E5
Strawberry La PO20 .... 120 B5
Stream CI PO18 .... 171 B5
Stream La RH10 .... 99 B1
Stream Pk RH19 .... 9 A3
Streatleigh Ct PO21 .... 195 A2
Streel's La GU28 .... 51 F5
Street End La PO20 .... 192 E3
Street End Rd PO20 .... 192 E3
Street Hill RH10 .... 19 E5
Street La RH17 .... 64 A8
Street The
  Albourne Green BN6 ...... 125 C6
  Boxgrove PO18, PO20 ... 154 D4
  Bramber BN44 .... 143 F2
  Bury RH20 .... 138 A7
  Charlwood RH6 .... 4 E7
  Clapham BN13 .... 160 E1
  East Preston BN16 .... 199 F6
  Lancing BN15 .... 183 F8
  Maltham RH20 .... 99 A2
  Patching BN13 .... 160 D2
  Plaistow RH14 .... 30 E2
  Rustington BN16 .... 199 C5
  Shoreham-by-Sea BN43 . 164 E1
  Slinfold RH13 .... 34 D4
  Stedham GU29 .... 70 A1
  Thakeham RH20 .... 120 B7
  Walberton BN18 .... 156 D1
  Walberton BN18 .... 176 E8
  Warninglid RH17 .... 82 F8

Street The
  Washington RH20 .... 141 D6
  West Itchenor PO20 .... 190 F7
  Westmeston BN6 .... 148 F8
Streete Ct 7 PO21 .... 195 B2
Streetfield Rd RH13 .... 34 E3
Stretch Hill RH20 .... 97 A5
Strettington La PO18 ...... 154 A3
Strettons Copse GU30 ...... 47 B2
Strickland CI RH17 .... 17 E5
Stringer Way BN1 .... 167 F3
Strone CI BN11 .... 181 E1
Strood La RH12 .... 35 C7
Stroud Green Dr PO21 ..... 194 F5
Stroudley CI RH10 .... 19 B5
Stroudley CI RH16 .... 199 E6
Strouds La PO21 .... 195 A1
Strugdate CI RH10 .... 19 B4
Stuart CI Crawley RH10 .... 19 D5
  Worthing BN11 .... 182 F4
Stuart Way RH19 .... 22 F7
Stuarts Meadow GU28 ... 114 C8
Stubbermere PO9 .... 149 B8
Stubcroft La PO20 .... 202 B7
Stubfield RH12 .... 36 A3
Stubpond La RH19, RH7 .... 8 D7
Stumblemead RH17 .... 41 A1
Stumblets RH10 .... 19 C7
Stumps End PO18 .... 171 C4
Stumps La PO18 .... 171 C4
Sturges Rd PO21 .... 195 C3
Sturt Ave GU27 .... 26 F5
Sturt Rd GU27 .... 26 F5
Sudbury CI PO21 .... 194 C1
Sudeley PI BN2 .... 188 D4
Sudeley St BN2 .... 188 D4
Sudeley Terr 6 BN2 .... 188 D4
Sudley Gdns PO21 .... 195 D3
Sudley Rd PO21 .... 195 D3
Suffolk CI RH6 .... 2 A2
Suffolk St BN3 .... 186 F8
Sugar La RH17 .... 65 C4
Sugden Rd BN11 .... 182 F3
Sugworth CI RH16 .... 85 D7
Sullington CI BN2 .... 168 F4
Sullington Copse RH16 ... 119 F2
Sullington Gdns BN14 .... 161 F3
Sullington Hill RH11 .... 18 D4
Sullington La RH20 .... 140 F7
Sullington Mead RH12 ..... 35 E3
Sullington Way BN43 ...... 185 A8
Sullivan Dr RH11 .... 17 E3
Sultan Rd PO10 .... 149 B1
Summer CI BN41 .... 186 A7
Summer La PO21 .... 193 F1
Summerdale Rd BN3 ...... 166 D2
Summerdown CI BN13 .... 181 B5
Summerdown St BN13 .... 181 B5
Summerfield Rd PO20 .... 190 C2
Summerfields BN14 .... 161 E6
Summerfield House Sch
  RH15 .... 107 A4
Summerhill CI
  Bognor Regis PO21 .... 196 B7
  Haywards Heath RH16 ..... 85 F7
Summerhill Dr
  Bognor Regis PO21 .... 196 C6
  Haywards Heath RH16 ..... 85 F7
Summerhill Grange RH16 . 85 F7
Summerhill La RH16 .... 85 F7
Summerlea Gdns 5
  BN17 .... 198 E5
Summerley La PO22 .... 196 B5
Summers Ho GU29 .... 92 D6
Summersdale CI PO19 .... 153 A1
Summersdale Rd PO19 ... 153 A1
Summersdeane BN42 ..... 165 F1
Summersvere CI RH10 ...... 6 A1
Sumners RH10 .... 64 B7
Sun Brow GU27 .... 27 A5
Sun Ct Chichester PO19 .. 173 A5
  10 Worthing BN11 .... 182 A1
Sun Park CI PO21 .... 195 A6
Sundale La GU27 .... 196 E5
Sunderland CI PO20 .... 154 D2
Sundew CI RH11 .... 18 A2
Sunneymead CI PO20 ..... 206 E6
Sunningdale Ct
  Crawley RH11 .... 18 D4
  Worthing BN12 .... 181 C3
Sunningdale Gdns
  East Wittering PO20 .... 201 D7
Sunningdale Rd BN13 .... 181 E6
Sunninghill Ave BN3 ...... 166 E2
Sunninghill CI BN3 .... 166 E2
Sunny Ave RH10 .... 21 A8
Sunny CI BN12 .... 181 E1
Sunny Way PO18 .... 171 B5
Sunnybox La BN18 .... 156 E4

Sunnycroft CI RH17 .... 86 E3
Sunnydale Ave BN1 .... 168 A6
Sunnydale CI BN1 .... 168 A6
Sunnydown Ct BN16 ...... 199 A3
Sunnyhill CI RH10 .... 21 A8
Sunnymead Crawley RH11 . 18 De
  Crawley Down RH10 .... 21 B8
Sunnymead CI PO22 ...... 197 A6
Sunnymead Dr PO20 ...... 206 E6
Sunnywood Dr RH16 .... 85 D7
Sunset La RH20 .... 119 C9
Sunte Ave RH16 .... 85 F2
Sunte CI RH16 .... 85 E2
Sunvale Ave GU27 .... 26 De
Sunvale CI GU27 .... 26 De
Surrenden CI BN1 .... 167 E4
Surrenden Cres BN1 .... 167 E4
Surrenden Holt BN1 .... 167 F2
Surrenden Lodge BN1 ..... 167 F2
Surrenden Pk BN1 .... 168 A4
Surrenden Rd BN1 .... 167 F7
Surrenden Rise RH11 .... 39 C8
Surrey Cott 5 BN17 .... 198 F4
Surrey Ho 12 BN2 .... 188 D4
Surrey St Arundel BN18 .. 158 A2
  Brighton BN1 .... 207 F6
  Littlehampton BN17 ...... 198 D5
  Worthing BN11 .... 182 C3
Surrey Wharf BN18 .... 158 B2
Surry St BN43 .... 184 F2
Sussex Bsns Village The
  PO22 .... 176 E6
Sussex Ct Elmer PO22 .... 197 B5
  2 Haywards Heath RH16 .. 85 E1
  Horsham RH13 .... 36 E1
  Hove BN3 .... 187 C6
Sussex Cty
  Cricket Gd BN3 .... 187 C4
Sussex Dr PO21 .... 194 A1
Sussex Eye Hospl BN2 ... 188 D4
Sussex Gdns
  Haywards Heath RH16 ..... 86 B3
  Rustington BN16 .... 199 C6
Sussex Hts 18 BN1 .... 187 E5
Sussex House Ind Est
  BN3 .... 186 F8
Sussex Lodge RH12 .... 36 C6
Sussex Manor Bsns Pk RH10 6 A2
Sussex Mews 9 BN2 .... 188 E4
Sussex Nuffield Hospl
  BN3 .... 186 F2
Sussex PI BN2 .... 207 B6
Sussex Rd
  Haywards Heath RH16 ..... 85 E7
  Hove BN3 .... 187 B6
  Nursted GU31 .... 88 D3
  Worthing BN11 .... 182 D3
Sussex Sq Brighton BN2 . 188 E4
  17 Haywards Heath RH16 85 E4
Sussex St
  Bognor Regis PO21 .... 195 D3
  Brighton BN2 .... 207 B5
  Littlehampton BN17 ...... 198 De
Sussex Terr BN2 .... 207 B6
Sussex Toy & Model Mus
  BN1 .... 207 A6
Sussex Village PO21 .... 197 B5
Sussex Way RH15 .... 106 E5
Sutherland CI
  Bognor Regis PO21 .... 195 C3
  Rustington BN16 .... 199 B5
Sutherland Ct 4 PO21 .... 195 C3
Sutherland Rd BN2 .... 188 C5
Sutton Ave BN16 .... 199 C4
Sutton CI PO22 .... 195 F6
Swainsthorpe CI RH10 .... 85 F3
Swaledale CI RH11 .... 18 C8
Swallow Rd RH11 .... 18 C8
Swallowfield CI RH13 ...... 59 C5
Swallows CI 3 BN15 ...... 184 C5
Swallows Green Dr BN3 .. 181 C5
Swallows La RH13 .... 101 F6
Swallows The BN17 .... 198 D4
Swallowtail Rd RH12 .... 36 E6
Swan Barn Rd GU27 .... 27 D6
Swan CI Emsworth PO10 . 169 C8
  Southwater RH13 .... 58 A2
  Storrington RH20 .... 119 C2
Swan Ct RH20 .... 98 B2
Swan Dene PO21 .... 204 F7
Swan La RH6 .... 4 F7
Swan Sq RH12 .... 36 C2
Swan View RH20 .... 98 C1
Swan Wlk RH12 .... 36 C2
Swanborough CI 7 BN43 . 184 F7
Swanborough Dr BN2 .... 188 F7
Swanborough PI BN2 ...... 188 F7
Swanbourne CI PO21 ...... 204 A8
Swanbourne Rd PO21 .... 204 A8
Swanbourne BN17 .... 178 D3
Swandean Hospl BN13 ... 181 D8
Swanfield Dr PO19 .... 173 C8

Swann Cl RH15 .... 107 D3
Swann Way RH12 .... 35 E3
Swans Ghyll RH18 .... 23 E3
Swanscombe Gdns PO21 .. 195 B2
Sweda Cl 🔟 BN2 .... 208 D8
Sweetlands BN6 .... 127 B5
Swift La RH11 .... 18 C8
Swift Rd PO10 .... 169 C3
Swift Way RH17 .... 178 C4
Swillage La BN16 .... 180 A8
Swindon Rd RH12 .... 36 B4
Swiss Gdns BN43 .... 184 E7
Swissland Hill RH19, RH7 .... 9 E7
Sycamore Ave RH12 .... 37 C6
Sycamore Cl
  Angmering BN16 .... 179 F4
  Crawley RH11 .... 5 C1
  Portslade-by-Sea BN41 .. 166 C3
Sycamore Dr RH19 .... 10 A1
Sycamore Rd PO22 .... 195 C7
Sycamores The
  Chichester PO19 .... 173 A7
  Sayers Common BN6 ..... 105 D1
Sydenham Terr PO10 ...... 149 D5
Sydney Rd RH16 .... 85 E6
Sydney St BN1 .... 207 A6
Sydney Tidy Ho 🔟 BN2 .. 188 C6
Syers Rd GU33 .... 45 B4
Sylvan Cl RH16 .... 86 B4
Sylvan Rd Crawley RH10 .... 19 A4
  Lancing BN15 .... 183 B6
Sylvan Way PO21 .... 195 B3
Sylvester Way BN3 .... 166 C3
Sylvia Cl PO21 .... 194 A1
Symbister Rd BN41 .... 186 C7
Syresham Gdns RH16 ...... 85 F4

Tabard Gate PO21 .... 194 B1
Tack Lee Rd BN18 .... 176 F3
Talbot Cres BN1 .... 168 D6
Talbot La RH12 .... 36 C1
Talbot Rd BN17 .... 198 C5
Tallis Cl RH11 .... 17 E5
Talman Cl RH11 .... 17 E5
Tamar Ave BN13 .... 181 C7
Tamar Cl Crawley RH10 ..... 19 C5
  Worthing BN13 .... 181 C7
Tamar Way PO20 .... 154 D2
Tamarisk Cl PO22 .... 195 C6
Tamarisk Way
  Ferring BN12 .... 200 F5
  Littlehampton BN16 ...... 199 F4
Tamarisk Wlk PO20 .... 201 F6
Tamworth Rd BN3 .... 186 F7
Tanbridge House Sch RH12 35 F2
Tanbridge Pk RH12 .... 36 B1
Tanbridge Pl RH12 .... 36 B1
Tandridge Rd BN3 .... 186 E6
Tanfield Ct RH12 .... 36 B2
Tangle Oak RH19 .... 8 E4
Tangmere Cty Prim Sch
  PO20 .... 194 C2
Tangmere Gdns PO21 ..... 194 D2
Tangmere Military Aviation
  Mus PO20 .... 154 D1
Tangmere Rd
  Brighton BN1 .... 168 A6
  Crawley RH11 .... 17 F6
  Oving PO20 .... 174 B8
Tankerdale La GU33 .... 45 A1
Tanners La GU27 .... 27 C7
Tanners Mead RH17 .... 61 E5
Tannery Cl RH13 .... 34 D3
Tansy Mead RH20 .... 119 B2
Tanyard Ave RH19 .... 23 A8
Tanyard Cl Crawley RH10 ... 19 C3
  Horsham RH13 .... 36 E1
Tanyard Cotts BN44 .... 143 C3
Tanyard La Danehill RH7 .... 66 C4
  Steyning BN44 .... 143 D3
Tanyard Way RH6 .... 2 B4
Tarham Cl RH6 .... 1 E5
Tarmount La BN43 .... 184 F7
Tarner Rd BN2 .... 207 B6
Tarragon Way BN43 .... 165 C1
Tarrant St BN18 .... 158 B3
Tarrant Wharf BN18 .... 158 B2
Tarring Gate BN13 .... 182 A4
Tarring Rd BN11 .... 182 B3
Tasman Cl BN13 .... 199 D4
Tasman Way BN13 .... 181 C6
Tatchells GU29 .... 92 D6
Tate Cres RH15 .... 106 F5
Tate's Way RH12 .... 33 D7
Tatham Ct RH11 .... 18 B1
Taunton Cl RH10 .... 19 D6
Taunton Rd BN2 .... 168 F1
Taverner Pl PO19 .... 173 B5
Tavistock Down BN1 ...... 168 C2
Tavistock & Summerhill Sch
  RH16 .... 85 F7

Tavy Cl BN13 .... 181 C6
Tavy Rd BN13 .... 181 C6
Taw Cl BN13 .... 181 D7
Taylor Wlk RH11 .... 18 C6
Taylor's La PO18 .... 171 C4
Taylors Field GU29 .... 92 E6
Taylors Rise GU29 .... 92 E6
Teal Cl RH12 .... 35 C5
Teal La PO20 .... 206 C8
Teasel Cl RH11 .... 18 B3
Teasdale RH11 .... 18 C3
Teign Wlk BN13 .... 181 C8
Teknol Ho RH15 .... 106 E2
Telegraph La GU31 .... 90 A3
Telegraph St 🔟 BN2 ..... 188 C4
Telford Pl RH10 .... 18 E5
Telgarth Rd BN12 .... 200 F4
Telham Ct 🔟 RH11 .... 17 F3
Templars Cl PO22 .... 196 D6
Templars Cty Fst Sch
  BN15 .... 183 B6
Temple Bar RH13 .... 188 E7
Temple Cl RH10 .... 19 D7
Temple Ct 🔟 BN17 .... 198 E5
Temple Gdns BN1, BN3 ... 187 E6
Temple Gr RH15 .... 106 D4
Temple La RH12 .... 3 A4
Temple Rd GU33 .... 45 C6
Temple St BN1 .... 187 E6
Templesheen Rd PO22 .... 197 B5
Ten Acres BN11 .... 183 A3
Tenacre Cl PO19 .... 173 C8
Tenantry Down Rd BN2 ... 188 E8
Tenantry Rd BN2 .... 188 D8
Tennis Rd BN3 .... 186 E6
Tennyson Ave BN16 .... 199 B5
Tennyson Cl Crawley RH10 . 19 B8
  Horsham RH12 .... 36 E6
Tennyson Cl 🔟 RH16 ..... 85 D5
Tennyson Rd
  Bognor Regis PO21 ...... 195 B3
  Worthing BN11 .... 182 C2
Tennyson Rise RH19 .... 22 C8
Tennyson's La GU27 .... 27 E4
Tennysons GU27 .... 27 E4
Terminus Mill PO19 .... 172 F5
Terminus Pl
  🔟 Brighton BN1 .... 207 F7
  Littlehampton BN17 ..... 198 D5
Terminus Rd Brighton BN1 207 F7
  Chichester PO19 .... 172 E5
  Littlehampton BN17 ..... 198 C5
Terminus Road Ind Est
  PO19 .... 172 F5
Terminus St BN1 .... 207 F6
Tern Rd RH11 .... 17 D5
Terrace The
  Crossbush BN18 .... 158 E1
  Lancing BN15 .... 183 E4
  Sidlesham PO20 .... 203 F7
  Worthing BN12 .... 181 C2
Terringes Ave BN13 .... 181 F5
Terry Rd RH11 .... 18 B1
Terry's Cross BN5 .... 124 C2
Terwick La GU31 .... 91 A8
Terwick Rise GU31 .... 68 D6
Test Rd BN15 .... 183 B6
Testers Cl RH13 .... 80 A7
Teville Gate BN14 .... 182 D3
Teville Inds BN14 .... 182 F5
Teville Pl BN11 .... 182 C3
Teville Rd BN11 .... 182 D3
Thackeray Rd BN14 .... 182 F4
Thakeham Cl
  East Preston BN16 ...... 180 B3
  Worthing BN12 .... 181 A2
Thakeham Copse RH12 .... 53 B1
Thakeham Cty Prim Sch
  RH20 .... 120 B7
Thakeham Dr BN12 .... 181 A2
Thakeham Rd RH20 .... 119 F2
Thalassa Rd BN11 .... 183 B3
Thames Cl Brighton BN2 .. 207 B5
  Littlehampton
    BN16, BN17 .... 199 A4
Thames Way BN13 .... 181 D7
Thatch Cott BN15 .... 183 F8
Thatcher Cl RH10 .... 18 D3
Thatchers Cl
  Burgess Hill RH15 .... 107 B2
  Horley RH6 .... 2 B5
  Horsham RH12 .... 36 E4
Thatchway Cl BN17 .... 198 D6
Thatchway The
  Angmering BN16 .... 179 F5
  Littlehampton BN16 ..... 199 D4
Theatre La PO19 .... 173 A6
Theatre Pl 🔟 PO19 .... 173 A6
Thelton Ave RH12 .... 35 D3
Theobalds Rd RH15 .... 107 D6

Theobold Ho 🔟 BN1 ..... 207 A6
Thesiger Cl BN11 .... 183 A4
Thesiger Rd BN11 .... 183 A4
Theydon Cl RH10 .... 19 A4
Thicket La PO18 .... 155 B5
Third Ave
  Almodington BN20 ...... 202 E8
  Bognor Regis PO22 ..... 196 B4
  Bracklesham PO20 ...... 202 B5
  Hove BN3 .... 187 B6
  Lancing BN15 .... 183 E7
  Worthing BN14 .... 182 D7
Thirlmere Cres
  BN14, BN15 .... 183 B5
Thirlmere Rd RH11 .... 17 D4
Thirlmere Way PO22 ...... 196 B6
Thistledowne Gdns PO10 . 169 D8
Thomas a'Becket Cty
  Fst Sch BN13 .... 182 A5
Thomas a'Becket Cty Mid Sch
  BN14 .... 182 A5
Thomas Bennett Com Coll
  RH10 .... 18 D3
Thomas Bennett Com Sch
  RH10 .... 18 E2
Thompson Cl 🔟 RH11 ... 18 B1
Thompson Rd BN1 .... 168 C1
Thompson's Hospital GU28 73 F1
Thorgate Rd BN17 .... 178 B3
Thorn Rd BN11 .... 182 C1
Thornberry Cty Middle Sch
  BN15 .... 183 F5
Thornbush Cres BN41 .... 166 B3
Thorncroft Rd BN17 ...... 198 F6
Thorndean Rd BN2 .... 168 D3
Thornden RH13 .... 81 E2
Thorndene Ave PO21 ..... 195 B4
Thorndyke Cl RH10 .... 19 D5
Thorney Dr PO20 .... 206 C7
Thorney Island Cty Prim Sch
  PO10 .... 169 C3
Thorney Old Pk PO10 .... 169 F1
Thorney Rd PO10 .... 169 D6
Thornham La PO10 .... 169 D6
Thornham Marina PO10 .. 169 E6
Thornhill Ave BN1 .... 168 A7
Thornhill Cl BN3 .... 166 E2
Thornhill Rise BN41 ...... 166 A4
Thornhill Way BN41 ...... 166 A3
Thornsdale 🔟 BN2 ...... 207 B6
Thornton Cl RH6 .... 1 E3
Thornton Ct 🔟 BN16 ... 199 E6
Thornton Meadow RH14 .. 76 B8
Thornton Pl RH6 .... 1 E5
Threal's La RH20 .... 119 E6
Threals Copse RH20 ...... 119 E5
Three Acres RH20 .... 36 A1
Three Bridges Cty Fst Sch
  RH10 .... 19 A7
Three Bridges Cty Mid Sch
  RH10 .... 19 A6
Three Bridges Rd RH10 ... 19 B6
Three Bridges Sta RH10 .. 19 B6
Three Gates La GU27 ..... 27 E8
Threestile Rd RH12 .... 14 F1
Thruslows PO21 .... 194 F3
Thurlow Rd BN11 .... 182 F3
Thurne Way RH12 .... 33 D7
Thyme Cl BN43 .... 165 C1
Ticehurst Cl RH10 .... 19 E6
Ticehurst Rd BN2 .... 188 F5
Tichborne Cotts RH16 .... 86 C6
Tichborne St BN1 .... 207 A5
Tideway BN16, BN17 ..... 199 A4
Tidy St BN1 .... 207 A6
Tilbury Pl BN2 .... 207 B5
Tilbury Way BN2 .... 207 B6
Tile Barn East PO20 ...... 191 C1
Tile Barn La PO20 .... 191 C1
Tilers Cl RH15 .... 114 A7
Tilgate Cl BN2 .... 188 D6
Tilgate Dr RH10, RH11 ... 18 E2
Tilgate Forest Bsns Ctr
  RH11 .... 19 A2
Tilgate Forest Golf Course
  RH11 .... 19 A2
Tilgate Forest Recn Ctr
  RH11 .... 19 A2
Tilgate Forest Row RH11 . 39 C5
Tilgate Par RH10 .... 18 E3
Tilgate Pl RH10 .... 18 E3
Tiletts La RH12 .... 35 E8
Tillinghurst La RH17 ...... 42 A2
Tillington Cotts BN18 .... 176 F3
Tillolston Cl RH10 .... 19 D5
Tillstone Cl BN2 .... 168 D2
Tillstone St BN2 .... 207 B5
Tiltwood Dr RH10 .... 21 C8

Timber Cl BN13 .... 181 C6
Timber Ct RH12 .... 36 C3
Timber Mill RH12 .... 57 F2
Timberham Farm Rd RH6 .. 5 D8
Timberham Link RH6 .... 5 E8
Timberham Way RH6 .... 5 E8
Timberlaine Ind Est PO19 173 C5
Timberlaine Trad Est
  BN14 .... 182 F5
Timberlands
  🔟 Crawley RH11 .... 18 B1
  Storrington RH20 .... 119 E2
Timberlea Cl RH20 .... 121 A5
Timberleys 🔟 BN17 ..... 199 A6
Timbermill Ct GU27 .... 26 F6
Timbers The RH13 .... 59 C6
Tindal Cl RH15 .... 107 D3
Tinghall PO21 .... 194 E3
Tinsley Gn RH10 .... 6 B4
Tinsley La RH10 .... 6 A1
Tinsley La N RH10 .... 6 B3
Tinsley La S RH10 .... 19 A8
Tintagel Ct Horsham RH13 . 36 D1
  🔟 Shoreham-by-Sea
    BN43 .... 184 F7
Tintern Cl RH11 .... 168 B1
Tintern Rd RH11 .... 18 A4
Tinwood La PO18 .... 154 E5
Tipper La GU31 .... 89 D3
Tiree Path RH11 .... 18 B3
Tisbury Rd BN3 .... 187 C6
Titch Hill BN15 .... 163 A3
Titchfield Cl RH15 .... 107 D1
Tithe Barn BN15 .... 183 E8
Tithe Barn Chalets PO20 . 206 B8
Tithe Barn Cl PO21 .... 205 B8
Tithe Barn Way PO21 .... 194 B1
Tithe Gn BN15 .... 199 B5
Tithe Orch RH19 .... 8 E4
Titian Rd BN3 .... 187 B6
Titnore Cl BN12, BN13 ... 181 A6
Titnore La BN12, BN13 ... 181 A6
Titnore Way BN12, BN13 181 A6
Tivoli 🔟 BN1 .... 167 E2
Tivoli Cres BN1 .... 167 D1
Tivoli Cres N BN1 .... 167 D2
Tivoli Pl BN1 .... 167 D2
Tivoli Rd BN1 .... 167 D2
Toat Hill RH13 .... 56 E8
Toat La RH20 .... 98 A8
Tobias Sch of Art RH19 ... 22 E6
Toddington La BN17 ...... 178 E4
Toddington Pk BN17 ...... 178 E3
Todds Cl RH6 .... 1 E5
Toftwood Cl RH10 .... 19 C5
Tollbridge Ho BN43 ...... 184 D8
Tollgate RH16 .... 86 B8
Tollgate Hill RH11 .... 18 C1
Tollgate La RH17 .... 64 E8
Tomset's Bank RH18 ...... 23 F1
Tongdean Ave BN3 .... 167 C2
Tongdean Ct BN1 .... 167 D4
Tongdean La
  Brighton BN1, BN3 ..... 167 C4
  Brighton BN1 .... 167 C4
Tongdean Rd BN3 .... 167 C3
Tongdean Rise BN1 ...... 167 C4
Toomey Rd BN14 .... 183 B5
Top Rd Sharpthorne RH19 .. 43 B5
  Slindon BN18 .... 156 C5
Top St RH17 .... 83 C4
Torcross Cl BN2 .... 168 E1
Toronto Cl BN13 .... 181 D6
Toronto Terr BN2 .... 188 C6
Torrance Cl BN3 .... 166 F1
Torridge Cl BN13 .... 181 C7
Torton Hill Rd BN18 ...... 157 F2
Tortula Cl GU29 .... 70 D6
Totland Rd BN2 .... 188 D7
Tott Hill RH6 .... 126 B5
Tottington Dr BN5 .... 144 F6
Tottington Way BN43 .... 165 B1
Tower Cl Chichester PO19 172 F7
  East Grinstead RH19 ..... 9 E2
  Horley RH6 .... 1 F3
  Liphook GU30 .... 25 B4
  Tower Hill RH12 .... 58 A8
Tower Ct RH19 .... 9 E2
Tower Hill RH12, RH13 ... 58 A8
Tower Ho
  🔟 Brighton BN1 .... 167 E2
  Burgess Hill RH15 ...... 107 B2
Tower House Cl RH17 ..... 84 E7
Tower Pl PO20 .... 201 F7
Tower Rd Brighton BN2 .. 188 C6
  Colgate RH12 .... 38 A7
  Lancing BN15 .... 183 D5
  Liphook GU30 .... 25 B4
  Worthing BN11 .... 182 E3

Swa – Tud **241**

Tower St Chichester PO19 172 F6
  Emsworth PO10 .... 169 C8
Towergate BN1 .... 167 E2
Towers Convent Sch The
  BN44 .... 144 B1
Towers Rd BN44 .... 144 B2
Town Barn Rd RH11 ...... 18 C7
Town Cross Ave PO21 ... 195 C4
Town La PO18 .... 133 C4
Town Mead RH11 .... 18 D7
Town Place Farm Cotts
  RH17 .... 87 C7
Townfield RH14 .... 53 B2
Townsend Cres BN17 .... 198 F6
Tozer Ct BN41 .... 186 B7
Tozer Way PO19 .... 173 B6
Trafalgar Ct
  🔟 Bognor Regis PO21 .. 195 B2
  Brighton BN1 .... 207 A6
Trafalgar Cty Inf Prim Sch
  RH12 .... 36 B4
Trafalgar Gate BN2 ...... 188 F3
Trafalgar La BN1 .... 207 A6
Trafalgar Pl BN1 .... 207 A6
Trafalgar Rd
  Horsham RH12 .... 36 C4
  Portslade-by-Sea BN41 . 186 B8
Trafalgar St BN1 .... 207 A6
Trafalgar Terr BN1 .... 207 A6
Tramway Cl PO20 .... 192 F8
Treadcroft Dr RH12 .... 36 E5
Treadwheel Rd PO8 ..... 128 D6
Tredcroft Rd BN3 .... 167 C2
Tree Ave GU27 .... 26 F8
Treemans Rd RH17 .... 65 B2
Treetops RH13 .... 79 F7
Treeview RH11 .... 18 C1
Trefoil Cl RH12 .... 36 E5
Trefoil Cres RH11 .... 18 B4
Tregarth Rd PO19 .... 153 A2
Tregenna Ho GU30 .... 25 B5
Treharne Cl BN13 .... 181 D7
Treloar Rd PO11 .... 189 B1
Trendle Gn PO21 .... 194 F2
Trenear Cl RH13 .... 36 E2
Trent Cl Crawley RH11 .... 17 F4
  Lancing BN15 .... 183 C6
Trent Rd BN11, BN12 .... 181 E2
Tretawn Gdns PO20 ..... 206 F6
Trevanne Plat RH10 .... 19 D7
Treveor Cl RH11 .... 182 C2
Treyford Cl RH11 .... 17 F6
Triangle Rd RH16 .... 85 E3
Triangle The BN15 .... 183 C4
Trinity Cl RH10 .... 19 C8
Trinity Rd BN6 .... 126 A6
Trinity St BN2 .... 207 B7
Trinity Way
  Bognor Regis PO21 ..... 194 F4
  Littlehampton BN17 .... 198 F4
Tripp Hill RH20 .... 116 F7
Tristram Cl BN15 .... 183 B7
Triton Cl PO22 .... 196 C5
Troon Cl RH11 .... 17 D5
Trotton Cl RH10 .... 19 C3
Trotton Rd GU29, GU31 .. 91 A7
Trotyn Croft PO21 .... 194 F2
Trout La RH13 .... 79 A7
Trout Rd GU27 .... 26 E6
Troymede RH17 .... 41 A1
True Blue Prec BN17 ..... 178 D3
Truggers RH17 .... 61 C8
Truleigh Cl BN44 .... 144 B2
Truleigh Dr BN44 .... 166 A4
Truleigh Rd BN44 .... 144 B2
Truleigh Way BN43 ...... 165 A1
Trumpers La GU28 .... 95 F8
Trundle Cl PO18 .... 152 E6
Trundle Mead RH12 ...... 36 C5
Trundle View Cl PO22 ... 176 B6
Truro Cl PO21 .... 152 F1
Truro Cres PO21 .... 194 E3
Trusler's Hill BN6 .... 124 F6
Tryndel Way PO22 .... 196 B4
Tudor Ave PO10 .... 149 A4
Tudor Cl Chichester PO19 . 173 C7
  Crawley RH10 .... 19 D5
  East Grinstead RH19 .... 22 F8
  Findon BN14 .... 161 E6
  Hove BN3 .... 166 F2
  Marehill RH20 .... 98 F1
  Middleton-on-Sea PO22 . 196 D5
Tudor Ct 🔟 PO22 .... 195 D4
Tudor Dr
  Upper Beeding BN44 ... 144 A3
  Westergate PO20 ...... 175 D8
Tudor Gdns RH15 .... 106 F4
Tudor Ho RH13 .... 36 F3

Tudor View BN17 .... 198 C4
Tudor Village RH20 .... 120 C3
Tuff's Hard PO18 .... 191 C7
Tufts Field GU29 .... 92 D6
Tufts Meadow GU29 .... 92 E6
Tuggles Plat RH12 .... 35 E7
Tulip Ct RH12 .... 36 C4
Tullett Rd RH10 .... 19 B2
Tunbridge Cres GU30 ...... 25 B5
Tunbridge La GU30 .... 25 B6
Tunnmeade RH11 .... 17 E5
Tungsate BN44 .... 143 D3
Tuppenny La PO10 .... 169 E8
Turkey La RH15 .... 107 B3
Turnberry Ct ⬛ RH16 ..... 85 E4
Turnbull Rd PO19 .... 173 B7
Turner Ct RH19 .... 10 A3
Turner Rd BN14 .... 182 E6
Turner Way PO20 .... 206 F7
Turner's Hill Rd RH19 ..... 22 B6
Turners Hill CE (C) Sch
RH10 .... 21 A3
Turners Hill Rd RH10 ...... 21 A7
Turners Mead RH20 .... 119 B2
Turners Mill Cl RH16 ...... 85 D7
Turners Mill Rd RH16 ..... 85 D6
Turners Way RH15 .... 106 F4
Turnpike Cl PO19 .... 172 F3
Turnpike Pl RH11 .... 18 D8
Turnpike Rd BN18 .... 138 F6
Turret Ct RH19 .... 9 C3
Turton Cl BN2 .... 188 D5
Tuscan Ave PO22 .... 196 F5
Tuscany Gdns RH10 .... 18 E8
Tushmore Ave RH10, RH11 ... 5 E1
Tushmore La RH10, RH11 ... 18 E8
Tushmore Rdbt RH11 ...... 18 D8
Tussock Cl RH11 .... 18 A4
Tuxford Cl RH10 .... 19 C4
Tweed La RH11 .... 4 F1
Twineham CE (C) Prim Sch
RH17 .... 105 A4
Twineham Cl BN2 .... 188 F7
Twineham La RH6, RH17 ... 105 A3
Twitten Cl ⬛ BN42 .... 185 E7
Twitten La RH19 .... 8 E4
Twitten The
Albourne Green BN6 ...... 125 C6
Burgess Hill RH15 .... 107 B4
Ditchling BN6 .... 127 D3
Southwick BN42 .... 185 E7
Twitten Way BN13, BN14 .. 182 A4
Two Barns La PO18 ...... 152 D6
Two Mile Ash Rd
RH12, RH13 .... 57 D3
Two Ways RH14 .... 32 A4
Twyford Cl BN13 .... 181 E6
Twyford Gdns BN13 ...... 181 E6
Twyford Rd
Brighton BN1 .... 168 E6
Worthing BN13 .... 181 E6
Twyhurst Ct RH19 .... 9 D3
Twyne Cl RH11 .... 17 F4
Twyner Ct RH6 .... 2 D4
Tye La BN18 .... 156 E1
Tylden Way RH12 .... 36 F6
Tyler Rd RH10 .... 18 D3
Tyler's Gn RH16, RH17 ... 85 B4
Tylston Meadow GU30 ..... 25 B5
Tymperley Ct RH13 .... 36 E3
Tyne Cl Crawley RH10 ..... 19 C5
Worthing BN13 .... 181 C7
Tyne Way PO21 .... 194 D4
Tynings The BN15 .... 183 E5
Tyson Pl ⬛ BN2 .... 207 B5
Tythe Barn RH17 .... 83 C3
Tythe Barn Rd PO20 ..... 206 E6

Uckfield Cl BN2 .... 188 F6
Ullswater Dr RH16 .... 179 A3
Ullswater Gr PO22 .... 196 B6
Ullswater Rd BN13 .... 183 B5
Underdown Rd BN42 ...... 185 E8
Underhill La
Clayton BN45, BN6 ...... 147 E8
Westmeston BN6 .... 148 C8
Undermill Rd BN44 .... 144 B2
Underwood Cl RH10 .... 21 B8
Underwood Rd GU27 ...... 26 F7
Unifax BN12 .... 181 C3
Union Pl BN11 .... 182 D2
Union Rd BN2 .... 207 B7
Union St BN1 .... 207 A5
Univ of Brighton (Belgrave
Street Annexe) BN2 ... 207 B6
Univ of Brighton (Cockcroft/
Watts Annexes) BN2 ... 168 D2

Univ of Brighton (Finsbury
Road Annexe) BN2 ...... 207 B6
Univ of Brighton (St Peter's
Ho)
BN2 .... 207 A6
Upfield RH6 .... 2 A1
Upfield Cl RH6 .... 2 A1
Upfield Villas RH14 .... 54 C2
Uphill Way PO20 .... 193 A8
Uplands Ave BN13 .... 181 F8
Uplands Cl GU27 .... 27 D8
Uplands Rd Brighton BN1 .. 168 C2
Rowland's Castle PO9 .. 128 E2
Uplands Sch BN2 .... 168 C2
Uppark GU31 .... 109 B8
Uppark Gdns RH12 .... 36 F6
Uppark Way PO22 .... 196 D7
Upper Abbey Rd BN2 ..... 188 D4
Upper Bedford St BN2 .... 188 C4
Upper Beeding Cty Prim Sch
BN44 .... 144 A2
Upper Bevendean Ave
BN2 .... 168 E1
Upper Bognor Rd 🔳
Bognor Regis
PO21, PO22 .... 195 D4
Bognor Regis PO21 ..... 195 E4
Upper Boundstone La
Lancing BN15 .... 183 D7
Lancing BN15 .... 183 D8
Upper Brighton Rd
Lancing BN15 .... 183 C8
Worthing BN14 .... 182 D7
Upper Chalvington Pl
BN2 .... 188 E5
Upper Cl RH18 .... 23 F2
Upper Dr BN16 .... 200 B4
Upper Dr The BN3 .... 187 D8
Upper Forecourt RH6 .... 6 B7
Upper Gardner St BN1 .... 207 A6
Upper Gloucester Rd BN1 .. 207 F6
Upper Hamilton Rd BN1 .. 207 F8
Upper High St BN11 ...... 182 E3
Upper Hollingdean Rd
BN1, BN2 .... 168 B1
Upper Kingston La
BN42, BN43 .... 165 D1
Upper Lewes Rd BN2 ..... 207 B7
Upper Lodges BN1 .... 168 D8
Upper Market St BN3 ..... 187 D5
Upper Mount GU33 .... 45 A3
Upper North St BN1 ...... 207 F5
Upper Park Pl 🔳 BN2 .... 207 B5
Upper Rock Gdns BN2 ... 207 B5
Upper Roedale Cotts BN1 .. 168 B4
Upper Shoreham Rd
BN43 .... 185 A8
Upper Sq RH18 .... 23 E3
Upper St RH20 .... 97 A3
Upper St James's St BN2 .. 207 B4
Upper St Johns Rd RH15 .. 107 A4
Upper Station Rd BN5 ... 123 D5
Upper Sudeley St ⬛ BN2 .. 188 D4
Upper Wellington Rd 🔳
BN2 .... 188 C7
Upper West Dr BN12 ..... 200 E5
Upper West La BN15 ..... 183 E8
Upper Winfield Ave BN1 .. 167 F6
Upperfield GU29 .... 70 F2
Upperton Rd GU28 .... 73 C1
Upton Ave BN42 .... 165 E1
Upton Cl BN13 .... 181 F3
Upton Gdns BN13 .... 181 F4
Upton Rd
Stockbridge PO19 ...... 172 F4
Worthing BN13 .... 181 F4
Upways Cl PO20 .... 203 F1
Ursula Ave PO20 .... 206 D6
Ursula Ave N PO20 .... 206 D6
Ursula Sq PO20 .... 206 D5

Vachery La GU6 .... 11 E7
Vale Ave Brighton BN1 ... 167 E7
Worthing BN14 .... 161 F2
Vale Cl BN41 .... 186 B7
Vale Cty Fst & Mid Sch
BN14 .... 161 F2
Vale Dr Horsham RH12 .... 36 B3
Worthing BN14 .... 161 F2
Vale Gdns BN41 .... 186 B7
Vale Rd
Haywards Heath RH16 .. 85 E2
Portslade-by-Sea
BN3, BN41 .... 186 C7
Vale Wlk BN14 .... 161 F1
Valebridge Cl RH15 ...... 107 C6
Valebridge Dr RH15 ...... 107 C5
Valebridge Rd RH15 ..... 107 C6
Valencia Rd BN11 .... 182 A3
Valentine Cl BN14 .... 182 B7
Valentine ⬛ BN3 .... 187 C7

Valentine Dr RH15 .... 106 E4
Valentines Gdns PO21 ... 194 C2
Valentines Lea GU28 ...... 51 A8
Valerie Cl BN41 .... 166 C2
Valeta Cl RH10 .... 19 C4
Valeta Ph PO10 .... 169 A8
Valeta Rd PO17 .... 169 F1
Valewood Cl RH14 .... 56 D1
Valewood La RH13, RH14 .. 56 D1
Valewood Rd GU27 .... 27 C4
Valiant Rd PO21 .... 169 F1
Vallance Cl RH15 .... 106 E4
Vallance Gdns BN3 ...... 187 A6
Vallance Rd BN3 .... 187 A6
Vallensdean Cotts BN41 .. 166 C2
Valley Cl BN1 .... 167 C4
Valley Dr BN1 .... 167 C4
Valley Rd Lancing BN15 .. 183 E8
Portslade-by-Sea BN41 .. 166 A2
Valley Side GU30 .... 25 B5
Valverde Ho 🔟 BN3 ..... 187 C7
Van Dyck Pl PO22 .... 195 A6
Van Gogh Pl PO22 .... 195 B6
Vanbrugh Cl RH11 .... 17 E3
Vanbrugh Ct PO22 .... 195 A6
Vancouver Cl BN13 ...... 181 D6
Vancouver Dr RH11 .... 5 D1
Vancouver Rd BN13 ..... 181 D6
Vann Bridge Cl GU27 ..... 49 A6
Vann Rd GU27 .... 49 A6
Vanners RH10 .... 18 E7
Vanzell Rd GU29 .... 71 A1
Varndean Cl BN1 .... 167 E3
Varndean Coll BN1 ...... 167 F3
Varndean Dr BN1 .... 167 E3
Varndean Gdns BN1 ..... 167 E3
Varndean Holt BN1 ...... 167 F3
Varndean Rd BN1 .... 167 E3
Varndean Sch BN1 ...... 168 A3
Varsity Rd BN1 .... 169 F1
Velyn Ave PO19 .... 173 B6
Ventnor Villas BN3 ...... 187 B6
Venus La PO21 .... 204 E7
Vera Wlk PO22 .... 195 A2
Verbania Way RH19 ..... 10 B1
Vere Rd BN1, BN2 .... 207 A8
Veric ⬛ BN2 .... 187 C7
Verica Ct PO19 .... 172 A7
Vermont Dr BN16 .... 200 A5
Vermont Way BN16 ...... 200 A5
Vernon Cl Horsham RH12 .. 37 A4
Rustington BN16 .... 199 C5
Vernon Ct ⬛ BN1 .... 187 E6
Vernon Terr BN1 .... 187 E7
Veronica Cl BN16 .... 200 A4
Veronica Way BN2 .... 207 B4
Viaduct Rd BN1, BN2 ..... 207 A7
Vicarage Fields BN13 .... 181 D7
Vicarage La
Bognor Regis PO22 ..... 196 A4
East Preston BN16 ...... 199 F5
Haslemere GU27 .... 26 F6
Horley RH6 .... 1 F4
Lodsworth GU28 .... 72 B2
Scaynes Hill RH17 ...... 86 F3
Steyning BN44 .... 143 D3
Vicarage Rd RH10 .... 21 A8
Vicars Cl 🔳 PO19 .... 173 A6
Viceroy Cl BN12 .... 200 E5
Viceroy Lodge 🔟 BN3 .. 187 A6
Victor Cl RH10 .... 6 D1
Victor Rd PO10 .... 169 F1
Victoria Ave
Burgess Hill RH15 ...... 106 E3
Easebourne GU29 .... 71 A1
Victoria Cl
Burgess Hill RH15 ...... 106 E3
Burgess Hill RH15 ...... 106 F2
Horley RH6 .... 2 A3
🔳 Midhurst GU29 ...... 92 E7
Victoria Cottage Hospl
PO10 .... 169 B8
Victoria Ct
🔟 Bognor Regis PO21 .. 195 B2
Horsham RH13 .... 36 D2
🔳 Hove BN3 .... 187 C6
Portslade-by-Sea
🔳 Shoreham-by-Sea
BN43 .... 184 E7
🔳 Worthing BN11 ...... 182 C3
Victoria Dr PO21 .... 195 B3
Victoria Gdns
Burgess Hill RH15 ...... 106 F2
Westergate PO20 .... 175 D7
Victoria Gr 🔳 BN3 ...... 187 C6
Victoria Ind Est RH15 ... 106 E2
Victoria Park Gdns 🔳
BN11 .... 182 C3
Victoria Pl 🔟 Hove BN3 .. 187 E6
Liphook GU30 .... 47 E8
Victoria Rd Balcombe RH17 .. 41 A1
Bognor Regis PO21 ..... 195 B2

Victoria Rd Brighton BN1 .. 187 E6
Burgess Hill RH15 ...... 106 E2
Chichester PO19 .... 173 C7
Crawley RH11 .... 18 D6
Emsworth PO10 .... 149 A1
Haywards Heath RH16 .. 86 A3
Horley RH6 .... 2 B2
Portslade-by-Sea
BN3, BN41 .... 186 C8
Shoreham-by-Sea BN43 .. 184 E7
Southwick BN41, BN42 .. 185 D7
Worthing BN11 .... 182 C3
Victoria Rd S PO21 ...... 195 B2
Victoria St Horsham RH13 .. 36 D2
Hove BN1 .... 187 E6
Victoria Terr
Bognor Regis PO22 ..... 195 F3
Lumley PO22 .... 149 C1
Westbourne PO10 .... 149 D3
Victoria Villas BN18 ..... 177 A3
Victoria Way
Burgess Hill RH15 ...... 106 F2
East Grinstead RH19 .... 22 F7
Victory Cl 🔟 PO21 ...... 195 B2
Victory Rd RH12 .... 36 B3
View Terr RH7 .... 10 A8
View The PO21 .... 205 A8
Views Path RH16 .... 86 B4
Villa Plage PO22 .... 197 A5
Village Barn The BN1 ... 167 E7
Villiers Cl BN1 .... 207 A6
Vinall Gdns RH13 .... 35 D4
Vincent Cl Horsham RH13 .. 36 F2
Lancing BN15 .... 183 D6
Vincent Rd PO20 .... 206 C6
Vine Pl BN1 .... 207 F6
Vine St BN1 .... 207 A6
Vineries Cl BN13 .... 182 A6
Vineries The
Burgess Hill RH15 ...... 107 D3
🔟 Hove BN3 .... 187 E6
Vinery Ct BN13 .... 182 A6
Vines Cross Rd BN2 ...... 188 F7
Vinnetrow Rd PO20 ..... 173 E3
Vinols Cross RH19 .... 42 F6
Vinson Rd GU33 .... 45 C4
Viscount Dr PO21 .... 205 B8
Vivienne Cl RH11 .... 5 D1
Volks Electric Rly
BN1, BN2 .... 188 C4
Vowels La RH19 .... 21 E2
Vulcan Cl RH11 .... 18 C2
Vulcan Rd PO21 .... 169 F1

Wad The PO20 .... 190 B1
Waddington Cl RH11 .... 18 A3
Wade End PO20 .... 206 C8
Wadeway The PO20 ..... 206 C8
Wadeys The RH14 .... 77 C8
Wadham Cl RH10 .... 6 C1
Wadhurst Cl PO21 .... 195 B4
Wadhurst Ct 🔳 BN13 .. 182 A3
Wadhurst Dr BN12 ...... 181 B2
Wadhurst Rise BN2 ..... 188 F5
Wadlands Brook Rd RH19 .. 9 D5
Wagg Cl RH10 .... 10 A1
Wagtail Cl RH12 .... 36 D7
Wain End RH12 .... 36 D5
Wainwrights RH11 .... 18 D3
Wakefield Rd BN2 .... 207 B8
Wakefield Way PO21 .... 194 E4
Wakehams Green Dr RH10 .. 6 D1
Wakehurst Dr RH10, RH11 .. 18 D3
Wakehurst La RH17 ...... 64 A8
Wakehurst Mews RH12 .. 35 F1
Wakehurst Pl RH16 ...... 199 C6
Wakehurst Place (Royal
Bot Gdn) RH17 .... 41 F3
Wakenhurst Ct BN11 ... 182 F3
Wakestone La RH20 ...... 75 A2
Walberton & Binstead CE (C)
Prim Sch BN18 .... 156 E1
Walberton Cl PO22 ...... 196 B5
Walberton Ct BN11 ..... 181 F1
Walberton Park BN18 ... 176 E8
Waldby Ct RH11 .... 18 A3
Waldegrave Rd BN1 ..... 168 A1
Walders Rd BN16 .... 199 B6
Waldron Ave BN1 .... 168 D6
Waldron Pl BN1 .... 168 D6
Walesbeech RH10 .... 19 A5
Walker Rd RH10 .... 19 C4
Wall Hill Rd RH18, RH19 .. 23 E5
Wallace Ave BN11 .... 181 F1
Wallace Ct 🔢 BN11 ..... 181 F2
Wallace Par 🔟 BN11 ... 181 F2
Wallace Rd BN13 .... 179 C3
Wallage La RH10 .... 20 D6
Walled Gdn The RH14 ... 31 F7
Wallfield PO21 .... 194 F2
Wallis Ct RH10 .... 5 D2

Wallis Ho RH19 .... 9 E1
Wallis Way
Burgess Hill RH15 ...... 106 E4
Horsham RH13 .... 37 A4
Wallner Cres PO22 ...... 196 C5
Wallrock Wlk PO10 ...... 149 B4
Walmer Cl RH13 .... 58 A2
Walmsleys Way PO20 ... 202 C5
Walnut Ave
Chichester PO19 .... 172 F8
Rustington BN16 .... 199 B5
Walnut Cl BN1 .... 167 E3
Walnut Ct RH13 .... 36 E1
Walnut La RH11 .... 5 B1
Walnut Lodge BN14 ..... 182 C4
Walnut Pk RH16 .... 86 B4
Walnut Tree Cotts RH14 .. 77 E2
Walnut Tree Dr PO10 ... 150 A3
Walnut Tree Way BN13 .. 181 B5
Walpole Ave BN12 .... 181 D2
Walpole Rd BN2 .... 188 D5
Walpole Terr BN2 .... 188 D5
Walsham Cl PO22 .... 195 F6
Walsingham Rd BN3 .... 186 F6
Walstead Ho 🔳 RH10 ... 18 D5
Walter May Ho 🔢 BN2 .. 188 F5
Waltham Park Rd RH20 .. 117 B6
Walton Ave PO21 .... 195 E3
Walton Bank BN1 .... 168 E5
Walton Cl BN13 .... 181 F6
Walton Heath RH10 ...... 19 D8
Walton La PO18 .... 171 C5
Walton Lodge BN13 ..... 181 F6
Walton Rd PO21 .... 195 E3
Wandle Cl RH10 .... 19 C5
Wandleys Cl BN20 ...... 155 F1
Wandleys Dr PO20 ...... 155 F1
Wandleys La BN18, PO20 .. 156 A2
Wandleys Lane Cvn Site
PO20 .... 155 F1
Wansford Way PO22 .... 196 C4
Wantage Cl RH10 .... 19 C3
Wantley Hill Est BN5 ... 123 F6
Wantley La RH20 .... 119 E2
Wantley Rd BN14 .... 162 A1
War Memorial Hospl
PO22 .... 195 C5
Warble Heath Cl PO18 .. 152 F6
Warblers Way PO22 .... 195 B7
Warbleton Cl BN2 .... 188 E5
Warbleton Ho 🔟 RH11 .. 17 F3
Warblington Rd PO10 ... 169 A8
Warblington Ct RH19 .... 23 A8
Ward Cres PO10 .... 149 C3
Warden Ct RH17 .... 85 A6
Warden Park Sch RH17 .. 85 A5
Wardley Cotts GU30 ..... 47 D4
Ware Ct RH15 .... 107 D3
Warelands RH15 .... 106 F1
Waremere Ct BN18 ...... 177 A3
Warenne Rd BN3 .... 166 C4
Warleigh Rd BN1, BN2 .. 207 A8
Warltersville Way RH6 ... 2 C1
Warmdene Ave BN1 ..... 167 F6
Warmdene Cl BN1 .... 167 F5
Warmdene Rd BN1 ...... 167 F6
Warmdene Way BN1 .... 167 F6
Warner Ct RH15 .... 107 A3
Warner Rd Selsey PO20 .. 206 C6
Worthing BN14 .... 182 F4
Warner's La PO20 .... 206 C8
Warnham CE (C) Prim Sch
RH12 .... 35 F8
Warnham Court Sch RH12 .. 35 F7
Warnham Ct BN1 .... 187 C5
Warnham Nature Reserve
RH12 .... 36 B6
Warnham Rd
Broadbridge Heath RH12 .. 35 D4
Crawley RH10 .... 19 B4
Horsham RH12 .... 36 B5
Worthing BN12 .... 181 D2
Warnham Rise BN1 ...... 168 A5
Warnham St Cl RH12 ..... 36 B3
Warnham St BN13 ...... 187 C5
Warnham Nature Reserve
RH12 .... 36 B6
Warnham Rd
Broadbridge Heath RH12 .. 35 D4
Horsham RH12 .... 36 B5
Worthing BN12 .... 181 D2
Warningcamp La RH13, RH17 .. 61 A2
Warninglid La RH13, RH17 .. 60 D2
Warren Cl RH19 .... 8 E3
Warren Cotts
Handcross RH17 .... 61 B8
West Dean PO18 .... 132 F6
Warren Cres PO10 .... 200 A6
Warren Croft RH20 .... 119 B1
Warren Ct Lancing BN15 .. 183 D5
Worthing BN14 .... 182 B7
Warren Dr Crawley RH11 .. 18 A8
Southwater Street RH13 .. 58 A3
Warren Farm La PO19 .. 152 F2
Warren Gdns BN14 ..... 182 B7
Warren Rd Brighton BN2 .. 188 E8
Liss Forest GU33 .... 45 E7

Warren Rd Worthing BN14 182 B7
Warren Side GU31 89 D3
Warren The
Burgess Hill RH15 107 C1
Ferring BN12 200 F4
Handcross RH17 60 E6
Warren Way PO22 176 B6
Warrington Cl RH11 17 E2
Warrior Cl BN41 166 B2
Warrs Hill La BN8 87 E1
Warwick Cl PO21 194 B2
Warwick Ct Arundel BN18 . 158 A2
5 Emsworth PO10 169 B8
4 Hove BN3 187 E7
Warwick Gdns BN11 182 E2
Warwick La BN11 182 E2
Warwick Mount 2 BN2 ... 188 C4
Warwick Pl
Bognor Regis PO22 196 D5
Worthing BN11 182 E2
Warwick Rd BN11 182 E2
Warwick St BN11 182 E2
Warwick Wlk 3 BN43 164 F1
Washbrooks Farm BN6 125 F5
Washington Bostal RH20 . 141 D5
Washington Cotts RH20 ... 141 D8
Washington Rd
Buncton BN44, RH20 142 E8
Crawley RH11 17 E3
Emsworth PO10 149 B1
Haywards Heath RH16 86 A5
Storrington RH20 119 E1
Washington RH20 141 A8
Washington St
Brighton BN2 207 B7
Chichester PO19 172 F7
Wassand Cl RH10 19 A6
Water La Angmering BN16 179 F5
Buncton BN44 142 C8
Littlehampton BN17 198 D6
Selden BN13, BN16 180 C7
Storrington RH20 119 F2
Water Lane Ind Est RH20 119 E3
Water Lea RH10 19 A5
Water Tower Bldgs 3
PO21 195 D3
Water View RH6 2 C3
Waterbury Hill RH17 65 B5
Waterdyke Ave BN42 185 E7
Waterfield Cl RH13 36 E3
Waterfield Cty Fst Sch
RH11 17 E4
Waterfield Gdns RH11 17 E4
Waterhall Golf Course
BN1 167 A7
Waterhall Rd BN1 167 C6
Waterlands La RH12 13 E1
Waterloo Pl 1 BN1 207 B6
Waterloo Rd PO22 196 A4
Waterloo Sq PO21 195 C2
Waterloo St BN3 187 D5
Waterplat The PO19 173 C8
Waters Edge PO21 194 E1
Waters Edge Gdns PO10 .. 169 B8
Watersfield Rd BN14 182 B5
Waterside
East Grinstead RH19 10 B1
Horley RH6 2 A5
Waterside Cl RH11 17 E4
Waterside Dr PO19, PO20 . 172 F4
Waterstone Cl PO20 191 A7
Watery La
Chichester PO20 173 A4
Funtington PO18 151 A4
Watling Cl 5 BN42 185 E7
Watling Ct 8 BN42 185 E7
Watling Rd BN42 185 E7
Watney Cotts RH17 42 E1
Watson Cl RH10 19 C4
Watts Lodge RH15 107 D3
Waveney Wlk RH10 19 B4
Waverley Cres BN1 168 C1
Waverley Ct RH12 36 B2
Waverley Rd
Bognor Regis PO21 195 A4
Rustington BN16 199 D5
Wavertree Rd BN12 181 D3
Way The BN16 200 A4
Wayfield Ave BN3 166 F1
Wayland Ave BN1 167 C3
Wayside Brighton BN1 167 D6
Crawley RH11 17 E4
Lancing BN15 183 C5
Wayside Ave BN13 181 D7
Weald Ave BN3 186 F8
Weald Cl Horsham RH13 58 E8
Hurstpierpoint BN6 125 F6
Weald Ct RH14 77 D7
Weald Day Hospl The
RH11 18 C6
Weald Dr RH10 19 A4
Weald Dyke BN43 184 F6
Weald Rd RH15 106 E3
Weald Rise RH16 85 E1
Weald Sch The RH14 77 D7
Weald The RH19 9 F4
Wealden Way RH16 85 D4
Wealdon Cl RH13 79 F7
Wear Cl BN13 181 C7
Wear Rd BN13 181 C7
Weare St RH5 14 D7
Weatherhill Cl RH6 2 F3
Weatherhill Rd RH6 2 F3
Weaver Cl RH11 17 E5
Weavers Cl
Burgess Hill RH15 107 D1
Easebourne GU29 70 F2
Weavers Hill BN16 180 A5
Weavers La BN5 123 E4
Weavers Ring BN16 180 A5
Webb Cl
Bognor Regis PO21 205 A7
Crawley RH11 18 B1
Weddell Rd RH10 18 F3
Wedges The RH13 56 D5
Wedgwood Rd PO22 196 A4
Weir Wood Resr (Nature
Reserve) RH19 22 D1
Weirbrook RH10 19 A3
Welbeck Ave BN3 186 E6
Welbeck Cl RH15 107 D4
Welbeck Dr RH15 107 D4
Welkin The RH16 86 B8
Well La GU27 27 D6
Well Lodge PO21 194 A2
Well Rd PO21 204 F7
Welland Cl BN13 181 D8
Welland Rd BN13 181 D8
Wellcroft Cotts BN6 125 C5
Weller Cl RH10 19 D5
Wellesey Ct BN11 181 F1
Wellesley Ave BN12 181 D2
Wellesley Ct 8 BN17 198 E4
Wellfield RH19 23 C7
Wellfield Cotts GU31 89 D3
Wellhouse La RH15 127 C7
Wellingham La BN13 161 E1
Wellington Cl RH10 6 E1
Wellington Gdns PO20 206 E8
Wellington Rd
Bognor Regis PO21 195 B3
Brighton BN2 207 B7
Chichester PO19 153 A1
Horsham RH12, RH13 36 D2
Portslade-by-Sea BN41 186 B6
Wellington St BN2 188 C7
Wellington Town Rd RH19 .. 9 D2
Wellington Way RH6 1 F5
Wellingtonia Cl 11 BN1 167 E3
Wells Cl RH12 35 F2
Wells Cres
Bognor Regis PO21 194 E4
Chichester PO19 152 F1
Wells Ho GU29 92 E6
Wells Lea RH19 9 D3
Wells Meadow RH19 9 D3
Wells Rd RH10 18 E2
Wells The GU27 27 C6
Wellsbourne 8 BN2 188 F5
Wellsfield PO20 190 C1
Wellswood Gdns PO9 128 E3
Wellsworth La PO9 128 E3
Wellwood Cl RH13 37 B4
Welwyn Cl RH11 17 E2
Wembley Ave BN15 183 D6
Wembley Gdns BN15 183 D6
Wembury Pk RH7 8 E8
Wenban Rd BN11 182 D3
Wenceling Cotts 4 BN15 184 C5
Wendover Grange 3
BN3 187 A6
Wendy Ridge BN16 199 B6
Wenlock Cl RH11 18 A4
Wensley Gdns PO10 149 B3
Wensleydale RH11 18 C3
Wentworth Cl
West Barnham PO22 176 B7
Worthing BN13 181 F8
Wentworth Ct BN16 200 A4
Wentworth Dr RH10 19 D7
Wentworth St BN2 207 B4
Weppons 2 BN43 184 F7
Wesley Cl Crawley RH11 17 E3
Horley RH6 2 A5
Wessex Ave
Bognor Regis PO21 195 B2
East Wittering PO20 202 A7
Wessex Ct 1 BN11 182 C2
Wessex Wlk 1 BN43 164 F1
West Ashling Rd
Hambrook PO18 150 D3
Hambrook PO18 150 E3
West Ave
Bognor Regis PO21 194 F3
Crawley RH10 19 A8
Middleton-on-Sea PO22 196 F6
Shoreham-by-Sea BN15 ... 184 A5
Worthing BN11 182 A2
West Bank BN18 177 A5
West Beach Rd BN43 184 D5
West Blatchington Inf Sch
BN3 166 E4
West Blatchington Jun Sch
BN3 166 E4
West Bldgs BN11 182 D1
West Bracklesham Dr
PO20 202 A6
West Brook Cl PO18 171 A5
West Broyle Dr PO19 152 C2
West Burton La RH20 137 E8
West Burton Rd RH20 137 D8
West Chiltington Cty
Prim Sch RH20 99 E1
West Chiltington La
Balls Green RH14 77 F2
Coneyhurst RH14, RH13 78 C6
West Chiltington Rd
West Chiltington RH20 100 A2
West Chiltington Common
RH20 119 D5
West Cl
Bognor Regis PO22 196 B4
Fernhurst GU27 49 B6
Middleton-on-Sea PO22 ... 196 D5
West Comm RH16 85 F6
West Common Dr RH16 86 A7
West Dean CE (C) Prim Sch
PO18 132 F5
West Dean Coll PO18 133 A6
West Dr Angmering BN16 . 179 D4
Bognor Regis PO21 194 B1
Brighton BN2 188 C6
Ferring BN12 200 E4
Middleton-on-Sea PO22 ... 197 A5
West End La
Ansteadbrook GU8 28 D8
Henfield BN5 123 B5
West End Way BN15 183 D3
West Front Rd PO21 204 F7
West Furlong Ct BN6 126 A5
West Furlong La BN6 126 A5
West Green Cty Fst Sch
RH11 18 C7
West Green Dr RH11 18 C6
West Gun Copse Rd RH13 . 57 D5
West Head BN17 198 F4
West Hill Ardingly RH17 63 E8
Dormans Park RH19 9 E6
East Grinstead RH19 22 D8
Worthing BN13 161 E2
West Hill Cl BN13 161 E2
West Hill Pl BN1 207 F6
West Hill Rd BN1 207 F6
West Hill St BN1 207 F7
West Hoathly CE (C)
Prim Sch RH19 42 E6
West Hoathly Rd RH19 22 D4
West Hove Cty Inf Sch
BN3 186 F7
West Hove Cty Jun Sch
BN3 186 F7
West Hove Golf Course
BN3 166 C5
West La
East Grinstead RH19 22 D8
Lancing BN15 183 E7
West Lavington CE (A)
Prim Sch GU29 93 A6
West Leigh RH19 22 E7
West Mallion RH16 85 F3
West Mare La RH20 98 F1
West Mead BN16 199 E4
West Mead Dr PO21 194 F4
West Meade GU30 47 B2
West Onslow Cl BN12 180 E3
West Pallant PO19 173 A6
West Par Horsham RH12 36 C4
Worthing BN11 182 A1
West Park CE (C) Fst &
Mid Sch BN12 181 D2
West Park Cres RH15 106 D4
West Park Rd
Domewood RH10 7 F5
Domewood RH7, RH10 8 B7
Handcross RH17 61 B7
West Preston Manor
BN16 199 E5
West Preston Mews BN16 199 E5
West Rd Emsworth PO10 .. 169 A8
Pyecombe BN45 146 E7
Southwick BN41 186 A7
West Ridings BN16 199 F4
West Sands Cvn Pk PO20 206 B8
West Sands La PO20 206 B7
West Side GU28 95 B8
West St Billingshurst RH14 . 77 C8
Bognor Regis PO21 195 C2
Brighton BN1 207 F5
Burgess Hill RH15 106 E4
Chichester PO19 172 F6
Crawley RH11 18 D5
Ditchling BN6 127 D3
East Grinstead RH19 22 E8
Emsworth PO10 169 B8
Haslemere GU27 27 C6
Horsham RH12 36 C2
Lancing BN15, BN14 183 B7
Midhurst GU29 92 F7
Portslade-by-Sea BN41 186 C7
Selsey PO20 206 C7
Shoreham-by-Sea BN43 ... 184 E7
Storrington RH20 119 D1
Worthing BN11 182 C1
West Stoke Rd PO19 152 C3
West Strand PO20 201 B8
West Tyne BN13 181 D5
West View
Fishbourne PO19 172 B6
Haywards Heath RH16 86 B6
Hove BN3 187 C8
West View Cotts
Breach PO10 150 A2
Haywards Heath RH16 86 B6
West View Dr BN18 176 F2
West View Gdns RH19 22 E8
West Walberton La BN18 . 156 C2
West Way
Chichester PO19 152 C2
Crawley RH10 19 A7
Hove BN3 166 D2
Littlehampton BN17 178 C3
Shoreham-by-Sea BN15 ... 184 B5
Slinfold RH13 34 D3
Worthing BN13 161 D1
West Wittering Parochial (C)
Prim Sch PO20 190 B2
West Worthing Sta BN13 . 182 A3
Westbourne Ave
New Brighton PO10 149 C2
Worthing BN14 182 D4
Westbourne Cl PO10 149 C2
Westbourne Cty Prim Sch
PO10 149 D4
Westbourne Gdns BN3 187 A7
Westbourne Gr BN3 187 A7
Westbourne House Sch
PO20 173 F7
Westbourne Pl BN3 187 A6
Westbourne Rd PO10 149 C3
Westbourne St BN3 187 A7
Westbourne Villas BN3 186 F6
Westbrook RH18 23 E3
Westbrook Field PO18 171 A5
Westbrook Way BN42 185 F7
Westbrooke BN11 182 D2
Westbury Ct 4 BN11 182 B2
Westcombe 1 BN1 187 E7
Westcott Cl RH11 39 C8
Westcourt Pl BN14 182 C3
Westcourt Rd BN14 182 C4
Westdean Rd BN14 182 B5
Westdene Cty Prim Sch
BN1 167 C5
Westdene Dr BN1 167 C5
Westdown Ct 2 BN11 182 A3
Westergate Cl BN12 200 F6
Westergate Com Coll
Westergate PO20 175 D6
Westergate PO20 175 E7
Westergate Mews PO20 ... 175 D8
Westergate Rd BN2 168 E4
Westergate St PO20 175 D6
Westerley Gdns PO20 202 B6
Western Apron Rd RH6 5 F8
Western Ave PO10 169 A8
Western Cl BN15 183 C4
Western Espl BN3, BN41 .. 186 D6
Western Lodge 2 BN15 .. 183 C7
Western Par PO10 169 A7
Western Pl BN11 182 C1
Western Rd
Burgess Hill RH15 106 E3
Haywards Heath RH16 85 F4
Hove BN1, BN3 187 E5
Hurstpierpoint BN6 125 F6
Lancing BN15 183 C4
Liss GU33 45 B4
Littlehampton BN17 198 F4
Selsey PO20 206 E6
Shoreham-by-Sea BN43 ... 184 F7
Western Rd N BN15 183 C6
Western Row BN11 182 C1
Western St BN1 187 D5
Western Terr 5 BN1 187 E5
Westfield PO22 195 B7
Westfield Ave BN16 200 A4
Westfield Cl BN1 168 A4
Westfield Cres BN1 168 A5
Westfield Ct 1 BN17 198 F4
Westfield Rd RH11 18 B6
Westgate PO19 172 E6
Westgate L Ctr PO19 172 F5
Westgrove Gdns 8 PO10 169 B8
Westhampnett Rd
Chichester PO19 173 C7
Westhampnett PO18 153 E1
Westhill Dr RH15 106 E3
Westingway PO21 195 A3
Westlake Cl BN13 181 E5
Westlake Gdns BN13 181 F5
Westland Ave BN14 182 A4
Westland Ct BN41 .. 186 A7
Westland's Copse La GU28 73 A4
Westlands Ferring BN12 ... 200 E5
Horsham RH13 36 E3
Littlehampton BN16 199 A6
Westlands La PO20 191 D5
Westlands Rd
Haywards Heath RH16 86 B5
Hunston PO20 193 A8
Westleas RH6 1 E5
Westloats Gdns PO21 195 A5
Westloats La PO21 195 B5
Westmead Gdns BN11 181 F2
Westmead Rd PO19 172 C6
Westminster Ct 1 BN11 . 182 F2
Westminster Dr PO21 194 E3
Westminster Rd RH10 19 C5
Westmorland Ct 12 BN1 .. 187 E7
Westmorland Dr PO22 196 B6
Westmorland Wlk 2
BN43 164 F1
Westmount 3 BN2 188 C6
Westmount Cl
BN42, BN43 185 D8
Weston La PO18 150 F5
Westons Cl RH12 36 D7
Westons Hill RH13 57 B6
Westpark La BN11, BN12 .. 181 E2
Westup Rd RH17 40 E2
Westview Terr BN14 161 E6
Westward Cl PO18 171 C5
Westward Ho PO19 172 C6
Westward La RH20 119 C6
Westway
Bognor Regis PO22 195 D5
Copthorne RH10 7 A3
Gatwick Airport RH6 6 B7
Westway Cl BN41 165 E4
Westway Gdns BN41 165 E4
Westwood Cl PO10 149 C3
Wey Hill GU27 27 A6
Wey Lodge Cl GU30 25 D4
Weycombe Rd GU27 27 C8
Weydown Ct GU27 27 B7
Weydown Ind Est GU27 27 B8
Weydown Rd GU27 27 B7
Weyland Cl GU30 25 C5
Weysprings GU27 27 A6
Whapple The 7 BN17 198 F4
Wharf Rd Hove BN3 186 D6
Littlehampton BN17 198 C5
Wharf The GU29 92 F7
Wheatcroft BN17 178 C3
Wheatfield Rd PO20 206 F8
Wheatfield Way
Brighton BN2 168 F3
Horley RH6 2 C4
Wheatlands Ave PO11 189 A1
Wheatlands Cres PO11 189 A1
Wheatsheaf Cl
Burgess Hill RH15 106 E5
Horsham RH12 36 E5
Wheatsheaf La RH17 85 A6
Wheatstone Cl RH10 6 B3
Wheelbarrow Castle GU29 . 71 A2
Wheeler Rd RH10 19 B4
Wheelers Way RH19 8 E3
Wheelwright La RH15 107 D1
Wheelwrights RH20 99 E1
Whichelo Pl BN2 188 C6
Whippingham Rd BN2 188 C7
Whippingham St BN2 188 C8
Whistler Ave PO19 153 A1
Whistler Cl RH10 18 F3
Whistler Ct BN1 167 F1
Whitaker Pl PO20 174 B7
White Acre BN17 178 C3
White City GU29 92 E7
White Hart Ct RH12 36 C4
White Horse Cnr PO20 175 A8
White Horse Ct 1 RH20 .. 119 D1

White Horse Sq BN44 .... 143 D3
White Horses Way BN16 .... 199 A5
White Lion Ct **5** BN43 ...... 184 E7
White Lodge Hove BN3 ...... 187 C8
 4 Littlehampton BN17 .... 198 E5
White St BN2 .... 207 B5
White Styles Cty Mid Sch
 BN15 .... 183 B6
White Styles Rd BN15 .... 183 B7
White Styles Terr BN15 ...... 183 B7
White's CI BN6 .... 126 A7
Whitebeam Rd BN13 .... 181 C5
Whitebeam Way
 Middleton-on-Sea PO22 .. 196 E6
 Tangmere PO20 .... 154 D3
Whitechimney Row PO10 149 D3
Whitecroft **5** BN16 .... 199 C5
Whitecross St BN1 .... 207 A6
Whitehall Dr RH11 .... 17 E6
Whitehawk CI BN2 .... 188 E5
Whitehawk Cres BN2 .... 188 E5
Whitehawk Cty Inf Sch
 BN2 .... 188 D5
Whitehawk Hill Rd BN2 .... 188 D5
Whitehawk Jun Sch BN2 . 188 E6
Whitehawk Rd
 Brighton BN2 .... 188 E6
 Brighton BN2 .... 188 F5
Whitehawk Way BN2 .... 188 E6
Whitehorse Rd RH12 .... 37 B6
Whitelands PO22 .... 196 A6
Whitelea Rd BN17 .... 198 D6
Whitelot CI BN42 .... 165 E2
Whitelot Way BN42 .... 165 E2
Whitely Hill RH10 .... 19 F1
Whiteman's CI RH17 .... 84 E8
Whitemans Gn RH17 .... 84 E8
Whiterock Pl BN42 .... 185 E7
Whites La GU27 .... 48 E3
Whiteside CI PO19 .... 173 B7
Whitethorn Dr BN1 .... 167 B4
Whitethroat La RH17 .... 62 D6
Whiteways PO22 .... 195 A6
Whiteways CI
 Bognor Regis PO22 .... 195 A6
 Littlehampton BN17 .... 198 D6
Whitfield CI PO22 .... 195 E5
Whitfield Rd GU27 .... 27 C8
Whitgift Wlk RH10 .... 18 D3
Whitley CI PO10 .... 149 D5
Whitmore Way RH6 .... 1 E3
Whittingehame Gdns BN1 167 F3
Whittington Coll RH19 ...... 9 A4
Whittington Ct **1** PO10 .. 169 B8
Whittington Rd RH10 .... 18 E3
Whitworth Rd RH11 .... 5 D2
Whitwer Cnr RH6 .... 4 F7
Whyke CI PO19 .... 173 B4
Whyke Ct PO19 .... 173 B4
Whyke La PO19 .... 173 B5
Whyke Rd PO19, PO20 ...... 173 B5
Whylands Ave BN13 .... 181 D8
Whylands CI BN13 .... 181 D8
Whylands Cres BN13 .... 181 D8
Whytemead Cty Fst Sch
 BN14 .... 182 E5
Whytings RH13 .... 59 C6
Wick CI PO22 .... 196 B5
Wick Farm Rd BN17 .... 198 C6
Wick Hall BN3 .... 187 D6
Wick La
 Bognor Regis PO22 .... 196 B5
 Easebourne GU29 .... 71 B4
Wick Par BN17 .... 178 D3
Wick St BN17 .... 178 D3
Wickbourne Cty Inf Sch
 BN17 .... 198 C6
Wickbourne Ho BN17 ...... 198 C6
Wickets The RH15 .... 106 F5
Wickham CI
 Haywards Heath RH16 .... 85 E7
 Horley RH6 .... 1 F4
Wickham Dr BN6 .... 126 C5
Wickham Hill BN6 .... 126 C4
Wickham Way RH16 .... 85 E7
Wickhurst CI BN41 .... 165 F2
Wickhurst Gdns RH12 ...... 35 E3
Wickhurst La RH12 .... 35 E3
Wickhurst Rd BN41 .... 166 A2
Wickhurst Rise BN41 .... 165 F3
Wickland Ct RH10 .... 18 D3
Wickor CI PO10 .... 149 C2
Wickor Way PO10 .... 149 C2
Wicks Cotts BN18 .... 177 C4
Wicks Rd RH14 .... 77 C8
Widdicombe Way BN2 ...... 168 E2
Widewater Ct **1** BN15 .... 184 C5
Widewater Ct **7** BN15 .... 184 C5

Widgeon CI PO20 .... 206 B8
Widgeon Way RH12 .... 36 C5
Widworthy Mews **7**
 PO21 .... 195 B3
Wigmore CI BN1 .... 168 B1
Wigmore Rd BN14 .... 182 D6
Wigmore Trad Est BN14 .. 182 F5
Wilberforce CI RH11 .... 39 C8
Wilbury Ave BN3 .... 187 C8
Wilbury Cres BN3 .... 187 D7
Wilbury Gdns BN3 .... 187 C8
Wilbury Gr BN3 .... 187 C6
Wilbury Grange **7** BN3 .. 187 C6
Wilbury Lodge **11** BN3 .. 187 C6
Wilbury Rd BN3 .... 187 C6
Wilbury Villas BN3 .... 187 C7
Wilby Ave BN42 .... 165 E1
Wild Orchid Way RH13 ...... 58 A3
Wild Park CI BN2 .... 168 E3
Wildacre CI RH14 .... 31 D3
Wilderness Rd BN6 .... 126 A6
Wilderness Rise RH19 ...... 10 A6
Wilderness The RH16 ...... 86 B8
Wilderwick Rd RH19, RH7 .. 10 A5
Wildgoose Dr RH12 .... 35 F3
Wildwood Golf Course
 GU6 .... 11 B3
Wildwood La GU6 .... 11 C5
Wilfrid Rd BN3 .... 166 D1
Wilkinson Ct **4** RH11 ...... 18 B1
Willett CI GU28 .... 115 B7
William Allen La RH16 ...... 86 B6
William Morris Way RH11 .. 39 C8
William Penn (C) Prim Sch
 RH13 .... 78 E2
William Rd PO19 .... 173 D6
William St
 Bognor Regis PO21 .... 195 D3
 Brighton BN2 .... 207 A5
 Southwick BN41 .... 186 B7
William Sutton Ho BN1 .... 207 A5
Williams Rd
 Broadbridge PO18 .... 171 C7
 Shoreham-by-Sea BN43 .. 185 C8
Williams Way RH10 .... 19 B5
Willingdon Rd BN2 .... 168 E1
Willmington Ct **2** BN11 .. 182 B1
Willow Ave BN16 .... 199 E5
Willow Brean RH6 .... 1 C5
Willow Brook BN17 .... 178 C3
Willow CI Crawley RH10 .. 18 E8
 East Grinstead RH19 ...... 9 D3
 Liphook GU30 .... 25 D3
 2 Shoreham-by-Sea
 BN15 .... 184 C5
 Steyning BN44 .... 143 D4
 West Chiltington Common
 RH20 .... 119 E6
Willow Cnr RH6 .... 4 F7
Willow Cres BN13 .... 181 C5
Willow Ct
 Chichester PO19 .... 172 D6
 Horley RH6 .... 2 B6
 4 Hove BN3 .... 187 D7
 Worthing BN11 .... 182 A3
Willow Dr RH14 .... 77 D8
Willow Gdns
 Hurstpierpoint BN6 .... 126 A7
 Liphook GU30 .... 25 D3
 Westbourne PO10 .... 150 A7
Willow Ho Hassocks BN6 .. 126 E5
 Worthing BN12 .... 181 A4
Willow Mead **8** RH19 .... 22 F4
Willow Pk RH10 .... 86 B4
Willow Rd Horsham RH12 .. 37 B5
 Liss GU33 .... 45 B4
Willow Ridge RH10 .... 21 A3
Willow Way
 Ashington RH20 .... 121 A4
 Bognor Regis PO21 .... 194 B1
 Hurstpierpoint BN6 .... 126 A7
Willow Wlk GU28 .... 95 E7
Willowbed Ave PO19 .... 173 C4
Willowbed Dr PO19 .... 173 C4
Willowbrook Pk BN15 ...... 184 C5
Willowbrook Rd BN14 ...... 183 A4
Willowbrook Way BN6 .... 127 A3
Willowfield **4** RH11 .... 18 D5
Willowhale Ave PO21 ...... 194 D2
Willowhale Gn PO21 .... 194 C2
Willowhayne Ave BN16 .. 200 A4
Willowhayne CI BN16 ...... 200 A4
Willowhayne Cres BN16 .. 200 A4
Willows Cty Fst Sch The
 BN15 .... 183 E7
Willows The
 Bognor Regis PO21 .... 195 C4
 2 Brighton BN2 .... 207 B8
 Burgess Hill RH15 .... 107 C5
 Findon BN14 .... 161 E6

Willows The
 Ford BN18 .... 177 E5
 Hassocks BN6 .... 126 E4
 Horsham RH12 .... 36 D5
 Lancing BN15 .... 183 E5
 Pulborough RH20 .... 98 A1
 Rustington BN16 .... 199 D6
 Selsey PO20 .... 206 E8
 Wills CI BN18 .... 177 B2
Wilman Gdns PO21 .... 194 D2
Wilmington CI
 Brighton BN1 .... 168 A5
 Crawley RH11 .... 18 C1
 Hassocks BN6 .... 126 F4
Wilmington Par BN1 .... 167 F5
Wilmington Way
 Brighton BN1 .... 168 A5
 Haywards Heath RH16 .... 86 A5
Wilmot CI **8** BN43 .... 185 C8
Wilmot Rd BN43 .... 185 C8
Wilson Ave BN2 .... 188 F6
Wilson C
 Chichester PO19 .... 172 D7
 Crawley RH10 .... 19 D3
Wilson Ct BN18 .... 177 B2
Wilton **1** RH16 .... 85 D6
Wilton C
 Bracklesham PO20 .... 202 C5
 Partridge Green RH13 .... 103 A3
Wilton Villas RH17 .... 41 A1
Wiltshire Ho **18** BN2 ...... 207 B5
Wimberhurst Ct RH12 ...... 36 C4
Wimblehurst Rd RH12 .... 36 C4
Wimborne CI BN11 .... 181 F2
Wimland Hill RH12 .... 16 D2
Wimland Rd Faygate RH12 . 16 D1
 Rusper RH12 .... 16 C4
Wimlands La RH12 .... 16 D2
Winchelsea CI **6** BN11 .. 182 A1
Winchelsea Gdns BN11 .. 182 A1
Winchester Dr PO19 .... 172 F8
Winchester Rd
 Crawley RH10 .... 18 E2
 Rustington BN16 .... 199 E6
 Worthing BN11 .... 182 C2
Winchester St BN1 .... 207 A8
Wincombe Rd BN1, BN3 .. 167 D1
Winden Ave PO19 .... 173 B6
Windermere Cres BN12 .. 181 D5
Windermere Ct **9** BN2 .. 188 C6
Windermere Rd RH16 ...... 85 F6
Windlesham Ave
 BN1, BN3 .... 187 E6
Windlesham CI BN41 ...... 166 A1
Windlesham Ct **10**
 Hove BN1 .... 187 E7
 Littlehampton BN17 ...... 178 D3
 5 Worthing BN11 .... 182 A1
Windlesham Gdns
 East Preston BN16 .... 200 A6
 Shoreham-by-Sea BN43 .. 184 F8
Windlesham House Sch
 BN14 .... 141 D3
Windlesham Rd Hove BN1 187 E6
 Shoreham-by-Sea BN43 .. 184 F8
 Worthing BN11 .... 182 A1
Windmill Ave BN6 .... 126 F3
Windmill CI
 Ashington RH20 .... 121 A5
 Bognor Regis PO21 .... 194 B1
 Horley RH6 .... 2 B3
 Horsham RH13 .... 37 A4
 Shaw BN5 .... 166 F2
 Upper Beeding BN44 ...... 144 B2
Windmill Copse RH20 ...... 119 E2
Windmill Ct Crawley RH11 . 18 D8
 Horsham RH13 .... 37 A4
Windmill Dr
 Brighton BN1 .... 167 D6
 Burgess Hill RH15 .... 107 A4
 Rustington BN16 .... 199 D6
Windmill Field PO18 .... 171 A5
Windmill La
 Ashurst Wood RH19 .... 23 C7
 East Grinstead RH19 ...... 9 D3
 Nep Town BN5 .... 123 E4
Windmill Par BN42 .... 165 E1
Windmill Platt RH17 .... 61 C8
Windmill Rd
 Littlehampton BN17 ...... 198 D4
 Southwick BN42 .... 165 E1
Windmill St BN2 .... 207 B6
Windmill Terr **16** BN2 .. 207 B6
Windmill View BN1 .... 168 B7
Windmills Cty Jun Sch
 BN6 .... 126 E4
Windrum CI RH12 .... 57 F8
Windrush CI Crawley RH11 . 17 F4
 Worthing BN13 .... 181 C8

Windsor CI
 Bognor Regis PO21 .... 194 E4
 Crawley RH11 .... 18 C2
 Hove BN3 .... 167 A3
 Southwater RH13 .... 58 A1
Windsor Ct Brighton BN1 .. 207 F5
 Brighton, Withdene BN1 .. 167 D4
 Horsham RH13 .... 36 F3
 Worthing BN11 .... 183 A2
Windsor Dr
 East Wittering PO20 .... 201 F7
 Rustington BN16 .... 179 B3
Windsor Lodge BN3 .... 187 B6
Windsor Pl RH19 .... 23 A8
Windsor Rd
 Chichester PO19 .... 173 D6
 Selsey PO20 .... 206 E6
 Worthing BN11 .... 183 A2
Windsor St BN1 .... 207 F5
Windsor Way BN15 .... 184 B6
Windward CI BN16, BN17 .. 199 A5
Windyridge RH11 .... 18 A5
Wineham La
 BN5, RH13, RH17 .... 104 D5
Winfield Ave BN1 .... 167 F6
Winfield CI Brighton BN1 .. 167 F5
 Portslade-by-Sea BN41 .. 166 A3
Winfield Gr RH5 .... 3 A8
Winfield Way RH10 .... 149 B4
Wingle Tye Rd RH15 .... 127 A8
Winkfield Ct RH16 .... 85 D5
Winkhurst Way RH15 ...... 107 D1
Winnals Pk RH16 .... 85 D5
Winner Way RH6 .... 5 D6
Winnet Way RH13 .... 58 A2
Winston Bsns Ctr BN15 .. 183 C5
Winston CI PO21 .... 194 F6
Winston Cres PO21 .... 194 F6
Winston Rd BN15 .... 183 D4
Winter Knoll The BN17 .... 198 F5
Winterbourne
 Horsham RH12 .... 36 F7
 Horsham RH12 .... 37 A7
Winterbourne CI BN13 .... 181 B5
Winterbourne Ct BN13 .... 181 B5
Winterbourne Rd PO19 .. 153 A2
Winterbourne Way BN13 .. 181 B5
Winterfold RH10 .... 19 A3
Winterpit CI RH13 .... 59 D6
Winterpit La RH13 .... 59 E6
Winters Cotts **6** GU29 .. 92 F7
Winters La GU29 .... 71 A4
Winterton Ct RH13 .... 36 D2
Winterton Lodge BN17 .... 198 E5
Winterton Way BN43 ...... 185 B6
Winton Pl BN1 .... 182 D3
Wire Mill La RH7 .... 8 F8
Wireless Mus RH16 .... 86 B7
Wisborough Ct
 Crawley RH11 .... 17 F3
 Worthing BN13 .... 181 F6
Wisborough Gdns RH14 .. 76 D8
Wisborough Green Cty
 Prim Sch RH14 .... 54 C1
Wisborough La RH20 ...... 119 E1
Wisden Ave RH15 .... 106 E5
Wish Ct BN3 .... 186 E8
Wish Rd BN3 .... 186 E6
Wiston Ave
 Stockbridge PO19 .... 172 E4
 Worthing BN13, BN14 .... 182 B5
Wiston CI BN14 .... 182 A5
Wiston Ct Crawley RH11 .. 17 F3
 12 Shoreham-by-Sea
 BN43 .... 185 C8
Wiston Rd BN2 .... 188 F6
Wiston Way BN2 .... 188 F7
Withdean Ave
 Brighton BN1 .... 167 D2
 Worthing BN11 .... 181 B1
Withdean CI BN1 .... 167 D3
Withdean Court Ave BN1 . 167 D3
Withdean Cres BN1 .... 167 E3
Withdean Ct **16** BN1 ...... 167 E3
Withdean Hall **3** BN1 .... 167 D3
Withdean Rise BN1 .... 167 E3
Wither Dale RH6 .... 1 E4
Withey Brook RH6 .... 1 D1
Withey Meadows RH6 ...... 1 D1
Withy Bush RH15 .... 106 E6
Withypitts RH10 .... 21 A3
Withypitts E RH10 .... 21 A3
Wittering Rd PO11 .... 189 B2
Wivelsfield Cty Prim Sch
 RH16 .... 107 F6
Wivelsfield Rd RH16 .... 107 E2
Wivelsfield Sta RH15 ...... 107 C4
Woburn CI BN1 .... 168 F5
Woburn Rd RH11 .... 18 A4
Woelfs CI RH20 .... 121 A5

Wold CI RH11 .... 17 F4
Woldhurstlea CI RH11 ...... 18 A4
Wolseley Rd Brighton BN1 168 D6
 Portslade-by-Sea BN41 .. 186 A8
Wolsey CI PO21 .... 194 D4
Wolstead Lodge **3** RH16 .. 85 F3
Wolstonbury Rd BN16 .... 179 C3
Wolstonbury CI
 Crawley RH11 .... 18 C4
 Hurstpierpoint BN6 .... 126 B4
Wolstonbury Ct RH15 ...... 107 B2
Wolstonbury Rd BN3 ...... 187 E7
Wolstonbury Way RH15 .. 107 B2
Wolstonbury Wlk **7**
 BN43 .... 164 F1
Wolverstone Dr BN1 .... 168 C2
Wolverton CI RH6 .... 1 F1
Wolverton Gdns RH6 ...... 1 F3
Wonford Way BN2 .... 2 A8
Wood End RH12 .... 37 C5
Wood La BN5 .... 144 F7
Wood Ride RH16 .... 85 D3
Wood St
 Bognor Regis PO21 .... 195 B2
 East Grinstead RH19 ...... 9 D1
Wood View BN18 .... 158 A2
Wood's Mill Countryside Ctr
 BN5 .... 144 F6
Woodard Rd BN15 .... 183 F7
Woodards View BN43 ...... 184 D5
Woodberry La
 Rowland's Castle PO9 .... 128 F3
 Stubbermere PO10, PO9 .. 149 B2
Woodbine Ct **7** PO21 .... 195 D4
Woodbourne Ave BN1 .... 168 A4
Woodbourne CI GU33 .... 45 C4
Woodbourne Ct RH12 ...... 37 A5
Woodbridge Pk RH16 ...... 200 A8
Woodbury Ave RH19 .... 10 B3
Woodbury CI RH10 .... 23 B8
Woodbury Lodge **5**
 Woodcock Hill RH19, RH7 .. 8 F4
Woodcote Graffham GU28 114 A8
 Horley RH6 .... 2 C4
Woodcote La
 Harwoods Green RH20 .... 97 D5
 Littlehampton BN17 ...... 178 D5
Woodcote Rd RH18 .... 23 F3
Woodcourt RH11 .... 18 C2
Woodcrest Rd RH15 .... 106 F7
Woodcroft RH15 .... 106 F5
Woodcutters RH17 .... 86 F3
Wooddale La RH14 .... 56 A2
Woodend
 Bognor Regis PO21 .... 195 A4
 West Ashling PO18 .... 151 C5
Woodend CI RH10 .... 19 A1
Woodfield RH13 .... 57 F2
Woodfield CI
 Bognor Regis PO21 .... 205 A2
 Crawley RH10 .... 18 E1
 Tangmere PO20 .... 154 D..
Woodfield Park Rd RH20 .. 169 D8
Woodfield Rd
 Crawley RH10 .... 18 E..
 Rudgwick RH12 ....
Woodfield Terr RH13 ...... 81 E..
Woodgate CI PO20 .... 175 D..
Woodgate Pk PO20 .... 175 D..
Woodgate Rd PO20 .... 175 D..
Woodgates CI RH13 .... 36 F..
Woodhall CI RH17 .... 84 F..
Woodhatch RH13 .... 57 F..
Woodhayes RH4 .... 19 B..
Woodhorn Cotts PO20 .... 174 E..
Woodhorn La PO20 .... 174 D..
Woodhouse CI BN3 .... 186 E..
Woodhouse La
 Blendworth PO8 .... 128 C..
 Rowland's Castle
 PO8, PO9 ....
Woodhouse Rd BN3 .... 186 E..
Wooding Gr **14** RH11 .... 18 B..
Woodland Ave
 Burgess Hill RH15 .... 107 C..
 Hove BN3 .... 167 B..
 Worthing BN13 .... 161 F..
Woodland CI
 Burgess Hill RH15 .... 107 C..
 Five Oaks RH14 .... 55 E..
 Horsham RH13 .... 37 B..
 Hove BN3 .... 167 B..
Woodland Cotts RH20 .... 120 A..
Woodland Cres RH15 ...... 107 C..
Woodland Dr
 Crawley Down RH10 ...... 21 B..
 Hove BN3 .... 167 B..
Woodland La RH13 .... 38 C..
Woodland Par BN3 .... 167 B..
Woodland Pl PO19 .... 153 A..

Woodland Rd P020 .... 206 D6
Woodland Villas P020 .... 155 F1
Woodland Way
 Brighton BN1 .... 167 F4
 Horsham RH13 .... 37 B4
Woodlands Crawley RH10 ... 19 D8
 Horley RH6 .... 2 C4
 Hove BN3 .... 167 C2
Woodlands Ave
 New Brighton PO10 .... 149 B3
 Rustington BN16 .... 199 C6
Woodlands Cl
 Angmering BN16 .... 180 A7
 Clapham BN13 .... 160 F1
 Crawley Down RH10 .... 21 B7
 Rustington BN16 .... 199 C6
Woodlands Cotts BN16 .... 199 C6
Woodlands La
 Chichester PO19 .... 172 F8
 Haslemere GU27 .... 26 F7
 Heath Common RH20 ...... 120 C3
 Hill Side GU33 .... 45 D3
 Walderton PO18 .... 130 B2
Woodlands Pk BN18 .... 176 F3
Woodlands Rd
 Bognor Regis PO22 .... 195 B6
 East Grinstead RH19 .... 10 A4
 Haywards Heath RH16 ..... 85 F4
 Littlehampton BN17 .... 198 E4
Woodlands The BN1 .... 167 E5
Woodlands Way
 Billingshurst RH14 .... 77 E6
 Southwater RH13 .... 79 E8
Woodlands Wlk RH13 ...... 59 C5
Woodlea Rd BN13 .... 182 A4
Woodleigh Rd RH15 .... 107 C4
Woodmancote Ct RH12 ... 36 D5
Woodmancote La
 PO10, PO18 .... 150 B4
Woodmancote Rd BN14 ... 182 B4
Woodmans Hill RH11 ...... 18 C2
Woodpecker Cres BN6 .... 106 D3
Woodpecker La RH20 ...... 119 E1
Woodpecker Rd GU28 ..... 95 E7
Woodpecker Way BN13 ... 181 C5
Woodridge Cl RH16 .... 86 A3
Woodroffe Wlk PO10 ...... 149 B4
Woodroyd Ave RH6 .... 1 F2

Woodroyd Gdns RH6 .... 1 F1
Woodruff Ave BN3 .... 167 C2
Woodruff Bsns Ctr The
 PO19 .... 172 E5
Woods Hill Cl RH19 .... 23 D6
Woods Hill La RH19 .... 23 D6
Woods Ho BN3 .... 187 A8
Woods Mill Cl BN5 .... 144 E6
Woods Way BN12 .... 181 C3
Woodside Horsham RH13 ... 37 B4
 West Barnham PO22 .... 176 B6
Woodside Ave BN1 .... 167 D2
Woodside Cl
 Cornerhouse RH13 .... 103 D4
 Storrington RH20 .... 119 E2
Woodside Ct 6 BN17 .... 198 E4
Woodside Lodge BN1 ...... 167 D2
Woodside Rd
 Crawley RH10 .... 18 F8
 Worthing BN14 .... 182 B4
Woodslands Cl BN6 .... 126 F4
Woodslands Rd BN6 .... 126 F4
Woodstock RH19 .... 9 C2
Woodstock Cl RH12 .... 36 D5
Woodstock Gdns PO21 .... 194 F2
Woodview BN43 .... 164 F1
Woodview Cl BN1 .... 168 D6
Woodwards RH11 .... 18 C1
Woodwards Cl RH15 .... 107 B1
Wool La GU29 .... 92 F7
Woolbeding La GU29 .... 70 B4
Woolborough Cl RH10 ...... 18 E7
Woolborough La
 Crawley RH10 .... 5 F1
 Crawley RH10 .... 19 A8
 Horley RH1 .... 2 F8
Woolborough Rd RH10 ..... 18 E7
Woolmer Hill Rd
 GU26, GU27 .... 26 D7
Woolmer Hill Sch GU27 ... 26 D7
Woolmer St PO10 .... 149 A8
Woolstaplers The PO19 ... 172 F6
Woolven Cl RH15 .... 106 E1
Woolven Row BN5 .... 123 F5
Wophams La PO20 .... 192 D7
Worcester Cl PO21 .... 194 E3
Worcester Ct 2 BN3 ...... 187 E6

Worcester Rd
 Chichester PO19 .... 152 F2
 Crawley RH10 .... 18 E2
Worcester Villas BN3 .... 186 C7
Wordsworth Cl RH10 .... 19 B8
Wordsworth Gdns PO22 ... 196 D6
Wordsworth Pl RH12 .... 36 E7
Wordsworth Rd BN11 .... 182 C1
Wordsworth Rise 8 RH19 ... 9 C1
Wordsworth St BN3 .... 187 A7
Worms La PO22 .... 196 E7
Worsted La RH19 .... 23 B8
Worth Abbey & Sch RH10 ... 20 B1
Worth Park Ave RH10 .... 19 C7
Worth Rd RH10 .... 19 C6
Worth Way RH10 .... 19 E5
Worthing Golf Course
 BN14 .... 162 B1
Worthing High Sch BN14 . 182 C4
Worthing Hospl BN11 ...... 182 E3
Worthing Rd
 Dial Post RH13 .... 101 E3
 East Preston BN16 .... 199 F6
 Littlehampton BN17 .... 178 E3
 Rustington BN16, BN17 ... 179 B3
 Southwater RH13 .... 57 F2
 Tower Hill RH12, RH13 .... 58 A7
 West Grinstead RH13 ..... 102 A6
Worthing Sixth Form Coll
 BN13 .... 181 E3
Worthing Sta BN11 .... 182 C3
Wray Cl RH19 .... 23 D6
Wraysbury Park Dr PO10 . 149 B4
Wren Cl Horsham RH12 ..... 36 D7
 Pulborough RH20 .... 98 B2
Wren Cres PO22 .... 195 B6
Wren Ct RH10 .... 18 E3
Wrenfield Pl 3 PO21 ...... 195 C2
Wrentham Ho RH15 .... 107 B3
Wroxham Way PO22 .... 145 E6
Wroxham Wlk RH10 .... 19 B4
Wyatt Cl RH14 .... 54 B1
Wyatt Ct PO20 .... 201 F7
Wyatts La RH7 .... 65 D5
Wyberlye Rd RH15 .... 107 A4
Wychcroft 4 BN14 .... 198 D5
Wycherry Rd RH16 .... 85 D5
Wychwood Cl PO21 .... 194 E1

Wychwood Gdns BN11 .... 183 B3
Wychwood Wlk PO21 ..... 194 E1
Wyck Ct BN41 .... 186 A7
Wycliffe Ct RH11 .... 17 E3
Wyde Feld PO21 .... 194 F2
Wye Cl RH11 .... 39 C8
Wye Ho BN11 .... 182 B2
Wyke Ave BN11 .... 182 E2
Wyke La N PO22 .... 196 C6
Wykeham Cl BN11 .... 182 C2
Wykeham Ct BN11 .... 182 C2
Wykeham Rd BN11 .... 182 C2
Wykeham Terr BN1 .... 207 F5
Wykeham Way RH15 .... 107 C2
Wykwood GU30 .... 25 D4
Wylde Green La GU33 ...... 45 D5
Wyncombe Cl RH20 .... 97 B3
Wyndham Lea RH20 .... 119 D6
Wyndham Pk GU29 .... 92 D7
Wyndham Rd GU28 .... 95 F7
Wyndham St BN2 .... 207 B4
Wynlea Cl RH10 .... 21 A8
Wynnes Mews BN3 .... 187 A7
Wynnstay RH15 .... 107 B2
Wysemead RH6 .... 2 C4
Wyshe The BN45 .... 147 C6
Wythering Cl PO21 .... 204 F7
Wythwood RH16 .... 85 E1
Wyvern Cl PO20 .... 154 E1
Wyvern Ct 6 BN11 .... 182 C1

Yachtsmens Cotts PO18 ... 171 A5
Yapton CE (C) Prim Sch
 BN18 .... 176 F4
Yapton La BN18 .... 176 F7
Yapton Rd
 Barnham BN18, PO22 ..... 176 D4
 Horsemere Green
  BN17, BN18 .... 177 C1
 Middleton-on-Sea
  BN18, PO22 .... 196 E7
Yarbrook PO18 .... 152 E7
Yardlea Cl PO9 .... 128 D1
Yardley St BN1 .... 207 A8
Yarmouth Cl RH10 .... 19 A4
Yarrow Cl RH12 .... 36 E5
Yattendon Rd RH6 .... 2 B3
Yattendon Sch RH6 .... 2 A4

Woo – Zac 245

Yeoman Rd BN12, BN13 ... 181 B5
Yeoman Way BN13 .... 181 B4
Yeomans Acre PO21 .... 194 F3
Yeomans Field PO18 .... 150 D1
Yeomans La GU30 .... 25 A4
Yew La RH19 .... 9 B3
Yew Tree Cl
 Bognor Regis PO22 .... 195 B6
 Horley RH6 .... 2 A4
 Lancing BN15 .... 183 E5
Yew Tree Cotts RH15 ...... 107 B3
Yew Tree Ct RH17 .... 84 F6
Yew Tree Pl GU33 .... 45 C4
Yew Tree Rd RH6 .... 4 E7
Yewlands Wlk RH11 .... 17 D4
Yewtree Cl RH13 .... 81 E2
York Ave
 East Grinstead RH19 .... 23 A8
 Hove BN3 .... 187 E6
York Chase PO19 .... 152 F1
York Cl Horsham RH13 ..... 36 F3
 Southwater RH13 .... 58 A1
York Ct 9 BN3 .... 187 E7
York Gdns BN17 .... 198 D5
York Gr BN1 .... 207 F7
York Hill BN1 .... 207 A7
York Ho BN41 .... 186 B8
York Pl BN1, BN2 .... 207 A6
York Rd
 Bognor Regis PO21 .... 195 D3
 Burgess Hill BN6, RH15 ... 106 D2
 Chichester PO19 .... 173 C5
 Crawley RH10 .... 18 E2
 Hove BN1, BN3 .... 187 E6
 Littlehampton BN17 .... 198 D5
 Selsey PO20 .... 206 E5
 Worthing BN11 .... 182 E2
York Villas BN1 .... 207 F7
Yorkhurst Hill PO18 .... 152 E7
Yorkwood GU33 .... 45 B4
Young St 4 PO19 .... 153 A2
Youngsmere Cl BN1 .... 168 C6

Zachary Merton Com Hospl
 BN16 .... 199 D4

Town and village index

Albourne 125 B5
Albourne Green 125 C6
Aldingbourne 175 A7
Aldsworth 149 F6
Alfold 31 F8
Alfold Crossways 11 A3
Almodington 202 F8
Amberley 138 D7
Angmering 179 E5
Ansteadbrook 28 C5
Ansty 84 C3
Apuldram 172 C3
Ardingly 64 A7
Arundel 158 C4
Ashington 121 B5
Ashurst 122 D5
Ashurst Wood 23 E6
Atherington 197 F6
Balcombe 40 F2
Balcombe Lane 40 A6
Balls Cross 52 B1
Balls Green 78 A3
Barlavington 115 E5
Barnham 176 D5
Barns Green 56 E3
Barnsnap 38 B3
Bepton 92 A1
Bignor 116 A2
Billingshurst 77 E7
Birdham 191 E5
Blackstone 124 E5
Blendworth 128 A7
Bognor Regis 195 D2
Bolney 83 C3
Bosham 171 C4
Bosham Hoe 191 C8
Botolphs 163 F8
Boxgrove 154 D3
Bracklesham 202 B6
Bramber 143 F2
Bramshott 25 C6
Breach 149 F1
Brighton 188 B4
Brighton 207 A4
Broadbridge 171 D7
Broadford Bridge 99 F8
Broadridge Heath 35 E4
Brook Street 62 F1
Broomer's Corner 100 F7
Bucks Green 33 B6
Buncton 142 C8
Burgess Hill 107 D2
Buriton 88 A5
Burndell 177 B3
Burpham 159 A7
Burstow 7 A7
Bury 138 A7
Byworth 96 B6
Charlton 133 F6
Charlwood 4 E7
Chelwood Gate 66 D8
Chichester 172 D7
Chidham 170 F4
Chilgrove 110 F1
Chithurst 69 C3
Church Norton 204 B4
Cinder Hill 65 B8
Clapham 160 F1
Clayton 147 E8
Climping 177 E1
Cocking 112 D8
Codmore Hill 98 D5
Coldwaltham 117 C6
Colgate 38 C6
Colworth 174 E2
Compton 109 A2

Coneyhurst 78 B4
Conford 24 E7
Coolham 78 D2
Coombes 164 A5
Cootham 119 B2
Copsale 80 C7
Copthorne 7 C3
Cowfold 81 F2
Cox Green 12 E1
Crabtree 82 A7
Crawley 18 F5
Crawley Down 21 C7
Crockerhill 155 B3
Crossbush 158 E1
Crosspost 83 B1
Cuckfield 84 F5
Cudworth 3 F8
Danehill 66 A4
Dial Post 101 E4
Ditchling 127 D3
Domewood 8 A5
Donnington 172 E1
Dormans Park 9 E6
Dormansland 10 B8
Dragons Green 79 C3
Dumpford 90 F8
Duncton 115 B7
Earnley 202 D6
Eartham 155 E7
Easebourne 71 B2
East Ashling 151 E4
East Beach 206 F8
East Dean 134 C6
East Grinstead 9 E2
East Lavant 153 A5
East Lavington 114 E5
East Liss 45 A4
East Marden 110 B2
East Preston 200 B6
East Wittering 201 E6
Eastergate 175 F8
Ebernoe 51 E4
Edburton 145 C4
Ellen's Green 13 A4
Elsted 90 D3
Emsworth 149 A1
Faygate 16 F1
Felbridge 8 F4
Felcourt 9 C8
Fernhill 6 E7
Fernhurst 49 B5
Ferring 200 F6
Finchdean 128 F6
Findon 161 F6
Fishbourne 172 A6
Fisherstreet 28 F3
Fittleworth 97 A2
Five Oaks 55 F5
Flansham 196 C7
Fontwell 156 A2
Forest Row 9 C7
Forestside 129 D6
Foxhill 74 E2
Fulking 145 F4
Funtington 151 A5
Furnace Wood 8 C4
Furner's Green 66 C1
Goddards' Green 106 A5
Graffham 114 B7
Greatham 118 A4
Halnaker 154 E5
Hambrook 150 C2
Hammerpot 179 F8
Handcross 61 C8
Hangleton 180 D4

Hardham 117 F7
Haslemere 27 D6
Hassocks 126 D4
Haywards Heath 85 C3
Heath Common 120 C2
Henfield 123 F5
Henley 71 B8
Hermitage 169 D8
Heyshott 93 B1
Hickstead 105 C5
High Cross 124 F7
Highbrook 42 E1
Highleigh 192 C1
Hill Brow 45 D2
Hill Side 24 D3
Hollywater 24 B8
Hookwood 1 D2
Horley 2 C3
Horsemere Green 177 C1
Horsham 36 C3
Horsted Keynes 65 D5
Houghton 138 B4
Hove 187 B5
Hunston 193 A8
Hurst Wickham 126 C6
Hurstpierpoint 126 B6
Ifold 31 D3
Iping 69 E2
Itchingfield 57 A6
Keymer 127 B4
Kingsfold 15 B5
Kingsley Green 27 B2
Kingston Gorse 200 D4
Kirdford 53 B2
Lambs Green 16 F6
Lancing 183 D5
Lickfold 72 A8
Linchmere 26 B2
Lindfield 84 E5
Liphook 25 C3
Liss 45 A4
Liss Forest 45 C6
Littlehampton 198 E3
Littleworth 103 A5
Lodsworth 72 A3
Lower Beeding 60 A3
Lower Fittleworth 97 A2
Loxwood 31 F4
Lumley 149 C1
Lurgashall 50 C3
Lyminster 178 D6
Madehurst 137 B1
Mannings Heath 59 D6
Maplehurst 80 F6
Marehill 98 E1
Mark Street 66 F3
Marley Heights 27 A1
Maudlin 153 F1
Merston 174 B3
Mid Lavant 152 E5
Middleton-on-Sea 196 E4
Midhurst 92 F6
Milland 89 D3
Monk's Gate 59 C4
Navant Hill 50 E5
Nep Town 123 E4
Nepcote 161 F5
New Brighton 149 C2
Newgate 3 D8
Newpound Common 54 E2
North End 177 A5
North Heath 98 F7
North Lancing 183 F8
North Marden 110 B5
North Mundham 173 D1

North Stoke 138 C2
Northchapel 51 A7
Norton 155 B1
Nursted 88 E7
Nutbourne Common 99 B1
Nutbourne
  (nr Emsworth) 170 C2
Nutbourne
  (nr Pulborough) 99 B2
Nuthurst 59 A1
Nyewood 90 A8
Nyton 175 D8
Oakwoodhill 14 A7
Oving 174 C7
Pagham 204 E8
Park Street 34 C4
Partridge Green 103 B3
Patching 160 D2
Paynes Green 14 D8
Pease Pottage 39 B6
Petworth 95 E7
Plaistow 30 F2
Poling 179 B6
Portslade-by-Sea 186 B5
Poynings 146 C5
Prince's Marsh 45 A2
Prinsted 169 F7
Pulborough 98 D1
Pyecombe 147 B6
Rackham 139 C8
Rake 46 B4
Red Hill 128 D1
River 72 D3
Rogate 68 B4
Roundstreet Common 54 C6
Rowhook 13 E1
Rowland's Castle 128 F2
Rudgwick 33 C7
Runcton 173 E1
Rusper 16 D7
Rustington 199 B4
Salfords 2 A8
Sayers Common 105 D1
Scaynes Hill 86 E3
Selden 180 C8
Selham 94 C6
Selsey 206 D7
Sharpthorne 43 A6
Shipley 101 D8
Shipton Green 191 A4
Shopwyke 173 F7
Shoreham-by-Sea 184 E5
Shripney 175 C1
Sidlesham 192 F1
Singleton 133 D6
Slaugham 61 B5
Slindon 156 C6
Slinfold 34 D3
Slough Green 62 A1
Small Dole 144 F6
Somerley 191 D2
Sompting 183 B7
South Ambersham 93 F6
South Harting 89 D3
South Hayling 189 B1
South Mundham 193 D5
South Stoke 158 D8
Southbourne 170 A8
Southwater 57 E1
Southwater Street 58 A3
Southwick 185 F7
Staplefield 61 F5
Stedham 70 A1
Steyning 143 C3
Stopham 97 D3
Storrington 119 D2

Stoughton 131 A5
Street End 192 D1
Strettington 154 A4
Strood Green 35 A4
Stubbermere 149 E8
Sullington 140 A8
Sutton 115 A9
Tangmere 154 C1
Terwick Common 68 D2
Thakeham 120 B8
Tillington 95 C6
Tinsley Green 6 C5
Tisman's Common 32 F6
Toddington 178 E3
Tortington 177 F2
Tower Hill 55 B4
Treyford 90 B7
Trotton 69 A8
Turners Hill 21 A6
Twineham 105 B2
Twineham Green 105 B1
Upper Beeding 144 A4
Upperton 73 B6
Upwaltham 135 B8
Walberton 156 D6
Walderton 130 B4
Wallis Wood 13 D5
Warminghurst 120 D2
Warnham 35 E7
Warningcamp 158 A5
Warninglid 61 A4
Washington 141 B3
Watersfield 117 A6
Wepham 159 A7
West Ashling 151 E5
West Barnham 176 A6
West Burton 137 D7
West Chiltington 99 B6
West Chiltington
  Common 119 C8
West Dean 133 A3
West Grinstead 102 C8
West Harting 89 D7
West Hoathly 42 B4
West Itchenor 190 H5
West Kingston 200 B6
West Lavington 93 A2
West Liss 45 B5
West Marden 130 A6
West Stoke 151 F6
West Thorney 169 F4
West Wittering 190 C1
Westbourne 149 D2
Westergate 175 D8
Westerton 153 B3
Westhampnett 153 E5
Westlands 191 E1
Westmeston 148 F2
Whitemans Green 84 E4
Wick 178 D4
Wiggonholt 118 E3
Wineham 104 D1
Wisborough Green 76 B7
Wiston 121 D7
Woodgate 175 E5
Woodmancote
  (nr Emsworth) 150 A3
Woodmancote
  (nr Henfield) 124 C2
Woolbeding 70 C3
Worthing 182 E2
Wrays 1 B4
Yapton 176 F3

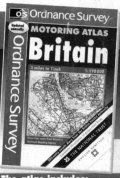

STREET ATLASES ORDER FORM

The Street Atlases are available from all good bookshops or by mail order direct from the publisher. Orders can be made in the following ways. **By phone** Ring our special Credit Card Hotline on **01933 443863** during office hours (9am to 5pm) or leave a message on the answering machine, quoting your full credit card number plus expir date and your full name and address. **By post or fax** Fill out the order form below (you may photocopy it) and post it to: **Philip's Direct, 27 Sanders Road, Wellingborough Northants NN8 4NL** or fax it to: **01933 443849.** Before placing an order by post, by fax or on the answering machine, please telephone to check availability and prices.

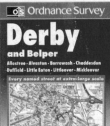

COLOUR LOCAL ATLASES	PAPERBACK	Quantity @ £3.50 each	£ Total
CANNOCK, LICHFIELD, RUGELEY		☐ 0 540 07625 2 ➤	
DERBY AND BELPER		☐ 0 540 07608 2 ➤	
NORTHWICH, WINSFORD, MIDDLEWICH		☐ 0 540 07589 2 ➤	
PEAK DISTRICT TOWNS		☐ 0 540 07609 0 ➤	
STAFFORD, STONE, UTTOXETER		☐ 0 540 07626 0 ➤	
WARRINGTON, WIDNES, RUNCORN		☐ 0 540 07588 4 ➤	

COLOUR REGIONAL ATLASES	HARDBACK	SPIRAL	POCKET	
	Quantity @ £10.99 each	Quantity @ £8.99 each	Quantity @ £4.99 each	£ Total
MERSEYSIDE	☐ 0 540 06480 7	☐ 0 540 06481 5	☐ 0 540 06482 3 ➤	
	Quantity @ £12.99 each	Quantity @ £8.99 each	Quantity @ £5.99 each	£ Total
BERKSHIRE	☐ 0 540 06170 0	☐ 0 540 06172 7	☐ 0 540 06173 5 ➤	
	Quantity @ £12.99 each	Quantity @ £9.99 each	Quantity @ £4.99 each	£ Total
DURHAM	☐ 0 540 06365 7	☐ 0 540 06366 5	☐ 0 540 06367 3 ➤	
	Quantity @ £12.99 each	Quantity @ £9.99 each	Quantity @ £5.50 each	£ Total
GREATER MANCHESTER	☐ 0 540 06485 8	☐ 0 540 06486 6	☐ 0 540 06487 4 ➤	
TYNE AND WEAR	☐ 0 540 06370 3	☐ 0 540 06371 1	☐ 0 540 06372 X ➤	
	Quantity @ £12.99 each	Quantity @ £9.99 each	Quantity @ £5.99 each	£ Total
BEDFORDSHIRE	☐ 0 540 07801 8	☐ 0 540 07802 6	☐ 0 540 07803 4 ➤	
BIRMINGHAM & WEST MIDLANDS	☐ 0 540 07603 1	☐ 0 540 07604 X	☐ 0 540 07605 8 ➤	
BUCKINGHAMSHIRE	☐ 0 540 07466 7	☐ 0 540 07467 5	☐ 0 540 07468 3 ➤	
CHESHIRE	☐ 0 540 07507 8	☐ 0 540 07508 6	☐ 0 540 07509 4 ➤	
DERBYSHIRE	☐ 0 540 07531 0	☐ 0 540 07532 9	☐ 0 540 07533 7 ➤	
EDINBURGH & East Central Scotland	☐ 0 540 07653 8	☐ 0 540 07654 6	☐ 0 540 07656 2 ➤	
NORTH ESSEX	☐ 0 540 07289 3	☐ 0 540 07290 7	☐ 0 540 07292 3 ➤	
SOUTH ESSEX	☐ 0 540 07294 X	☐ 0 540 07295 8	☐ 0 540 07297 4 ➤	
GLASGOW & West Central Scotland	☐ 0 540 07648 1	☐ 0 540 07649 X	☐ 0 540 07651 1 ➤	
NORTH HAMPSHIRE	☐ 0 540 07471 3	☐ 0 540 07472 1	☐ 0 540 07473 X ➤	

PHILIP'S